DRUNK ON POWER
VOLUME ONE

(Swiss Federal Archives)

HEINRICH PFEIFER
WRITING AS HEINRICH ORB

Drunk On Power

A Senior Defector's Inside Account
of the Nazi Secret Police State

Translated by Bernhard Rest
Edited with Commentary by Robert Temple

VOLUME ONE

eglantyne books

Published by Eglantyne Books ltd,
The Club Room, Conway Hall, 25 Red Lion Square, London WC1R 4RL.
www.eglantynebooks.com

ISBN 978-1-913378-10-3
Printed in the UK by Imprint Digital ltd.
A CIP record for this title is available from the British Library.

Book layout and design by Eric Wright
Production team:
Robert and Olivia Temple, Michael Lee, Eric Wright and Bernhard Rest

No photos in this book have been sourced from a picture agency. Many are from original prints or negatives, most of them never before published in a book or at all. Most of the signed photos were given by the subjects to their friends and relations, subsequently sold off, and purchased on the commercial market. No photos have been sourced directly from the German Bundesrachiv, since an attempt to contact that Archive resulted in an automatic reply stating that they could not deal with correspondence. Nevertheless, when photos from intermediary sources have obviously originated from the Bundesarchiv, picture credits of 'Bundesarchiv' have been added. Some images taken from original prints are identical with images held by the Bundesarchiv, in which case they exist in duplicate outside of that Archive. Some images taken from other sources may have originated with the Bundesarchiv, but there is no evidence of such origin, and those have not been given picture credits of 'Bundesarchiv' because of the uncertainty. Every effort has been made to identify any possible copyright holders, and the publishers are happy to add appropriate picture credits to future editions if contacted by any persons having evidence of copyright, but due to the age of the photos, this is highly unlikely. Anyone in doubt should contact the publishers.

A BOOK OF NAZI REVELATIONS

An Introduction by Robert Temple

The search for who the true author of this book was, trying to unpick his various disguises, aliases, and false identities, was a needle-in-a-haystack operation. Even getting hold of a rare copy of the book relied upon good luck and prolonged searching. Most copies were apparently destroyed by Nazi sympathisers at the time of its publication in Switzerland. The author had much to tell. And there were plenty of people who did not want him to tell any of it.

This is truly the book the Nazis hoped would never happen. Written by the most important defector from the Nazis' 'Deep State', it gives a detailed account of the people, the projects, the institutional structure, and the operating methods of the SS security police, known as the SD (for *Sicherheitsdienst*, 'security service'). It names names, and even gives the rude nicknames of some of the highest Nazis and describes their worst murderous deeds and often their disgusting personal habits.

The book was written under the strictest possible limitations. Because the author was living as a political exile in Switzerland, he had to submit his text to the Swiss Government and obtain their official written permission to publish. This was considered at the highest levels. The Attorney General of Switzerland personally insisted that the author must not mention the name of Switzerland in the book and must not make any polemical anti-Nazi statements, despite the fact that by 1945 the Nazis had already lost the war. The author had been assisting the Swiss intelligence services for years and he was aware of many other things he must suppress. He worked for the Intelligence Department of the General Staff of the Swiss Army from the autumn of 1938 until September 1, 1941, providing detailed information on the Hitler regime and identifying its spies abroad. Although the book is full of astonishing revelations, and has no rival as a source of information about the Nazi 'Deep State' as experienced from the inside, the author could only drop mere hints about many things which he wished he could explain at length. It was necessary to follow many of these hints to where they led, as the author clearly wished. The names of the Gestapo's key foreign agents are often given, and the author 'ran' several of them because he was in charge of many aspects of Nazi counterintelligence as Chief of Heydrich's Bureau for Foreign Deployment, and was himself a brilliant field agent who had worked with them in many foreign countries, especially France. He was multilingual and a master of disguise.

The author was truly 'the man of a thousand names and a thousand faces'. He had so many aliases that the people who knew his true identity could be counted on the fingers of one hand. Ever since he entered the Nazi service in 1929, he worked under a false name even in the SA, the Abwehr, and the SD, and it is thought that even Himmler did not know his real name. This paranoid secrecy was initially at the insistence of Alfred Rosenberg, and continued under Himmler and Heydrich. The author worked intimately with Heydrich, whom he frankly describes as 'satanic' and the most dangerous of all the Nazis. Compared to Heydrich, Himmler was a 'softie', our author insists.

This book was published under the pseudonym of Heinrich Orb. Only the most experienced historians and researchers have known that it existed, and not all of them have properly read it or been able to obtain a copy. It sometimes appears listed in bibliographies without any comment or citation, which suggests it has not been actually read. Most copies appear to have been bought up and destroyed. There were plenty of Nazis left at the time of its publication in 1945, and their enthusiasm for destroying books had not diminished. Nor had their enthusiasm for destroying people, for the author was assassinated in 1949.

The original German edition of this book was published without illustrations. This translated edition has been greatly enlarged, with more than 250 illustrations, and with very extensive commentary. And now it is possible to bring forward absolute proof of the identity of the author, and to give his real name. As already mentioned, this book was published under the pseudonym of Heinrich Orb. However, 'Heinrich Orb' never existed. The real author of this volume was named Heinrich Pfeifer.

WHO WAS HEINRICH PFEIFER?

The pseudonym used to disguise the author of this book has from time to time provided occasions for the intentional spread of disinformation. The few people aware of the book, of whom some are suspiciously anonymous and placed disinformation on the internet, have put forward various possible authors, some of whom have been ridiculous and discredited persons. This enabled the book to be dismissed because a straw dog had been created who could easily be knocked over as an unreliable supposed author. Such nonsense is now entirely at an end.

The initial breakthrough occurred when I was able at last to buy a copy of this book from a Swiss book dealer and discovered that it was signed by the author at the time of publication. I could thus at last prove the true identity of the author because I had a signed copy of the book in which the author inscribes it as 'Heinrich Pfeifer called Orb'. Why Orb? The author's grandfather was born in the spa town of Bad Orb in Hesse, east of Frankfurt and Hanau. (In German the word *bad* does not mean what it does in English, but means 'spa'.) Today it has a population of between 9,000 and 10,000. Pfeifer probably adopted Orb as a pseudonym because of its early family associations. It seems doubtful that Orb was otherwise ever used as a surname.

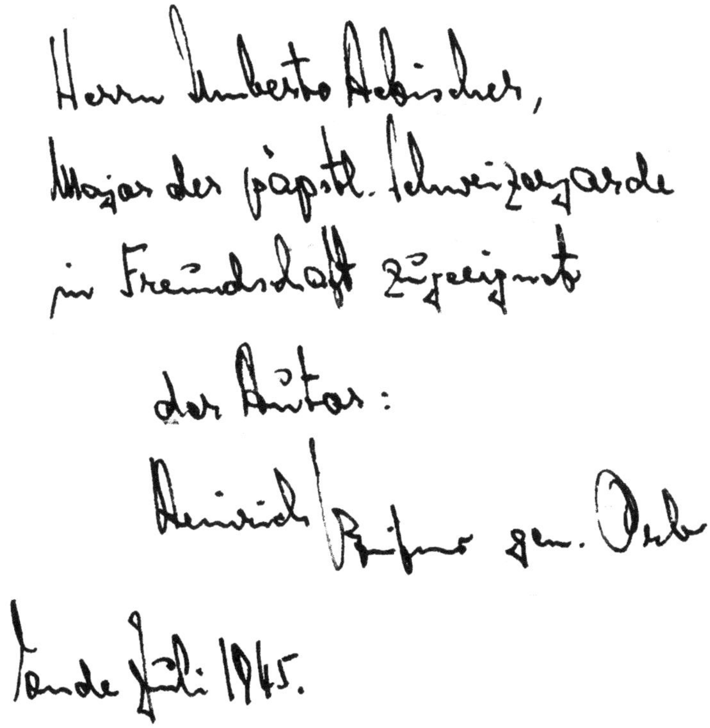
Herrn Umberto Aebischer,
Major der päpstl. Schweizergarde
in Freundschaft zugeeignet
der Autor:
Heinrich Pfeifer gen. Orb
Ende Juli 1945.

The inscription inside Eglantyne's copy of this book. It reads in English: 'To Herr Umberto Aebischer, Major of the Papal Swiss Guards [at the Vatican], in friendship, from the author: Heinrich Pfeifer called Orb. End of July 1945.'

The abbreviation *gen.* appearing before Orb is the abbreviation for *genannt*, which means 'named' or 'called'. Umberto Aebischer was Swiss, and later rose to become Colonel and Commander of the Pope's Swiss Guards. As a Swiss German, his first name would really have been Umbert (a traditional name in the Aebischer family going far back in time), but as his work was in Rome, Umbert became 'Umberto'. Pfeifer was himself a Catholic, from a Catholic family, and he mixed in Swiss Catholic circles after his defection. Indeed, the publisher of his book was a well known Swiss Catholic publishing house, which is one reason why the Swiss Government reluctantly allowed the book's publication.

Heinrich Pfeifer was assassinated in 1949 by a hit squad of postwar 'Vengeance Nazis' in very strange circumstances, involving his being taken away by two 'policemen' who turned out not to be policemen and who disappeared, the police claiming they had never heard of them and they were nothing to do with them.

So who was the mysterious Heinrich Pfeifer who wrote this book? His full name was Heinrich Franz Pfeifer. Sometimes his surname is spelled with a double-f, but that is incorrect. He was born on March 21, 1905, at Frankfurt am Main in Germany. His father Heinrich Pfeifer was a senior postmaster who died in 1916, apparently killed in the First World War, when the boy was only eleven. His mother was Theresa Katherina, née Schad. Mrs. Pfeifer eked out a survival on her husband's war pension. Heinrich attended secondary school where one of his friends and fellow students was a boy two years older named Werner Best, who later became the Deputy Head of the Gestapo. This was during the time when the young Best's family were living in Mainz. (Best's father was a postmaster, and maybe the boys became friendly because both their fathers were postmasters, and could have known each other professionally.) The famous Oberrealschule which they both attended was evidently Das Gymnasium am Kurfürstluchen Schloss in Mainz. Pfeifer may have boarded with his Schad relatives in their traditional town of Wiesbaden, just across the river from Mainz. Pfeifer's mother presumably wanted this opportunity for her boy to go to a superior school, as she was existing in penury at Frankfurt. Although Heinrich was very clever, one might even say brilliant, after graduating from secondary school there was no money for him to go to university. So he entered a commercial apprenticeship in Frankfurt and simultaneously took evening classes at the University of Frankfurt in economics. That only lasted for three semesters, however, for after that he moved to Milan where he worked in the Milan branch of his employers, Bamberger, Leroi & Co. The company manufactured bathrooms for hotels, schools, private homes, and offices. It was a big company. Pfeifer continued to work for them in Milan for three years and became fluent in Italian. His Italian became so good that he was later to be used as an Italian translator in the secret dealings between the Nazi SS and the Italian secret police. Pfeifer then accepted a position in the Milan office of Villeroy & Boch, a German manufacturer of ceramics who were partially a competitor of his earlier employers. This company was owned by Franz von Papen, a leading political figure with whom Pfeifer would interact later when he became a spy, as related in the book. Von Papen briefly became Chancellor of Germany in 1932 and later became Vice Chancellor under Hitler in 1933. From 1934 to 1938 he was Germany's Ambassador to Austria, and Pfeifer liaised with him in Vienna during his mission there, an adventure which is told in Volume Two. But he was soon sent to work in Villeroy & Boch's Barcelona office, where he began learning Spanish. After seven months there, the German-Spanish Trade Treaty expired and there was little work for him, so he was transferred to his company's offices in Marseille and in Lyon, where he improved his French. These language abilities were to be crucial for his later work in espionage. When his company wanted to call him back to Germany to work in their Dresden headquarters, he quit his job and went to stay with his mother in Frankfurt and plan what to do next with his life.

As early as his time in Milan, Pfeifer began a side career in journalism. (Hence he accurately described himself as a professional journalist when he defected to Switzerland.) The way in which this happened is rather comical. Because Pfeifer was working at that time in a company which made bathroom appliances, he met a visitor named Benno Reifenberg, who was then a manufacturer of toilet seats. Reifenberg (1892-1970) was to become a famous journalist and art critic, writing under the pseudonym of 'Florestan'. He became Editor of the features section of the *Frankfurter Zeitung*, the newspaper of Pfeifer's home town. Reifenberg and Pfeifer struck up a friendship and Reifenberg asked Pfeifer to write a piece about the famous Ambrosian

Library in Milan for the arts section of the Frankfurt paper. The article was a big success, and from then on wherever he was, Pfeifer was a regular foreign freelance contributor to the arts sections of many German newspapers. He always did this in his spare time and never used his real name. It was thus at this time that he began what was to become a dominant feature of his life, the use of pseudonyms and aliases.

Having arrived in Frankfurt and with foreign travel in his blood, Pfeifer conceived a plan to migrate to Japan, where one of his school friends had an important position in the city of Kobe and was prepared to help him establish himself there. Pfeifer journeyed to Hamburg to take a steamship to Japan, but Fate unexpectedly intervened. Destiny had other plans for him.

In Hamburg while he waited for his boat to Japan, Pfeifer met with his friend Reinhold Schünzel (1886-1954), a half-Jewish actor who had been acting in films since 1915 and directing them since 1918. Hamburg was Schünzel's home town. They had come to know each other previously through Pfeifer's multifarious journalistic activities. It was Schünzel who persuaded Pfeifer not to go to Japan, but instead to go with him to Berlin and join in the film business. He said Pfeifer could easily write some film scripts, and so Pfeifer moved to Berlin and during the winter of 1927/1928 commenced his brief career as a screenwriter. His first film was entitled *Gustav Mond, Du Gehst So Stille* (*Gustav Mond, You Walk So Quietly*, 1928), in which the lead role of Gustav Mond was played by Schünzel, who also directed the film. Pfeifer used the pseudonym of Friedrich Stein, a surname which was to stick with him for years to come, in his spy work. He wrote the script jointly with an old timer named Heinz Gordon (born 1871), who was 35 years older than Pfeifer and had been in the film business since he wrote his first short in 1913. In their collaboration, he showed Pfeifer how to write scripts. This film was released in English as *You Walk So Softly*.

After this, Pfeifer co-wrote three more films under the name of Friedrich Stein. They were: *Die Wochendbraut* (*The Week-End Bride*, 1928), directed by Georg Jacoby and produced by Orplid-Film Gmbh. The English version, *The Week-End Bride*, was released in 1930; *Meine Schwester und Ich* (*My Sister and I*, adapted from a play, 1929), directed by Manfred Noa and produced by National-Film; and *Wer Wird Denn Weinen Wenn Man Auseinandergeht?* (*Why Cry if You Are Leaving*/ aka *No Use Crying*, 1929) directed by Richard Eichberg, filmed at Babelsberg studios at Potsdam. This was a joint production by Universum Film (UFA), Richard Eichberg Film Gmbh, and British International Pictures, who released the English version as *No Use Crying*. Sound had come in by then and the song on the soundtrack was sung by Marlene Dietrich.

Pfeifer's film connections would come in very handy when he was later responsible for monitoring the bugged flat of the famous film actress Brigitte Helm, who had starred in the film *Metropolis*. As he listened to the conversations he would have known many of the names mentioned and would have met many of the people speaking. Indeed, he was possibly the only person in the Nazi organisation other than Josef Goebbels who would have had this much background knowledge of the film business. And, ironically, another of Pfeifer's espionage duties was, at the request of Himmler and

Heydrich, to monitor the bugged residence of their hated rival, Goebbels himself!

Pfeifer made a lot of money from his screen-writing, but did not otherwise enjoy this work very much. He continued his freelance journalism with pieces on art criticism and socio-critical reports. He then became involved in founding the famous afternoon newspaper *Tempo* for the publishing house Ullstein Verlag, but it did not last very long (it was published between 1928 and 1933), ceasing within months of Hitler's accession to power. *Tempo* had a specially large section on the film industry, to which Pfeifer contributed and probably partially edited. Its arts coverage made it necessary reading in Berlin at that time for everyone in show business. The newspaper was also strongly anti-communist, but was left-liberal in its orientation rather than nationalistic. It later became specifically anti-Nazi. Its Managing Editor was Manfred George, who was Jewish and whose full name was Manfred Georg Cohn. This is another example of one of Pfeifer's closest friends and working colleagues being a Jew. It was during this period that Pfeifer began to study political issues very seriously. He read most or all of Karl Marx, Engels, and Lenin. He found all of their writings spiritually empty and become convinced that the movement they had started was very dangerous. He thus became a passionate anti-Communist, which was to lead to his next big adventure, which would be decisive for the rest of his life.

In the spring of 1929, Pfeifer gave up film-writing and went to the Nazi Party headquarters in Berlin to offer himself as a fighter in the struggle against communism. And that led to his meeting Alfred Rosenberg, the influential Nazi ideologue. Rosenberg stopped Pfeifer from publicly declaring and identifying himself in the fight against communism and, seeing that he was highly intelligent, gave him a job instead as an important advisor for the theoretical and scientific resistance against communism in his own organisation. (Rosenberg must have been impressed that such a young man had read the works of Marx, Engels, and Lenin and rejected their ideas!) His official appointment was thus to the Bureau Rosenberg for Counterintelligence against Communism, acting as Aide to Rosenberg. Pfeifer was told he must use a pseudonym, so he decided to continue to be called by the surname of Stein which he had used in the movies, but instead of Friedrich, he chose the first name of Heinz, which is one of the two nicknames for Heinrich, the other being Hans. So from then on, Pfeifer became Herr Heinz Stein.

It must in some ways have been an unpleasant physical experience for Pfeifer to have to work with Alfred Rosenberg. Rosenberg had very dirty personal habits. He never washed and, as a result, he stank so badly that no one could bear to sit next to him. If Nazi leaders gathered, Rosenberg could be guaranteed to have empty chairs to either side of him, or perhaps even his own side of the table to himself. He never seemed to 'catch on' as to why people avoided close proximity to him. He also whistled all the time, often whistling between words while he spoke. And he had another awful habit: he never changed his shirt until it fell practically to rags. So he would be in the same shirt every day for many months, as it got dirtier and smellier. Then it would fall apart and he would reluctantly replace it.

Rosenberg had a personal torment, which was that he was not a native German speaker. He had been born and raised in Estonia and educated in Latvia. His first language was Russian and for his entire life in Germany he spoke German imperfectly, and with an accent. The presence of the young Pfeifer would have been a great psychological relief to him, because even in his early twenties Pfeifer was fluent in Italian, French, and English, and semi-fluent in Spanish. He had lived abroad for many years, just as Rosenberg had, and did not find accents disturbing, but instead expected them. Pfeifer was also perfect at formal 'literary German', and Rosenberg could imbibe tips for proper speaking from him without any humiliation, and Pfeifer could correct Rosenberg's written German for him and nobody else need know. With the clever young anti-communist Pfeifer, Rosenberg could relax in the company of a multi-lingual disciple. Pfeifer was a devout Catholic from a Catholic family. But this was not at all unusual amongst the Nazis at this stage. Heinrich Himmler, after all, was a devout Catholic. And even Adolf Hitler himself had been raised as a Catholic by his loving, misty-eyed mother who adored him just as she did the Virgin Mary.

It is important to realize that the secret to Pfeifer's lightning success and rapid rise in the hierarchy of the Nazi 'Deep State' was due to his being recognised as a protégé of Arthur Rosenberg. Rosenberg was an immensely powerful senior leader of the Nazis who had a strong influence on Hitler himself. The fact that Rosenberg was a virulent and ranting anti-Semite may have been unpleasant to the young Pfeifer, who seems never to have been anti-Semitic himself, and who had Jewish or part-Jewish friends in the film and newspaper businesses. But this was Pfeifer's first sponsor within Nazism, and perhaps he initially regarded Rosenberg's rants as an eccentric feature of someone who had come from the Baltic regions. Pfeifer only gradually came to realize the thoroughly evil nature of the system which he had joined. And he was slow to 'snap'. His de-conversion experience was to happen only as a result of the Night of the Long Knives, a ghastly massacre which happened June 30 - July 2, 1934. He was personally present with Himmler at the special dinner for Ernst Röhm the night before Röhm was murdered. The shock of those events made Pfeifer's eventual defection inevitable. But the certainty that he had to 'get out' was slow to mature, as we shall see. After all, how does one 'get out' of the Nazi 'Deep State' when one is in charge of part of it? He himself admitted later that he was the only one of the six key people who were eye-witnesses of every central aspect of the Night of the Long Knives who had escaped being murdered in order to shut them up.

Pfeifer worked for Rosenberg as a communist theory expert for several months and then in August, 1929, he joined the Nazi Party in Berlin under the name of Heinz Stein, which he had adopted from the beginning. All membership records relating to him from then on were under that name. The Party was never officially informed of his true identity. The Party leadership, recognising his unique abilities, instructed him to remain 'Heinz Stein' and never to reveal his real name. The only people who knew who he really was were Alfred Rosenberg and Werner Best. It is possible that Kurt Daluege and Josef Bürckel (both discussed in a moment) learned his real name, but equally possible that they did not. It is even likely that Pfeifer's later bosses Reinhard Heydrich and Heinrich Himmler did not even know his true identity. This paranoid secrecy would later be most useful to Pfeifer after his defection, because the vengeance squads would be looking for Heinz Stein, who was always fictitious. Pfeifer had truly entered the world of mirrors.

And there would be many more false names, so many that in order to remember them all himself, he adopted a system of giving himself first names in different varieties of Heinrich. Sometimes he was Hans, as when he used the alias of Hans Tisch, sometimes he was Heinz, sometimes he was Heinrich, and his French alias was Henri Bauer, so that he even had a French version of Heinrich available to him. And he was called Henry sometimes, which is the English version. Another of his aliases, Karl Henri, used Henri as a surname, and sometimes he was Henri Karl, reversing it. And another, Franz Fischer, used his real middle name as a first name. These recyclings of his own names in different variations would have helped him call his various aliases to mind more quickly than if each alias was entirely invented. As he himself specifically states: 'At the request of the party leadership, I maintained this pseudonym [Heinz Stein] for the whole of the duration of my services to the NSDAP [Nazi Party]; indeed, it was the only name by which I was known to other party members.' Pfeifer's choices of aliases were ingenious. Somehow, he even managed to obtain a genuine French passport in the name of Henri Bauer. Although he was fluent in French, he seems to have lacked a perfect pronunciation. He thus gave himself a German surname and claimed to be from Alsace, a region which had repeatedly switched between being part of Germany and part of France. The French were used to Alsatians. After all, it was Alsatians who created most of the Paris brasseries, where they served their native sauerkraut, and still do. Also, Bauer was a name which some Jews had. (Bauers who came to England often changed the spelling to Bower, as it sounds exactly the same.) No one would suspect an Alsatian with a French first name and a German surname and a slight accent, and especially one with a surname which might even be Jewish. How could such a person possibly be a German spy? And Pfeifer even infiltrated the French security service, the Deuxième Bureau, becoming 'their' agent but really being a double-agent. But that was just one of his many adventures.

And the secrecy extended even further than false names. As Pfeifer explains in his book, even the files and records of 'Heinz Stein' were, at the insistence of Heydrich, kept entirely separate from those of the normal employees of the SS and SD. As he was only 24 years old, his first rank was as a Sturmführer (Second Lieutenant), rising soon to Obersturmführer (senior first lieutenant). But then he rose very quickly to the rank of Sturmbannführer (Major), being one of the youngest officers of that rank in Germany. But all of his military ranks, his awards, his commendations and citations, were listed as those of Heinz Stein, and were kept apart from the official personnel records and stored in a special underground hideaway in Berlin where the top super-spies' records were kept safe from prying eyes in a place so secure that Pfeifer said it was superior to any bank vault and could never under any circumstances be accessed by anyone without authority. He states that he himself had constant access to it for his work. That was where the most secret special operations and foreign intelligence material was kept. It is a depository which has never been found, and is probably still intact, having never been discovered. (Unless, as explained later, it was never 'lost' to the true inheritors of the Nazi legacy.) The voluminous SS files seized by the Americans after the War were only the routine and standard files. The records of most of the top security officers and the top counterintelligence operations were not in them. They may still be underground somewhere, waiting, waiting, waiting ...

In discussing the people who were really running the security police affairs of Nazi Germany at this time, we need to keep in mind what few people seem to realize, namely, how young they were. I have already commented on the youth of Pfeifer, but Heydrich was only one year older than Pfeifer, and Werner Best was only two years older. Hermann Behrends ('the dachshund', see the main text), Heydrich's childhood chum who became his favourite assassin, was three years younger than Heydrich. We are talking here of men who were all in their twenties and yet they had an unlimited licence to kill. In fact, they were barely men at all but were really still boys, very bloodthirsty boys, bullying boys, deciding who could live and who could die. The extreme youth of these powerful Nazis is simply not properly realized. And Heinrich Himmler was only five years older than Pfeifer and four years older than Heydrich. They were all so young.

Let's look at it like this: Pfeifer was 24 when he became Rosenberg's Aide and advisor on communist theory; Behrends then was 21 and still in his home town as a hoodlum, Heydrich was 25, Best was 26, and Heinrich Himmler was only 29. We are used to thinking of these people as mature men, but that is illusory. They were still practically children, the kind that pull the wings off of flies. I doubt that many people have ever stopped to think about the fact that the Nazi 'Deep State' at the beginning was manned by boys in their twenties. We generally think of Himmler as a grown-up. But was he really ever grown up? If he could indulge his fantasies from the time of his late twenties, why change? Why not stay a spoilt brat and have lots of fun becoming one of the greatest mass murderers in history?

The security police of the SS known as the SD (initials for *Sicherheitsdienst*) had a public face and a private face. The public figures such as Himmler and Heydrich could not be incognito, as their true identities were so well known. But numerous top officials of the SD worked under pseudonyms in the same way that Pfeifer did. For instance, Pfeifer's close friend and colleague SS Oberführer (later SS Brigadeführer) Karl Albert's real name was Karl Albrecht. Pfeifer knew this because they were such good chums, and he tells us his real name in the book. The true identities of several other heads of departments and divisions in the SD are unknown. Pfeifer calls them by their pseudonyms which were their work names, either because he did not know their real names or to protect those who were his friends from being exposed. Another close colleague and friend of Pfeifer's was SS Brigadeführer Günther Palten, whose real name was Günther Patschowsky, and he adopted the name change on October 6, 1937. He was registered in the SS under two different numbers: 40064 (in 1935) and 36005 (in 1934). So he not only had two different names, he even had two different SS numbers. These things were all done on purpose to disguise the spies' identities and create a hopeless web of confusion. Sometimes even the most senior Nazis changed their names, for good reason. Robert Ley's real surname was Levi, and he was Jewish, but he managed to hide this fact during his Nazi career, aided by his being one of the loudest, most disgusting, and most violent of the Party's anti-Semites. Pfeifer despised him and took delight in exposing this hypocrisy. And of course the most famous name change of all was that of Hitler. His real name was Adolf Shickelgrüber (aka Shicklgrüber), which somehow does not have much of a ring to it, for someone intending to rule the world. Hitler was a genuine family name which he therefore adopted, possibly because it was short and snappy. For similar reasons, one presumes, Stalin ('Man of Steel') and Lenin were adopted as snappy names by those dictators. After all, Stalin's true Georgian surname was long and cumbersome, just like Shickelgrüber. It seems that Evil likes an easy name, and Satan is certainly one.

One of Pfeifer's aliases is particularly strange, and it doubtless has a story behind it which we can probably never fully know. He called himself at one point Baron Karl von Walther. This seems at first sight to be entirely unexpected and with no thread connecting it to anyone or any thing real. But it is likely that it arose because of his friendship (and perhaps they were much more than friends) with the young film actress Hertha von Walther, who was two years older than him and whom he would inevitably have met during his year of film work. She was one of the German film industry's wild girls at precisely the time Pfeifer was working in films. She had run away from her boarding school at the age of 17 to become an actress. She joined Max Reinhardt's theatre company and became his mistress. She then made a transition into films and was given her first film role by the famous director G. W. Pabst, and became his mistress and appeared in his film *The Love of Jeanne Ney* (1927), in which she played Margot. Her friend Brigitte Helm played Gabrielle in that film. In 1921, Hertha had even co-directed a film entitled *Julot der Apache* (*apache* here meaning 'gangster'). She was in many films, including some famous ones such as Fritz Lang's M with Peter Lorre (in which she played a prostitute). Her full name was Hertha Fema Elfrieda Stern und Walther von Monbary. That is an aristocratic name, and although her father was apparently not a baron, there was a genuine Baron von Walther who was a professor of chemistry, and doubtless a relation of some kind. Hertha herself was part Polish by descent. Hertha's father had been a Major General in the Kaiser's army and died in 1917. Hertha's older brother Kurt had been killed in the War in 1915. He had been born in Frankfurt, as had Pfeifer. Could there have been an earlier connection? It would seem to be impossible for Pfeifer to have used the alias von Walther without the knowledge and connivance of Hertha, for otherwise she would have protested at it and drawn unwelcome attention to him. Was he masquerading as Hertha's cousin? Had she been suborned as a spy? Were they working together? The field of speculation is wide open. One speculation I might put forward is that she may have assisted him in having incognito personal access to Josef Goebbels, who from 1933 became master of the German film industry and slept with all the actresses, probably including her. We know from Pfeifer's own testimony in this book that he was in charge of bugging and monitoring the private life of Goebbels on the direct orders of Heydrich and Himmler, who hated Goebbels. Pfeifer used to listen to Goebbels's bedroom activities through concealed microphones, so the surveillance was intense. If Pfeifer had been 'Hertha's young cousin' whom she brought along to soirées held by Goebbels he would have had perfect cover. But we shall probably never know. Pfeifer would never have revealed this, because to do so would have opened Hertha to dangerous reprisals and could even have resulted in her murder. She lived until 1987, 38 years longer than Pfeifer himself. At a later date, Pfeifer used a variation of this alias and called himself simply Karl Walter.

Pfeifer did not remain with Rosenberg, but was assigned to the staff of the SS Group East under SS-Gruppenführer Kurt Daluege. It was then that Pfeifer received his first military officer's commission, aged 25. Daluege had suppressed the 'Stennes Revolt' against Hitler in 1929, and this resulted in his rise in prominence and his command of this important Group of what was to become the new SS. Technically speaking, Daluege was probably officially in the SA, and it is likely that Pfeifer's first commission was actually an SA one. He became an aide to Daluege and was raised in rank to Obersturmführer. Daluege was a protégé and great favourite of Hermann Göring, and, like Göring, he loved mixing with high society. Pfeifer came to know Daluege intimately and ended up hating and despising him. He describes him well in the book. He was of large size, 'a giant of a man' and very upright in his bearing. Pfeifer seems to delight in telling us that Daluege's job for many years had been to manage rubbish collection in Berlin. In other words, he was a garbage collection supervisor. Pfeifer says he was 'a not especially bright, but hardworking and tenacious individual.' And he adds: 'This Kurt Daluege may have been a rowdy hooligan, but a very disciplined one, who never acted without or against an order "from above". Because of his insolent character he never managed to be accepted into the SD ... he needed to be able to brag and boast, while playing the role of an upright man of integrity ... he lacked personal initiative ... and in his case, fawning servility – which also formed a major part of his character – was not combined with a talent for independent thought and action. He ... was endowed with obnoxious bumptiousness. ... a bootlicker and unrestrained self-centred egotist who paid tribute to his super-ego-god in the currency of brutal terror, who compensated for his inferiority complexes with pushy ambition and a propensity for petty personal revenge, and made up for his lack of intellect with brashness and pluck – that was Kurt Daluege,'

What a letter of reference! And nor was Pfeifer the only person who thought that Daluege was a pompous idiot. Former Gestapo chief Rudolf Diels called him 'the idiot Daluege' in his memoir, *Lucifer ante Portas*, Stuttgart, 1950, p. 321.

So we can see that Pfeifer was no boot-licker. But he worked earnestly under his boss in countering communism. He was involved in the roundup of communists and closing-down of communist printing shops during the night of January 30-21, 1933, which as he informs us began with the raiding team meeting in Daluege's private residence, and then setting off from there. Presumably this was done to ensure secrecy concerning the planned operation.

Pfeifer tells us that his previous boss Alfred Rosenberg was scheming against Daluege, and attempting to replace him. It is difficult to know which one of the two men Pfeifer hoped would win the struggle. After all, Rosenberg hated Christianity, and Pfeifer was a devout Catholic. Rosenberg also coined the term *Untermensch* ('sub-human') to describe the Jews, and Pfeifer does not seem ever to have been an anti-Semite. For which of the two men did he have the greater contempt? Pfeifer explains what happened and that Rosenberg lost the struggle because he was 'much too primitive and clumsy a manipulator to succeed'. Rosenberg's plan was a disastrous failure, as Pfeifer explains in his book.

Pfeifer was active as a field agent, commencing in these early days. His bold personality and his complete mastery of the various Marxist and Communist texts, dogmas, and sects, enabled him to infiltrate several of their groups and speak with authority. He was so successful at this that he was asked to become the head of one of the Trotskyite groups! Another of his activities was to wander round in rags disguised as a beggar, gathering information. He was never spotted. He seemed to be able to be anybody with complete ease. For him, an alias was not just a name, it was a person, and he became that person. Apparently, he never failed in any of his daring missions speaking in foreign languages, being an impostor, lying convincingly, and infiltrating any organisation effortlessly. Everybody always believed him. He had so many identities, he was a spy version of the Portuguese author Fernando Pessoa, who wrote under so many pseudonyms. One wonders whether Pfeifer ever wondered who he really was.

In 1929 or 1930, Pfeifer fell in love and married Mrs. Helene Lichte, a divorcee, née Wolf. She had a daughter by her first marriage, Ursula Lichte. Pfeifer was very fond of his step daughter. He and Helene had a son, Hans Pfeifer, who was born December 19, 1931, in Berlin. Things did not work out after a while, and Pfeifer and Helene agreed to a divorce. However, the Nazi Party intervened and prohibited the divorce. Important Nazis were not allowed to divorce. So strict was this Puritanical rule that Hitler personally intervened to prevent Josef Goebbels from doing so, and ensured that he never saw the girl in question again. Pfeifer in his book remarks upon this control of the private lives of Nazi officials by the Party, without specifying his own situation. Years later, he would fall in love again with Elspeth Kober, and they would have two sons. But Pfeifer's divorce from his first wife only became possible after the War was over and the Nazi regime no longer existed. So at last he could marry Elspeth, which he did in Switzerland.

Pfeifer's second wife, Elspeth Kober. She was Swiss, not German. The story of who Elspeth Kober was, how he met her, who her father was, and all the other circumstances of that time will be told in Volume Two. (State Archive Basel)

Hans Pfeifer, Heinrich's Pfeifer's eldest son, who was born in 1931. His full name was really Johannes-Heinrich, but he used the nickname Hans when he grew up, and that is how he signed official documents. (State Archive Basel)

In the early 1930s, as the Nazis were getting their security agents recruited and organised, it was common for strong German nationalists who were not members of the Nazi Party, and also for many devout Catholics, to be brought into the spy services. The two books by historian George C. Browder about the German secret police (in which Pfeifer is not mentioned, by the way, for this name did not appear in the 'normal' files which Browder consulted, or, indeed, in any of the undiscovered secret files either) give an excellent description of the general situation at that time. Pfeifer admits to having been a strong Nationalist, but he was not a member of the Nazi Party until he was forced to join by Rosenberg, he was not an anti-Semite, he was very religious, and he developed a violent hatred of the Nazi concentration camps with which he later became familiar. But none of this was allowed to get in the way of his being useful, as far as Pfeifer's ultimate boss Reinhard Heydrich, Himmler's deputy and the head of the SD, was concerned. Yes, they seem to have had their quarrels, some real and some simulated. An example of a simulated quarrel between them was Heydrich's Order for Pfeifer's arrest in 1936. It was spurious and clearly a cover for his planned defection to Poland, and could not even have been carried out, considering that Pfeifer's true identity was not known to any arresting authorities. Furthermore, the SD did not deal with people in such a 'normal' fashion. They did not issue Arrest Orders, they just seized people and shot them. As Pfeifer himself has said of Heydrich's treatment of his enemies: 'he annihilated them'. Nor were arrest orders necessary to Heydrich's squad of ruthless killers known as the Alarm Command. All that was necessary were a nod and a wink, a name and address. So that 'quarrel' was just a setup.

One of Pfeifer's closest friends was Fritz Ponath, whom he recruited as his chief clerk in the Stein Office to save Ponath from arrest by the Nazis, as he describes in the book. Ponath was later killed fighting in France. Pfeifer writes a passionate elegy to his friend, and stresses that 'Nazism was entirely alien and abhorrent' to him. We may assume the same about Pfeifer himself, and his strident denunciations of the Nazis make his true feelings clear.

Pfeifer's true importance began under his bosses Himmler and Heydrich. 'Himmler and Heydrich' in real terms often means just Heydrich, since in Munich, when Pfeifer joined them, Himmler sat quietly in his inner office, the entrance to which was blocked by Heydrich, who dealt with almost all business and prevented people going in to see Himmler because he thought Himmler was "too soft", as Himmler would burst into tears if a widow and orphan pleaded with him to release someone. Pfeifer was running his own secret office under their direction in 1933-4. As Heinz Stein, his office was known as the *Büro Stein* (Stein Office) or *Sonderbüro Stein* (Special Office Stein). As he himself tells us, at the time of his appointment he held the rank of Sturmbannführer, or Major, on 'the secret ranking list of the Reichswehrministerium'. In other words, the Nazi Government kept a secret list of its covert agents and employees working under false names, so that even Pfeifer's post and rank were kept secret, in addition to his identity, as has already been mentioned. He was valuable because of his extraordinary abilities, verging on the super-human, in counter-intelligence work. He had been introduced to Himmler and Heydrich by his old school friend, mentor and

The author's Swiss friend Umbert ('Umberto') Aebischer, Major of the Papal Swiss Guards in 1945, and later its Colonel and Commander, seen here sitting at his desk in the Vatican.

This book was written

out of obligation to the friends who fought against Nazism and militarism and the comrades who were murdered and tortured.

This book is dedicated to

my son Johannes-Heinrich and his mother, after more than ten years of separation.

HEINRICH ORB

PERSONAL QUOTE FROM HEINRICH PFEIFER:

With each passing page, the task upon which I had embarked increasingly turned into an obligation towards my friends who had remained in Germany and who continued their stoical fight against the Nazi regime despite all the terror, and to my comrades and all like-minded individuals who were being tortured to death in the concentration camps. All of them were good Germans, as I believe myself to be.

PREFACE

The power of Nazism is a *power of yesterday*. The whole world, as it awakens from astonishment and horror, has resolved to do everything it can do to prevent this power from returning, in some guise, as a *power of tomorrow*. And yet – even as many resounding voices are crying "Never again!" – various mechanisms are in motion that might encourage that very return. The same was true in the period following World War I, and cautionary voices could be heard then, too. For what was true then still holds true today: some preventative measures are likely to encourage, or even bring about, the very thing they are designed to prevent! Unfeasible paragraphs in enforced treaties, suppression, burden. What is imposed through myopic *Realpolitik* in the hour of one-sided supremacy can have quite the opposite effect – because such measures betray the essence of the word "peace". Thus many a conflict is brought merely to a temporary halt through a crushing force that imposes a *"peace of power" – only for the conflict to erupt again after some time.* The world is still waiting for the first true *"peace of conviction"*.

Those who think in all too "realistic" terms fail to understand the *disposition* through which power coalesces and collapses, how *disposition* can give rise to conflict and catastrophe, but also lead to harmony and reconciliation. The "business of today", which – thanks to the current distribution of power can be carried out with minimal resistance – does not offer clues to this disposition. One has to dig deep and identify the deepest root causes in order to find the correct medicine. It is *imperative* to do so – for ultimately the inner disposition is always the prime factor. Mundane everyday life is already rearing its head; the panic-fuelled horrors of yesterday will soon be forgotten and glossed over, and already we fall back into habits that we abjured during the hours of fear. Already there are many zealous and righteous judges who use harsh words to pronounce the entire German people guilty – and among them there is no shortage of individuals who were quite accommodating to the powers of Nazism during the critical years of 1940 and 1941. It is an old and bad habit to utter sweeping condemnations of others, of entire peoples, fellow humans that were caught in the centre of a political typhoon. Those who were sitting in the storm shelters as the tempests ravaged the lands find it easier to pronounce judgement on others.

Mental short-sightedness is a dangerous condition. It is true that everything possible has to be done to prevent a return of the scourge of the National Socialist demon (by whichever name it might be known), but it is equally true that these endeavours must be of a proper, careful and just kind. Experience has taught us that generalisations (which are always unjust), words of compulsion and deeds of hatred often achieve the opposite. What should be repelled instead is fostered, what should be thrust to the ground instead is strengthened, and what one forevermore seeks to avoid instead is brought to pass. Favoured by the power constellations of this hour, such emotive and myopic actions in reality lead to counterproductive effects. The two main political mistakes that result from such actions have parallels in the field of education, where pedagogical rather than political principles are violated. Firstly, a teacher or educator who persistently demands more than can possibly be achieved even with the utmost exertion will necessarily ruin individual pupils and the whole class. The bitterness of the imposed experience of failure will gradually lead to stubborn hostility, hatred, despair and utter denial! The second mistake is the suppression of available energies, such as the energy of youth. If such energies are not channelled and targeted toward decent aims, but merely supressed, they will fuel a core of inner tension that eventually will erupt in incalculable destruction. Both these mistakes in the treatment of people and nations are invariably made at points when power is absolute and when there is no opposition to keep it in check. Posterity pays the price.

The first step in any sensible attempt to prevent a grave, recently overcome threat from reawakening must be to gain an understanding of the nature of that threat. The essence of societal threats is mental. People act according to their mental constitution and in response to the prevailing situation. The situation – defined by geographical, economic or historical conditions, advantageous or debilitating traditions or disappointing events – *induces* action. The type of reaction, the manner of action chosen, corresponds to the character of the people and the nation.

Therefore, if one wants to avert the return of a peril one has just lived through, one has to get to know this peril. While this getting to know must *start* with the facts – with external markers serving as identifiers – it must go *beyond*. It must permeate the events right through to their root causes, that is to say, their sources of strength and guiding factors. Only when one sees these for what they are can one efficiently embark on a cure. Remedies are only efficacious in the hands of a doctor who *diagnoses*, but not when administered by some quack who merely attacks the symptoms and makes everything worse in the course of doing so.

How could National Socialism overpower a great cultural nation such as the German one to such an extent that after the seizure of power no major uprising or significant passive resistance was visible to anyone on the outside, that this nation accepted such sacrifices, such subjugation and such bondage, inexplicably endured coercion of conscience and conviction, silently consented to atrocities beyond measure inflicted on itself and others, and then launched a war of aggression which led to a new World War, and persisted in it even when the fortunes of war turned away from the ensign of the swastika? How could a people not only entrust itself to such leaders, but also stay true to them when their promises so often were laid bare as deception and their vows revealed as delusion? And how could it muster such heroism, loyalty in the face of suffering and death, the virtues of the best soldier – efforts almost beyond belief – for five years and more, all for a new class of master which in the main was composed of criminals and outcasts who on a daily basis compromised themselves through crudity, depravity, gluttony and immoral enrichment of the most nauseating kind? *Never before had a nation waged war against itself more profoundly than Germany when it fought for Hitler.* Moreover, how was it possible for power to grow so strong that it became possible to bat away the resistance of its opponents in a matter of weeks – that is to say the resistance of Poland, Belgium, Holland, France (with its reputed "strongest army in the world"), the Balkan nations, and, at times, that of England and Russia?

This is the inquiry into the secret of a power that first overawes its own nation and then, using its people as its instrument, a large part of the world. How did Hitler, Himmler, Heydrich and the others do it? How was it possible? A paltry and toxic movement – irrelevant at first, made up of insignificant individuals with primitive slogans and pathetic thoughts, berating everything, promising everything, a gathering of bullies, convicts and virulent characters – grew by recruiting hangers-on from the growing ranks of the discontented, using coarse words and violent tactics. A few years later the whole of Europe was shuddering before the ogre that had grown – and with good reason! Millions dead, hundreds of thousands tortured, countless millions expelled and displaced – how could it happen? Everyone is familiar with the external events, but how it all became possible and real, I fear, very few people have understood.

The present book seeks to offer a first approach to gaining an insight. Fundamentally it is a factual report. As has already been said, comprehension must start with the facts. Not the facts that everyone lived through, but the hidden facts unearthed here. How did the Nazis build up their power? How did they force the German people so effectively down under their yoke? In these pages this is exposed by a man who was part of it all. There can be no doubt that the pseudonymous author had a vantage point from which he could observe the system from the inside in all its intricacies. Not only that, but for a while he actively participated in its construction – until the hour of his "Damascus" experience, until the days when his eyes were opened as to the whence and whither of that edifice. This epiphany happened only just in time to search his soul and, after severe examination and many an adventure, to escape from the grip of the power he himself, intoxicated like so many, had helped to create.

Perhaps the author will tell at a different time – thus lifting his secret – at which position he stood as he worked (it would appear on a daily basis) with Himmler, Heydrich and similar characters, how his eyes were opened, what he subsequently experienced and what he did to combat the threat after recognising it for what it was. For now, we will witness in astonishment and horror the emergence of the National Socialist power, whose innermost operatives – the likes of the "superhumans", the people in the Security Service (*Sicherheitsdienst*, SD) – have never been exposed to the world. We will learn about the precise mechanisms through which the German people were ensnared in the network. They were inextricably caught before they knew themselves. And for mere mortals there was no way out of the web the powers had woven, except for death under horrific ordeals. Now the world is crying out about these ordeals, and it is right to do so. But why only now? When hundreds of thousands of Germans, the actual and potential resistance, disappeared in the horror camps, as the persecution of the Jews was raging, the same world that is now crying out did not want to be disturbed in its everyday life by such reports. Those reporting were said to be telling fairy tales, and they were told in no uncertain terms that one *did not want to hear* that sort of thing. The victims' screams slammed into unyielding rock, and false wisdom lead to mercilessness. Foreign governments, too, knew what was taking place in Germany – but they did not want to disrupt the successful relations they maintained with the savage potentates. They made deals with them, entered into agreements, strengthened the Nazis' power through recognition and censored their accusers. It was a conspiracy of silence. And yet, the plans laid out in Hitler's book aroused the world's vociferous and universal anger only when he was – almost – able to realise them. The details of the concentration camps were well known long before the beginning of the war.

REPUBLIC OF POLAND

Ministry of Foreign Affairs

THE MASS EXTERMINATION of JEWS in GERMAN OCCUPIED POLAND

NOTE

addressed to the Governments of the United Nations on December 10th, 1942, and other documents

Published on behalf of the Polish Ministry of Foreign Affairs by

HUTCHINSON & CO. (Publishers) LTD.

LONDON : NEW YORK : MELBOURNE

Price: Threepence Net.

The Polish Government in Exile in December 1942 presented clear evidence of the Nazi plans to exterminate the Jews. This evidence was presented to all the world through the United Nations. But no one wanted to know.

This book – despite the important and largely new material it contains – would be of less value if the aura of the very spirit that created these facts was not discernible behind the facts. A spirit of immense prowess, but one on a corrupted course! Or, to put it another way, a demon and liar, one endowed with organisational mastery, iron discipline, an arid, obstinate ardour – and yes, with an evil kind of warped virtue.

But – let us talk no more, *let us read!*

At the end of the book the reader may, in quiet contemplation and with watchful conscience, ask himself: Had I been caught in this web – at first well-nigh unsuspecting and then horrifically and hopelessly entangled – would I have had the strength to sacrifice wife, children, family, position, every earthly asset (and this without the slightest humanly imaginable possibility of achieving anything), to disentangle myself from the web of power only to suffer an agonising death? Anyone who, before God and in clear conscience, is able to answer in the affirmative, who is sure of himself to be equal to all of life's trials and able to resist all seduction of power, habit, utility and lust, and moreover can claim to have mercy on his side – such a person has the right to throw stones at the average German who was not equally capable.

A publisher who presents such a book to the general public is taking on a responsibility. Not for every word and every belief that is uttered in these pages – only someone who was part of it all could do that, and the minutiae are the author's concern. The publisher, however, would like to clarify why the publication of this text was taken on. The reason is this: the hope that a better world can be rebuilt from the ruins. Finding the strength to do this in the face of utter devastation must be based on the purest of intentions. If one wants to change things for the better, one has to see them as they are, and not distorted by habit, fervour or prejudice. A contribution to a survey of the facts as well as clarification as a basis for the formation of judgement that has to precede any action – that is what the publisher has sought to provide.

(A friend of the publishing house)

INTRODUCTION

THE *WEHRMACHT* AND THE PARTY

Militarism or national defence?

It is not the intention – and neither would it be possible – to tackle the issue of "*Wehrmacht* and party" in a single chapter. Investigating the secrets of National Socialist power in some measure involves disentangling the threads that were spun from the party to the *Wehrmacht* and vice versa, and it is these threads, in their many interconnections and divergences, that constitute the actual authoritarian state that was the *Third Reich*. The following chapter specifically deals mainly with the *Wehrmacht*, the German officer class, the "avatars of Old Prussian officer virtue". A series of accusations will be made, which – in such stark exposition – will paint a purely negative picture, a rather one-sided black-and-white sketch. It is therefore necessary to include some opening explanations and definitions, which in no way are intended as excuses for the wrongs that have been committed, but rather are an attempt to do justice to people whose hand had been forced. This concerns in the main the aforementioned "avatars of Old Prussian officer virtue", who will shortly enter the stage. But first, a word about the party and its ideology.

In these pages, National Socialism will be described as "hopefully the last and at the same time most dangerous exponent of German militarism", but also as "the bastard of German militarism". The latter description may at first seem more plausible, but in reality they are both justified. The political programme of the NSDAP, the myth of National Socialism, the depravity of its racial theory and the notion of the "master race" that emerges from it – all these and similar topics have filled the pages of countless books and publications. It is not our intention to contribute to that type of literature, for we mainly want the facts to speak. But we do have to briefly characterise National Socialism for what it is.

What is the innermost core of National Socialism? What is its ideological root from which it emerged in all its power and weakness, the mainspring that could hold the key to an understanding of its demeanour, its development and also its demise?

National Socialism is a pseudo-religion. The essence of a true religion is belief in the absolute, in something that does not depend on us mortals or the passage of time, nor the whims and ambitions of individual powerful nations – that is to say it is the belief in something that does not depend on anything that is of this Earth or exists in space and time. It is man's calling to seek that which is "detached" and "unconditional"; it is our purpose in life, we can not change it, we can only set out to seek it. The cognizant spirit strives for truth that exists within itself, and for an ideal – the eternally immutable commandments of justice and love.

The great French thinker René Descartes, making the notion of methodic doubt the cornerstone of his philosophy, came to the conclusion that human self-awareness is the most certain evidence that contributes to our cognition. "*Cogito, ergo sum* – I am self-aware, therefore I am." This fundamental tenet gained immense importance. It achieved much that is good, but also misled when it was stretched too far. When left to stand by itself, it incorporates a dangerous corollary: individual human consciousness can be elevated to form the basis of all cognition and all ethical norms; a corollary that can lead (and has led) to unconditional individual liberalism. Descartes himself did not go there; he remained a life-long devout Christian and bowed to the absolute.

As is made plain in its myths and key literature and manifest in all its teachings and deeds, National Socialism preaches "*cogitamus ergo sumus*" (albeit without actually uttering these words). As a race, we, the Aryans, are becoming aware of ourselves, our life, our "blood and soil". Race functions as the super-ego, and it becomes self-aware within its leaders. This is the fundamental tenet, the *ur-truth* by which all else is defined. Anything that acknowledges this foundation – this thinking consciousness of the awakening race – must be true; anything that benefits it must be good. An absolute and higher category, independent of the racial super-ego, does not exist. The notion of "objectivity" becomes absurd, and "justice" metamorphoses into whatever is deemed advantageous.

This, however, is the ultimate and most fundamental and irreconcilable difference with true religion. The god of Nazism emanates from the notion of race itself, he is a vitalistic concept, a god that emerges from the soil and flows like blood in arteries; a god who only wants himself and nothing else, who tolerates only what benefits him. What does not serve him must be destroyed.

Anyone who understood this – sadly it dawned on most people only when it was too late – would have known where the path would lead; would have understood why things had to take the terrible turns they did; would have been aware that any gestures of acquiescence displayed or any dialogue sought by National Socialism were mere delaying tactics; would have known that in reality every treaty would ultimately be violated and every partner betrayed as soon as it seemed opportune to do so. Every step in the unfolding events, the internal and external machinations of power, would have seemed clear, logical, and even inevitable to anyone who held that key.

What is more, it is a fundamental feud with the Christian belief in God: the vitalistic super-ego-god of race will never *get al.*ng with the eternal, all-gracious, compassionate, redeeming Father-God of *all* humanity, who preaches peace, love, justice, compassion, sacrifice and belief in the hereafter. The super-ego-god may try to deceive, betray and paralyse the servants of Christianity. Well, he has done that in abundance. He may enter into a concordat, perhaps a naval treaty – – – but merely as a political feint, for he is forever incapable of being serious about such agreements.

Of course there were a few who understood all of this early on, but those who proclaimed it were not believed. In the forthcoming expositions on the essence of National Socialism I have been following the writings of a German scholar that at the time were, sadly, largely ignored. Let us call to mind once again the main point: a pseudo-religion that means nothing less than a raised fist against the Christian God! And when Adolf Hitler praises "divine providence", and at the same time allows himself to be idolised as the "leader of all Germans chosen by divine providence", this so-called "divine providence" is nothing more than the vitalistic "Aryan" race-god, who instructs members of the National Socialist master race to seize power over other peoples and nations. Thus it has absolutely nothing to do with the notion of "divine providence" in the Christian sense – indeed, Hitler's invocation of *his* divine providence is synonymous with that very fist raised against God. And, characteristically, the National Socialist master race has invented the concept of "sub-humans", a term used not only to designate Communists or members of other races, such as Jews, Slavs and Negroes, but one also applied to anyone who is unwilling to recognise the notion of a master race.

National Socialism is the most horrifying manifestation of man's delusion of grandeur – the belief that he can live and act without God. The more these "master humans" were driven by their master-race god, the super-ego, into an obsessive delirium of wanting to (and eventually having to) rule, the more relentlessly they had to rage with a rule of coercion and terror not only against other races and nations, but also against those members of their own kind who had not yet succumbed to the same delirium and, as non-National Socialists, were compelled to worship and serve a system of a master race that they abhorred.

The "avatars of Old Prussian officer virtue", that is to say the officers of the newly founded German *Wehrmacht*, in some sense were also "master humans", but it would be incorrect to designate them as such in the strictly National Socialist sense. For while they were always eager to serve the authoritarian state and happy to contribute to its glorification, their kind of societal supremacy (as they saw it) had not yet fully been estranged from God. Despite all their dutifulness towards the authoritarian state and their iron discipline, they had a conscience, a sense of responsibility not only towards the state, but also towards God. This conscience could be numbed, at times even switched off altogether, but it could not be completely supressed or expunged. An absolute, a "higher being", did exist and therefore the existence of divinity was acknowledged, and – despite all aberrations – never negated. The deep tragedy and the turmoil of the German character were often manifest in these "avatars of Old Prussian officer virtue", their actions and eccentric "virtuousness". On the one hand there was the "iron sense of duty", the inexorable sternness and rigid discipline with which this guild of war craftsmen went about their craft; on the other hand there was the strictly segregated "private sphere", in which it was quite possible, in an hour of silent contemplation, to fold one's hand in prayer and to meditate upon one's desire for nearness to God. (In National Socialism prayer was replaced by racial ceremonies.)

It is interesting to note that, of all people, the creator of the military aristocracy and founder of the first German officer corps, the King of the Prussians, Frederick II, established the Grand Old Prussian Masonic lodge "*Zu den drei Weltkugeln*" ("The Three Globes"), whose first Grand Master he was. Incidentally, all subsequent Prussian kings followed his example in this respect. (These Old Prussian lodges – until 1934 there were three of them – under no circumstances must be confused or identified with the international Masonic lodges, who – unlike the Prussian lodges – permitted Jews.) The members of the Old Prussian lodges were either Prussian officers or Prussian civil servants (who also would have previously served as officers). Prominent representatives of "Old Prussian officer virtue", such as Scharnhorst, Blücher, Gneisenau, Moltke, Schlieffen *et al.*, were all members of the Old Prussian lodges. Even Field Marshal von Hindenburg's father had been the "Worshipful Master" of an Old Prussian "*Feldloge*" (a Masonic lodge whose membership was made up exclusively of serving military officers), which is why Hitler, upon assumption of power, had to promise to the aged *Reichspräsident* that he would not dissolve the Old Prussian lodges (as opposed to the Jewish-international ones); a promise that – naturally – he did not keep. It is not the purpose of this book to pick a fight with the Freemasons. In any case, these Old Prussian Freemasons were not atheists, for they acknowledged God as the "Great Architect of the Universe", they understood the imperfection in all human endeavour and believed in the absolute that cannot be attained during earthly existence.

This is the "logo" of the Old Prussian Masonic Lodge "The Three Globes", founded in Berlin in 1740 by King Frederick II of Prussia. He was its first Grand Master according to the author, though that is denied today. Jews were not admitted. Hitler closed the Lodge in 1935, but the lodge reopened in 1946 and is still going strong. The name of the Lodge really means "The Three World-Globes" (*Drei Weltkugeln*). The meaning is, as shown in the logo, mounted globes depicting the Earth or the night sky, such as used to be found in most classrooms in the days when geography was taught in schools and when gentlemen always had globes in their studies. Why the Prussian Masons felt thay they needed three of them is a mystery.

This is not the place to judge why National Socialism arose in Germany (as opposed to any other nation) and why the attempts to make the Germans into democrats failed during the time of the Weimar Republic; indeed, why they had to fail. Chanting anti-German slogans of hatred and satisfying the cravings for revenge for the wrongs and atrocities committed by the Germans will not be conducive to Germany's renewal and will not help to rebuild Germany, Europe or the wider world. Germany – and with it Europe – can only be saved if the German people can successfully be turned into good Christians once again! Yet this urgent task can only be accomplished through genuine Christian ambition, in true Christian spirit. The more the victorious nations display this Christian spirit, the more easily such a spirit will be able to develop in a defeated and occupied Germany. All you faint-hearted sceptics, hear this: pessimism, as a fundamental attitude, is altogether un-Christian. Pessimism and faintheartedness can no more be reconciled with honest Christianity than gullibility – in the sense of irresponsibility – and jingoism. In order to tackle the difficult and important task of reconstruction and renewal, one requires above all genuine knowledge of the nature of past mistakes and their repercussions, and an understanding of the historical context of even the most recent times – as it were, an inventory of facts as they truly are and not as they might seem. It is therefore our duty to report on the facts in all details known to us, without glossing over anything or engaging in wild and dubious speculation; it will be necessary to investigate the mentality that led to mistakes and atrocities. In order to better illustrate the following, we shall briefly give the floor to a man who has made a name for himself as a moral philosopher and pedagogue, but whose political "excursions" have attracted severe criticism: Prof. Dr. Friedrich Wilhelm Förster [1869-1966). In reference to the war of 1914–18 he writes in his chapter "The Solidarity of the Two Germanies":

"Who bridged the immense chasm between the pure spirit and the corrupted one, between German culture and neo-German barbarism? It was German philosophy – Kant, Fichte, Hegel. As they were drowning in subjectivity, the most profound and earnest Germans yearned to be rescued onto the *terra firma* of normative and universal principles. The whole phenomenon of a nationalist Germany can only be understood if one views the fusion of German idealism with the affairs of the German state and its politics – i.e. the whole "materialisation" of the German soul – from the correct psychological angle. Other nations, too, underwent such a "materialisation" process; the reason that in the case of the German people it led to delusion and disease is not that Germans are essentially more "material" than other nations, but precisely because the German nation's extreme mental tension from a particular moment onwards had been poured in its entirety into the realm of the *material* (Wagner's Wotan) and the nation state, and thus gave birth to a peculiar form of "materialism" and national cult, namely one motivated by idealism. The German spirit had been won for the state in a peculiarly "cerebral" fashion, and this very state was now becoming heavily steeped in German metaphysics and notions of "totality", and thus – much like Jehovah in the Old Testament – became an all-consuming fire. The nation and the national community absorbed all of German poetry and music; and thus the "immeasurable" within the German character was absorbed by the body politic, where it inflated all that is by its nature plain, administrative and even obsequious – that is to say the entity which is only ever meant to be a mere means to promote human perfection. In the process of becoming infused with the "immeasurable", the state aggrandised itself to unbounded entitlement; to a point where the collision of the absolute, state-controlled spirit with the reality of the existence of "the other" could no longer be avoided.

"The rest of the world, startled and frightened, as if awoken from a deep slumber by the terrible collision, asked: 'But where is the Germany of Goethe, Bach, Beethoven?' The answer: the old orchestra has by no means vanished, but has engaged a different bandmaster and is now playing the *Hohenfriedberger Marsch*...

"I once had a Catholic student, who, during the war, had been entirely unaffected by such developments. In the trenches at Douaumont he read a French biography of Saint Thérèse of Lisieux, and he remained forever on my side. It was plain to see that aberrations of the spirit as described above only could occur where deep and universal Christianity no longer governed thought and conscience.

"Many of my pupils were killed at Verdun or in the Vosges. During their brief periods of home leave many of them would have visited me and poured their hearts out, and so I was able to gain a deep insight into the wholly peculiar process that for a century has been ruthlessly selling German idealists to Prussianism, and marrying a pure spirit to a corrupted one, in life and death. One of them wrote: 'What matters in the end is always the willingness to make sacrifices, and not that which the sacrifice is made for... And so once again we sang the old patriotic songs, in a wholly new spirit.' It was the Kantian concept of duty that had forged the connection between their spiritual longing and their fate on the battlefield: an ancient religious spirit of sacrifice born in a Christian wellspring, vastly amplified in the German character, then – owing to a scarcity of material nourishment – grown pale and emaciated into abstract idealism and the vague desire to lose oneself in something higher. The ancient German longing of the fragment for the whole, of the particular for the universal – now cast into the cramped confines of the nation state's limited horizon!

"... Undoubtedly, German philosophy of the 19th century – which in its barren abstractions haughtily thought itself superior to Christianity, but yet nourished the inner lives of German youths with mere rocks instead of bread – must bear overwhelming blame for the derailment of the German people. The entire 19th century is filled with the tendency of souls increasingly deserted by God and Christ to be infatuated with earthly *ersatz* objects substituting for the spiritual wealth they had lost."

After this attempt of an interpretation of the "Solidarity of the two Germanies" – which we shall leave to Prof. Dr. Friedrich Wilhelm Förster without commentary, even though one might easily take exception to the term "solidarity" – we must now turn to a definition of the term "militarism".

On the issue of "militarism or national defence" it has to be noted that the former is certainly not identical with the latter and that national defence by no means requires militarism. Under normal circumstances, no nation can be denied its right to national defence; indeed, if a nation was denied the right to defend its borders it would cease to be a free and independent nation. This is why nations justify national defence by specifically using as a pretext the need to defend the freedom and independence of its people against a foreign aggressor. Defending oneself against an aggressor stands to reason, whereas provocative attacks have nothing to do with national defence.

Militarism will always be synonymous with an offensive stance – offensive not only in a military but also in a political sense. Militarism means governing in the sense of domination – it inevitably fosters an authoritarian state and is incompatible with democracy. The officer class under militarism cannot be compared to that in democratic nations. It may well be a large grouping in a democracy and relatively small under militarism (the Weimar Republic had an army of a mere 100,000 men!), but the officer corps in a state with militarist leanings plays an entirely different role compared to its equivalent in a true democracy. "Militarism" cannot exist in a healthy democracy. The attempts to establish a democracy in the Weimar Republic were thwarted not least by the failure to liquidate the militarism whose continued existence after World War 1 was ensured by the officer corps within the relatively small 100,000-strong army. The offensive spirit of the officer corps was undiminished and its craving for revenge for "the humiliation inflicted by the Treaty of Versailles" was continually nourished by the Weimar Republic's political opponents, through the disappointments of the peace agreement, the blunders made by other nations and, finally, by National Socialism. Militarism and its aggressive disposition bred a class of officer that referred to itself as the "bearers of the nation's defiance". It is the misfortune of the German people that its officer corps, time and again, purported to be representatives of this defiance, but that such defiance was not content with national defence, and, according to tradition, culture and world view, repeatedly incited the German people to attack its neighbours, allegedly in order to regain that which had been lost (such as the Polish Corridor or Danzig). The entire concept of militarism cannot be assessed correctly without a clear understanding of its nucleus, the officer class. This officer class is synonymous with the *guild of war craftsmen*. This guild with its *esprit de corps*, its duteousness and incorruptibility (these attributes will be investigated more fully below) not only was elevated to the status of a superior caste but they became the idols of an entire nation. It was regarded as the noblest civic duty to be obliging to this caste and the greatest honour to be commended by it or even accepted into its ranks. In the end, war craft is cultivated for its own sake, it is no longer a means for national defence but becomes an end in itself, the incarnation of all that is "heroic". The authoritarian state recruits its paladins preferably from the guild of war craftsmen and invests them with the splendour of "heroism" (and these heroes at the same time are seen as heroes of virtue!). And only when the state ceased to do this, the guild of war craftsmen rebelled against the authoritarian state that was the Third Reich.

SS-Oberstgruppenführer Philipp Bouhler [1899-1945] was one of Adolf Hitler's closest collaborators and, though less in the public eye than others, one of the most important advocates of National Socialism. Under the orders of his Führer he wrote a book on Napoleon [*published in 1942*], in which he compares Hitler to Napoleon – and indeed Napoleon's cravings for power were not unlike Hitler's.

SS Reichsleiter Philipp Bouhler (1899-1945, suicide) according to the author "was one of Adolf Hitler's closest collaborators". He had an unusual background, in that he had lived for some time in Brazil and spoke fluent Portuguese. He became Hitler's Chief of Chancellery and planned and organised the execution of 250,000 disabled people, including children, and between 15,000 and 20,000 concentration camp prisoners. Hitler ordered him to write a book comparing Hitler to Napoleon, which was published in 1942. Always willing to oblige his Führer …

The notorious "T4" killing institution, dedicated to murdering men, women and children who were disabled, "mentally unfit", or judged to be "inferiors" who must be eliminated from a society to be composed of perfect Aryans. More than 250,000 persons were murdered in this way, all of them Germans. (The murders of the Jews took place separately.) The reason why this harmless-looking building and the murderous organisation within were called "T4" was because its dreaded address was Tiergartenstrasse 4 in Berlin. The campaign of mass murder was known as "Aktion T4". The euphemism for the mass murder was "special treatment".

One of the most outstanding polemic pamphlets against Napoleon was published in 1813 by Benjamin Constant (born in Lausanne, Switzerland in 1767). The text, entitled *"De l'esprit de Conquête et de l'Usurpation"*, aptly characterises the offensive spirit of militarism, and everything that is said against Napoleon can be applied word for word to Hitler and his National Socialism. In Section 1, Chapter 10, Constant writes:

"When faced with the duty to repel an aggressor, all qualms have to be silenced. All classes of people have to rush to the scene, for everyone is equally endangered. As they are not spurred on by villainous looting, they will not degenerate, and as their fervour stems from true conviction, no compulsion is required. As the disruption of normal social activities is justified by the most sacred duty and the most precious interests, it does not have the same consequences as the usurper's arbitrary interference. The people are able to see an end to the disruption; they submit to it freely as a means to return to a quiet life... But it is one thing to defend one's homeland, and an altogether different matter to attack other people, who in turn have a homeland to defend. The spirit of conquest seeks to confuse these two ideas. When certain regimes send their legions from one of Earth's poles to another, they are still talking about defence of their homeland; it would seem they call homeland wherever they choose to start a fire."

Militarism and its officer class thought it had to refrain from outwardly getting involved in the "political" sphere. For that reason alone militarism cannot be straightforwardly identified with the ruling political system (in our case National Socialism). But the officer class views itself as the first and most noble servant of any authoritarian state and carefully guards the privileges of its guild. But it must be said again and again that – given their traditions and upbringing – the spirit of these war craftsmen could never be anything other than offensive. The fact that these war craftsmen did not engage in politics, that to a certain extent they even despised politics, does not alter the fact that naturally their ultimate desire was to not lose their fighting spirit or become weak, but rather to have an opportunity to put into action their fighting spirit! Yet this fighting spirit could not be actualized in any other way than the one described by Constant in Part 1, Chapter 8 of his polemic:

"Nowadays, when war is merely a source of deprivation and suffering and does not bestow any advantage on any nation, a political system based on conquest can only be based on lies and deception... Entirely possessed by its extreme plans, no government (i.e. that system based on conquest) would have the courage to say to its people: Onwards, to conquer the world! Instead, it would talk of national independence, of national honour and a "smoothing" of the borders, of trade interests, of far-sighted precaution, and I don't know what else. For the vocabulary of hypocrisy and injustice is inexhaustible... Using 'far-sighted precaution' as a pretext, such a regime would attack its most peaceful neighbours or modest allies by accusing them of hostile intentions and asserting the need to pre-empt their preconceived plans of attack."

We have little intention of singing the praises of Benjamin Constant, the "father of liberalism", with whose other opinions we by no means always agree. But when studying his polemic against Napoleon, one seems to be listening to a visionary, a warning prophet who had seen the immense catastrophe of National Socialism and raised his voice against it in vain. To conclude, an excerpt from Part 2, Chapter 4:

"Think of the events that have coalesced in front of our eyes over the past six months. The conquest had established an illegitimate power throughout large swathes of Europe, and this usurping regime – which was acknowledged even by those who had every reason to never accept it – had done everything to consolidate its power. At times it had threatened other nations, at times it had flattered them: it successfully gathered enormous forces in order to intimidate, invented sophisms designed to deceive, and entered treaties in order to soothe consciences. In doing so, it had gained a few years during which its origins grew somewhat obscure. The governments it had destroyed – republican or monarchist in nature – were seemingly without hope, and yet they lived on in the hearts of their peoples; even twenty lost battles could not tear out those roots. But only one battle lost by the illegitimate power, and it was harried from all sides and forced to retreat."

After these considerations – which we consider to be worthwhile – we would like to allow the facts to speak. Just one more essential explanation:

In order for the German people to recover – and only if that nation in the heart of Europe recovers will the rest of Europe be able to do the same – not only National Socialism but also German militarism has to be eradicated, root and branch. The internal logic that makes the aforementioned considerations inevitable is the following: war, and therefore the suffering of entire peoples, is an inevitable and forgone conclusion when the craft of war is elevated to an heroic ideal and the guild of the warriors anointed as the nobility of a people. The legal concept of self-defence, the protection of people and homeland, is a bitter and sad necessity in our imperfect world. But to make war craft, or the art of annihilation (a means that should only ever be used with a bleeding heart), into the highest, independent goal of ambition; for a state to make it into a vocation: that is militarism as we have met it in Germany. When war craft is idealised – and it is a mental process, much like anything else of fundamental import – then that nation's idol will continually lead that nation into attack and into war, with all its terrible consequences.

Two Junctures

There are two turning points that mark the most recent history of the German *Wehrmacht* and *Reichswehr* respectively: June 30, 1934 and August 8, 1944. (It is not July 20, 1944 that is decisive – the day on which the officers' assassination attempt on Hitler became public knowledge – but the date on which its consequences were felt, namely August 8, 1944.) The public is only vaguely aware that June 30, 1934 was the day of the *Wehrmacht's* victory over the party. The hesitant generalissimo Freiherr von Fritsch was unable to capitalise on the hand that he had been dealt on June 30, 1934 – he preferred instead to forge a compromise with Hitler, surmising correctly that only Hitler and his National Socialism would be able to give the generals the war machinery they wanted – a war machinery on an unprecedented scale. The general's expectations were fulfilled in this respect, but it was a miscalculation to believe that Hitler would honour the homogeneity of the *Wehrmacht*; despite his assurances to the contrary, Hitler soon began to politicise the *Wehrmacht* and in doing so disempowered the generals.

Baron (*Freiherr*) Thomas Ludwig Werner [*always called Werner*] von Fritsch (1880-1939), Commander in Chief of the German Army [*the Reichswehr*] until 1938. According to the author, he was 'unable to capitalise on the hand he had been dealt' in 1934 and was outmanoeuvred by Hitler.

The events in the run-up to June 30, 1934 will be dealt with separately and at some length; what follows here is merely a brief summary of the facts:

In March 1934, the commander of the *SA*, Ernst Röhm, presented a carefully worked-out plan to Hitler (who was not only the leader of the party and *SA* but also Röhm's close personal friend), detailing the necessary steps for the dismantling of the *Reichswehr* and the establishment of a so-called *Volksheer* (people's army). Under the plan, all undesirable generals and conservative officers would be arrested, all barracks and military depots would be occupied, and the *Reichswehr*'s 100,000-strong army would be newly structured and staffed with men from the various *SA* divisions. Hitler responded with neither a "yes" nor a "no" to his best friend's proposals, and for months stalled Röhm and the handful of other *SA* leaders that were in on the plan, until eventually the planned putsch in all its details was betrayed to General Fritsch at army command.

SA Leader Ernst Julius Günther Röhm (1887-1934), Hitler's close friend whom Hitler condemned to death without a qualm. He was killed in the aftermath of "the Night of the Long Knives", as described in detail later in this book. Röhm had spent considerable time in Bolivia as a mercenary soldier and military instructor before returning to Germany to take part in the Nazi activities there. Compromising letters describing his homosexual activities in Bolivia, brought to Germany by a blackmailer, complicated his career in the SA but were suppressed until after his murder. The very evening of his arrest in 1934, not long before he was taken into custody, he said to his friends that if he could not succeed in his attempts to make the SA part of the Reichswehr, he would resign and return to Bolivia. He was very ill at the time, with severe neuralgia, and was under specialist treatment for extreme pain.

On June 29, 1934 General Fritsch made his historic call to the then Minister President of Prussia, Hermann Göring: "Either Röhm and all involved *SA* leaders are immediately sentenced by a special court, or the Berlin garrison will get its marching orders on July 1, 1934!" Göring rushed to see Goebbels, and agitated discussions with Hess ensued, who, in his capacity as deputy leader, at that point held the actual party leadership in his hands. *Reichsführer SS* Heinrich Himmler (at the time in fact still officially Röhm's subordinate and outwardly on excellent terms with him) also happened to be present in Berlin and was taken into the men's confidence. Hess also ordered Major [Dr. Walter] Buch, Head of the Supreme Party Court, to be brought to Berlin by plane. The result of these discussions: Goebbels, at that time Hitler's favourite, and Major Buch flew to Godesberg, where Hitler had retreated to in order to escape his friend Röhm's petitions. Under the influence of Goebbels and Buch, Hitler decided to betray Ernst Röhm, who had never intended a coup against Hitler himself, but rather a takeover of the *Reichswehr* in co-operation with Hitler and the party. In influential party circles Hitler's decision was seen as proof of his statesmanlike shrewdness, and the subsequent executions of the *SA* leaders as a political necessity to avoid civil war. The chief of the army command staff, General von Fritsch, was granted his wish, and in the courtyard of the former military college Lichterfelde (later the "*Leibstandarte* Adolf Hitler" barracks) a so-called revolution tribunal was improvised. The army command, that is to say the ministry of defence, detached two generals to oversee the executions, which were carried out under the command of [Josef] Sepp Dietrich (the commander of Hitler's body guard). The names of two generals involved in this revolutionary tribunal: General [Gerd] von Rundstedt (1875-1953) and General [Erwin] von Witzleben (1881-1944, executed)!

General (later Field Marshal) Karl Rudolf Gerd von Rundstedt (1875–1953). He retired as a *Generaloberst* (Colonel General) in 1938 but was brought back into service when the War started and appointed Field Marshal. The author points out that Rundstedt was one of the two generals who in 1934 oversaw the executions of the SA men, as part of the "Night of the Long Knives". He did this to prevent the SA from forcibly disbanding the *Reichswehr* (German Army) and replacing it with their own soldiers. Rundstedt was a passionate Nazi fanatic, who towards the end of World War II made a speech saying that the present war (which he could see was being lost) was only a prelulde to a World War III, which he dearly wished for, and meanwhile, maximum destruction in all the Nazi occupied countries should be pursued urgently, so that they could easily be reconquered.

Colonel General (later Field Marshal) Job Wilhelm Georg Erdmann Erwin von Witzleben (1881-1944). He was the other general who, with Rundstedt, supervised the 1934 executions of the SA men. In 1941 he was appointed Field Marshal to succeed Rundstedt. For years, he had taken part in many plots to remove Hitler, whom he despised. He was thrown out of the Army for criticising Hitler, but then brought back because his military expertise was needed. In 1944, his anti-Hitler sentiments were proved to the ultimate extent by his taking part in the July plot to kill Hitler. If it had succeeded, Witzleben would have taken the supreme command of the entire German Army. He was subsequently executed in prison on Hitler's direct order by being hung from a meat hook on August 8, 1944. It is possible that Witzleben was the intimate friend of the author who took part in that particular plot, and whose execution on that exact date he mentions, without naming the friend. Only eight of the plotters were executed on that day. So the author's friend had to be one of the eight, several of whom are highly unlikely.

The rampaging by the *SS*, and in particular the men of the *SD*, carried on for weeks and months beyond June 30, 1934. Their hunger for vengeance was satisfied, and private disagreements were settled with the gun. Meanwhile, at his speech to the *Reichstag* on July 13, 1934, Hitler only mentioned the executions at Lichterfelde – i.e. those that had officially been sanctioned by the generals of the *Reichswehr*. In accordance with the compromise he had forged with the generals of the *Reichswehr*, Hitler declared at the *Reichstag* [the Parliament]: "In our state there is only one authority that bears arms – the Wehrmacht! And there is only one authority that bears the political will – the National Socialist party! Having given my word and following my innermost conviction, I am committed to my promise to the President of the *Reich* [General von Hindenburg] to preserve the army as an apolitical instrument." Yet, even though Hitler had already been sworn in as the *Reichswehr's* Commander in Chief on the day before Hindenburg's death, the generals were still strong enough for Hitler to be compelled, when he announced universal conscription in March 1935, to pass a law that stated: "During his time of service, no soldier must be a member of any political organisation!"

The Chief of the Army Command Staff, General von Fritsch, resigned shortly before the annexation of Austria in March 1938, and with him other prominent members of the new German *Wehrmacht*. General [Werner] von Blomberg at the same time also resigned as a minister; the resignation of this clutch of generals was seen as a protest against Hitler's annexation of Austria. In reality the resignations of General Fritsch and his followers occurred because Hitler no longer was keeping the promises he had made in 1934 and had started – against a pledge made to Hindenburg and Fritsch – with his infamous "ideological instruction" in the barracks of the *Wehrmacht.* This was decidedly unpopular with the generals, who remonstrated not only with Hitler, who had not been true to his word, but especially with General von Blomberg, the minister in charge. The generals declared openly that a "politicisation" of the army was incompatible with the *professional honour* of a German officer, and when that same general committed a further – and very public – breach of what was considered professional honour by marrying his secretary, even Hitler had to drop him, as none of the remaining army leaders and members of the general staff would have carried on working with a man such as Blomberg. (Tellingly, Blomberg could not even be reactivated at the outbreak of war, as so many others were.)

Field Marshal Werner von Blomberg. He resigned as Minister in protest because Hitler was politicising the Army, along with other generals. However, he lost respect because he married his secretary, which was considered an offence against the dignity and honour of the German officer corps. His first wife Charlotte Helmich (1880-1932) whom he had married in 1904 had died of tuberculosis in 1932. (They had five children together.) The secretary whom he married was Luise Margarethe Gruhn, who was called by the nickname Erna. The quiet wedding to Miss Gruhn was held on 12 January 1938, with Hitler and Göring as witnesses, Göring having encouraged Blomberg to go ahead and marry a second wife of the lower classes, as he had done himself. It was later claimed that Miss Gruhn had been arrested for having been a prostitute when younger, and a naked photo of her wearing only a pearl necklace was produced anonymously to the police. Was she being "framed" to get rid of Blomberg and the photo was really one intended just for him as a gift from her? Some skulduggery was certainly involved, for a photo of her taken in 1948 was later circulated and claimed to be a Gestapo file photo of her as a prostitute in the 1930s, so that attempts to smear her and Blomberg were definitely still being made years after the War had ended. She and Blomberg had indeed been arrested in a hotel room by the Gestapo *before* their marriage. This is one of those murky matters so typical of the Nazi era where dirty tricks and disinformation make it impossible for us to disentangle the truth about who was plotting against whom, and why. But in any case, the immediate result was to "cancel" Blomberg, to use today's phrase, and eliminate the possibility of his being listened to in any further criticisms of Hitler.

Erna Gruhn, the second wife of Field Marshal Werner von Blomberg.

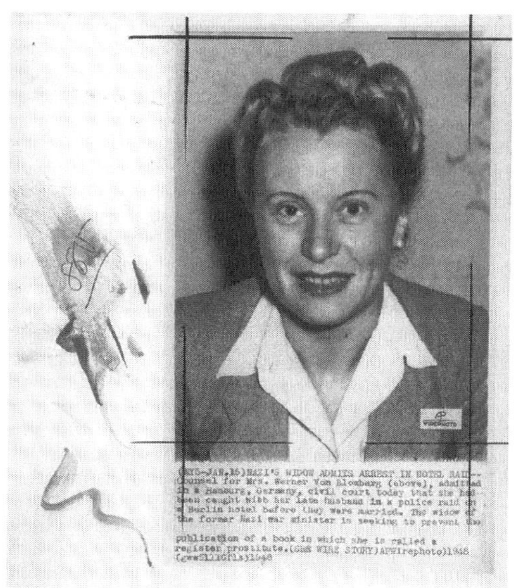

Another photo of Erna Gruhn, in 1948, with news text attached.

Prior to his being "dumped", von Blomberg had been key to the Nazi plans. Here we see Mussolini delighted to chat jovially with him. Mussolini spoke German fluently, with an Italian accent which the Germans found charming. He suffered from a serious ulcer condition, and continually swallowed flasks of yoghurt and ate dry rusks in order to try to keep it under control and reduce the pain.

General von Fritsch and the other generals that had resigned had, without doubt, been first-class members of the general staff, but they were of an almost primitive straightness and narrow-mindedness. There were other generals who, though no less able, were nevertheless somewhat more "unscrupulous" in their non-military thoughts and actions. One such man was General [Fedor] von Bock. When, on October 30, 1938, even General Rundstedt retired as Commander of the 1st Army Group in Berlin because he was unable to stand up to the political "educators" the party had installed (the so-called *Schulungsleiter* – training managers), it was

General von Bock who replaced von Rundstedt and, without hesitation, strictly banned the party political officials from entering any barracks in Berlin, yet at the same time establishing a good relationship with Hitler. General von Bock's stock answer, with which he dismissed all party officials, *Reich* leaders, and even the *Reich* Minister of Propaganda, Josef Goebbels, is infamous. In his grating voice, without a hint of scorn or mockery, he would exclaim: "My *Führer* does not wish it!" And for a while even the *Führer* himself had to bow to these relentless invocations of "my *Führer*" by von Bock, because the Prussian General was a master at taking Hitler at his word.

General Albrecht Franz Friedrich Fedor von Bock (1880-1945, killed by air attack) 'was a master at taking Hitler at his word.' Here they are together.

The Chief of the General Staff, Ludwig Beck, retired at the same time as General von Rundstedt. For several months prior to his resignation a rumour had circulated in Berlin, according to which the Chief of the General Staff had not agreed with the annexations of Austria and then Czechoslovakia; indeed, that he had not even been familiar with the invasion plans, as Hitler was alleged to have worked these out personally and without Beck's knowledge. Now, anyone who understands the role of a chief of the general staff will immediately realise that such rumours must have been nonsense; clearly Beck would have been intimately familiar with the design of these invasion plans. And of course it was not Hitler who had drawn them up, but General von Reichenau, in his capacity as Commander of the 7th Army Corps in Munich. He had designed the invasion plan for Austria and, after newly being appointed Commander of the 4th Army Group in Leipzig, drew up the invasion plans for Czechoslovakia and Poland.

General Walter Karl Ernst August von Reichenau (1884–1942) in 1933. According to the author, he drew up the invasion plans for Austria, Czechoslovakia, and Poland. Later as Field Marshal he commanded the German 6th Army which conquered Ukraine. He was murdered on the orders of Himmler on January 17, 1942, at his own headquarters, by three visiting SS officers: Fritz Leine, Paul Radunski, and Max Pelke. The false story was put about that he had died of a stroke, caused by his habit of going for long runs in the ice cold weather of Russia. He had notifed Himmler on January 11 that he would not accept Himmler's demand that SS officers be appointed at all levels within the Army, thereby giving Himmler joint, and eventually total, control of the Army. Himmler did not like to be refused, so Reichenau paid the price. It should be noted that Reichenau was a fanatical anti-Semite who also thought all Jews were communists.

All of this would naturally have happened in close co-operation with the Grand General Staff, whose chief General Beck had been. It is also incorrect to portray Becks's retirement as a protest against the party's attempts to politicise the *Wehrmacht*. The fact that Beck was not opposed to National Socialism had been made clear when, as Commanding Officer at Ulm, he vigorously supported a group of Nazi officers who had been put on trial by the Weimar government for political agitation within the *Reichswehr* (the affair around Scheringer, Schulz *et al.* in 1930). Beck was neither opposed to war nor opposed to the Nazis, but… he was an artilleryman and fortress specialist. As a modern member of the general staff he was indeed in favour of the motorisation of the infantry and the expansion of the *Luftwaffe* and was a fervent supporter of the upgrading of all offensive weaponry, but he warned with increasing urgency of neglecting the heavy artillery, and was not ready to concede that the heavy artillery could in principle be entirely replaced by dive bombers (the so-called *Stukas*). Beck cautioned his friends as well as Hitler against an over-hasty arms build-up and premature aggression, because as he, in his capacity as Chief of the General Staff, assessed the newly created *Wehrmacht*, there was no way that it should be involved in a new World War before the end of 1945 (!), and he saw clearly that any military embroilment would inevitably lead to a World War. As a fortress specialist, Beck demanded the construction of giant fortresses around Germany's perimeter and vigorously advocated the upgrading of the heavy artillery, whose importance, in his assessment, remained undiminished however successfully it might be possible to wage a *Blitzkrieg*. Despite all of these warnings and protestations, Hitler in part neglected and in part ignored the demands of the Chief of the General Staff, and it was because of this that Beck resigned. In some sense he foresaw the outcome of the war and the final annihilation of the *Wehrmacht* that he had helped to establish. On the one hand, this *Wehrmacht* was insufficiently armed for a defensive war, and on the other, it had – in Beck's view – gone too soon into a war that it was only able to wage as *Blitzkrieg*.

The biggest loss for the new *Wehrmacht* was the discharge of the Commander of the War Academy, General [Curt, or Kurt] Liebmann (1881-1960), who tendered his resignation on April 30, 1939. General Liebmann was the most outstanding member of the general staff available to the new German *Wehrmacht*. The only other man of the same standing was perhaps General von Reichenau; but in his impetuousness he was no match for the conciliatory calm and wisdom of that military scientist *par excellence*, General Liebmann. Much like General von Beck, Liebmann demanded that the *Wehrmacht* would not be involved in a war before the end of 1945. Naturally Liebmann was in favour of *Blitzkrieg*, desired it and prepared for it. Yet time and again he personally lodged energetic complaints with Hitler and pointed out the potentiality of a defensive war and thereby the distinct possibility of a war on several fronts. Such a war should be avoided if at all possible, as – in his assessment – the *Wehrmacht* would not be equal to such an eventuality before the end of 1945. Thus the Generals Beck and Liebmann were of the same opinion, but it must be pointed out that the Chief of the General Staff von Beck obtained his knowledge from the Commander of the War Academy, General Liebmann.

General Curt Liebmann (1881-1960), was the son of the Prussian Major General Konrad Liebmann (1846-1917), and had been brought up in a military background, with the Army "in his bones". The author praises him highly for his intelligence and expertise. He was Commander of the War Academy. But he resigned at the same time as his friend General Beck in 1939, as they both thought Hitler's plans would lead to a catastrophic world war which Germany would inevitably lose. (Bundesarchiv)

All the aforementioned generals could justifiably claim that they *personally* were never Nazis out of conviction (this even goes for von Reichenau, who notoriously had the reputation of being a Nazi general through and through – more on that later). Indeed, these generals can even invoke their warnings, objections and retirements in protest as proof of their anti-Nazi stance. But – and let us include this pre-emptive and precautionary "but" at this point – in line with their tradition, their upbringing and their *esprit de corps*, all of these generals, these war craftsmen, worshipped and were servants of the authoritarian state that forced the "Prussian spirit" onto the German people and with it the blind obedience of their caste. Whoever made available the best tools of war and the largest war machinery to these war craftsmen would be "their man", and Hitler put a war machinery at their disposal, the scale of which would have never been sanctioned by the people or parliament and could only have been made possible by a dictatorship or a regime of terror.

The more Hitler and his henchmen indoctrinated the entire German people with Prussianness in its distilled form of the modern Nazi spirit, and the more he proletarianised the German people, the less could he allow the war craftsmen to retain their guild and *esprit de corps*. The *Gleichschaltung* of the people (the enforced conformity) inevitably had to go hand in hand with a *Gleichschaltung* of the officer class. With his National Socialism, Hitler had carried out a "uniformisation" of the entire people and had created a new type of "party nobility" that oversaw and indeed made this uniformisation possible in the first place: the *Gauleiter*, *Reichsleiter*, and the *SS*- and *SA* Commanders of all ranks. This party nobility begrudged the guild of the war craftsmen its privileged position and would never forgive the generals the proceedings of June 30, 1934, when the generals demanded and pushed through the liquidation of an important component of the party nobility – i.e. the executions of Röhm and his *SA* Commanders. For a while the need for the expansion of the *Wehrmacht* and the breakneck speed and colossal scale of armament inevitably united the divided brothers, and in the rapture of the great victories at the very outset of the war there was no time for feuds, revenge or disdainful resignations. But the day of reckoning would come when one brother would assault the other and either the "party nobility" or the "noble guild" of the war craftsmen would be liquidated. When, in time, victories turned into defeats and the war revealed itself more and more clearly as a catastrophe for the German people, the old fault lines spontaneously burst open again. To preserve itself, the party had to try to dissolve the guild of the war craftsmen and to exterminate the *esprit de corps* of the Old Prussian general class. And all the pent up hatred and thirst for revenge of the "party nobility" erupted on August 8, 1944, and the defeat suffered on June 30, 1934 was avenged. With every inch that the catastrophe of war edged towards total defeat, the attempts to turn the generals' *Wehrmacht* into a *Volksheer* (a people's army) intensified – just as Röhm in his capacity as Commander of the *SA* had envisaged before June 30, 1934.

In order to fully understand the significance of the officers' revolt on July 20, 1944 and the party's devastating revenge strike against the generals of the *Wehrmacht* on August 8, 1944, a number of cross connections have to be made. Prominent "avatars of Old Prussian officer virtue" and members of the general staff from the guild of war craftsmen were forced to establish a so-called "honour tribunal" (because only by taking part could they save their own skins), and had to sit in judgement on their comrades and personal friends. General von Rundstedt was forced to divest his closest friend, General von Witzleben, of his military honours. General [Heinz Wilhelm] Guderian (1888-1954) – whose previous appointment as Commander of the *Panzerwaffe* (replacing General Lutz) had in no small part been made possible by the two friends von Rundstedt and von Witzleben – was compelled, in his new capacity as Chief of the General Staff, to expel his former mentor from the *Wehrmacht*. General Schroth, previously Commander of the 12th Army Corps in Wiesbaden, was forced to condemn his revered superior General von Witzleben (previously Commander of the 2nd Army Group in Frankfurt/Main). And next to von Witzleben there were other distinguished comrades and eminent members of the general staff who, together with the Field Marshal, had to be handed over to the hatred and vindictiveness of the party grandees.

In order to fully comprehend the full tragedy of August 8, 1944, one has to be aware of these ties and interconnections and appreciate the importance of comradeship to the military caste's spirit. It should be made absolutely clear that execution by hanging was not just a violation of the executed person, but also a violation of the sentencing judges and, in addition, a provocative violation of the entire German officer class. June 30, 1934 was a victory by the *Wehrmacht* over the party. August 8, 1944 was a terrible retaliation by the party over the *Wehrmacht*; and even if the *Wehrmacht* had been able to recover from that blow, it would have perished in the wake of the deathblows dealt from the outside by the Allied armies.

Old Prussian Officer virtue

National Socialism was the most dangerous and hopefully the last manifestation of German militarism, and at the same its most vile degeneracy. To destroy National Socialism while allowing German militarism to survive in any form whatsoever would be a crime against the German people, and thereby a crime against Europe and the entire civilised world. German militarism is the fundamental and hereditary evil under which the German people have been suffering for centuries (!), and from which it can only be cured if that militarism can be successfully exterminated, root and branch.

To exterminate German militarism means to liberate the German people from the so-called "Prussian spirit". It is National Socialism's dubious achievement that it popularised this Prussian spirit as the Nazi spirit, and forced it upon people of all social strata and in all regions, indoctrinating the German youth with special fervour. This Prussian spirit, with all its misunderstood virtuousness and grotesque sense of honour, was, in its incarnation as Nazi spirit, made into the idol for a generation of young people who have virtually no opportunity for comparison, do not know any counteracting forces from former times, and will therefore not be able to develop their own defence mechanisms against that spirit. Deliverance from the Prussian spirit, aka Nazi spirit, and thereby the extermination of German militarism will therefore depend primarily on the extent to which the education problem can be solved in the years that will follow the war. The problem of education will be settled in a Christian spirit, in which everyone approaches the difficult task ahead with courage and a deep sense of responsibility, free not only from maudlin sentimentality, but also free from un-Christian scepticism, and inspired by God's true love, which alone can conquer hatred and overcome the deepest troubles in inner joy and freedom.

In order to defeat the Prussian spirit, aka Nazi spirit, it is vitally important to thoroughly examine these avatars of the so-called "Old Prussian officer virtue". But first, let us hear some useful insights by former US Vice President Henry Agard Wallace, who, in a regrettably overlooked speech given in Delaware, Ohio on March 9, 1943, said:

"The Prussian philosophy teaches many of the loftiest ideals to its adherents, but time and again we have witnessed how these ideals in the end are appropriated by the forces of evil... I do not mean to say that Prussia is the world's only villain, for neither England, France, Russia, Spain, nor the USA have always been perfect. But it is the case that Prussia and Japan are the only two nations that have systematically, from generation to generation, abused their citizens' highest virtues for the glorification of the state as well as ruthless warfare."

The American Vice President Henry Agard Wallace (1888-1965) in a speech of 1943 criticised the Prussian philosophy, and said that its "ideals in the end are appropriated by the forces of evil". The author says he wished that more people had taken note of that truth expressed by Wallace.

Who, then, are these "avatars of Old Prussian officer virtue", and what is so special about this "Old Prussian officer virtue"? The avatars of Old Prussian officer virtue are all the aforementioned generals, i.e. von Bock, von Witzleben, von Rundstedt, Halder, Brauchitsch, Guderian, Liebmann, [Erich von] Manstein, Model and all the rest; as well as Hindenburg, Blücher, Gneisenau, Clausewitz; furthermore the military leaders under "The Old Fritz" (Frederick the Great) and the officers under The Great Elector (Frederick William), not forgetting the generals during the time of Bismarck, in World War 1, and those of the war that started in 1939. All of these "avatars of Old Prussian officer virtue" are not devoid of a certain tragic stature. The "Old Prussian officer virtue" comprises a wealth of altogether honourable characteristics, such as incorruptibility, honesty, dutifulness and simplicity. Only in their synthesis do these characteristics amount to "Old Prussian officer virtue", and the Prussian generals have been its embodiment since time immemorial until this day.

Yet "Old Prussian officer virtue" differs from true virtue by the very fact that it can be abused for any purpose, without protest, with a simple order, without asking why and to what end. Indeed such questioning alone would be considered a disgrace for this most peculiar of all "virtues", which has an element of "zombie obedience" about it. Old Prussian officer virtue knows only one aim: enlargement and glorification of the authoritarian state, a warped version of the concept of a "*Vaterland*" at whose core is the army, the custodian of a powerful, controlling and dominant Greater Germany!

To achieve this end, every means is justified, and every "order from above" will be carried out. It started with the Knights of the Teutonic Order of the March of Brandenburg, but those Christian monks only too quickly forgot prayer and God when they became embroiled in the craft of warfare. Their descendants became Prussian grenadiers, and the freedom fighters from 1813 turned into drilled soldiers; and eventually the post-war revolutionaries from the years 1918/19 were recast as Nazi soldiers. Then and now the spiritual fathers were always these paragons of virtue with their glorious "Old Prussian officer virtue", which has caused so much pain, death, suffering and crime.

The "Old Prussian officer virtue" is held in dangerously high esteem not only in Germany but also abroad. Yet it requires a rather limited mental horizon of its adored avatars, almost completely precluding regular, independent examination and thought processes. German officers and Prussian generals wait for orders "from above" and then execute those orders with every possible thoroughness and care. For such individuals the craft of warfare is the most sublime science, whose study becomes their *raison d'être* and whose application their purpose in life. The sciences and arts are considered mere accessories that are only of interest to the extent that they can be made useful for the craft of warfare – and thereby a possible war. To give an order, having himself been given an order to do so, is the epitome of earthly bliss for the German militarist, and the robotic report "Order executed!" is the sweetest music to his ears.

Early on in the Nazi regime, virtually all avatars of "Old Prussian officer virtue" viewed the National Socialists as impertinent bandits, who, with sacrilegious hands, reached for the hallowed "cultural assets of the forefathers". But these paragons of virtue were quite happy to quickly reconcile themselves with the "evil Nazis" when they began to advocate, without restraint, a new and grandiose type of pan-Germanism, the likes of which the war craftsmen had not dared to imagine in their wildest dreams. And when Adolf Hitler as head of government gave the generals a war machinery of hitherto unknown dimensions and grandeur, the guild of war craftsmen accepted him as their lord and master and agreed – albeit reluctantly – to the farce of Private Adolf Hitler being elevated to the position of Supreme Leader of the newly created *Wehrmacht* (however, neither Fritsch, nor Beck, Bock, Rundstedt, Witzleben etc. resigned because of it!). They only asked of him that he would abide by the guild's rules, acknowledge the professional honour of the officer class, guarantee the guild's homogeneity vis-à-vis the party and state, and supply ever newer and better tools. Yet at the beginning of the war, Hitler had not only become the highest master of the generals and the *Führer* of the German people "chosen by divine providence", he was infinitely more: Hitler had become "*Führer* of the German will to win"! And the fact that every "decent" German always wants to win is the most self-evident truth for those avatars of Old Prussian officer virtue.

The party leader Adolf Hitler had promoted "his" generals to positions of colonel general and field marshal, and they carried the banner of National Socialism from victory to victory. As long as the victorious campaigns continued, they believed in his "ingenious intuition" and happily praised his military genius. It has to be spelled out in no uncertain terms that the generals were more than content as long as "*their* brave German boys" charged victoriously under *their* command, attacked other peoples with artillery and tanks, bombed foreign cities, and inflicted their fury of war on other, peace-loving nations. Cultural assets were destroyed, people were deported, hostages were shot in huge numbers, and the Jews were "exterminated"

– all of this happened for the avatars of "Old Prussian officer virtue". It was brought about to a large extent "for the glory of Germany", with and through these generals, whose consciences had been numbed by a sense of duty that commanded them to "win". Only when the fortunes of war turned, when the victorious charges reversed into backward surges, only when German cities started to be bombed and German cultural assets were destroyed, a kind of "conscience for Germany" was stirred. Suddenly there was disapproval – at first hidden, then open – of the leadership of "Private Hitler"; their old *esprit de corps* was aroused against the party. That *esprit de corps* of theirs... in its seclusiveness it had always been ill disposed towards popular mass movements and never could identify with the "plebs". (They applied the term "plebs" to National Socialism, just as they had applied it to Marxism under Bismarck and Wilhelm II, and all democratic parties and trade unions in the Weimar Republic.)

A famous Swiss publicist once wrote: "There is no such thing as war crime; it is clear that there is only murder and slaughter of civilians and prisoners." Guilt demands punishment, and murder is punishable by death even in Christian nations. But if anyone has ever sinned according to the principle "the end justifies the means", surely it was the avatars of "Old Prussian officer virtue".

Following the successful Anglo-Saxon invasion on the west coast of France, the British Prime Minister Winston Churchill said of the German officers and Nazi leaders in a speech to the landing troops: "They are killing each other!" He said this with reference to the officers' assassination attempt on Hitler on July 20, 1944. It is too gruesome a drama – full, as it is, of torture, murder, looting and hangings – to be called a tragicomedy: German militarism begets a bastard, namely National Socialism. This National Socialism turns into the most dangerous exponent of German militarism and recasts the Prussian spirit as the Nazi sprit. National Socialism forces uniformisation on an entire nation for the sake of German militarism, and then goes on to strip that very militarism's generals of their uniforms! It assaults the traditional creators and guardians of German militarism, the conservative officers, abuses them, leads them to the gallows, dishonours them. The avatars of "Old Prussian officer virtue" and German militarism had but one opportunity to cleanse their honour thus besmirched, by taking resolute action with drawn swords against the insulter, against the National Socialism that had long become the very lifeblood of German militarism. It would take Shakespearean eloquence and creative power to portray this drama in all its tragedy, and to draw out all the apparent contradictions of the inexorable and inescapable turn of events.

After the World War of 1914-18, the defeated German militarists and their political friends created the so-called "*Dolchstoss-Legende*" ("the legend of the stab in the back"), and ultimately it was National Socialism that came to power thanks to this *Dolchstoss-Legende* and, in the *Wehrmacht*, was able to create a new German militarism for the militarists.

After the final defeat of the German armies and the annihilation of the power of the party, the fear that a new *Dolchstoss-Legende* might re-emerge seems unfounded. The avatars of "Old Prussian officer virtue" are facing extinction now, but – even though the NSDAP has officially been dissolved in Germany – there is still a danger that the Prussian spirit could live on in the German people as the Nazi spirit. To prevent this from happening is the responsibility of re-education; and such re-education can only succeed through resolutely setting examples of democratic and Christian virtues. Before turning our attention to the modern guardians of the Nazi spirit, let us once more investigate the particular activities of the avatars of "Old Prussian officer virtue".

Commander, General Staff and War Academies

Frederick II of Prussia, as one of the leading military commanders in history, created and maintained a general staff in the modern sense. Out of a sealed-off state entrenched behind ramparts grew the specifically Prussian attacking spirit that went on to control Frederickian Prussia. This King, named "The Great", stands at the beginning of an evolution which, in the moral domain, developed a very particular "soldierly code of honour", and, in the material domain, for the very first time demanded the exploitation of all scientific and industrial innovations for warfare. In his general staff, the King of the Prussians created a new military aristocracy, which was given exhaustive training in all tactical and strategic matters, while, with pitiless sternness against itself, breeding an *esprit de corps*, unfamiliar with and immune to most of life's pleasures – for a certain mental deficiency is as much part of that *esprit de corps* as is material (corporeal) frugality. Extreme restraint, dutifulness and fitness in all military matters were inherent characteristics of these new officers, as was a non-negotiable discipline that demanded blind obedience from all subordinates.

Frederick the Great (i.e., Frederick II, King of Prussia; 1712-1786). He reorganised the Prussian army, and was Hitler's greatest hero. Hitler kept an oil portrait of Frederick the Great in his private office. Hitler was an omnivorous reader of history books, especially ones which agreed with his own compulsions for militarism or bold and brazen use of force. Hitler said the only two Englishmen he admired were King Henry VIII and Oliver Cromwell. Hitler had an original oil portrait of Frederick the Great in his private office and gazed upon his hero every day, presumably determined not just to emulate but to surpass him.

Here we see Hitler signing a document in his private apartments, beneath an original oil portrait of his hero Frederick the Great. According to Erich Kempka, Hitler took this portrait with him to his Berlin bunker, where he died. In his memoir, Kempka records: "The pistols of Adolf and Eva lay on the red carpet. The Führer's blood lay pooled on the table and floor coverings. Also on the table lay the overturned vase. To one side was an image of Hitler's mother as a young woman. The portrait of Frederick the Great hung above the writing table." So Hitler died in front of the image of his hero.

The first major historic test for this Prussian general staff created by Frederick II came in the years leading up to the war of liberation against Napoleon. Gerhard von Scharnhorst emerged as the creator of an officer corps that was welded together through the privilege of birth and a meticulous selection process. In its exceptional position as the brains of an army that, for the time being, was purely fictional, it segregated itself from the rest of the populace and led a life quite apart from it. When, in 1812, the party that advocated rapprochement with Napoleon won the upper hand in Berlin, the leading members of the general staff went to Russia with Baron vom Stein and there started to prepare for a retaliatory strike against the usurper. When Napoleon's defeated armies flooded back into Germany, Baron [Heinrich Friedrich Karl] vom [and zum] Stein (1757-1831) and the officers of the newly created general corps also returned, and the King of Prussia was forced into action by the members of the general corps. The negotiator who convinced General Yorck von Wartenburg to sign the Convention of Tauroggen (ignoring the fact that in 1813 the Prussian king was still in a formal alliance with Napoleon) was no other than a young officer in the general corps and favourite pupil of [General Gerhard von] Scharnhorst (1755-1813), namely Carl von Clausewitz, who later went on to become the grand instructor of the Prussian general staff.

Under the leadership of generals Blücher and Gneisenau, the liberation war of 1814-15 turned into an enthusiastically fought people's war, but in the years of peace that followed, 1815-1848, the state rather neglected the expansion of military assets (much like it had done after the death of Frederick II). And again it was a small group of career officers who, under the leadership of the new Chief of the General Staff, Clausewitz, preserved the tradition of the military nobility. Not only that, Clausewitz and his collaborators established a grand military "science", which not only concerned itself with the instruction of soldiers, but developed an entirely novel moral foundation that demanded unconditionality in all military matters – if necessary, going as far as "honourable demise". The unyielding will for the "annihilation of the enemy at any cost" (Clausewitz) was formed, and thereby the foundation was laid for Total War. Clausewitz's fundamental work "*Vom Kriege*" ("On War") remains the catechism of all members of the general staff to this day. In Book 1, Chapter 1 Clausewitz lectures:

"War is never an isolated act. War does not emerge suddenly; its propagation does not take place in an instant..."

When the German War Academy in Berlin was reopened in 1935, General Liebmann celebrated Carl von Clausewitz (who had died in 1831) as the "spiritual father" of the newly created German *Wehrmacht*.

General Carl Philipp Gottfried von Clausewitz (1780-1831), the "spiritual father" of Hitler's newly created German Wehrmacht. Hitler idolised him, as did the Wehrmacht generals. His famous book *On War* appealed to Hitler's greatest passion, which was to wage relentless war and conquer the world. Hitler could quote whole pages of text of the book from memory. According to the author, Hitler followed Clausewitz's military rules but also "applied them to politics", namely, "to crush the enemy". Thousands of his political opponents met with death and ruthless elimination.

Scharnhorst, Gneisenau and Clausewitz were the guardians of the "Old Prussian officer virtue" and the creators of an officer corps whose generals ultimately made it possible for Moltke, the famous Chief of the General Staff, to muster a pan-German army for the "Iron Chancellor" Bismarck, which became not only the guarantor of victory over Napoleon III, but also the guarantor of the new German *Reich* and its unity. The continuous fragmentation of Germany could only be contained through the kind of military authority that the Prussian general corps had quietly created and implemented in all the major military units of the various *Länder*. Without Count Moltke's general staff, Bismarck would not have been able to achieve the unification of the *Reich*.

Count Schlieffen was Chief of the General Staff from 1891 until 1905, and it was he who created the actual pan-German general staff, which under him consisted of no fewer than 160 elite officers. He perfected the art of "manoeuvring with armies of millions", and he became the grand theorist of a World War which he would not live to see himself, but about which he declared that "entire armies will capitulate" in the battles of annihilation that will have to be fought. Hindenburg and Ludendorff subsequently tried, without success, to continue their master Count Schlieffen's *magnum opus*.

General Erich Friedrich Ludendorff (1865-1937) at his desk during World War One. He and Hindenburg tried to implement Count Schlieffen's military theories during that war, but they did not work as they had hoped.

When they failed, again it fell to the generals of defeated German militarism – just as in 1812 – to keep the old Frederickian attacking spirit and its officer corps alive. According to its traditions, it would continue, even in the face of defeat, to diligently train itself in the art of war and to perfect its weaponry according to the latest scientific developments.

This officer corps only ever viewed the Weimar Republic as an interim stage and never fully accepted it, because the Weimar Republic did not want to concern itself with revenge and an attacking spirit, and because – in line with the stipulations of the Treaty of Versailles – it had imposed a mere 100,000-strong army on the officer corps. Yet, the sinister General von Seeckt, the organiser of that 100,000-strong army, recast it as a core unit for a later army of millions, and, through a most harsh and exacting selection process, bred an officer corps in which each individual was a master of the craft of warfare. This General von Seeckt was accurately compared to Scharnhorst, and following his death in late 1936 was buried alongside Scharnhorst in the Invalids' Cemetery in Berlin.

When, under Adolf Hitler, the 100,000-strong army was transformed into an army of millions, the newly created general corps tried to faithfully follow the four fundamental rules established by von Seeckt, or at least to comply with them at the outbreak of war:

1. Surprise in itself is a moral power. (Clausewitz.)

2. In order to crush the enemy, one must organise one's efforts in accordance with the enemy's power of resistance. This can be expressed as the product of two inseparable factors: the magnitude of the available means and the intensity of will power. (Clausewitz.)

3. In war, action is never solely directed against matter, but also always against the moral power it is endowed with. (Clausewitz.)

4. In a war on several fronts, it is desirable to annihilate one enemy after the other. (Schlieffen.)

In actual fact, in 1938 Adolf Hitler followed the very same military rules but applied them to politics. At the beginning of the war, the general staff's strategy, in accordance with the four rules, led the German *Wehrmacht* "from Warsaw to Paris and Athens". But in Russia all their rules and good intentions shattered; indeed, to be precise, they had already been wrecked at the cliffs of Dover.

The first approach that General von Seeckt had earlier made to a foreign armed force was to the Red Army. Even before the Japanese, the Bolsheviks had enlisted German generals as their instructors and had these masters establish their war academies in Moscow, St. Petersburg, in the Ukraine and in Siberia. They were the first to request that an officer from the general staff be sent to Russia from Berlin, to co-operate with Russian military men in the translation of the three volumes of General von Clausewitz's textbook "On War". And when the friendship with Russia turned into war with Russia, the Soviet generals proved themselves such able students of their German instructors that they ultimately beat their former masters and eclipsed their achievements. In any case, the Russians – and with them the Japanese – were the only ones to understand early enough the significance of the German war academies and eagerly tried to emulate them.

The German war academies are of special significance. Neither German politicians, nor the politicians of other nations (to whom those academies were equally relevant), understood the significance of the war academies of that small 100,000-strong army; but neither did the military in France, England or America really comprehend what was going on in those educational institutions. There was nothing like them anywhere in the world – not even in

Russia or Japan – and they were much more than simply specialised educational facilities. For some time these war academies were ostensibly run as "sports academies", and even once that disguise had been dropped, they were viewed merely as some form of higher cadet school.

The politicians of the Weimar Republic – to the extent that they were honestly invested in attempts to realise a democracy in Germany – can be accused of never managing to gain a deep enough insight in the machinations of the *Reichswehr* and never bringing the officer corps under their control, and thereby that of the public and the people. The only politician who had any chance of becoming *Reichswehr* minister was one who the officer corps would regard as a guarantor of their institution's homogeneity, and one who would deny access to military installations and documents to any non-military person. The *Reichswehr* minister not only acted as the departmental minister for all other members of the government and parliament, he was also the guardian of the "military secret" and would put on appropriate airs. German politicians were in such awe of the guild of the war craftsmen that they did not dare to exercise any stringent control in the first place; and when an investigation did become necessary, it was handed over to a special commission – or even referred to the imperial court! – with whom the officer corps and the generals responsible had an easy job. For those politicians all military matters of the *Reichswehr* were written in "a book sealed sevenfold", and they would never feel entitled to break those seals for fear of being accused of a "betrayal of military secrets". The most serious crime a politician could commit was precisely such a "betrayal of military secrets", and the imperial court in Leipzig was quick to press charges and impose prison sentences in such matters, which inevitably would mean the end of any political career.

One of the Weimar Republic's most brazen contradictions was rooted in the fact that, while the Versailles Treaty prohibited any rearmament and the Weimar government was trying to destroy the old "attacking spirit", the imperial court in Leipzig was allowed to conduct grandiose court cases in which the "betrayal of military secrets" relating to any such rearmament and "attacking spirit" was punished with incarceration in a prison or penitentiary. Either the terms of the peace treaty are complied with and there is no rearmament (in which case there are no military secrets that could be "betrayed"), or the attacking spirit, rather than being exterminated, is given a new lease of life that has to be kept secret (in which case democracy is being betrayed and an irresponsible war of revenge is encouraged). It verged on the tragicomic that in the Weimar Republic not only German, but also foreign intelligence officers were dragged in front of and sentenced by the imperial court for "betrayal of military secrets" (such as the French Capitaine Morand) – that is to say, officers from the powers that had been victorious 1918/19, who had dictated the Versailles Treaty and whose duty it should have been not only to prevent renewed armament, but also make impossible the cultivation of the *Reichswehr's* attacking spirit in the German war academies.

What, then, was the true nature of these German war academies? Admittance was reserved for especially gifted and reliable officers. Upon entry, the newly appointed officer would become a sworn member of the staff of whichever commanding general was in charge in that particular territory. The students of the academy were given substantial assignments by that staff, and were expected to solve special tasks over the course of a semester or more, and to complete projects that would count as final assessments or graduating examinations. The completed assignments were marked, improved or rejected by the staff of the commanding general (or, under the 100,000 army's command structure, the staff of the division commander), and assignments deemed to be of sufficient quality were passed on to the general staff in the Ministry of the *Reichswehr*.

Crucially, it was at these German war academies that the plans for the entire German *Blitzkrieg* strategy were painstakingly compiled over the course of many months and years. The academic assignments were reworked, re-sifted and reviewed a dozen times or more, and finally stored in the secret archives at Berlin's Bendlerstrasse (the site of the Ministry of the *Reichswehr*, later the *Reich* War Ministry) – ready and in anticipation of their implementation. It was only thanks to this work carried out at the war academies that the German generals – and thereby the German leadership – again and again were able to rapidly carry out the invasion of any given country once the decision had been made. Invasion plans had, in peace times, not only been drawn up for neighbouring countries, but even for German campaigns straight across Russia to East Asia on the one hand, and, via Asia Minor and North Africa, as far as India on the other! It would be wrong to assume that the preparation of such plans only started after Hitler assumed power. No! Such plans had already been drawn up many years earlier during the Weimar Republic, and were simply revised at certain intervals, brought up to date in line with the latest developments in warfare technology, and fine-tuned to the current "potential for war". Prior to the establishment of German military sovereignty, only a purely fictitious magnitude of the "potential for war" was available for such considerations, but the plans worked out at the war academies allowed a more precise calculation of how strong the German *Wehrmacht* would have to be for any given war scenario.

In each general staff, alongside the chief of the general staff himself, the chief of the operations department is the most important man – the chief of the general staff's "right hand", as it were. But as the 100,000-strong *Reichswehr* was officially not permitted to incorporate an operations department, for a while the chief of the general army office (*Truppenamt*) instead played the role of the chief of the operations department. When Hitler "threw off the mask", and the *Reichswehr* became the *Wehrmacht*, General Freiherr [Gustav Anton] von Wietersheim (who later served as Commander of the 14th Army Corps in Magdeburg) became the first official chief of the operations department. He was the first grand instructor who taught Hitler "strategy and tactics".

General Baron (*Freiherr*) Gustav Anton von Wietersheim (1884–1974). He was the man who taught Hitler "strategy and tactics".

When Hitler promoted General von Blomberg to the office of Minister of War, not only

Blomberg moved to the department, but also his Chief of Staff, General von Reichenau. This General von Reichenau had, for a short time, served as Chief of the Army Ordnance Office (as had General [Paul] Otto), and went on to become the early grand organiser of the German *Wehrmacht*. Ultimately, as Commander of the 4th Army Corps in Leipzig, he was responsible for the deployment of offensive weaponry, the heavy motorised units of which the *Panzer* Division was but one part. (The establishment of the 4th Army Corps in Leipzig – in the immediate vicinity of the 3rd Army Corps in Dresden, whose Commander was General Blaskowitz, a close friend of General Reichenau – was exclusively for purposes of co-ordination of the heavy motorised units; the 4th Army Corps, unlike all other army corps, was not territorially limited. In his capacity as organiser and first inspector of the new attacking force, the Commander of the 4th Army Corps in Leipzig, General Reichenau, was responsible for the entire *Reich's* territory.) It was that same General von Reichenau who, while still serving as Commander of the 7th Army Corps in Munich at the war academy located there, had drawn up the invasion plans for Austria (which were based on many earlier studies carried out by *his* pupils) and Czechoslovakia, and later – as Commander of the 4th Army Corps and in co-operation with the war academy in Dresden – designed the plan of attack against Poland.

It was telling that in the Weimar Republic, of all people, it had to be the Chief of the General Army Offices – who in reality was the chief of the operations department – who was in charge of the office of the inspector of the war academies. And when, at a later date, an independent inspectorate of the war academies was established, this office was still subordinate to the chief of the operations department. The great master at the war academies was none other than General Liebmann, who, after the declaration of "military sovereignty" in 1935, was appointed as the first commander of the newly established war academy in Berlin. General Seeckt had identified Liebmann's military-pedagogical genius long ago; he not only went on to become the mentor for many young officers in the general staff, but also the inspiration for Beck, Halder, Wietersheim, Bock, Rundstedt, Witzleben, Guderian and all the rest of them.

"General staff", "operations department", "plan of attack" etc. are all terms with which a trained military person will be very familiar but ones that a layperson at times might form an entirely wrong idea about. A plan of attack requires lengthy work at the general staff, taking months, often years. Men and material have to be provided, lines of supply have to be organised and issues of transport solved, reserves have to be readied, consumption of munitions and potential loss of human life have to be calculated, and the enemy's strength as well as the nature of his resistance and the extent of his war potential have to be taken into account. To list all details of an attack plan would fill the pages of a separate book. By the time the invasion starts, the real work of the general staff must have been accomplished. The attack itself is not the job of the general staff, whose work is of a preparatory nature, but the task of the commanding army leader and his command staff. It therefore is not essential for the planning general staff to retain supreme command once fighting has started (as was the case with Reichenau); however, in most cases it is desirable, so that the general staff has control over the implementation of its plans, is able to monitor the supply lines as planned and, should unforeseen resistance be encountered, is able to immediately initiate countermeasures by revising the original plans. The general staff – those are the architects with their slide rules, drawing boards and rulers, and the mathematicians, who are required to solve algebraic problems containing the huge unknown factor "X". Once the architects have finished their work, the carpenters, bricklayers, foremen and a whole motley crowd of artisans are called upon to put their plans into action; the work of the master builder begins: that of the commanding general and his commanding staff.

At the beginning of the war, laypeople looked at the military genius of the German officer corps in wonder. These German officers and generals were transformed into invincible gods, who only had to utter the command, "Let there be victory!" and —— there was victory! The German armies seemed to be unstoppable in their forward charges, and it appeared that they could decide, from one day to the next, to march into any other foreign country, without having to worry one iota about the implementation of such an invasion. Reality, however, looked very different to the picture astounded laypeople had formed in their minds. In reality – given current techniques of war and the incredibly complicated nature of the apparatus that makes up today's war machinery – there is no single invasion or attack of any kind that has not been prepared in painstaking work lasting weeks, months or years and calculated and planned down to the minutest detail. Without the invasion plans (whose official designation was simply "*A.-Plan*") that had been pre-prepared in the German war academies over years and decades – continuously reworked, improved and perfected and now filed, ready to be implemented, in the archives of the war ministry – no invasion and no attack could have been executed successfully from one day to the next, even if there had been only minimal resistance.

This is one of the fundamental differences between a democracy and a military authoritarian state: in countries with a healthy democracy, such as Switzerland, England, or the USA, the officer corps, under constant control of parliament and accountable to it, is not permitted to work on invasion plans against foreign nations; indeed, it would be considered a crime against the nation's democracy to draw up invasion plans in times of peace, against friendly nations and states with which one lives in peace and wants to continue living in peace. This assertion can be proven, and the proof has a name: invasion! In early 1944, the commanders-in-chief for a forthcoming major continental campaign by the English and Americans were appointed. General Eisenhower and his staff were called to London, where they found no such thing as a completed invasion plan, but instead had to draw up such a plan over the course of many months of detailed and intensive work, the extent of which only a specialist can fully appreciate. The mammoth task of an invasion can only be successful if it has been perfectly prepared in all its military-scientific details. The evidence to the contrary is perfectly clear: the sudden German invasion of Austria and Czechoslovakia, the attack on Poland, the occupation of Denmark and Norway, the *Blitzkrieg* against Holland, Belgium and France, the first successful campaign against Russia and the rapid occupation of Yugoslavia and Greece etc. – none of this would have been possible to implement successfully without the painstaking work and preparatory planning at the German war academies, which had already been initiated during the days of the Weimar Republic and the 100.000-strong army, that is, before Hitler's takeover.

To produce yet more evidence and counter-evidence: when, following the campaign in North Africa and after Badoglio's capitulation, the Allies were faced with the task of a rapid occupation of Italy, the members of the general staff of the grand democracies were not in possession of the crucial plans for such an invasion. Again, such a plan had to be painstakingly drawn up over the course of months; to improvise instead was not an option. On the other hand, the complete lack of any planning for retreat or disengagement had catastrophic consequences for the German general staff during the war against Russia, then against France, and finally all theatres of war. German militarism certainly had first-rate generals at its disposal, real luminaries in their field, and as long as German warfare happened according to "plans", namely meticulously drawn-up *invasion* plans, the German war machinery rushed forward and ever forward. But when – as it did in Russia – the first unscheduled stop occurred, when suddenly the great unknown "X" could no longer be calculated by the military mathematicians and therefore the equations could no longer be balanced, for the first time there was no plan.

To complete any disengagement plan would have required many months of work by the generals, and any such plan would, once ready for implementation, likely have been rendered obsolete by the passing of time. But a lack of planned retreat strategies could, in the long run, not be replaced by improvisations, however ingenious, such as the one by General von Manstein in Southern Russia.

Field Marshal Fritz Erich Georg ("Erich") von Manstein (1887-1973). He was born Fritz Erich Georg Eduard von Lewinski but changed his surname because of being adopted by his aunt and her husband (von Manstein), who could not have children. Manstein tried very hard to save the situation in Russia for the Germans, and furiously opposed the idiotic decisions by Hitler, who sacked him in 1944.

At the beginning of the war, the Allies' complete lack of planning for invasion – and thereby their unreadiness for war – was interpreted as weakness, and the German attacking spirit was undeservedly glorified. Today that glory has faded into nothing. Now, after the end of the war, rid the German attacking spirit of the war debt, and thus German militarism will be crushed!

PART ONE

THE SYSTEM

THE FACTORS OF POWER

A. THE SECURITY SERVICE OF THE *REICHSFÜHRER SS*; THE *SD-RFSS*

I. Ideology
The "*Sonnenmenschen*"

After the officers' assassination attempt on Hitler on July 20, 1944, the British Foreign Minister [Anthony] Eden gave a speech in London (on July 24, 1944). Instead of expressing sympathy for the revolting generals, he dealt them a blunt rebuff by declaring:

"Hitler is the actual symbol of the German attacking spirit. Even if that symbol were to vanish, the spirit that remains would still have to be exterminated. —— This time round we have to make sure that any possibility of further aggression is removed."

Anthony Eden, as British Foreign Minister in 1944, said that the spirit of Hitler "would have to be exterminated".

The "outdated" Prussian spirit was turned into the modern, much more aggressive Nazi spirit; the number of avatars of "Old Prussian officer virtue" gradually diminished, and their positions were gradually occupied by the so-called "*Sonnenmenschen*" ("men of the sun"). These "men of the sun" are a no less exclusive grouping than was the former Prussian officer corps; indeed, they could almost be described as a secret society. Not only did they operate their own secret tribunal system, but even during the heyday of National Socialism they lived a strictly guarded existence in the background, so that until the very end they remained virtually or completely unknown in Germany and for a long time the public was entirely ignorant of their very existence. These "men of the sun" appeared publicly in official positions as little as possible, and they were prohibited from playing any role in society in their capacity as members of the aforementioned secret society.

The term "*Sonnenmensch*" was initially intended as a derisive moniker, and indeed it seems like mockery that, of all people, these "men of the sun" were required by higher authorities to avoid the "light of day", i.e. the glare of publicity. Such mockery was dished out by high-level Nazi officials and insiders, but they lost their appetite for ridicule as soon as they had any dealings with the "men of the sun". These "*Sonnenmenschen*" were required to have all the characteristics that had also defined the avatars of "Old Prussian officer virtue": honesty, incorruptibility, bravery, dutifulness, a straightforward way of living, and – this deserves special attention, for it was an explicit requirement – an impeccable family life, which, while a matter of course for Prussian officers and German members of the general staff, could not necessarily be taken for granted when it came to high-level Nazi leaders. A new attribute was a maniacal obsession with power that was characteristic of each and every one of these "men of the sun", which manifested itself in personally exerted terror with all its cruel consequences. What was also new was unconditional and blind obedience towards the person of the political leader, Adolf Hitler, and his representative, Heinrich Himmler.

The "*Sonnenmenschen*" did not include all of the *SS*-troops of the *Reichsführer SS*, Heinrich Himmler, but only a very particular and hermetically secluded section, namely the "*Sicherheitsdienst*" (security service) of the *Reichsführer SS* (abbreviated as "*SD*"), which was affiliated to the *SD* Main Office. As is well known, the *SS* was subdivided into three main groups, which were subordinate to and led by the three so-called main offices:

1. The *SS* Main Office, to which all active and reserve *Schutz-Staffeln* (protection squadrons) were subordinate, including the frequently mentioned *SS-Verfügungstruppen* (combat support forces).

2. The Race and Settlement Main Office, whose remit included *SS*-selection, ideological instruction ("blood and soil") and – as its name suggests – political competency for all matters of settlement. It also incorporated the Ministry for Agriculture.

3. The *SD* Main Office, which will be the subject of detailed investigation in the pages below.

Each of these main offices was run by its own chief. Until the start of war, they were:

For the *SS* Main Office: *SS-Obergruppenführer* [August] Heissmeyer, the later head of the Gestapo in Norway;

For the Race and Settlement Main Office: the former Minister for Agriculture, [Richard Walter] Darré, and alongside him (but formally in a subordinate position) the often overlooked *SS-Obergruppenführer* [Werner] Lorenz, who played a pivotal role in all "resettlement" issues and was a very popular figure in Berlin's diplomatic circles until the outbreak of war;

SS Obergruppenführer Werner Lorenz, who was 'very popular in Berlin's diplomatic circles' according to the author. From his expression here one can imagine that he was good at sardonic humour at diplomatic receptions.

For the *SD* Main Office: *SS-Obergruppenführer* Reinhard Heydrich (who was later murdered in Prague), and his deputy Dr Werner Best, author of the infamous Boxheim documents and later the *Reich's* Plenipotentiary for Denmark in Copenhagen.

Reinhard Heydrich in his Munich office in early 1934, before he and Himmler were able to relocate to Berlin for their headquarters. By this time, the author was working immediately under him and reported directly to him, disguised by the pseudonym of Heinz Stein so that no one (especially not their rivals Admiral Canaris and Hermann Göring) would know his true identity. Heydrich's office blocked the way to Himmler's inner office, so that no one could get through to Himmler without Heydrich's consent. Heydrich was worried about Himmler being "too soft". The author normally only saw Heydrich, and met with Himmler only on important occasions when a project of major importance was being planned.

The chiefs of the three main offices were directly and immediately subordinate to *Reichsführer SS* Heinrich Himmler, as opposed to the "staff of the *Reichsführer SS*".

Heinrich Himmler and his wife Margarete {"Marga"), a nurse (who was seven years older than him). They used to go for strolls like this looking like Mr. and Mrs. Nobody. No one passing him in the street would imagine that he was Western Europe's most cold blooded mass murderer, quite on a par with Josef Stalin. Eglantyne was able to acquire this original snapshot, but another print of it exists in the Bundesarchiv, which is of inferior quality to this one.

The *SS* (*"Schutz-Staffeln"*) was founded in 1929, as a special component of the *SA* (*"Sturm-Abteilungen"*), with a dedicated *"Reichsführer"*. Until June 30, 1934, this *Reichsführer SS* was directly subordinate to the Chief of Staff of the *SA*, Ernst Röhm, and only after the *SS* gained formal independence in 1934, the *Reichsführer SS* was appointed "*Reichsleiter* of the NSDAP", and from that point onwards was subordinate directly and personally only to the leader of the party, Adolf Hitler. While the Race and Settlement Main Office had already played an important role within the party following the foundation of the *SS* in 1929, the *SS* main offices were only created in the wake of June 30, 1934. The *SD-RFSS* (the Security Service of the *Reichsführer SS*) was founded two years after the creation of the *SS*, at the request of the "leader's deputy", Rudolf Hess – at that time second only to Hitler in the party's power structure and therefore his presumptive successor.

The *SD*, the infamous informer organisation operating within the party and later the entire state, was shrouded in mystery from its inception. The *SD* men had to undergo an exceptionally rigorous selection process, and had to be especially trustworthy, discreet and loyal to the party. Tellingly, the *SD* was founded not for purposes of surveillance of enemies of the party, but in order to monitor the party loyalty and reliability of prominent party leaders. The small elite of devoted and reliable party officials who made up the SD (who through their commissions alone had already gained exceptional importance within the party and ultimately tremendous power within the National Socialist state), formed the "brain of the party and state" – a rather questionable honorary title, first bestowed onto them by Rudolf Hess and later affirmed by Hitler himself.

The organisation of the *SD* Main Office and its *SD* Senior Districts (*Oberabschnitte*)

Before detailing the organisational structure of the *SD*, it is worth noting that almost all important posts within the secret police, the Gestapo, were filled by *SD* men. It would be wrong to view the Gestapo as the actual instrument of power of the National Socialist state, for in reality it was the *SD* with its *SD* Main Office. The Gestapo was nothing more than the executive of the *SD*, and it is significant that even the Gestapo officials themselves were not allowed to know who among them was actually a member of the *SD* and who was not. (Conversely, of course, such secrecy did not apply to *SD* men who were also members of the Gestapo.) There was equal fear of the *SD* within the ranks of secret police officials as there was among the circle of corrupt Nazi-officials of the highest levels, all the way up to *Gauleiter*, *Reichsleiter* and *Reichsminister*. Without fail, the two letters "*SD*" would make even the highest-ranking Nazi leaders shudder with fear. There is an anecdote around Hitler's former close Munich friend Ernst ['Putzi'] Hanfstängl. The story goes that "good friends" of Hanfstängl had a bet that even that minion of the *Führer* would make himself scarce if he was told that the *SD* was after him. No sooner said than done! One of the "friends" called Hanfstängl at his apartment late one evening to insinuate that the *SD* had "asked after him" and that he could expect a visit at his address in the morning. Hanfstaengl is said to have cleared out in a mad rush, and for fear of the *SD* ultimately went as far as America. Well, … *"se non è vero, è ben trovato"*.

Ernst Franz Sedgwick Hanfstängl [*the surname means "hemp stalk"*], universally known as "Putzi" Hanfstängl (1887-1975) was one of the most unusual characters of his time. He was half American and half German. He attended Harvard, where his fellow students called him "Hanfy", but otherwise from childhood he was always "Putzi", which in Bavarian peasant dialect means "Little Fellow". He grew to be very tall (six feet four inches), so that his nickname was always a source of amusement. He had huge hands and was an excellent pianist who could thump away with big chords convincingly. He could instantaneously transpose any melody to any key or style, and could convincingly turn a Bach fugue into a Viennese waltz with complete ease. His bizarre friendship with Adolf Hitler, whom he met in the 1920s when Hitler was an unknown beer hall orator, flourished in particular because Putzi was expert at playing piano transcriptions of Wagner's music, which Hitler continually asked him to do for him. They would spend whole evenings when Putzi would play through the entire two hand piano transcription of Wagner's *Meistersinger*, for instance, and Hitler would sit entranced. The *Meistersinger* was Hitler's favourite opera, and Wagner's *Liebestod* melody was Hitler's favourite aria. He would always call for one or the other, or both, to be played, to calm him down after giving a fiery speech. Eventually, they fell out because Putzi kept trying to "civilise" Hitler and restrain his murderous impulses. But then there was a very real danger that Hitler's killers would murder him, so he realized he would have to flee Germany and return to America, where he moved in very high social circles and would be safe. It is doubtful that Putzi ever knew that the SD had played a prank on him, and it is equally doubtful that the author knew of what serious danger Putzi really was in, having irritated Hitler so much with "helpful criticisms". Apparently the "prank" is only recorded by Pfeifer, who knew the men personally who teased Putzi with the phone call. The fact is that Putzi had every reason to be terrified of the SD anyway, and he did indeed flee Germany, via Switzerland, and after many difficult years he wrote a fascinating memoir revealing the details of Hitler's beginnings and early life as a political figure, and giving details of many of the key people and incidents of Nazi Germany up until 1939. There is no other highly personal memoir of the period of comparable intimacy and value.

The *chief of the SD* also held the post of chief of the secret state police. This amalgamation of posts ensured that no friction would arise between the *SD's* secret service and the executive of the Gestapo in the first place. The chief of the *SD* was superior to the *SD* Main Office. He maintained his own personal staff and a so-called "*SD* raiding squad" (*Rollkommando*), which must not be confused with the raiding squad of the office of the secret state police. This "*SD* raiding squad" was not used in general police raids, and therefore was not continuously on standby. Its role was rather to carry out special investigative missions for the chief of the *SD*. Until the outbreak of war, the commander of that "*SD* raiding squad" was *SS-Standartenführer* [Hanns] Johst (1890-1978), a reckless daredevil who already as a young officer during the previous World War had been decorated with the highest medals. Johst was also known as a competent amateur photographer who secretly made various photocopies and photographs for his boss – always on occasions when such images should not even have been shown in the *SD* Main Office.

Hanns Johst (1890-1978), whom the author knew intimately, and whom he describes as "a reckless daredevil". Although he was a poet and playwright, he was passionately pro-Nazi and joined the SD. He eventually rose to be a Gruppenführer and became President of the Reich Chamber of Literature, enforcing Nazi ideology upon authors. But before that, the author reveals that he was Commander of the SD Raiding Squad (*SD Rollkommando*) and in charge of carrying out executions. The author said he "also hurtled up and down the motorway between Munich and Berlin in his red Bugatti, delivering encrypted orders and reports of those orders having been carried out" and "procured the often rather substantial amounts of bribe money and expenses for the various *SD* senior districts." Clearly, in between executing enemies of the Reich and collecting bribes, he only engaged in the most "divinely poetic" of activities, being the model of a Nazi literary figure and also head of the German Academy of Poetry. [*Note: Hanns Johst should not be confused with Heinz Jost, another prominent Nazi, who is discussed elsewhere.*] (Bundesarchiv)

Within the personal staff of the chief of the SD, a high-ranking member of the *SD* functioned as the liaison officer to the Main Division V (espionage and counterintelligence) in the *Reich* Ministry of War. Officially, this liaison officer acted for the secret state police office, but in reality he was a member of the *SD* staff. Until the start of the war this post was filled by [SS] Police Major [Kurt] Pomme (1899-1964). It deserves special mention that a police officer could simultaneously also be a secret member of the *SD*, even though the uniformed regular police force was not subordinate to the chief of the *SD* (not even in his capacity as chief of the Gestapo and chief of the criminal police of the *Reich*). Police Major Pomme was formally detached to the chief of the Gestapo by the regular (uniformed) police, and only some insiders knew that he was actually a member of the *SD*.

The post of *aide-de-camp* to Heydrich (both in his capacity as chief of the *SD* and chief of the Gestapo) until 1938 was filled by an infamous *SD* member, *SS-Standartenführer* [Walter] Potzelt, a shady and unscrupulous Bavarian, who would later became chief of the *SD* Senior District West, in Frankfurt/Main.

SS-Gruppenführer Reinhard Heydrich – in his multiple capacities as chief of the *SD*, the Gestapo and the criminal police of the Reich, as well as later "acting" *Reichsprotektor* of Bohemia and Moravia – will be the subject of closer investigation, for he was not only the co-founder and first chief of the *SD*, but also its sinister and ingenious mastermind; one of the most dangerous protectors and reinforcers of power in the National Socialist state. In the same context, his longstanding and congenial deputy, *SS-Oberführer* Dr Werner Best, will also be closely scrutinised.

The *SD* headquarters were situated in Berlin's Wilhelmstrasse 112, in the former Prinz-Albrecht-Palais, where, as recently as during the days of the Weimar Republic, King Aman-Ullah (*Ghazi Amanullah Khan, reigned 1919-1926*; 1892-1960) of Afghanistan resided during a state visit to Berlin. The extensive basements were of such bulk that it is likely they will have survived all the bombardment during this recent war. These subterranean structures extended as far as the Ministry for Aviation and the People's Court (formerly home to the Federal State Parliament) in one direction, and as far as the offices of the secret state police (formerly home to the Labour Court) and the seat of the *SS* offices in the Hotel Prinz Albrecht in Prinz-Albrecht-Strasse in the other direction. There was a gigantic subterranean labyrinth beneath the entire complex of buildings between Wilhelmstrasse-Saarlandstrasse (formerly Königgrätzerstrasse) and Anhaltstrasse-Prinz-Albrecht-Strasse, all of whose entrances and exits were connected to the *SD* Main Office, the Prinz-Albrecht-Palais.

The Prinz Albrecht Palais in Berlin, at Wilhelmstrasse 112, which became the headquarters of the SD. The building was destroyed in an air raid by the RAF in November 1944. The building had also for some time housed the Nazi Party Museum, which helped to disguise its SD connection. The SD were based on the third floor ("second floor" in British usage). The building was linked to a vast labyrinthine system of secret underground tunnels described by the author, one of which led directly to the SS Headquarters in Prinz-Albrecht-Strasse, so that it was possible to go between the SD Headquarters and the SS Headquarters without being seen.

The SS Headquarters of Heinrich Himmler in Berlin from November 1934 was based here in this hotel named the Hotel Prinz Albrecht, on what was then named Prinz-Albrecht-Strasse. Himmler's office was on the second floor ("first floor" in British usage). The street is today called Niederkirchnerstrasse. Much of the hotel was destroyed in November of 1943 in an air raid, and the rest in 1945. The author did not need to use the street to enter this buiding because he could walk underground and unseen through the tunnel connecting it with the SD Headquarters in a nearby street. Much or possibly all of the gigantic underground complex in this area, which the author describes, probably still survives, as he himself believed to be the case. The most secret archives of the SS and SD were kept underground in "impenetrable" security conditions. As the author says: "The vaults of any major bank would seem like a child's plaything compared to the installations that housed the secret archive." Not all of them have been found. For instance, the author's own files and lists of assignments and aliases is specifically said by him to have been excluded from the main SS and SD files and kept in one of the 'impenetrable' special locations. This would apply also to some of his closest colleagues working under Heydrich on counter-intelligence and special operations. It certainly seems to have been the case also with SS *Oberführer* Wilhelm Albert (real name: Albrecht), the author's close friend and collaborator. Albert, as a lieutenant, had been the first full-time and salaried head of Group West of the SD in late 1933, but after he subsequently became Head of Office V, the Foreign Section, all of his and the author's secret work was separated from the SD main files by a strict firewall, as a security precaution by the paranoid Reinhard Heydrich, who never allowed the author to use or reveal his real name to the organisation. It is possible that only Heydrich, Himmler, Werner Best, and presumably also Albert, knew the author's true identity. There may have been several such SD operatives who were thus "untraceable and unidentifiable", employed and operating under false names. Ironically, it was this very policy which worked to protect the author after his defection, since those searching for him did not know who he was either. As regards the "secret" personnel lists and files of the SD and SS which have never been found, they may survive in the unlikely location of a leafy suburban street in Berlin named Königsallee, a lengthy and somnolent street of quiet villas. In 1939 the villa at 11 Königsallee was acquired by the SS and SD as a secret suburban out-station, and was used as a school for training saboteurs and spies preparing for foreign missions or for carrying out Fehme assassinations. In May of 1943, the building was expanded to act also as an operations base for the secret evacuation plans for forming an underground Nazi International in exile, creating the rat lines to Spain, South America, etc., the ODESSA operation, and other such plans. (The main foreign headquarters for such operations after the War was prepared at Madrid, still to be safely under the control of Franco for decades to come.) A secret and ultra-secure underground bunker was constructed at Königsallee, where precious files were stored, especially files detailing all the escape routes and contacts, who took them and who welcomed them. If you go to Google and try to see the street view of this building today, you will encounter a security block which prevents you seeing it. (The block is like a shiny silver wall constructed in front of the camera solely for that portion of the street view which looks towards that building. But this extends all the way from Number 3 to Number 13, indicating a considerable extension of this security complex and now incorporating a succession of separate but linked buildings.) It therefore seems to have a security agency connection today. It may be that the contemporary German security agency has all the "missing" files which were stored at that location, but just keeps them to themselves. Maybe that is where the personnel files of Heinrich Pfeifer as 'Heinz Stein' may be found. (Bundesarchiv)

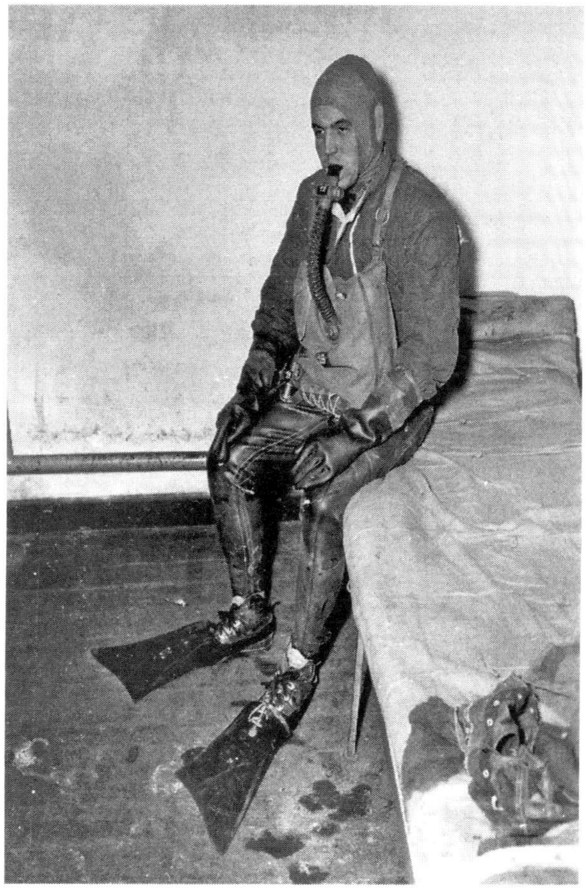

This is a photo of a German saboteur frogman who was captured by the Allies during the War and photographed in his entire German frogman outfit. He would have been trained at the Sabotage School at 11 Königsallee in Berlin under SS General Werner Heissmeyer (a cousin of August Heissmeyer, mentioned later), and then given specialist frogman training after he had completed his general sabotage course. Such frogmen were used to attach mines to ships and carry out numerous secret underwater tasks including blowing up docks and wharves. Heissmeyer trained most of the saboteurs sent to foreign countries and from 1938 was the head of the Sabotage School of the SS, SD, and Gestapo, the main headquarters of which was at 11 Königsallee in Berlin, but had subsidiaries in many towns and cities. The "cover name" for these schools was *Deutsche Heimschulen* ("German Home Schools"). But that was some idea of a Nazi joke, as they were sabotage and intelligence schools and nothing to do with any home. As for Berlin, the complex of buildings from Number 3 to Number 13 Königsallee apparently remains a secret installation complex to this day, and has numerous different underground bunkers. Presumably the entire records of all the Nazi foreign saboteurs are preserved and kept there still.

The *SD* Main Office was the centre of administration for the important *SD* senior districts, which covered the entire area of the *Reich*. It was subdivided into five, and later seven, main departments, the so-called *SD* offices, which were all headed by a so-called *SD* head official. While on paper these *SD* head officials were of equal rank to the chiefs of the *SD* senior districts, in reality they did not have nearly the same clout. One exception was the head official of the *SD* Office V, (Foreign Section), whose influence was perhaps even greater than that of a chief of an *SD* senior district. Until the outbreak of war, that post was held by *SS-Oberführer* [*a paramilitary rank roughly equivalent to a "senior colonel"*] Albrecht [Wilhelm Albrecht aka Albert, 1898-1960], who hailed from Frankfurt/Main, and previously – as predecessor to the aforementioned [Walter] Potzelt – had been the chief of the *SD* Senior District in Frankfurt/Main ["Group West"]. This Albrecht – generally called "Albert" – had been an officer both in World War 1, and then in the *Schwarze Reichswehr*, namely the illegal *Reichswehr* squadron that led the fight against Polish insurgents in 1920/21. He also played a role in the secret resistance movement against the French occupation of the Rhineland, and already at that time maintained excellent relations with the *Reich* War Ministry. This man possessed an organisational genius for all manner of secret units; a quality detected early on by Heydrich (the chief of the *SD*), who deployed him in the highly senior position of Chief of the Senior Division West in Frankfurt/Main. There, Albrecht immediately organised successful espionage against France, which was applauded even within *Reichswehr* circles, despite the underlying rivalry that still existed between the institutions. After the establishment of the *SD* Main Office in Berlin, Heydrich sent for Albrecht and, by installing him as the head official of the *SD* Office V (Foreign Section) within the *SD* Main Office, promoted him to the position of supreme commander of all the so-called *"V. Kolonnen"* ("Columns V."), which to a large extent still had to be created by Albrecht. (Incidentally, the term *"V. Kolonne"* was never in common use in Germany; it was derived from the name "*SD Office* V", whose first – and possibly only – chief was Albrecht.)

It is worth discussing this individual, Albrecht, a little further. His whole life story seemed to make him predestined to become the grand organiser of all manner of conspiratorial groups, subversive gangs and espionage organisations. He was the creator of the *"V. Kolonnen"*, and yet, on the inside, remained a strangely "decent chap", as absurd as this may sound. Of course Albrecht was also obsessed and intoxicated with power, but he was more of a servant of that power, which he wished to deploy not for its own sake, but for a misguided notion of "greatness of the fatherland". The "humiliation inflicted on his fatherland", as he perceived it, was what drove him into the arms of National Socialism. What made this man "internally decent" was his inability to tolerate personal injustice or to acquiesce wrongdoing against others. He was enraged about the lies and deception of June 30, 1934, when he learned, while he was in Frankfurt/Main, that it was only his special status that had saved his skin on that day. And while all other chiefs of the *SD* senior districts in the *Reich* used June 30, 1934 as a pretext to satisfy their own lust for revenge and to settle personal vendettas, under Albrecht no such brutalities were committed in Frankfurt/Main. On one occasion, however, he did give a real piece of his mind to *SA Führer* [Adolf-Heinz] Beckerle (who later became police president in Frankfurt and then German envoy in Sofia) and warned him, revolver in hand, not to carry out the smallest malicious act ever again. From that point forward there was no man that Beckerle had higher respect for than Albrecht.

SA Obergruppenführer Adolf-Heinz Beckerle (1902-1976). The author's friend Karl-Wilhelm Albrecht (aka Albert) pointed his revolver at him and warned him to stop abusing his power by carrying out malicious acts. Beckerle respected him a great deal after that. But later, as Ambassador to Bulgaria, Beckerle was one of the worst persecutors of the Jews and promoters of their extermination.

Later, when Albrecht heard from a friend who had returned from a concentration camp about what was actually going on there, he expressed his abhorrence with such vigour that Heydrich felt compelled to place him under house arrest. (Yes, indeed: there were even high-ranking party officials and *SD* chiefs who, before the major pogroms in 1938, did not want to believe – because they were unable to believe – what horrors were taking place in *their* concentration camps!) The full contradiction of the two Germanies, the decent and the barbaric, are manifest in this man, Albrecht. It will come as no surprise to hear that he was always a kind, gentle and forever caring family man. He, the creator of the *"V. Kolonnen"*; he, Heydrich's closest associate; he, the most important member of the truly notorious and satanic "Security Service of the *Reichsführer SS*".

The author's friend and closest colleague, SS Oberführer [later Brigadeführer] Karl Wilhelm Albert [properly Albrecht but called Albert, which is a more modern form of Albrecht] (1898-1960). The author says he was "a kind, gentle, forever caring family man". Albert became Heydrich's closest associate, and it was Albert, as Head of the SD Foreign Section, who dispatched the author on his foreign missions (see Volume Two), which the three of them planned meticulously in advance. It is probable that Albert helped the author to defect.

This photo from a military history forum of the internet is described there as "Unknown *Oberführer*". It seems to be an official file photo of Wilhelm Albert (aka Albrecht). But it was clearly filed without any name attached, hence the description "unknown", which accords with Heydrich's policy of secrecy concerning the names of his top spies. (Indeed, the use of the name Albert in place of Albrecht was in itself sufficient to make his birth records untraceable; only an intimate colleague such as the author could have known that he was really named Albrecht.) Albert/Albrecht was an older man than his SD colleagues, and had been an officer in the First World War. Notice that he is wearing service ribbons from his earlier action in the field. Two of them match the two worn in the other photo. The service ribbon with two wide vertical white stripes on a black background is the 1914 Iron Cross ribbon, and it matches the one worn also by Admiral Canaris. (See his photo below.) The cleft in this man's chin matches in both photos.

The *SD* Office II (Archive) was of even greater importance within the SD Main Office hierarchy than the *SD* Office V (Foreign Section), even though its head official was little more than a registry clerk or vault administrator. This secret archive of the *SD* Main Office was the actual "brain of the party and the state". The vaults of any major bank would seem like a child's plaything compared to the installations that housed the secret archive. "It is easier to get access to heaven than to the archive in the *SD* Main Office," a high-ranking *SS* officer and member of the *SD* once said to Albrecht. Not only did the facility have cutting-edge security installations and a sophisticated control system for each document and every last single piece of paper; the entire gigantic secret archive could, in a matter of minutes and at the push of a button, be utterly destroyed using hydraulic presses.

Anything and everything could be unearthed in this archive. Ministers were spied upon, and all good and bad deeds by any *Gauleiter*, *Reichsleiter*, prominent and entirely unknown Nazis and Nazi opponents were registered there. The habits, love lives, financial expenditures and monetary requirements of insignificant and grand personalities were recorded; the gains and losses of industry bosses, bankers and all notables from the party, state, society, church and any other association; their carnal desires and small human weaknesses; their correspondences and the company they kept. Suspects and such individuals who might turn into suspects were documented; friends and like-minded people were regarded with suspicion; and any instance of corruption could be proven using documents from the *SD* Main Office's secret archive. Diplomats, foreign statesmen and politicians each had their own file, as did eminent foreign personalities who at one time had played even the smallest role in politics or might be persuaded to do so in the future. An exaggeration? No – the sad truth! Only the fact that it was the Nazis themselves who compiled reams upon reams of incriminating evidence, of an extent and accuracy that subsequently would have been impossible to obtain, provides some measure of comfort.

Of all the documents and records that were kept in the secret archive of the *SD*, two further duplicates were kept in facsimile. One of these was kept at the *SD* senior district responsible for that particular territory, while the other was stored by that same *SD* senior district at a secret location, one which was only known to the chief of the *SD* senior district and his adjutant and deputy.

It should be pointed out that of course each of the five (or later seven) *SD* offices within the *SD* Main Office was itself composed of a myriad of subordinate offices and bureaux. A mere glance at the designation of any such department is enough to bring to mind the image of an unsolvable algebraic riddle, and only a well-trained mental acrobat would find his way to the actual *SD* office through a veritable labyrinth of letters and numbers. Imagine an upper-case Roman numeral II, followed by a hyphen and A2 with a lower-case d or g in superscript and below it some Arabic numeral with a dash and a new upper- or lower-case letter. Perhaps now you begin to develop a notion of German organisational prowess, and the manner in which offices and bureaux, main and secondary departments and so on and so forth – where each officer and each lowly runner also was a special kind of number or letter and most definitely belonged to some "category" – were organised. There, at the *SD* Main Office, the German bureaucratic, paper-pushing genius reached its most dizzying heights, and, after playing too much hide-and-seek behind all those letters and numbers and all that secret-mongering, in the end even the initiated could hardly navigate that labyrinthine edifice of secrecy.

The *SD* senior districts were at the most important administrative level within the security service – far more influential than the purely technical apparatus that was formed by the *SD* Main Office. The chief of an *SD* senior district was able to act largely independently, was able to issue his own directives and orders, and personally and directly was subordinate only to the actual chief of the *SD*, and no-one else within the administrative apparatus of the *SD* Main Office (the only exception being the *SD* Office V, Foreign Section).

The size of the *SD* senior districts varied from region to region. Initially there were seven *SD* senior districts (later that number rose to nine), and territorially they coincided with the Reich's military districts. There were, however, fifteen military districts, which corresponded to the fifteen army corps, plus three "commando corps": the 14th Army Corps in Magdeburg, the 15th Army Corps in Jena and the 16th Army Corps in Berlin (which did not have their own military district). The 17th and 18th Army Corps, which in turn did have their own military districts, were stationed in Vienna and Salzburg respectively.

The *SD* senior districts were organised as follows:

SD Senior District EAST, based in Berlin, territorially responsible for the 1st Army Corps in Königsberg, the 2nd Army Corps in Stettin, and the 3rd Army Corps in Berlin;

SD Senior District WEST, based in Frankfurt/Main, territorially responsible for the 9th Army Corps in Kassel and the 7th Army Corps in Wiesbaden;

SD Senior District SOUTHWEST, based in Stuttgart, territorially responsible for the 5th Army Corps in Stuttgart;

SD Senior District NORTHWEST, based in Hannover, territorially responsible for the 6th Army Corps in Münster and the 11th Army Corps in Hannover;

SD Senior District HAMBURG, based in Hamburg, territorially responsible for the 10th Army Corps in Hamburg;

SD Senior District CENTRE, based in Dresden, territorially responsible for the 4th Army Corps in Dresden;

SD Senior District SOUTH, based in Munich, territorially responsible for the 7th Army Corps in Munich and the 13th Army Corp in Nuremberg;

SD Senior District OSTMARK, based in Vienna, territorially responsible for the 17th Army Corps in Vienna and the 18th Army Corps in Salzburg.

When the *SD* Senior District OSTMARK was incorporated into the *Reich*, the *SD* Senior District SOUTHEAST (whose territory had previously been part of the much too large *SD* Senior District EAST) was created:

SD Senior District SOUTHEAST, based in Breslau, territorially responsible for the 8th Army Corps in Breslau.

SD-RFSS and the commanders of the military districts

Of course not the whole army corps (*AK*) was barracked in the respective cities, but only certain troop units along with the commanding general of a particular *AK* and his staff; in this case, the general staff of the *AK*. The military districts were the administrative areas of the general command, from which the troops for that army corps were conscripted. In times of peace, the commanding general also served as the military district's commander in chief; in times of war, when the commanding general went to the front with his corps, another commander – whose responsibility was the recruitment of reserve troops – was appointed to remain in the military district. During the war, all the commanders of the military districts together with the reserve troops stationed in the barracks for training formed the so-called "home forces" (*"Heimatheer"*), that is to say, troops that were on the whole not yet ready for combat. Those "home forces" had their own supreme commander – at first this was General [Friedrich] Fromm (1888-1945, executed}, replaced in July 1944 by *Reichsführer SS* Heinrich Himmler – to whom all commanders of the military districts were subordinate and who, in turn, was a prominent member of the Great General Staff and formally subordinate to the army general staff. By convention, in times of war, older and decommissioned generals were appointed as the commanders of the military districts. However, as the war dragged on, they gained more and more importance, as it was they who were responsible for the essential task of replenishing – at any cost – missing troops at the frontline of *their* army corps; a task that was often only possible using increasingly drastic recruiting measures. Two conflicting factors led to increasing tension between the party and the leadership of the military districts: on the one hand, as per party decree, young party officials were not to be drafted; on the other hand, as time went on, it became almost impossible for the commanders of the military districts to provide enough troops to make up for the severe shortages at their respective fronts. On occasion these tensions escalated, and the Gestapo – and with it, in the background, the *SD*! – had to protect party officials from the grasp of the recruiting commanders. The *SD* was in turn ordered to examine and monitor the recruiting commanders' "loyalty towards the *Führer*". Eventually, following Himmler's representations at Hitler's headquarters several weeks before July 20, 1944 (!) – that is to say before Himmler became supreme commander of the home forces – no fewer than 117 prominent officers were removed from their posts and replaced by "reliable" officers and generals. The majority of these deposed officers were commanders of military districts and recruiting officers for the home forces.

In the days immediately leading up to July 20, 1944, General von Unruh, a man of advanced years, also was forced to resign his post, though news of this deposition never reached the general public. General von Unruh had been a kind of "inspector of the commands of the military districts" and, in close co-operation with Ernst Sauckel, the "*Reich* Plenipotentiary for Labour Deployment", *Gauleiter* and *Reich* Governor for Thuringia, was responsible for the replenishment of the home forces (in effect, the reserve forces) through continuously and repeatedly sifting and combing through the workforce. This hardened general was infamous and feared for employing drastic and rigorous measures against the workforce. The party bureaux used him as a buffer against the protests of industrialists and company directors, and at the same time he was a useful conduit to the commanders of the military districts, who held him in high esteem. In performing his thankless recruiting task it was inevitable that he, too, would repeatedly "lay his hands on" young party officials and friends of high Nazi leaders, and so even this old general, who had served his party and state in such important roles, was dismissed.

As per a decree issued by the *Reich* administration at the start of war, all Nazi leaders and party officials – with the sole exception of the ranks of *Gauleiter*, *Reich* governor and minister – were required to serve at the front for at least three months in each year. It was common practice for the gentlemen of the party to take part in an officers' training course somewhere behind the front (they were even allowed to choose a particular branch within the armed services!), and after three months would return home as newly minted officers of the *Wehrmacht*. Particularly popular branches were the *Luftwaffe* or Air Defence. The gentlemen would fly a quick "mission" and then proudly have a medal pinned to their chests, for in the early stages of the war the business of flying was not all that dangerous for such gentlemen. But for party officials who had already risen to officer rank during the war of 1914-18, it was better to play it safe and take part in a "retraining course" at a different army branch (most often also at the *Luftwaffe*), because conveniently such courses also took up the required three months. Yet, the more dangerous the war games became over the years, the more these "also-officers", as they were called by the soldiers on the front, became "indispensible" for the party, even for three months per year. A further "retraining course" was not really an option during the years 1942, 1943 and 1944 – the commanders of the military districts simply did not allow it. So, when there were no other options left, one had oneself deployed as an "administrative official" in some occupied territory (preferably in Russia), because administrative service in occupied territories counted as "war service" and therefore as service at the front, and, besides, one could enjoy the welcome prospect of enriching oneself at the cost of a foreign nation.

Even before the invasion and the summer offensive by the Red Army at the end of 1944, General

[Walter Rudolf Moritz] von Unruh (1877-1956) had an audience with Hitler, during which he demanded – in his own name and those of nearly all commanders of the military districts who with their signatures supported the general's demands – the conscription of all minor and major party officials who for more than a year had seen no real action, and for those individuals to catch up on their service with the units at the front; especially all those party officials who had in the meantime lost their administrative posts in Russia and for the most part were now stationed at provisional administrative posts within *Reich* territory, somewhere in Poland, Bohemia, Moravia or in the Balkans. As most of them had not served "at the front" for two years or more, it essentially meant that they could be sent to the front with their units for at least six months. Allegedly almost 100,000 party officials owed service at the front in this way! (In times of peace, an army corps is made up of two or three divisions, equal to approximately 40,000 men.) The outcome of the protest lodged by General von Unruh and his commanders of the military districts is well known: 117 officers and generals were stripped of their commands, and on July 20, 1944, Heinrich Himmler became supreme commander of the home forces. Through Himmler's secret state police, but mainly through the "efficiency" of the *SD*, the party had achieved a decisive "victory" over the *Wehrmacht*. The home forces were under the control of Himmler, and the command of the military districts was turned into the executive branch of the *SD* within the *Wehrmacht*, in the same way that the Gestapo had been the executive branch of the *SD* in the civilian domain since 1934. From that point forward, the *SD* senior districts' grip of power on the homeland seemed well nigh unlimited.

General of the Infantry Walter Rudolf Moritz von Unruh (1877-1956). After he laid his demands before Hitler in 1944, 117 officers and generals were stripped of their commands, and Heinrich Himmler was elevated to be Supreme Commander of the Home Forces. But it was too late to make any difference.

II. RAMIFICATIONS
Dr Werner Best, the organiser

Much nonsense has been written, sometimes out of pure sensationalism, but often in good faith and with honest, fervent eagerness to set the record straight; many a yarn about a prominent or not-so-prominent Nazi leader has been spun, many a horror story invented and naively repeated. Sadly, and all too often in the past, National Socialism and its leaders have thereby been done a great favour, because it was all too easy to condemn the entire so-called "literature written in exile" because of some misreporting and to write it off as "lies" *en bloc*. The authors of such texts can be accused of making things too easy for themselves and seeing reality too simplistically. Not only do they frequently – and with shocking primitiveness – paint black on black and white on white, but sadly they also merely produce farcical caricatures that have little to do with reality. For reality is much more complicated, and the facts are much more incriminating than even the most horrific scare stories could ever be. Dr Werner Best is a prime example.

Without doubt, Dr Werner Best was a clever man with a keen sensibility for the direction and strength of the "political wind". As a student he had played a role during the occupation of the Rhineland, not as a National Socialist, but as the student leader of the German National People's Party at the University of Frankfurt/Main. It was only as the NSDAP grew that his personal ambition drove him into the arms of the National Socialists. He hastened to prove his radical views by authoring the infamous Boxheim documents, for which he was indicted in 1932 by the Prussian Minister for the Interior, Severing; however, no verdict was ever reached. Upon Hitler's assumption of power, Dr Best became Minister for Policing for Hesse-Darmstadt under *Gauleiter* Sprenger. Dr Best hoped to bring down Sprenger in order to improve his own position, and overeagerly collected incriminating materials, especially regarding his superior's excessive drinking sprees. Sprenger was summoned to Berlin and was given an official warning by Rudolf Hess; but Dr Best – a relatively recent party member – had celebrated too soon and schemed all too brazenly and was forced to resign as Minister for Policing. Despite all this, *Reichsführer SS* Heinrich Himmler – still furious about the fact that he had not been elevated to the position of chief of the entire political police of the *Reich* upon Hitler's takeover, and ranting in impotent rage against the "highest federal state authority in the *Reich*", i.e. Dr Diels' secret state police – had Dr Best join him in Munich at Heydrich's suggestion. (At that time, Himmler was merely Chief of the Political Police in Bavaria, but later, after the Reichstag Fire, he widened his sphere of influence to include Baden and Württemberg, and eventually all *Länder* except Prussia!) Dr Best was introduced into the *SD* by Heydrich personally and was tasked with the establishment and organisation of the new *SD* Senior District Southwest in Stuttgart. As the "Chief of the *SD* Senior District Southwest" – as was his official title – Dr Best had been gifted an instrument of power unlike any he had had access to during his time as Minister for Policing for Hesse-Darmstadt; and he promptly demonstrated that he knew how to put it to use. He immediately recognised that close co-operation between the *SD* and the *Reichswehr* in all areas of espionage and counter-intelligence was an imperative, and his connections to the *Reichswehr's* counter-intelligence bureau in Darmstadt, as well as his personal acquaintance with the chief of the later Main Division V, Admiral Canaris (which he had made during the French occupation of the Rhineland), came in very useful. Dr Best made himself at home in the former Crown Prince's Palace in Stuttgart, and set about building the *SD's* first major transmitting station, which could compete with any police radio system.

SS Obergruppenführer Dr. Karl Rudolf Werner (always called 'Werner') Best (1903-1989), the author's early friend and sponsor, who first introduced him to Himmler and Heydrich and got him his job with the SD. But Best afterwards 'went on a frenzied power rampage of the most repulsive kind', being solely responsible for all killings in the South of Germany, according to the author. It was Best who personally handed a revolver to Ernst Röhm and ordered him to kill himself. When Röhm refused, Best had him gunned down by his SD men. The author was present and an eyewitness of this, and before long he and Best were the only two eyewitnesses of Röhm's death who remained alive, the others having been done away with because they knew too much.

In Stuttgart Dr Best played the diplomat and proved his considerable talent for negotiation. With feigned modesty he won over the powerful and was able to bring about reconciliation between Himmler and the *Gauleiter* of the Palatinate and Saarland regions and later *Reichskommissar* Josef Bürckel – a man with a reputation for being "wild" and "red". Bürckel had often vociferously criticised the "shenanigans" perpetrated by the men of the *SS* in Munich (which we shall talk about in more detail later), and had, for all intents and purposes, taken away all executive power from Himmler's police within the territory of his *Gau*, despite the fact that the Palatinate region was part of Bavaria. Dr Best ensured that Bürckel would from now also send his own personal opponents and party enemies to Dachau for "re-education" and would henceforth closely co-operate with Himmler-Heydrich in all police matters.

In 1934, Himmler and Heydrich triumphantly took over the offices of the secret police in Berlin. (Himmler was by then officially "inspector" of the Gestapo and the *de facto* chief of all branches of the political police in the entire *Reich*, and Heydrich had replaced Dr Diels, though formally the Gestapo remained subordinate to Hermann Göring, the Minister President of Prussia.) At the same time, Dr Best took over the *SD* Senior District South in Munich and was appointed "Deputy Chief of the Political Police in Bavaria". This meant that he became the outright holder of police power in the whole of Southern Germany, because holding the offices of chief of both the *SD* Senior Districts South and Southwest amounted to controlling the whole of Southern Germany.

On June 30, 1934, Dr Best, having been promoted to the rank of *SS-Standartenführer*, went on a frenzied power rampage of the most repulsive kind; he was responsible for every single execution, both "legal" and "illegal", within the territories of the *SD* Senior Districts South and Southwest. He personally oversaw the executions that took place in the courtyard of the police prison in Munich and in the Wittelsbacher Palais; under his command [Gustav Ritter von] Kahr (1862-1934, murdered), [General Ferdinand]von Bredow (1884-1934) and all the others were executed.

Gustav Ritter von Kahr (1862-1934, murdered) He was President of Bavaria and was murdered in the Night of the Long Knives for opposing Hitler.

General Ferdinand von Bredow (1884-1934, murdered). He was shot in the face at point-blank range on his own doorstep in Berlin in the Night of the Long Knives massacre. He was head of the Abwehr (military intelligence service) and was the Deputy Defence Minister to Defence Minister General Kurt von Schleicher, who with his wife had been shot dead in their own house a little while earlier by the SD hit-man Johannes Schmidt.

He, Dr Best, also personally took a pistol to the cell of *SA* Chief of Staff Röhm, with which Röhm was supposed to shoot himself. When he refused to do so, he was mowed down by Dr Best's *SD* men, who had been waiting at the door of the cell with their sub-machine guns.

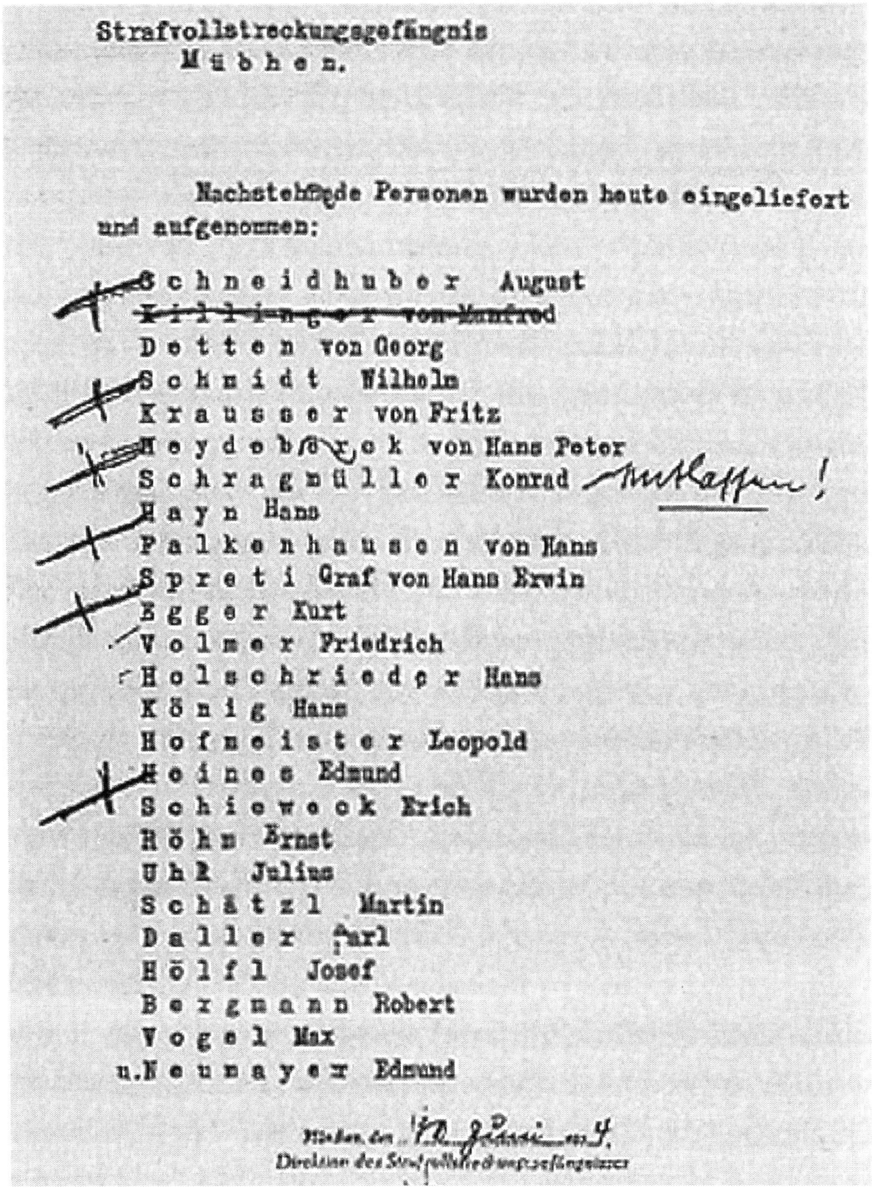

Strafvollstreckungsgefängnis
Mübhen.

Nachstehende Personen wurden heute eingeliefert und aufgenommen:

Schneidhuber August
~~Killinger von Manfred~~
Detten von Georg
Schmidt Wilhelm
Krausser von Fritz
Heydebreck von Hans Peter
Schragmüller Konrad — Mitläufer!
Hayn Hans
Falkenhausen von Hans
Spreti Graf von Hans Erwin
Egger Kurt
Volmer Friedrich
Holzschrieder Hans
König Hans
Hofmeister Leopold
Heines Edmund
Schiewock Erich
Röhm Ernst
Uhl Julius
Schätzl Martin
Daller Karl
Hölfl Josef
Bergmann Robert
Vogel Max
u. Neumayer Edmund

München, den ...
Direktion des Strafvollstreckungsgefängnisses

A prisoner list from Stadelheim Prison in Munich immediately prior to the Night of the Long Knives. Of the persons named in this book, Edmund Heines and Ernst Röhm appear on the list. Both were executed shortly after this list was made. This document was reproduced on an internet discussion website without a reference, and its original source is unknown. The heading means "Penal Incarceration List, Munich" (with the "n" missing from Munich because of a typing error). The next sentence means: "The persons hereunder were today delivered up and received (into custody)." Also on this list is Gruppenführer Wilhelm ("Willy") Schmidt, who had been Head of the Personnel Division of the SA and was one of the fiercest and most determined of the SA leaders, who was determined to proceed with a *putsch* without Röhm if Röhm backed out and resigned. And in addition, Röhm's official boyfriend Count (*Graf*) Hans Erwin von Spreti appears; he had been sleeping with Röhm at the time of their arrest in the early hours of the morning. Also on the list is SS Gruppenführer Robert Bergmann; he, Röhm and Röhm's doctor (Dr. Emil Ketterer) had dinner together and then stayed up until 11 PM playing the Bavarian three-handed card game named Tarok on the evening of June 29, only hours before the arrests were made at 5 AM. It is somewhat strange that Bergmann was so close to Röhm, Head of the SA, when Bergmann himself was an officer of the SS. The explanation for this apparent contradiction has apparently not been forthcoming, but in any case, we can see from the list above that Bergmann was arrested and treated as if he were one of the SA men.

In the background is the notorious Stadelheim Prison at Munich. The man in the photo is the poet and playwright Ernst Toller, who was imprisoned there in solitary confinement from 1919 to 1924. While there he wrote the long poem *The Swallow Book* about the pair of swallows who flew through the bars of his cell and made a next in his cell, his only companions, who helped him keep his sanity over the five long years. That poem was published in English in 2022 by Eglantyne Books. Adolf Hitler was imprisoned there for one month in 1922. It was to be the place of death for Ernst Röhm, machined gunned to death in his cell. Our author was an eye-witness to this murder, as he explains.

As reward for the atrocities he committed in Bavaria, Württemberg and Baden, Dr Best was promoted to the position of Deputy Chief of the *SD*. He moved to Berlin with his family, where he became Heydrich's deputy in all areas, which included the position of Deputy Chief of the Gestapo, in his capacity as chief of its "legal department". Dr Best immediately went to work in Berlin, and orchestrated the first joint "social evening" that involved both the secret state police and Admiral Canaris' Main Division V. The two chiefs of the police and the military intelligence service turned up at the former "House of the Aviators" (latterly the "People's Court" and Prussian Federal State Parliament) with a large entourage. In order to fully appreciate the significance of that day, one has to bear in mind that the *Reichswehr* had only recently won its victory over the party (on June 30, 1934), and that it was now a member of the Grand General Staff, namely Admiral Canaris, who made the journey to Prinz-Albrecht-Strasse (because the Federal State Parliament was situated directly opposite the headquarters of the secret state police). It was a veritable "peace festival", celebrated with much ceremoniousness. The young former First Sea Lieutenant Reinhard Heydrich, who had just been promoted from *SS-Brigadeführer* to *SS-Gruppenführer*, embraced Admiral Canaris, who greatly outranked him, in front of the assembled staff; they introduced their chiefs of staff to each other, toasted each other, and their marvellous comradeship was sealed "for eternity". The shady, power-hungry Heydrich, the chief of the "men of the sun" of his *SD*, was the triumphant victor; and next to him, smiling obligingly, stood the "modest" *regisseur* of the event, Dr Werner Best. This festival of reconciliation between the devious Admiral Canaris and the reckless, ingenious chief of the *SD*, Heydrich, took place in Spring 1936. The two men had learned to appreciate and respect each other during the course of the espionage affair around the Polish Major Sosnowski, because it was thanks to the intervention by the *SD* that Admiral Canaris and his *Reichswehr* department were unable to downgrade the *SD* chief Heydrich's police force to mere stooges. Heydrich had got wise to Admiral Canaris' schemes, but was unable to deprive him of his power or to trick him into officially disclosing his secrets.

Admiral Wilhelm Franz Canaris (1887-1945, executed for high treason), Chief of the *Abwehr*, the Military Intelligence Service, from 1933 to 1944. Canaris had complete contempt for Adolf Hitler. He was the great intelligence rival to Himmler, Heydrich, and the SD. Heydrich hated him and referred to him as "the geriatric" and "the grumpy old bear". It was partly to ensure that Canaris could not identify who was running the SD's counter-intelligence operations and carrying out special secret missions abroad that the author had to operate under a bewildering number of aliases, at the insistence of Heydrich. It is thus probable that Canaris and his organisation never knew the name "Heinrich Pfeifer", especially as the SD's secret archive was impenetrable, as described by the author, who used it regularly. Canaris's murder was ordered by Himmler, and it involved Canaris being forced to walk naked to the scaffold where he was hung, his body being then immediately burned, with a few pieces of his unburnt skin left flying in the prison air, according to one inmate who survived (a detail quoted by Hugh Thomas in his book on Himmler).

Orchestrating the "social evening Heydrich-Canaris" was not Dr Best's last great feat. It was customary for the post of deputy police chief to be filled by a lawyer, whose job it was to ensure that no conflict would arise between the executive and the judiciary. But now Dr Best was commissioned by Himmler and Heydrich to legalise the Gestapo's regime of terror, in other words, to create a legal basis for it, and thus became the personal representative of

Himmler-Heydrich and of the entire *SD* within the newly created "Academy for German Law". Much too little attention has been given to the fact that it was not the president of that academy and *Reichsleiter* for all legal matters of the NSDAP, Minister Dr Hans Frank II, but rather the *SD* representative and Deputy Chief of the Secret State Police, Dr Werner Best, who established (and justified at length during one of the academy's plenary sessions) the legal tenet: "Whatever serves the state is lawful and right."

Lay people did not grasp the outrageousness of installing that tenet as one of the fundamental pillars of all new German law. By stating "whatever serves the state is lawful and right", all police despotism could be justified, and any amount of terror inflicted by the state would be legalised by default. "Whatever serves the state is lawful and right" – that was characteristic of Dr Best, the representative of the *SD* and secret state police, but also of Dr Best, the private citizen, unscrupulous careerist and man of sharp elbows.

The *SD-RFSS* at work

There are other Nazi personalities who, when viewed from the outside, appear to have played much more important roles and whose personal power seemed much greater; men such as Göring, Goebbels, [Robert] Ley, and others. And yet there is a crucial difference between them and men such as Himmler, Heydrich and Best. To get straight to the point: we believe the men in the latter category to be much more dangerous! It was not because its operatives were stuck in an obsessive power delirium that the *SD* became a truly satanic instrument of power; after all, the same goes for other Nazi officials, too. The men of the Himmler-Heydrich-Best-Kaltenbrunner ilk became so exceptionally dangerous because, as typical fanatics, they were able to bring to bear both an incredibly systematic approach and a peculiar strength of character. Let us refer back to the remarks about the "men of the sun" at the beginning of this chapter. The *SD* officials did not carouse and debauch and did not have affairs; the usual pleasures in life meant nothing to them or played a very minor role in their private lives. They stayed in the background and whenever possible avoided the public glare, having correctly identified the fact that it was much better to indulge their power mania away from the limelight; the audience is not supposed to see the puppeteer pulling the strings. Until the start of war, the *SD's* regulations stipulated that its officials should be paid a monthly stipend of no more than 1,000 *Reichsmark*, and that sum is what they lived on. At the same time, all the chiefs of the *SD* senior districts would have handled thousands, sometimes hundreds of thousands of *Reichsmark* in bribes each month. But no auditor in the world would have been able to carry out more stringent controls than the accounting department within the *SD Main Office*. Even the smallest discrepancy that could not be fully explained would inevitably lead to highly embarrassing legal proceedings at an *SD* tribunal, where draconian penalties were handed out. This internal secret tribunal system only dealt with registered *SD* members and was not subordinate to the "Supreme Party Court", which was presided over by the infamous retired Major *SS-Obergruppenführer* and NSDAP *Reichsleiter* Walter Buch. Whenever the *SD* "court of honour" handed out a death penalty, this was carried out by the aforementioned *SS-Standartenführer* Johst, in his capacity as commander of the "*SD* raiding squad".

It has already been mentioned that *SD* members were expected to lead impeccable family lives, and one can rest assured that men like Dr Best indeed were exemplary family men. Incidentally, every chief of an *SD* senior district was obliged – by means of the influential ancillary "Department I" (where "I" stands for "information") – to scrutinise the private lives of his *SD* members and to watch out for any aberrations. If an *SD* man was accused of a misdemeanour by, say, his wife, a first warning was given by the responsible chief of the district, while the second warning would have come from the chief of the *SD* senior district; being summoned to the *SD* senior district was already a very precarious matter for any *SD* man. There was no third warning; the matter would have led straight to proceedings at the *SD* "court of honour", initiated by the responsible *SD* senior district.

One has to know this peculiar "sense of honour", this iron discipline and inward sternness, this grotesque "virtuousness", paired with a delirium of power and brutal fanaticism, in order to be able to correctly gauge and appreciate the menace of the *SD*, its officials and members. Cold, sober calculation of the enemy's weaknesses, slithery pliancy and seeming connivance when unexpected difficulties arose, brutal aggression when the timing seemed most right, all combined with the downright satanic and cunning organisation of the *SD* and its police executive, with all the horrors of terror: that was the power instrument *par excellence* of the National Socialist state.

Two examples will for now serve to expand on the above:

Reinhard Heydrich is appointed deputy *Reichsprotektor* for Bohemia and Moravia. He immediately puts a stop to the crude rampages waged by the leader of the Sudeten Germans and Minister for the Interior in Prague, Frank I. An intricate network of informers is established, and prominent Czech personalities are corrupted and forced into submission either with money or through the threat of information about their personal weaknesses being leaked to Heydrich. Soon a substantial number of prominent personalities find themselves ensnared. But where the "carrot" is not accepted, the "stick" will come crashing down suddenly and unexpectedly, and a terror of unprecedented organised brutality rips apart body and limb. This is the motto according to which Heydrich acts: "Buy people! Any amount of money spent on your opponent's honour will be worth it! But when he refuses to bargain, then strike him without mercy!" Machiavellianism? No, given Heydrich's genius and the context of the *SD* it is much more: it is the Satanism of a sophisticated organisation that believes it can play politics with human weakness and go unpunished. Two stock phrases were always on the lips of this man in the dealings with his staff: "Discontent does no harm – just don't let it organise itself!"; and the seemingly banal sentence, "If you know it, it is well, but you have to know it!". Especially this second sentence harbours the secret of the power of a man like Heydrich and his *SD*.

The second example:

Dr Werner Best, colleague to Himmler-Heydrich, is appointed *Reichskommissar* for Denmark, and there, in Copenhagen, again proves his talent for negotiation. What seems paradoxical becomes reality; the Gestapo chief Dr Best gives the impression of being more "lenient" than the responsible military governor, General [Hermann Konstantin Albert Julius] von Hanneken (1890-1981). Indeed, there is open antagonism between the two men: the stubborn general and nobleman von Hanneken demands the declaration of a state of emergency, but the Deputy Chief of the *SD* and the Secret State Police, Dr Best, immediately decrees its lifting.

General Hermann von Hanneken (1890–1981), who became Military Governor of Occupied Denmark, where he declared a state of national emergency. Dr. Werner Best of the SD, as Reichscommissar of Denmark, immediately lifted it, thus behaving more leniently than the Army general. The two men did not get on at all. (*Photo from 1942*)

Time and again he employs corruption as his tool of choice, until he switches to the instrument of terror. It was certainly not for lack of talent on Dr Best's part, but due to the inviolable untaintedness of the Danes that Mephisto's methods were ineffectual. Dr Best's mission was bound to fail, much like the mission of Heydrich and his successors, and all similar missions in foreign lands, for nowhere in Europe will a whole nation allow itself to be corrupted and to be oppressed and dominated by power-hungry invaders, even if the most brutal methods of terror are applied.

The tentacles of the polyp: the informers

At the outbreak of war, the membership of the *SD* in the entire *Reich* (including Austria) was probably no larger than 120,000 men; if anything, this estimate is on the high side. Despite the enormous manpower required in the occupied territories during the time of the Nazi military machine's greatest successes, it is estimated that during the war the membership of the *SD* only increased to around 250,000 men. This relatively small number becomes comprehensible as soon as one gains an overview of the additional army of intelligence officers, informers, snitches and denunciators.

The men of the *SD* wore a standard *SS* uniform, but the collar patches only incorporated the rank insignia (on both sides for *Standartenführer* and above), and for lower ranks contained no designation for the specific *Standarte* or *Sturmbann* (as was required for all other *SA* or *SS* uniforms). On the left forearm of the black surcoats a small diamond shape containing the letters "*SD*" was embroidered in silver thread. As further credentials, each *SD* man also carried a membership card, which had to be personally signed by Himmler or the chief of the relevant *SD* senior district and on the back included a membership stamp (for the monthly membership fee of one *Reichsmark*!), which had to be renewed every month with a stamp of a new colour and a new date, and without which the membership card lost its validity.

A single *SD* man was often the sole *SD* representative within the party cell of his residential district. Each *SD* man belonged to an *SD* district with its own *SD* district chief, from whom he had to take orders and to whom he was personally responsible. Each *SD* district was run from a private apartment, rather than from party- or state premises. The *SD* districts comprised a certain area within the territory of the *SD* senior district; the district chief was subordinate to the chief of the senior district, and it was his duty to immediately hand over all information materials, documents and informer reports to the *SD* senior district, which in turn issued the notorious triplicate: the original went to the secret archive in the *SD* Main Office in Prinz-Albrecht-Strasse in Berlin, one copy remained with the *SD* senior district, and a final copy was stored strictly privately, in a location that was only known to the chief of the *SD* senior district and his adjutant. It is also worth mentioning that the first adjutant of each chief of an *SD* senior district served as his official deputy and in his absence had full authority of command. In particular, this power encompassed authority over all *SD* members who were also officials in the secret state police or had other senior functions within the party or state. In such instances it did not matter if in another commission they far outranked the adjutant or even the chief of the *SD* himself; either way, they had to follow his orders. Much like with the officers in the military intelligence service, the ranks in the *SD* were kept intentionally low until the outbreak of war. When Hitler took power, no chief of any *SD* senior district was of a rank higher than *SS-Obersturmführer*; indeed, Dr Best did not manage that rank until Spring 1934, and Heydrich, Chief of the *SD* and the Secret State Police, was only promoted from *SS-Brigadeführer* to *SS-Gruppenführer* after June 30, 1934. But already at the outbreak of war, all these chiefs of *SD* senior districts were at least *SS-Standartenführer* or *SS-Oberführer*, and within the first years of the war rose to the highest ranks, such as *SS-Gruppenführer*, *SS-Obergruppenführer* and *SS-Oberstgruppenführer*.

The additional army of "staff members" that was directed by the *SD* and was subordinate to the chiefs of the *SD* – much like an army corps is subordinate to a commanding general – comprised five categories. This subdivision into five categories was strictly the business of each *SD* senior district. Usually a particular *SD* man would not know how "his" staff members had been classified by the *SD* senior district, indeed, often even the responsible chief of the *SD* district was left in the dark as to the particular categorisation of "staff members". The five categories were:

1. V-men *("Vertrauensleute")*: "trusted men", who were almost always recruited from the ranks of tried and tested members of the NSDAP or one of its ancillary organisations, and who, while they were not members of the *SD* themselves, enjoyed its full confidence.

2. A-men *("Agenten")*: "agents", who did not necessarily have to be National Socialists, but nevertheless were seen as unconditionally reliable by the *SD*, and were deployed, on a case-by-case basis and often for a fee, in investigations of treason and espionage, but also within industry, at administrative bodies and even at ministries.

3. Z-men *("Zubringer")*: "informers", or snitches and denunciators, who could be found everywhere and typically only had their own interests at heart. These "informers" were in constant service at the *SD* and often received a fixed monthly salary plus bonuses for exceptional service.

4. H-men *("Helfershelfer")*: "accessories", occasional informers, who – for reasons of personal revenge, professional jealousy or false ambition and with clearly dishonest motives – denounced their colleagues and fellow men.

5. U-men *("Unzuverlässige")*: "unreliables", who were seen as corrupt and – while from time to time carried out valuable informer services for the *SD* and were paid handsomely for it – were under constant surveillance. Often they were career criminals and not merely "unreliable" in a strictly "political" sense.

It is significant that none of these "staff members" knew for certain which category they had been put in, and often they were ignorant of the very existence of such a classification system. The "accessories" and "unreliables" of categories 4 and 5 had next to no chance of advancing into a higher category, while for members of categories 2 and 3 this was a distinct possibility, even though they themselves were completely unaware of it. Naturally, the "trusted men" of category 1 were on the whole highly respected "members of staff" and were frequently in direct contact with the chief of the *SD* senior district. (This is significant, considering the fact that even *SD* men in their own district had no possibility of direct contact with the chief of their *SD* senior district. Indeed, often an *SD* man would not even personally know his highest superior, and until 1936 it was customary that he should not even know where the seat of the *SD* senior district was located!) It was mentioned above that the "trusted men" of category 1 were "almost always recruited from the ranks of tried and tested members of the NSDAP". This, however, does in no way mean that party membership alone was enough to be accepted into or registered with category 1. There was no shortage of party members – some of whom were prominent officials – in the other categories (including the fifth) who would never be trusted by the *SD*. Individuals belonging to category 2 (which was highly respected by the *SD*), were not "agents" in the usual sense, but captains of industry, bank directors and renowned scientists, who were deployed by the *SD* as consultants and advisors to produce expert reports.

Two examples will serve to demonstrate quite how difficult it was to become a full member of the *SD*, even for V-men and A-men:

In the "factory protection service" of the company Siemens & Halske AG (about which more will be said below), there was a former senior boatswain's mate by the name of Becker, who had acted for many years as the middleman between his boss, the head of the personnel department under Herr [Ludwig] von Winterfeldt, the retired naval captain Schumacher, and the *Reich* War Ministry and subsequently also the *SD*. In the spring of 1934 Becker applied to be accepted as a full member of the *SD* at the *SD* Senior District East in Berlin. Until that point he had done extremely important service for the *SD* as an expert in matters of counter intelligence, and as such had been a member of category 2. The political reliability of this man was beyond doubt; however, to test him further, he was "tempted" by certain "ladies" within the *SD* (who always were available for such services and others), and, lo and behold, Becker resisted, even though he was married to an old hag and had no children. Then followed a series of invitations to lavish dinners, and again the candidate conducted himself in a very civilised manner, just as would be tacitly expected. Finally, a few V-men – who of course did not know what was going on – were instructed to get him thoroughly drunk and --- Becker did the stupidest thing he could have done in his situation: he began to show off and bragged about his excellent connections to the *SD*. The candidate utterly and irrevocably failed his examination, and henceforth there was no way for him to ever become a member of the *SD*. Indeed, unbeknownst to himself, he had slipped from category 2 into category 3, had been downgraded from a respected "agent" to an "informer", and could count himself lucky that his bragging about the *SD* did not land him in a concentration camp. He was in fact told in no uncertain terms that a repeat performance of similar grandstanding would earn him a few months in a camp.

A similar case is that of Councillor (and later Senior Councillor and Undersecretary) Wilfrid [Albert Karl] Bade (1906-1945). Even before Hitler's takeover, he had made a name for himself in party circles as a young journalist and bootlicker of Goebbels, had published two books with the help of Goebbels, and then followed him to the Ministry of Propaganda. [*Note: in 1933 Bade even published a biography of Goebbels. And the same year, he published a book entitled (in translation)* The SA Took Berlin by Storm: A Factual Report.] Under the Head of the Ministry, Jahnke (the later editor of the newspaper DAZ, *"Deutsche Allgemeine Zeitung"* and head of the publishing company Rudolf-Mosse-Verlag), Councillor Bade was responsible for the monitoring of foreign journalists accredited in Berlin. Josef Goebbels, the *Gauleiter* of Berlin, himself was unaware that his subordinate Bade was a prominent V-man, that is to say a "trusted man" of the *SD*, who performed valuable service for the *SD* in monitoring and spying on the foreign journalists and all individuals that came and went at the Ministry of Propaganda. Bade was also a senior *SA Führer*, and after June 30, 1934, applied to be accepted as a full *SD* member at the *SD* Senior District East in Berlin. His application was very politely but firmly rejected, and Bade remained simply one of the *SD's* "trusted men", albeit a very prominent one. And why is it that Councillor Bade was not accepted into the ranks of the *SD*? He had not been able to resist the charms of the "ladies" of the *SD*, despite the fact that he had a nice wife and two young children in Berlin-Tempelhof. A report on the "ladies" of the *SD* would warrant its own chapter. They were categorised by the *SD* just like the men, and almost exclusively came from so-called "polite society" and often from old German nobility. These "ladies" time and again performed valuable services for the *SD* for considerable amounts of money, and investigating their stories would mean facing up to one of the saddest and at the same time most repulsive aspects of the breakdown of the prevailing – or now, rather, disintegrated – social order.

Wilfrid Albert Karl Bade (1906-1945). He was a notorious "boot-licker of Goebbels" who entered the Ministry of Propaganda. But unknown to his boss, Bade was secretly a spy for Heydrich's SD as a trusted SD "V-man".

The significance of the *SD* Senior District East: Berlin

Territorially, the *SD* Senior District East was hardly larger than the *SD* Senior District South, but it was by far the most important *SD* Senior District. Not only because it contained the regions East Prussia, Pomerania, the March of Brandenburg, parts of the province of Saxony (and formerly even Silesia and Upper Silesia), but because its seat was located in Berlin and it encompassed the area of Greater Berlin with the capital's 4.5 million inhabitants, and – crucially – all the ministries, offices and central departments of industry, economy and commerce. It is impossible to imagine the *immense* variety of institutions and individuals the *SD* Senior District East had to spy on, monitor, control, delegate and register. When Hitler took power, until just before war broke out, the chief of the *SD* Senior District East was Dr [Hermann] Behrends, who must not be confused with several other senior party officials and officers in the *Reichswehr* of the same name. Dr Behrends was the youngest of all the chiefs of the *SD* senior districts. He was born in Wilhelmshaven in 1907, the same place where he later met the chief of the *SD*, Reinhard Heydrich, who was then still a lowly first lieutenant in the navy. Dr Behrends' parents ran a seamen's tavern, where First Lieutenant Heydrich was a regular and often ran up a bill, which his Herr Papa in Halle an der Saale would duly pay off at regular intervals. The young, tall, slender, handsome, blond naval officer was idolised by the short, bowlegged, red-haired high school student Behrends, and when First Lieutenant Heydrich had to resign his commission in the navy because of a duelling affair and soon joined the NSDAP, the youthful Behrends, who had only just left school, enthusiastically followed him.

Dr. Jur. (Doctor of Law) Hermann Johann Heinrich Behrends (1907-1948, hanged at Belgrade). He eventually became an SS Gruppenführer. Heydrich knew him since he was a boy. His nickname in the SD was "the dachshund" because he was short and bow-legged. He was red-headed, and he idolised the tall, blond Heydrich. Early on, according to the author who worked closely with both of them, Behrends and Heydrich were connected by an exclusive secret telephone line which was unknown to the secret police, and was thus untappable. But according to the author, Behrends "was not exactly the sharpest tool in the box" and his special skills were for extortion, intrigue, blackmail, and snooping on people. Although he obtained a Doctor of Law degree, he "had help" with his doctoral thesis, as Heydrich wanted him to have that official qualification.

When the brilliant Reinhard Heydrich was commissioned with the establishment of the *SD* by Himmler, Heydrich sent for the young Behrends, appointed him chief of the all-important *SD* Senior District East in Berlin, and moreover made sure that his loyal assistant would gain his doctorate – "on the side", as it were – and sit his exam as a Prussian probationary judge. In general, Heydrich, as the Chief of the *SD*, was very keen on members of his staff having a doctorate and having passed all state examinations, which would qualify them well as lawyers. One of the few *SD* officials who was not an academic or a lawyer was the aforementioned Albrecht, who at least could produce an officer's certificate, which he gained with distinction during World War 1. Heydrich's requirement of a law degree meant that his *SD* chiefs would later find easy admission to the highest offices at the Ministry for Interior and the police, and soon there was no undersecretary, no chief of a central office, no head of department at the secret police, and no district chief at the criminal police who was not also a senior *SD* official. It has to always be borne in mind, however, that *SD* membership was of primary importance, and holding a public office came second.

Without a shadow of a doubt, there were many senior officials in the *SD* who were far more intelligent than Dr Behrends of the *SD* Senior District East. But Dr Behrends had not only stayed loyal to his boss Heydrich, he was downright submissively dependent on him, and Heydrich possessed in Behrends a useful tool that he could deploy without any qualms whenever he saw fit. By appointing a man such as Dr Behrends as the Chief of the *SD* Senior District East in Berlin, it was in practice he, Heydrich, who personally led that *SD* senior district. This was especially important before Himmler-Heydrich were appointed as chiefs of the secret state police in Berlin, because at that time (until March 1934) Himmler-Heydrich were still far away in Munich and held little power in Berlin. All the more reason to install in Berlin a man who could be trusted unconditionally! It is testimony to Heydrich's skill that he knew how – through a man such as Dr Behrends – to weave the threads in Berlin that in the end inevitably led to the downfall of Dr Diels and to the disempowerment in all police matters of Göring in his own stronghold of Berlin. It was Dr [Hermann] Behrends who, in his capacity as Chief of the *SD* Senior District East in Berlin and under constant instruction by Heydrich, compiled such a large amount of material against Göring and Dr Diels, that in the end it was possible to convince the party leadership under Rudolf Hess just how dangerous it would be to continue to entrust men such as Göring and Dr Diels with the running of the secret police as the highest authority in the state of Prussia. Meanwhile, during this "time of struggle", Heydrich in Munich and Dr Behrends in Berlin were connected by a secret phone line, which not even the secret police bureau knew about, and therefore could not intercept. No day passed without endless telephone calls between Heydrich and Dr Behrends; and, for good measure, the aforementioned Commander Johst of *SD*-raiding-squad-fame also hurtled up and down the motorway between Munich and Berlin in his red Bugatti, delivering encrypted orders and reports of those orders having been carried out. In order to procure the often rather substantial amounts of bribe money and expenses for the various *SD* senior districts, the Chief of the *SD* issued the rather laconic directive: "If you need money, kindly go and get it yourselves!" In saying this, Heydrich was in effect sanctioning blackmail. How such "self-procurement" manifested itself, for instance, at the *SD* Senior District East, can be seen in the affair around "Eduard Winter AG", a company with its seat in Berlin:

Eduard Winter AG in Berlin, Kurfürstendamm, is a wholesale and distribution company for automobiles, which, at the time of Hitler's assumption of power, was Greater Berlin's sole distributor of all car models manufactured both by the American General Motors Company and the German Opel factory. As is well known, General Motors and Opel were virtually merged in 1932, only to be separated again at a later date. Eduard Winter personally oversaw the sales of the American General Motors luxury vehicles, while the sales of the far less well-established Opel automobiles were handled by his associate Herr [Wolf-Werner] von Blumenthal (1889-1965). This individual, Herr von Blumenthal, was a young ne'er-do-well from a highly respectable family, for whom a position at Eduard Winter AG had been, as it were, "bought"; this had been done as much in order to provide the *enfant terrible* with a position befitting his social status as to get rid of him. The Prussian Field Marshall and Chief of General Staff to Crown Prince Frederic during the campaign of 1870/71, Leonhard Graf von Blumenthal (1810-1900), was an uncle or great uncle to the Eduard Winter associate. One of the company's senior salesmen, who was a member of the *SD* as early as 1932, reported instances of serious misconduct on the part of Eduard Winter to the then newly established *SD* Senior District East. These allegations were partly of a personal nature, and partly related to business manipulations – mainly foreign currency transfers of a dubious nature, through which Eduard Winter had invested a portion of his wealth in London. In the immediate aftermath of Hitler's takeover it was not the "less-than-pure Aryan" Eduard Winter, but his "honourable" associate Herr von Blumenthal who was "invited" to visit Dr Behrends at the security service. There he was presented with a host of facsimile documents, all of which would have led to the certain annihilation of Eduard Winter AG, had a case been brought at the public prosecutor's office. At the same time it was intimated to the head of the Opel branch of the company that it would be the sales of Opel vehicles – as opposed to those of automobiles manufactured by General Motors – that would thrive in the National Socialist state; all the more if an organisation such as the *SD* were to officially champion the acquisition of those vehicles. It was further insinuated that the *SD* was the only institution in the newly established state that had the powers to avert prosecution of the present transgressions, if – – – ! Herr von Blumenthal was a clever man, and did not see the need even to confer with his boss and associate Eduard Winter, but asked with gusto how much that "if" would cost. Well, in the first instance that "if" cost the firm Eduard Winter AG a handsome pile of gold, but it turned out to be good deal in the long run, because due to the volume of orders placed by the state and police, the sales of Opel vehicles rocketed like never before. Herr von Blumenthal personally profited immensely from that "if", because his associate Eduard Winter went abroad "temporarily" and later dropped out of the firm altogether. The firm, meanwhile, was forced to install the denunciator, a member of the *SD*, as an authorised signatory at the firm, and was required to supply, at no cost and at a moment's notice, any number of Opel vehicles to the *SD* Senior District East. Herr von Blumenthal turned into a kind of private banker for the *SD* Senior District East: if the chief of the *SD* Senior District quickly required a larger sum of money which he was unable to get his hands on right away, all he had to do was call his "friend" Blumenthal, who was only too happy to provide any amount of money, which would have been reimbursed as agreed. And just to make sure that this ungainly story of blackmail is not devoid of a jolly punchline we should mention that after one year, in February 1934, the blackmailed Herr von Blumenthal was made a "V-man" by the *SD*, a "trusted man" highly respected at the *SD* Senior District. In the autumn of 1934 the *SD* Senior District East was offered a further 200,000 *Reichsmark* by their trusted man Blumenthal, "encouraging" the *SD* to push through, on behalf of the firm Eduard Winter AG, the approval of the construction of a major automobile repair centre on the Kurfürstendamm while circumventing the relevant building regulations. Naturally, the 200,000 *Reichsmark* were not offered as a bribe but as a "charitable donation". The former ne'er-do-well Herr von Blumenthal had blossomed into a "first-rate" businessman, one who was destined to succeed in the National Socialist state. But it has to be reaffirmed again and again that of such bribery and extortion monies not a *Pfennig* would have "stuck to the fingers" of a chief of an *SD* senior district. The six-figure-sums "donated" by the firm Eduard Winter AG seem paltry compared to the vast sums of money that flowed from big business (say, the Siemens corporation) into the coffers of the *SD*. But that is the story of a later chapter.

The firm Eduard Winter AG still thrives today, though whether anyone knows of or remembers the strange events concerning that company which our author relates is not known.

Even though the Chief of the *SD* Senior District East, Dr Behrends, was not exactly the sharpest tool in the box, he did possess some useful talent as an extortionist, intriguer and snooper with a certain *Fingerspitzengefühl*, an instinctive situational awareness, and, like all *SD* men, was overambitious, pushy and obsessed with power. June 30, 1934, gave Dr Behrends an opportunity to go on an unparalleled power rampage; only Dr Werner Best in his *SD* Senior District South would have had a similar opportunity. Dr Behrends was responsible for the murder of Gregor Strasser, for the murder of Undersecretary Klausener, the head of the group *Katholische Aktion*, the murders of Bose, Jung and all the others, who were "illegally" murdered and shot in Greater Berlin and the area of the *SD* Senior District East. He was also responsible for the murder of General von Schleicher, despite the fact that the execution was not personally commanded or carried out by Dr Behrends, but instead by one of his henchmen.

Importantly, on June 30, 1934, Dr Behrends, in his capacity as Chief of the *SD* Senior Section East, was formally appointed "Special Gestapa Commissioner for the liquidation of the Röhm Affair" (this was the actual official name of the appointment) and invested with exceptional powers and authority. (Gestapa = *Geheimes-Staatspolizei-Amt*, the Secret State Police Bureau.) He held the post of Special Gestapo / Gestapa Commissioner until late September 1934, and at the end of July 1934 personally travelled to East Prussia and Silesia with Heydrich in order to carry out the "clean-up operations" within the party and the *SA* that were deemed necessary; and the "cleaning up" only happened revolver in hand. The number of executions carried out by Special Commissioner Dr Behrends between June 30 and late September 1934 exceeds that of the "official" executions carried out in the military college Lichterfelde in Berlin many times over.

Next to the short, pompous Dr Behrends, his adjutant [Richard] Pruchtnow, a tall, older man who seemed to be calmness personified, cut a strange figure. He had not only been an officer in the last World War of 1914-18 but still very much looked the part, and was appointed one of the head officials in the *SD Main Office*.

A photo taken 29 January 1937, showing Richard Reinhard Ferdinand Pruchtnow (1892-1943) standing in the centre of this photo. To our right is Reinhard Heydrich, to our left is Heinrich Himmler. At far left is Lina Heydrich. Between her and Himmler is Karl Wolff (Hitler's "perfect Aryan" whom he called Wolffie). Pruchtnow's wife is between him and Heydrich.

Next to Pruchtnow, the most important man at the *SD* Senior District East was Dr Hans Schmidt [i.e., SS Sturmbahnführer Dr. Jur. Johannes Schmidt called "Hans"; SS number 36232; 1908-1976], the head of "Department I", the information department, a man of the same age as Dr Behrends. He murdered General [Kurt] von Schleicher [*and his wife*] with his own hands by shooting him [*them*] on June 30, 1934 [*in their own home*].

SS Sturmbannführer Dr. Jur. Johannes "Hans" Schmidt (1908-1976; SS number 36232), who murdered General von Schleicher and his wife personally. He was put in charge of the Information Department of the SD Senior District East.

Another photo in profile of the elusive SD operative Dr. Johannes "Hans" Schmidt.

Like all *SD* senior districts, the *SD* Senior District East was located in a well-disguised private apartment. Even the neighbours of the unassuming small villa in Berlin-Westend, Eichenallee 2, which is where the offices were located until 1936, knew nothing of the presence of the *SD* senior district in their immediate vicinity. [*Note: Google street view of this building is blocked, suggesting that it remains a secret building today, as is pretty clearly the case also with the series of buildings on Königsallee, as discussed elsewhere.*] Later on, the *SD* Senior District East was relocated from Eichenallee 2 to a palatial villa in Berlin-Grunewald, Jagowstrasse 18. There, in a large complex of villas with shared gardens, was also located the residential villa belonging to *Reichsführer SS* Heinrich Himmler, and, in a separate villa, the infamous *"SD-Führer-Schule"*, which was – in order to differentiate it from other schools – often referred to as the *"SD-Akademie"*.

This is Jagowstrasse 18 in Berlin today. Previously, on this spot was the personal villa of Heinrich Himmler "in a large complex of villas with shared gardens", and in the same villa complex was also the feared SD's Training Academy.

This *"SD-Akademie"* had been founded by Dr Best in 1935 at the behest of the Chief of the *SD*, Reinhard Heydrich, and only accepted senior *SD* officials, or those who aspired to such a position. The teachers were all prominent *SD* members, but other first-grade party officials and *SS-Führer* who were not *SD* members would also be invited to give lectures or run special courses. Until the outbreak of war, one famous instructor had been *SS-Obergruppenführer* Lorenz, who was later in charge of "relocations". The first commander of the *"SD-Akademie"* until the outbreak of war was *SS-Standartenführer* and *SD-Führer* Graf, who had previously been a head of department at the *SD* Senior District East.

Just like all other *SD* senior districts in the *Reich*, the *SD* Senior District East also had its own telephone connection to the *SD* Main Office and the office of the secret state police, which was only to be used by the chief of the *SD* senior district and his adjutant, who were the only two persons who knew the secret telephone number. Even the official telephone connection at the *SD* senior district was secret; it could not be found in any telephone directory under the name of the *SD* office, as it was listed under the name of some stooge. The *SD* senior district also had a well-disguised postal address in the name of some private individual, so that any office in the *Reich* or even abroad could write to a certain Herr "X" of Jagowstrasse 18 in Berlin-Grunewald, and the mail would reliably and directly be handed to the chief of the *SD* Senior District East. Similarly, the chief of the *SD* and the *Reichsführer SS* had their own well-disguised postal addresses, so that a letter to Himmler only needed to contain a code word in the postal address to ensure that the mail item would be handed to and opened and read personally by *Reichsführer SS* Heinrich Himmler. In order to preclude any acts of treason, from time to time the cover address, code word and even the number of the telephone line would be changed.

III. Retrospection

The end of this chapter all but demands a review of the various forces and powers portrayed in this witness report, which is entirely based on first-hand experience and sadly all-too-real events.

The *SD-RFSS*, the security service of the Reichsführer *SS*, was the most important instrument of power the National Socialist rulers possessed; indeed, the leaders of the *SD* were the true holders of power within the state and the most dangerous individuals obsessed and intoxicated with National Socialist power. In the same way that "Old Prussian officer virtue" was reduced to absurdity by these "men of the sun", the state's power was reduced to absurdity by the *SD*. The *SD* was truly sadistic in its sophistication and indeed "the brain of party and state", as Rudolf Hess had put it. But every work of man, anything created by human hands – with good or ill intentions – is imperfect. Nothing was holy or sacred to the *SD*; it suspected, monitored, and watched everyone, including the highest Nazi officials, and faithfully registered their weaknesses, both insignificant and serious. And in the end this diabolic spy system, like *Moloch*, devoured its own children. Through the *SD*, the Aryan super-ego-god of race transformed itself into a demon that wrought its suicidal horrors against its own kind. The *SD-RFSS* is testament to what human organisational genius, without God, without belief in the absolute and a "higher being", must inevitably give rise to; namely self-laceration and self-destruction. It was not least through the activities of the *SD* that National Socialism drove Machiavellianism – the mechanisms designed to preserve the unity of the state, as outlined by Machiavelli in his "*Principe*" *(The Prince)* – to convulsing excesses and transformed it into a perverted satanic effigy of itself. Under National Socialism, "*Realpolitik*", the politics of "*Sacro Egoismo*", celebrated its highest triumphs and, through it and with it, experienced its greatest, and hopefully final, defeat. With the help of an instrument of power such as the *SD*, the Nazi potentates thought they could pursue "high politics" through the weaknesses of their fellow human beings, and their false god would lead them on to conquer the world. But such political machinations always fail in the end; one cannot play off the weaknesses of one man against those of another and pursue such "politics" without ultimately falling victim to one's own weaknesses. Plato once called politics "the art of interweaving dispositions". The Nazis never knew such art, just as they never knew or were able to comprehend the God of Christianity – God, who is love itself.

God, the embodiment of love.

And all that is lovable, loving, noble, beautiful and good in us – that is the divine in humans.

Hatred – that is of the devil.

All that is hideous in us, envy, malevolence, petty grievances and the false ambition they beget, the thirst for power, tyranny – that is the diabolical in humans.

Oh, pitiful and insignificant humans, you, who think you can live without God, you, who have never cultivated the divine – love! – within, but who rage in diabolical hatred against your fellow humans and against yourselves, you, who intoxicate yourselves in the fires of a contemptuous and self-consuming delirium of hate!

Hatred sown by man has by no means lethal consequences merely for the enemy, but it comes back to devastate those who have sown it. May this sober account of facts – gruesome facts – find its conclusion in such self-reflection.

PART ONE

THE SYSTEM

THE FACTORS OF POWER

B. THE SECRET STATE POLICE

I. Inception
The police in the Weimar Republic

The abbreviation "Gestapo" is understood by all, and everybody knows that it refers to the political police in Nazi Germany, or, more specifically, the secret state police. A less well-known fact is that initially – and even as late as 1934 – no such thing as the Gestapo existed, but merely the "Gestapa", that is to say the Secret State Police Bureau (*Das Geheime-Staatspolizei-Amt)* in Berlin. This Gestapa only had jurisdiction in the state of Prussia, and by no means the entire *Reich.* At the same time, until 1936 – when Heinrich Himmler was officially appointed Chief of the German Police – "The Gestapo", in its capacity as the secret state police, remained the official title of the political police of the state of Prussia. Alongside it there existed an independent "political police" in each and every German *Land* and *Gau* – that is for Bavaria, Württemberg, Baden, etc., and indeed even an independent "political police" for Hamburg! It is worth noting, however, that from 1934 the head of each of these separate police forces was *Reichsführer SS* Heinrich Himmler, who also acted as Chief of the Secret State Police Bureau. Himmler had been appointed "Inspector" of the Gestapa in late March 1934, and Reinhard Heydrich, the chief of the *SD*, was appointed as its actual chief, replacing Dr [Rudolf] Diels.

Dr. Jur. [*Doctor of Law*] Rudolf Diels (1900-1957). In 1933-1934, he was head of the Gestapa [*later called the Gestapo*] but in April 1934 he was replaced by Reinhard Heydrich. "Gestapa" was an acronym for *Das Geheime-Staatspolizei-Amt,* which in English means "Secret State Police Bureau". The "*Ge*" in both Gestapa and Gestapo stands for *Geheime,* which means "secret". The author tells us of the relationship between Hermann Göring and Diels: "Certainly Göring and Diels were closer than even Nazi insiders were aware." (The author had access to all the secret recordings of all the Nazi leaders and knew all their most personal secrets. However, the author had a Puritanical streak and often speaks elliptically of sexual matters, apparently finding it difficult to use direct language about such things.)

However, Hermann Göring, in his capacity as Minister President of Prussia, remained – until 1936 – the official superior of Himmler-Heydrich in the state of Prussia, and thereby the supreme lord and master of the Gestapa, which will be the subject of further investigation below. During the Weimar Republic, the *Reich* Ministry for the Interior was a purely administrative body, without its own executive, for there was no such thing as a *Reich* Police. Executive power, that is to say police power, resided exclusively within the individual *Länder*; in Prussia this was the Ministry of the Interior for Prussia in Berlin, Unter den Linden, diagonally opposite the Hotel Adlon. The entire *Schutzpolizei* (protection police) and the police headquarters in all larger cities with their respective police presidents were directly subordinate to the Ministry of the Interior for Prussia. (The police headquarters of Southern Germany were not known as *"Polizeipräsidium"*, but instead as *"Polizeidirektion"*.) Among the police chiefs in the *Reich*, the police president of Berlin had special status, inasmuch as he also had a ministerial rank (to be precise, a "second-rank minister"), and hence was remunerated according to his position as a Prussian undersecretary, i.e. a "second-rank minister". His official car carried a ministerial insignia, and he was entitled to personally take part in sessions of the Prussian government when police matters were being discussed. All personnel matters within the police corps and at police headquarters – such as promotion, recruitment and salaries – were the responsibility of the Ministry of the Interior for Prussia.

It is worth noting that in the days of the Weimar Republic, despite the fact that all police power in Prussia resided with the Ministry of the Interior for Prussia, the police executive always remained merely a "subsidiary body of the public prosecution department", in other words, a subsidiary body of the official and public judiciary. This provided a safeguard against police despotism, as the police force was accountable to the judiciary in all instances when police power was being exercised at the behest of the legal authorities, that is to say, in the name of ordinary jurisdiction. The police force was the "custodian of public order and safety", and it was mandatory that the "consequences" of any measures taken by the police force in order to maintain this public order and safety were brought before a judge. Any delinquent – no matter if the alleged case was of a political or criminal nature – had the right to be heard by an investigative judge within 24 hours, and no person was to be held in police custody without judicial assent. Certainly there were cases of inexcusable acts of police arbitrariness even during the times of the Weimar Republic; some instances of "judicial error" can be found at any time and everywhere. But such errors were indictable offences and remained the exceptions that proved the rule according to which every citizen should enjoy the protection of the law to safeguard against police arbitrariness. This is not the place to condemn judicial harshness or the severity of police measures – they are possible in every nation and at all times, and hence also in the Weimar Republic – but it is right to explicate the fundamental truth that protection of the law did exist at that time.

Following Hitler's power grab, the Secret State Police Bureau, the Gestapa, was created on Göring's orders and declared "supreme authority in the state of Prussia". This opened the floodgates for police despotism, for the executive police powers of this Gestapa no longer were under the control of the judicial authorities, and the interdependent relationship between the police force (until then a "subsidiary body") and the public prosecution department was severed. In order to carry out arrests, Gestapa officials no longer required the arrest warrants – signed and issued by the public prosecution department – that had been an absolute requisite under the Weimar government. Impartial protection of the law, as had previously been guaranteed for every citizen by an official and public judiciary, was rendered null and void. The political executive was now in a position to detain arrestees for arbitrary lengths of time in prison, or, worse, in one of the concentration camps (which at that time were still provisional institutions).

In order to bestow the pretence of legality on such political police terror, it was vested in a flimsy, twofold juridical overcoat: the "*Reich* directive for the protection of the state" and the (tragicomically entitled) "*Reich* directive for the protection of the private citizen", both of which were created and signed off by *Reichspräsident* Hindenburg. Using justifications such as *"for personal protection"* or *"for protection from public anger"*, political suspects were arrested and subjected to relentless police terror lasting months or years. Instead of using the former system of arrest warrants issued by the public prosecution department, the Gestapa now smugly issued its own warrants that used such "justifications".

The Social Democrat Carl Severing was one of the most prominent Prussian Ministers for the Interior of the Weimar Republic. He appointed a personal consultant, a certain Dr. [Rudolf] Diels, who held a post at the political department of the Prussian Ministry for the Interior. Dr Diels, a young assistant judge "from a good family" and without party ties, had excellent connections to the Rhineland-Westphalian heavy industry and assumed his role as Severing's personal consultant for political issues (!) with the grade of senior councillor. Dr Diels, who had graduated from law school with distinction, was married to the daughter of the boss of the Mannesmann steelworks in Cologne.

Carl Wilhelm Severing (1875-1952). He was a Social Democrat Member of Parliament and Minister of the Interior of Prussia. He spotted a promising young lawyer in the Ministry of the Interior and promoted him to be a Senior Councillor and act as his personal advisor for political affairs. The young man was Dr. Rudolf Diels, later to be the Head of the Gestapa. Not quite what Severing had in mind, we can be sure, as Severing was a declared enemy of the Nazis and had at one time actually ordered the arrest of Adolf Hitler. (Bundesarchiv)

Very soon Dr Diels demonstrated that he knew very well how to pursue "high politics" on his own initiative. He made connections to Franz von Papen, a member of the Prussian parliament on the radical right-wing of the Catholic Centre Party, sidled up to leading circles within the *Reichswehr* via the "Association of Former Cavalry Men", and showed himself very sympathetic towards the pressing personal financial woes of that association's secretary, the cavalry-man-turned-show-jumper [Major General Hartwig] von Platen (1878-1938). Alongside senior *Reichswehr* officers, such as General von Fritsch and General [Günther von] Progrell (1879-1944) (Fritsch had not yet been appointed Chief of Army Command; at that time the post was still held by General [Kurt] von Hammerstein-Equord (1878-1943), other eager members of the association included Count von Helldorff, the later chief of the *SA* in Berlin and police chief in the opulent city of Potsdam and eventually police chief of Berlin; Joachim von Ribbentrop, at that time still a purveyor of German sparkling wine and old French liqueurs and cognacs; and Hermann Göring, formerly – in the World War of 1914-18 – also a cavalry officer, then active with the air force. Naturally, Franz von Papen could not be missing from that circle.

Herr von Papen was appointed *Reich* Chancellor on June 1, 1932 and made peace with the "wild" National Socialists. However, this peace was short-lived, and von Papen had to resign as early as December 2, 1932.

We should also recount a little episode, which, despite the fact that it is not devoid of a certain tragedy, seems like some sort of a hoax. For Franz von Papen, as German *Reich* Chancellor, it was simply a "matter of honour" to expel the hated "Marxists" from their government posts in the "ancestral homeland of Prussia". By a decree issued on July 20, 1932, von Papen had himself appointed "*Reich* Commissioner for the State of Prussia" by the *Reichspräsident*, and on the very same day dissolved the Social Democrat government of the venerable Prussian Minister President Otto Braun. (In times of political unrest – such as the ones provoked by Herr von Papen by repealing the ban on NSDAP uniforming – the government of the *Reich*, or more specifically, the *Reichspräsident*, was able to appoint a so-called *Reich* Commissioner for the relevant state, who was endowed with dictatorial authority for "the upkeep of public order and security".) Herr von Papen pulled off his *coup de main* in deposing Carl Severing. Herr von Papen, the newly appointed *Reich* Commissioner, sent a young officer accompanied by eight men to the ministry, who ordered Minister Severing to leave the ministry and to resign his ministerial commission. The minister would only have had to press a button, and the young officer and his entourage of eight would have had to turn tail and run, lest they were arrested by the *Schutzpolizei* (the protection police), which at time was loyal to Herr Severing. Especially the Berlin corps of the *Schutzpolizei*, under its commander Colonel Heimannsberg, a die-hard Social Democrat, was staunchly loyal to the Prussian Minister of the Interior. The Herr Minister exclaimed valiantly, "I only yield to power!", to which the young officer glibly retorted, "Herr Minister, I am that power!" After that, Minster Severing vacated his ministry.

This is not a made-up story, but a factual account of the inglorious end of the Social Democratic government in Prussia, that is to say, the end of a minister who had unlimited authority but did not know how to use it, or perhaps did not want to use it. On July 20, 1932, the Weimar Republic perished. The name of the undertaker: Franz von Papen.

Reich Commissioner and *Reich* Chancellor Franz von Papen had put Baron von Bracht in charge of the "official duties of the Prussian Ministry for the Interior". Despite the fact that it was the young undersecretary Dr Diels who had wheedled his superior, Herr von Bracht, into issuing a ridiculous (and widely ridiculed) decree on swimwear regulations *("Zwickelerlass"* – "gusset decree"), Dr Diels was able to consolidate his position, and even then began to spin the first connecting threads between Papen-Göring-Hitler on the one hand, and Hitler-Kirdorf on the other. Emil Kirdorf was a major tycoon in the Rhine-Ruhr area, owner of the Gelsenkirchen smelting works, and president of the steel industry association, which was no less significant a player than the Krupp steel works. The friendship between Hitler and Thiessen was forged thanks to Dr Diels' capabilities. The "young man", who always kept himself in the background, later also managed to arrange the fateful meeting between Hitler, Papen and Göring in the Cologne residence of the banker Schröder. Apart from their political significance, the meetings that Dr Diels put in place also were of considerable financial importance and consequence for the NSDAP; the large deficit the party's campaign and propaganda funds had accrued could be balanced thanks to Dr Diels' successful scheming. Herr von Papen's "cabinet of barons" and General von Schleicher's brief chancellorship was finally followed by Hitler's seizure of power on January 30, 1933.

General Kurt von Schleicher (left) and Franz von Papen together in 1933 when they thought they might have the situation under control, but it all soon unravelled. A year later, von Schleicher was shot dead in his home and von Papen had his two front teeth knocked out and was fortunate to survive assassination as well. Martha von Papen here stands beside her husband.

The promise made by the German Field Marshall General Paul von Hindenburg – a pledge he had made in his capacity as *Reichspräsident* as late as the autumn of 1932, namely, "I will never appoint that Bohemian *private* as *Reich* Chancellor" – had been broken.

Hitler was *Reich* Chancellor, Herr von Papen was Vice Chancellor, and, as such, also the *Reich* Commissioner for Prussia. Like Baron von Bracht before, the National Socialist Hermann Göring was now put in charge of the "official duties of the Prussian Ministry for the Interior", again by *Reich* Commissioner Herr von Papen. Only a few months later Hermann Göring was officially confirmed in his post as Minster President of Prussia and at the same time Minister for the Interior of Prussia.

At that time, Göring was one of a very small number of National Socialists who were seen as "socially acceptable" in conservative circles and who enjoyed a good reputation in "polite society" (where, strangely, Hermann Göring was classed as a "moderate politician", whereas in party circles he was seen as a "reactionary").

Hermann Göring on the occasion of his 45th birthday. He was seen as "socially acceptable" in conservative circles. Although he was an apoplectic and violent buffoon, and a faker, he was an expert at unctuous simulations of bonhomie, good cheer, affability, and good will. None of it was real. For much of his life, Göring was addicted to morphinee and opioid painkillers, which had a huge effect upon his personality and behaviour. He was only five feet 7 inches tall (170 cm), but he became so obese that he could not even see his own feet, much less put his own shoes on. His jovial exterior concealed a vicious hidden self, which gloated on observing people being tortured and listening to their screams of agony, and then seeing them die.

PUNCH OR THE LONDON CHARIVARI—JANUARY 31 1940

THE GREAT PROTECTOR

[Field-Marshal Goering has confiscated all property in Poland "in order to safeguard it."]

Göring's obesity was so extreme that it became a feature used to mock him in cartoons. Here we see a British cartoon of 1940 portraying him as a fat, rotund human blimp. (*From Punch, the London Charivari, January 30, 1940.*)

He managed to stay in the good books of the old *Reichspräsident* Hindenburg, because not only was he a master at playing the active officer, but he was one of only a few Nazis who had been awarded the highest military honour of the Wilhelmine Period, namely the medal *"Pour le Mérite"*. Göring insinuated to Hindenburg that National Socialism was not averse to a restoration of the Hohenzollern monarchy, and undoubtedly there were certain sympathies on the part of the Hohenzollerns towards National Socialism. One of the Hohenzollern princes was a very eager member of the NSDAP and a prominent *SA* leader – his Royal Highness Prince August Wilhelm, known as Auwi, *SA Gruppenführer* in the staff of *SA* Chief of Staff Ernst Röhm.

At right of the photo is the tall, forbidding and serious figure of Prince August Wilhelm Heinrich Günther Viktor ("Auwi") of Prussia (1887-1949) in his role as a Gruppenführer of the SA. He was the fourth son of the Kaiser. Because Hitler tried to lure the Prussian and Bavarian monarchists to support him, by promising to restore their monarchies, the Kaiser asked Auwi to join the Nazis and act as his liaison with Hitler and facilitate the envisaged restoration of the exiled Kaiser to his throne. After the War Auwi was imprisoned as a war criminal and died in an internment camp.

Hermann Göring had the affectations of a *grand seigneur* and the bearing of a Prussian officer. He enjoyed a certain popularity among large swathes of the population due to his "human weaknesses": his pomposity, his penchant for fine uniforms, titles, medals and badges of honour, and his coarse sense of humour. He was the prototype of the kind of German man depicted in satirical magazines at home and abroad, long before there was such a thing as National Socialism. Many politically immature Germans imagined a "leader" to look like Hermann Göring. He was an all-out opponent of Marxism with every fibre of his being, and he displayed a reactionary demeanour that in many led to the erroneous belief that this man Göring perhaps was a political "reactionary" after all and should therefore not be identified with the "wild" Nazis. In truth, Hermann Göring was one of National Socialism's most vicious sabre-rattlers from the beginning, one of the dictator Adolf Hitler's most servile supporters, and at the same time one of the most unscrupulous plotters within the NSDAP, a careerist and overachiever beyond measure and of the worst imaginable kind. After the

Reichstag Fire trials, Göring was nicknamed "The Bloodhound" by the Communists. As awful as such a moniker may be, in Hermann Göring's case it was justified, because this "jovial" and imperious Nazi potentate was one of the most brutal terrorists among all Nazi officials. He indulged his blood-fuelled intoxication with power without restraint and "on a case-by-case basis". A cynic, morphinee addict and domineering braggart: that was the *"Herrenmensch"* Hermann Göring, a cunning schemer and forever a faithful and useful servant to his lord and master Adolf Hitler. This hedonistic egotist – a man of plump corpulence but also a certain sharpness of mind – enjoyed conducting spineless "diplomacy" similar to that of the Westphalian nobleman Franz von Papen. His great self-assurance and irascible bravado, his over-confidence in his dealings with others, as was instilled in all officers during their active service in Wilhelmine Germany, and his greed for money and ostentatiousness all sharply distinguished Hermann Göring from other individuals intoxicated and obsessed with power, such as Heinrich Himmler, or the "men of the sun", who unconsciously might always have felt a certain envy towards Göring, driven and haunted, as they were, by feelings of inferiority, distrust and resentment. General von Progrell once coined the phrase: "They would give their little finger for the privilege of chopping off a personal foe's thumb in order to gain favour with their *Führer.*" If ever there was a Nazi leader to whom these words could rightfully be applied, it is Hermann Göring. Power always creates a certain mystique, but the mystique surrounding the "jovial and moderate" Minister President and *Reichsmarschall* Göring makes a mockery of the facts. Göring liked to wear the disguise of "plain conservatism"; this made him all the more dangerous and downright repulsive.

During the contest for power in Germany between 1930 and 1932, Hermann Göring was one of Hitler's most influential advisors. Despite the fact that the NSDAP in Berlin had their *Gauleiter* Josef Goebbels, Göring was appointed "Political Commissioner for the NSDAP" as early as 1930, and in that capacity conducted for Hitler all important negotiations with various departments and the "circle around Hindenburg". When Hitler took power, none of the Nazi leaders even for a moment entertained the thought that their power grab would be disrupted or stymied by non-National Socialists. To be sure, *Reichspräsident* Hindenburg had stipulated that Hitler had to include a large number of reactionary "co-regents" in his government, who were to form a kind of bulwark against National Socialist excesses. In order to placate the "old gentleman", Hindenburg's *protégé* Franz von Papen was made not only Vice Chancellor, but also *Reich* Commissioner in Prussia. If truth be told, it has to be said that Papen never had an opportunity to wield the authority invested in him by his office or even to use it against the Nazis. It is an open question whether he was too weak, too unprincipled or simply too afraid. "*Reich* Commissioner" in his case was no more than an empty title, because from the outs*et al.* affairs were dealt with by Göring, in the typical imperious, arrogant and brutal manner for which he eventually was made official Minister for the Interior in Prussia. Then Göring was given an additional title, one that conferred on him the appropriate grandeur for the execution of his ministry, and bestowed on him the proper stature, especially for Prussia and in Prussia: Göring was appointed General of the Infantry (!) by Field Marshall General and *Reichspräsident* Paul von Hindenburg. This is a fact that was hardly noticed and not assessed correctly at home or abroad: a previously active, but now retired German captain, airman and holder of the order *"Pour le Mérite"*, was made "General of the Infantry", from one day to the next, bypassing all service regulations. It caused an unimaginable sensation among the entire officer corps of the *Reichswehr* and all long-serving professional soldiers. But as the appointment had been made by Field Marshall General Hindenburg, who was highly respected among the officer class, there were no protests or even serious misgivings. To be perfectly clear: there is a fundamental difference between an "active" officer and a so-called reserve officer. An active officer, even one with the relatively low rank of captain, is a career officer, which means that he will have had professional training (cadet school, general staff instruction), whereas an officer of the reserve will only have performed standard military service, that is to say he would have been a one-year volunteer and then advanced through the non-commissioned officer ranks at great speed.

A State Commissioner "for special deployment"

Adolf Hitler became *Reich* Chancellor on January 30, 1933, and on the very same night, following a huge torchlight procession, the *SA* and *SS* went on the rampage in Berlin and began to terrorise the German people. Delegates at the *Reichstag* and the *Landtag* (the national and regional assemblies, respectively), local councillors and union leaders were abducted, beaten and vanished without a trace. At first, the *SA* and *SS* gangs had it especially in for "the Reds", the Marxists, and later, in the weeks to follow, they turned their "attention" to Catholics and "reactionaries".

The police headquarters in Berlin were home to the so-called "Division I. A.", whose main task it was to restrain the Communists, and to monitor the *KPD* (the German Communist Party) at their central offices in Karl-Liebknecht-Haus. As early as January 31, the new state authorities "ordered" the "Division I. A." to arrest many prominent Communist leaders, but most could not be found – some had been abducted and taken to unknown locations, others had already fled. The "Division I. A." had to admit its impotence, the police force had lost its grip and all control, and the police executive remained ineffective.

Initially Hermann Göring entered the Prussian Ministry for the Interior, Unter den Linden, under the title of "commissioner", but in truth he already held absolute power in the state of Prussia. When Göring moved to the Prussian Ministry for the Interior, he was accompanied by *SS-Obergruppenführer* Kurt Daluege, chief of the active *SS-Obergruppe East* (Greater Berlin, Brandenburg, Pomerania, East Prussia) and leader of the National Socialist group in the *Landtag*.

Kurt Daluege, a giant of a man who was feared as a rowdy hooligan, had volunteered for service in the World War of 1914-18, then served as a first lieutenant in the so-called *"Schwarze Reichswehr"*, and subsequently participated as a volunteer corps fighter in the "Assault on Annaberg" in Upper Silesia. (In 1921, under the Catholic *Reich* Chancellor Dr Josef Wirth, open, albeit illegal, armed campaigns were carried out against the Polish insurgents, who were ousted from Upper Silesia along with their leader, Adalbert (aka Wofciech) Korfanty. Korfanty and his Polish insurgents had attempted to forcefully annex certain German territory that even the Treaty of Versailles had awarded to the *Reich*.) Daluege founded and led the so-called *"Frontbann"*, which later became the first *SA* group in Berlin, and, on Hitler's orders, quelled the "Stennes Revolt" in Berlin, when in 1929 the then leader of the *SA*, Walter Stennes, had begun to revolt against the party leader, Adolf Hitler. This revolt marked the birth of the uniformed *SS*, the *"Schutz-Staffel"*, which until that point had merely been a security force with special privileges within the *SA*, but without its own uniform or service regulations. Ernst Röhm became *SA* Chief of Staff, and Heinrich Himmler became *Reichsführer SS*, but Himmler initially remained subordinate to Chief of Staff Röhm, as the *SS* only gained its independence following the events of June 30, 1934, when *Reichsführer SS* Himmler was appointed *Reichsleiter* of the NSDAP. In reward for the liquidation of the "Stennes Revolt", Kurt Daluege was appointed as the first and most senior *SS* leader in Berlin. In his civilian life, Daluege was a graduate engineer and had for a long time been employed at the municipal rubbish collection service in Berlin.

A not especially bright, but hardworking and tenacious individual, Kurt Daluege had shared a veneration of the *Reichswehr* and all things military with Hermann Göring ever since the days of World War 1, and he was able – soon after Hitler's takeover and with explicit approval by the *Reichswehr* Ministry – to advance to the position of police general. As commander of the uniformed police in Germany and chief of the *Ordnungspolizei* (the uniformed regular police force, one of the two subdivisions of the total police force in the German *Reich*), in 1936 Daluege formally became Deputy Chief of the German Police and thereby deputy to Heinrich Himmler, the Chief of the German Police. The official post of "Chief of the German Police" had been created and enshrined in law in 1936 through a decision by the *Reich* government. Following the assassination of Reinhard Heydrich, who had been chief of the *SD* and "Chief of the Criminal Police" (the second subdivision within the *Reich's* police force), Kurt Daluege was appointed *Reichsprotektor* for Bohemia and Moravia, ahead of Baron Neurath (whose "deputy" Heydrich had been).

This Kurt Daluege may have been a rowdy hooligan, but a very disciplined one, who never acted without or against an order "from above". Because of his insolent character he never managed to be accepted into the *SD*, the security service of the *Reichsführer SS*, and he would have never accepted a background role, even one that would have presented him with an abundance of personal power. Much like his mentor Hermann Göring, he needed to be able to brag and boast, while playing the role of an upright man of integrity. It was one of his ambitions to be seen as "socially acceptable", and he enjoyed keeping up the pretence of an honourable family man. He adored titles, medals and all badges of honour, but still could never attain the full "greatness" of his idol Göring, because he lacked personal initiative; and in his case, fawning servility – which also formed a major part of his character – was not combined with a talent for independent thought and action. He lacked the overbearing self-assuredness of a man like Göring and was merely endowed with obnoxious bumptiousness. Externally, a dauntless officer; internally, a bootlicker and unrestrained self-centred egotist who paid tribute to his super-ego-god in the currency of brutal terror, who compensated for his inferiority complexes with pushy ambition and a propensity for petty personal revenge, and made up for his lack of intellect with brashness and pluck – that was Kurt Daluege. A man such as this was able to advance to the position of commander of the uniformed regular police and was allowed to "solemnly" deputise for the highest police chief, Heinrich Himmler. In his capacity as *Reichsprotektor* for Bohemia and Moravia, endowed with imposing authority, he was able to indulge his intoxication with power. Yet he was never entrusted with the subtler tool of the criminal police – to wield that tool, this ambitious toady was not considered smart or sharp enough, and he lacked both in ideas and the required deviousness.

Kurt Max Franz Daluege (1897-1946; executed) succeeded Reinhard Heydrich in charge of Bohemia and Moravia. According to the author, who knew him well, he was 'a giant of a man who was feared as a rowdy hooligan … he needed to be able to brag and boast … a boot-licker and unrestrained self-centred egotist … brutal terror … and a propensity for petty personal revenge … made up for his lack of intellect'. In other words, the author did not think very highly of him. (This photo was posted on the internet by an anonymous person named 'Fred'.)

On January 30, 1933, the offices of the *SS-Obergruppe* East were located in a private apartment on the corner of Potsdamerstrasse and Lützowstrasse in Berlin, which Daluege had rented in his capacity as a member of the regional assembly, the *Landtag*. Like all members of that assembly, Daluege enjoyed parliamentary immunity; i.e. he was granted protection against criminal liability in the course of exercising his parliamentary duties. The National Socialists always attached great importance to this guarantee given by the Weimar Republic – that is, until they found themselves in a position of authority. They trampled all over this right as soon as they wielded power in the state – or, more accurately, as soon as they had arrogated power to themselves, and before they were even formally fully mandated. They simply mandated themselves, and subsequently invented laws to build a flimsy and spurious legal basis for their takeover. In any case: immunity not only protected the individual Kurt Daluege in the times before the power grab, it also protected his apartment from unannounced and unwelcome searches. And so it was from the "private residence" of *Landtag*-member Kurt Daluege that in the night from January 30 to January 31, 1933, the first "hauls" (as they were called by the *SS* staff) against Communists were orchestrated without delay, especially against illegal printing shops that produced newspapers and flyers. These "printings shops" were by no means large-scale, industrial typesetting or graphic design companies, but in most cases simply primitive manual rolling presses in some humble worker's apartment.

As early as February 1, 1933, Kurt Daluege sat down with Göring at the Prussian Ministry for the Interior and, as the "reorganiser" of the Prussian Police force, was given the interim title of "State Commissioner for Special Deployment", and was furnished by Göring (!) – who at that time himself was merely a "commissioner" in the services of *Reich* Commissioner Papen – with extraordinary powers. But even then, Daluege did not take a single step without prior consultation with Göring, without his approval or order.

Undersecretary Hall became Daluege's advisor in all matters of personnel, while, for the time being, the retired Captain Gourdet, adjutant of the *SS* Staff of the *SS-Obergruppe* East, remained in his post as Daluege's first adjutant (later to be replaced by Police Captain Schlange). The position of the all-too-openly corrupt Nazi lawyer Undersecretary Luettgenbrunn – the newly appointed head of the legal department and Daluege's great rival in the Prussian Ministry for the Interior – quickly became untenable, and the disastrous *"Nordwolle"* case finally put an end to his tenure. For his impudent acts of blackmail, with extortion monies running into the hundreds of thousands of *Reichsmark*, he was even put on remand for a brief period, but he was never charged nor did he have to forfeit any of his quickly amassed wealth. Luettgenbrunn, the sly fox, was one of many who could not understand why the young and intellectually challenged but outwardly very "soldierly" Daluege had been allowed to rise through the ranks so quickly, soon surpassing them all. But Kurt Daluege, with his splendidly upright military figure, always ready to receive orders, would always be valued more highly by Hitler and Göring than a so-called "egghead", even if that "egghead" – like Luettgenbrunn – was the more senior National Socialist. Those notorious political "bicyclists" who obsequiously hunch their backs to those "above" them while vigorously treading onto those "below" them: they always have the greatest and most secure opportunities for advancement in any totalitarian regime.

Here is the Associated Press announcement of Kurt Daluege succeeding to the position of Reichs Protector of Bohemia and Moravia. Heydrich was not yet dead but 'lay gravely wounded from would-be assassin's bullets.'

Another man who felt an inner calling to become police chief, and from the very first day tried to challenge Kurt Daluege in his position, was a Baltic German from Riga by the name of – – – Alfred Rosenberg. Yes, indeed: the infamous Germanic-Aryan ideologue and dilettante "philosopher" of National Socialism and author of *"The Myth of the Twentieth Century"* had ambitions to become police chief!

Alfred Rosenberg was clever enough to know not to plot against Hermann Göring, the "Commissioner" of the Prussian State and at that time one of Hitler's closest confidants. He foresaw that Göring would soon be Minister President of Prussia, and he, Alfred Rosenberg, had his eye on the position of Minister for the Interior of Prussia. That office – and the concomitant control over the police executive – would enable him to turn his "ideas" into reality, to serve his super-ego-god in the best possible way, and to indulge his intoxication with power without any distractions.

Alfred Ernst Rosenberg (1893-1946, hanged). This is the notorious author of *The Myth of the Twentieth Century* (1930) who was instrumental in making Anti-Semitism and persecution of the Jews a fundamental tenet of Nazism. He introduced the term *Untermensch* ("sub-human") to describe Jews and blacks. He also violently hated Christianity and considered modern art "degenerate". Rosenberg was born January 12, 1893, in Tallinn (then called 'Reval'), Estonia, where he attended school. He studied architecture at the Technical College in Riga, Latvia, and for some time also in Moscow. He moved to Germany in 1918 when he was 25 years old and settled in Munich, where he became affiliated with the Nazi Party by 1921. He went on to become the chief Nazi theorist and ideologue. From 1933 to 1945 he was Head of the Nazi Office for Foreign Affairs and from 1934 to 1945 he was Head of the Rosenberg Bureau which determined culutural policy for the Nazi state. Earlier, he had wanted to be in charge of the police in Prussia and to be Prussia's Minister of the Interior. The author tells the tale of how that all went wrong. It is interesting to know that Rosenberg spoke Russian better than he spoke German; this is recorded by Putzi Hanfstängl in his memoir, as Putzi knew Rosenberg intimately from a very early date, and despised him for his fanatical anti-Semitism, egomania, and crazy notions of all kinds. Hanfstängl also says that Rosenberg had a maddening habit of whistling through his teeth when people spoke to him, a habit which he shared with Rudolf Hess, whom he described as "another whistler like Rosenberg". Hanfstängl shared an office with Rosenberg for a long time because early on they were joint editors of the Nazi newspaper the *Völkischer Beobachter* (*The Peoples' Observer*), and their desks were diagonally opposite one another in the same small office. Hanfstängl came to hate him more than any other Nazi. He has written in his memoir: "Rosenberg was such an unappetizing fellow. He had only recently married, but his colleagues on the paper recounted innumerable stories about his unsavoury love life, which usually involved multiple intercourse with half a dozen men and women compaions at a time in some grubby back-street flat. It must have been the Tartar in him. In dress he had the taste of a costermonger's donkey, and on this occasion I remember very well he was wearing a violet shirt with a scarlet tie, with a brown waistcoat and blue suit. He had some theory about it being a waste of money to wash shirts and used to throw them away when they became unwearable even by his standards." Rosenberg always kept a loaded revolver prominently displayed on his desk, to suggest that he was ready to become a man of action at a moment's notice.

But suddenly it seemed that Daluege might be the person to challenge his position and the one who would stand in his way. Consequently Alfred Rosenberg had to get rid of Daluege and simultaneously weaken Göring's grip on power! The plot failed – had to fail – for Rosenberg was much too primitive and clumsy a machinator to succeed against a man like Göring (who, of course, was watching over Daluege and very quickly understood the game that was being played against him via Daluege). What is more, Alfred Rosenberg had a pitiful informant and wretched advisor, namely Harald Siebert. [*Note: This was Dr. Harald Georg Karl Siebert, a German born in Latvia in 1886, died 1936. He had been a psychiatrist and an intelligence officer for a Russian army corps during World War One. He sold secrets to the Russians and the French while also loyally serving the Nazis as Rosenberg's childhood friend.*]

Harald Siebert had been Alfred Rosenberg's friend during their schooldays back in Riga and then his close ally during the days when he was still officially "working" for the social-democrat ministers [Gustav] Noske (1868-1946), [Philipp] Scheidemann (1865-1939} and [Carl] Severing (1875-1952), and on the side performed valuable informer tasks for the Communists [Fritz] Heckert and [Hans] Kippenberger. Heckert was the leader of the *KPD's* trade union and a member of the *Comintern* politburo in Moscow, while Kippenberger was the chief of the German branches of both the Communist intelligence service and the GPU (the Soviet State Political Directorate).

Fritz Heckert (1884-1936, died in Moscow), co-founder of the Communist Party of Germany. (Image from Wikipedia.)

Hans Kippenberger (1898-1937), Communist member of the Reichstag. He had nearly as many aliases and false identities as the author. He was the head of the Soviet spy network in Germany, according to the author, part of whose duties were to carry out intensive and continual counter-espionage against him. (Image from Wikipedia.)

The "journalist" Harald Siebert (who for many years was a resident of Südwest-Corso in Berlin) was a specialist for political intelligence and for counterfeit documents of all kinds, and was entangled in many a dubious affair. During the times of the Weimar Republic, there was no intelligence bureau that he had not approached to offer his services. The British intelligence service knew him just as well as did the Soviet GPU or the official French intelligence service *Deuxième Bureau.* He was held in equal disrepute at the *Schwarze Reichswehr*, the *Reichswehr* Ministry, and at nearly every party headquarters in post-war Germany. There was a reason why Harald Siebert concerned himself so thoroughly with informing services: as an intelligence officer he had fought *against* Germany during World War 1 in a Russian-Tsarist army corps.

For decades, one of Harald Siebert's loyal assistants and friends had been a certain Ernst Döffinger, who, in 1932, at Siebert's behest, opened a "commercial credit agency" and became a middleman not only to the Communists and Italian fascists, but also to the French *Deuxième Bureau.* Thanks to Siebert's close friendship with the "great philosopher" Alfred Rosenberg, Döffinger's and Siebert's pasts could be covered up, and they became eager National Socialists.

Harald Siebert produced a dumb and impertinent report for Alfred Rosenberg, in which Kurt Daluege was most severely attacked. In February 1933 Rosenberg handed this report to the party leader and the leader's "deputy" Rudolf Hess. Daluege was accused of being involved with a shady individual by the name of Ary Marr, a fraudster and swindler well known to the legal authorities, who had no fewer than eight or ten previous convictions to his name. It was alleged that this Ary Marr had been invited – albeit unofficially – to the Prussian Ministry for the Interior, in order to oust long-serving officials from their offices through denunciation and spying, and to play a major role in the department's "reorganisation" with which Daluege had been tasked. What Siebert and Rosenberg failed to mention in their report was the fact that Siebert's ally, Ernst Doeffinger, was an old friend of Ary Marr's, who had done many a shady deal with him in the past. Marr had bragged to Doeffinger about his "summoning" to the Ministry for the Interior, and with much posturing and self-praise, perhaps a little blackmail and the odd threat, had not only aroused Doeffinger's envy and resentment but also instilled fear in the two comrades Siebert and Doeffinger. Of course it was easy for a crook such as Marr to fabricate "incriminating materials" against even the most senior state officials, to pass these on to Daluege, and to perform some welcome tasks for him. The "philosopher" Rosenberg – completely divorced, as he was, from reality, and who, at that time, still had a reputation amongst party grandees for being incorruptible – seriously thought that arguments such as "involvement with a fraudster and swindler well known to the legal authorities" would be enough to harm Kurt Daluege in the eyes of "his *Führer* Adolf Hitler".

The outcome of Rosenberg's foray: Ary Marr eventually ended up in a concentration camp; Captain [Carl August Wilhelm, "Willi"] Gourdet (born 1884), Daluege's adjutant, lost his newly won position because of his exorbitant ignorance and gullibility; and Alfred Rosenberg's informers, Herr Siebert and Herr Döffinger, were immediately arrested (still at Ary Marr's instigation!), and sent to the torture chambers operated by the *Feldpolizei* in General-Pape-Strasse. Even before Hitler's takeover, Hermann Göring, in his capacity as NSDAP Commissioner in Berlin, had created his own security detail, the so-called *Feldpolizei* ("field police"), which should not be confused with a later force by the same name that operated as part of the *Wehrmacht*. Göring's "Praetorian Guard" was dissolved in 1934, and its members were given the opportunity to join the traffic police, where they were used as part of special police patrols but no longer formed a unified corps. After Göring had been appointed as Minister President of Prussia, he was quite happy to rid himself of this *Feldpolizei*, and instead created his own personal police force, namely the *"Landespolizeitruppe Hermann Göring"*, a sort of well-equipped infantry regiment. But even this *"Landespolizeitruppe Hermann Göring"* became redundant when power was consolidated in 1936, and so it was remodelled as the so-called *"Flak-Regiment"* of the new *Luftwaffe*, which was barracked in Brandenburg near Berlin.

The two chiefs of Hermann Göring's *Feldpolizei* were Captain Weiss and Major [Eric] Schneider (both decommissioned) from the *"Brigade Ehrhardt"*, one of many irregular militia groups from the years following World War 1 who were wreaking havoc in Germany until 1923, when they were for the most part subsumed into the NSDAP and became the core of the *SA* and *SS*. Yet the *Feldpolizei* was infamous and feared especially in *SA* and even in *SS* circles, for its members did not shy away from taking action against *SA* and *SS* men when disputes or even physical brawls arose between them. Especially in the east of Berlin, in Wedding and Neukölln this was not a rarity, for in these working-class districts entire Communist cells had defected to the NSDAP *en bloc* and had been welcomed into the *SA*. It was – in no small part – thanks to Göring's *"Feldpolizei"* that immediately after Hitler's takeover in the Spring of 1933 party discipline was re-tightened and all random maverick actions by minor *SA* and *SS* leaders were finally stamped out. However, one would be profoundly mistaken to view this *"Feldpolizei"* as a fair and even-handed law enforcement agency. There are no methods of torture more horrendous than the ones employed at the *"Feldpolizei"* headquarters in Berlin's General-Pape-Strasse during the years of 1933-34; the boundless orgies of sadism the ex-officers Weiss and Schneider engaged in could only have been dreamt up by sick and deviant minds and cannot be described in words.

Major Eric Schneider, who according to the author, with his colleague Captain Weiss carried out "boundles orgies of sadism" which "could only be dreamt up by sick and deviant minds and cannot be described in words". All of this was done on behalf of Hermann Göring, who liked carefully planning the torture sessions every morning, and Schneider and Weiss would then carry out his sick and demented plans with great glee. Göring often went to watch.

However, there was a difference between the torture regime of the *SA* and *SS*, and that of Hermann Göring's *"Feldpolizei"*, namely the fact that while the *SA* and *SS* often singled out their victims at random, at the *"Feldpolizei"* headquarters in General-Pape-Strasse only such individuals were allowed to be tortured who had been taken there on the express orders of Hermann Göring or one of his closest associates or confidants (such as Kurt Daluege). Not a single person was tortured there without Hermann Göring's knowledge, for every morning one of his two *"Feldpolizei"* commanders would produce a list of all detainees, and Göring would personally determine the kind of ordeal that would be inflicted on them! This fact is one of the most dismal aspects of the barbarity of Hermann Göring; a man who so mendaciously disguised himself as a "gentleman of integrity" and fooled those around him with his charade of the "moderate reactionary". While his bloodlust knew no bounds in the subterranean torture chambers of the *"Feldpolizei"* headquarters in General-Pape-Strasse in Berlin, at the same time he passed new, stringent animal rights laws in his new capacity as *Reich* Hunting Commissioner and outlawed vivisection. In General-Pape-Strasse the most gruesome and bloody human sacrifices were offered at the altar of the super-ego-god, and then – perhaps on the same night – the "theatre buff" Göring would enjoy lyrical and profound theatre productions, would relish in peppering his oratory in polite society with quotes by Goethe and Schiller, bestowing charming flattery on the ladies and generally engaging in witty conversation. Alfred Rosenberg's friends, the two shady characters Siebert and Doeffinger, were not tortured in General-Pape-Strasse, but, after Rosenberg's representations with Rudolf Hess, after only a few days' detention were transferred to Munich. This was in effect equivalent to their release, for in Munich it was not Hermann Göring who held the reins, but his adversaries Heinrich Himmler and the chief of the *SD*, Reinhard Heydrich, neither of whom were at the time at all predisposed towards "the competition in Berlin". Doeffinger returned to Berlin, while Harald Siewert, for reasons of precaution, chose to remain in Munich for the time being, and contrived to win Heydrich's personal protection by becoming his "associate" as a spy and "high calibre" informer. In his capacity as a purveyor of information for the *SD*, he and Doeffinger, without knowing it, were classified as Z-men and put into "category 3", i.e. the category for informers, "superior" spies and denunciators "for personal gain".

All the attacks made on Daluege by either Rosenberg or Luettgenbrunn were immediately rebuffed in the days and weeks following Hitler's takeover. Having been taken under Hermann Göring's wing, Kurt Daluege saw himself as the chief of the entire Prussian police force, and duly was officially appointed *Ministerialdirektor* in the Prussian Ministry for the Interior. The erstwhile "State Commissioner for Special Deployment" had turned into one of the most powerful Prussian officials. Not only were all police chiefs and the entire criminal police force subordinate to the new Herr *Ministerialdirektor*; in addition he was commandant of the Prussian *Schutzpolizei*, the protection police, and as such its first and later highest general and commander – initially only in Prussia, later throughout the entire *Reich*. But suddenly there appeared on Daluege's horizon a new pretender who seemed to have his own eyes on the position of police chief: the lowly senior councillor Dr [Rudolf] Diels, who had just been promoted to the rank of undersecretary by Göring.

The formation of the Gestapa

Hermann Göring loved to hold meetings, gathering the faithful around him, having them report to him, and dispensing orders to them. During the months of February and March 1933, not a single day passed without endless cabinet meetings taking place in the conference rooms of the Prussian Ministry for the Interior; Göring, surrounded by his staff and assistants, basking in the abundance of his own power like a personified super-ego-god.

Like a shadow, a diminutive, reserved man was always sitting close by his new master; the newly appointed Nazi officials paid precious little attention to him. Neither was any importance ascribed to the fact that at the end of each session this nondescript non-National-Socialist was asked by the great lord and master to remain in the room for further consultation. An advisor, one of many, whose services were required by the newly appointed minister who wanted to get up to speed with the unfamiliar intricacies of the new ministerial portfolio, a man with expertise and an excellent memory for names and faces: to the freshly-minted Nazi officials, this unimposing man – Dr [Rudolf] Diels by name – appeared to be nothing more and nothing less. Because about the recent goings-on behind the scenes, the acts leading up to Hitler's takeover, these Nazi functionaries knew precious little; and they were certainly unaware that Dr Diels had played a decisive role in the various scene changes that had taken place.

Hermann Göring had promoted Kurt Daluege to the position of his deputy in the state of Prussia, despite the fact that Berlin at the time was home to a considerable number of party grandees, all of whom were more senior and more prominent than Daluege. The reason Göring chose Daluege, of all people, as his highest police official was not only the aforementioned personal aptitude of the man, but, more importantly, the fact that Daluege, in his capacity as *SS-Obergruppenführer* of Greater Berlin, had at his disposal a well-equipped and – in contrast to the forces of the *SA* in Berlin – tightly disciplined private army, which was composed in the main of the hopeful offspring of the well-to-do *petit bourgeois*. One of the first and most pressing tasks given to Daluege by his master Göring was to equip the *SS* with the tools of power of the police, to amalgamate it with the uniformed police force, and thereby to integrate it into the overall police apparatus. Such an approach would safeguard against any possible labour unrest and revolts within the *SA*.

Already during the first few days and weeks after the takeover it soon became clear that even the *SS* and Kurt Daluege's police troops would not be able to quell the chaotic unrest (which was rife especially in Berlin), and to put a stop to the numerous abductions or return those who had already been abducted. During the Weimar Republic there had never existed an actual political police; there were only the various subdivisions within the individual police headquarters and the respective criminal police forces, such as the "Division I. A.", a subdivision of Berlin's police headquarters on Alexanderplatz.

After long and frequently rather tumultuous sessions at the Prussian Ministry for the Interior, during which the tinny voice of the new lord and master Hermann Göring at times grew to a shrill and unpleasantly loud crescendo, it was decided that "Division I. A." should be detached from the Berlin police headquarters and its offices be relocated to the site of the former Communist headquarters in Karl-Liebknecht-Haus on Bülowplatz (but not before hastily renaming the ex-Communist premises as "Horst-Wessel-Haus", and changing the name of the square on which they were located from Bülowplatz to "Horst-Wessel-Platz"). Bülowplatz was in the immediate vicinity of Alexanderplatz, and even more centrally located in Berlin's east than were the police headquarters. For all intents and purposes, "Division I. A." had been dissolved and now provisionally existed under the designation "political police".

Much like the various police headquarters with their criminal police divisions and the uniformed police force, this new "political police" should naturally have been answerable to Kurt Daluege, the responsible head of department in the Prussian Ministry for the Interior. It was therefore all the more astonishing when Hermann Göring assigned an independent chief to this political police force, namely Dr Diels, who was directly and immediately subordinate to Hermann Göring, and, unlike other undersecretaries, was not under the control of the higher-ranking ministerial head of department. It took all of Hermann Göring's authority to keep at bay the pent-up anger, envy and resentment of Kurt Daluege and the legions of new officials in the ministry who had been longstanding party members against the non-National-Socialist Dr Diels. Certainly Göring and Diels were closer than even Nazi insiders were aware, but the deciding factor in the appointment of the chief of the political police must have been that Göring saw clearly that a man like Daluege did not possess the skills that would be needed to create a tool of all the subtlety that the new political police would require. Dr Diels was an exceptionally smart man, very quick-witted and, with his diplomatic cunning and slyness, equal to any challenges that might arise. But for Göring there was another inestimable advantage that Diels brought to his new office: as a former non-National-Socialist, he would never venture to plot against Göring within the Nazi hierarchy, or even to oust him from his high office. There was no way that Göring could have found a more compliant, yet highly intelligent and able tool than Dr Diels. (When Göring eventually did have to rid himself of Diels in order to replace him with party grandees such as Himmler and Heydrich, Göring was very quickly forced to relinquish his authority over the police in Prussia; his own party comrades challenged him for the control of the executive and eventually wrought it from him.)

As the newly appointed chief of the political police, Dr Diels immediately set to work. Understandably there was a shortage of officials who were blindly devoted to National Socialism, and so Dr Diels at first brought in officials who were personally known to him and whom he thought he could trust. One such man, who had previously been with "Division I. A.", was the slightly stuffy detective Reinhold Heller (1885-1945, suicide), who, at Dr Diels' recommendation, was promoted to the rank of detective superintendent and temporarily moved into offices in Horst-Wessel-Haus. It was Dr Diels who immediately saw that the creation of a political police force alone would not be enough, especially as long as that political police had to carry out its office as a "subsidiary of the public prosecution department" and the police executive was controlled by ordinary jurisdiction. Herr Dr Diels was certainly no less unscrupulous than other Nazi functionaries, but, being a smart man, he thought it important at the very least to maintain the pretence of justice. And so, in late February / early March 1933, Göring proposed to detach the political police from the public prosecution department also on a formal level.

By the end of March 1933, the desired independence had finally been achieved and the necessary framework for Dr Diels' political police had been found: the Secret State Police Office (Gestapa) was founded and, on Göring's orders, was declared "highest federal state authority" in the state of Prussia. Complete independence from the public prosecution department and public jurisdiction had been achieved; indeed, it was now the Gestapa that was superior to the public prosecution department, that is to say, as a police force it was ranked ahead of the judicial authorities.

Not only were the premises at Horst-Wessel-Haus not large enough for the Gestapa, but Göring wanted to have his police force in the immediate vicinity of his private Berlin villa; he had taken up residence in a large Prussian mansion, tucked away in gardens at the corner of Leipzigerstrasse and Leipzigerplatz. And so the Gestapa requisitioned the premises of the new Labour Court in Berlin and relocated from Bülowplatz (Horst-Wessel-Platz) to Prinz-Albrecht-Strasse 7, opposite the Prussian state parliament, which then became the "House of the Aviators" and later the seat of the Berlin People's Court.

The Gestapa – as is obvious from its designation "highest federal state authority in the state of Prussia" – only had jurisdiction in Prussia. The responsibility for the political police across the rest of Germany lay with *Reichsführer SS* Heinrich Himmler and the Chief of the *SD*, Reinhard Heydrich, who would soon enough bring about the utter downfall of their rival, Dr Diels, and ensure that there would be no "comeback" and no political resurrection for the man.

Initially the Gestapa in Berlin did not have separate offices in the provinces around the capital, but merely a sub-branch within the criminal police force that formed part of each of the police headquarters in the regions. These sub-branches – as was the case already during the Weimar Republic – would deal with political criminals, "political disturbances" and the like. This meant that a rudimentary basis for a unified political police corps already existed, but an expansion on a large scale and the creation of so-called *"Stapo-Dienststellen"* (state police offices) and thereby of a regular political secret state police – the Gestapo – only happened under Himmler-Heydrich, that is to say following the events of June 30, 1934. While the Gestapa (the Secret State Police Office) continued to exist beyond the creation of an independent Gestapo (the Secret State Police), it was then downgraded to the status of a mere administrative office and highest central department. With Himmler's appointment as Chief of the German Police, the Gestapo gained jurisdiction for the territory of the entire *Reich* and only then – i.e. since 1936 – was its sphere of influence no longer limited to the state of Prussia.

With his Gestapa, Dr Diels was able to establish a semblance of "state order" relatively quickly and to put a stop to the indiscriminate and haphazard regime of abduction and private terror inflicted by minor *SA* and *SS* men. Crucially, he also built up his agency's prestige among the lower party structures. Indiscriminate attacks had been banned "by order from the highest authority", and in order to, as it were, recompense the *SA* and the *SS* and to stop the thugs from carrying out beatings and acts of terror at a whim, the Gestapa hired, *ex officio*, the most savage and brutal *SA* and *SS* men as prison guards and put them to work in the quickly constructed concentration camps. These concentration camps were facilities belonging to the party – in effect, private prisons run by marauding hordes of party supporters – but the new political police, the Gestapa, was keen to take over the running of these camps because it was impossible to jail all political "criminals" and other detainees in regular police prisons. Police prisons were usually relatively small (with the exception of the central police prison in the police headquarters on Alexanderplatz); they were not designed for lengthy detainment, as during the time of the Weimar Republic arrested persons still had to be referred to a regular court, which would either rescind the arrest or, on the strength of an arrest warrant issued by the public prosecution department, would hand the detainee over to an investigative judge, who in turn would transfer the individual in question from the police prison to a regular prison. Police prisons had only ever been intended as temporary holding facilities; only on occasion would they have been used to accommodate individuals serving a short police sentence of no more than one month in duration. Now, however, police prisons suddenly were expected to take in the Gestapa's political prisoners for many weeks or months at a time, which was logistically impossible. In the premises of the former Labour Court, the headquarters of the Gestapa in Prinz-Albrecht-Strasse, twelve new prison cells were constructed, but that number was only just sufficient to temporarily detain a small number of individuals who had to be kept on site for personal interrogation. Therefore the concentration camps established by the *SA* and *SS* were a welcome asset for the Gestapa. The first large concentration camp in the Berlin area (on a site in Oranienburg) was taken over by the Gestapa, as well as several others in the provinces.

One of the earliest concentration camps, operated in the years 1933-1934, situated in a disused brewery in the centre of the town of Oranienburg near Berlin. It held 3000 prisoners, mostly communists, social democrats, and homosexuals. The roundup of the Jews had not yet started at this period. This camp was replaced by a larger and more professional one nearby at Sachsenhausen in 1936.

In addition, the Gestapa quickly appropriated the police prison on Alexanderplatz, and instructed the *SS* to open a new concentration camp in the former military prison belonging to the Berlin garrison in Columbiastrasse, the infamous *"Columbiahaus"*. For its unfortunate inmates, this *"Columbiahaus"* was again more a temporary holding facility for investigative custody than an actual concentration camp.

In all of these camps the *SA* and *SS* were at liberty to arbitrarily torment and torture the Gestapa's victims, and occasionally – as long as it was not done by Gestapa officials personally – to shoot a detainee during an "escape attempt". While acts of torture previously had been the manifestation of random depravity and the sadistic excesses of solitary evildoers and sexual deviants, now a diabolical and systematic approach was dreamt up, which made the agonies of torture the norm. There were no exceptions and no possibility of escape. By tightening the organisation of the *SS*, the organisational genius of Himmler-Heydrich very quickly proved successful also in the state of Prussia, long before Himmler-Heydrich had assumed police authority there. In his own defence, Herr Dr Diels was able to assert that during his tenure as chief of the Gestapa it was almost exclusively "infamous Communist pigs" who were handed over to the party thugs for "treatment" in the concentration camps, and that therefore only "Communist pigs" sometimes "snuffed it" there. These were the words with which Dr Diels tried to distance himself from Himmler-Heydrich's terror methods in a conversation with an industry boss from the Rhineland region in the days after June 30, 1934, when Himmler-Heydrich had "dared" to send several prominent masonic colleagues of that tycoon (members of the so-called "Old Prussian Great Lodge") to a concentration camp.

Diels' deputy, the Deputy Chief of the Gestapa, was an eminent lawyer by the name of Dr Folck (who must not be confused with "Volck, the bomb planter", who was in Himmler's service for a while). Dr Folck initially feigned complete ignorance after the *Reichstag* fire, but in the end did depart, having decided that as a lawyer he could no longer consent to the all-too-extreme acts of despotism perpetrated by the Gestapa.

A baptism of fire: The burning of the *Reichstag*

Kurt Daluege was at the Prussian Ministry for the Interior, still a "State Commissioner for Special Deployment"; Dr Diels, also at the Prussian Ministry for the Interior, was a newly appointed undersecretary and leader of a political police that was not yet called the Gestapo and could not yet act as the "highest federal state authority"; and the "Secret State Police Office" had yet to be established, so that Detective Superintendent Heller for now had to make do with a liaison officer in the Ministry for the Interior, who would every day convey the orders by his new boss, Dr Diels, whom he often would not see face-to-face for days on end. The actions by the provisional political police were limited to the execution of search warrants and occasional, often random arrests. Full of repulsive vengefulness, lawless *SA* and *SS* hordes were still going on the rampage against minor and entirely insignificant Communist and Socialist party officials.

At the time of Hitler's takeover, Dr Diels was rightly seen as a specialist in the defence against Communism and Marxism. Now he had to convince his new employers that "unfortunately" neither the Communists nor the Socialists posed any sort of "clandestine" threat, and that an armed revolt by the "Reds" in Berlin was very unlikely. Undoubtedly Dr Diels knew the politicians on Germany's radical left better than they even knew each other, and he was convinced that their "revolutionary ardour" was not all it was cracked up to be. But elections to the *Reichstag* were just around the corner and there was a fear that the Communists and Socialists would emerge with a large majority and triumphantly take over the *Reichstag*. This had to be avoided at all costs.

In February 1933, a grand "council of war" was held in the Prussian Ministry for the Interior, and a major strike against the Soviet trade mission in Berlin, Lindenstrasse, was resolved upon and preparation began immediately. But before the plan came to fruition, the members of the government from the German National faction under the leadership of the *Reichsminister* for the economy, Alfred Hugenberg, as well as the Ministry of Foreign Affairs under Foreign Minister Freiherr von Neurath, opposed it in parliament. The strike was not executed for economic and foreign-policy reasons; for the time being, the reliable stream of substantial Soviet state contracts worth millions was still required, along with the shiny gold bullion which the Soviets liked to use for payment. At a later date, the new Nazi police run by the non-National-Socialist Dr Diels would instigate a different plot; however, the target was not the Russian trade mission, but merely a German-Russian oil and petroleum corporation by the name of "DEROP", which had its seat in Berlin's Budapesterstrasse. It had been possible to demonstrate that DEROP's extensive fleet of lorries, which delivered oil to every corner of Germany, was being misused for the distribution of Communist flyers and brochures ahead of the impending elections. These pamphlets were transported *en masse* by DEROP's lorry drivers, who were on the whole signed up members of the Communist party. DEROP was temporarily closed, and, after the Russian-Soviet portion of the company shares had been transferred into the ownership of the German state, was re-opened as a "purely German" firm. The Soviet Union hurriedly, openly and clearly distanced itself from the KPD, the German Communists, and left them to their own fate.

At the end of February 1933, Adolf Hitler needed to prove that an "acute Communist threat" was imminent, even though in reality no such thing as a Bolshevik insurrectionist movement existed. Yet National Socialism needed such an "imminent Communist threat" in order to document – both at home and abroad – its long-propagated role as liberator and saviour. The Communists, on the other hand, seriously believed that they would be able to bring down

Hitler's government by legal means. There were elections just around corner, so all that needed to happen, in their minds, was to emerge with a suitable majority from these elections, and then, using a vote of no confidence, to force Hitler's government to step down; in the same way that the Nazis – in cahoots with the left-wing opposition – had successfully ousted both *Reich* Chancellor Franz von Papen and *Reich* Chancellor General von Schleicher. Despite being carried out with much fervour, the house searches – including ones in the fictitious "secret basements" of Karl-Liebknecht-Haus – did not produce enough incriminating material to gain sufficient leverage to ban the Communist and Marxist parties. But Hitler was anxious about losing his leadership position, which was already under threat from the other non-National-Socialist factions in parliament and which could easily have been derailed by a victory of the radical left-wing parties. Göring, Goebbels and their henchmen were fearful that they might lose the position of trust they enjoyed with that very same *Reich* Chancellor and party leader, Adolf Hitler, and so they came up with the absurd idea of setting fire to the *Reichstag*. Later, the trial would show that the burning of the *Reichstag* was carried out in the most clumsy and crude manner. There had not been enough time for preparation and indeed not much planning had gone into it. It was a *coup de force*, an audacious makeshift stunt dreamt up at the last minute in order to prove an "imminent Communist threat" to Adolf Hitler, to the German electorate, and to the troublesome non-National-Socialist factions in parliament. The initiator of the idea to set fire to the *Reichstag* was Goebbels, who at the time was not a minister, but only Chief of *Reich* Propaganda and NSDAP *Gauleiter* of Greater Berlin. Göring was a mere "Commissioner" of the state of Prussia, and both men – Göring and Goebbels – were summoned by their master, *Reich* Chancellor Adolf Hitler, to a meeting during which yet again they were given a dressing down like two schoolboys. Literally "foaming with rage", that is to say, *actually* foaming at the mouth in a screaming tantrum, Adolf Hitler threw himself to the floor during that meeting. Fearful of an NSDAP defeat in the impending elections, fearful of the loss of their high positions within the party and possibly soon within the state, and fearful of the loss of their leader's benevolence, Goebbels and Göring forged an interim alliance of necessity which would last but a few weeks or months. In order to overcome the depression and glumness that had descended on the two unequal comrades after they had left the meeting with Hitler, on the staircase between the first floor and ground floor of the *Reich* Chancellery Goebbels quipped to Göring: "We should burn down the *Reichstag*; that would solve our problems!" No sooner said than done! Hermann Göring and his party comrade Josef Goebbels drove to the offices that had been put at Göring's disposal as *Reichstagspräsident* (and which at the time also served as his residence). There they locked themselves away for several hours and, on the same evening – in their capacities as *SAObergruppenführer* and most senior *SAFührer* in Greater Berlin respectively – summoned two *SA* leaders: Count von Helldorff (then the party's official *SAGruppenführer* for Berlin) and *SAOberführer* Ernst (whose *SA* section was responsible for the government quarter in Berlin). Incidentally, von Helldorff would be hanged by party comrades in 1944, while Ernst would be shot on June 30, 1934.

There is no doubt that during this first "intimate" meeting – which took place in the offices that at the time were occupied by *Reichstagspräsident* Hermann Göring and were situated in a building directly behind the large *Reichstag* – the plan to burn down the *Reichstag* was hatched. For two days Hermann Göring was not to be seen at the Ministry for the Interior, Unter den Linden. The department officials were murmuring about rumours of an expected major "Communist assault"; their highest boss was said to have personally taken on the co-ordination of the necessary countermeasures, the planning of which he was said to be currently engaged in, hence his absence. The entire police apparatus was put on the highest alert which was maintained for four days, until finally a "beacon" was s*et al.*ght in the form of the *Reichstag* fire, and with it the signal to brutally attack anything that was Communist or Marxist. It was now possible to ban the KPD and SPD, and thus the NSDAP went on to secure its absolute majority in parliament.

The German Parliament building, the Reichstag, on fire in 1933. The fire was blamed on the communists, as an act of terror, but it was a false flag operation, because the Nazis themselves did it, as described in detail by the author. In fact, it was originally Josef Goebbels who thought of doing it, saying to Göring: "That would solve all our problems." They had both had a disturbing meeting with Adolf Hitler, who had foamed at the mouth in one of his fits of rage and thrown himself to the floor screaming. That had left them somewhat on edge. (From an original negative)

The semi-ruined Reichstag as it appeared at the end of the War. (From an original Russian print)

The Reichstag before the 1933 fire and after the War. (From an original press photo.)

From his exile in Switzerland, the eminent Communist propagandist, publisher, journalist and general wheeler-dealer Willi Münzenberg published and distributed the so-called *"Braunbuch"* (*"The Brown Book"*), in which the *Reichstag* fire trials – and the act of arson itself, as it was alleged to have happened – were described. At this point we need only make this observation: neither Kurt Daluege nor Dr Diels were let in on the secret plot in advance or played any role in its planning, and neither did the entire Berlin police corps have the slightest inkling before February 27, 1933. To be sure, they had been placed on the highest alert and everyone felt that something was "afoot", but everyone expected that this "something" would in fact come from the side of the Communists – simply because one wished it; the wish was the "father of the thought". However, Göring-Goebbels-Helldorff-Ernst were clever enough not to enlist any accessories within the Prussian Ministry for the Interior or the Berlin police headquarters prior to the execution of their deceptive and deceitful manoeuvre, the burning of the *Reichstag*. Setting fire to the *Reichstag* was the last "illegal" act of arson, murder and terror carried out by the marauding party thugs for which no officials, not even Nazi officials, were required. The day would arrive soon enough when it would be these officials who would have to "do their duty", and it would not be long before they would have to be put under pressure in order to "do their duty" in a manner that would please and benefit National Socialism and the new state authorities.

The police received an order from Hermann Göring to seek out the arsonists among the Communists —— and they set to work. But after only a few interrogations the inspectors tasked with the investigation realised that something "was not right". The stolid detective superintendent Reinhold Heller, a rather plain and old-fashioned sort of official, found himself tasked with the solving of a riddle that for him was unsolvable. And when one of the accused Communist leaders, Ernst Torgler, unexpectedly came forward in order to assist with the police investigation, a bewildered Herr Heller called his superior Dr Diels to ask what an earth he should do with that man. The brusque answer was: "Detective Superintendent, you are required to do your duty – get that into your head!" And suddenly Herr Heller knew what his duty was, and he arrested Torgler.

The Chairman of the Communist Member group of the Reichstag, Ernst Torgler (1893-1963). He naively came forward after the Reichstag Fire to offer his help in finding the guilty parties, unaware that the false flag Fire was a plot to incriminate himself and the other communists. The investigator, Detective Superintendant Reinhold Heller [1885-1945; he later became SS *Obersturmbannführer* on 10 September 1939, his fourth SS promotion in a year and a half], was astounded when Torgler showed up, and did not know what to do. He phoned Dr. Diels, who ordered him to arrest Torgler, which he then did. Torgler did not "hand himself over to the police" as stated on Wikipedia, but instead, according to the author, came to offer his help to the police in their investigations into the Fire. The author knew Heller well as a close SD colleague and was told this story by him personally. (*Portrait drawing by Emil Stump, 1932. From Wikipedia.*)

The police officers tasked with the investigation had a choice: either risk their commissions, state pension entitlement and even their liberty, or, against their better judgement – or rather against their personal hunch – seek out and find the arsonists among the ranks of the Communists. The police officers knew the Communists and their actions very well, because for years – and not only since Hitler's takeover – they had been their state-appointed adversaries and persecutors. They thought the Communists capable of little good, but much evil. And so, even when in the course of the investigation those trained police officers saw increasingly clearly that the burning of the *Reichstag* had not been carried on orders issued by the German Communist Party, it took little effort on the police officers' part to pin the arson on the Communists, and in that way to be of use to their new masters in the state, the ruthless National Socialists, and to secure their own official positions. They knew the Communists and were convinced of their impenitence and deceitfulness. As "plain and simple" officials they had no difficulty at all in identifying the Communists as arsonists, knowing that they were not guilty, but "perhaps could have been".

With this fabricated tracking down of the arsonists Dr Diels' political police had provided the first tangible proof of its usefulness, and – as the burning of the *Reichstag* from the outset was designed to be nothing other than the signal "to attack", to start open and "legal" terror against Communists and Marxists – this political police now set out to demonstrate its prowess in the execution of the desired terror. Political parties were banned and the immunity of undesirable members of parliament was rescinded, with the result that those individuals were "officially" declared "fair game". Over night, the "imminent Communist threat" had vaporised into nothing – all because of a fire that the Communists had absolutely nothing to do with.

The members of the factions that had opposed National Socialism until this point realised they had to save their own skins, and a spirit of "every man for himself" took hold. These upright, virtuous German parliamentarians – sofa revolutionaries, as they once had been dubbed by a French Communist – were helpless like children in the face of the collective terror waged by the police and party. They had stubbornly held on to the idea that it would be possible to fight Hitler with the ballot paper, but they were powerless against the armed police forces and party troops, and did not even dare to employ the weapon of a general strike. Not even Berlin's traffic- and transport workers went on strike, even though they had been regarded as the "most dangerous Reds". The sentiment "every man for himself" turned into a delusional idea; it led to many prominent politicians performing gushing contortions of devotion in front of the new authorities, proving their rapturous and consummate enthusiasm for National Socialism. It was the start of the time of the so-called *"März-Gefallene"* (a term meaning "killed in action in March", which had originally been applied to the victims of the revolutions of March 1848 in Vienna and Berlin). This was the name given to those who hastily – during the month of March 1933 – became members of the NSDAP, and, through their newfound party membership, sought and found association with National Socialism. The *"März-Gefallene"* to a large part were made up of previously non-National-Socialist officials and state employees, civic and local officials, and many radical right-wing politicians who had not yet become Nazis. Only a few were prepared to bear the severe hardship of exile and to go abroad.

Another *"März-Gefallener"* was the chief of the new political police, Herr Dr Diels, who had recently formally sealed his affiliation with the party. While he did not know about the plans to burn down the *Reichstag*, as a clever man he soon realised what the deal was, and he demonstrated that he was exactly the man Hermann Göring wished him to be, and that he was ready to be used for anything and everything. It was not least the *Reichstag* fire and its aftermath that enabled Dr Diels to create the secret state police office, the Gestapa, and, by elevating it to the status of "the highest federal state authority", to provide it with all the required striking power.

The management of the arson at the *Reichstag* had been pitiful, as there had been insufficient time for careful preparation. But the "managers" Göring and Goebbels not only knew how to disseminate barefaced and often contradictory lies, but also how to keep their preparations secret, even amongst their closest circle of friends. Like all notorious liars and cheats, eventually they believed their own lies. Hitler himself had so often talked about the "imminent Communist threat", posed as the saviour, and, prophet-like, invoked the spectre of Bolshevism in front of a gullible audience so many times, that in the end he not only believed his own lies, but, after endlessly ranting against his opponents and talking himself into a frenzy of utter conviction, he eventually was able to rid himself of all opposition with untold brutality and unscrupulousness.

Were Göring and Goebbels pitiful "managers"? Yes, and no! Despite all their blunders they had achieved what they had wanted: for their *Führer*, they had secured dictatorial power, and for themselves and their party cronies they had secured governmental positions large and small, authority and power. In the *Reichstag* fire, the first major burnt offering had been laid on the altar of the super-ego-god. Being a fire-devouring god, he would grant his disciples no peace until they would bring him the offering of war. Imperiously, this super-ego-god would demand lies, bluffs and terror; and he demanded the worst of all deception, namely self-deception. But self-deception inevitably leads to a mortification of conscience, to unscrupulousness, an utter lack of restraint, and it seduces into blind hatred and delusion, which in the end maul the individual's ego.

For the sake of even-handedness, it is necessary at this point to recognise the following facts: Detective Superintendent [Reinhold] Heller "turned" and became a *"März-Gefallener"* and NSDAP bootlicker. But, in the matter of the *Reichstag* fire, he did everything in his power to shield Torgler and Georgi Dimitrov with his two compatriots from the fury and hatred of the party troops, and managed to avert torture and ordeal for "his" detainees. The mentally disordered Marinus van der Lubbe, on the other hand, the innocent victim of a vile miscarriage of justice, was not subject to protection by Detective Superintendent Heller, and was "dealt with" by party cohorts, by Helldorff and his henchmen, and by the clairvoyant Erik Jan Hanussen, at the time a close friend of Count Helldorff, who was in financial debt to him.

Erik Jan Hanussen (born Hermann Steinschneider, 1889-1933, assassinated). Hanussen was a master hypnotist, an occultist, a clairvoyant, a mind reader in public performances, and one of the most extraordinary characters of his time. From the early 1920s he coached Hitler on how to speak and gesture at his political rallies, and taught him about mass psychology. Several feature films have been made about him, he was the basis for a novel by Leon Feuchtwanger, and he seems to have held an endless fascination for people no matter how many decades have elapsed since his murder. In 1988, István Szabó made the feature film *Hanussen* in which the hypnotist was played with terrifying conviction by Klaus Maria Brandauer in a performance which ranks in cinema history. Hanussen walked a tightrope with the Nazis, but it was fated to end badly for him, not least because he tried to disguise the fact that he was a Jew and didn't get away with it. (Others did: for instance, Dr. Robert Ley, one of the prominent Nazi leaders, was really named Levi and was Jewish. Some win, some lose when they play dice with people like the Nazis.)

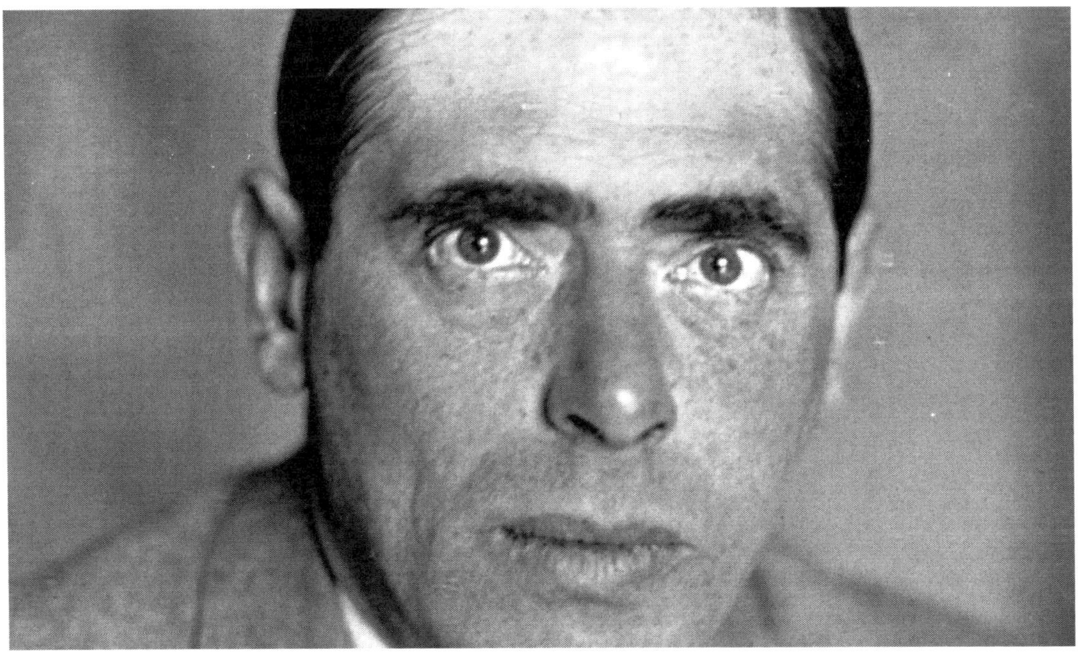

Hanussen had a very powerful gaze which could hold people spellbound. He claimed to see into the future, and to be able to read people's minds. Some of his claims to clairvoyant powers appear to have been genuine. For his stage performances he often employed trickery such as secret signalling techniques from planted members of the theatre audience. He does seem to have had abilities of a telepathic nature as well, but because they were intermittent, they could not be sustained for an entire evening, and occasionally erupted without conscious control.

Hanussen helped Hitler learn to whip himself up into manic fury at his rallies by what was effectively a process of self-hypnosis. Because of Hitler's severe sexual dysfunction, with his withered genitals and extreme sexual psychoses and frustrations, the final portions of his public speeches turned into orgasmic explosions of rage which were substitutes for sexual orgasms.

At the personal instruction of Hermann Göring (via Dr Diels), Heller was not even able to personally question van der Lubbe. Dr Diels – and not Heller – ensured that all "experiments" performed on the unfortunate van der Lubbe would be covered up. Heller ensured that Dimitrov would reliably receive all the packages that were sent to him in prison by his supporters, and, after the trial, indeed it was again Detective Superintendent Heller who personally flew with Dimitrov and the two other Bulgarians from Halle-Leipzig to Königsberg [*today called Kaliningrad*], where they were met by a Soviet aircraft and triumphantly taken to Moscow. So it was Heller who took the personal risk to get Dimitrov to safety and to personally prevent party members from taking out their anger – at the last minute – on the man whom they despised so much. Hermann Göring himself had threatened Dimitrov with the promise of destroying him, even if he was "unexpectedly" acquitted.

Marinus van der Lubbe (1909-1934), who was falsely blamed for the Reichstag Fire. He was guillotined in a Leipzig prison yard on January 10, 1934. He was a young Dutch communist, and was a scapegoat for the false flag attack which had actually been thought up by Josef Goebbels and carried out by the Nazis to justify their seizure of complete power "to keep Germany safe from communism", but really to secure Hitler's complete power. The author says that van der Lubbe was mentally disturbed and was "the innocent victim of a vile miscarriage of justice".

Dr. Jur. Karl Werner, the Chief Public Prosecutor at the trial of the five communists accused of starting the Reichstag Fire. He must have been aware of the innocence of the defendants.

Change of command

Owing to Dr Diels' intelligence and unhesitating "efficiency" it was possible to transform the Gestapa into an instrument of power the likes of which could not be found anywhere else in the Reich. It was only natural, then, that the non-Prussian police commanders Himmler and Heydrich were keen to get their hands on that exquisite instrument as soon as possible. In their attempts to wrench police authority from Dr Diels (and with him from Göring), they had at their disposal a resource that not even Dr Diels could prevail against, namely a first-rate secret spy- and informer organisation, the *SD-RFSS*, the Security Service of the *Reichsführer SS*. A power struggle erupted between the Gestapa and the *SS*, which ended with the subjugation of the Gestapa by the *SD*, and the creation of the *SD's* own police force: the Gestapo, the Secret State Police. The fight had not been fair: on the one side, the non-National-Socialist Dr Diels, who could only count on the protection of the powerful Hermann Göring and his own intellect and deviousness; on the other side, Heinrich Himmler's organisational talent and the go-getter Heydrich, who would stop at nothing and who had at his disposal the fearsome weapon that was the *SD*. In the struggle for supreme police power, Dr Diels was forced to act openly and lay his cards on the table. Himmler-Heydrich, on the other hand, obtained invaluable help from sources entirely unknown to Dr Diels, namely the spies and informers of the *SD* in the state of Prussia. Neither Dr Diels nor Hermann Göring could have known who in their immediate vicinity was a member or agent of the *SD*, monitoring their every step and sending reports of their movements to Himmler-Heydrich in Munich. Heydrich's motto, "If you know it, it is well, but you have to know it!" would prove its worth, for conjecture is one thing, but effective knowledge is a different matter altogether.

Heydrich's first successful breach of the opposition's citadel occurred when he managed to install the then *SS-Hauptsturmführer* [Hanns] Johst, commander of the *SD-Rollkommando*, as a permanent liaison officer in the Secret State Police Office in Berlin, Prinz-Albrecht-Strasse; that is to say as the official liaison officer to the Bavarian Political Police, whose chief was Heydrich himself. Johst immediately contacted Dr Behrends at the *SD* Senior District East, and three reliable *SD* members were detached to the Gestapa for office duties, to act as worthy deputies while Johst was travelling back and forth between Berlin and Munich. The leader of the three men, and Johst's first deputy, was a notorious *SD* man by the name of Pospischil, a Sudeten-German who had fled Czechoslovakia following the manslaughter of a border official, and who would later – posing as a certain "Baron Wronski" – play a heinous role in various *SD* spy operations.

A second successful blow was landed when Dr Diels – "at a recommendation" – contacted the police headquarters in Breslau [Wrocław], summoned Senior Councillor [Günther] Patschowsky [1903-1945, death while a POW; he changed his name to Dr. Günther Palten on 6 October 1937. By the time of the War, he became SS-Brigadeführer under this name. He probably used other aliases as well in his work in the SD, where he was an intimaate colleague of the author, a fellow Christian, who also did not use his real name.], a counter-espionage specialist, and appointed him chief of the newly created "Main Division III" (counter-espionage and treason). Senior Councillor Dr Patschowsky arrived at the Gestapa with an entire entourage of assistants, among them Detective Superintendent Kubitzky, who was indeed a seasoned criminal investigator and specialist for industrial counter-espionage, but also, just like Dr Patschowsky, a trusted member of the *SD*. With the appointment of Patschowsky as the chief of a main division, Dr Diels had undermined his own position; his days as leader of the Gestapa were numbered. The fact that, of all people, the then *SS-Hauptsturmführer* in the *SD*-RFSS, Dr Patschowsky, was able to lodge himself in the

Secret State Police Office can be explained thus: through Johst, Heydrich was aware of Dr Diels' intentions to incorporate in the Gestapa a special section for counter-espionage and to elevate it to the position of a main division. It was to be expected that Dr Diels, when it came to selecting a specialist, would contact the counter-espionage division in the *Reichswehr* Ministry. In choosing a person acceptable to the ministry, so the thinking went, co-operation in matters of counter-espionage would run with the least possible amount of friction. And so Himmler-Heydrich in Munich mobilised their friend and confidant *SS-Gruppenführer* [Udo von] Woyrsch (the son of Field Marshal Remus von Woyrsch), who at the *Reichswehr* Ministry touted Senior Councillor Patschowsky as a first-rate police specialist for counter-espionage. When Dr Diels turned to the *Reichswehr* Ministry for a recommendation of just such a specialist, it was only "natural" that Dr Patschowsky should be put forward. Of course neither Dr Diels nor the *Reichswehr* Ministry had any inkling of the interconnection between Dr Patschowsky and Himmler-Heydrich in Munich. The eventual uncovering of the feint to all concerned parties caused much indignation at the *Reichswehr* Ministry about the abuse of its recommendation.

[*Note:* Like his friend Heinrich Pfeifer, Patschowsky was a true man of mystery. He was registered in the SS under two different numbers: 40064 (in 1935) and 36005 (in 1934). So within a period of three years, he had two official SS numbers on file and two official names on file. Once again, we see a chamaeleon at work in the SD counter-espionage department, whose identity was disguised not only by an official name change, as well as probable multiple unofficial aliases, but also obscured by a fictitious double-registration in the SS. Anyone searching the SS files could not possibly have identified him unambiguously, if only because he would be filed partially under 40064 and partially under 36005. And those were merely the official files. As we know from the author, the secret files were the real files, and they were stored somewhere "impenetrable", so that the official files were all just a "cover".]

At the trial of the Polish spymaster Major Jerzy ("Jurek") von Sosnowski, the tensions between Himmler-Heydrich and the Division for Espionage and Counter-espionage (Admiral Canaris' Main Division V) at the *Reichswehr* Ministry became publicly evident, and it required all of Dr Best's cunning to smooth over these tensions and to establish a sustainable working relationship. Dr Patschowsky had to be let go by the new masters of the Gestapa, as his position as the chief of the Main Division III had become untenable. Instead, a special counter-espionage position against Poland was created for him in Upper Silesia (a position within the Gestapa, and not the *Reichswehr* Ministry).

One case of espionage investigated by Patschowsky provided the external trigger for the fall of Dr Diels and the appointment of Himmler-Heydrich in Berlin. The combined efforts, intrigues and spy activities by Johst, Patschowsky and Dr Behrends (the aforementioned Dr Behrends from the *SD* Senior District in Berlin) had finally succeeded in paving the way for Himmler's and Heydrich's triumphant entry into the Secret State Police Office in Berlin's Prinz-Albrecht-Strasse. The *SD-RFSS* had won a decisive victory over Dr Diels and his protector and master Hermann Göring; the *SD-RFSS* had performed splendidly in the internal party tussles for supreme authority in the state, and the *SD-RFSS*, until then one of many "private" party organisation, became the foremost and most important instrument of power in the *Reich* and the "brain of the party and state".

At the end of 1934, Heinrich Himmler, *Reichsführer SS* and chief of the political police in all German *Länder* bar Prussia, was appointed "Inspector of the Secret State Police Office" in Berlin; and Himmler's most faithful and loyal assistant, the Chief of the *SD*, Reinhard Heydrich, was appointed as chief of the Gestapa. It was then that the apposite phrase was coined: "Without Himmler, no Heydrich; without Heydrich, no Himmler!" Himmler, the *Reichsführer SS*, remained the *Führer's protégé*. Heydrich, the more recent party member, remained the man in the background, Himmler's backbone, nerve centre and pair of hands. Hermann Göring remained – until 1936 – the highest chief of the Gestapa, and in the meantime also the titular Minister President of Prussia, and thereby the highest authority in the state of Prussia, to whom Heinrich Himmler, in his capacity as "Inspector", was subordinate. Yet the actual chief of the Gestapa – in a much wider sense than Dr Diels had ever been – was now the Chief of the *SD*, Reinhard Heydrich. Only a few weeks after his appointment as Chief of the Secret State Police Office there was not a single position of importance that was not under the control of tried-and-tested *SD* members. Heydrich had brought an enormous entourage of assistants from Munich, and a large number of Dr Diels' "old" Gestapa officials were immediately dismissed or transferred to the provinces, where, under Heydrich's direction, the so-called "Stapo offices" were expanded and spatially separated from the various police headquarters. The next chapter will give a detailed account of what the Gestapa looked liked soon after Heydrich's "assumption of power", that is to say in July 1934, immediately after the "Röhm revolt", which was not a revolt at all.

Hermann Göring had lost his fight against Himmler (whom he was forced to appoint as "Inspector"), and Dr Diels had been replaced by Heydrich. In the final stages of the power struggle, when there was an unending deluge of complaints against Dr Diels on grounds of "arbitrary measures" taken against the Gestapa (which by and large were skilfully fomented by Himmler-Heydrich in Munich), Hermann Göring staged a "glittering pyrotechnic display" of justice, which was not devoid of a certain tragicomedy. Enraged and distraught about his impending and unpreventable deprivation of power, Göring, the Prussian Minister President, rushed to Stettin [Szczecin] in order to personally relieve no fewer than fifteen detectives of their duties. He had them incarcerated and dragged in front of a summary court – for beating up detainees during interrogations! An act of justice? No! Rather, a temper tantrum on the part of the Herr *Ministerpräsident*, who used the pretext of a "minor misdemeanour" (namely the mistreatment of detainees) to fire a warning shot, a conscious and calculated threatening gesture, which would be clearly understood by those it was directed at; that is to say, Himmler-Heydrich in Munich: "Do not dare to cross me or to disrespect my position of *Ministerpräsident*! Because that is how powerful I am, and I will use my power also against you!"

The fifteen detectives at the police headquarters in Stettin [Szczecin] had acted on the orders of *SA-Führer* [Helmuth] Friedrichs, who was temporarily placed in "honourable detainment" but soon released and — promoted to the rank of *SA-Gruppenführer*. The fifteen officers were given prison sentences by the summary court, and it turned out that they were *not* long-standing party members, but *"März-Gefallene"*, who before Hitler's takeover had been members of the "German State Party" under the democrat Artur Mahraun. Despite their former anti-National-Socialist activities, they had been appointed by the then *Gauleiter* of Stettin [Szczecin] Wilhelm Karpenstein, which is why the *SA* leadership in Stettin [Szczecin] rebelled against their own *Gauleiter*. Karpenstein, already disliked in party circles because of his "moderate" stance and actions, was accused of "embezzlement of party funds" and spent some time incarcerated by the Gestapa in Berlin, only to be released after his innocence was proven. He did however lose his position as *Gauleiter*. That is what Hermann Göring's "justice" looked like.

The deployment of the *SD-RFSS* as the most excellent instrument of power in the National Socialist state was a question of principle. Apart from that, the claims to power by prominent Nazi officials rarely were questions of principle, but purely personal matters satisfying a personal lust for power, and matters of egomaniacal ambition for power. One has to correctly assess the scheming of the National Socialist potentates in order to fully understand why one day Göring was best of friends with Goebbels, only to start a contest for the *Führer's* favour the next day, in which his opponent would be discredited or vilified by any means necessary in order to gain a personal advantage. Himmler-Heydrich allied themselves with the "red" Bürckel, and the next day they were close to throwing him into prison. Goebbels worked hand in glove with the "Catholic" Franz von Papen while at the very same time preparing his toppling as Vice Chancellor. Göring fraternised with *SA* Chief of Staff Ernst Röhm, and soon after used the collective force of his police apparatus to destroy Röhm. The schemes glistened in all colours of the rainbow and were more multifaceted than the number of senior Nazi leaders, and nearly as numerous as all possible permutations of the "for" and "against" of all the individuals involved, aligning with one another and fighting against each other. Meanwhile, the *SD-RFSS*, whose most senior members almost without exception also were high-ranking police officers, registered, incited and stoked these intrigues, all with Hitler's full knowledge and approval. The *SD* established a system of informers, which, in conjunction with its police apparatus, was as dangerous for opponents of National Socialism as it was for its own party members. This fire-breathing, fire-devouring Moloch and asphyxiating super-ego-god was both inflated and hollow, so that in the end it inevitably had to collapse in on itself. The *Götterdämmerung* led to the collapse of the idol, who was crushed by the hands of his own servants, the self-indulgent and hubristic high priests of the swastika. Human intoxication with power, pitted against God, negating the absolute and transcendental being… lay in ashes!

"The gang's all here." At extreme right is General von Fritsch, Commander in Chief of the German Army, and next to him chatting to Hitler is Field Marshal Werner von Blomberg, Minister of War. To Hitler's right are successively Rudolf Hess, Heinrich Himmler leaning forward, Josef Goebbels (pointedly ignoring his hated rival Himmler), and SS Obergruppenführer Richard Darré, Reichs Minister of Food and Agriculture, looking off to his right. This photo dates sometime between 1935 and 1938.

II. Organisation
Key figures

A soon as *Reichsführer SS* Heinrich Himmler had been appointed "Inspector" of the Gestapa, and the then leader of the *SD*, Reinhard Heydrich, had been appointed as its "Chief", the two men immediately set out to consolidate the legal basis of their new positions within the state of Prussia by enacting new legislation on April 26, 1934. While another law passed on November 30, 1933 had already enshrined the status of the Gestapa as the "highest federal state authority" – that is to say many months after Göring arbitrarily "nominated" it as such! – Heinrich Himmler was clever enough to have his special status as "Inspector" enshrined in law within a few days after his move from Munich to Berlin, and thereby to make it impossible for Hermann Göring (who had in the meantime advanced to the position of Minister for the Interior of Prussia) to dismiss him at the first opportunity.

Der Reichsführer SS

H H

Heinrich Himmler became Reichsführer and Chief of the German Police, thus making it impossible for Hermann Göring to sack him. He then stole the Gestapa, later called the Gestapo, from Göring and became all-powerful. Note the unmistakable handwriting of his initials "H. H.". It was his habit to write them on all memos of which he approved, including in this case his photo. When Himmler looked you in the eye, it was essential not to show fear. This was difficult, because his penetrating stare was that of a man capable of mass murder without a qualm. And yet, widows and orphans could make him cry when they appealed to him pathetically, which infuriated and worried Heydrich. Himmler had been "the school sneak" when he was a boy. He was obsessed with archaeology, but that was a side of him of which the author had no experience, so he never mentions it. The same is true of Himmler's elaborate occult rituals, of which the author knew nothing. After the War, Hitler's architect Albert Speer said that he had a sense of dread whenever he met Himmler, and avoided meeting Himmler's eyes. Instead, he made a point of fixing his gaze just below Himmler's spectacles. Himmler had a small old duelling scar near his cheek bone. Speer noticed that whenever Himmler rubbed the scar thoughtfully with the index finger of his right hand, it meant that he was annoyed about something. Others have said that whenever Himmler was enraged, his face would go white and his duelling scar would turn red. The dental assistant to Hitler's and Himmler's personal dentist Professor Hugo Johannes Blaschke (1881-1959) was Käthé Heusermann. After the War, she had this to say about Himmler: "Himmler had very, very good teeth, very white. He was very proud of them. Their whiteness, it was quite unusual, …He only had two fillings, and you couldn't see those when he smiled. He had no teeth lost … His teeth were almost perfect. … Himmler was not a man you would ever forget." Otto Strasser knew Himmler at an early stage in Munich and wrote of him that he was "an unemployed agriculturalist, who had once vainly hoped to become an officer. 'You'll remain infantile all your life', and 'You've got the soul and sensibilities of a butcher', were two of the things that my brother Gregor used to say to him. Himmler was not cruel, but he was incapable of emotion or suffering. Later he arrested his own brother at the Führer's orders, and he would have killed his parents without a moment's hesitation if the Führer had ordered him to do so. With regard to women, Himmler always reminded me of Gretchen's phrase in *Faust*, 'Heinrich, you inspire me with horror'. He had had only one sexual adenture, which he described to me himself. This, he said, was at the age of thirty-two. He spent a night at an inn, where he was seduced by the landlady, who was ten years older than he. He remained attached to the woman who performed this miracle."

According to a *Reich* law passed on February 10, 1936, the Gestapa – previously merely the "highest federal state authority" in the state of Prussia – widened its influence to become "highest *Reich* authority" for all remaining *Länder*, and *Reichsführer SS* Heinrich Himmler was appointed Chief of the German Police.

Chief of the German Police:
Reichsführer SS **Heinrich Himmler**

I.	II.
Chief of the Regular Police Force:	Chief of the Security Police:
Police General Kurt Daluege	*SS-Gruppenführer* Heydrich
(also Deputy Chief of the German Police)	(also Chief of the *SS* Security Service *SD-RFSS*, and leader of the Gestapa in Berlin

Kurt Daluege – despite the fact that he was the deputy of the Chief of the German Police – had no authority over the political police and the criminal police in the entire *Reich.* Given his predisposition and aptitude, Reinhard Heydrich, who would later be assassinated in Prague, was the most terrifying holder of police authority in the Hitler regime, and became the driving force behind practically everything that Himmler did and planned. The adage "Without Heydrich, no Himmler; without Himmler, no Heydrich" was entirely justified, especially during the time of the constitution and expansion of the political police – and especially of the *SD* – with its enormous network of spies and denouncers and its terror.

Reichsführer SS Heinrich Himmler, the Chief of the German Police, later the *Reich* Minister for the Interior and eventually even the "Supreme Commander of the *Heimatheer*" (the "domestic army"), is often wrongly seen as a single-minded and ingenious demon, holding unlimited police authority. An inaccurate picture is painted, one that much more resembles a man like Göring rather than a man like Himmler, for the morphine addict Göring actually had something of the bloodhound about him, was someone who had to indulge his intoxication with power in excesses of blood, and, in the fullest sense of the word, became the "beast incarnate" as he raged like an animal. Heinrich Himmler had very little or nothing of a powerful personality about him, neither in a positive nor a negative sense. Heinrich Himmler initially rose to power within the NSDAP as the secretary of Gregor Strasser (Dr Ley's predecessor as NSDAP *"Organisationsleiter"*), whom he murdered on June 30, 1934. As if to add insult to injury, until his appointment as Chief of the German Police, Himmler was thought of by his friends and in senior Nazi circles as "very correct" and "highly sensitive", which earned him the sobriquet "Gentle Heinrich". Himmler's "correctness" manifested itself in extreme pedantry: trivialities such as a speck of dust or an open button on a uniform were enough to put him into a blind rage. The slightest disorder on his desk would set him off, and woe betide the personal adjutant who failed to ensure that all pencils were sharpened and set out in exact alignment on the desk. Himmler's "highly sensitive" nature, on the other hand, was in evidence as a somewhat lachrymose state of mind; begging and pleading by women and children would drive the man to floods of tears. For that reason it was strictly forbidden to grant a personal audience with Himmler to any supplicant, especially to women petitioning for their husbands, because in a spontaneous fit of compassion he might order a release from a concentration camp or the like. The sadistic weakling and unscrupulous wimp Heinrich Himmler was mistaken for a despotic tyrant. Instead, he was a calculating cynic racked with inferiority complexes, and it was this very emotional instability that drove him to weave the threads of his web with apparent outward restraint and cool, satanic cunning, while giving free rein to his organisational genius. Himmler neither had the qualities required of a military commander nor those of a master builder; he was a mere schemer who loved the gloom of the sidelines, for he knew that he was not cut out to be a tribune of the people and that he should avoid public appearances as much as possible. At the throne of his lord and master, Adolf Hitler, this smarmy intriguer and wimpish, spineless fanatic obsessed with power was much more dangerous than a strong-minded go-getter could have ever been. Quite how dangerous this unscrupulous weakling could be was not only felt by opponents of National Socialism, but also his competitors in the contest for power in the state – among them the seemingly omnipotent Hermann Göring.

Hitler's power grab in 1933 marked the onset of Himmler's wooing of the *Reichswehr*, but although obvious preferential treatment was given by the then *Reichswehrminister* von Blomberg, Himmler's advances came to nothing because of unrelenting rejection by Colonel General Fritsch and his generals. Despite repeated pleas and interviews, Himmler was not even promoted to permanent major general, even though as *Reichsführer SS* and commander-in-chief of the military *SS* dispositional troops he was due that very title. [Konstantin] Hierl (Chief of the *Reich* Labour Service) and [Adolf aka Hans] Hühnlein (Chief of the *NSKK*, National Socialist Motor Corps) were both given the rank of a general of the *Wehrmacht*, and according to a decree by the Reich government every *Gauleiter* was promoted to the rank of major general. But despite all his efforts, Heinrich Himmler was not promoted to the rank of general; his name did not even appear on the register of the *Reichswehr* Ministry (later the *Reich* War Ministry). Over time, a ferocious hatred for the "reactionary generals" built up within Heinrich Himmler, which would inevitably erupt at the first opportunity. At the outbreak of war, his non-commissioned officers, the commanders of the SS divisions, were promoted to the rank of lieutenant general, or even deployed as commanding generals, but the *Reichsführer SS* only became a permanent "general of the *Wehrmacht"* when he succeeded in exposing and brutally suppressing a "general's plot" against Adolf Hitler and subsequently having himself appointed "Supreme Commander of the *Heimatheer*" (the "domestic army"). For years, Heinrich Himmler had to grudgingly suffer the fact that his deputy, Police General Kurt Daluege, was recognised by the *Wehrmacht* generals as a "commanding general", while he, Himmler, was not even able to call himself a major general. It suited the "Supreme Commander of the German *Wehrmacht*", the party leader Adolf Hitler, very well to restrain his police chief Himmler in unfulfilled envy for a long time, in order to unleash him on the high-handed generals with deadly accuracy at a later date. *Reichsführer SS* Heinrich Himmler was Hitler's fawning adulator, and through inexhaustible unscrupulousness, flattery, pliancy and nauseating zeal he had made himself ever more indispensible. He had won Hitler's personal favour by suggesting to him – even before his advent to power – the idea of a special "Race and Settlement Office", on the basis of which the actual *SS* would later be created. At first he gained influence over Hitler through his ability to tell jokes and by becoming one of Hitler's favourite entertainers and companions. But it was not until he had established his security service for "party and state" and turned the *SD* Main Office into the "brain of the party and state" that he became indispensible. However, the ingenious broker of police power in the Third Reich, who for a long time had held all the threads in his hands and knew how to weave an ever-finer web of informers and spies, was not Himmler and not Daluege, but the first chief of the *SD-RFSS* and *Reichsführer SS* Reinhard Heydrich, who would meet a terrible fate in Prague.

Reinhard Heydrich was a Lucifer figure; he was not only the leader but the creator of the secret club of the *"Sonnenmenschen"* ("the men of the sun"). It was he who dreamt up the satanic organisation which "governed" the concentration camps and through which barbarous cruelty against humans was turned into an elaborate systematic operation. He, Reinhard Heydrich – and not Himmler, not Hess or Göring – had cast a web of spies, informers, denouncers and overseers that covered Germany in its entirety. A furious beast in human form? No, this man Heydrich was a Lucifer, who would apply the most rigorous standards not only to himself but all his subordinates, who would extract every last scintilla of energy out of himself and all those around him, and demanded rigid discipline of himself and his peers. For his people he was the epitome of a *"Herrenmensch"*; he was not only their boss, he was the most capable, hardworking and fanatical among them; to them he appeared like the incarnation of the super-ego-god; he was a truly satanic genius: the most obsessive, brutal and unrelenting wielder of police power the Third Reich ever produced. Reinhard Heydrich was the counterpart to Heinrich Himmler. He was too clever to ever replace that man, Himmler; rather, he used him as a go-between to the super-ego-god incarnate, Adolf Hitler, and as such Himmler was no more than a stooge to Heydrich. Reinhard Heydrich was a relatively recent party member, had not been "part of it all" from the beginning, and was fully aware that during his lifetime – or, more precisely, that of Hitler – he would never be able to take Himmler's place. He was obsessed with power but loved to lead an existence in the background and shunned the glare of publicity, of the so-called "society", having correctly realised that puppets need to be pulled by threads invisible to the audience, if the melodrama, the cruel play about power and with power, was to be a success. To Heydrich, power was synonymous with the exertion of violence and organised terror in its most brutal form.

Reinhard Tristan Eugen Heydrich (1904–1942, assassinated), Deputy of Heinrich Himmler. The author, who worked under him and reported to him, calls him "a Lucifer figure … who dreamt up the satanic organisation which 'governed' the concentration camps … he was obsessed with power … To Heydrich, power was synonymous with the exertion of violence and organised terror in its most brutal form." On the other hand, the author points out that Heydrich was "a gifted performer of Mozart on the piano", and: "the delicacy and tenderness with which this violent madman was able to interpret Mozart or Chopin on a grand piano was utterly staggering." Heydrich also played the violin beautifully.

Reinhard Heydrich's father had been a member of an Old Prussian lodge in Halle / Saale, and in his parents' house Heydrich became acquainted with the splendid Old Prussian officer virtue. He himself became an officer; a Navy officer in the small post-war *Reichsmarine* that existed after 1918. As a First Navy Lieutenant he had to take his leave, not because of "National Socialist activities", as is often wrongly suggested, and also not because of embezzlement or some such misdemeanour, as his opponents allege, but because of a duelling incident following some affairs with women. Perhaps that is why later, as Chief of the *SD*, he demanded impeccable family lives of his *"Sonnenmenschen"*; perhaps this duelling affair was the reason why he required respectable "moral conduct" of each and every *SD* member and even made such conduct a prerequisite for acceptance into the *SD*. One thing is for certain: his departure from the *Reichsmarine* and expulsion from the officer corps was the root of the hatred and contempt that Heydrich felt for the "reactionary dogs", for the conservative generals, for the Old Prussian officers. But at the same time, his unconscious veneration for the "Old Prussian officer virtue" forever led him to seek and find contact with its avatars. Before the young Heydrich joined the *Reichsmarine* as a cadet, he had wanted to study music. Indeed, he was a fine musician, and the delicacy and tenderness with which this violent madman was able to interpret Mozart or Chopin on a grand piano was utterly staggering. He often asserted that only a person with "artistic intuition" would be able, for example, to discover or weave a spy network down to its most intricate threads; he believed in his musical ear, which he insisted enabled him to register the slightest stirrings in his enemies; he made much of his instinctive *"Fingerspitzengefühl"*, with which he was able to search out his opponents' weak points. Heydrich was truly a Lucifer character, a wielder of police power ingenious and dangerous in equal measure, a man who appeared as an *Übermensch* to his friends and confidants, and as a *"Herrenmensch"* was arguably one of the most brilliant and abominable high priests of the National Socialist super-ego-god. As the leader of the *"Sonnenmenschen"* he became the creator of the most subtle instrument of terror of National Socialism, was one of the most cruel fanatics among these godless people, and the adversary of the loving God of Christianity. And the unfathomable and infinite love of the God of the Christians was so immense that He allowed the violent madman Reinhard Heydrich to repent on his deathbed: Heydrich – according to reliable eyewitness accounts – returned to the fold of the Christian God moments before his end. At the hour of his death, the man who had been the virtually omnipotent police chief during his earthly existence did not lie in a bed, however, but rather in a bathtub. His spinal cord had been shattered and the flowing waters were supposed to alleviate his pain. The agonising pangs of conscience under which Heydrich eventually died in the hospital in Prague after that assassination are said to have been infinitely greater than the physical torments he had to endure. God's ways are wondrous and His love is infinite! God cannot be mocked, but He will even have mercy on the most unrighteous of men, for every man carries within him an immortal soul that comes from God and wishes to return to God. —— Heydrich's funeral gave occasion to hold a grandiose celebration in honour of the super-ego-god of National Socialism, which at that time was at its zenith. In truth, at the hour of Heydrich's death, this super-ego-god collapsed into nothing.

The headquarters

In his capacity as *Reich* Minister of the Interior, Heinrich Himmler expanded the organisation of the police apparatus in such a way that an entire cellular hive-like construct emerged, made up of divisions, sections, offices, main offices and so forth, the complexity of which can not be disentangled here. The *SD* (with its *SD* Main Office and thereby also the Secret State Police Office) formed the core of this super-organised Nazi police apparatus. The chief of the *SD* was also the chief of the German Security Police, that is to say the entire *Reich* Criminal

Police, including the Political Police, the Gestapo. In the same way that Reinhard Heydrich became "Deputy *Reichsprotektor* of Bohemia and Moravia" after the outbreak of war, and his deputy Dr Best became *Reich* Commissioner and eventually plenipotentiary in Denmark, virtually all former chiefs of the Gestapa offices became senior Nazi officials in the occupied territories and for the largest part were personally responsible for the terror waged there and the crimes perpetrated by the Nazi police.

When Himmler and Heydrich arrived at the Secret State Police Office in Berlin in 1934, a purge – as already described earlier in these pages – was carried out, and the most important posts within the Gestapa were filled with *SD* officials whom the two men had brought with them from Munich. The following section will provide an outline of the composition of the Gestapa in Prinz-Albrecht-Strasse in Berlin shortly after Himmler's appointment as Inspector and Heydrich's appointment as Chief of the Secret State Police Office, namely at the end of June 1934. While Heinrich Himmler's appointment as Chief of the German Police in 1936 brought with it substantial expansion and reorganisation, the leading figures in the Gestapa offices remained the same, and in some sense the Gestapa of 1934/35 was the trunk from which a number of new branches and offshoots sprang forth. The following outline therefore is a representation of the bloodline that gave rise to the Nazi police apparatus of the years of war.

When on June 30, 1934, the ostensible "Röhm revolt" took place, the Secret State Police Office in Berlin's Prinz-Albrecht-Strasse 7 was structured as follows:

> *Inspector*, and as such personally responsible to the Prussian Minister of the Interior Hermann Göring: *Reichsführer SS* Heinrich Himmler.
>
> *Chief*, and as such subordinate to Inspector Heinrich Himmler: *SS-Gruppenführer* Reinhard Heydrich.
>
> *Deputy Chief*, with the rank of undersecretary of the Prussian Ministry for the Interior (since 1935): *SS-Oberführer* Dr Werner Best.

(Following Himmler's appointment as Chief of the German Police in 1936, Dr Best was installed as chairman of the Commission for Police Law in the Academy for German Law.)

Reinhard Heydrich continued in his post as Chief of the *SD-RFSS*. Dr Werner Best also acted as Deputy Chief of the *SD*.

The Secret State Police Office, the so-called Gestapa, was composed of three main divisions:

Main Division I: Administration, finance, personnel, archive, and correspondence with the Stapo offices across the *Reich*, which to a large part had yet to be established and at first were merely the political police's subdivisions within the various police headquarters across Prussia.

Main Division II: The various sections within this main division were tasked with recording and combating all domestic political trends and movements of the opponents of National Socialism.

Main Division III: Treason and counter-espionage.

The adjutancy of the Chief of the Gestapa

Heydrich's adjutancy, in its capacity as his headquarters, was superordinate to the three main divisions. The "Adjutancy Heydrich" maintained its own special armoury, and it was in charge of the office's *SS* guards, which were composed of *SS* dispositional troops and relieved on a weekly basis.

The post of chief adjutant was held by *SS Sturmbannführer* Potzelt, a sinister misanthropic Bavarian, who, in any case, was soon promoted to the post of Chief of the *SD* Senior District West in Frankfurt/Main. His place as chief adjutant was taken over by Police Captain [Kurt] Pomme (born 1899), who was swiftly promoted to the rank of major on June 30, 1934.

Heydrich had at his disposal a special police commando (*"Sonderkommissariat"*) that could only be summoned and deployed by the Chief of the Gestapa personally. It was on constant standby – on continuous duty day and night – and was a sort of personal raiding squad for the Gestapa chief. At Heydrich's express orders, any reports of assassination attempts on senior Nazi leaders had to be referred to that special police commando. Heydrich had compiled a list of persons whose correspondence was to be closely monitored; the running of this operation also fell into the remit of the special police commando. A journal kept about this surveillance operation was only to be viewed and checked by the Gestapa chief Heydrich personally. Any letters with potentially incriminating content were immediately photocopied on a designated Siemens device in the special police commando's offices and were filed in a secret archive, which was separate from the general Gestapa archive and could only be accessed through the special police commando. After the establishment of the *SD* Main Office in the Prinz-Albrecht-Palais, this Gestapa secret archive was subsumed in the secret archive run by the *SD-RFSS*.

The chief of that special police commando (with the rank of detective superintendent) was *SS-Hauptsturmführer* and *SD* member Wippert, who himself was only a youthful go-getter, but led his subordinates with rigorous discipline and did not tolerate any arbitrary excesses.

(Until 1936, the premises of the Gestapa were also home – with offices on the 4th floor – to the earlier mentioned *"SD-RFSS Rollkommando"* which, after the establishment of the *SD* Main Office, relocated to the Prinz-Albrecht-Palais in Wilhelmstrasse. This "*SD* raiding squad", with its commander Johst, must not be confused with the "special police commando" at the Gestapa.)

Main Division I

The official designation was "administration".

The heads of this division were: one senior clerk, one detective inspector (*"Kriminalinspektor"*), one detective sergeant (*"Kriminalsekretär"*), and one detective superintendent (*"Kriminalrat"*). Main Division I controlled the administrative correspondence with the various offices of the Political Police, and, until 1936, was accountable to the Prussian Ministry for the Interior. One of its subdivisions was the so-called "division for protective custody". This is where all concentration camp detainees were registered, and where an index file was kept, which detailed not only all those currently detained in "protective custody" (complete with photographs, fingerprints, records of conduct etc.), but also all politically suspect persons who had ever been in "protective custody" (i.e. in a concentration camp) but had been released as "reformed".

This "division for protective custody" however had no right of disposal and no influence whatsoever on the "political cases", for it was not a criminal division but purely an administrative body. Matters such as release, punishment and transfer of prisoners were decided by Main Division II.

Main Division I (administration) did not have its own head, but was subordinate to and received orders from the "Adjutancy Heydrich".

Main Division II

This was the actual political executive of the Gestapa; its heads were directly and immediately subordinate to the Chief of the Gestapa, and were required to report at Heydrich's office for a daily briefing between 9am and 10am. The individual divisions, as established between 1934 and 1936, were the following:

Division: KPD and SPD (Communists and Social Democrats) and Marxist splinter groups. This did not include organised labour factions.

Chief: *SS-Standartenführer* [Heinrich] Müller II, a long-standing member of the *SD* with the rank of detective superintendent. A brutal and sadistic Bavarian, whom Heydrich had brought with him from Munich.

SS Standartenführer Heinrich Müller (1900–date of death unknown; vanished in 1945, probably defected to Russia). He became Chief of the Gestapo and was central to the planning and execution of the Holocaust. The author calls him "a brutal and sadistic Bavarian whom Heydrich had brought with him from Munich."(Bundesarchiv)

Division: Illegal trade unions, illegal organised labour.

Chief: Detective Superintendent Reinhold Heller, a long-serving official from Division I. A. in the Berlin police headquarters. Until 1933 not a member of the NSDAP and never a member of the *SD-RFSS*. He was promised the post of Chief of the Main Division by Göring and Diels, but had lost a lot of influence and standing after Diels' departure. Under Heydrich he only just managed to hang on to his position, as at Heydrich's takeover he had initially been included on the list of officials to be dismissed, but was then kept in office thanks to his in-depth knowledge of the Berlin scene.

Division: Associations and trade associations (including the German Labour Front!). Monitoring of existing, legal organisations.

Chief: *SS-Sturmbannführer* Flechtner (or similar), who, as a long-standing member of the *SD*, had been brought to Berlin from Munich by Heydrich. Before 1933 he had to resign his post as a detective in Bavaria because of "National Socialist activities", but was reinstated after Hitler's takeover as a detective superintendent with the Political Police in Munich. [*Note: It is probable that "Flechtner" was an alias and that this man's real name was Reinhard Flesch, who was head of B4 of this Main Division (Section) II, and was a former policeman from Bavaria; he returned to Bavaria in 1935 and was succeeded by Gerhard Flesch (1909-1948, executed). The fact that the author does not reveal his real name suggests a close friendship between them, and that he wishes to protect him by concealing his true identity. Another reason for protecting him might be to avoid him being recognised as connected with the SS man Gerhard Friedrich Flesch who was probably his brother, who succeeded Reinhard in his post in 1935, and who was executed in Norway after the War. As long as Pfeifer continued to refer to him under his alias of Flechtner, he could describe his position without compromising him or endangering his life and possibly exposing him to the same fate as Gerhard Flesch.*]

Division: Reaction and church. "Stahlhelm" (a WW1 veteran's organisation), all non-Marxist factions, "political Catholicism and Protestantism".

Chief: *SS-Obersturmbannführer* [Franz Josef] Huber, a prominent member of the *SD* and particular favourite of Heydrich, valued for his intelligence and unscrupulousness. A Bavarian whom Heydrich had brought to Berlin, he was a devious investigator who, as a "special Gestapa commissioner" had been invested with extraordinary powers.

SS Obersturmbannführer Franz Josef Huber (1902-1975). In 1938 he was made Head of the Gestapo and State Police for Vienna. After the War, he was recruited by the CIA, who concealed his criminal past, and from 1955 to 1964 he served in the West German Inteligence Service, retiring on a civil service pension. He was responsible for the mass deportation of the Jews of Austria, and for the interrogation and torture of an estimated 500,000 people at his headquarters in Vienna, but he was never held to account or punished for his genocidal crimes because he was "protected".

Division: Freemasons and religious sects.

Chief: Councillor Dr [Karl] Haselbacher (1904-1938), who had previously worked at the Prussian Ministry for the Interior and until 1933 had not been a member of the NSDAP. He was treated with hostility by the *SD* members in the Gestapa.

Division: NSDAP and homosexuality. (Homosexuals were only persecuted after June 30, 1934 and the "Case Röhm".) This division was tasked with the monitoring of suspect elements within the party.

Chief: *SS-Obersturmbannführer* [Josef Albert] Meisinger, a prominent *SD* member and detective superintendent (a rank he had already held in Munich). Meisinger was not only tasked with the monitoring of the NSDAP, but also of its ancillary bodies, such as the *SA*, the Labour Service etc. (but not including the German Labour Front). His division also incorporated the infamous "Division for the Control of Jews".

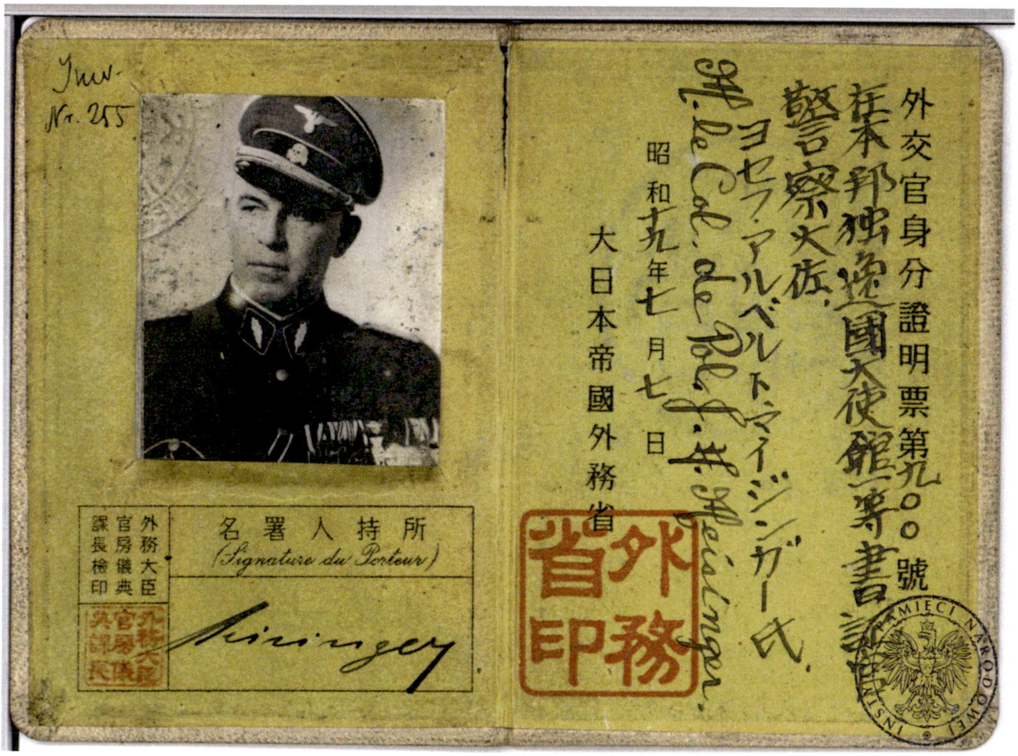

SS Standartenführer Josef Albert Meisinger (1899-1947, executed in Warsaw). In 1941 he was the Gestapo liaison officer at the German Embassy in Tokyo, where he tried to persuade the Japanese to kill the 18,000 European Jews who had escaped to Japanese-occupied Shanghai. This Japanese visa bears his photo and signature.

The three division heads in the Main Division II of the Gestapa, [Heinrich] Müller II, [Franz Josef] Huber and [Josef Albert] Meisinger, were very senior SD officials and had been unconscionable and cruel oppressors of the German people long before they became infamous terrorists in the occupied territories after the start of war in 1939. Years before there were "war criminals", they had become murderers of Germans and committed the most heinous crimes within Germany. If at this point only these three individuals are named as criminals and murderers, and their names are singled out, this is done because these three names will without doubt be found on future lists of "war criminals". Those three men belong to a guild of criminals who, unnoticed by other nations, were allowed to rage in Germany against Germans; indeed, until the start of the war, it was almost frowned upon or seen as "improper" to report on the crimes of these monsters outside of Germany and to try to stir up the world's conscience. All political refugees from these years can bear witness to this fact; almost all of their attempts – *then*, long before the outbreak of war – to alert people around them, the foreign press, in short, decent humanity, to the atrocities committed by the Nazi regime, were in vain. These admonishers and forewarners, who pointed out that the hands of those criminals were not only dripping with the blood of Jews, but also with the blood of their own countrymen who had disagreed with them, ran the risk of being vilified as "dangerous liars". The other nations did business with the new rulers in Germany, accepted them into society, entered into treaties with them, and sought their favour; because they were powerful. Any requests made to leading politicians or to the so-called "polite society" in England, the United States, France, Poland, Norway, Holland, Belgium, Denmark, in the Balkans and elsewhere to comment on the terror inflicted in Germany and on the horrendous atrocities committed against Germans in Germany, fell on deaf ears. It therefore seems like an irony of fate that now, at the end of the war, those very same politicians and that very same so-called "polite society" make the entire German people accountable for the crimes committed abroad by the Nazis and to declare the entire German people as complicitous, after trying their best for years, with dubious probity, to ignore the anguished screams of pain by Germans tortured and tormented by the Nazis, so as to not have to take any notice of them.

Main Division III

The officials of Main Divisions I and II spoke half mockingly, half enviously of the "secret-mongering" going on in Main Division III (counter-espionage and treason), for that department was strictly segregated within the Gestapa building and secured with additional grates and grilles, dedicated guards and a separate reception. There was only one entrance and exit, which even the other officials in the building could not pass without being checked. Unlike the other divisions, Main Division III had its own chief, who was able to meet and communicate with Heydrich at any time without prior appointment.

Until the summer of 1935, the Chief of Main Division III was the seasoned *SD* man *SS-Standartenführer* and Senior Councillor Dr Patschowsky, who had previously been stationed in Breslau [Wrocław] and already under Dr Diels was the leader of the main division; later he would play a central role in Dr Diels' downfall. In order to placate the *Reichswehr* Ministry (whose officials had recommended him to Dr Diels against their better judgement) he had to be retired and was transferred to Upper Silesia where, in a new role as a Gestapa special commissioner, he carried out successful secret missions against Poland for the *SD-RFSS*. Later he was appointed chief of the newly established *SD* Senior District South East in Breslau [Wrocław].

In 1935, Patschowsky was succeeded as Chief of Main Division III by the Deputy Chief of the *SD-RFSS*, Dr Werner Best, who until that point had been Deputy Chief of the Bavarian Political Police in Munich. (Heydrich had officially remained as its chief, despite the fact that he had long since left Munich and was stationed in Berlin.)

As Chief of Main Division III, Dr Best at the same time became Deputy Chief of the Gestapa and leader of the "legal department".

The Deputy Chief of Main Division III was another seasoned administrative official, Councillor Damzog, whom Patschowsky had brought with him from Breslau [Wrocław]. Damzog had been a clandestine National Socialist and signed-up member of the NSDAP even before 1933, but was not a member of the *SD*.

The various subsections of Main Division III (counter-espionage and treason) dealt with cases of espionage directed at foreign nations and the espionage carried out by those nations. Naturally these subsections also engaged in first attempts at active civil espionage. Before describing the various subsections in greater detail, it is necessary for the sake of greater clarity to make the following explanatory remarks.

Treason and espionage in point of fact are one and the same thing; the only difference being the relationship between the person and the perpetrator. High treason, on the other hand, has nothing to do with espionage; it is the overthrowing of an existing government with violent means.

Treason consists in the betrayal of political, military or economic secrets, carried out by a German against Germany for the benefit of a foreign power.

Espionage consists in the reconnaissance of political, military or economic secrets, carried out by a foreign national in Germany, for the benefit of his own nation or that of a third power in whose service he is.

In general, treason is seen as highly dishonourable, as individuals betraying their mother countries usually act purely for their personal advantage and gain. (Under the Nazi regime a special type of treason was born, where the "traitor" might have acted on "idealistic" grounds.)

While espionage carried out by agents remunerated by a foreign power is also seen as dishonourable, it lacks the element of "betrayal of the motherland". A spy operating in a foreign land on behalf of his own nation often would be an honourable intelligence officer who had turned into a spy out of patriotism.

Until 1936 (and probably beyond), the various subsections of Main Division III who dealt with espionage and counter-espionage were:

Subdivision East: Poland, Russia, Hungary, and all nations of the Balkans, as well as the Far East.

Chief: Detective Superintendent Dr [Walter] Kubitzky (1891-1945), a long-serving, experienced specialist from Breslau [Wrocław], and recent recruit of the *SD-RFSS*.

The case officer for Poland, Czechoslovakia, Hungary and the Balkan nations was Detective Superintendent Dr [Kurt] Riedel, a young and relatively "proper" official, who had been a member of the NSDAP prior to 1933, but was not a member of the *SD*.

The case officer for Russia and the Far East was Detective Superintendent Fenner, a Baltic German, who as student under the Tsarist regime is said to have been active for the Okhrana (a secret-police force of the Russian Empire). He was considered an eminent specialist in all matters relating to the GPU (the Soviet intelligence service). An unpleasant careerist and busybody.

Subdivision West: France, Belgium, Holland, Luxembourg, England (including Scotland, but excluding Northern Ireland).

Chief: Detective Superintendent Gross (or Grohs?). A seasoned criminalist with much experience in the area of counter-intelligence, who played a role during the occupation of the Rhineland by the Allies (1923). Born in Rhineland, he was brought from Cologne to Berlin by Patschowsky. Not a party member.

The case officer for France was Detective Superintendent [Dr. Jur. Ludwig] Fischer, who had previously been an officer in a corps of volunteers. He was appointed to the Gestapa together with Detective

Superintendent Gross and was seen as an authority on the French *Deuxième Bureau.* A member of the NSDAP since 1932, but not a member of the *SD*.

Until 1935, Belgium, Holland and Luxembourg "provisionally" fell under the remit of Detective Superintendent Fischer. A special case officer was only appointed in 1935.

Detective Superintendent (later Gruppenführer) Dr. Jur. Ludwig Fischer (1905-1947, executed). In 1937 he was elected to the Reichstag. In 1939 he was appointed Chief Administrator (and in 1941 Governor) of the Warsaw District of occupied Poland. He established the Warsaw Ghetto and carried out mass executions of Jews and other horrendous acts of sadism and violence. He was hung for war crimes in Warsaw in 1947.

Until the spring of 1935, the Gestapa did not appoint a separate case officer for England-Scotland, as the British Isles fell under the remit of the Political Police in Hamburg. In February 1935 a dedicated case officer was appointed, despite the protestations made by the "Bureau Ribbentrop", where an envoy by the name of Raumer had reserved the portfolio for "England" for himself, including all matters relating to espionage and counter-espionage.

Subdivision Coast: States around the Baltic Sea, including Finland and Scandinavia and Denmark. At first handled by a clerk; a case officer with the rank of Detective Superintendent was appointed only in 1935.

Chief: Detective Superintendent Manns (or Manz / Mahns?), an individual from Northern Germany. He also functioned as "commissioned" case officer for Northern Ireland.

Subdivision Overseas: This was only relocated from Hamburg to the Gestapa in Berlin in 1936.

Subdivision South: Mediterranean nations, including Portugal. This was handled by the Bavarian Political Police (Chief: Heydrich; Deputy: Dr Best), and only relocated to Berlin in 1936.

Subdivision Industrial Espionage: Industrial espionage in major industrial enterprises, if there was no associated element of "betrayal of military secrets".

Chief: Dr [Johannes] Hans Schmidt, who was not a criminal investigator, but a prominent member of the *SD* and candidate for a senior civil service position (senior councillor). He had previously held the post of "Chief of Department I" (Information) in the *SD* Senior District East in Berlin, and already in the autumn of 1934 was seen as the presumptive successor of Councillor Damzog as the Deputy Chief of Main Division III. A young, dangerous, power-hungry Nazi official, who, as the murderer of General Schleicher, will be the topic of further discussion later.

III. Retrospective

Most emphatically: this is what the Secret State Police Office, the so-called Gestapa, looked like in the summer of 1934.

Each division had its special file references, which had the appearance of difficult problems of algebra. Each official was a letter, each case that needed to be processed was a number, subdivided into categories, arranged into a myriad of schemata. Heinrich Himmler's obsession with organisation reached truly orgiastic dimensions.

The segmentation of the *SS* into three so-called main offices has been detailed above: the *SS* Main Office of the active *SS* troops, whose chief was the notorious *SS-Obergruppenführer* [August] Heissmeyer, who would go on to become the Chief of the Gestapo in Norway; the Race and Settlement Main Office; and the SD Main Office, whose chief Reinhard Heydrich was killed in Prague and replaced by the Austrian Ernst Kaltenbrunner.

SS Lieutenant General (*Gruppenführer*) Ernst ("Fritz") Kaltenbrunner (1903-1946, executed), who succeeded Reinhard Heydrich, whose right hand man he had been, as Head of the SD Main Office, thus becoming Himmler's chief deputy. He was known as "the Gorilla", and his ruthless ferocity was just as terrifying as a gorilla looks (real gorillas, ironically, are not particularly violent). Kaltenbrunner was six feet seven inches (2 metres) tall, a lumbering fellow who moved awkwardly. He was an Austrian who joined the Nazi Party in Austria. As a student at the University of Vienna, he organised gangs to attack and murder Jewish students there and enjoyed throwing them down long stone steps and beating them to a pulp. He closest friends and colleagues were all violent thugs, two of whom were hanged for murdering the Austrian Chancellor Dolfuss. He assisted with the Anschluss in 1938, and the author got to know him intimately in Vienna in connection with those events, as he was Kaltenbrunner's superior and directed his role in that highly complex plot. Kaltenbrunner was then put in charge of the Austrian SS as a reward, and steadily moved up the ladder of promotion. He was a fanatical anti-Semite and advocated and assisted in the extermination of the Jews. He also had a hatred of homosexuality so intense that he advocated the forcible castration of all homosexual men. From May, 1942, Kaltenbrunner was the key organiser of Himmler and Martin Bormann's secret plans for a postwar Nazi International Underground, and he presided over the SS and SD's secret suburban outstation in Berlin at 11 Königsallee where all those preparations were carried out, the rat lines of escape were decided, the coordinating office in Madrid was set up, and support for future escaping SS men was arranged in Sweden, Spain, Argentina, Chile, and the other welcoming countries. Kaltenbrunner had vast files detailing every Nazi sympathiser in the United States, and he laid a lot of the groundwork for the exit of SS men to America after his own death, in the many operations such as Project Paperclip which secretly took thousands of SS men there against strict Presidential orders, giving them new identities and expunging their Nazi backgrounds from the official records. (An example was Baron Jesco von Puttkammer of NASA, 1933-2012; the fact that his father, also named Baron Jesco von Puttkammer, was a personal aide to Hitler was not publicly known.)

In order to complete the picture, it has to be mentioned that when Heinrich Himmler was appointed as Minister for the Interior (replacing Frick), he added two administrative *SS* main offices to the three existing "political" main offices, and in so doing transformed the *Reich* Ministry for the Interior into an *SS* stronghold:

SS Main Office for Budget and Construction, whose chief became *SS*-Gruppenführer and Undersecretary in the *Reich* Ministry for the Interior, Oswald Pohl.

SS Gruppenführer Oswald Ludwig Pohl (1892-1951, executed). He later oversaw the organisation of the concentration camps and devised the practice of extracting the gold from the teeth of the dead Jews, and selling it and their hair. He organised the "rental" of Jews for slave labour purposes and was one of the most passionate advocates and practicioners of genocide in the camps.

SS Main Economic Office, which was also led by *SS*-Gruppenführer [Oswald] Pohl, with *SS*-Brigadeführer [Fritz] Bracht [1899-1945, suicide] head of a section in the *Reich* Ministry for the Interior, acting as deputy.

These two new *SS* main offices were established in May 1939.

Of these men looking at a table model of a concentration camp, the man at right is SS Brigadeführer Fritz Bracht (1899-1945, suicide by cyanide), the deputy to Oswald Pohl. In 1944 he became Obergruppenführer and was Gauleiter (Governor) of Upper Silesia, a region which included Auschwitz. (Bundesarchiv)

When *Reichsführer SS* Heinrich Himmler, the Chief of the German Police, was appointed *Reich* Minister for the Interior, executive power was taken away from the ministries for the interior of each separate *Land* (Prussia, Bavaria, Saxony, Württemberg etc.) even on an administrative level and instead transferred to the *Reich* Ministry for the Interior in Berlin. A "central power" had been created. In effect, this central power had already come into existence with Himmler's move to Berlin and his installation as Inspector of the Gestapa, but initially only by virtue of the fact that Himmler-Heydrich had become the chiefs of every single police department in the various *Länder*. When Himmler was promoted to the position of Chief of the German Police, a *Reichspolizei* had been created and formalised for the first time. With Himmler's appointment as *Reich* Minister for the Interior, it was further unified and centralised on an administrative level, and the "incorporation" of the *SS* into the new police apparatus of the German *Reich* was completed. The *Gleichschaltung* (forcible co-ordination) had been accomplished. There still were the various *"Gaue"* (districts), but the *Gauleiter* and *Reich* governors were required by the party and by the state to ensure smooth implementation of the standardised uniformisation of the German people, and to follow the orders issued by the central authorities in Berlin to the letter. The originally "Prussian" Gestapo had become the *Reich's* stooge; the *SD-RFSS*, the "brain of the state and party", controlled the police; the entire police apparatus, whose role in the past it had been to maintain public order and safety on behalf of the judiciary, had become a terrible instrument of terror, which was wielded by vicious personified devils: the "protection squads" controlled by *Reichsführer* Heinrich Himmler.

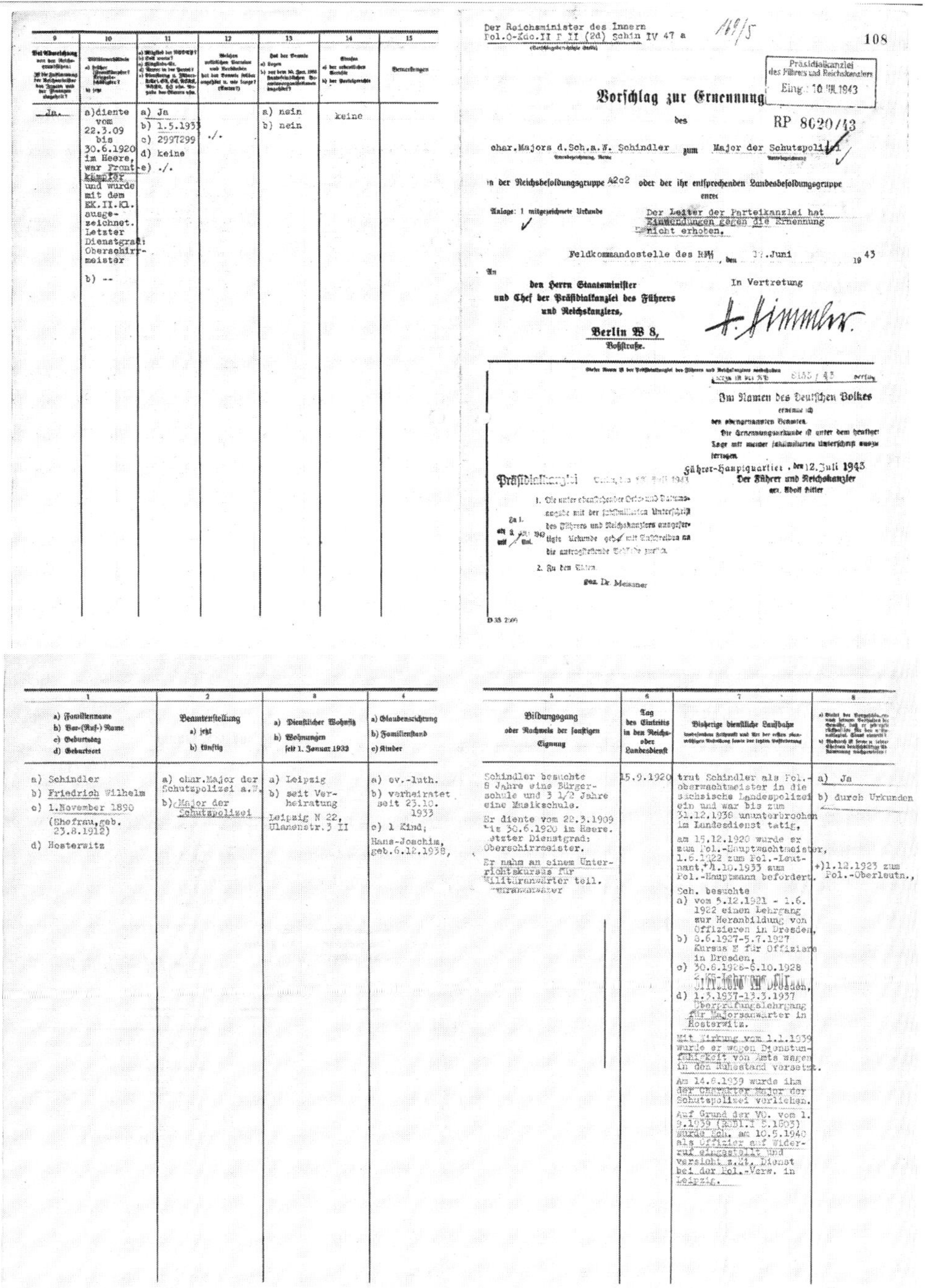

Der Reichsminister des Innern
Pol.O-Kdo.II F II (2d) Schin IV 47 a
149/5
108

Präsidialkanzlei des Führers und Reichskanzlers Eing.: 10 VII 1943

Vorschlag zur Ernennung

des

RP 8020/43

char.Majors d.Sch.a.W. Schindler zum Major der Schutzpolizei

in der Reichsbesoldungsgruppe A2c2 oder der ihr entsprechenden Landesbesoldungsgruppe

Anlage: 1 mitgezeichnete Urkunde

Der Leiter der Parteikanzlei hat Einwendungen gegen die Ernennung nicht erhoben.

Feldkommandostelle des RFSS, den 27.Juni 1943

An

den Herrn Staatsminister
und Chef der Präsidialkanzlei des Führers
und Reichskanzlers,

Berlin W 8,
Voßstraße.

In Vertretung
H. Himmler.

Im Namen des Deutschen Volkes
ernenne ich
den obengenannten Beamten.
Die Ernennungsurkunde ist unter dem heutigen Tage mit meiner faksimilierten Unterschrift auszufertigen.

Führer-Hauptquartier, den 12. Juli 1943
Der Führer und Reichskanzler
gez. Adolf Hitler

Präsidialkanzlei

1. Die unter obenstehender Orts- und Datumsangabe mit der faksimilierten Unterschrift des Führers und Reichskanzlers ausgefertigte Urkunde geht mit Zuschreiben an die antragstellende Behörde zurück.
2. Zu den Akten.

gez. Dr. Meissner

D 35 2/69

1	2	3	4
a) Familienname b) Vor-(Ruf-) Name c) Geburtstag d) Geburtsort	Beamtenstellung a) jetzt b) künftig	a) Dienstlicher Wohnsitz b) Wohnungen seit 1. Januar 1932	a) Glaubensrichtung b) Familienstand c) Kinder
a) Schindler b) Friedrich Wilhelm c) 1.November 1890 (Ehefrau,geb. 23.8.1912) d) Hosterwitz	a) char.Major der Schutzpolizei a.W. b) Major der Schutzpolizei	a) Leipzig b) seit Verheiratung Leipzig N 22, Ulanenstr.3 II	a) ev.-luth. b) verheiratet seit 23.10. 1933 c) 1 Kind; Hans-Joachim, geb.6.12.1938,

5	6	7	8
Bildungsgang oder Nachweis der sonstigen Eignung	Tag des Eintritts in den Reichs- oder Landesdienst	Bisherige dienstliche Laufbahn	
Schindler besuchte 8 Jahre eine Bürgerschule und 3 1/2 Jahre eine Musikschule. Er diente vom 22.3.1909 bis 30.6.1920 im Heere. Letzter Dienstgrad: Oberschirrmeister. Er nahm an einem Unterrichtskursus für Militäranwärter teil.	15.9.1920	trat Schindler als Pol.-Oberwachtmeister in die sächsische Landespolizei ein und war bis zum 31.12.1938 ununterbrochen im Landesdienst tätig. am 15.12.1920 wurde er zum Pol.-Hauptwachtmeister, 1.6.1922 zum Pol.-Leutnant,+) 1.10.1933 zum Pol.-Hauptmann befördert. Sch. besuchte a) vom 5.12.1921 - 1.6. 1922 einen Lehrgang zur Heranbildung von Offizieren in Dresden, b) 8.6.1927-5.7.1927 Kursus E für Offiziere in Dresden, c) 30.8.1928-6.10.1928 2.KS-Lehrgang für Offiziere in Dresden, d) 1.3.1937-13.3.1937 Überprüfungslehrgang für Majorsanwärter in Hosterwitz. Mit Wirkung vom 1.1.1939 wurde er wegen Dienstunfähigkeit von Amts wegen in den Ruhestand versetzt. Am 14.8.1939 wurde ihm der Charakter Major der Schutzpolizei verliehen. Auf Grund der VO. vom 1.9.1939 (RGBl.I S.1603) wurde Sch. am 10.5.1940 als Offizier auf Widerruf eingestellt und versieht z.Zt. Dienst bei der Pol.-Verw. in Leipzig.	a) Ja b) durch Urkunden +) 1.12.1923 zum Pol.-Oberleutn.,

9	10	11	12	13	14	15
	Militärverhältnis a) früher b) jetzt	a) Mitglied der NSDAP? b) Seit wann? c) Mitglieds-Nr. d) Ämter in der Partei? e) ...	Welchen politischen Parteien und Verbänden hat der Beamte früher angehört u. wie lange?	Hat der Beamte a) Logen b) ... angehört?	Strafen a) der ordentlichen Gerichte b) der Parteigerichte	Bemerkungen
Ja.	a) diente vom 22.3.09 bis 30.6.1920 im Heere, war Frontkämpfer und wurde mit dem EK.II.Kl. ausgezeichnet. Letzter Dienstgrad: Oberschirrmeister b) --	a) Ja b) 1.5.1933 c) 2997299 d) keine e) ./.	./.	a) nein b) nein	keine	

An official document in the Eglantyne Collection signed by Heinrich Himmler. Although Himmler did not formally replace Dr. Wilhelm Frick as Minister of the Interior until August 1943, we see here clear evidence that he was acting as Minister of the Interior when he signed the above document on June 27, 1943. He qualified his signature with the words "*In Vertretung*", which means "by proxy" or "as representative of" the Minister. So he had clearly taken over the Ministry weeks before his official appointment was documented, and Frick was already kicked out. This document is entitled "Recommendation for Appointment" and concerns a police officer of the Protection Service named Friedrich Wilhelm Schindler (born November 1, 1890, at Hosterwitz). Another important detail about this document is that it embodies a subsidiary document dated July 12, 1943, which is stampted "*gez. Dr. Meissner*". *Gez.* Is an abbreviation for *gezeichnet* and means "signed by". The signatory was Dr. Otto Lebrecht Eduard Daniel Meissner (1880–1953) in his role as Head of the Office of the President, as may be seen because the document is from the Führer's Headquarters. So Himmler as merely Acting Minister had sent his document through to Meissner for Hitler's approval, in order to make his act official.

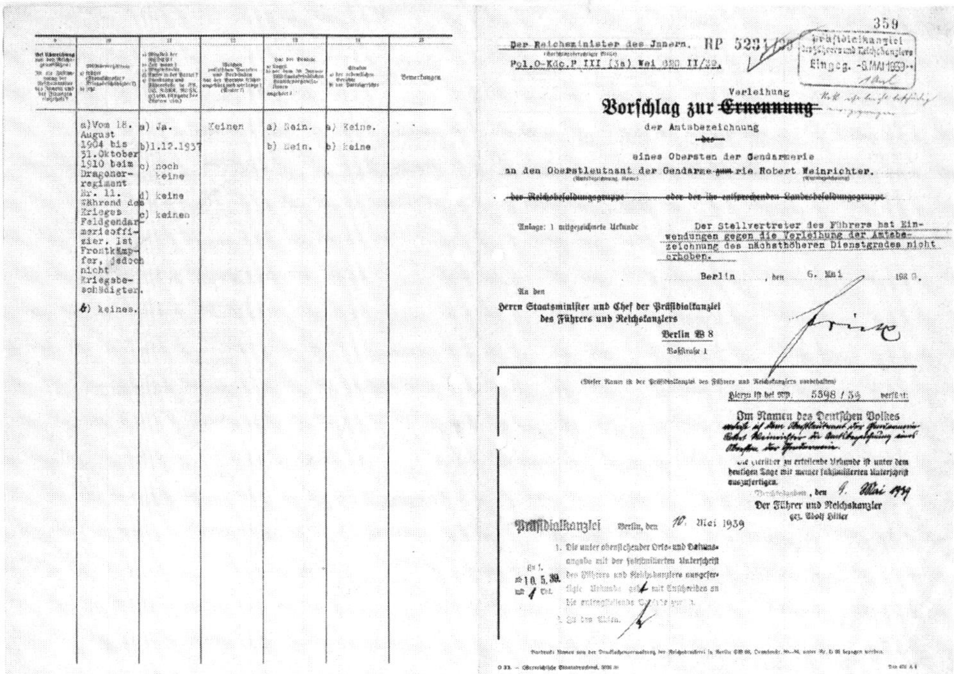

359

Der Reichsminister des Innern. RP 5231/39
Pol.O-Kdo.P III (3a) Wei 820 II/39.

Präsidialkanzlei des Führers und Reichskanzlers
Eingeg. -8.MAI 1939-

Verleihung
Vorschlag zur ~~Ernennung~~
der Amtsbezeichnung
~~der~~
eines Obersten der Gendarmerie
an den Oberstleutnant der Gendarmerie Robert Weinrichter.

~~der Reichsbesoldungsgruppe oder der ihr entsprechenden Landesbesoldungsgruppe~~

Anlage: 1 mitgezeichnete Urkunde

Der Stellvertreter des Führers hat Einwendungen gegen die Verleihung der Amtsbezeichnung des nächsthöheren Dienstgrades nicht erhoben.

Berlin, den 6. Mai 1939.

An den
Herrn Staatsminister und Chef der Präsidialkanzlei des Führers und Reichskanzlers
Berlin W 8
Voßstraße 1

Frick

(Dieser Raum ist der Präsidialkanzlei des Führers und Reichskanzlers vorbehalten)

Hierzu ist bei RP. 5398 / 39 verfügt:

Im Namen des Deutschen Volkes

Die hierüber zu erteilende Urkunde ist unter dem heutigen Tage mit meiner faksimilierten Unterschrift auszufertigen.

, den 9. Mai 1939
Der Führer und Reichskanzler
gez. Adolf Hitler

Präsidialkanzlei Berlin, den 10. Mai 1939

1. Die unter obenstehender Orts- und Datumsangabe mit der faksimilierten Unterschrift des Führers und Reichskanzlers ausgefertigte Urkunde geht mit Anschreiben an die antragstellende Behörde zurück.

10. 5. 39.

2. Zu den Akten.

a) Von 18. August 1904 bis 31. Oktober 1910 beim Dragonerregiment Nr. 11. Während des Krieges Feldgendarmerieoffizier. Ist Frontkämpfer, jedoch nicht Kriegsbeschädigter. b) keines.	a) Ja. b) 1.12.1937 c) noch keine d) keine e) keinen	Keinen	a) Nein. b) Nein.	a) Keine. b) keine	Bemerkungen

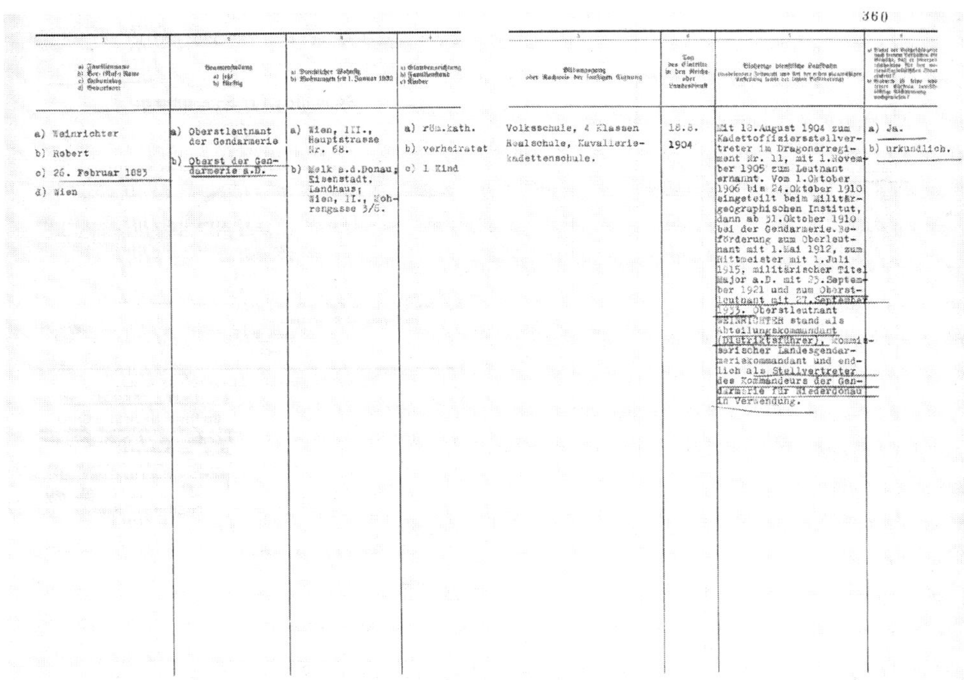

360

a) Familienname b) Vor- (Ruf-) Name c) Geburtstag d) Geburtsort	Beamtenstellung a) jetzt b) künftig	a) Dienstlicher Wohnsitz b) Wohnungen seit 1. Januar 1932	a) Glaubensrichtung b) Familienstand c) Kinder	Bildungsgang oder Nachweis der sonstigen Eignung	Tag des Eintritts in den Reichs- oder Landesdienst	Bisherige dienstliche Laufbahn	
a) Weinrichter b) Robert c) 26. Februar 1883 d) Wien	a) Oberstleutnant der Gendarmerie b) Oberst der Gendarmerie a.D.	a) Wien, III., Hauptstrasse Nr. 68. b) Melk a.d.Donau; Eisenstadt, Landhaus; Wien, II., Mohrengasse 3/8.	a) röm.kath. b) verheiratet c) 1 Kind	Volksschule, 4 Klassen Realschule, Kavalleriekadettenschule.	18.8. 1904	Mit 18.August 1904 zum Kadettoffiziersstellvertreter im Dragonerregiment Nr. 11, mit 1.November 1905 zum Leutnant ernannt. Vom 1.Oktober 1906 bis 24.Oktober 1910 eingeteilt beim Militärgeographischen Institut, dann ab 31.Oktober 1910 bei der Gendarmerie. Beförderung zum Oberleutnant mit 1.Mai 1912, zum Rittmeister mit 1.Juli 1915, militärischer Titel Major a.D. mit 23.September 1921 und zum Oberstleutnant mit 27.September 1933. Oberstleutnant WEINRICHTER stand als Abteilungskommandant (Distriktsführer), kommissarischer Landesgendarmeriekommandant und endlich als Stellvertreter des Kommandeurs der Gendarmerie für Niederdonau in Verwendung.	a) Ja. b) urkundlich.

In comparison with the Himmler document, we see here a document in the Eglantyne Collection signed by the previous Minister of the Interior, Dr. Wilhelm Frick, on May 9, 1939. This document is entitled "Recommendation for an Award" and concerns Robert Weinrichter (born February 26, 1883, at Vienna), who is a Lieutenant Colonel of the Austrian Gendarmes living in Vienna, and who is being promoted to full Colonel. (It is noted that he is a Roman Catholic. This somewhat older man, aged 54, is noted as having served in the Austrian Dragoons from 1904 to 1910 and then acted as an officer of the military police in the First World War.)

PART ONE

THE SYSTEM

THE FACTORS OF POWER

C. THE CONCENTRATION CAMPS

PREFACE

It is no coincidence that the most stirring literary works on the last Great War (1914-18) could only be written several years after the end of that war. The writers themselves had to deal with all the horror, misery and suffering they had lived through and had to come to terms with the terrible events they had witnessed, before being able to relate them in a coherent fashion to the wider public. It took many sleepless and troubled nights before Freiherr Vieth von der Golssenau (better known under his literary pseudonym Ludwig Renn) was able to complete the manuscript for his book "*War*"; and Erich Maria Remarque, a.k.a. Kramer, again and again reached for the brandy bottle in order to find some sleep and oblivion after writing down a few pages of his work "*All Quiet on the Western Front*".

It is the author's opinion that providing a report on the concentration camps is even more difficult than writing about one's experiences of war. How can it be possible to write about the cruellest atrocities, the most repulsive perversions, the most terrible suffering and the most satanic methods of torture in the concentration camps, without turning the manuscript into an abhorrent and sickening document?

One's own experiences are now several years in the past. And yet the hand falters and the head flounders with any attempt to recount the experiences in the concentration camps. It requires the utmost willpower to remain calm and objective, and the deepest concentration to be able to produce a sober report on the facts, and to resist sliding into emotional narrative exuberance and delivering mere accusatory and inculpating judgement. Despite all the atrocities of war and Nazi terror, a report on the concentration camps will – to this day – seem inconceivable and therefore incredible to many German readers. To any genuine doubters we say this: anything and everything that you have heard about the conditions, the murdering and the barbarous torturing in the concentration camps is true, and in fact is only ever a small fraction and snippet of what actually happened! To non-German readers, on the other hand, we emphatically say this: the Nazis first tested and perfected their methods of torture on honest, oppositional Germans, before inflicting them on members of other nationalities. Hundreds, thousands, tens of thousands of Germans were dragged into the concentration camps and were tortured and murdered there, before Jews, Czechs, Poles, Russians, the Dutch, Belgians, the French, Norwegians, Danes and whoever else were sent to the camps. The screams of terror and cries for help uttered by Germans fell on deaf ears abroad; foreign statesmen, diplomats and government officials did not care a jot. But today, after the Nazis' evils have been laid bare in front of the whole world, some voices abroad dare to declare: "There is and never has been a German opposition to National Socialism!" Or, even more fatuous: "The entire German nation is guilty!"

May our report on the concentration camps turn out to be a sober one. Like all other reports in this book, it is intended to be a report on the facts. In putting aside one's own personal experience, it is an attempt to portray the satanic organisation for what it was. We do not want to provide a brief extract from one particular concentration camp, but instead will give a brief sketch, including an historical account of the development of the concentration camps.

I. The origin of the concentration camps
The establishment of the first "official" concentration camp

In the earlier chapter on the foundation of the Secret State Police, an account was given of the events following January 30, 1933, the day of the "seizure of power", when countless Nazi opponents were arbitrarily abducted by local *SA* and *SS* units. These victims of the *SA* and

SS were mostly taken to the local haunts of the various storm trooper units, that is to say to public taverns or inns. This is where the mistreatment and torture of the first days of the Nazi regime took place. In order not to "alarm" the local residents, the captured political opponents were dragged into basements or isolated outbuildings, but in larger cities the victims' cries could still be heard even from those remote places. Therefore "orders" were given to use derelict warehouses or factory buildings wherever possible as locations for "dealing with the enemy". For example, on the outskirts of Berlin, near the little town of Oranienburg, a derelict factory that had fallen out of use years ago was found for this purpose; in Hamburg the *SA* requisitioned a disused warehouse near the Chaussee Hamburg-Elshorn; and the *SS* in Munich set up camp in disused barracks in a gravel pit in the immediate vicinity of Dachau. However, these were not yet actual "concentration camps", but rather private interrogation sites, where political opponents were beaten with truncheons, tortured with pliers and irons, and occasionally wounded or murdered by being shot. Eventually, the Political Police run by *Reichsführer SS* Heinrich Himmler was established in all German regions, except in Prussia, where until the end of March 1934 Dr Diels' Secret State Police was "operating" as the highest federal authority, without the involvement of the *SS*. The Political Police took note of the "interrogations" carried out by the *SA* and *SS* and, as there was insufficient space in the available police prisons to accommodate political prisoners, the Political Police "officially" handed over their "less serious" cases to the *SA* and *SS* for detention and "processing". The Secret State Police Office in Berlin took its first detainees to Oranienburg and handed them over to the *SA* for "custody" in a dilapidated factory building, which afforded almost no protection against wind and weather. However, the first detention camp that was under the direct and exclusive authority of the Political Police and carried the official designation "concentration camp" (*"Konzentrationslager"*, abbreviated to *KZ*) was not located in Oranienburg but was to be established in Dachau.

Until April 1934, *Reichsführer SS* Heinrich Himmler and his *SD*-chief Reinhard Heydrich were headquartered in Munich. At the Wittelsbacher Palais, Himmler acted as Chief of the Political Police forces of all *Länder* (except Prussia), while Heydrich was Chief of the Bavarian Political Police. (The Wittelsbacher Palais would continue to function as the headquarters of the Political Police in Munich beyond April 1934.) The satanic genius Heydrich was the first to recognise the police forces' need for dedicated concentration camps. He prevailed upon *Reichsführer SS* Himmler to task *SS-Obersturmbannführer* Eicke (who had fled from Ludwigshafen to Munich!) with the establishment of the concentration camp Dachau. Eicke was promoted to the rank of *SS-Standartenführer* and was put in charge of the newly assembled *SS-Totenkopfstandarte* (literally "skull regiment"). With the exception of Adolf Hitler's *Leibstandarte* (body guard), this *SS-Totenkopfstandarte* was the first professional *SS Polizeiverfügungstruppe* (police dispositional troop) whose members received a fixed salary.

At the time of the "assumption of power", Munich was home to an ever-growing number of political fugitives, who, being displaced from their homes and unemployed, had been a financial burden on the NSDAP for some time. They were the Austrian "legionaries", an illegal grouping of violent and marauding Austrian individuals who had only been able to escape Chancellor Dollfuss's energetic grasp and imprisonment in Austria by quickly crossing the border into the *Reich*; rough, coarse and burly youths who in the main hailed from Tyrol. They had hung around Munich and its vicinity, and then had been incorporated into the Munich branch of the *SS*, where, in the months leading up to the "takeover", they had been the rowdiest hooligans at the NSDAP's party events. Now, these former "legionaries" were again pulled out of the local *SS* branches and, using them and other unemployed *SS* men from Munich, a completely new type of *SS* unit was created: the *SS-Totenkopfstandarte*!

The chosen site for the base of the *SS-Totenkopfstandarte* was —— the gravel pit in Dachau with its disused barracks! The *SS-Totenkopfstandarte* became the first state-run *SS* dispositional police unit, and as such was an inherent part of the Bavarian Political Police. Its members' wages were paid by the Bavarian Ministry for the Interior, much like those of every policeman and police official. The tasks assigned to that new police unit were, on the one hand, the custody of the Bavarian Political Police's *Schutzhäftlinge* (literally "protective custody prisoners"), and, on the other, the construction and expansion of the gravel pit Dachau into the police force's first "concentration camp for *Schutzhäftlinge*".

"*KZ* Dachau" had been founded – the first official concentration camp in the entire *Reich*. It was used by no means exclusively by the state of Bavaria; to begin with, the *SD-RFSS* hauled all of "its" detainees into the new *KZ* Dachau. During the course of the year 1933, the *SD-RFSS* brought its victims from Berlin, Hamburg, Königsberg [Kaliningrad], Breslau [Wrocław] and Kiel, from the Rhineland and from all over Southern Germany to Dachau, sometimes openly, sometimes secretly. (It was done secretly when the *SD-RFSS* thought that it had to evade the grasp of the Secret State Police Office, the "highest authority in the state of Prussia", that is to say, Göring and Dr Diels. Until the end of March 1934, the most frenzied manhunts took place in the state of Prussia, with one "hunter" trying to snatch the "prey" from another. While the Bavarian Political Police – in its capacity as state executive and thanks to Reinhard Heydrich's dual leadership role – backed all operations carried out by the *SD-RFSS*, there was a certain amount of inter-regional rivalry between the Secret State Police Office in Berlin and the Bavarian Political Police. This was eclipsed, however, by the often much more ferocious disputes over authority between Hermann Göring's body guard, the so-called *"Feldpolizei"*, and the *SD-RFSS*.)

While in other concentration camps (which were at first less "official") just as much torturing and just as many brutal beatings and murders took place as in *KZ* Dachau, that place Dachau was to become the embodiment of Nazi terror. Indeed, *KZ* Dachau was the point of origin of a diabolical system of torture and maltreatment, and it became a testing ground for elaborate methods of torture, "organised" down to the last detail. *KZ* Dachau became a "model camp", along the lines of which similar concentration camps were soon established and "nationalised" all over the *Reich* territory. The *SS-Totenkopfstandarte* was the slave keeper installed by the state. The slaves, whose official designation was *"Schutzhäftlinge"*, had to repair barracks, erect shelters and workshops, and work until they dropped to build grand houses and villas, in which the most senior *SS* leaders would take up permanent residence. The gravel pit Dachau was turned into the first "*SS* town", whose constructors were kept strictly isolated in remote barracks in worse conditions than filthy cattle.

As was mentioned in an earlier chapter, the detainees in the concentration camps were political opponents of National Socialism, who either could not be convicted by an ordinary court due to a complete lack of factual evidence, or were those who had served a sentence and had been released from prison, immediately to be taken into "protective custody" and sent to a concentration camp. "Protective custody" was imposed "for personal protection from anger of the people"! That, in any case, was the "legal justification" that had been given in 1933 to the aged *Reichspräsident* von Hindenburg. It goes without saying that the "anger of the people" was nothing more than the anger of the party – especially that of the *SA* and *SS* – directed at political opponents. Eventually the NSDAP introduced into the law the notion of "re-education" for the "protection of the people and the state". We shall investigate at a later point how such "re-education" was carried out in the concentration camps.

The commander of the *SS-Totenkopfstandarte*

The actual "founder" of the concentration camps was neither Himmler nor Eicke, but – in so far as he had been the originator of the idea of police-run concentration camps – *SS-Brigadeführer* Reinhard Heydrich: the satanic Chief of the *SD-RFSS* and, at that time, still the Chief of the Bavarian Political Police; later Chief of the Secret State Police Office in Berlin; Chief of the Security Police in the entire *Reich*; and eventually Deputy *Reichsprotektor* of Bohemia and Moravia, as well as *SS-Gruppenführer* and later *SS-Obergruppenführer*; and, on top of all that, until his death in Prague, Chief of the *SD-RFSS*. However, at this point we shall refer to the Commander of the *SS-Totenkopfstandarte*, [Theodor] Eicke, as the "founder of the *KZ* Dachau", for it was he who, in line with orders and directives given by Himmler-Heydrich, established and constituted *KZ* Dachau and was in charge of the organisation of the "supervision of the detainees".

SS Obergruppenführer Theodor Eicke (1892-1943). He was head of the especially vicious Totenkopf ("skull") Division of the Waffen-SS. He later became Commandant of Dachau Concentration Camp as well as being named Inspector of the Concentration Camps, so that he supervised eight of of them.

An unknown Rifleman from the Third Elite Division of the Totenkopf ("skull") force, serving under Theodor Eicke. This photo is to show the insignia of the skull worn by these troops, which here is clearly seen on his collar. The soldiers were very proud to wear the sign of the skull, to boast of their ferocity and that they were elite.

In 1934, after paying a visit to *KZ* Dachau, an American lady who was stationed in Berlin as an officially accredited foreign correspondent for an American newspaper composed a multicolumn report of stirring prose, in which she praised the "order, discipline and cleanliness" and the "perhaps harsh, but always fair treatment of the detainees". She was particularly "enchanted" with the courtesy afforded to her by Commander Eicke, who took it upon himself to personally show her around and to "demonstrate and clearly explain all the camp's facilities in minute detail". The American journalist wrote: "Herr Eicke is a charming personality with a profound sense of responsibility for the detainees in his care, who safeguards strong discipline amongst the prison guards." This report was published in a major American newspaper in the spring of 1934 and was reprinted by several magazines and by many outlets of the foreign press. On the basis of such an "authentic" report authored by a highly reputable and "neutral" journalist, the entire world's conscience was able to fall into a tranquil slumber. It was a time of paranoia regarding Bolshevism and fear of labour unrest in Europe, where "discipline and cleanliness" and "calm and orderliness" were equated with "lawfulness and justice". Former Communist leaders were paraded like tamed wild animals and the most beastly Nazi terrorists were praised as the heroic guardians and protectors of civic order; by no means only in Germany itself, but also, to no less a degree, abroad.

Who, then, was this "charming and gracious" Herr Eicke, commander of the first official concentration camp in Dachau and head of the newly established *SS-Totenkopfstandarte*? At the time of the "seizure of power" on January 30, 1933, Eicke held the rank of *SS-Obersturmbannführer* in Ludwigshafen am Rhein and led the *SS-Sturmbann* Ludwigshafen of the 10th *SS-Standarte* under the leadership of *SS-Standartenführer* [Willy, or Willi] Schmelcher in Neustadt a.d. Hardt. The 10th *SS-Standarte* was the only *SS* unit in the entire governmental district of Bavaria and the *Gau* of Rhenish Palatinate where the "red" *Gauleiter* Josef Bürckel had assumed absolute power after Hitler's takeover of government. *SS-Standartenführer* Schmelcher was a loyal factotum to *Gauleiter* Bürckel, who, much to the chagrin of *Reichsführer SS* Heinrich Himmler, unduly claimed authority over the *SS-Standarte* of his *Gau*. Due to his friendship with Robert Ley, *Gauleiter* Bürckel enjoyed the special patronage not only of Rudolf Hess, but indirectly also that of *Reich* Chancellor Adolf Hitler, and was therefore untouchable to Himmler-Heydrich in Munich. Instead, they had to grin and bear Bürckel's all-too-often (for them) rather unpleasant manoeuvres.

Here Himmler, with his arm raised, is reviewing some SS troops. The man in the civilian suit is Gauleiter Josef Bürckel, the tall man behind his right shoulder is Reinhard Heydrich, and the next man, standing in profile, is Bürckel's loyal supporter, SS Standartenführer Willy (or Willi) Schmelcher (born 1894), who at this time was President of Police for Saarbrucken. (The officer standing at rear after Schmelcher was named Prützmann, and he is not mentioned by our author.) This photo was taken in the Saarland in 1937 or 1938. The author knew both Bürckel and Schmelcher intimately from his earlier time in the Saarland.

SS-Sturmbannführer [Georg] Kemmet (1893-1969), the adjutant of the 10th *SS-Standarte*, occupied a position of particular intimacy with *Gauleiter* Josef Bürckel. An old drinking buddy of Bürckel's, he was a former foreman in the "I.G. Farbenindustrie" (a chemical and pharmaceutical conglomerate) in Ludwigshafen, but had lost his job in 1929 due to his National Socialist activities. Nevertheless, Kemmet was held in some esteem by the workers in Ludwigshafen, in complete contrast to the overbearing Eicke, who, with his *Sturmbann*, was the responsible *SS* leader for Ludwigshafen.

In the first days of February 1933 the workers in Ludwigshafen witnessed a strange spectacle. At the behest of *Gauleiter* Bürckel, the adjutant of the 10th *SS Standarte* appeared in front of a group of former Social Democratic union leaders in order to negotiate the "handing over" of the Social Democratic party press and the existing printing works of *"Vorwärts"*, a Social Democratic newspaper published in Ludwigshafen. The leadership of the *Gau*

Rhenish Palatinate had given assurances that the existing printing works would be allowed to continue to operate and that the workforce would be kept on, if they agreed to "hand over" their workshops to the *Gauleiter*, and to transform the Social Democratic publication into a National Socialist mouthpiece. Kemmet's negotiations were in full swing, when suddenly *Obersturmbannführer* Eicke appeared with his *SS-Sturmbann* and demanded the immediate detainment of the Social Democratic party officials and the dismissal without notice of all Social Democratic members of the workforce – in stark contrast to the "negotiations" conducted by the adjutant of the *SS-Standarte* and the *Gauleiter's* representative, *SS-Sturmbannführer* Kemmet. The Social Democratic workforce witnessed the most exquisitely tragicomic scenes between *SS-Obersturmbannführer* Eicke and *SS-Sturmbannführer* Kemmet, which eventually ended in a physical fight. In the end, the *Gauleiter*, who had been informed of the altercation on the phone by Kemmet, had to deploy the local police in Ludwigshafen – who, under the leadership of Police Captain Buchmann, turned up in three tanks! – in order to separate the two fighting cocks Eicke and Kemmet, and to enforce his will (which had been expressed by Kemmet) on the furious *SS-Obersturmbannführer* Eicke. Eicke and "his men" were "routed out", Eicke had to immediately leave the area of the *Gau* Rhenish Palatinate, and Bürckel imposed permanent banishment from the *Land* on the recalcitrant *SS* leader. Eicke, however, went immediately to Munich in order to lodge a complaint against Kemmet and Bürckel with the *Reichsführer SS*, claiming that all he had wanted to do was to execute Heinrich Himmler's "orders", which in turn, according to Eicke, had been sabotaged by Kemmet and his *Gauleiter*. Given the power constellations at the time, the *Reichsführer SS* was not in a position to challenge the "red" *Gauleiter* Josef Bürckel in any way whatsoever, and therefore had to, as it were, consign the 10th *SS-Standarte* to its fate, namely to be a useful tool for the sole use of *Gauleiter* Bürckel. Neither was it possible for Himmler to reprimand *SS-Sturmbannführer* Kemmet or *SS-Standartenführer* Schmelcher, but he would ensure that neither *SS* leader was promoted for years to come after the incident. As far as *SS-Obersturmbannführer* Eicke was concerned, Himmler saw no other option than to take under his wings the man who had come running to him, if only to signal some form of protest. While Eicke would not be able to set foot in the *Gau* of Rhenish Palatinate (as it turned out, until 1938!), he was rewarded by Himmler for his unconditional loyalty to the *SS* leadership with a promotion to the rank of *SS-Standartenführer*.

At the suggestion of the Chief of the *SD-RFSS* and Chief of the Bavarian Political Police, Reinhard Heydrich, *SS-Standartenführer* Eicke was appointed as the first commander of the newly established *SS-Totenkopfstandarte* and the first commander of the concentration camp Dachau. Heydrich had seen clearly that party leaders who had fallen out with their local party branches – and especially with a *Gauleiter*, who wielded almost absolute authority in his territory – would make the most useful (i.e. compliant and submissive) *SS* leaders. Along similar lines, Heydrich would soon bring Dr Werner Best – who had fought a bitter but ultimately futile fight against the *Gauleiter* of Hesse, Jakob Sprenger – into his inner circle and appoint him as Deputy Chief of the Bavarian Police. Dr Best was an intelligent man and a sly fox and would not only become a close ally of Heydrich's, but eventually rise to the position of Deputy Chief of the *SD-RFSS* and, during the war, Plenipotentiary for Denmark in Copenhagen. Eicke, on the other hand, remained "only" a general employee of the *SD-RFSS* and the incumbent police chief. He was not even worthy of membership of the *SD-RFSS*, and even as Commander of the *SS-Totenkopfstandarte* (which had in the meantime grown into a full-blown army corps) and being remunerated by the *Wehrmacht* according to the rank of a general, in the *SS* hierarchy he remained one rank below that of the Chief of the *SD*, who was his superior and responsible official.

The office of "Inspector of the Concentration Camps"

When Himmler-Heydrich arrived in Berlin in March 1934, took over the Secret State Police Office Berlin, and created a Secret State Police with competency for the entire territory of the German *Reich*, they did not forget about Herr Eicke, now *SS-Brigadeführer* and Commander of the *SS-Totenkopfstandarte*. He, amongst others, was summoned to Berlin, where in the autumn of 1934 the office of "Inspector of the Concentration Camps" was created. In the same way that Himmler had created for himself the title of "Inspector of the Secret State Police" and thereby had become its highest chief, the first commander of *KZ* Dachau – in his new capacity as "Inspector of the Concentration Camps" – assumed the role of chief of all concentration camps in Germany. It is important to note, however, that this newly appointed "Inspector" was more dependent than ever on the Chief of the *SD*, Heydrich, in his capacity as leader of the Secret State Police. The office of Inspector of the Concentration Camps was an administrative one, a kind of inspection body. Under no circumstances would the Inspector of the Concentration Camps have been able to order the release of a detainee in one of the concentration camps; only the Secret State Police had that authority. But, together with his camp commanders, he was allowed, at his discretion, to torment, torture, beat to death or "shoot during attempted escapes" the detainees, knowing that such "treatment" would be entirely consistent with Himmler-Heydrich's intentions, knowing that he was acting "according to the orders". Yet to make the judgement to release a prisoner was beyond the authority of camp commanders, and even the Inspector of the Concentration Camps himself. The Inspector's subordination to the Chief of the Secret State Police was given further outward expression by assigning him only a small number of rooms on the ground floor of the premises of the Secret State Police Office in Berlin, Prinz-Albrecht-Strasse 7, and also by the fact that it was not Herr Eicke who was put in charge of the Protective Custody Department in that building, but instead some detective superintendent, who was directly answerable to the "Chief", the leader of the *SD*, Heydrich.

Even when Eicke had been made Inspector of the Concentration Camps, he remained Commander of the *SS-Totenkopf* units. The *SS-Totenkopfstandarte*, with a capacity similar to that of an infantry regiment, had grown into an *SS* dispositional police force, the so-called "*SS-Totenkopfverbände*", which had a capacity similar to that of an infantry division. The official function of that police unit continued to be the guarding of the concentration camps. The command offices were relocated from Dachau to Oranienburg near Berlin; in other words, the "*SS* town" that had sprung up on the outskirts of little Oranienburg became the staff headquarters of the *SS-Totenkopfverbände*. In the same way that –despite his dual roles as Chief of the Secret State Police Office and Chief of the *SD-RFSS* – Heydrich insisted on meticulous separation of the two offices, the offices of the "Inspectorate of the Concentration Camps" and the "Command of the *SS-Totenkopfverbände*" were strictly separated, according to Eicke's dual roles there.

As far as Himmler-Heydrich were concerned, Inspector Eicke would guarantee that all concentration camps, which were now controlled by the state, would be established and "run" according to the *KZ* Dachau blueprint. Only men who had been schooled as *SS-Führer* in KZ Dachau and had proven themselves to be "suitably energetic" would be eligible to become commander of one of the other concentration camps.

When he assumed office, the Inspector of the Concentration Camps in the Secret State Police Office in Berlin took over eight concentration camps. The following camps had been established as state-run institutions by the autumn of 1934, when the Office of the Inspector of the Concentration Camps took over their administration and running:

1. *KZ* Dachau, then with "facilities" for approx. 10,000 detainees;

2. *KZ* Sachsenhausen near Oranienburg, then with "facilities" for "only" approx. 8–10,000 detainees;

3. *KZ* Papenburg near the Dutch border, together with the labour camps Esterwege, Neu-Sustrum, Boergermoor and Aschendorf, where as early as autumn 1934 a total of more than 15,000 detainees were forced to labour in the marshes;

4. *KZ* Fuhlsbüttel near Hamburg, where at that time approx. 4–5,000 individuals were detained;

5. *KZ* Lichtenburg in Silesia, then with "facilities" for approx. 3,000 detainees;

6. *KZ* Buchenwald, at that time still a relatively small (i.e. "normal-sized") camp where approx. 4,000 individuals were detained;

7. *KZ* Moringen in the Ruhr region, with "facilities" for approx. 3,000 detainees, dismantled in 1937/38;

8. *KZ* Columbiahaus in Berlin, the former military prison of the Berlin garrison, where approx. 180–200 individuals were detained.

These were the eight concentration camps that Inspector Eicke inherited when he took office. In total, therefore, he "took over" at least 47,000 detainees, for whose "welfare" or otherwise he was responsible!

It must be made clear again that the figures given above for the numbers of detainees in the eight concentration camps are only accurate at the point at which the Inspector of the Concentration Camps took office, that is to say in the autumn of 1934. Over the course of the following years a large number of other concentration camps were established in Germany, especially after the *Anschluss* (annexation) of Austria, Bohemia and Moravia and the "re-integration into the *Reich*" of Danzig [Gdansk] and Warthegau (the Polish province of Posen [Poznań]). Furthermore, after only a few months' activities by Inspector Eicke (or rather, by Himmler-Heydrich, in their capacity as the responsible police chiefs), the existing concentration camps were expanded. For instance, after the pogroms of November 1938, *KZ* Buchenwald was designated as a "camp for Jews" and its capacity expanded to 30,000 and later even 40,000. At the outbreak of war in 1939, *KZ* Sachsenhausen housed 20,000 detainees, *KZ* Lichtenburg "only" 8,000 and so on and so forth…

KZ Columbiahaus occupied a special position insofar as it was not an actual camp, but rather a sort of remand centre for the Secret State Police Office, which until 1938, at its premises in the Prinz-Albrecht-Strasse, had available only 12 single cells, which were in addition to a small (and also insufficient) number of cells belonging to the police prison on Alexanderplatz. *KZ* Columbiahaus was a veritable labyrinth of prison cells, which was demolished in 1938 during the course of the expansion of the airport Tempelhof.

II. The treatment of the detainees
The guards

In the World War of 1914–18, *SS-Standartenführer* Eicke had been a plucky German officer. When he took over the newly established *SS-Totenkopfstandarte*, he first of all ensured that this first *SS* dispositional police unit was in no way inferior to any *Reichswehr-* or Protection Police unit in terms of military efficiency. He implemented such a harsh military drill that "his lads" were dead on their feet after every military exercise. One of the *Herr Kommandeur's* favourite pronouncements was the old Prussian barracks dictum: "I will rack you until water boils in your a . . . !" And, always the brash *SS-Führer*, he would add: "So that you will turn into real German men, hard as steel, and won't stand like pansies in front of those sub-humans."

The average age of an *SS* man in the *SS-Totenkopfstandarte* was 17–19 years! They were young, feral kids, just out of puberty, of the age when a nascent male is prone to excessive behaviour and keen to prove himself as "especially manly" and to emulate some sort of "heroic ideal". It should not be necessary to expound what sort of "heroic ideal" was dangled in front of the *SS*-men by their *SS-Führer*.

Eicke managed to turn the *SS-Totenkopfstandarte* into a highly disciplined police unit. Three weeks in every month "his lads" were drilled using all the chicanery of neo-German military training, three weeks in every month these boys were continuously exercised, with shouts of "Lie down! — Get up! — Quick march!", hours of crawling on their stomachs through thick mud and filth, hours of exercises with the bayonet and light and heavy machine guns, so that by the end of the day they were covered in bruises and bloody grazes. For three weeks, after every exhausting march there were hours of scrubbing and brushing, until the last tiniest speck of dust was removed. For three weeks, the *SS* men were given "military" instruction and ground down until they could not feel the bones in their own bodies. For three weeks — — — ; and in the fourth week, these 17-, 18- and 19-year-olds were let loose on the detainees. Now they, who had been tormented in military drills for three weeks, were themselves allowed to torment and torture. Now they were allowed, after three weeks of having to follow even the harshest order without the slightest protest, to finally give orders themselves, to bully and harass, and to watch like hawks if "their" orders were carried out "snappily" and "according to the instructions".

So what, if the detainees thus tormented and harassed by the youthful *SS* men were utterly dejected, feeble, starving, fatigued, overworked individuals, often well-nigh driven to madness through entirely warranted fear? "They are 'sub-humans', but you are the elite of the German nation!" This is what the young *SS* men would have been told a dozen times every day by their *Kommandant*, their company commander, or their *Truppenführer*. They were told again and again, until the words permeated their very flesh and blood and became second nature. And did the detainees not look exactly like the *SS* men pictured "sub-humans"? Unshaven, unkempt, bedraggled, with crazed and unsteady expressions, in stained, shabby clothing, patched and darned all over, sunken-cheeked and with the sallow complexions of basement dwellers?

The most evil brutes do not necessarily have to be idiots, and so even some *SS* men might have spared a few thoughts on the why and wherefore of it all. But provisions had been made for that eventuality, too. During his "watch", no *SS* man was to be in contact with one and the same detainee for more than two hours. According to a schedule, every two hours there was a "change of guard", after which each *SS* man would spend the next two hours with a different group of detainees, on a different floor of the camp, in different barracks, at another "work place". The schedule ensured that an *SS* man would hardly ever return to the same place within the eight-day period of "guard duty", and thereby the establishment of personal contact with individual detainees was avoided where possible.

Merciless preparatory military drills of the *SS* lads; indoctrination with the notion of their status as superior humans; praise for inflicting the cruellest practices when they were let loose on the helpless detainees; and a watch schedule that made any personal connection between guard and detainee impossible – that was the ingenious and devilish system that was inflicted on the detained opponents of the NSDAP.

When the *SS-Totenkopfstandarte* was assembled in 1933, as already mentioned, the majority of the *SS* men consisted of former Austrian "legionaries" and out-of-work *SS* members from Munich. Initially they had to sign a service contract for a year. After that initial period they were able to sign up for a further five years, and they were tempted with the possibility of a "glittering career" as an *SS-Unterführer* (junior squad leader) in the course of general armament. Only one year later (in 1934), the *SS-Totenkopfstandarte* was transformed into an *SS* police unit with the size of an entire division, which inevitably led to a shortage of personnel, and so many a young *SS-Unterführer* was unexpectedly rapidly promoted to the rank of *SS-Rottenführer* (section leader), *SS-Scharführer* (squad leader) or *SS-Truppführer* (troop leader). Especially "capable" candidates – that is, "capable" according to National Socialism and the "*SS* spirit" – were sent on special training courses and were able to "try their luck" as *SS* officer candidates, of course only after having "proven" and "distinguished" themselves for some time as *SS* non-commissioned officers. The pinnacle for these young men was the prospect of one day wearing the shiny silver insignia of a *"UVD"* (*"Unteroffizier vom Dienst"* – non-commissioned duty officer) on their uniforms. As a matter of fact, at the end of 1934, most *SS-Unterführer* in the *SS* dispositional police unit *"Totenkopf"* (which by that time was division-sized and distributed over concentration camps all across the *Reich*) hailed from Tyrol or Bavaria. The Tyroleans were largely the "legionaries", the scum of the Austrian people, who had betrayed their own country and people. It is shameful to think that the cruellest oppressors of humanity came from formerly Catholic countries and families. Many youth educators – especially in rural areas – must have utterly failed. Many clergymen and teachers were no longer truly Catholic in the bottoms of their hearts, no longer suffused by the sacred law of Christian love for God and their fellow men, and therefore were unable to gift the Christian ideal of life to the impetuous youth in time. This failing we must and are willing to recognise. It is also true, however, that the German resistance movement was strongest especially in the Bavarian and Austrian territories, a fact that demonstrates the extent to which a dichotomous character of a people – a peculiar bonhomie mixed with sternness, and forbearance mixed with a propensity for flying into a temper – can give birth to the most diverse range of individuals. At their worst, these people are stubborn, at their best, willing to make sacrifices verging on self-abandonment. But we can also see where apostasy leads, and where people and nations end up who stray off the predestined righteous path towards God, who intentionally turn their backs on God and raise their fists against the God of Christianity, against love, which is God Himself. Humans made in the image of God had turned into beasts and ungodly monsters – with the very same consequentiality that turned the angels that had fallen away from God into devils.

As early as 1934, barracks were erected all across Germany for the use by the *SS* dispositional police unit *"Totenkopf"*. Before universal conscription was re-introduced (on March 16, 1935), which only after August 24, 1936 was synonymous with compulsory active duty lasting for two years, potential recruits for the party troops were tempted with the promise that by signing up for a year with an *SS* dispositional police unit they would be able to avoid the impending two-year conscription at the *Wehrmacht*. This led to many a father taking his son out of school and signing him up with an *SS-Totenkopfverband* (which could already be joined at the age of 17), in the mistaken belief that after one year he would be "free" and would not have to interrupt his vocational training in some workshop, factory or office.

In Württemberg and the Province of Hanover, during the year 1934, the *SS* dispositional police unit "Totenkopf" must have had especially able recruiters, for at the beginning of 1935 youths from those regions formed a significant percentage of the new conscripts. While very few good things can be said about certain Tyroleans and Bavarians, especially the legionaries, who as SS men would later do "service" in the concentration camps, in general more positive things can be said about the recruits from Württemberg and the Province of Hanover. On the whole, they were deemed "unsuitable" for guard duties in the concentration camps and were eventually – of course with some exceptions – withdrawn from service in the *SS-Totenkopfverbände*. In the years before the start of the war (1939), it was unusual for one of these individuals to extend their service beyond the period they had initially signed up for, and it was a rarity for one of them to rise to the rank of *SS-Unterführer*. Of course this does not mean that all Württembergians and all Hanoverians are good people and that all Tyroleans and Bavarians are bad people. The author counts many Bavarians among his friends, who have proven themselves as loyal companions and during the heyday of National Socialism remained staunch opponents of the Nazi regime. However, we should spare a thought for the Württembergians and Hanoverians at this point, for many of these lads were stripped of their black *SS* uniforms in front of the specially assembled troops on grounds of "treason". Such "treason" usually consisted of nothing more than decent – and thereby "transgressive"! – treatment of a detainee by the "traitor". And it was not enough to strip the "traitor" of his *SS* uniform, he would immediately be sent to a concentration camp himself and given a punishment – which had to be administered immediately by one of his comrades – of at least 25 blows with a truncheon. In the space of two months, January and February 1934, in the small KZ Columbiahaus this fate befell nine Württembergians and five Hanoverians! In other, less confined concentration camps, the beatings of "treasonous" *SS* men were usually carried out away from the main camp, so that the camp's detainees would not notice them. All they knew was that on the following day a "new face" with a shaved head, beaten and bloody, would arrive.

The "official" forms of punishment in the camps

A mere "report" by a young *SS* man was enough for punishment to be handed out to a detainee. Perhaps the detainee, in the opinion of the guard, had not pushed his heavily laden wheelbarrow in double-time, perhaps at the morning roll call his straw mattress had not been folded into an exact square or the blanket had not been placed according to the precise regulations, perhaps at an inspection an *SS* boy found a speck of dust that in reality was not even there. The possibilities for getting "reported" were endless. The "reported" individual was called in front of the camp commander. If he "pleaded guilty", we would receive 25 truncheon blows, but if he denied his guilt in honest conviction of his innocence, the "obstinate bastard" would receive 50 blows, or much worse. In any case, the detainees were entirely at the mercy (or lack thereof) of the youthful *SS* men. Unconscionable mental torture was inflicted on the "condemned" by making them wait for days or weeks for their "punishment"; they would arrive at each morning inspection not knowing if that day the "punishment" would be carried out or not. Hundreds, thousands of emaciated wretched individuals would muster in the courtyard, shaking with fear, waiting for the latest proclamation by the *SS* camp commander.

Execution squads were standing at the ready to carry out each punishment, but not until an *SS Führer* (usually the officer in charge) had read out in a grating voice the relevant written "order" by the *Reichsführer SS*. This, too, is significant: each of these "orders", written on a bright red official form, started with the sentence: "The *Reichsführer SS* has ordered…" (Instead of, say, "the Inspector of the Concentration Camps", or "the Camp Commander" etc. No, the orders came from — — — the *Reichsführer SS* himself!)

The different types of punishment thus announced with much ceremoniousness before being handed out were these:

i. *The bench*: The detainee would be strapped to a bench, so that the buttocks would be firmly pressed against it. To the left and to the right of the detainee, two *SS* men would take turns in inflicting regular blows to the naked buttocks, taking a short run-up each time. The *SS Führer* who had read out the flogging order would stand to one side and count out loud with each blow. Also present would be the camp doctor, an *SS Führer* usually with the rank of *Obersturmführer*. Even though the blood would be flowing after only a few blows, the camp doctor would only raise an objection if the detainee lost consciousness, in which case the flogging would be halted until the detainee had regained consciousness after a bucket of water had been thrown over his head. Detainees were not removed from the "bench" if they lost consciousness.

Often the camp doctor would brush iodine on the utterly raw buttocks while the tortured individual was still strapped to the bench, thus causing yet more excruciating pain. Once the detainee was released from the bench, he had to immediately stand in file again and, despite the bleeding and agonies, set to work straight away. Any hesitation or writhing in agony would have been grounds for yet more, much worse, punishment. 25 blows were the usual penalty for "less serious cases"; it was the punishment handed out most often in the camps. 50 blows were handed out to "obstinate bastards", who dared to deny their guilt during the interrogation that followed a "report", or dared to gloss over their "misdeeds". Truncheon blows were only ever handed out after a "single report", as punishment for "less serious offences against the camp regulations" – about which the accused most often knew absolutely nothing.

ii. *The tree*: Usually right in the centre of the camp, there would be a post, rammed deep into the earth, perhaps three metres high. At the top, instead of a horizontal bar, there would merely be a sturdy hook. The detainee sentenced to punishment on the "tree" would climb a ladder and his hands would be tied together above his head with steel wire. The steel shackle would be fastened into the hook and the ladder would be removed from below the condemned man. He would drop down, but his feet would not reach the ground, and he would now be hanging from the "tree" from dislocated arms. Punishment on this torture stake was preferably handed out during spells of baking heat or a storm.

The "allocated" punishment on the "tree" usually lasted one, two or three hours and was most often handed out to detainees who had made themselves "guilty" of the same "misdemeanour" more than once, and had previously been sentenced to truncheon blows on the "bench" – however, without "success", in the opinion of the camp command.

The carrying out of the punishment on the "tree" was also "supervised" by the *SS* camp doctor. That is to say, the *SS* camp doctor ensured that the detainee would not temporarily evade his punishment through unconsciousness. Loss of consciousness was no reason to be prematurely taken down from the "tree"; the *SS* camp doctor would merely order for the detainee to be woken from his oblivion by having water poured over him, after which he was left hanging from the "tree" for much longer than the spell of unconsciousness had lasted.

The "tree" was only introduced as an official form of punishment in all concentration camps in 1938, following the pogroms against the Jews.

In addition to the two forms of punishment "bench" and "tree", which were, on "order by *Reichsführer SS*", solemnly proclaimed and executed in front of the assembled camp internees, there were other "official punishments" which did not necessarily have to be formally announced according to an "order" by the *Reichsführer SS*. They could also be imposed by the camp commander directly, or, more often, by the Gestapo official responsible for the detainee who would receive the "punishment", the "case handler". These other "official" forms of punishment included:

iii. Confinement in a darkened cell: A completely dark, small cell, bare walls, concrete floor; depending on the severity of the punishment, with a plank bed or without (in which case the detainee had to lie on the concrete floor). Under no circumstances was the detainee given a straw mattress or a blanket, even in the harshest winter. No chair or table. Reduced rations, usually only a piece of bread and a cup of water per day; in "aggravating circumstances" alternatingly two days of complete food deprivation, on the third day a cup of so-called "coffee" and a slice of bread in the morning, and nothing else; and after that another two days without any nourishment. Often the thirst was much worse than the hunger. In "special cases", on the third day the detainee would be handed a piece of heavily salted herring, no bread, and not a drop of water of coffee.

The minimum sentence for such confinement in the dark was a week, and in some cases the punishment would last for an entire month! Once a week the camp doctor would check if the detainee had not yet "snuffed it", thus fulfilling his duties as a doctor.

Most blackout cells did not have any sanitary facilities. The detainee would be given a bucket without a lid – so that he would not be able to use it as a seat – and it was ensured that there was not a drop of water in the bucket to begin with. In addition, the detainees were not allowed to have even a scrap of paper on them. Every morning when the cell was unlocked for the "morning inspection", the bucket would be emptied by the *"Scheisshausfritz"* (the *SS* man on lavatory duties). As soon as the door was opened for the morning inspection, the detainee had to stand to attention in front of the visiting *SS* man and to report: "Blackout cell occupied by detainee number such and such!" If, due to exhaustion, the posture or the report were not carried out "according to the regulations", an aggravation or increase of the penalty might follow.

After some incidents where detainees had attacked a visiting *SS* man in a blind rage during the morning inspection, a rule was introduced whereby detainees who had spent more than eight days in such confinement could only be visited in the presence of an *SS Führer* or the *UVD* (the non-commissioned duty officer). If the exhausted detainee fell over while attempting to stand to attention, he would simply be shot.

iv. Confinement in a "light" cell: everything that was said about confinement in a darkened cell also applies to confinement in a "light" cell, with the difference that instead of being in complete darkness, the cell was filled with an unbearable abundance of light, day and night. The walls of these "light cells" had been whitewashed, and two, three or even four powerful floodlights were mounted on the ceiling in such a way that the detainee could not possibly reach or damage them. In the confinement of the unventilated cells, these lights created an unbearable heat, threatening to burst the detainee's lungs and heart.

v. The "spider": in order to increase the severity of the punishment, the detainee in the "light cell" would be handcuffed. Thick steel ropes were threaded through the handcuffs and the detainee was thrown onto a bench. His legs would be spread apart, and each leg would be tied to one of the legs of the bench. The handcuffs would be tied to the opposite side of the bench beyond his head, making any movement impossible. Then the floodlights would be pointed directly at the face of the tied down detainee, who would be dressed only in a pair of trousers, without shoes or socks. The minimum sentence was 24 hours, but this could be extended at a whim. Of course no food or drink was administered for the duration of the torture on the "spider". Each morning, the detainee would be untied in the presence of an *SS Führer* and several *SS* men, and was ordered to relieve himself into a bucket, after which he would be tied up again. While being untied and tied up again, he would be subjected to beating and kicking; often bones would be shattered. A practice very "popular" with the *SS* men, say, during an interrogation, was to break the manacled individuals' nose, or to kick him in the stomach, so that he would inadvertently try to pull up his knees in pain, with the result that the shackles at his feet would cut deep into the flesh or the ankles would fracture.

The "spider" almost always was a torture to death, for after only a few days the detainee would go insane and, using his very last energy, would jump at his tormentors after being untied at the morning inspection, who would stand ready with unlocked rifles and simply shoot him down. As the detainee would only be untied once in every 24-hour period, he would have soiled himself, and was taunted and beaten even more because of it. Of course he would not be given a fresh pair of trousers.

The *SS* men visiting the detainees subjected to the "spider" were accompanied by the *SS* camp doctor, who would be there to "do his official duty", for this was an "official" form of punishment (despite the fact that it was almost always ordered by the Gestapo).

vi. Mock execution: The detainee was told that he would be executed at such and such a time on such and such a day. He was allowed to write a farewell letter to his relatives and then was put against a wall in handcuffs. An execution commando would muster, *SS* men in steel helmets. Military commands would sound. The detainee was blindfolded. The rifles were loaded, the metal of the catches clinked rhythmically. "Attention! — Aim! — — — — Fire!" A salvo of blank cartridges would crack. The blindfold would be torn off the detainee's face accompanied by a barrage of taunts and gibes.

During his detainment in the *KZ* Columbiahaus in Berlin, the present author witnessed three incidents where robust, strong men, who had withstood the most cruel methods of torture during the toughest interrogations, yet after such mock executions were reduced to tears, crying uncontrollably like children and ready to confess anything. The *SS* camp doctor would also have been present during such mock executions!

The six methods of punishment described above – it must be emphasised again – were official forms of punishment, which were imposed either on orders by *Reichsführer SS* Heinrich Himmler, by a Gestapo official in charge, or by a camp commander, and implemented by the *SS* men of the *SS-Totenkopfverbände*.

The *SS* men's "pranks"

Apart from the official forms of punishment in the camps, there was a whole range of "pranks" the young *SS* lads liked to play on the detainees, with those in solitary confinement being the preferred targets.

A young *SS* man's watch, on a long, narrow corridor, might have lasted from, say, 1.00am until 3.00am. That is boring. Or perhaps the young lad was afraid of his bad conscience and wanted to chase away some dreadful vision. In any case, he would unlock a cell and fetch a detainee to "while the time away". Now the usual "pranks" would start, with much shouting and swearing on part of the *SS* man, punches and slaps in the face would rain down on the drowsy detainee, and, "just for fun", he would be kicked and beaten with the butt of a rifle. In addition, there might have been a "little" military drill. The detainee was ordered to fetch his plank bed from his cell. Then he was put up against a wall, and ordered to "stand to attention", with his hands against the seams of his trousers. Now the top edge of the wooden plank was leant against the bridge of his nose, and the detainee, who was not allowed to move, was ordered to count out loud. He was told that if he managed to get to 100, he would be allowed to return to his cell. Of course the *SS* man knew perfectly well that it would be well nigh impossible to endure the incredible pain for such a long time and to remain standing still. If the detainee dared to move a hand away from the seam of his trousers in order to slightly lift the sharp edge of the plank away from the bridge of his nose, a violent beating would follow, and further "pranks" would be "tried out" to while away the *SS* man's time. Perhaps the detainee would be ordered to empty his straw mattress and to perform a "sack race" along the corridor. Of course the detainee would repeatedly fall to the ground, where he would be kicked and beaten until he had managed to get back to his feet. Even worse: the torn sack would inevitably lead to a "report" the next morning, with the result of being "punished" on the "bench" or "tree". And for the entire duration of such "drills" or "pranks", other exhausted detainees in cells along the same corridor, who would have been woken by the noise, were waiting in unbearable terror, fearing that they might be picked on next by the *SS* man, to take the place of their fellow sufferer.

Y*et al.* such "pranks" seem almost harmless compared to the bestial sexual crimes that were perpetrated on the defenceless detainees. It is impossible to describe all these perversities, but we have decided – despite all our misgivings and reluctance – to outline some of these disgusting atrocities in more detail. This is most certainly not done for the sake of a kind of tragic "sensationalism". These atrocities are part of the satanic system with which the "enemy's resistance" was to be "broken". Where beatings and torture did not easily yield results, attempts were made to convulse and shatter the enemy's inner, moral resistance. Physical blows – even the most ferocious and terrible – which hit the fragile body from the outside, sometimes can even toughen the inner, healthy core of a human, can beat moral resistance "into" the tortured individual and all but purify his soul. One needs only to recall the Christian martyrs, who through their suffering and plight, through the cross and death often received ultimate purification and thus attained true greatness and transcendent Christian heroism. As part of their satanic system, the Nazi monsters therefore used sexual crimes to break – as it were, from the inside – the moral resistance of those opposed to their beliefs, and to maim not only their physical bodies, but even more so their souls. Such infernal practices were inflicted especially on clergymen.

It was almost always the *SS* camp doctors who would "distinguish" themselves in the perpetration of such perversities and sexual crimes in the German concentration camps! These academically trained *SS* camp doctors were the worst imaginable monsters and, in their cruelty, their sadism and their brutality, eclipsed even the most evil *SS* men. For the entertainment of a few *SS*-

Unterführer the most unspeakable "operations" were carried out on the healthy penis or testes of a detainee; prostate "massages" were conducted as "exercises", in the course of which the tied up internee's colon would be torn to shreds; as an "experiment", corrosive acid would be applied to an injured penis by the *SS* camp doctor, to much jeering by the assembled *SS* men. All such defilements of humans were no isolated excesses, however, but run-of-the-mill "pranks" by *SS* men and their *SS-Unterführer*, led on by the *SS* camp doctors.

Within the space of a week, that is to say during a single watch, specifically in the week around March 20, 1935 (!), in *KZ* Columbiahaus in Berlin three of eleven internees detained in solitary confinement on a single corridor (on the right-hand side of the ground floor) hanged themselves from their underwear out of pain and shame, following "treatment" by the *SS* camp doctor of the sort described above. The responsible camp commander of *KZ* Columbiahaus at the time was *SS-Oberführer* Dr. [Alexander] Reiner [born 1885], formerly a dentist in Danzig [Gdansk]. The *SS* camp doctor, whose name the author has not able to ascertain, was a Bavarian of some thirty years of age, who had just "celebrated" his engagement to an innkeeper's daughter from Berlin. The responsible *UVD* (non-commissioned officer in charge), who was present at all instances of abuse, spurring on the proceedings, was *SS-Hauptscharführer* Josef Meyer, also known as *"der hagere Sepp"* ("skinny Joe"), who hailed from Pasing near Munich. Apart from Meyer, three *SS-Unterführer* from Tyrol were also present. On one occasion, one interested observer and contributor was the responsible *SS* camp leader (the camp commander's aide), *SS-Obersturmführer* Callio [*probably a mistaken spelling for Kallio, which is a Finnish surname*], who, until January 1, 1934, had been part of the adjutancy of *SS-Obergruppenführer* [Fritz Philip] Weitzel [1904-1940, killed], the police president of Düsseldorf.

SS Obergruppenführer Fritz Philip Weitzel (1904–1940, killed at Düsseldorf). The Police President of Düsseldorf, Weitzel assisted Heinrich Himmler with advice on ancient Germanic paganism. SS Obersturmführer Callio, one of Columbiahaus's sadists, had been his adjutant.

All these *SS* men, including the camp doctor, were members of the *SS* dispositional police unit *"Totenkopf"*, with its headquarters (in 1935) in Oranienburg. The camp commander *SS-Oberführer* Dr Reiner – the only member of the *"Totenkopf"* unit, apart from Eicke, who held such a high *SS* rank – was a voyeuristic sadist. He praised the participating *SS-Unterführer* in front of the assembled detainees, and gave orders for a number of internees from other cells to be locked up in the room where one of their fellow detainees, who had just committed suicide, was still hanging from the ceiling. The cell door was unlocked, an unsuspecting detainee was pushed in, and, standing out on the corridor, *SS* camp commander Dr Reiner and *SS-Obersturmführer* Callio would watch through the spyhole and take delight in the detainee's horror. Shortly after, the detainee would be released from the death cell by the camp commander himself, with the remark: "Now you bastard know how it's done! Get back to your cell, take your underpants, and have a go yourself!"

Apparently the only known photo of Dr. Alexander Reiner (born 1885), the "voyeuristic sadist", Commander of Combiahaus Camp, who loved to watch the prisoners being tortured and had a "prank" of locking prisoners in a cell where another prisoner was hanging dead.

Once again it has to be stressed: At that time (in March 1935!), in all of Germany's concentration camps there were no Czechs, no Poles, no Austrians etc., there were no foreigners in "protective custody"; and Jews constituted an extremely small percentage of the detainees in the concentration camps! It was Germans who were being tortured and murdered by the Nazis, and it was the German opposition that languished in the camps!!

Many upstanding German Communists and Social Democrats and many formerly well-known German trade union leaders were locked up in the various *KZs*. But – especially after the appointment of Himmler-Heydrich in Berlin (late March 1934) and the massive wave of arrests that followed the events of June 30, 1934 – there were also a large number of democrats and common citizens, who by late 1934 already formed the majority of the detainees (that is, relative to the Marxists). Freemasons, Protestants and Catholics were also taken into "protective custody". In May / June 1934 the first priests and monks arrived in the *KZ* Columbiahaus, and were detained together with artists from a cabaret show in Berlin (*"[Werner] Finck und Genossen"*).

At this point, we would like to commemorate two men who were able to get out of the concentration camps with unbroken spirits and over the course of their lives proved themselves to be outstanding personalities, helping to lift the souls of many individuals who had been mortified in the camps and saving them from finding an end in suicide. Both were exemplary chaplains, offering not only consolation but also material help in the hour of the greatest human misery and anguish. The two men, outwardly so dissimilar and belonging to entirely different schools of thought, did not know each other and had no personal contact during their internment, and yet they acted in the same spirit and accomplished so much:

Pater Spieker, a Jesuit and pulpit orator in the cathedral at Cologne, who for many months had done the most severe physical labour in the swamps of *KZ* Papenburg, always in good spirits, before being transferred to *KZ* Columbiahaus in June 1934. He must have been one of the very first clergymen to be detained in a concentration camp. In *KZ* Columbiahaus the Jesuit Pater Spieker for a short time worked as the *"Scheisshausfritz"* and so was able, now and then, to exchange a few words, without being overheard, with the detainees on Corridor III (first floor, right-hand wing) through closed cell doors, or in the lavatories on the corridor was able to render some small service to a fellow detainee by lifting him up physically or spiritually. This priest – perhaps without ever knowing it – performed miracles and was the guardian spirit of his fellow sufferers, among whom there would have been many a die-hard Marxist. This short and stout man never alluded to the privileges of his priesthood, and never derived any personal benefits from it. Not only was he made to labour like the other detainees, he laboured more than them, taking on the work of those too exhausted to carry on themselves.

Dr. Otto Bordes [*a Berlin dentist*], Grand Master of the Old Prussian Lodge *"Zu den drei Weltkugeln"* [*Three World Globes*], had refused to "voluntarily" dissolve his lodge and therefore – despite Hindenburg's appeal for the lodge – was sent to *KZ* Columbiahaus. After months of solitary confinement he was engaged as an "assistant architect" and so, in the course of carrying out surveys, worked in every part of the building. The tall septuagenarian with his shock of white hair by no means only cared for his detained masonic brothers, but found encouraging and warm words for all the desperate internees, and somehow he would always find an apple, a piece of bread or something else edible which he would – often at a considerable risk to his own life – slip into the cell of a starving detainee. Incidentally, this Grand Master of an Old Prussian Grand Lodge was a very active member of the Christian-Protestant church!

When on April 1, 1934 *SS-Oberführer* Dr Reiner was succeeded as camp commander by *SS-Obersturmbannführer* [Karl-Otto] Koch, the detainees in *KZ* Columbiahaus breathed a collective sigh of relief. However, the impression that the new camp commander, compared to the diabolical Dr Reiner, was some sort of an angel soon vanished.

When *SS-Obersturmbannführer* Koch took over, the first "foreign exchange racketeers", that is to say, Franciscan monks in their brown habits, arrived at the camp. The Franciscan prior from Paderborn, Father Meinhard (von der Heidt), who in discussions with his bishop had always advocated amicable co-operation with the Nazis, suffered a nervous breakdown when he witnessed the treatment his *confratres* received. At the orders of the Secret State Police Office he was given "preferential" treatment, was designated a "seriously ill person", and sent to the infirmary, which was an extremely rare privilege.

The *SS* camp doctor, in cahoots with camp commander Koch, dreamt up a new fiendish "treatment" for many clergymen: they were wrongly accused of being afflicted with pubic lice! They were denied any so-called work clothes for many days and instead had to keep wearing their habits. Then, after being hauled in front of a bawling posse of *SS* men, the *SS* camp doctor gave them a cream to treat the imputed pubic lice. While the *SS* men told the most repulsive dirty jokes, read from pornographic books and passed around obscene pictures, the clergymen were forced to rub the cream onto their sexual organs and thereby seemingly performed acts of masturbation. The monks were then called "filthy pigs", sworn at in the most obscene fashion and, under a barrage of punches, were herded back into their cells.

Such abuse took place for the first time in June 1935 in the *KZ* Columbiahaus, under the command of *SS-Obersturmbannführer* [Karl-Otto] Koch (1897-1945, executed). This type of "treatment" for fictitious pubic lice soon became a favourite "prank", which was systematically inflicted on clergymen in the German concentration camps.

SS-Obersturmbannführer Karl-Otto Koch, the sadistic commandant of the Columbiahaus Concentration Camp at Berlin in 1935. His favourite joke was to torture and torment imprisoned clergymen with pornographic images and force them to carry out sexual acts against their will in front of himself and the guards.

The work of the detainees

The building of barracks, houses and even villas has already been mentioned. This was in addition to other forms of outdoor labour, which were to be performed at any time of the year and in even the worst weather conditions. Most of the detainees toiled in quarries, gravel pits, in the fields, or draining swamps (for example, in the labour camps of *KZ* Papenburg"). In addition, every *KZ* had its own carpenter's-, tailor's-, and shoemaker's workshops, and suchlike. Skilled craftspeople at intervals enjoyed preferential treatment, as during such times that they were employed carrying out artisanal work for a high *SS* leader, they were given fewer beatings and rarely subjected to the aforementioned camp punishments, as these would have diminished their capacity for work and curtailed services which directly benefitted an *SS* leader. In any case, the *SS* leaders of the *SS* dispositional police unit *"Totenkopf"* had entire apartments furnished by the carpenters among "their" detainees" and had bespoke uniforms and civilian clothes tailored for them. Some resourceful individuals among the beaten and mistreated convicts produced beautiful artisanal gifts for the highest *SS* leaders in the staff of *Reichsführer SS* Heinrich Himmler and the heads of department and officials of the Secret State Police and the *SD-RFSS.*

As part of the general armament of the German *Wehrmacht*, and for the requirements of the *SS* dispositional police units, entire incorporated companies were established on the back of the detainees' manpower. The very existence and the profits of many newly established corporations of textile-, leatherworking-, food processing-, and even aeronautical industry, as well as agricultural research institutes and chemical laboratories were based entirely on the labour carried out by the detainees in the concentration camps. Some of these businesses were state-run (entrusted to the *SS* by the *Reich* Ministries for the Interior, Agriculture or Aviation); others, whose shares were held by *SS* leaders and the running of which had been turned over to the *SS* dispositional police unit *"Totenkopf"*, were in "private" hands; still others were owned by the *SS* itself, with the *SS* Main Office acting as "legal entity" and title bearer. Following the appropriation of the *Reich* Ministry for the Interior by Heinrich Himmler and the appointment of the *Reichsführer SS* as *Reichsminister* for the Interior (replacing Dr Frick), a new *SS* Main Economic and Administrative Office was created, under whose remit also fell the accounting and administration of all the businesses run by the *SS-Totenkopf* units. *SS-Obergruppenführer* Pohl (who also held the post of head of department in the *Reich* Ministry for the Interior and owned a palatial villa within the *SS* town Dachau) was appointed as chief of that new *SS* Main Economic and Administrative Office. Neither the Office of the Inspector of the Concentration Camps in Prinz-Albrecht-Strasse in Berlin, nor the command of the *SS Totenkopf* units in Oranienburg were charged with the financial administration of those companies and certainly were not their proprietors. The Office of the Inspector of the Concentration Camps merely was "in charge of the running" of those companies, and the command of the *SS Totenkopf* units in Oranienburg and its *SS* men ensured uninterrupted "cultivation and exploitation". Of course, strictly speaking, the *"Totenkopf"* command had nothing at all to do with those companies, as it was only in charge of the *SS* men, but not the detainees themselves. It was the Office of the Inspector of the Concentration Camps that was responsible for the convicts working in the companies.

III. Urgent questions and some answers

Where is the German opposition?

When the Office of the Inspector of the Concentration Camps was created in the autumn of 1934, Inspector [Theodor] Eicke (1892-1943, shot down in the Battle of Kharkhov] took over eight concentration camps in which a total of at least 47,000 detainees were held. That means

47,000 members of the opposition! Among them were no foreign nationals and almost no Jews. It can be justifiably claimed that by 1936/37, that is to say before the *Anschluss* of Austria and the pogroms against the Jews in November 1938, the number of German detainees languishing in the concentration camps would have risen to at least 60,000. This number does not include the political prisoners and convicts in German prisons or any of the individuals in "protective custody" who were awaiting their fate in overcrowded police cells.

60,000 German oppositionists! At first sight, this might seem a small number for the 70-million-strong population of the Old *Reich* – even when one considers that almost all of these 60,000 individuals were men of conscription age. It might seem a small number even if one were to add an estimated 40,000 individuals who had been convicted of political crimes, in addition to all the dead, who had made space for the living. Even that would not add up to two in a thousand Germans, of either sex or any age.

It is necessary to make an observation that may at first seem somewhat fallacious:

Each detainee was committed to a concentration camp and thereby "entrusted" to the Office of the Inspector of the Concentration Camps with a registered docket number. The detainee's docket slip would contain personal information, with the rubric "remarks" either indicating "minor case", "severe case", or "solitary confinement until further notice". Neither the inspector nor the camp commander were able to enquire after the political disposition, the origins, or the particular nature of the "political case" of the detainee brought to the camp or to consult with the police. Such enquiries were expressly forbidden in accordance with an order given by the *Reichsführer SS*, which was rigorously enforced. Neither did the inspector and the camp commander (and least of all the detainee himself!) know how long the detainment in the camp would last. By contrast, the camp command did have the right, and even the duty, to recommend the release or further detainment of an internee every three months. However, sole competence in making final decisions based on such recommendations resided with the responsible case workers at the Secret State Police who had ordered detainment in the first place, that is to say with the Department for Protective Custody at the Secret State Police Office. In practice, the process played itself out in a much less "individual" approach than might have been assumed, and, in 99 out of a 100 cases, was handled in a purely perfunctory manner. Nevertheless: every three months a new decision was to be made on the further fate of each detainee in the concentration camp, irrespective of whether those had been the first three months of his detainment or whether he had already been detained for a year or more. (It was part of the fate of the "privileged" skilled workers that no camp commander would readily recommend the release of such cheap, yet sought-after, workers.)

For the financial year 1935/36 (i.e. April 1, 1935 – March 31, 1936), the Secret State Police Office submitted the following statistics to the Prussian Ministry for the Interior (which was still in existence at that point and to whom the Secret State Police Office was accountable):

Detainees in "protective custody" in the State of Prussia:
11% detained for three months,
47% detained for six months,
29% detained for one year,
13% detained for more than one year.

What went for the state of Prussia can be assumed to be correct with only minor variations for the remaining territory of the *Reich*. These figures demonstrate that more than half of the "detainees" spent "only" six months or less in a concentration camp. It follows that it would be no exaggeration to assume that until the start of the war in 1939 well over 500,000 honourable Germans, who were loyal opponents of National Socialism, were dragged through the concentration camps, not counting Jews, Austrians, Czechs, Poles, the Dutch, Norwegians, the French, Belgians etc. etc.

Half a million Germans who had to endure all the horrors of Nazi terror! Half a million Germans, violated by German Nazis! Half a million honourable German men, helplessly at the mercy of their political opponents! Half a million oppositional Germans, on whom the Nazi gangs' methods of torture were practised and rehearsed, long before being inflicted on Jews and foreign nationals! 500,000 oppositionists! And that is a conservative estimate! To this number one has to add the legions of detainees, convicts, and hanged and shot individuals, who had been dragged in front of the Nazi courts because of their honest political convictions!

After the start of the war in 1939 the rest of the world only ever heard about foreign nationals and Jews being tortured and murdered in the German concentration camps, and it is true that relatively few German oppositionists could have been found in the concentration camps at Dachau, Buchenwalde, Belsen, Sachsenhausen etc. And straight away statesmen and journalists jumped to conclusions and asked: "Where is the German opposition, if not detained in concentration camps?"

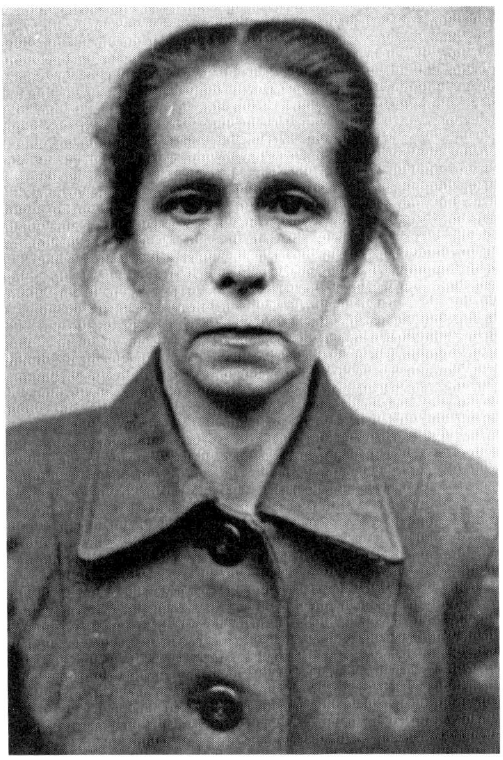

Juana Bormann, (1893–1945, executed). Commencing in 1938, she was a prison guard at several Nazi concentration camps including Lichtenburg, Auschwitz, Belsen, and Ravensbrück. She was a crazed, sadistic murderess who used to release her fierce "big bad wolfhound" and watch it savage and kill prisoners for her pleasure. Abusing and murdering prisoners was her passion and chief delight. She was hanged in 1945.

In the winter of 1938/39, the largest German concentration camp, *KZ* Papenburg, with its four separate labour camps, was formally dissolved. However, this "termination" only manifested itself as the camp's transfer from the police authorities to the judicial authorities, who continued to run it as a labour- and penitentiary camp for convicted "political criminals", as all prisons were so overcrowded that it was no longer possible to detain political prisoners there. In the "former" *KZ* Papenburg there was space for at least 40,000 German men who had been detained due to their honest political convictions, and now were used to labour in the swamps at Papenburg.

But where were German detainees held after the winter of 1938/39? Were they "released"? Had the police authorities ceased to detain Germans; were there no appreciable numbers of arrests of Germans? Were German detainees now simply handed over to the ordinary jurisdiction (that is to say the Nazi courts) as "political suspects" for sentencing, instead of being sent to concentration camps? Had some form of lawfulness – albeit a rather flimsy one – been established? Or was there really no longer any German opposition after the outbreak of war, had every last German turned into an enthusiastic Nazi?

On February 4, 1938, after the forced resignations of General Fritsch as Commander-in-Chief of the German Army and his generals, Adolf Hitler assumed direct authority over the entire German *Wehrmacht*, the office of War Minister was abolished, and shortly afterwards, on March 13, 1938, the invasion of Austria started. At the same time the so-called *"Westwall"* (the "Siegfried Line", a defensive line along Germany's western border) and other major defensive lines were constructed at breakneck speed. The new German *Wehrmacht* not only needed soldiers, but also an army of cheap workers, legions of submissive, tightly disciplined drudges. A large-scale "sifting" of the German concentration camps ensued, in an attempt to identify workers for the construction of the defensive lines. A small proportion of the detainees were taken into the *Wehrmacht*, however not as regular members, but as "second-class soldiers"! So-called "punishment battalions" were formed, made up of detainees who were treated as convicts rather than soldiers. The larger proportion of the detainees, however, went from the concentration camps straight into the forced labour battalions that formed part of *"Organisation Todt"* (an engineering organisation using largely forced labour). Any "release" after three or six months, or one or two years, was now out of the question; that possibility remained open only to those detainees who were left in the concentration camps.

Dr. Fritz Todt (1891-1942, assassinated by senior Nazi colleagues). The Todt Organisation was founded by him and bore his name. He was an engineering genius who built the German autobahns and then became Reich Minister for Armaments and Ammunition. When he told Hitler that Germany could not possibly win the War against Russia, he was looked upon as unreliable and suspect. His main rival Albert Speer is believed to have been party to his murder.

According to a report compiled by the Chief of Field Marshal von Reichenau's operations department, the contingent of "second-class soldiers" in the entire *Wehrmacht* at the beginning of 1940 did not exceed 17,000 men. By the beginning of 1945 that figure is estimated to have increased ten-fold, as there were no "departures" – other than through death – but plenty of "arrivals", with the Gestapo "taking care" of meeting the ever-increasing demand for trench labourers.

On April 1, 1939 – that is to say, *before* the start of the war – *"Organisation Todt"* had 320,000 "second-class" excavators and trench workers at its disposal. These are workers that had not been referred by the *Reich* Labour Service. Within *"Organisation Todt"*, the category "second class" did not exclusively apply to former concentration camp detainees; it applied to all unskilled German labourers. It is possible that a certain percentage of those "second-class" labourers would have been supplied by unemployment offices, but the majority certainly was "allocated" by the concentration camps.

According to entirely plausible estimates, the contingent of "second-class" German soldiers and "second-class" excavators and trench workers that was made up entirely of former "protective custody" prisoners and "political suspects" easily exceeded one million (!) men during the course of the war. We readily admit that these men had it a lot easier than the detainees who had remained in the concentration camps. Not only was it not permitted to senselessly beat, kick and torture them, for this would have reduced their capacity for work, but they were also fed better. On the other hand, they had to carry out the heaviest forms of work, often at risk to their lives. The "second-class" soldiers were worse off than the "second-class" excavators and trench workers in *"Organisation Todt"*, inasmuch as for them "military drills during leisure time" had been introduced, which were incomparably harsher than the drills for the labour battalions in *"Organisation Todt"*.

The men in the penal battalions both of the *Wehrmacht* and *"Organisation Todt"* were not allowed any holidays. They were permitted to write one letter per month and one postcard per week (at the outbreak of war in 1939), which were of course subjected to strict censorship. Penal authority (smoking bans, pack drills, medium detention, aggravated detention with only water and bread, etc.) rested with their immediate superiors. Deserters were immediately shot. The most severe form of punishment, however, was a transfer to *KZ* [*Konzentrationslager* = Concentration Camp] Lichtenburg [at Prettin]. Since the winter of 1938/39, this camp had been designated to exclusively receive those who had been transferred for disciplinary reasons either from *"Organisation Todt"* or from within the ranks of the "second-class" soldiers within the *Wehrmacht*, who had already served their sentences at the *Wehrmacht* and for their transfer to *KZ* Lichtenburg had been specifically excluded from the *Wehrmacht* units.

The answer to the question, "At the beginning of the war, where was the German opposition, if not in the concentration camps?" is this: the very substantial German opposition – inasmuch as it was able to make its presence felt – could be found in the "punishment battalions" of the *Wehrmacht* and *"Organisation Todt"*! (For the so-called "civil" opposition, and especially for the opposition within the NSDAP, the *SS* additionally established the so-called "probation battalions".) Any "second-class" soldiers, any members of *"Organisation Todt"*, or any members of the *SS* "probation battalions" who were taken prisoners of war by English [sic], American, Russian [sic] or French troops could bear witness to that fact!

What did the German people know about the concentration camps?

These days, the following question has come back into vogue: "If a loving God did exist, how could He allow so much suffering?" To answer this question fully would require a definition of the concept of God, which would go beyond the scope of this book. We assume the existence of the triune God of Christianity to be an immutable fact. We further believe that it is indeed possible – even without too much theological theorising – to answer the above question, for it is indeed a sorry proposition to suddenly saddle "God" with responsibility for the mess that we, pathetic humans that we are, have got ourselves into through our very "renunciation of God".

It would be a similarly sorry proposition to suddenly blame the entire German people for all the crimes perpetrated by the Nazis, and further to declare National Socialism to be the sole source of all misery and suffering in the world. There is no doubt that National Socialism – and not the entire German people! – must chiefly be blamed for inciting the war, and we will hold it accountable with unwavering and stern justice. The National Socialists launched the boomerang of hate, which always circles back to strike down the agitator.

Yet we – all of us, who neglected or even entirely disregarded the sacred law of Christian charity – are to a certain extent complicit in the demise of this world. And that is why, again and again, we demand that every single one of us should beat his breast in remorse and humbly speak the words: *"Mea culpa, mea culpa, mea maxima culpa!"*

If the question of guilt for the criminal workings of National Socialism were ever to be fully investigated, the following incontestable fact must not be overlooked: all the civilised nations of the world, their leading statesmen and influential social classes for many years studiously ignored the cries for help by German (!) Nazi-opponents locked up in concentration camps and prisons. In his confessional work *"Mein Kampf"*, Adolf Hitler had precisely foretold how he would use power, once he had seized it, against his opponents in Germany and the nations of Europe, and y*et al.* the concerned parties abroad forever tried to ignore the very public avowals that had been made by the *Führer* of National Socialism. Even just before his assumption of power, in August 1932, Adolf Hitler expressed his solidarity with the perpetrators of the *Potempa* murders in front of the whole world by sending them a telegram, congratulating the murderous *SA* youths on this most heinous crime carried out against a defenceless opponent. And even after Hitler's power grab, foreign diplomats and statesmen bent over backwards to establish friendly relations with Hitler and his National Socialism. Until the autumn of 1939, all attempts by German oppositionists to mobilise other nations' moral and ethical strength against National Socialism failed because of the complacent business interests of those who wanted to do "business" at any cost, no matter if that "business" was political or purely commercial in nature.

All the Nazi atrocities carried out in the occupied territories had for years already been tested and rehearsed on oppositional German men, women and children. And it is beyond doubt that other nations *could* have known about these crimes, *must* have been able to know about these crimes, but simply did not *want* to know! As long as the Nazi crimes were "only" perpetrated against Germans, they were happy to stand idly by! Only when there was a threat to their own life and limb did they scream blue murder!

Today one hears: "The entire German people is guilty! For we have felt the onslaught of the cumulative force of the German people!" In saying this, the question of guilt is dumbed down, any conscience is numbed, and an appealing catchphrase is created for all fools, of which there are many among every people and race on earth!

Crime demands punishment, and it is a self-evident Christian duty to demand punishment for every perpetrator, no matter if he was wearing a brown Nazi shirt or the uniform of the *Wehrmacht.* In this context especially we would like to stress yet again that in no way do we seek to exculpate

German militarism, and that we will hold it to account wherever it made itself available as a loyal vassal to the Nazi regime in the form of jingoism, and wherever it was guilty of perpetrating war crimes during the times of National Socialist victories.

Yet at the same time we venture to propagate the "apostolate of God's love in politics", knowing that we run the risk of being decried as "cranky idealists". Hatred in this world can only be overcome through love, through that magnificent "love for God and humankind" which has nothing to do with facile optimism or escapist rhapsody, but is deeply rooted in unshakeable Christian faith. Justice, atonement for wrongs committed, expiation for crimes perpetrated – all these are self-evident elements of this love, a love that is God Himself! Let us seek justice, but let us beware of the heathen concept of "an eye for an eye, a tooth for a tooth", for in following it we would only respond to a crime with another crime.

What is taking place today among the German people under the Nazi regime has been labelled by Professor Dr Wilhelm Röpke (1899-1966; author of many books from 1936 onwards, and a social, political, and economic critic of fascism) "a tragedy in which guilt and fate are intertwined, a tragedy the likes of which the world has never seen before". And, letting Professor Dr Wilhelm Röpke's ideas resonate, we want to add the following for consideration:

If it is the case that a nation's economic and social histories cohere with its political history, then we have to reach far back in time in order to find the roots of the current German problem. Two characteristics have to be highlighted: during the 1,000 years of the German *Reich's* existence (from 843 until 1866) it was not possible to implement any sort of federalism, for the "transfeudal" sections, towns and bourgeoisie, were ruptured in Germany in the Middle Ages. Another decisive attribute of the social development of Germany is the denominational schism, with the subsequent demise of German urban culture and the ruin of the antifeudal peasantry. The result was —— — the German "subject"! Proud erstwhile *"Bürger"* (townsmen) had been replaced – with laudable exceptions – by pitiful *"Spiessbürger"* (conformist petit-bourgeoisie).

Let us, on the other hand, consider the development of Prussianism. The rivers Elbe and Saale form the boundary between the ancestral German homeland and colonial Germany. The eastern territories gave rise to the character of the "colonial Germans" – conquering, and eastward bound, but ultimately the archetypal victims of the nemesis of imperialism, who, in enslaving other nations and peoples, eventually end up unfree themselves. Their agricultural system knew no intermediary peasantry; the bulk of people were "held" by feudal aristocrats, in the same way that Negroes were "held" in the colonial Negro-plantations that were being established at around the same time. These Prussian conquerors placed themselves in diametrical opposition to the peasantry that was on the rise in western nations. Karl Freiherr vom Stein and Karl August von Hardenberg sought to make concessions to the influence of western agricultural systems by abolishing serfdom and feudal bondage, but the reforms were stopped in their tracks by the infamous "Edict of Regulation" of 1816 [this is wrong, should be 1811], and Prussia became a nation not only deficient in farmers, but also towns. Out of necessity, feudal Prussianism was averse to any form of individualism and tended more towards collectivism. In Prussia, the struggle against absolutism and feudalism started very, very late.

Absolutism and feudalism were arguably the collective fate of all of Germany, albeit in a somewhat milder form outside of Prussia. In Prussia, absolutism and feudalism ultimately achieved full mechanisation of the state, which consequently intensified into a demonic menace. This is where the Prussian obsession with organisation with its much lauded "thoroughness and discipline" comes from. The ensuing psychological reaction leads to progressive narcissism and self-aggrandisement on the one hand, and to dangerous delusions of persecution on the other.

Professor Dr Röpke refers to Bismarck as a "grand sorcerer", who was able to unite the two components, the conformist petit-bourgeoisie and Prussianism, so that after 1866 Germany was transformed into a Greater Prussia. In truth, Bismarck's achievement is an unparalleled violation of a nation, which necessarily had to lead to Nazism and the current catastrophe. Stirred by the French Revolution, Germans had learned about the ideals of liberty and the yearning for a nation state, but they sacrificed liberty for a Bismarckian type of "unity". A certain brand of historical narrative of the sort written in Berlin has distorted these processes to such an extent that it will be necessary to completely re-write the German history of the last centuries.

Worn down through the grind of internal tariffs, Germans in Prussia, with its customs union, would welcome someone who would promise to liberate them from economic hardship. Even outstanding men and combative "liberals" caved in to Prussia, which, since 1818, appeared "sympathetic" through its customs policies. Using deception and seduction, trickery and force, Bismarck subjected Germany to the rule of Greater Prussia, but already in the 1870s Germany found herself at the mercy of a diametrically opposed set of economic policies, which brought the "liberal era" to an end. Germany's capitalism developed against a backdrop of interventionist and monopolistic economic policies, which had started with a transition to protectionism following the imposition of the "Bismarck" tariffs in 1879.

The same year of 1879 was a fateful year for Germany far beyond the economic sphere. The Prussian doctrine became prevalent; Berlin and everything Prussian were systematically promoted and favoured. Statism, monopolism and subventionism united with a rigorous form of centralism; the entire German banking system was concentrated in Berlin in ever fewer hands. German heavy industry took on an unmistakably feudal character and became one of the pillars of Prussianism.

The Bismarckian unified state presented to the world not only the prototypes of monopolist capitalism and of the "proletariat", but inevitably also created organised socialism. Professor Dr Röpke considers organised socialism to be a typical product of German social and intellectual history. Rapid population growth, proletarianisation and sharply separated social classes are among its essential prerequisites. The only possible forms of protest against Greater Prussianism were the founding and subsequent membership of the Social Democratic Party; yet, despite all its democratic trappings, this party was a decidedly Prussian construct.

To conclude his analysis, Professor Dr Röpke asks: "Should the world have its path dictated by countries with a singularly pathological social history?" And, with Professor Dr Röpke, we would like to answer: "Certainly not!"

Yet, does this mean that, based on Röpke's deliberations, we would answer in the affirmative to this question: "Is the German people in its entirety complicit in and accountable for all the crimes perpetrated by the Nazis?" We shall answer, with the same fervour: "Certainly not!"

Even the gravest guilt of those responsible cannot be equated with the collective guilt of an entire people; and the German people in its entirety is not worse than any other people. In every nation, among every people, there are both good and bad individuals. But wherever anti-social elements, downright evil individuals, the scum of a nation, are able – through external circumstances and a tragic sequence of strokes of fate – to suddenly seize power in a state, something akin to "what happened in Germany" becomes possible.

A share of the blame for the fact that such antisocial elements were able to seize power in Germany lies with those responsible for creating desperate conditions in Germany, as well as with those who stood idly by and allowed it to happen; this applies to responsible actors and agents abroad as well as within Germany.

We reject the notion of collective responsibility and liability of the German people for the perpetrated Nazi crimes. However, we are well aware of the negative character attributes of the Germans, the hubristic arrogance and narcissism that inevitably lead to a persecution complex; we are well aware of the dangerous ideals of "order and discipline", those much-lauded characteristics one may well respect, despite the fact that individuals with personalities thus endowed are not necessarily always particularly likeable. After all, it is not by accident that we have chosen to allude to Professor Dr Röpke's "tragedy in which guilt and fate are intertwined" in these pages. But we are also well aware of the positive and likeable character traits of the German people, as unreasonable as it may seem to speak of them at this point in history and in the face of the immense suffering recently caused by Germans. We know about the "childlike disposition" of the German people. Indeed, much more than is the case with other nations, the German national character resembles an adolescent boy, who easily tends towards provocative insolence and cocky impertinence if he finds himself in the hands of an unsuitable teacher, and in whom criminal tendencies are stirred as soon as he is put in the uniform of a loveless educational institution.

And so: should the German people atone for its narcissism, its intoxication with power, its hubris?

Truly, Germans have had to pay bitter penance under the terror of the Nazi regime, and, during the last years of the war, had first-hand experience of the entire brutal reality of the suffering of war, lived through all the horrors of anguish and misery, hunger and homelessness, were scourged by all the fury of warfare unleashed by the Nazis, and were mercilessly driven through the hellfire of that conflict. After such horrors of war, to speak to the German people in its entirety of "penance", verges on dubious pharisaism! Expiation for committed Nazi crimes, just punishment of all perpetrators: yes, a thousand times, yes! But who would dare, after this war, to revile the deeply suffering and fatally injured German people, to talk of "penance", and in the same breath, call himself a Christian?

How much do German people know about the Nazi crimes perpetrated during the war in the occupied territories? How much do they know about the conditions in the German concentration camps?

The answer, alarmingly, is: very little!

After his own release from the *KZ* Columbiahaus, the present author spoke with various people in Berlin who lived in the immediate vicinity of that camp and passed by it on a daily basis, and on Sundays (long before the outbreak of war) even went for walks up there, along the edge of the Tempelhof parade ground. None of these people had the slightest inkling of the cruelties committed by the Nazis, in *KZ* Columbiahaus or elsewhere. They all honestly believed – even those who didn't approve of it – that the Nazis applied the notion of "tough, but just", as they claimed. Yet, even years after his release, the author still had not managed to tell his wife or children of the true conditions in the concentration camps; and most former concentration camp detainees presumably shared a similar fate in this respect.

To conclude, an example:

After the liberation of France, mass graves of murdered, mutilated Nazi victims were discovered and excavated at Lyon airport, a short distance away from the landing strip. At the same time, young German prisoners of war were working nearby. When asked by a Swiss journalist to comment on these atrocities committed by the Nazis, the young German prisoners of war answered in unison: "We do not believe it! This can't have been done by Germans! This is vile French inflammatory propaganda!" And this was no excuse, it was – as the Swiss journalist was aghast to realise – the honest and firm belief of these German prisoners of war!

The question of guilt cannot be solved in this book, we can merely report on the facts. Every non-German reader of the factual report on the concentration camps may ask himself this question: "Could something like this have happened in my country?"

We venture to answer this question:

Wherever Christianity has been reduced to a formality and the teachings of Christ have turned into vacuous formulae; wherever humaneness is merely a stale phrase and no longer a conviction; wherever human rights are disregarded; wherever an "upright citizen", who was not personally affected, utters the words: "These Nazi perpetrators must not simply be hanged or shot, but must be tortured in the same way that they tortured their victims, so that they can learn what it feels like!" —— in all these places

"something like this could have happened"!

He who does not respect human dignity, he who desecrates God's own image in another human being, whoever that human being may be, lends his name to a form of differentiation – and with it, discriminative treatment! – that is as dangerous as were the Nazi's racial laws and their *Herrenmenschen* delirium.

Every perpetrator must be held to account in a clear and just way; but he must not be tortured and abased!

And beware of simply modifying the National Socialist concept of the "subhuman" and suddenly applying it to the Nazis themselves, or even to all Germans! Because then, yes then, "something like this could have also happened in your country"!

There are no "sub-humans",

there are no "super-humans";

there are only poor, erring humans, full of sin and fault.

No-one should misunderstand these deliberations: not a single crime is to be palliated, and not a single criminal must be exculpated!

He who has perpetrated a crime must be punished. — The penalty for murder and defilement is death.

As judges, we want to be harsh but just!

PART ONE

THE SYSTEM

THE FACTORS OF POWER

D. THE NATIONAL SOCIALIST SCHOOLS

I. The educational problem
Not Christianity, but we Christians have failed.

It sounds like a fairy tale when our fathers and grandfathers tell us of a time before the World War of 1914-18 when it was possible to travel to foreign countries without holding a passport, visa or certificate of citizenship, and without the clutch of forms and formalities that are required nowadays by every nation – not only of foreign travellers, even those just passing through, but also of their own citizens. Following the Russian Revolution of 1917, even a man such as Fridtjof Nansen had to deploy all of his international standing, his reputation and his well-earned esteem to secure Nansen passports (a document originally intended for stateless persons, named after Nansen) for hundreds and thousands of Russian refugees. Few sophisticated people in the so-called "civilised" countries of this Earth would have taken offence when – in the years before the outbreak of war in 1939 – refugees seeking protection were frisked at the border by distrusting policemen, in a manner in which no farmer would proceed at the cattle market. Émigrés and political refugees were penned up in mass camps like herds of mutton, and they had to be thankful not to be returned to the border immediately and delivered back into the hands of their persecutors. Of course there is a juridical term for this practice: national emergency! There are motives such as "self protection" and "self-preservation instinct". But perhaps it would be more to the point to say: The people of this Earth do not respect and love one another any longer!

We humans of today, who overwhelmingly – in Europe – still refer to ourselves as "Christians", who formally still belong to a Christian confession and a Christian church, who still believe in God: have we not lost sight of God's highest commandment, the commandment of love for our neighbour, as is written in the Gospel according to Matthew (22, 34)?

"But when the Pharisees had heard that he had put the Sadducees to silence, they were gathered together. Then one of them, who was a lawyer, asked him a question, tempting him, and saying, 'Master, which is the great commandment in the law?' Jesus said unto him, 'Thou shalt love the Lord thy God with all thy heart, and with all thy soul, and with all thy mind.' This is the first and great commandment. And the second is like unto it, 'Thou shalt love thy neighbour as thyself.' On these two commandments hang all the law and the prophets."

All of us, who still today call ourselves "Christians" and perhaps even argue about theological subtleties, have forgotten the fundamental difference between the Old Covenant and the New Covenant:

Under the Old Covenant, God was Justice!

Under the New Covenant, God is Love!

And all Justice, all Law and all Duty is contained in this Love, is contained in God, who is love itself.

How can an honest Christian talk or think of his "love for God", and at the same time disregard his love for his neighbour?

How can a Christian profess to love God, but neglect love and benevolence towards his nearest, or even be a despiser of mankind?

This type of question leads us straight to the heart of the educational problem. Go and talk to your youth educators, go and talk to the pulpit orators and the preachers, and find out how often, during the course of a week, a month, a year they talk of the highest and most noble commandment: of love for God and one's neighbour. Nearly everywhere, your enquiries will yield deeply saddening and shameful results.

Over the course of the past decades and centuries, the Roman Catholic Church has been blessed with many great popes, bishops and priests. The Protestant, Evangelical, Lutheran and Anglican Churches and all other confessions have produced heroes of faith in recent times, and in oppressed nations all over the world martyrs and true warriors of God have risen. They all deeply lived the love for God and their fellow men, they all found words of love – at times heart-wrenching – in the midst of a world of hate, and with their truly heroic love overcame hatred. We are mindful of the hortatory words on the topic of such love that can be found in the papal and episcopal encyclicals. It would be desirable if these beautiful pastoral letters and valuable epistles were read from the pulpits in Catholic churches in a way that does not send the "rapt" congregation to sleep.

Nowadays most of us Christians are jaded; many of us are hollow and empty! Our so-called "religious inner life" in reality often no longer truly springs from within, encouraging, enriching, a driving force in our daily life with all its joy and anguish: we no longer carry the holy fire of love within us, the love that is God Himself. We no longer carry God within us, and therefore neither the love for God and our neighbours! We are deprived of love, or even depleted of love. At best, our religious life has been reduced to a small element of our Sunday routine, a modest addendum to our lives, without impact or meaning. We have to learn to direct our lives inwards again, hold communion with ourselves and thereby with God, and turn towards love and benevolence for our fellow humans. If we truly hold communion with ourselves, we do not run the risk of self-righteously counting ourselves among the "commendable exceptions", who certainly do exist and have existed at all times, constituting Christianity's avant-garde, without knowing it or striving for it, driven by egotism and ambition.

Friedrich Nietzsche, the ingenious fool, was compelled, though he was an atheist, to testify for God with this most powerful and trenchant eloquence: "Once upon a time, he who is love itself peered into the hearts of humans, but they did not understand him." Just try and speak – dressed in civilian clothes – of love, of God's love and the love for God and for fellow humans, and you will reap scorn and derision, or a pitying shrug of the shoulders and murmuring and whispering behind your back, along the lines of: "Dumb and unfounded fantasies of an idealist! How can he be so unworldly and these days talk of love!"

But how do you suggest we overcome hatred, if not through love? Most of all: how do you suggest we bring up our young, if not through and with love? How do you want to win over the young, if not through love? How do you think you can enthuse the young, if not for the deeds of love, for an active love for God and our fellow humans?

Has Christianity failed?

No! Christianity has never failed once in two thousand years! Only those who wrongly have called themselves Christians have failed.

We have failed, because our religious life for a long time has not been synonymous with the innermost experience of God.

We have failed, because we were not able to instil positive Christian ideals in our youth, to convey to our young the highest and most noble commandments and to win them over with their fire of youthful enthusiasm: Thou shalt love the Lord thy God and thy neighbour as thyself!

The book "*Life, Nature, Religion*", published in 1926 by [the publishing house of Friedrich] Cohen in Bonn, has sadly received much too little attention and is not widely available these days. In it, one can find the following passage:

"If thoughts of God, the afterlife, justice and love derived from God, and salvation and blessedness were to correspond to a reality; if the matter of these thoughts was – in the parlance of everyday people – as real as the rocks and the sea, as gravity that binds us, and as the light that shines for us, and if consequently there were laws to be derived from these realities, —— undoubtedly it would be magnificent, beautiful, powerful and sublime, an inextinguishable blazing light of hope, an unfailing source of optimism, and a decisive factor for all our actions." (Friedrich Dessauer) (1881-1963) [*The author is referring to Freidrich Dessauer's book* Leben, Natur, Religion: Das Problem der Transzenden Wirklichkeit, *originally published in 1924 by Friedrich Cohen of Bonn, and reprinted in 1926.*]

Has the German youth been irremediably contaminated?

On January 30, 1939, the anniversary of the "assumption of power" (the last before the outbreak of war), Dr Josef Goebbels, *Reich* Propaganda Minister and *Gauleiter* of Berlin, gave a propaganda speech in front of the assembled youth of the Berlin working-class district of Wedding, in which he reflected on the following thoughts, among others:

"Even we, now grown men, once went to school and sat at what are now your desks. But we didn't have it as good as you, my German boys and girls. We did not have any ideals relating to the present, which we could get excited about and for which we could work and fight. We lived in a state then that no longer had any future objectives and that was satiated in its purpose. It also was no longer able to teach us about any ideals. If we were yearning for ideals, we had to seek them out ourselves."

Propaganda Minister Josef Goebbels enjoyed lecturing German schoolchildren, saying to them: "Even we, now grown men, once went to school and sat at what are now your desks. But we didn't have it as good as you, my German boys and girls." That was in 1939, just before the outbreak of a world war, which was doubtless his concept of a better world for children, in which so many of them would be mercilessly slaughtered fighting for their Führer.

Now, we all know with what horrendous ideals the Nazi regime not only enthused but also fanaticised the German youth. — To begin with, the German youth was made to believe: "Christianity has failed!" And today, the German youth no longer knows Christianity, most of them do not even know about God, not to speak of the "love for God and fellow humans".

National Socialism offered to the German youth more than bare "historical materialism", as was preached in the Soviet Union. It created the ideal of the "heroic human" and the racial ideal of the "German super-human". The German youth should not be deprived of a cult, and as the Christian cultus was not useful for the authoritarian Nazi state, an *ersatz* concept was forged and an "Old German", heathen mysticism was created, which was simultaneously astonishingly weird and, for the German youth, very dangerous. "A clenched fist against God, against the God of Christianity," once said a truly great man. — The super-human Nietzsche seemed to have been born and, despite all the mysticism, was still nothing more than an automaton.

(How many more times will we have to listen to some jaded know-all telling us: "Yes, well, it's all Nietzsche's fault! And the French encyclopaedists'! And Hegel's! And Haeckel's! And Darwin's! And — — —" We would like to ask: what did our "moral philistines" do about any of it? They only fought negatively against it, but were not able to read the signs of the times.)

Yet, what seems to us to be more important than the instilling of heathen "content", however dangerous this might have been, and more important than any so-called "ideals" that the Nazis deluded the German youth with, is the fact that National Socialism spurred the German youth into *action*. The German youth after the Great War wanted to embrace the meaning of life not through thought, but through deeds. This youth did not want to think and talk *about* object and deed, but wanted object and deed immediately and directly. It would be interesting in this context to investigate why people today so abruptly turn away from philosophy and towards technology, a circumstance that leads many "ideologues" to wrongly conclude that technology is the fundamental evil. In this respect, too, we could like to refer to the aforementioned book "*Life, Nature, Religion*", and the groundbreaking text "*Philosophy of Technology*" by the same author.

In Switzerland, a remarkable essay entitled "On the problem of re-educating the German people" was published in the Jesuit magazine *"Apologetische Blätter"* (Nr. 19 / October 15, 1944). While we do believe in the bitter necessity of a re-education (unlike the essay's author, who rejects it in an overly optimistic manner), for our consideration we would like to quote from some of the article's excellent sections:

"For the 'revolutionaries' (among the National Socialists – author's note) the decisive factor, in a positive sense, was the conviction that the old bourgeois order was a thing of the past. They had not arrived at this viewpoint through schooling or lengthy consideration, in the way the organised working classes had, but as a result of the unemployment that had suddenly befallen them and the visceral symptoms of disintegration of the bourgeois order that most of them originated from. They were not only members of the *petit bourgeoisie*, employees and workers, but also intellectuals and – above all – *adolescents*. They had not connected with the Marxism of Social Democracy or that of Communism, for they did not want to be 'materialists'. Besides, they were not at all looking for 'ideologies', but 'deeds'. They were tired of the 'political parties' useless talk' and instead wanted to 'break through' to a new order of social and public life. And especially the adolescents among them were given much to do by the National Socialist movement, which suited their youthful temperament. The National Socialist movement called them to arms not theoretically, but actually, appealed to their 'heroism and loyalty', promised 'greatness', and gave them specific and concrete tasks."

We can and must win over the German youth for a positive form of Christianity, for a Christianity of action. We have to enthuse our young for the deeds of Christian charity and have to demand concrete "heroic deeds" of love from them. Indeed, we must deploy the youth of the world, and especially the youth of Germany, for the "apostolate of God's love in politics" and make them into veritable champions of Christ! These are no hollow figures of speech and no bleary pipe dreams, but the harsh and inexorable reality we face; it is the challenge that every youth educator must rise to after this war.

The question "has the German youth been contaminated?" still requires an answer. Yes, our young have been poisoned and corrupted by the Nazi leaders; worse than that, they have been violated.

In their upbringing as "heroic humans", the German youth was brutalised against "those of other race and blood"; with the biggest brutes becoming the biggest "heroes". The established notions of decency and morality were turned on their heads. In order to breed a racially pure population, extramarital sexual intercourse was not only tolerated, but it was encouraged, and in some specific areas this encouragement turned into insistence and even coercion. After this war, the task ahead for educators and every honest Christian is immense, and to accomplish it will at times require true Christian heroism. (Devout Christians will rightly assert: without God's grace this enormous task cannot be accomplished! And, more than ever, the old adage holds: God's blessing gained, all is obtained!)

The German youth is contaminated! We now need to answer the question: has the German youth been irremediably contaminated? — In a way, we have already answered this question.

In highly un-Christian pessimism, a well-known Swiss publicist and editor of a renowned Catholic magazine once declared in all seriousness that the girls of the *BDM (Bund Deutscher Mädel* – the National Socialist "League of German Girls") and large swathes of the morally degenerate male Hitler Youth should be exterminated; as in his view there was no other solution to the problem of the German youth! If anyone were to point out to the man that his proposal is no different to the most vile methods dreamt up by Hitler, he would be outraged, for had he not always been an upstanding fighter against the Hitler regime?

Apart from the aforementioned brutalisation, the German youth has also been fanaticised for the aims of a barbarous authoritarian state and is caught in a youthfully exuberant intoxication with power and delusion of race. But by no means is the German youth *irremediably* contaminated! We do not wish to contrast that Swiss publicist's dark pessimism with rose-tinted optimism when it comes to the recuperation of the German youth. The disease has been inculcated, it is growing rampant in the blood. It will require a lengthy recuperation process, until even the first signs of a recovery will be noticeable. What such a recovery process will need more than anything else is love, much love, kindness and patience. Not a love that forgives all, but a love that understands all, without misplaced consideration and mawkishness.

The German youth has not been irremediably contaminated! We would like to express the hope that this generation is currently living through its last febrile delirium, and that the germs of the disease are being expelled by means of this very fever. What will remain, however, will be the seriously weakened body of a fatally injured youth. With the end of the war the false ideals have been destroyed. War, the experience of war, the outcome of the war and the collapse of Nazism have buried these "ideals"; the Nazi leaders themselves have crushed them in their pitiful failure. This did not occur during the war, not at a time when the last drops of courage and readiness for self-sacrifice were being wrung out of every individual. Only when the horrendous murdering and burning suddenly came to an end did a reaction occur, did disillusionment set in and self-reflection commence. The German youth is exhausted, it is empty within. To recognise this fact is terrifying and devastating.

To this young generation, who were ready for action and fighting until the end, and who have sacrificed and failed in equal measure, we want to say this, quoting from the book *"Die Nachfolge Christi"* ("Christian Discipleship") by Thomas von Kempen (Thomas à Kempis):

"Son, in every place, and with every external action and pursuit, diligently strive to be *internally* free and in control of yourself. May your deeds be subject to you and not the other way around, and may you be their master and judge, and not their slave and mercenary."

II. The youth organisations of the NSDAP

The Hitler Youth and *BDM*, *SA*, *NSKK*, *NSFK* and the *Reich* Labour Service

The National Socialist state correctly understood that parents and family play a decisive role in the upbringing of the young, and therefore the Nazi regime ensured that German youths became largely estranged from their families. Parents' right of co-determination in educational matters was reduced to a minimum and in many cases eliminated altogether. Parents were powerless against an "order" a 12- or 14-year-old troop leader might have given to their 8- or 10-year-old son. The war tore families apart in two respects: not only were male family members of conscription age absent while serving at the front, but weary mothers, having toiled all day long carrying out heavy physical labour, would return to an empty home at the end of the day. Most children of school age were "forcibly evacuated" with their schools during the course of the war, usually far away from their homes. As a result, practically all opportunities to bring up their children had been removed from parents. Children were – insofar as they did not already have to perform war duties "helping" in the *Wehrmacht* or the arms industries – completely at the mercy of the Nazi-educators appointed by the state. Children were robbed of their childhoods, to some extent already before the war, but all the more so during the war. The Nazi regime, which once had been so proud of the freshness and health of its Hitler Youth, exploited the health of the German youth in an utterly irresponsible manner, a fact that cannot be justified with any "imperatives of war", however well documented they may have been. Today's young generation in Germany is completely devoid of youthful carefreeness.

The so-called "Hitler Youth", usually abbreviated to *HJ ("Hitlerjugend")*, was founded by the NSDAP in 1926, and a *Reich* law passed in 1939 made membership compulsory for all young Germans. This forced uniformisation of the young – unparalleled in history – robbed the German youth of virtually every potential for individual development. The Hitler Youth, a state institution run according to the National Socialist *Führer* principle, was under the control of the *Reichsjugendführer*, who was directly subordinate to Adolf Hitler and, in the exercise of his office, was not answerable to any other ministry or party agency. Within the NSDAP, the *Reichsjugendführer* occupied the highest rank, namely that of a *Reichsleiter*. The first *Reichsjugendführer* was the "poet" Baldur von Schirach, who had previously been the leader of the National Socialist German Students' League. Later, when he was appointed *Gauleiter* of Vienna, he ceded the post of *Reichsjugendführer* to his "chief of staff" Hartmann Lauterbacher, but remained NSDAP *Reichsleiter* and as such was tasked by Adolf Hitler in 1941 with the youth evacuations from "threatened cities" and the creation of suitable youth encampments.

Baldur Benedikt von Schirach (1907-1974) was the Head of the Hitler Youth. Here he is saluting them from a vehicle with a Hitler salute as they march past him in Nuremberg. In case you notice how young the children are, it is worth knowing that it was compulsory for every German child to join the Hitler Youth from the age of ten. These appear the to be the latest "crop". The bald man standing and smiling at them is SA Obergruppenführer Julius Streicher (1885-1946, executed at Nuremberg), the most virulent and fanatical anti-Semite in the entire Hitler regime, whose anti-Jewish excesses shocked even his colleagues. He was even worse than Alfred Rosenberg. He himself destroyed the Grand Synagogue at Nuremberg as his contribution to *Kristallnacht.* He edited the violently anti-semitic newspaper *Der Stürmer* (*The Attacker*), which was so disgusting that Hermann Göring prohibited his staff from even reading it. His nickname was "King of Nuremberg", so here he is welcoming the children to his city, where he hopes quickly to make good little Jew-haters of all of them.

Here is Baldur von Schirach standing demurely behind his Führer. Schirach has proudly signed this photo. His title is *Reichsjugendführer*, or "Führer of the Nation's Youth". One thing about Schirach which is little known is that he spoke English fluently, which not many of the Nazis did.

The Hitler Youth was structured thus:

Deutsches Jungvolk (German Youngsters), for youths aged 10-14 years. The members of this group, a preliminary stage of the actual Hitler Youth, were called *"Pimpfe"* ("little nippers").

Hitler Youth, for youths aged 14-18 years.

A similar arrangement applied for girls, who were members of the umbrella organisation *"Bund Deutscher Mädels" (BDM)*:

Deutsche Jungmädels (Young Girls' League), for youths aged 10-14 years, a preliminary stage to membership of the actual *BDM*.

Bund Deutscher Mädels (League of German Girls), for youths aged 14-21 (!) years.

Parents or legal guardians were required by law to register their child with the Hitler Youth leader responsible for their residential district by March 15 of the calendar year within which their son or daughter turned 10.

The subdivisions of the Hitler Youth (including the *BDM*) were these:

Kameradschaft, led by an *HJ-Kameradschaftsführer* (in the *Jungvolk*, the equivalent subdivision was *"Fähnlein"*);

Schar, led by an *HJ-Scharführer*;

Gefolgschaft, led by an *HJ-Gefolgschaftsführer*;

Unterbann, led by an *HJ-Unterbannführer*;

Bann, led by an *HJ-Bannführer*;

Gebiet, led by an *HJ-Gebietsführer*.

Until the outbreak of war, a boy would leave the Hitler Youth aged 18, join the *Reich* Labour Service, and then serve in the military for two years. Following active service in the *Wehrmacht*, the former Hitler Youth boy would be subject to so-called "post-conscription military education" by the *SA*. According to a "Führer's order" from January 27, 1939, a special *SA* unit (led by the former *Reichswehr* officer *SABrigadeführer* Georg von Neufville) was created for this purpose.

SA Brigadeführer Georg von Neufville (1883-1941, killed fighting in Russia). He was appointed Head of Postconscription Military Education for all young Germans after they had completed their compulsory two years of active service in the Army.

A model Hitler Youth, trained to salute his Führer at the age of ten. Those aged ten to fourteen were called *Pimpfe*, "Little Nippers" The sign says "In memory of my schooldays. 1933." (Unknown boy.)

By the time they reached their teens, the Hitler Youth were all rigged up in their uniforms with their swastika armbands, ready for action, and with the necessary looks of stalwart determination on their faces, ready to fight, ready to kill. (Unknown boys.)

An unidentified girl in her uniform of the German Maidens' League.

Here we see another unidentified girl in her uniform of the German Maidens' League, but in this photo we can see the swastika on her sleeve and read that she is from the South Swabian branch of the League.

Other members of the general staff of that unit were Lieutenant Colonel [Kurt] Denke (1892-1945) from the army supreme command, Corvette Captain [Karl/Carl, born 1906] Nahrath [*later Bereichsleiter*] from the marine command, and Major Siegerstetter [*probably Ludwig Siegerstetter, 1890-1945*) from the *Luftwaffe* general staff. The organisation of this "pre- and post-conscription military education" was of fundamental importance, which was neither recognised nor appreciated by military experts abroad. Without this novel organisation it would have been an impossibility, in the autumn of 1944, to seemingly pluck out of thin air the so-called *"Volkssturm"* ("People's Storm", a national militia set up by the Nazi party) and the *"Volksgrenadier"* divisions (newly formed infantry divisions). All reserve officers who had long retired from military service were called up as part of these efforts and deployed as military instructors.

Youngsters who had "proven" themselves in the Hitler Youth had the additional option of completing their active military service in one of the *SS* dispositional police units. One of the "ultimate aims" of a certain section of the members of the Hitler Youth was to be admitted into the *SS* later on. Only if they failed in that endeavour due to the rigorous selection criteria would they join, as new party members, the regular *SA* or one of the NSDAP's ancillary organisations. (The above-mentioned "military education" by the *SA* was compulsory and not synonymous with membership of the *SA*.) Apart from the *SS*, the favourite unit for fanatical former members of the Hitler Youth was not the *SA*, but the *NSKK*, the National Socialist Motor Corps, and even more so the *NSFK*, the National Socialist Flyers Corps. Both were responsible – always under the leadership of the *SA* military authority – for a part of the "post-conscription military education":

– the *NSKK* for recruits released from the *Panzerwaffe* (tank forces) and other motorised units of the *Wehrmacht*; and

– the *NSFK* for recruits released from the *Luftwaffe* (air force).

The following section will give an overview of the various organisations that took in Hitler Youth boys when they had reached the age threshold (usually after completion of a stint in the *Reich* Labour Service and compulsory military service), imparting final and decisive education and instruction in the National Socialist spirit. As the *SS* and the *SA* had the same organisational structure, and as we have already repeatedly concerned ourselves with the *SS* in previous chapters, we will only deal with the *SA* at this point.

The National Socialist Motor Corps was launched by a "*Führer's* decree" on August 23, 1933. It was formed out of the *SA* motorised units and elevated to the status of an autonomous subdivision within the NSDAP. Hans Hühnlein [*Note: the author is referring to Adolf Hühnlein, 1881-1942, died of cancer; Hans must have been his nickname, a fact otherwise apparently unrecorded.*], who had until then led the motorised units within the *SA*, was appointed as chief of corps. Hühnlein was a former officer and an old comrade in arms of Hitler's from the early days in Munich, who reached the highest rank within the party when he was appointed *Reichsleiter* of the NSDAP in his capacity as chief of corps of the *NSKK*. In addition, he was made a major general of the *Wehrmacht*. The *NSKK* was structured exactly like the *SA* and the *SS*, except for the fact that between the organisational levels of "motorised groups" and "motorised brigades" a further level of so-called "motorised inspections" was inserted into its hierarchy. [*Various lists of people chosen for assassination at the time of the SA purge existed, and on at least one of them the name of Hühnlein is known to have appeared. However, he was not murdered, and by and large Hühnlein seems to have kept out of politics and concentrated on his vehicles.*]

Major General Adolf ("Hans") Hühnlein, Hitler's old friend from 1923 and the Beer Hall Putsch. He became Korpsführer of the Nazi Motor Corps from 1933 until his death from cancer in 1942.

The organisation of the three major party subdivisions, the *SA*, *SS* and the *NSKK*, can be best illustrated using the example of the *SA*, whose organisational structure was used as the template for the other two branches:

Rotte = 3 men;

Schar = 2-4 *Rotten;*

Trupp = 3-4 *Scharen;*

Sturm = 3-4 *Trupps.* (A *"Sturm"* is the lowest independent unit and equivalent to a company in the *Wehrmacht.*)

Sturmbann (equivalent to a battalion) = 3-5 *Stürme.* A *Sturmbann* had its own ensign.

Standarte (equivalent to a regiment) = 3-5 *Sturmbanner.*

The higher subdivisions were *Brigade, Gruppe,* and ultimately the Supreme *SA* Leadership. The Supreme *SA* Leadership was under the control of the *SA* Chief of Staff, but Adolf Hitler himself was the actual leader of the *SA.*

The first notable *SA* Chief of Staff, Captain [Walter Franz Maria] Stennes (1895-1983), rebelled against Hitler in 1929. That revolt, which was quashed by *SA Gruppenführer* Kurt

Daluege, resulted in the creation of the *SS* (albeit initially as a mere subdivision of the *SA*). Captain Stennes went abroad and found employment in Chongqing organising the bodyguard of Chiang-Kai-shek, the supreme commander and head of state of China.

After the failure of his revolt against Hitler in 1929, Captain Walter Stennes found work elsewhere. Since Hitler was not yet in power and could not seize him or kill him, he was able to flee to China where he organised the personal bodyguard of President Chiang Kai-shek (1887-1975, who is seen above).

Captain Stennes' successor at the *SA* was Captain Ernst Röhm, under whose leadership the *SA* experienced an unprecedented upturn. Apart from Julius Streicher, Ernst Röhm was the only man to be on first-name terms with Hitler. He was shot following the events of June 30, 1934, which were wrongly referred to as an *SA* revolt. Following these developments, the *SS* was made independent of and formally separated from the *SA*. The *Reichsführer SS* was elevated to the rank of a *Reichsleiter* of the NSDAP, and as such was no longer subordinate to the *SA* Chief of Staff. Following Röhm's death, *SA Obergruppenführer* and *Oberpräsident* of Hanover, Victor Lutze, was appointed as *SA* Chief of Staff, succeeded by *SA Obergruppenführer* Schepmann. Both men had been officers in the World War of 1914-18.

The passionate Jew-hater, Julius Streicher (1885-1946, executed), who according to the author was one of only two men on first name terms with Hitler, the other being Ernst Röhm (whom Hitler ordered to be murdered). (It is probable that Rudolf Hess was also technically on first name terms with Hitler, but out of his disproportionate respect and hero-worship declined to call him Adolf.) Streicher was one of the most fanatical anti-Semites in Germany, and was often referred to as 'Jew-Baiter Number One'. He was hanged after the War for cimes against humanity. Otto Strasser, who knew him all too well, said he was a "sexual maniac" and wrote of him: "Never have I met a man more haunted by erotic fantasies. For Streicher the racial theories of National-Socialism were merely an excuse for unloading into the *Stürmer [Note: a weekly tabloid Nazi newspaper edited by Streicher]* the dangerous outpourings of his diseased imagination. 'A sexual crime committed by a Jew on the front page of my paper is like a delicious cocktail, a meal starting with caviar,' he once said to me. He was a man whose ugliness was repulsive to women. During the war he was degraded for an indecent assault upon a young French governess." Hitler's psychoanalyst, Dr. Kurt Krüger, who knew Streicher very well, in his memoir says of him that he "has always given me the impression of an animal badly in need of a bath" and consequently "it would be impossible to understand him if one had no sense of smell." And regarding Streicher's maniacal anti-Semitism, Krüger provides this illuminating account: "Streicher first discovered his hatred of Israel, and the need for racial purity, when the girl with whom he was in love turned him down in favour of a Jew. ... Oddly enough, I have never heard him say anything against the Jews except when he was ranting from a platform. What is in the make-up of such a man that makes Jews palatable to him on an ordinary level, and obnoxious when he has managed to climb several feet in the air? Is it a simple maladjustment of the affections, or a more complicated piece of fraud?"

Victor (aka Viktor) Lutze (1890-1943). He joined the Nazi Party in 1922. After Ernst Röhm was murdered, Lutze succeeded him as head of the SA, where he supervised a reduction and "cleaning up" of the SA's forces and was named a Reichsleiter (Leader of the Reich). He had only one eye, having lost the other in combat in the First World War. During the War, he was appointed Chief of Police for the Province of Hanover. In 1943 he was driving too fast and crashed into a tree, killing his older daughter and receiving injuries of which he died later in hospital.

The National Socialist Flyers Corps was launched, at Hermann Göring's instigation, by a "*Führer's* decree" on April 17, 1937, in order "to keep alive and intensify the aeronautical spirit in the German people, to provide aviation training prior to military service, and to combine and unify all aeronautical activities". A general of the *Luftwaffe*, namely Lieutenant General Friedrich Christiansen, was appointed as Chief of Corps of the *NSFK*. Christiansen had been a famous flying ace in the World War of 1914-18 and had been awarded Prussia's highest military medal of honour, the *"Pour le mérite"*. Unusually, his route into aviation was not via the cavalry, but via the navy, where he had served as a marine lieutenant and well-known *U-Boot* captain. General Christiansen, a personal friend of [Luftwaffe Colonel-General Ernst] Udet (1896-1941, suicide) [the famous World War I flying ace] and Göring, was not a long-standing party member and therefore was not appointed *Reichsleiter* of the NSDAP. In 1940/41, when an invasion of the British Isles seemed to be imminent – an operation in which the *Luftwaffe* was meant to play a major role – *Luftwaffe* General Christiansen was appointed military governor of Holland.

Despite the fact that the responsibility for *pre*-military education had also been given over to the newly created *SA* unit (as per a *Führer's* decree from January 27, 1939), the *Reich* Labour Service continued to be the organisation that every Hitler Youth boy was required to join before commencing his military service with the *Wehrmacht*. The chief of the *Reich* Labour Service was a retired *Reichswehr* colonel, who had left the *Reichswehr* in 1924 with the rank of major general, since 1929 had acted as a head of department and consultant in the NSDAP, and immediately after Hitler's takeover took over the organisation of the *Reich* Labour Service. Konstantin Hierl by name, he was a long-standing party member and one of the 19 *Reichsleiter* of the NSDAP.

Konstantin Hierl (1875-1955) was an old chum of Hitler's before he came to power. He joined the Nazi Party in 1929. He was Head of the Reich Labour Service and State Secretary of the Ministry of Labour. He then transferred to the Ministry of the Interior as Reichscommissar, being State Secretary for the Ministry. In 1943 he became Minister without Portfolio and was a Reichsleiter (Leader of the Reich). He was appointed Major General, which explains his uniform here. He is wearing the First World War Iron Cross, first and second class, which he won on the Western Front as a Colonel in the previous war. He helped keep the Reich running by organising its labour force, supplying workers to repair roads and runways, laying mines, constructing fortifications, keeping the supplies of food and ammunition flowing to the front, etc.

The *Reich* Labour Service was a purely state-run civil organisation and as such was under the control of the *Reich* Ministry for the Interior, where Hierl occupied the post of state secretary. The Chief of the *Reich* Labour Service was also in charge of seven inspectors, who each headed one of the seven departments within the *Reich* Labour Service:

– the department for service, personnel, education and instruction;

– the department for work performance;
– the administrative and commercial department;
– the legal department;
– the department for press and propaganda;
– the department for health; and
– the department for conscription and registration.

The *Reich* Labour Service comprised 36 so-called *Arbeitsgaue* (labour districts), which were each headed by an *Arbeitsgauführer* with the rank of a *Generalarbeitsführer* or *Oberstarbeitsführer*. The inspectors of the seven aforementioned departments usually held the rank of *Obergeneralarbeitsführer*, the second highest rank after *Reichsarbeitsführer*. Much like in most Nazi organisations, this organisation, too, was subdivided into a vast number of branches and offices and was structured according to a hierarchy that mirrored that of the *Wehrmacht*:

Arbeitsmann, *Vormann*, *Obervormann*, *Truppführer*, *Obertruppführer*, *Unterfeldmeister*;
followed by the ranks equivalent to "officer" status:
Feldmeister, *Oberfeldmeister*, *Oberstfeldmeister*;
and the ranks equivalent to the "generals":
Arbeitsführer, *Oberarbeitsführer*, *Oberstarbeitsführer*, *Generalarbeitsführer*, *Obergeneralarbeitsführer*.

It is not insignificant that a large number of Prussian squires and German noblemen were represented in the highest echelons of the *Reich* Labour Service.

Within the Hitler Youth, there was a myriad of special groups and factions, all of course with their accompanying bureaus, branches, main departments and the many other offices that had been created for the endless numbers of careerists in the party. Apart from the usual war games, which the German youth was to be enthused about, there was much "cultivation of customs and traditions" and much ado about the *BLUBO* ideology *("Blut und Boden"* – blood and soil). The *HJ* choirs dug out many old *Landsknecht* (mercenary) songs, and the *HJ* theatre troupes rehearsed coarse folksy plays full of fascist undertones and staged them up and down the country. The poison of National Socialist ideology was propagated very skilfully and instilled in the so often unaware participants. The German youth was not only threatened with the cane, and was not only drilled and exercised, but this generation of young German people was also flattered in an unprecedented manner, awakening a hubristic arrogance in this "cream of the German race". Folk art was also cultivated in the Hitler Youth, sometimes even yielding commendable results. The systematic coarsening and barbarisation, led by the Nazi-appointed educators and party officials, at times produced very peculiar "graduates".

It is no coincidence that there was only ever talk of the Hitler Youth, and that it was taken for granted that this was synonymous with the male half of the German youth. Indeed, the female youth was only a sort of appendage of the dominant and primary Hitler Youth. The girls were meant to serve and their purpose was to ensure the preservation and procreation of the German race. Having reached her 14th birthday, a German girl would be transferred from *Deutsche Jungmädel* to the *Bund Deutscher Mädel*. There she would serve her so-called *Landjahr* ("country year"), was trained in home economics, cooking and sewing etc., and, after the outbreak of war, enjoyed the "special privilege" of being drafted for labour service, or even being "allowed" to become an auxiliary volunteer with the *Wehrmacht*. After her 21st birthday, the *Mädel* could be received into the National Socialist Women's League, which was an adjunct to the German Labour Front. Gertrud Scholz-Klink was the *Reichsleiterin* of the National Socialist Women's League (as well as *"Deutsche Frauenführerin"* – German Women's Leader). As she was a woman, she never rose to the highest rank of the NSDAP, that of *Reichsleiter*, despite all her titles and offices. Under the Nazi regime, German girls and women never had equal status, not even when they carried out the heaviest of labour and, with their service at the home front, were required to fully stand in for their brothers, fathers and husbands who were at the front. And yet, National Socialism managed to use and fanaticise girls and women for its ends in vast numbers. At mass rallies, the enthusiasm shown for their *Führer* by National Socialist girls and women all too often verged on hysteria. Anyone who would have witnessed, for example, the conduct of National Socialist girls and women in front of the *Reich* Chancellery in Berlin on the evening of January 30, 1933, the day before Hitler's takeover, knows what fanaticised women are capable of.

Ordensburgen **("order castles") und** ***Junkerschulen*** **("*****Junker*** **schools")**

In general, the Hitler Youth did not maintain its own schools, it only ran instructions camps, which were on the whole mobile and not tied to a geographical location. Anyone who especially distinguished himself in the Hitler Youth, and after serving in the *Wehrmacht*, or, in such cases, more likely in an *SS* unit, would have the chance to be "blessed with the incomparable honour" of being admitted into one of the *Ordensburgen*. In addition, the candidate would have had to have served for at least three years in a party unit in a leadership role (say, as an *SS-Sturmführer*, or, in the *HJ*, at least as an *Unterbannführer*) and distinguished himself in doing so.

At the beginning of 1939, the NSDAP maintained three so-called *Ordensburgen*:
Krössinsee in Pomerania
Vogelsang in the Rhineland
Sonthofen in Bavaria.

In these schools, each of which had a capacity for 1,000 students, the next generation of National Socialist leaders was groomed. This means that there were at that time only 3,000 young men in the entire territory of the *Reich* who were deemed worthy of receiving a special education as future "leaders of the German people" in the academies run by the party.

Anyone admitted to an *Ordensburg* became a *Junker*! A *Junker* had to enlist for a training period of three years, one year in each of the three *Ordensburgen*, during which time he would have been almost completely isolated from the outside world. At the point of admission, a *Junker* had to be between 25 and 30 years of age, and, after graduation, a *Junker* would become a high party official. The curriculum for the *Ordensburgen* was compiled by *Reichsleiter* Alfred Rosenberg, the "*Führer's* commissary for the supervision of the entire spiritual and ideological education of the NSDAP and its ancillary organisations". Prominent party grandees and NSDAP *Reichsleiter* would personally give frequent lectures according to Alfred Rosenberg's curriculum.

The three NSDAP *Ordensburgen* enjoyed an unparalleled position of privilege among all the party's schools, and any *Junker* who had graduated from these *Ordensburgen* automatically held a privileged position compared to a graduate of any of the other *Junker* schools run by the *SS* or *SA*.

The most distinguished school after the three *Ordensburgen* was the *SS Junker* School

Braunschweig. Unlike the *Ordensburgen*, it was purely a military school, a sort of war academy run by the *SS*, where *SS* leaders, who would later be put to use as officers in the *SS* dispositional police units, were trained in military matters. The *SS Junker* School Braunschweig, the first one of its kind, was founded in November 1934, and its first commander was the former Lieutenant General *SS-Brigadeführer* [Paul] Hausser (1880-1972).

General Paul Hausser (180-1972). In 1934 he was appointed the first Head of the first SS War Academy at Braunschweig. (Bundesarchiv)

The organisation of the former cadet schools served as a model for the *SS Junker* School Braunschweig. Every *SS-Junker*, before being elevated to the rank of an officer, had to take an exam in front of a board comprised of members of the general staff of the *Reichswehr* (!) and later the *Wehrmacht*. Consequently, all those who emerged as *SS* leaders from the *SS Junker* School Braunschweig were recognised as officers by the *Wehrmacht*.

Hausser, the first commander of the *SS Junker* School Braunschweig, was a noteworthy man. Until 1932 he had been a member of the *Reichswehr*, where he had served as a regimental commander in Dresden and ultimately as commander of the 4th infantry regiment. After his departure from the *Reichswehr* with the rank of Lieutenant General, he served as Chief of the *SA* Reservist Brigade in Berlin Brandenburg with the rank of *SABrigadeführer*, until Himmler brought him into the *SS* and appointed him as the commander of the first *SS Junker* school. In March 1936, the former Lieutenant General Hausser, having now been reappointed as *SS-Brigadeführer*, became inspector of all *SS* dispositional troops and as such was responsible for the training of the new *SS* military regiments, the *SS-Standarten "Adolf Hitler", "Deutschland", "Germania"* and *"Der Führer"*, as well as the technical units *SS* Signal Corps "Adlershof" near Berlin and the *SS* Engineers Corps "Dresden" (one battalion each). The newly appointed inspector was *not* in charge of the *SS* dispositional unit *"Totenkopf"* and the *"Leibstandarte* Adolf Hitler*"*. It is to the credit of the former Lieutenant General Hausser that the *SS* dispositional units for whose military training he was responsible turned into true elite units, equal in combat value and fighting power to the very best military units. After the outbreak of war, Hausser was promoted to the ranks *SS-Gruppenführer* and then *SS-Obergruppenführer* and distinguished himself as a capable commander on the eastern, south-eastern and western fronts. He and Sepp Dietrich, the commander of the *"Leibstandarte Adolf Hitler"*, were the only two *SS* leaders who, with the ranks of Colonel General, made it to the very top of the *Wehrmacht* hierarchy. Colonel General *SS-Obergruppenführer* Hausser was wounded while leading an army unit during the German retreat out of France in the area of Falaise, but despite his injuries he stayed at the head of his unit and managed to breach the Anglo-American encirclement. Afterwards he spent many months gravely ill in a military hospital near Heidelberg. Hausser's military career is described in a lot of detail here because it was he who was selected as the supreme commander of the planned national redoubt in the Alps of Bavaria and Tyrol.

The most important *SA* school was the *SA Reichsführerschule* in Dresden, which was also a sort of military academy, and in actual fact had been founded as a branch of the famous *"Kriegsschule Dresden"* (a renowned *Reichswehr* war academy) for the military training of *SA* leaders. The offices of *SA Gruppenführer* Ivers, the Chief of the Department for the *Reichsschulen* of the Supreme *SA* Command, were located within the *SA Reichsschule* Dresden.

It would be pointless within the context of this book to list even just the names of all the schools run by the *SS, SA, NSKK, NSFK* and all other party subdivisions. At the beginning of 1939, the *Reich* Labour Service alone maintained – apart from a so-called *Reichsschule* – no fewer than:

9 district schools

5 *Feldmeister* schools

3 administrative schools

19 *Truppführer* schools

from which the *Reich* Labour Service recruited each new generation of leaders and where its *Unterführer* were trained.

Alongside the *Ordensburgen*, the Junker schools of the *SS* and the *SA*, which usually had a military character, and the schools of the *Reich* Labour Service listed above, there existed the so-called "national-political educational establishments". These were official state-run schools, which therefore did not belong to the party or one of its subdivisions, but were directly subordinated to the *Reich* Ministry for Science, Education and Public and Culture. (In the past, the running of the schools had fallen under the remit of the responsible ministry in each *Land*. The *Gleichschaltung* laws of March 31 and April 7, 1934, which sought to further the "spirit of a centralised state", transferred all responsibility to the *Reich* Ministry for Science, Education and Public and Culture). *Reichsminister* Bernhard Rust, one of the most obnoxious Nazis, who has in general been given much too little attention, was appointed as chief of these "national-political educational establishments".

Reichsminister Bernhard Rust (1883-1945,suicide), 'one of the most obnoxious of the Nazis' according to the author.

In 1933, while Rust was still Prussian Minister for Cultural Affairs, at his personal instigation the first three "national-political educational establishments" were founded in the state of Prussia, namely in Ploen, Koeslin [Koszalin] and Potsdam. These three institutions were followed by others; before the year 1933 was out, for example, the "Great Orphanage" in Potsdam was remodelled as a national-political educational establishment (though already in 1937 it was returned to its original purpose and reinstated as a military orphanage run by the Supreme Command of the *Wehrmacht*). The cadet school Wahlstatt met a similar fate; it was abandoned also in 1937 due to "difficulties relating to space and terrain". When the first of these schools were established, the central theme was to "work towards the actualisation of National Socialist principles".

During the year 1934, national-political educational establishments were founded in the following locations:

Berlin-Spandau,

Naumburg-Saale,

Ilfeld-Harz, Oranienstein near Diez/Lahn,

Stuhm-Danzig [Gdansk].

Further institutions were opened in Württemberg (Backnang), Anhalt (Ballenstedt-Harz) and in Saxony (Klotzsche, near Dresden), followed by Schulpforta and Bensberg/Rhine in 1935. In 1936, *Ministerpräsident* Mergenthaler opened a second national-political educational establishment in the *Land* of Württemberg, namely in Rottweil, and the then *Ministerpräsident* of Anhalt opened a second institution in Koethen. In 1938, the tenth Prussian school, Neuzelle, was founded in Brandenburg.

After the Nazi assault on Austria, the four existing Austrian educational establishments – Theresianum (Vienna), Breitensee (Vienna), Boerhavegasse (Vienna, a girls' school), and Traiskirchen (near Vienna) – were taken over and, in 1939, to "commemorate the takeover", re-opened as national-political educational establishments for the *Gau Ostmark*. The girls' school was relocated away from Vienna into the Starhemberg mansion Hubertendorf. In the autumn of 1940 the first establishment of the *Gau Sudetenland* was founded in Ploschkowitz [Ploskovice] Castle near Leitmeritz [Litoměřice], and the first such establishment of the *Warthegau* was founded in a castle previously belonging to Count Sułkowski, in Reisen [Rydzyna] near Lissa [Leszno].

[*Note: Prince Ernst Rüdiger Camillo von Starhemberg, 1899-1956, was an Austrian fascist whom Hitler accused of plotting with Ernst Röhm and Gregor Strasser in support of the SA. Starhemberg became Vice-Chancellor of Austria as well as its Minister of Public Security. When the Anschluss of Austria happened, Starhemberg fled to Switzerland, and became an open opponent of the Nazis, collaborating both with the Western Allies and with the Russians. The seizing of the Starhemberg mansion and its use for a girls' school was obviously part of the Nazis' punishment for the Prince's political stance.*]

No fewer than ten "national-political educational establishments" were newly opened to mark the occasion of the *Führer's* birthday on April 20, 1941:

Putbus on the Island of Rügen,
Lublinitz [Lubliniec] in Upper Silesia,
Seckau and Vorau in Styria,
St. Paul in Carinthia,
St. Wendel in the *Westmark* (Saarland),
Reichenau on Lake Constance,
Rufach [Rouffach] in the Alsace region,
Achern in the Baden region,
Colmar-Berg in Luxembourg.

The fact that almost all of the "national-political educational establishments" were installed in "expropriated" castles, mansions or monasteries formed part of the National Socialists' usual practice.

The prevailing spirit within these schools and the manner in which the occupants of these establishments were treated can best be illustrated with reference to the following fact:

The chief of the powerful *SS Main Office, SS-Obergruppenführer* [August] Heissmeyer (who had gained notoriety as the Gestapo Chief of Norway and who at times scared *Reichskommissar* Terboven nearly as much as he intimidated Herr Quisling) also acted as Inspector of all National Socialist educational establishments. As inspector of the schools, it was *SS-Obergruppenführer*

Heissmeyer's responsibility to ensure that only tried and tested *SS* leaders were admitted into the teaching staff. The chief of the educational establishments, *Reichsminister* [Bernhard] Rust, was not entrusted with the drawing up of the curricula; this task fell entirely under Inspector Heissmeyer's remit. The *Reichsminister* was only responsible for "financial administration". During the official ceremonies held on April 22, 1941 at the "national-political educational establishment" Backnang-Württemberg, celebrating the opening of the ten new schools, *Reichsminister* Rust spoke the following "fine" words: "It is the *Führer's* deepest conviction that to deploy men in combative roles is to fulfil God's highest commandment, and that only he who fulfils this commandment may expect the blessings of providence!"

The "short and bow-legged" SS Obergruppenführer August Heissmeyer (1897-1979) was put in charge of German education. All teachers had to be SS-approved and he personally drew up the curricula. He married the notorious Gertrud Scholtz-Klink, the Reich Women's Leader (for her see Volume Two.) According to the author, Heissmeyer became head of the Gestapo in Norway for some time under the Quisling regime, though this does not seem to be recorded anywhere on the internet. According to the author, he was so scary that he terrified even Quisling himself. He also became Chief of the SS Main Office and was always ready to "crack down". Heissmeyer was one of the most brutal and violent of all the Nazis. He was an incredible daredevil, undertaking hundreds of desperate and dangerous missions as a Lieutenant in the First World War, so that his pursuit of violence and danger could genuinely be considered compulsive and uncontrollable. After the First World War, Heissmeyer became one of the main assassins active in the revived Fehme Movement, and we shall never know how many moderate, centre and left politicians he personally assassinated. He joined the Nazi Party in 1922 and became a spy who infiltrated the trade unions, apparently using various aliases and even physical disguises. (He should not be confused with his cousin SS General Werner Heissmeyer, who is discussed elsewhere.)

Inspector Heissmeyer had left no doubt about how "God's highest commandment", as seen by Adolf Hitler, was to be understood and interpreted.

Within the *SS* hierarchy, *SS-Obergruppenführer* Heissmeyer, in his capacity as Chief of the *SS* Main Office, was ranked just below *Reichsführer SS* Heinrich Himmler. After the death of Heydrich, the Chief of the *SD*, Heissmeyer was seen as Himmler's closest ally. Within the hierarchy of the state, however, there were two *SS* leaders that outranked Heissmeyer, namely *SS-Oberstgruppenführer* Kurt Daluege and *SS-Obergruppenführer* Kaltenbrunner. Kurt Daluege was chief of the German regular police force, and as such the deputy of Himmler, in his capacity as chief of the German police; furthermore, after Heydrichs's death and the dismissal of Baron Neurath, Daluege was appointed as *Reichsprotektor* for Bohemia and Moravia. Kaltenbrunner, on the other hand, succeeded Heydrich as chief of the German security police and – much more importantly – as chief of the *SD-RFSS*. Nevertheless, he never attained Heydrich's significance and his influence on Himmler is said to have been very limited.

Yet the man who would become the most popular *SS* leader, and whose power should not be underestimated, was *SS-Obergruppenführer* and Colonel General of the *Wehrmacht*, Sepp Dietrich. Even when he was deployed at the front he never relinquished his leadership of the *"Leibstandarte Adolf Hitler"*, and in some sense he could be seen as Himmler's antagonist. For Sepp Dietrich not only enjoyed the personal confidence of Adolf Hitler, but he was also the military representative of the triumvirate Bouhler-Bormann-Amann, the head and heart of the entire party apparatus. He could also count on Xaver Schwarz, *Reich* treasurer and Hitler's personal asset manager, and the party's supreme judge, retired Major Buch. While the two men were very close associates of Dietrich, they by no means always agreed with Himmler.

SS-Obergruppenführer Heissmeyer was seen as one of Himmler's most reliable friends and was deployed by Himmler whenever a "merciless crackdown" was deemed necessary. Indeed it was Heissmeyer who would break the resistance of the brave Norwegians. The appointment of this man who physically in no way conformed to the Nazi racial ideal (he was short and bowlegged) as "inspector of the national-political educational establishments" illustrates in the starkest terms the conditions youth education found itself in under the Nazi regime.

PART TWO

THE FIRST EXPANSION OF POWER

THE WORKINGS OF NATIONAL SOCIALISM

I. Introductory remarks

It has already been suggested that the author seeks to report on facts, not "connections". There are good reasons to reiterate this point at the beginning of the present chapter. June 30, 1934 is seen as a turning point in the fate of modern German history. Other writers also share this point of view; much has been written in the press, in magazines, brochures and books about June 30, 1934. Unfortunately the authors of such articles oftentimes lost themselves in "connections", and their imagination at times strayed into the most exalted spheres, only to then burrow into the lowest depths. Concrete details were thin on the ground; the authors relied on hearsay and a few official communiqués. The less information there was available, the more abundantly did the "connections" sprout and multiply.

The present author knows that it was not more than perhaps a dozen men who knew – through their own direct experience – the precise interconnection between the events that would turn out to be a turning point in German history.

Or more precisely: only perhaps a dozen men who precisely understood the circumstances that led to the events of June 30, 1934 survived that day. One of them is the author of these pages. By the end of the war, the last survivors from that group of insiders could likely be counted on the fingers of one hand. And yet there are many who only knew one detail or another, and on the basis of such limited knowledge drew the wrong conclusions, because they were unaware of the interconnections.

As the following report is one of the few sources that will be available to future generations, it has been deemed necessary to include many details, some even of an embarrassing nature. It is a simple fact that pathological tendencies and their exploitation played a significant role in the events that brought about June 30, 1934, and that Nazism abundantly exploited the associated dependencies for its purposes. One of the three female protagonists that deserve special mention, Baroness Biel, was a conscious and salaried agent of the *SD-RFSS*, whereas Miss Isabel St. and Fräulein Jucki de L. were exploited and unsuspecting victims.

II. The path to June 30, 1934
The *Reichswehr*

The German *Reichswehr* had been created on the basis of the Treaty of Versailles; officially it came into existence on January 1, 1921. It was then transformed into the new German *Wehrmacht* on March 16, 1935, when a *Reich* law was passed reintroducing universal "conscription", in direct contravention of the terms of the Treaty of Versailles. As per the peace dictate, the *Reichswehr* was to be comprised of 100,000 men in the *Reichsheer* (land forces), including 4,000 officers, and 15,000 men in the so-called *Reichsmarine*, including 1,500 officers. On March 16, 1935, the order of the day to the soldiers of the new German *Wehrmacht* included the words: "Despite all the shackles put upon it, the *Reichswehr* has been able to rescue the venerated and ancient soldierly spirit and the willingness to sacrifice, and to preserve these for the new German *Wehrmacht*!"

The *Reichspräsident* was the Supreme Commander of the *Reichsheer* and the *Reichsmarine*; until 1925 this was the Social Democrat Friedrich Ebert, and, from April 26, 1925 until August 2, 1934, Field Marshall General von Hindenburg. The *Reichswehrminister*, who was directly subordinate to the *Reichspräsident*, had authority of command. The special position of the *Reichswehrminister* was evidenced by the fact that, in his capacity as the commander of the *Reichswehr*, he was not answerable to the government of the *Reich* or the responsible *Reich*

Chancellor, but only to the *Reichspräsident.* This arrangement ensured from the outset the *Reichswehr's* homogeneity and inviolability vis-à-vis the *Reich* government and the *Reichstag. Reichspräsident* Ebert has the dubious distinction that he practically never exercised his authority of command and instead let the *Reichswehr's* generals have free rein. Field Marshall General von Hindenburg, on the other hand, considered it a matter of honour to promote the *Reichswehr* under his command in any way possible. According to the terms of the Treaty of Versailles, no state-run arms industry was allowed to exist; yet under *Reichspräsident* von Hindenburg the foundations of a new arms industry were laid. Without it, the gigantic expansion of armament that began under Hitler could not have been accomplished in such a short time. A commanding general, the "Chief of the Army Command", was at the head of the *Reichswehr.* The general staff of this army command did a thorough job in preparing the 100,000-strong *Reichswehr* as the core of a future army that would be a million strong.

The Chiefs in Command of the *Reichswehr* were:
1921–1926: General Hans von Seeckt,
1926–1930: General Wilhelm Heye,
1930–1934: Kurt Gebhard Freiherr von Hammerstein-Equord,
1934–1935: Werner Freiherr von Fritsch.

When the *Reichswehr* was transformed into the new German *Wehrmacht,* General von Fritsch was appointed "Supreme Commander of the Army", only to be replaced, after his dismissal, by General Walther von Brauchitsch in 1938.

Field Marshal Walther Heinrich Alfred Hermann von Brauchitsch (1881-1948). He replaced von Fritsch as Supreme Commander of the Army in 1938.

While formally the authority of command over both elements of the *Reichswehr*, the *Reichsheer* and the *Reichsmarine*, rested with the *Reichswehrminister*, his office played a largely administrative role. The person with actual authority over the *Reichsheer* was the "Chief of the Army Command".

The *Reichswehrminister* were:
1920–1928: Dr Otto Gessler,
1928–1932: Dr Wilhelm Groener,
1932–1933: General [Kurt] von Schleicher,
1933–1938: General [Werner] von Blomberg.

General Dr. Wilhelm Groener (1867-1939), Reichswehrminister 1928-1932. He and Hindenburg were the two people who advised the Kaiser to abdicate at the end of the first World War, advice which the Kaiser took. He threw Army support to the Social Democrats after the First World War and helped to prevent a communist revolution in Germany. He was a determined opponent of the Nazis, but he lost power in 1932 because of trying to stop them.

The command over the small German navy was exercised for the *Reichswehrminister* by an admiral acting as "Chief of the Navy Command". These chiefs were:
1920–1924: Admiral [Paul] Behncke,
1924–1928: Admiral [Hans] Zenker,
1928–1935: Admiral Dr [Erich] Räder.

In the same way that General Fritsch had been put in command of the land troops, Admiral Dr Räder was appointed "Supreme Commander of the *Kriegsmarine*" when the new German *Wehrmacht* was created.

Grand Admiral Erich Johann Albert Räder (1876-1960), who commanded the German Navy until 1943, when he was replaced by Admiral Karl Dönitz. In his youth, before the First World War, he had been the Captain of the Kaiser's private yacht, a yacht which later was bought by Atwater ("Attie") Kent in America.

The office and title of *Reichskriegsminister* (*Reich* Minister of War) were also created as early as 1935, which means that in actual fact General von Blomberg was *Reichswehrminister* only until 1935, and then was given the new title of *Reichskriegsminister*. Much like the *Reichswehrminister* before him, the *Reichskriegsminister* was formally the supreme commander of the three newly created constituent elements of the *Wehrmacht*: army, navy and – a new addition – the *Luftwaffe*. When Hitler took over the supreme command of the *Wehrmacht* in 1938, not only was that authority withdrawn from the *Reichskriegsminister*, but that office was dissolved altogether and all responsibilities (that is to say, the purely administrative responsibilities) were taken over by the newly appointed "Chief of the Supreme Command of the *Wehrmacht*". From 1938 that post was held by General Wilhelm Keitel.

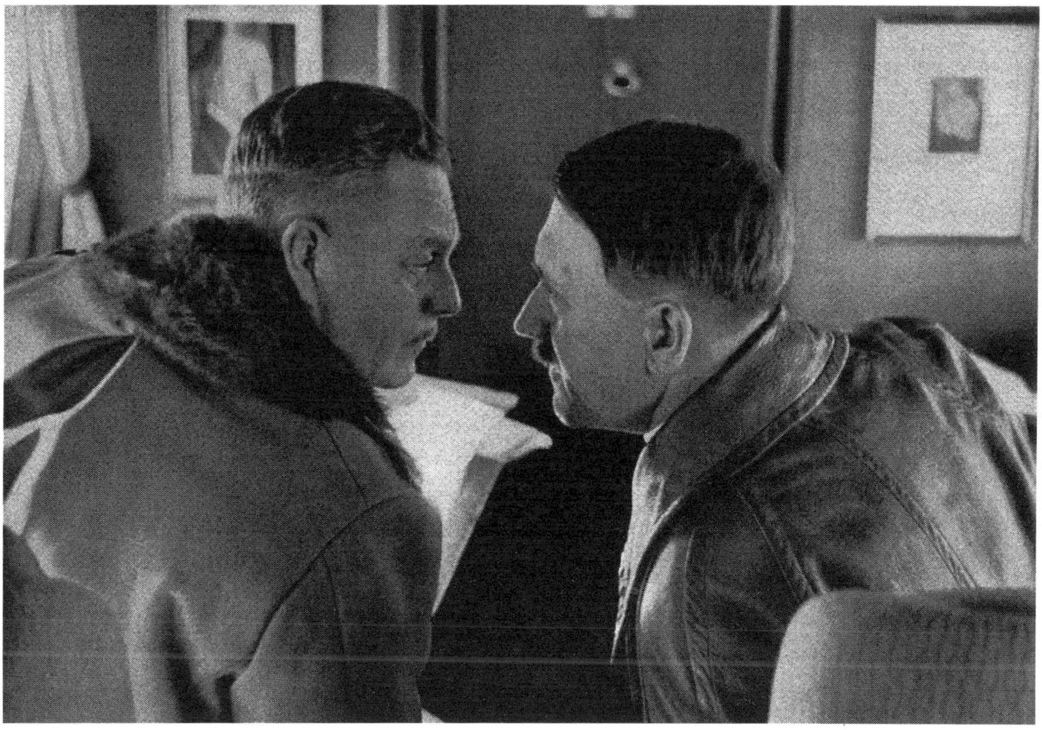

Hitler and General Wilhelm Keitel in earnest conversation. Being obliging and a good listener got Keitel very far, and he became Supreme Commander of the German Army.

Germany was divided into seven *Wehrkreise* (military districts), each with its own division. The divisions were later turned into army corps, and the division commanders – the commanding generals – became army corps commanders. In addition to the seven army corps there were three cavalry divisions.

With its "cavalry academy", the city of Hanover was a stronghold of the cavalry, where, even before the creation of the new German *Wehrmacht*, substantial troop numbers, far exceeding a single cavalry division, were stationed. For many years, General von Pogrell (who has since attracted much too little attention both within Germany and abroad) acted as the commander of that cavalry academy. He strove to preserve the "attacking spirit of the cavalry" and made sure that "his cavalry" would form the core of the newly created tank units. Until his dismissal in 1938, General von Pogrell was – much like General von Fritsch – a firm opponent of National Socialism, who frequently and openly expressed his contempt for the

Nazis. It was to him – and not, say, to Gregor Strasser – that the promise was made in 1932 by Field Marshal General von Hindenburg (a man whom he revered) that he, *Reichspräsident* Hindenburg, would never appoint "the Bohemian Private [Hitler]" as *Reich* Chancellor. For these gentlemen, the term "Bohemian" was synonymous with all that was unsound, gypsy-like, of obscure heritage, lacking tradition and devoid of a "sense of honour".

The organisational mind behind the creation of the *Reichswehr* was General Hans von Seeckt, a tough, taciturn sort of man, who would doggedly perform his duties and was forever resentful about the outcome of the war of 1914–18. General von Seeckt was rightfully regarded as a second Gneisenau of the Prussian-German army and revered as such even during his lifetime. During the war of 1914–18, he was first Chief of the General Staff of the 11th Army, being involved in the breakthrough at Gorlice, when between April and September 1915 the Russian Front was pushed back from the direction of the Carpathian Mountains. The commander of the 11th Army was August von Mackensen, whose Chief of General Staff, General von Seeckt, remained in position when Mackensen was given the command over the Army Group South, which penetrated deep into the Caucasus via Turkey and eventually even seized the Russian oil fields. When the magnificent Chief of General Staff, Hans von Seeckt, was appointed as "Chief of the Army Command" in the newly founded *Reichswehrministerium*, the entire German officer corps of the old army knew that at Bendlerstrasse, the seat of the new *Reichswehrministerium*, the most thorough kind of military work would be carried out from then on, far exceeding the scope required for a 100,000-strong army. Seeckt not only implemented a strict regimen and tight discipline, but he also introduced a 12-year conscription period for every single one of his 100,000 men. In so doing, he created a new type of professional soldier who would receive training that surpassed even that received by longstanding staff sergeants in the "glory days" of old, and was in no way inferior to the training given to career officers. Von Seeckt created an army of technicians, specialists and members of the general staff, which would lay the foundations for a new German *Wehrmacht*. But von Seeckt was not only an organisational genius, who knew how to avail himself of all technical resources and would carefully examine every innovation and invention and assess its military usefulness for his 100,000-stong army. Above all, he ensured that the attacking attitude and a soldierly spirit, honouring the revered master of all war craft, Carl von Clausewitz, would be kept alive. General von Seeckt created an officer corps that was firmly rooted in the old traditions but was intimately familiar with all innovations of the craft of war. He founded the aforementioned war academies and cultivated a general corps that at the time was unrivalled anywhere in the world. He himself was a great instructor and military pedagogue, who, with his deep misanthropy, was able to pick out a set of especially gifted officers whom he made his closest allies. Despite the fact that a general staff was not allowed to exist, under General von Seeckt a team of generals established itself at the *Reichswehrministerium*, whose members carefully and jealously guarded "the secret of the *Reichswehr*" and were at great pains to preserve the inviolability and homogeneity of the small officer corps. No member of parliament, no minister, no leading politician – if he was not also a "confidant of the *Reichswehr*" – ever gained access to the *Reichswehrministerium* during the times of the Weimar Republic. The *Reichswehr's* generals formed a highly respected but hermetically sealed guild, which would not admit any *Reich* Chancellor, or any "disagreeable" politician of any stripe into their round, or even allow anyone to gain any sort of insight into their activities. Yet at the same time, General von Seeckt acted strictly and fastidiously according to the principle that the small *Reichswehr* should not be "exploited" for political ends, and he allowed no "political experimentation".

The Generals Ludendorff and Hoffmann in Munich

After the war of 1914–18, there were large numbers of professional low-ranking officers, of whom many had been promoted, with much enthusiasm, to officer rank only during the war. As "active officers" in their divisions they had served the army well, but now found themselves without a position. Their pension payments, which had been guaranteed by the Weimar Republic, were insufficient to live on, and the end of war had not only taken away their positions as career officers but in many cases entirely uprooted them, so that they were no longer able to find their way in the social and professional circumstances of the post-war years, which were not only chaotic in and of themselves but were further worsened by the prevailing economic hardship of the times. While a retired general might have just been able to subsist on his meagre pensions payments, a retired captain, major, lieutenant-colonel or colonel would have rightly said about his pension payments: "Too much to starve on, too little to live on!" Given the prevailing war-weariness, only a few found positions as military advisors abroad, among them, for a period of time, Captain Ernst Röhm as a military instructor in Bolivia, and Colonel [Max Hermann] Bauer (1869-1929 in Shanghai) and his comrades as military inspectors in China for the new leader, Chiang Kai-shek.

In 1918, the supreme commander Paul von Hindenburg, together with the Quartermaster General, the Württembergian General Wilhelm Groener, had not only been able to bring the German Emperor to safety in Holland, he also managed, after the armistice, to return the German troops home in some semblance of order. (From 1928 to 1932, Quartermaster General Groener proved himself an especially talented *Reichswehrminister*, and rather openly pursued renewed armament.)

In 1918, shortly before the signing of the armistice agreement, General Ludendorff had lost his mind to such an extent that there was talk of a nervous breakdown. In a sulk, he retired to Munich, where he soon began to plot against the "Berlin faction" in the *Reichswehr* and against the *Reichswehrministerium* in general. His craving for recognition, his aggrieved vanity and his unbounded ambition drove him to conduct a highly questionable form of "standalone politics" and a short-term fraternisation with the fledgling National Socialism of Adolf Hitler, which came to an inglorious end in the unsuccessful coup attempt of November 9, 1923.

The monstrously vain General Erich Friedrich Wilhelm Ludendorff (1865-1937), famous from his exploits in the First World War. He sulked and pouted and annoyed absolutely everybody.

Also in retirement in Munich was the Prussian General [Carl Adolf Maximilian] Max Hoffmann (1869-1927), who during the World War of 1914–18 had been Hindenburg's First Officer of the General Staff, since 1916 was Chief of the General Staff *Ober-Ost*, and had represented the "Supreme Army Command" at the peace negotiations in Brest-Litovsk in 1917. As a man of similarly great ambition as Ludendorff – their cravings for recognition never allowing the men to become good friends – he frequently came into personal conflict with the "Berlin faction" within the *Reichswehr*. He was the inspiration for the *"Schwarze Reichswehr"*, a motley collection of various irregular militia groups that made a nuisance of themselves in Germany in 1922–23. For a time, the *Reichswehrministerium* and the generals residing in Berlin led by General von Seeckt were quite happy to see these militia groups operating against the Polish insurgents in Upper Silesia. They not only tolerated but indirectly supported these militia groups, because, according to the terms of the peace treaty, the *Reichswehr* was not allowed itself to act and at the time was still too weak to successfully revolt against or defy the provisions of the Treaty of Versailles. However, when the militia groups had – successfully – done their part, General von Seeckt was first among those who categorically demanded and eventually secured their disbanding.

The following two episodes deserve special attention. General Max Hoffmann was the mysterious *regisseur* who not only directed General von Goltz's army (not to be confused with another general of the same name, who was the organiser of the Turkish army) in the Baltics against the Bolsheviks, but also had encouraged the Caucasian Prince Paul Avalov-Bermondt [correctly, Prince Pavel Rafalovich Avalov-Bermondt; 1877-1973] to assemble an army made up of Tsarist soldiers and officers that had been captured in Germany and to lead it against the Bolsheviks. Prince Paul, a former cavalry captain and controversial adventurer – who had appointed himself colonel and subsequently was made into a general and army commander by General Hoffmann – had the "Baltic Goltz" fight his war, and, for a short period of time, resided in Riga like a Byzantine pasha entirely unchallenged. He even had his own Avalov roubles minted, but then disappeared as suddenly as he had arrived. After his getaway from Riga, the Foreign Office in Berlin's Wilhelmstrasse had paid him an enormous "sum of acquittance". Having quickly squandered this, he began to borrow money far and wide, and, in 1933/34 organised a "Tsarist-National-Socialist" movement. His attempts at ingratiating himself to the new regime in Germany failed. He spent a brief period in a concentration camp and eventually fled to Yugoslavia, where he found refuge with Prince Paul of Yugoslavia in Bled Castle, thanks to his romantic liaison with the Duchess of Mecklenburg, who had also effectuated his release from the concentration camp.

The dashing Cossack, Prince Pavel ("Paul") Avalov-Bermondt (1877-1973). Alternative spellings: Bermont and Avaloff, and sometimes called Bermondt-Avalov instead of Avalov-Bermondt. He even minted his own currency. But he did not defeat the Bolsheviks.

General Max Hoffmann, in the meantime, even after his failed Baltic experiment with Prince Paul Avalov-Bermondt, did not refrain from carrying on with his own brand of "Eastern politics", which was futile and dangerous in equal measures. He encouraged [Schalwa Alexander] Karumidze and his associates to produce forged paper *chervonets*, which were to be smuggled into the Soviet Union in order to destabilise the Russian currency and to create an occasion for the overthrow of the Soviet regime! However, during the trials in Munich in the wake of the *chervonets* forgery affair, which were conducted following presentations made by the Soviet regime but before a single forged banknote had found its way into Russia, General Hoffmann's name was not to be mentioned. As a reward for their reticence, the accused individuals, who feigned to accept the court's ruling in order to keep up the pretence, never had to serve their sentences. The individual who betrayed the *chervonets* forgery to the Soviets via a go-between was none other than the aforementioned Harald Siewert. General Max Hoffmann, who had caused so many problems and headaches for the *Reichswehrministerium* in Berlin, died in 1927.

The account of the second episode illustrates the hubris of General Erich Ludendorff – "aggrieved vanity" personified:

At the defeat of the German army in October/November 1918, Ludendorff suffered a personal breakdown of such intensity, that his friends were so worried about his state of mind that they feared he might live in a state of permanent mental derangement. Ludendorff never forgave his superior Paul von Hindenburg the fact that not he, Ludendorff, had been allowed to lead the troops home after the armistice, but instead General Quartermaster Wilhelm Groener had been given that honour. From that time onwards Ludendorff hated Hindenburg and accused him of Masonry; indeed, his hatred of Hindenburg, which he was not able to display openly, turned into an unbounded hatred of the Freemasons, which was not only directed against the "Jewish" lodges, but mainly against the Old Prussian lodges, which he would fight furiously, as it was they who were supported by Hindenburg. (As has already been mentioned, Hindenburg's father had been a prominent Masonic master, and most Prussian officers were members of one of the three Old Prussian Grand Lodges.) After the failed Munich putsch of 1923, a simmering hatred for Hitler was also growing in Ludendorff, despite the fact that the NSDAP, which had been resurrected in 1925, made far-reaching concessions to the man's vanity and treated him like a capricious diva. They needed him – with his renunciation of God and church – as one of the standard bearers of National Socialism and one of the most prominent priests of the new super-ego-God. When Hindenburg died on August 2, 1934, Ludendorff found within himself not a single word or gesture of condolence, yet he was not going to miss the funeral of the hero of the German people, which was to be held in Tannenberg. However, he did not take the place of honour among the funeral guests that had been reserved for him, but instead kept himself apart, visibly sulking, and even denied his former superior and friend a wreath, and did not bid farewell at the grave. His hatred, fury and aggrieved vanity lasted beyond the grave.

VON HINDENBURG DIES AT 86 AFTER A DAY UNCONSCIOUS; HITLER TAKES PRESIDENCY

Times Wide World Photos.

PRESIDENT PAUL von HINDENBURG

END COMES AT 9 A. M.

Reich President Dies at His Home in East Prussia.

MADE A VALIANT FIGHT.

Disappearance of House Flag at Neudeck Announces News to World.

THERE HAD BEEN NO HOPE

He Lapsed Into Coma After Hitler Reached Bedside for Last Meeting.

By The Associated Press.

NEUDECK, Germany, Thursday, Aug. 2.—President von Hindenburg died at 9 A. M. today.

The President's death was indicated to correspondents by the disappearance of the house flag from the flagstaff.

Death came to the 86-year-old leader of the German people and former war marshal after a valiant fight against a complication of ailments.

Chancellor Hitler has assumed the Presidency.

Old General Ludendorf sulked and refused to lay a wreath at Hindenburg's funeral. Hitler meanwhile took over the government and assumed the position of President.

The "Munich faction" versus the *Reichswehrministerium*

Seeckt and his generals in the *Reichswehrministerium* were called the "Berlin faction" within the *Reichswehr*; the "Munich faction", in contrast, had essentially very little to do with the *Reichswehr*. Rather, this so-called" Munich faction" was made up of career officers that had been retired after the World War of 1914–18, had now grouped themselves around the two sulking and sparring generals Ludendorff and Hoffmann, and, for want of a regular occupation, made eager forays into politics and – encouraged partly by Ludendorff, partly by Hoffmann –became more and more entangled in political squabbles. The *"Organisation Consul"*, the infamous *"O.C."*, was founded, as well as the *"Captain Ehrhardt Freikorps"*, the *"Freikorps Oberland"*, the *"Freikorps Rossbach"*, and a whole range of other *Freikorps* (militia groups) and secret organisations that harboured thoughts of revenge for the lost World War of 1914–18. *"Freikorps Epp"* stamped out the "Bavarian Soviet Republic" that had sprung up in Munich; that particular *Freikorps* was almost exclusively made up of front soldiers of the famous "Bavarian Infantry Lifeguards Regiment", whose last commander, at the end of the war in 1918, had been Franz Ritter von Epp. Before disbanding at home after the armistice, he led the regiment against the putschists of Eisner's "Soviet government" in 1919 and thus became Munich's "liberator". The *"Freikorps Oberland"* was also involved in the "liberation" of Munich, but gained public notoriety mainly through its "storming of Annaberg", which led to a decisive victory in 1921 against the Polish insurgents in Upper Silesia. The *"Brigade Ehrhardt"* and the *"Organisation Consul"* played a major role in the "passive resistance" during the French occupation of the Rhineland in 1923. All of these militia groups implemented their own secret and ad-hoc forms of "justice", under which not only "traitors" of their organisations, but also "traitors of the *Vaterland*" (such as the venerable *Reichsminister* Walter Rathenau and Matthias Erzberger) were simply lynched. The appellation *"Fehme-Mörder"* ("Fehme murderers", named after a form of German medieval vigilantism) became a veritable honorary title for all those mercenaries and members of the secret militias, who, without being called upon, grandstanded as "avatars of the German will for resistance".

Matthias Erzberger (1875-1921) was lynched by a pre-Nazi fascist militia mob called Organisation Consul on 26 August 1921. He was a Catholic Centre Party MP in the Reichstag. He had been Germany's Minister of Finance from 1919 to 1921. He signed the Armistice between Germany and the Allies to end World War I. In the eyes of the far right, this made him "an enemy of the Fatherland". But his murder was "a *fehme* murder", of which there were 6000 following the end of World War I whereby poliicians hostile to the extreme nationalists were murdered. The secret and deadly *Fehme Court* which ordered the deaths of their enemies (often sewn into sacks or left standing vertically in their graves) was an ancient tradition of the Teutonic Knights, of the Teutonic Order, which was founded in 1190. The *fehme* tradition never ceased but it was revived in earnest in the 20th century. The execution of the *fehme* murders under Hitler was a task carried out by the author's boss, Reinhard Heydrich of the SD. He had a special squad of brutal assassins for the task, called the Special Service Alarm Command, or "Heydrich's Killers", the commander of whom was the violent and psychopathic thug SS Walter Sohst (later Standartenführer, promoted for being so good at killing people; 1898-1964), who, suitably, was an East Prussian steeped in the *Fehme* tradiitions of vengeance and murder. Twice he had to be temporarily suspended because of his extreme cruelty, which even the SD and Gestapo found too much to take. He was tall, slim, well-dressed, and looked like a typical Prussian officer. These killers had their office on the fourth floor of the Gestapo building and were technically part of the Berlin Special Service, but in practice this special branch belonged personally to Heydrich alone. Anyone who dared to speak of the *Fehme* or give evidence was inevitably assassinated. The *Fehme* is in fact a thousand year-old secret of the Prussian aristocratic *Junker* military class. Even by mentioning the *Fehme* just a few times in passing in his book, considering that it was from a position of personal knowledge of it, the author had possibly signed his own death warrant, at least as things stood in 1945. In order to understand the Hitler regime, it is essential to know the thousand-year Prussian tradition of secretive assassinations, often of a ritual nature, which preceded it. Sewing *Fehme* victims in sacks reminds us of the mysterious murder of the British MI6 intelligence agent Gareth Williams, who was conspicuously left dead in a locked holdall. There is no doubt that that was a ritual "message" left by the killers, exactly in the way the *Fehme* victims were left sewn in sacks, also a "message" which was as clear as day to those in the know. Putzi Hanfstängl has recorded the detail that it was "a slightly mysterious man named Lieutenant Klintsch" who "had a hand in the murders of Erzberger and Rathenau." Our author does not mention Klintsch, who had been an officer of the SA and had taken part in the Kapp Putsch in Berlin in 1920. His full name seems to have been Johan Ulrich Klintsch of the Second Marine Brigade Ehehardt and of the Organization Consul. It appears that he was one of the original SA founders. Since he disappeared from events, it is likely that he was killed in connection with the Night of the Long Knives. (Postcard photo dated 1919)

It is said that it was during a stay in a field hospital in Pasewalk in 1918 that Hitler decided to become a politician. It is still unclear how a lowly private and runner in the *"Regiment List"* was able to become a "training officer" in Traunstein. In any case, he managed to be accepted as a member of the "Special Unit for the Overthrow of the Bavarian Soviet Republic" in May 1919. His close ties to the commander of that "special unit", General [Franz] Ritter von Epp (1868-1947), the later *"Führer* of the *Reich* Colonial League", leader of the Colonial Policy Office of the NSDAP and *Reich* Governor of Bavaria, were first established during that period. It was also at that time that Adolf Hitler began to build his connections to the well-known geopolitician General Karl Haushofer, whose teachings he would enthusiastically apply in the drawing up of his party- and later *Reich* policies.

General Franz Ritter von Epp (1868-1947). From 1933 he was a Reichsleiter of the Nazi Party. From May 1919 in Bavaria, close ties between von Epp and Hitler had commenced, and von Epp helped Hitler in his early career.

Röhm, Römer, Göring, Kriebel, Hess and various other decommissioned officers, whatever their names may have been, gathered around Ludendorff and Hoffmann and waited for "their hour", which would enable them to once again become active officers in a new German *Wehrmacht*. Until that time, they were active in the various militia groups with various levels of "success". What they all lacked was a unified and clear political objective. A wild mercenarism had been established in Munich, with each individual "doing politics" on his own terms, oftentimes coming into conflict with the laws of the Weimar Republic, but without being pursued too harshly by the courts, due to his distinguished war record and the medals of honour he had collected. The word *"völkisch"* [an amorphous term combining national, racial, populist and traditional notions] was rattling around in many of their heads, but they were all far removed from any sort of "people's movement" and were alienated from and decidedly hostile towards the actual mass movements within their nation (such as Social Democracy, Marxist and Christian unions, etc.). The people, fatigued by war, did not care about notions of revenge and perceived these insolent mercenaries as alien bodies that needed to be absorbed.

Adolf Hitler recognised his opportunity early on and seized the moment. He formed his pact with Ludendorff and sidled up to all the generals politicising in Southwest Germany, such as Hoffmann, Epp and List. He gained the sympathies and readiness for collaboration of the entire wild coterie of officers, of Lieutenant Colonel Kriebel, the *"Pour le mérite"* awardee Göring, and Captain Ernst Röhm, and succeeded, in a relatively short space of time, to subsume all the existing groups, associations, secret clubs and militia units into the newly established National Socialist Party of Germany, the NSDAP, or at least bring them under direct or indirect interim party control. The affiliation to the new party, the absorption into the NSDAP, in many cases only happened after its resurrection in 1925, after the "martyr" Hitler had served his sentence in Landsberg.

The "Berlin faction" included Seeckt, Pogrell, Bock, Rundstedt, Fritsch – the "conservatives" – whose only interest it was to retain, according to old traditions, the small *Reichswehr* and its officer corps as a homogenous body and a hermetic guild, and to shield it from all political influences, in order to preserve it as the inviolable core of a new German apolitical army of millions, and to be able to prepare it, without distractions by external influences, for the impending "great task". There could be no doubt that this "great task" could be nothing other than a "glorious war", through which Germany would be restored to its former size and significance, and, as a "global military power" that controlled the continent, would realise a grandiose "pan-Germanism". Headed by General von Seeckt, the cold, sober and calculating men in the *Reichswehrministerium* approached their self-imposed task with dogged tenacity and steely determination. They harboured no illusions, and calculated the enemy's strengths with the same precision they applied in the evaluation of their own weaknesses and imperfections. It was in the nature of these "venerable *Herrenmenschen*", instilled through ancestry and upbringing, to abhor popular mass movements and to view them as harmful for the sort of Germany they had in mind. They were undeterred by clamour and impetuousness, and knew only too well that any political experimentation would be detrimental to their designs. Therefore within the *Reichswehrministerium* in Berlin there was no real opposition towards the "Munich faction"; the esteemed generals were much too self-assured and confident to take the "Munich faction" seriously or to even see it as any sort of threat to their own positions. On the contrary: they used the "Munich faction" whenever it seemed opportune to do so for the implementation of their plans, and quickly commanded *"Halt!"* when the southerners were at danger of overstepping the mark. This is the only explanation for why, on the one hand, a man like Adolf Hitler was able to advance to the position of "training officer" in the *Reichswehr* in southwestern Germany, while at the same time the attempted National Socialist putsch was quelled by the very same *Reichswehr* in November 1923. It is also the only explanation for why General Hoffmann was able to direct, with the approval of the *Reichswehrministerium*, the militia groups and to orchestrate the forging of *chervonets*, only for the militia groups to be dissolved at the behest of the *Reichswehrministerium* and the forgers to be put on trial.

By contrast, the "Munich faction" consisted of political hotheads, dare-devils and mercenaries who did not want and were not able to wait for the *Reichswehrministerium* in Berlin to conclude its preparations following years of quiet, thorough and protracted work by the generals. They were unable to wait, for they were without gainful employment and had to create some form of income; their self-preservation instinct demanded it. As they were not in a position to take up a civilian profession, they resorted to politicising and setting up secret societies, and sometimes did some odd jobs for the noble gentlemen in Berlin's Bendlerstrasse. When Hitler arrived and slowly but surely welded them together to give them a unified objective, using their rowdyism for his political ends, the "noble gentlemen" in the *Reichswehrministerium* considered Hitler with his NSDAP also to be a mere dogsbody, who could sometimes be used for their own ends, but who could be brought back into line at any time should he, the *Reichswehrministerium's* loyal servant, overreach in the execution of his task. The over-confident generals only realised when it was too late, to what extent they had underestimated Hitler with his NSDAP, and how badly they had miscalculated.

In Prussia there existed the *"Stahlhelm"*, an organisation of front soldiers founded in 1918 by Franz Seldte in Magdeburg. This *"Stahlhelm"* was a tightly disciplined militaristic organisation staunchly loyal to the *Reichswehrministerium*, that is to say the "conservatives". Why should it not be possible to use the "Munich faction" in the same way the *"Stahlhelm"* was being used? Even the fact that the "Munich faction" was largely made up of brash hotheads seemed advantageous to the *Reichswehrministerium*, for it would be easy – so the thinking went – to distance oneself from those hotheads if anything should go wrong, if anything should happen that could not be endorsed publicly for reasons of precaution and morals, but could secretly be supported if it could be seen as useful in the achievement of one's goals.

"Organisation Consul", *"Brigade Ehrhardt"*, *"Freikorps Oberland"*, *"Jungdo" (Junddeutscher Order)*, *"Völkische Freiheitsbewegung"*, *"Tannenbergbund"*, Admiral Trotha's *"Bündlerbewegung*, and a good dozen other associations and groupings: at first the NSDAP was nothing more than another such splinter group, another party that was not to be taken all too seriously, without any support in the wider German population. It has been forgotten nowadays that in the time after the First World War the overwhelming majority of Germans were truly peaceable. Hitler was party member number 7 of the NSDAP, and it was undoubtedly his unscrupulous demagogy that eventually transformed one of these minor groups – namely the NSDAP – into the mass movement of National Socialism.

The plight and deprivation of the post-war years, the insecurity, the powerlessness and disunity of the democratic parties of government, and the injustice and misconjecture of the victorious powers were exploited by the agitators of the new party. With lies, bluffs, threats and reckless promises they operated without conscience and were able to rouse the suffering German people from their oppressive and drab monotony. They created the heroic notion of "victorious" party soldiers and deluded the people with lustrous images of a "glorious tradition" that needed to be perpetuated in splendour. The idol of the super-ego-god was created; past and future heroic deeds were alluded to. The German people was exhausted, oppressed, and, in its political immaturity, split into many parties who often fought each other over trivialities and only exacerbated the fragmentation of the German people instead of fostering healthy conciliation. The parties were no match for Adolf Hitler and his NSDAP because, in order to mount a successful fight against National Socialism, they were much too finical about their methods and quite frankly too decent.

The *SA* and *SS*: the party soldiery

It is a well-known fact that he who gets the laughs will emerge victorious from any debate; nothing can harm a political opponent more than a well-timed joke. But a sense of humour was something the National Socialists never had – indeed, were incapable of ever having. A good sense of humour requires wit, but the Nazis had always despised intellectuals and those possessing wit.

Early on in his political career, Adolf Hitler had learned that any of the arguments he advanced in his speeches at political gatherings could easily be refuted with wit and humour and thus rendered ineffectual. In response, he promptly employed so-called "marshals", whose job it was to stop any witty hecklers by simply removing them from his gatherings and throwing them out into the street. Humour and wit cannot flourish when they are being brutally supressed. "We've wiped the smiles off their faces," Hitler would say during his gatherings, when his "marshals" had restored "order", thus snuffing out any possibility of "dangerous" debate.

Once Hitler had recognised the usefulness of the various militia groups and covert units, he ensured that they would form the core of his party soldiery. The "marshals" would form the *SA*, the "storm detachments" for the "protection" of mass gatherings. The most brutal thugs could quickly be enlisted to use their fists for Hitler's movement; the more moderate elements hesitated a little, and many eccentric loners only joined the NSDAP after Hitler's power grab. The militia groups of the so-called *"Schwarze Reichswehr"*, having witnessed the scenes of fraternisation between their revered General Ludendorff and Hitler, in effect felt called upon to officially join the NSDAP. Faced with increasing resistance from the *Reichswehrministerium* in Berlin, their opportunities for action had been dwindling, and their raison d'être as militia groups and covert units had been increasingly undermined.

The party chronicles proudly recount the success of the first major mass gathering that took place on November 4, 1921 in the *Hofbräuhaus* in Munich. Before the start of the event, Hitler gathered his "marshals" around him, and addressed them with these words:

"Today, for the first time, you are called upon to keep faith with our movement, come hell or high water. None of us will leave the hall, unless they carry us out dead. I will personally tear the armband and badge off any coward who dares to retreat like a deserter. Should there be the slightest attempt to break apart our gathering, remember that attack is the best defence!"

The party chronicles go on to say: "46 marshals eject 800 opponents from the hall. From this day on, the marshals shall be known by the honorific title *Sturm-Abteilung*."

The infamous *SA* had been founded and was given a kind of uniform that consisted of a windbreaker, a ski cap and a red armband emblazoned with a black swastika on a white background. The fight, the terrorising of political opponents, was taken beyond the beer halls and out onto the streets. The new *SA* was subdivided into *"Stürme"* and given its own flags, the so-called *"Standarten"*. In October 1922, the "entry" into Koburg took place, followed closely by the first party convention in Munich in January 1923, where the *"Führer"* Adolf Hitler ceremoniously "bestowed" four *"Standarten"* on the *SA*, which had mustered 6000 men for the occasion.

After the failed putsch in November 1923 the party was banned. Air Force Captain Hermann Göring escaped the grasp of the police by fleeing to Sweden, and the Captain of the General Staff, Ernst Röhm, hired himself out as a military instructor in Bolivia. Adolf Hitler wrote his book *"Mein Kampf"*, the theoretical foundation of his system, while serving his sentence in Landsberg prison, rather enjoying the role of a martyr. Front officer Rudolf Hess shared the fate of his *"Führer"* Adolf Hitler, and became his secretary and adjutant.

In 1925 the NSDAP was able to celebrate its political resurrection. Even more so than before, the *SA* was styled as a veritable combat- and terror unit. For the personal protection of individual speakers and party leaders a special bodyguard was created from within the ranks of the *SA*, namely the *SS*. The so-called *Schutz-Staffeln* (protection squadrons) developed as subdivisions of the *SA*. At the party conference in Nuremberg in 1927, the *SA* mustered 30,000 men; and at the party conference in 1929 there were already 60,000 of them, yelling hoarsely: "Germany awake! Death to the Jews!" – a battle cry that had come into existence between 1923 and 1925, the years of the party ban.

1929 saw deep divisions within the party leadership, following Adolf Hitler's refusal to curb the thuggery, to reshape the party and its leadership in order to present it as being capable of governing. In Berlin, *SA Führer* [Walter Franz Maria] Stennes revolted against Hitler, but the revolt was quashed by the then *SAGruppenführer* Kurt Daluege in Berlin. *SA Führer* Stennes went to China where he became the commander of the bodyguard of the Chinese supreme leader Chiang Kai-shek.

SA Führer for Berlin, Walter Franz Maria Stennes (1895-1983). He led the Stennes Revolts against Hitler in August 1930 and March-April 1931, but they failed. After the Nazis came to power in 1933, Stennes fled to China and became military advisor to Chiang Kai-Shek until 1949, attempting to remodel the Kuomintang forces along the lines of the Prussian Army. He returned to Germany in 1949, where he lived until his death 34 years later. (Bundesarchiv)

In order to prevent any attacks from within the *SA* or any other party factions, the *SS* – which until that point had functioned as the bodyguard for party leaders – was retrained as a special protection unit, and given its own uniform. Its members were selected from the legions of volunteers, following extremely strict selection criteria. Heinrich Himmler put the idea of a "Race and Settlement Office" into the head of his Führer and was appointed *Reichsführer* of the *Schutz-Staffeln*. Though the *SS* was still part of the *SA*, it had become an independent and self-contained unit. At the head of the *SA*, the putschist Stennes was replaced by the retired Captain and member of the General Staff, Ernst Röhm. Hitler appointed himself "Supreme Commander of the *SA*", thus assuming personal authority over the entire *SA*. This in turn led to the creation of the post of *SA* Chief of Staff, an office that was subordinate only to Adolf Hitler, and not the party leadership itself. The first *SA* Chief of Staff was that very man Ernst Röhm. Until June 30, 1934, *SS Reichsführer* Himmler was directly subordinate to Röhm.

Ernst Röhm was an organisational genius, and Heinrich Himmler would become his new master's eager pupil. Before a year was up, Röhm was able to provide a private army of 110,000 men for his close friend and *"Führer"* Adolf Hitler. He introduced a soldierly regime of discipline and drilled his *SA* men like army recruits. In plain sight of the Weimar government these private troops were armed: every *SA* and *SS* man was issued with a pistol (or, in certain units, even a rifle) and received firearms training. While the association *"Stahlhelm"* (which was run by [Franz] Seldte, [Theodor] Duesterberg and [Franz von] Stefanie) was a purely military training group, in which basic training for future soldiers was provided by officers of the *Reichswehr*, the *SA*, now run by Chief of Staff Ernst Röhm, was a political private army unparalleled in its size and scope.

100,000 well-equipped and armed (!) *SA* and *SS* men publicly marched in Braunschweig in 1932, following Hitler's appointment as a councillor by the (legally appointed) Nazi Interior Minister for Braunschweig, Dietrich Klagges.

Hitler's party took full advantage of all democratic rights provided by the Weimar constitution, but simply disregarded any of the associated obligations, and, in so doing, was able to create a private army of unprecedented magnitude. This party, which seemed to be able to get away with well-nigh anything, would go on to terrorise an entire people.

1932 – the election year

With five major rounds of voting taking place, the year of 1932 was an extraordinary election year. It turned out to be an endurance test that the parliamentary system of the Weimar Republic was not equal to. It was an almost foregone conclusion that the party that was willing to conduct its campaign in the most unscrupulous manner would be the one to benefit most from the electoral process. With 230 seats, the NSDAP emerged from the elections to the *Reichstag* on July 31, 1932 as the strongest party (up from 107 seats in 1930). In the second presidential election, Adolf Hitler received 13.4 million votes, behind Field Marshal General Paul von Hindenburg, who received 16 million votes and was thus re-elected as *Reichspräsident*. Nevertheless, the NSDAP had reached and passed its zenith, losing some of its vote share in the last of the five election rounds. It was a small loss, but political insiders recognised it as the unmistakeable first sign of an impending decline. In leading Nazi circles that sign was indeed read and understood, and thus, despite all outward electoral success, there was considerable concern about the future, which led to a crisis within the party in the winter of 1932.

Not only were the party coffers empty and propaganda and campaign funds depleted, but the NSDAP had emerged from the elections saddled with debts of almost 20 million *Reichsmark* (!), which were entirely unsecured. The party's financial genius, *Reichsleiter* and treasurer Franz Xaver Schwarz, was completely stumped, as were the director of the "Franz Eher" publishing company, *Reichsleiter* M. [Max] Amann, and every other *Reichsleiter* of the NSDAP.

Franz Xaver Schwarz (1875-1947, Party Member Number 6 of the Nazi Party, was the financial genius who kept the Party going, but in 1932 he was 'stumped' as to what to do. He held a high position in the SS and went on to become the "National Treasurer" (*Reichsschatzmeister*) of Germany.

The then *Reichsorganisationsleiter* of the party, Gregor Strasser, not only voiced concerns regarding the party's finances, but also expressed his deep political worries. As founder and leader of the *NSBO*, the National Socialist Factory Cell Organisation, he was well aware of a change of mood within the workforce and feared the rise of a communist or socialist "people's front" in the wake of the NSDAP's parliamentary successes. There were many heated exchanges between Gregor Strasser and Adolf Hitler, who was coming under increasing pressure (not only from Strasser himself but also other prominent Nazi officials) to send National Socialist delegates to the *Reich* government, even if he, Hitler, was not to be accepted as *Reich* Chancellor by *Reichspräsident* Hindenburg. As a representative of the "left wing" of the NSDAP, Gregor Strasser engaged in negotiations with the new *Reich* Chancellor General von Schleicher on his own authority, and declared his willingness to join Schleicher's cabinet as a *Reichsminister*, particularly in view of the fact that Hitler kept putting off making a decision in the matter. Hitler's hesitancy encouraged Gregor Strasser to accept either the post of Minister for Employment, or the post of a *Reich* Minister for the Interior, which at the time was a merely administrative office devoid of executive power. But no sooner had he sent his acceptance to *Reich* Chancellor General von Schleicher than Hitler disavowed him. Not only did Strasser withdraw his plan to include National Socialists in the existing *Reichskabinett*, but, as a matter of personal probity, he also offered his resignation from all his party offices to Adolf Hitler, and was more than a little surprised when his demission was accepted fully.

As is generally known, Gregor Strasser was murdered by his party comrades on June 30, 1934. As *Reichsorganisationsleiter* he had played a leading role in the establishment and rise of the NSDAP, but nevertheless he had already been betrayed by his party in the winter of 1932. In Strasser's defence it must be mentioned at this point that – despite Hitler's disavowal – the then *Reich* Chancellor General von Schleicher did offer a ministerial post in his cabinet to Gregor Strasser, an offer which Strasser however declined. Joining Schleicher's government would have been tantamount to splitting the party, for the idea was for Strasser not only to resign his membership of the NSDAP, but also to set up a breakaway National Socialist opposition party. This is not the place to debate, with the benefit of hindsight, the pros and cons of such secessionist schemes. The fact is that at the time Gregor Strasser felt bound to "keep faith with his *Führer* Adolf Hitler". (In any case, that is the reason he gave when he declined *Reich* Chancellor Schleicher's offer.)

Gregor Strasser (1892-1934). He was one of the founding Nazis. Josef Goebbels had been his private secretary and Heinrich Himmler had been his Adjutant. But he was murdered by the SS during the Night of the Long Knives, of which the author was an eye-witness. He had expressed "his deep political worries" before his death. Gregor's brother Otto (Otto Johann Maximilian Strasser, 1897-1974) had been a member of the Nazi Party since 1924 but was expelled by Hitler in 1930. He and his brother were socialists and represented a "left wing" of the Nazis, opposed to the Nazi racial theories. He left Germany in 1933 and lived in various countries as an emigrant from his homeland. After the War commenced, Otto Strasser became active in writing books opposing the Hitler regime. He founded the Free German Movement in France and he published his first book of revelations and harsh commentary, *Hitler et Moi* [*Hitler and Me*], Grasset, Paris, 1940. This appeared soon afterwards in English translation as *Hitler and I* (Jonathan Cape, 1941). In that book he gives a detailed description of the murder of his brother Gregor: "My brother Gregor was having lunch with his family when eight Gestapo men came and took him away without any explanation. He was taken to the Prinz Albrecht-Strasse prison and thrown into a cell. After twelve hours of solitude, darkness and uncertainty, he suddenly saw a revolver pointed at him through the grating. The first shot missed, and Gregor took refuge in a corner of the cell; but three gunmen, including Heydrich and [Theodor] Eicke, the killer now in charge of all the concentration camps in Germany, came in, and Gregor, riddled with bullets, fell to the ground. He was still breathing when Heydrich administred the *coup-de-grace* with a shot in the back of the head. I had these details from the man who wiped the blood from the walls and removed the traces of the shooting. He was able to escape after the execution, and joined me in Prague." The unnamed third shooter was apparently Heydrich's special protege Hermann Behrends, the SD's cunning short-legged criminal known as "the dachshund". (Bundesarchiv)

Otto Strasser, brother of Gregor Strasser. An intimate friend and colleague of Hitler and the other leading Nazis from the 1920s, he fled Germany in 1933 in time to save his life, and begged his brother to come with him, but Gregor declined, and was killed. This photo was taken in Paris in early 1940 before the Nazis entered Paris in May. It appears to be unknown, and is here scanned from an original presented by Otto to some friends. It was pasted into a signed copy of Otto's first book, *Hitler et Moi*, published in Paris in 1940.

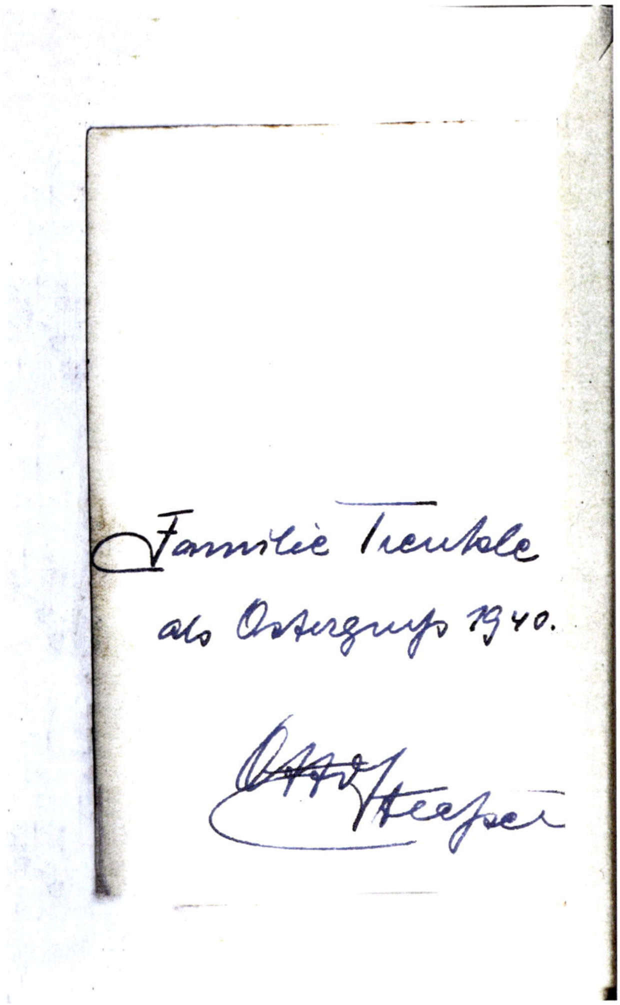

The inscription on the back of the photo reads: 'To the Treukle Family as Ostergrup 1940. Otto Strasser'. *Oster* means 'Easter' and Strasser was in Paris for Easter, 1940. So by 'Easter group', Strasser presumably means that the Treukle family invited him to have Easter lunch with them.

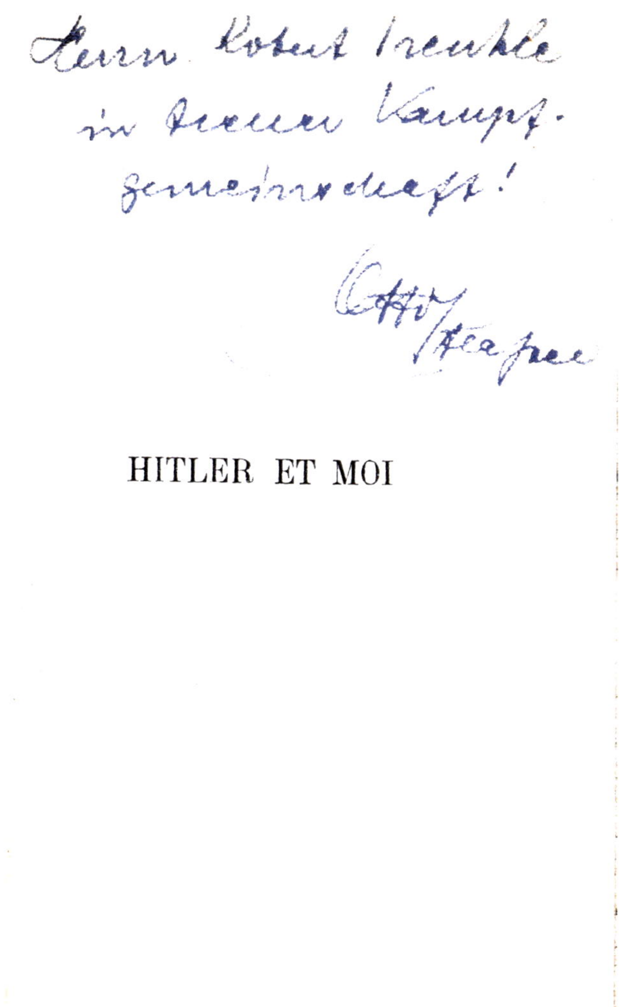
Herrn Robert Treukle
in unserer Kampf-
gemeinschaft!

Otto
Strasser

HITLER ET MOI

The signed pre-title page of Otto Strasser's *Hitler et Moi* (Paris, 1940). The inscription reads: 'To Herr Robert Treukle in our common struggle! Otto Strasser'

The cover of the original edition of *Hitler et Moi* (*Hitler and Me*) published by Grasset in Paris in the early spring of 1940, just before the Nazis came. The book was translated into English and published the same year as *Hitler and I* in both Britain and America. An expanded version of this book was subsequently published in America as *Flight from Terror*, with co-authorship credit given to the American journalist Michael Stern (1910-2009), who enlarged Strasser's descriptions of events, either by getting more detail from Strasser or simply made them up for dramatic efect.

This expanded version of Otto Strasser's book *Hitler et Moi* was enlarged with the American journalist Michael Stern. It is unknown whether the expansions of the text can be considered entirely reliable. This book was published by McBride & Company, New York, 1943. Otto Strasser went on to write several further books, living as an exile in Canada from 1942, where he was for years in constant fear of assassination. He died in 1974.

The man chosen to replace Gregor Strasser as *Reichsorganisationsleiter* of the NSDAP was his deputy, Dr Robert Ley. From 1932 until 1936, however, Dr Ley performed his duties only provisionally, and was only officially appointed and promoted to *Reichsleiter* of the NSDAP in 1936.

The "people's front" that Gregor Strasser had so feared manifested itself neither in 1932 nor in 1933, after Hitler's takeover. At any rate, the term "people's front" only emerged much later, as a consequence of the rise of German National Socialism, and it originated not in Germany, but in France, under the government of Léon Blum.

In the winter of 1931/32, the Communist Party of Germany, known as KPD, had been able to gain significant influence over the trade unions, splitting some of the Social Democrat organised labour groups. The KPD won decisive victories in the works council elections of 1931/32 at Berlin's leading newspaper groups (Ullstein, Mosse, Scherl), as Communist candidates received some 60 per cent of the total vote. This was all the more significant as the printing trade had always been at the avant-garde of the organised labour movement. However, instead of making the most of its victories, the KPD became embroiled in fierce internal arguments over the "party line". In the factories and party assemblies endless doctrinal discussions were held; resolutions were passed and overturned, and soon old and new party members were excluded from the KPD in ever larger numbers for allegedly not "towing the party line". In the end, no worker really knew what that party line actually was, particularly in view of the fact that many expelled members presented themselves to the workforce in splinter groups, each of which claimed to be the only true "Leninist" grouping, and that all others, including the Stalinist KPD, had betrayed the teachings of Marx and Lenin. Trotskyism, Leninism, the Fourth International etc. were flourishing, but the official KPD denounced as a *Sozialfaschist* anyone who did not bow to its ideological party terror.

Johannes R. Becher, the chairman of the "Association of Proletarian-Revolutionary writers", an especially faithful party member and author, threatened the Communist propaganda poet Erich Weinert with the term *Sozialfaschist*, after which the good-natured and naïve Herr Weinert began to ask any party grandee he could get hold of whether his latest poems had been truly "faithful to the party line". He would read his verses to modest factory workers, waiting anxiously for their reactions, before taking his work to mass party gatherings where he would declaim his poems with much pathos. Most of the honest working folk did not care much about poetry, but they had a soft spot for "their Erich", because often, when he was bellowing his poetry from the podium, he would include the most delightfully colourful language in his rhymes. And so they calmed him down, while his party comrades in the Communist writers' association would jealously call him a "deranged petit bourgeois". It is still a mystery why Erich Weinert – this meek-as-a-lamb Communist, whose appearances in the Saarland will be discussed later on – was able to rise to the position of "President of the National Committee for a Free Germany" in Moscow; a man whose political judgement and personal decision-making ability were disputed by his own party comrades.

But the poet Erich Weinert was not the only one running around looking for clues as to what the party line actually was; even the KPD's highest party officials were in the same position. Among them was Wilhelm Pieck, a man especially faithful to the party line, who was seen by his party comrades as being rather phlegmatic and was thought to have tenaciously survived every crisis within the party precisely because of that character trait. Back in 1932, Pieck and [Fritz] Heckert had held significant positions as the KPD's representatives to Komintern, the Communist International in Moscow. Werner Hirsch, chief editor of *"Rote Fahne"*, the KPD's official journal in Berlin (a very intelligent journalist who would later be murdered), said about Pieck that he was one of those typical "plush sofa Communists", who, as faithful party officials, only had one concern: not to stray from the party line. Still, Wilhelm Pieck was a top-flight KPD party official, and so it is not overly surprising that he was appointed by Moscow as Erich Weinert's deputy in the headquarters of the "National Committee for a Free Germany". Even more unsure about his "faithfulness to the party line" than Wilhelm Pieck was Peter Maslowski, the son of an East Prussian pastor and advisor on cultural matters to the Communist faction in the *Reichstag*. In 1932, he made no secret of the fact that he was very worried that he might lose his parliamentary seat by not being reselected as a candidate by the KDP, despite the fact that his wife occupied an important position at the Russian trade mission in Berlin. Indeed, in the autumn of 1932 Peter Maslowski was not nominated for election by his party, and he is said to have been shot by the Nazis "during an escape attempt" only a few months later. The life of this principled and upright man – like so many others – was ended at the hands of murderers.

It was not only the Communists' internal fragmentation and the blatant bafflement of many prominent KPD leaders that weakened, at a crucial moment, the organised labour movement's opposition against the Nazis. In addition, during the election campaign of 1932, the KPD had officially chosen the slogan: "Our greatest enemy, the public enemy number one of the workers, is not the Fascist (i.e. Nazi), but the *Sozialfaschist*, the Social Democrat and Christian Social trade unionist!" As absurd as it may sound, this was the distressing and tragic reality: the KPD engaged in fierce in-fighting against the Social Democrat and Christian Social workforce, and at times even saw fit to make common cause with the Nazis in the factories, in order to harm the SPD and the *Zentrum* party! (Even in parliament, at the *Reichstag* and *Landtag*, there were some instances where the Nazis and Communists joined forces against the parties loyal to the government, such as the SPD and the *Zentrum* party. There was a certain logic to such alliances, as both parties aimed to torpedo all practical measures put forward by the Weimar government, in order to topple the democratic system. With the help of the German National Party led by Alfred Hugenberg, as well as other splinter groups, these destructive manoeuvres succeeded all too often.)

In the election campaign of 1932 the Communists' conduct was no less unscrupulous than that of the Nazis. They vilified their "public enemy number one" wherever they could, battering the Social Democratic and Christian Social parties with torrents of abuse. Yet in its dependency on directives from Moscow, the KPD leadership lacked a sense of purpose for the development of clear domestic policies and was unable to adapt to local circumstances. The Nazis always had possessed a sense of purpose in the form of a desire for destruction, but the German Communists were hampered by certain social requirements. A venerable trade union leader in Luxembourg once put it very succinctly: "They (the KPD leaders) shouted 'Down!' all too often and 'Forward!' all too little. With their stereotypical programme of tearing things down they had to lose out against the Nazis. They were mere would-be-revolutionaries who were unable to take new ideas to the people."

It is not the purpose of this book to lay bare the faults of the various political parties of the Weimar Republic. In the *Reichstag*, the Communists sat on the extreme left and the Nazis on the extreme right. They were polar opposites, yet still shared some characteristics. Nearly all other political parties were also internally fragmented, but in a different manner. There were strong religious impulses that opposed National Socialism, some of which found expression in the policies of the *Zentrum* party. But the political centre had to fight against the Nazis with a considerable handicap: the strong emphasis on nationalism and the Nazis' disguise of quasi-religious language ("We are rooted in Christianity!") confused many ordinary German people. In the most powerful stakeholders in the country – namely the major landowners, heavy industry, the generals, the nobility and the state bureaucracy – these traits also helped to create an attitude towards the Nazis that was, if not always outright sympathetic, then at least temporising and acquiescing. Whenever National Socialism came under severe fire, it could expect the support from those quarters, that is to say, from society's highest echelons. The traditional northern and eastern German hostility towards Catholics also played a major role in this. And so, discounting a few feeble gestures by the *Demokraten*, a party whose support had melted away in successive elections, the *Zentrum* party was almost alone in its fight against Nazism. The Social Democrats, natural opponents of the Nazis, were not led well, and any co-operation with the *Zentrum* party would inevitably lead to rapprochement between the right wing of the governing parties and the Nazis. Nevertheless, the *Zentrum* party was the only major party to emerge with roughly the same share of the vote from the various rounds of voting. It has to be mentioned again and again that the democratic parties, which refused to fight with unfair means, were defeated by the Nazis' unscrupulousness. And many an upright and far-sighted politician was ignored by his own party leadership when he called for an energetic fight against National Socialism and berated its demagogy.

After an episcopal conference in Fulda, the archbishop of Mainz, who had excommunicated members of the NSDAP and had publicly denied the Holy Communion to those who wore the Nazi party's insignia (in 1932!), was forced to revoke the excommunications. Sadly he did not live to see the day when, only a few years later, the bishops who during his lifetime had tended towards caution and indulgence in their view of Nazism, came together as a compact bloc that would bravely oppose National Socialism and, ignoring all danger to their own lives, would speak out against racial fanaticism and Nazi crimes. Many thousands of outspoken critics of National Socialism were martyred; among them many thousands of lowly clerics of all Christian denominations, monks, priests and pious nuns. The German bishops became heroes at a time when the Nazis were already inflicting unbounded terror on the German people all across the nation.

Hitler's seizure of power

Breaking his own word (which he had given only months previously), *Reichspräsident* Field Marshal General Paul von Hindenburg appointed the party leader Adolf Hitler as *Reich* Chancellor.

Seated in the centre of this gathering is President Field Marshal von Hindenburg. He is looking paternally towards his young friend Adolph Hitler, who sits smiling beside him, holding a top hat. On the other side of Hindenburg sits Hermann Göring, Minister without Portfolio, who is engrossed in some paperwork. The date is August 27, 1933, and the location is Tannenberg in Saxony. It is the occasion of a Great Demonstration of Faith in Tannenberg (*Die grosse Treuekundgebung in Tannenberg*). Hindenburg had however broken faith with the public by appointing Hitler Chancellor seven months earlier. Within less than a year of this photo, Hindenburg would be dead and Hitler would seize total power. The actual occasion seen in this photo was the 19th anniversary of the Second Battle of Tannenberg which was fought between Germany and Russia, which resulted in the amost complete destruction of the Russian Second Army. It was Hindenburg himself who had been the German commander of that national triumph. (He saw himself as avenging the defeat of the Teutonic Knights of Prussia at the First Battle of Tannenburg 500 years earlier.) (*From an official photo issued for the occasion.*)

The "circle around Hindenburg" imposed a cabinet on Hitler that was largely made up of non-National Socialists; it is an often-overlooked fact that only three (!) of the *Reich* ministers in Adolf Hitler's first cabinet, formed on January 30, 1933, were National Socialists:

1. Adolf Hitler, *Reich* Chancellor;
2. Wilhelm Frick, *Reich* Minister for the Interior;
3. Hermann Göring, initially *Reich* Minister without portfolio.

Dr. Wilhelm Frick (1877-1946, executed), who was Minister of the Interior (*Der Reichsminister des Innern*) from January 30, 1933, to 1943, in which year he was replaced by Heinrich Himmler. He introduced many of the laws against Jews and also the law for forcible sterilization of "unsuitables", as well as the authorising of their euthanasia. He became Protector of Bohemia and Moravia, where he was ruthless in suppressing dissent. He remained as a Reichsminister without Portfolio until the end of the War. He was hanged at Nuremberg in 1946.

The non-National Socialist *Reich* ministers were:

Franz [Joseph Hermann Michael Maria] von Papen (1879-1969), Vice Chancellor and *Reich* Commissioner for the State of Prussia;

Konstantin Freiherr von Neurath (1873-1956), Foreign Minister;

Alfred [Ernst Christian Alexander] Hugenberg (1865-1951), Minister for Economics and Agriculture;

Lutz Graf Schwerin von Krosigk (1887-1977), Finance Minister;

Franz Gürtner (1881-1941), Justice Minister;

Paul Freiherr von Eltz-Rübenach (1875-1943, while under surveillance from the Gestapo), Postal Minister and Minister for Transport;

Franz Seldte (1882-1947), Labour Minister;

General Werner von Blomberg(1878-1946), Minister of Defence;

Hjalmar Schacht (1877-1970), President of the *Reichsbank*, and as such a member of the cabinet.

The conservatives around Hugenberg – with whom some insightful parliamentarians, such as Treviranus and Lejeune-Jung, had severed ties – were jubilant; they earnestly believed that they had trapped Hitler. They felt sure that they had checkmated the NSDAP not only through Hitler's participation in a government that included Hugenberg and Franz Seldte as influential ministers (leaders of the German National People's Party and the *"Stahlhelm"* respectively), but also through an overwhelming non-National Socialist, and decidedly conservative, majority in the cabinet. Furthermore, Adolf Hitler had been appointed as *Reich* Chancellor with the explicit caveat that he was not to dismiss any member of his cabinet.

Adolf Hitler and all high Nazi officials naturally did *not* intend to keep any promises that had been made "under duress". This "duress" was to be understood in the sense that Hitler had had to accept von Hindenburg's conditions in order to finally become *Reich* Chancellor and thereby to save his party from financial ruin and impending bankruptcy due to its debt burden. The first act of the newly appointed *Reich* Chancellor Adolf Hitler was to mobilise his party soldiery, and, using the *SA* and *SS*, to appropriate executive power in all parts of the country, an act that was in clear violation of the law. In the state of Prussia this appropriation was organised by Hermann Göring, in his capacity as a "commissioner in charge of the affairs of a Prussian Minister for the Interior", despite the fact that it was not the National Socialist Göring, but rather the "gentleman equestrian" Franz von Papen who actually held the post of *Reich* Commissioner for Prussia. (This appointment had been one of the *Reichspräsident's* explicit conditions, in an attempt to save "his" Prussia from the grasp of National Socialism.) *Reichsführer SS* Heinrich Himmler appropriated the police executive in the other regions, among them Bavaria, Württemberg and Baden, where he was confirmed in the office of police chief only weeks later and retrospectively! The only Nazi minister with an actual portfolio, *Reich* Minister for the Interior Frick, claimed powers that he was in no way entitled to. In direct contravention of the constitution, he decreed the seizure of the executive power in the *Länder*. A retrospective legal basis for this unauthorised assumption of authority could only be created months later.

The NSDAP leadership staged a "National Socialist uprising" and justified it by invoking an "imminent Communist threat". The non-National Socialists protested vigorously against this abuse of authority and blatant infringement of the law by the Nazi *Reich* Minister for the Interior. As an "imminent Communist threat" as propagated by the Nazis did not exist at all, it had to be constructed as fast as possible, in order to placate the non-National Socialist ministers (who had become wary of Hitler's machinations), or, even better, to get rid of them altogether, in order to free up suitable positions for all the Nazi officials who were eagerly waiting to be installed in government posts. Thereupon Göring-Goebbels and their entourage came up with the idea of the Reichstag Fire.

Wilhelm Frick (1877-1946, hung at Nuremberg), appointed Reich Minister of the Interior on January 30, 1933. He defied the constitution and seized powers he was not entitled to. This laid the groundwork for Hitler's takeover. However, Otto Strasser believed that Frick was not personally a wicked man: "Frick was honest, straightforward and without malice. ... He was a skilful lawyer and rendered great services to the Party, and he was the oldest of the [Nazi beer hall] plotters, practically the only one of them who had a home, a job, and a settled life." It should be noted however that these comments were made by Strasser while in exile in 1940 *before* Frick became Protector of Bohemia and Moravia and committed so many horrible war crimes, and it is to be doubted that Strasser would have said a favourable word about him if he had known the monster he would turn into.

The Reichstag Fire was the dawn of the "official" party terror of National Socialism. In its immediate aftermath – on March 31 and April 4, 1933 – the *Gleichschaltung* laws were passed and thereby the assumption of authority by *Reich* Minister for the Interior, Wilhelm Frick, was sanctioned. The Communist Party was now officially banned; in practice, it had ceased to exist weeks earlier, as – notwithstanding parliamentary immunity and the fact that the KPD had not yet been banned – all KPD party leaders that could be found had been hauled into concentration camps, murdered, or kidnapped, never to be seen again. The Communists played no further role in the impending elections to the *Reichstag*. Of the Social Democrats, whose election campaign was seriously impeded, only a small fraction returned to the *Reichstag*; some had been arrested or mistreated, while others were simply not issued with rail tickets and were thus unable to travel. Other parties, too, were strong-armed in various ways —

until the Enabling Act was finally extorted from the "rump parliament", using threats and promises in equal measure. Then the *Reichstag* was dissolved and, making a mockery of the promises given, all parties, their organisations, their newspapers, all the structures of their political and social power and tools for shaping public opinion were destroyed.

And the workers? —— The Marxists' contradictory election slogans and the Communists' dictum "Not the fascist, but the *Sozialfaschist* is our enemy!" (Autumn 1932) bore golden fruits for National Socialism. The workers were irritated, and believed – because they wanted to believe – that the conservatives had effectively trapped Adolf Hitler. According to a German proverb, "one uses bacon to catch mice", but the fact that National Socialism could in no way be compared to a mouse was overlooked; rather, it was the most dangerous predator of German domestic and foreign politics! It was assumed that it would be possible to pursue a temporising approach, to wait and see how things would develop. In keeping with its often-expressed opinion that National Socialism was its "forerunner", the KPD's watchword was: The fact that the Nazis are in government advances the imminent rule of the proletariat! —— There was no industrial action anywhere; none of the trade unions called for a general strike. Little wonder, then, that the unnerved workers simply deserted their inept party leaders, and, changing allegiance, joined the NSBO (the Nationalist Socialist Factory Cell Organisation) in droves, and entire Communist party units in the Berlin working class districts of Wedding and Neukölln sought and found admission to the *SA*. When a frustrated and angry ticket inspector in Berlin's underground station *Kochstrasse* asked the Communist parliamentarian and writer Karl Grünberg when the KPD would get its act together and would call for a general strike, Grünberg answered resignedly: "What do you expect, comrade – the messenger from Moscow has not yet arrived, so the party can't pass a resolution!" Karl Grünberg had only recently returned from his travels in Russia and had effusively praised the Soviet regime in meetings with the municipal transport workers of Berlin.

Following the elections to the *Reichstag* in 1933, and as a result of the ruthlessness with which the Nazis – in clear violation of the constitution – passed laws to "legalise" their presumption of power, *Reich* Minister for Economics and Agriculture, Alfred Hugenberg, resigned on June 30, 1933. He had been the conservatives' great hope, a sly fox, who thus far had managed to outwit everyone, as his friends said jokingly of him.

Hugenberg's replacement in the *Reichskabinett* and as *Reichsminister* were: Richard Walther Darré (succeeded during the war by Herbert Backe), who was appointed Minister of Agriculture, leader of the *RNS* (a government body set up to regulate food production) and *Reich* Farmers Leader. As *SS-Obergruppenführer*, he was the chief of the *SS* Main Office for Race and Settlement, and authored the works "New nobility from blood and soil" and "Peasantry as life source of the Nordic race".

SS-Obergruppenführer Richard Walther Oscar Darré (1895-1953), Miister for Food and Agriculture.

Hitler and Darré greeting one another at a train station. Presumably, Darré has just arrived and is being greeted by his Führer.

SS-Obergruppenführer Herbert Friedrich Wilhelm Backe (1896-1947) who succeeded his friend Richard Darré during the War as Minister of Food and Agriculture. Backe was a close friend of Reinhard Heydrich and a fanatical anti-Semite. He had been born and brought up in Bakumi, Georgia, where after the Russian Revolution he was imprisoned for being a German, which bred in him a violent hatred of the Soviet Communists.

Hjalmar Schacht, who, after initially overseeing the Ministry for Economy on a provisional basis, was officially appointed *Reich* Minster for the Economy. He held the post from 1934 until 1938, when he was succeeded by the Vice President of the *Reich* Chamber of Culture, undersecretary in the Ministry of Propaganda and *Reich* Chief Press Officer of the government, Walther Funk, a.k.a. *"Theater-Funk"*. Funk not only replaced Schacht as *Reich* Minister for the Economy, but also took over his position of President of the *Reichsbank*.

Walther Funk (1890-1960), at left. He became Reich Minister for the Economy in 1938. Here he is with Raffaello Riccardi (1899-1977), Italian Minister for Exchanges and Currencies (1939-1943), and with Dino Alfieri (1886-1966), a photo taken apparently in 1940, during Afieri's time as Italian Ambassador to Germany. Three happy fascist chums together, all smiles and jollity.

The ministers who remained in the government were:

Lutz Count (*Graf*) Schwerin von Krosigk, as *Reich* Finance Minister.

A signed portrait photo of Finance Minister Count Johann Ludwig ('Lutz') Schwerin von Krosigk (1887-1977), sitting at his desk in the Finance Ministry. He served as Finance Minister from 1932 to 1945. (Eglantyne Collection)

Franz Seldte as *Reich* Labour Minister, who in 1935 was required to reinvent his association of former front fighters, *"Stahlhelm"*, as the "Association of National Socialist Front Fighters", which subsequently vanished into thin air.

Franz Seldte (1882-1947, died a prisoner in a US military hospital), Reich Minister for Labour from 1933 to 1945.

The *Reich* Minister of Defence, General Werner von Blomberg, was appointed *Reich* Minister of War in 1935. After his resignation, which was forced on him by the generals in 1938, the *Reich* Ministry of War was dissolved.

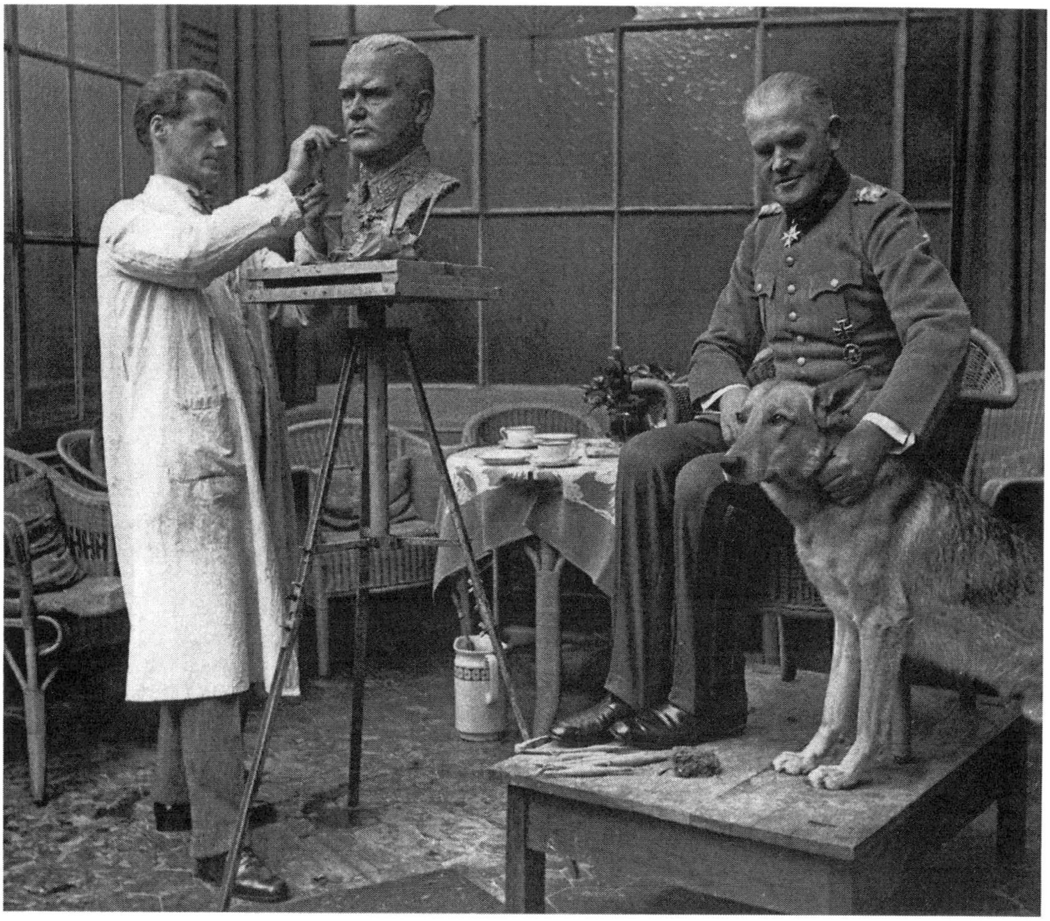

Field Marshal Werner von Blomberg with his dog.

The *Reich* Foreign Minister Konstantin Freiherr von Neurath was dismissed in 1938 (he had been Foreign Minister since 1932, that is to say since before Hitler's takeover), but he remained as *Reich* Minister without portfolio, and for a brief period acted as *Reichsprotektor* for Bohemia and Moravia as well as President of the Secret Cabinet Council, a position without any real significance. Freiherr von Neurath was replaced as Foreign Minister by *SS-Gruppenführer* Joachim von Ribbentrop.

At left is Baron (*Freiherr*) Konstantin von Neurath (1873-1956), German Foreign Minister from 1932 to 1938. In this photo he is apparently in London, with his and Nazi Germany's friend Montagu Norman (1871-1950, created Baron Norman in 1944), Governor of the Bank of England from 1920 to 1944. Norman was an enthusiastic member of the Anglo-German Fellowship and a close friend of Hjalmar Schacht, President of the Reichsbank and Minister of Economics under Hitler. Norman behaved disgracefully in transferring Czech gold, which was on deposit in England, to the Bank of International Settlements in Basel, of which he was a director, for distribution on to Hitler's regime. Two months after the outbreak of War he agreed to transfer more Czech gold direct to Hitler's regime, but this was blocked by the British Government. He nevertheless remained as Governor of the Bank of England for the duration of the War and was raised to the peerage despite his pro-Nazi sentiments and actions. It is one of the mysteries of the Second World War why he was allowed to remain in place despite his sympathies for the enemy. Churchill throughout the War was desperate to get rid of him, but was prevented time and again from doing so. Here Norman and Neurath (who was not originally von Neurath, because he bought his "von") are apparently planning something or other. (Whatever it was, it was not anything good!)

Franz von Papen remained as Vice Chancellor until 1934, but had to resign his post as *Reich* Commissioner for Prussia as early as March 31, 1933, when Hermann Göring was appointed as Minister President of Prussia.

Hermann Göring also became *Reich* Minister for Aviation, was installed as chief of the *Reich* Forestry Office and German Hunting Society, and collected countless official titles, medals of honour and other decorations.

New additions to the *Reich* government were:

Rudolf Hess, as "Deputy of the *Führer* and *Reich* Chancellor" and Minister without portfolio, in April 1933.

Rudolph [Walter Richard] Hess (1894–"1987?") became Deputy Führer and Chancellor of Germany in April of 1933. He wrote much or all of Hitler's book *Mein Kampf* for him when they shared a prison cell. Hitler was Hess's "god" and many have suggested that they formed a homosexual relationship during that time, where Hess literally fell in love with Hitler. This has been discussed in books treating Hitler's sexuality. Hess had many personal peculiarities. Putzi Hanfstängl says that he had "the exasperating habit of fooling around with the chair he was sitting on. He would sit on it the wrong way around, pass it through his legs, sit on the back, twirl it on one leg, like an amateur acrobat trying to show off." Hess was one of the few top Nazi leaders who had had a university education, so that he was highly literate, but he was a complete fanatic with narrow views which were held obsessively. Otto Strasser, who knew him well, said of him: "Of Rudolf Hess there is little to say. He was a handsome young man, an intellectual, and an artist, an officer and a poet. He was enthusiastic and faithful. He never faltered in his passion for Adolf Hitler. So great, in fact, was his sentimental admiration for Adolf that evil tongues used to call him 'Fräulein Hess'. I myself believe, however, that the relationship was absolutely pure." It was, by the way, Hess who introduced the name *Führer* for Hitler. Prior to their being in prison together, Hitler was only ever called "Herr Hitler". Then in prison Hess started calling him *Mein Chef* ["My Boss"]. But that did not catch on. And so Hess thought to call him *Mein Führer* ["My Leader"], and that stuck. And Ernst Röhm in his role as the head of the SA made a decree that Hitler was thereafter always to be referred to as *Mein Führer*. So it became a rule for National Socialism. As for the use of the word *Heil*, that was not invented by Hess. It was a common greeting in Austria in those days; if you ran into a friend named Ernst, say, on the street, you might casually say "Heil Ernst!" and he would "Heil" you back. Hitler himself was an Austrian, although he had by a devious and questionable route obtained instant German citizenship just in time to be named Chancellor of Germany by Hindenburg.

Hans Frank II was appointed as *Reich* Minister without portfolio for "re-organisation of the German legal system" and President of the Academy for German Law, and during the war took up the post of *Reich* Commissioner for Poland.

This is a photo of Niklas Frank holding up a photo of his father Hans Michael Frank (1900-1946, died in prison), the notorious Nazi "butcher of Poland" who rounded up all the Polish Jews and sent them to their deaths, and who earlier had reorganised the legal system of Nazi Germany for Hitler, whose friend he had been since the early days. Niklas Frank very bravely and courageously published a book in 1987 condemning his father for his terrible crimes and is a strong opponent of the Nazi legacy. He appeared in the film *Hitler's Children* in 2012 and in the film *My Nazi Legacy: What Our Fathers Did* in 2016, which is one of the most extraordinary documentary films ever made and should really be viewed by everyone. It is so emotionally powerful and psychologically illuminating that one watches it mesmerised, and it takes a long time to recover from the experience. Niklas Frank's behaviour has been truly heroic.

SA Chief of Staff Ernst Röhm (who would be murdered on June 30, 1934) also became a minister without portfolio.

Bernhard Rust (1883-1945, suicide) hitherto Prussian Minister for Culture, was promoted to the position of *Reich* Minister for Science, Education and National Culture.

Hanns Kerrl (1887-1941), leader of the *Reich* Office for Regional Planning and since 1933 Prussian Minister for Justice, was appointed *Reich* Minister for Church Affairs.

Paul Freiherr von Eltz-Rübenach (1875-1943), who held the post of *Reich* Postal and Transport Minister, was compelled to withdraw from the cabinet in 1937. The Ministry was divided and the new appointees were:

Julius [Heinrich] Dorpmüller (1869-1945) as *Reich* Minister of Transport, and

Wilhelm Ohnesorge as *Reich* Postal Minister.

Franz Gürtner, the Bavarian Justice Minister to whom Adolf Hitler was greatly indebted, and who had held the office of President of the Supreme Court of the *Reich* in Leipzig since 1929, was appointed *Reich* Minister of Justice in 1933 (to be succeeded at his death by Erwin Bumke, who in turn was succeeded at his death by Otto Thierack.)

On March 30, 1933 a new *Reich* Ministry was created, whose activities would be of great significance for Germany under National Socialism:

The *Reich* Ministry for Propaganda, which was led by Dr Paul Josef Goebbels, propaganda chief of the NSDAP and *Gauleiter* of Berlin.

The scope of this book would not be sufficient to report fully on Dr Goebbels' sinister character and activities. At this point it is merely to be noted that the idea of the Reichstag Fire, which was translated into action by Göring, emanated from Goebbels' mind, and that he was the *spiritus rector* of the betrayal of his party comrade Ernst Röhm and the subsequent propagation of the lie of the so-called "Röhm Revolt".

Paul Josef Goebbels (1887-1945, suicide), Minister of Propaganda from 1933 to 1945. He was the person who first conceived the idea for the Reichstag Fire, according to the author, one of whose jobs was to monitor Goebbels secretly by informants, tapping of his phone, bugging his office, etc., on the orders of Heydrich and Himmler, as Goebbels was their hated rival. Goebbels was an outrageous skirt-chaser and so out of control with his erotic obsessions that Hitler had to intervene at one point to end one of his trysts. Because Goebbels had the power to decide who could and who could not appear in a film, many actresses cast their glances upon him, and their gazes were more than met. Because the author was party to the monitoring of Goebbels, he knew all the details and all the dirty secrets of this man whom Himmler and Heydrich despised. Goebbels had a club foot, which he used to pretend was a war wound, until everyone learned the truth about it.

Two further *Reich* ministers without portfolio should also be mentioned:

Hans Heinrich Lammers (1879-1962), chief of the *Reich* Chancellery, and

Arthur Seyss-Inquart (1892-1946, executed), who in 1938/39 was *Reich* Governor of Austria and later was appointed as *Reich* Minister. He earned the Nazis' special gratitude through his betrayal of Austria following its annexation. After the outbreak of war, Seyss-Inquart as *Reich* Minister was appointed chief of the civil administration in Krakow and later chief of the civil administration in Holland.

Arthur Seyss-Inquart (1892-1946), Reich Governor of Austria, 'who earned the Nazis' special gratitude for his betrayal of Austria following its annexation', according to the author. He later became the Reich Commissioner for the German-occupied Netherlands, and carried out deportation of Jews and the shooting of hostages. He was hanged after the War.

Importantly, Heinrich Himmler, Chief of the German Police and *Reichsführer SS*, during the war succeeded the Nazi Minister Wilhelm Frick as *Reichsminister*. The German *Länder* had all but ceased to exist after the passing of the *Reichsstatthalter* (*Reich* Governors) law on January 30, 1935. The *Reichsgaue* law was created in 1939, according to which the *Reichsgaue* were designated "mid-level" administrative units, and as such were put under the direct command of the *Reich* government. At the same time all federal state agencies that still existed were converted into agencies of the *Reich*. The law from January 30, 1935 had already stated: "Within his administrative district, the *Reichsstatthalter* (*Reich* governor) is the permanent representative of the *Reich* government; he is appointed and recalled by the *Führer* and *Reich* Chancellor. It is the responsibility of the *Reichsstatthalter* to observe the guidelines of *Reich* policy devised by the *Führer* and *Reich* Chancellor; at his recommendation the *Führer* and *Reich* Chancellor appoints and dissolves the federal state government. Following the approval of the federal state government, the *Reichsstatthalter* issues and announces the federal state laws. The appointment of one *Reichsstatthalter* for several small *Länder* is acceptable."

The most feared signature in Nazi Germany. From an original document. (Eglantyne Collection) Himmler often endorsed documents with his initials "H H" in this clearly identifiable handwriting to signify that they were approved.

The "Island of the Respectable"

Immediately after the Reichstag Fire, at the end of February 1933, an association was formed in Berlin that called itself *"Die Insel der Anständigen"* ("Island of the Respectable"). It was not a registered association in the normal sense, but rather a group of notable personalities from Berlin society who met regularly and had no other aim than to devote themselves without distraction to a cultivated enjoyment of the arts. Among this group of friends, German classics would be read, the poets Hans Carossa (1878-1956) and Gerhart Hauptmann (1862-1946; he had won the Nobel Prize for Literature in 1912) (to name only two of many) would speak, refined chamber music would be masterfully interpreted, and lectures were given by renowned scholars. Most of these gatherings – if such a designation is at all appropriate – were held in the large, often palatial villas in the west of Berlin. Among the members of the "Island of the Respectable" were: the master conductor [Gustav Heinrich Ernst Martin] Wilhelm Furtwängler (1886-1954), the author Walter [Ritter] von Molo (1880-1958), the surgeon and privy councillor [Ernst] Ferdinand Sauerbruch (1875-1951), and the former German ambassador in Tokyo, an intellectual and well-known authority on East Asia, Wilhelm von Solf (1862-1936), whose sudden death in 1936 led to much speculation. [*Von Solf was anti-Nazi.*]

The intended purpose of the association "Island of the Respectable" was apolitical in nature; it was an informal gathering of members of the more refined parts of society who wanted to remain amongst themselves, and in their entire nature were markedly distanced from the parts of society that in those days had newly established themselves as predominant in Berlin. In a harmless and naïve way, the "Island of the Respectable" tried to oppose the brash upstarts, the National Socialists, and to distance itself from the leading Nazi clique, by declaring the new masters of the state as not "socially acceptable" and refusing them acceptance to this "Island of the Respectable".

Through this social boycott of Berlin's National Socialist leaders, a clear political bias was given to the association, despite its otherwise apolitical purpose of cliquish enjoyment of the arts. And so it was inevitable that the "Island of the Respectable" increasingly became a meeting place for those who stood in opposition to National Socialism. As members believed that during their soirées they were truly "amongst themselves", that is to say, amongst like-minded people, they made no secret of their "opposition" to Nazism, forcefully criticised the Nazis' machinations and openly expressed their outrage. After Alfred Hugenberg, the great hope of all conservatives, was ousted from Hitler's cabinet, hopes were increasingly pinned on the *Reichswehr*. Thus far, under the leadership of General von Fritsch, the *Reichswehr* had staunchly and at first seemingly successfully fended off all attempts by the Nazis to gain control over it, despite the fact that *Reichswehrminister* General von Blomberg was vociferously denounced as Hitler's dogsbody in conservative circles. The generals of the *Reichswehr* – along with the aged *Reichspräsident* Field Marshal General von Hindenburg – were seen as the most likely guarantors against overly brazen and insolent incursions into the state and society as a whole by the "plebeian" National Socialists.

The best possible relations were kept with the generals of the *Reichswehr* and the "circle around Hindenburg". General von Seeckt, now retired, sometimes attended the musical or literary events presented by the "Island of the Respectable". The general was on very friendly terms with the renowned composer and conductor [and violinist] Marta (aka Martá in Hungarian) Linz [von Kriegner] (1898-1982), who was an avid member of the "Island of the Respectable". [Count] Rudolf [*Graf*] von Bassewitz (1881-1951), the then leader of the department *"Protokoll"* (a sort of master of ceremonies in the Ministry for Foreign Affairs), was a regular attendee of the soirées organised by the "Island", as was the wife [Hildegard, née Roos; 1886-1952] of the fickle minister of state Otto [Lebrecht Eduard Daniel] Meissner (1880-1953), who had been in charge of the running of the *Reichspräsident's* office without interruption since 1920, and was at that time a prominent member of the "circle around Hindenburg". Quite generally, the "old guard" of the Ministry for Foreign Affairs was well represented. The youthful Baron von Gumpel of Munich was – wrongly – assumed to be a prominent representative of the association of young Catholics, while the popular Dr Edgar [Julius] Jung (1894-1934, murdered) was correctly seen as a close associate of the "Catholic" Franz von Papen, the man whom Adolf Hitler had had to accept as his vice chancellor, as he was a well-recognised favourite of the aged *Reichspräsident* von Hindenburg. Yes, even a man as reserved as Undersecretary Klausener, the leader of the group *Katholische Aktion*, would sometimes make an appearance in order to listen to Wilhelm Furtwängler, as he sat down at the grand piano to perform some of his own delicate impromptus, or to hear Michael Raucheisen accompany the contralto Sigrid Onégin on the grand piano. One of the initiators of the group's soirées was the star of *Universum Film*, Brigitte Helm – at the time the most successful German film actress.

A signed photo of the fim star Brigitte Helm, the most successful film star in Gemany at that time.

Brigitte Helm was a highly respected member of Berlin society due to her friendship with the well-known leader of the association *Stahlhelm*, the retired Major Franz von Stefanie, a man with especially close ties to the *Reichswehr* Ministry, on behalf of which he was in a position to award major arms contracts worth millions, which due to the terms of the Treaty of Versailles could not be acknowledged publicly. Members of the "Island of the Respectable" knew that in their personal rejection of National Socialism they were at one with the *Reichswehr* and the "circle around Hindenburg"; however, it would have been wrong to describe the group as a political opposition to the NSDAP, because nothing ever amounted to anything more than personal resentment. Socially, one was at pains to distance oneself from the Nazi leaders, but politically, a reserved, observant and therefore acquiescing stance was assumed, believing that it was possible to separate and isolate the personal and political spheres.

But neither could the "Island of the Respectable" be pigeonholed as "conservative" in the sense of the German National People's Party. Not only was there no talk of any specific party-political ties, but the names of the attendees at the various soirées stood testament to the diversity of the association's ideological make-up. They were gatherings of individuals who, *within* a certain stratum of society, stood in personal opposition to National Socialism, and who would later be labelled as "grumblers" by *Reichspropagandaminister* Dr Goebbels. And indeed, the political activities of the "Island of the Respectable" amounted to nothing more than "grumbling". Anything more, getting into any sort of tussle with the political hooligans of National Socialism, would have been frowned upon as quite "indecent". Finally, it must be emphasised that the "Island of the Respectable" was brought into being by women. It was the ladies of Berlin's society who organised these soirées that were peppered with exquisite artistic performances. And it was these same ladies who were at great pains to ensure that no "unworthy" individuals (that is to say, Nazis) would appear at "their" gatherings, so that one could truly be amongst "one's own kind".

Dangerous machinations?

In 1933/34, sensational reports concerning secret German rearmament – the reconstruction of the German *Wehrmacht* in violation of the terms of the Treaty of Versailles – were printed in the foreign press. Naturally, all such reports were immediately rejected by the Nazis, but the abundance of official denials could not hide the fact that the various reports that had made their way abroad were only too correct. They were much more than mere rumours, and the relevant German authorities were certain that it must have been a highly efficient espionage operation that had successfully laid bare the top-secret German rearmament efforts. Most of the dispatches that appeared in the foreign press started with the words: "Reports have emerged from within the circle around Hindenburg, according to which..."

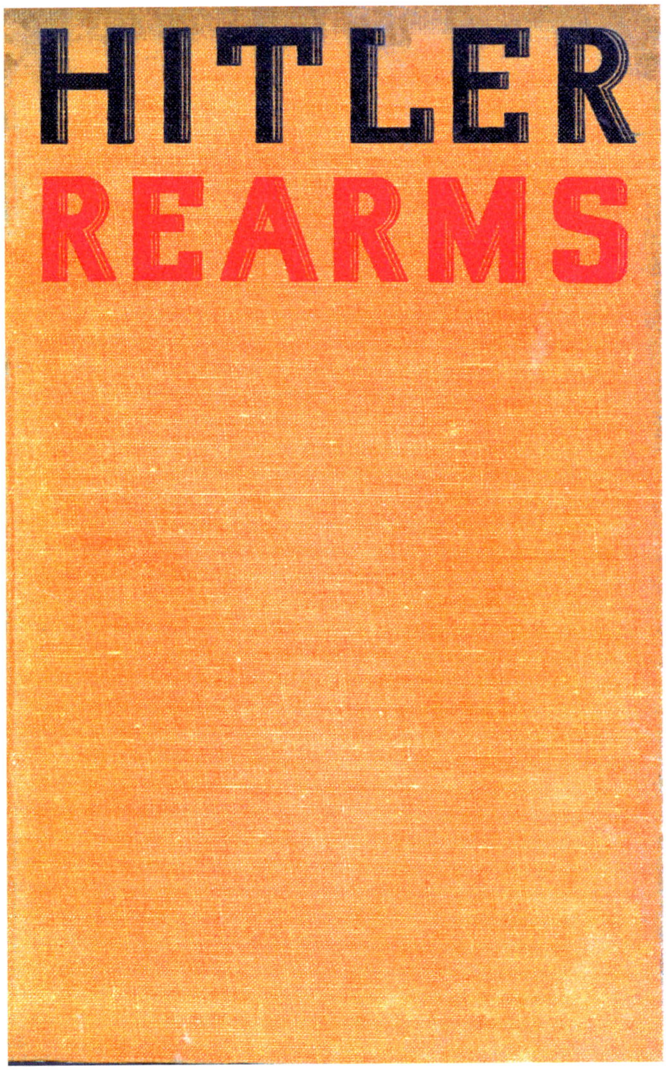

This book was published in London in 1934, edited by Dorothy Woodman (1902-1970), who worked as a journalist in Berlin in 1933 and covered the Reichstag Fire. The book was 336 pages long and contained clear proof, with photographs, that Germany was rearming in defiance of the Versaille Treaty and was turning into a militaristic state. She even published lists of all the factories that were making arms, tanks, armoured cars, warships, and planes. And she meticulously listed precisely which armaments which factories were making. (As an example, 15 cm. shells were being manufactured by Baer und Stein Metallwarenfabrik in Berlin.) The details of her lists were truly extraordinary. Many blind eyes were turned in Britain to this embarrassing information.

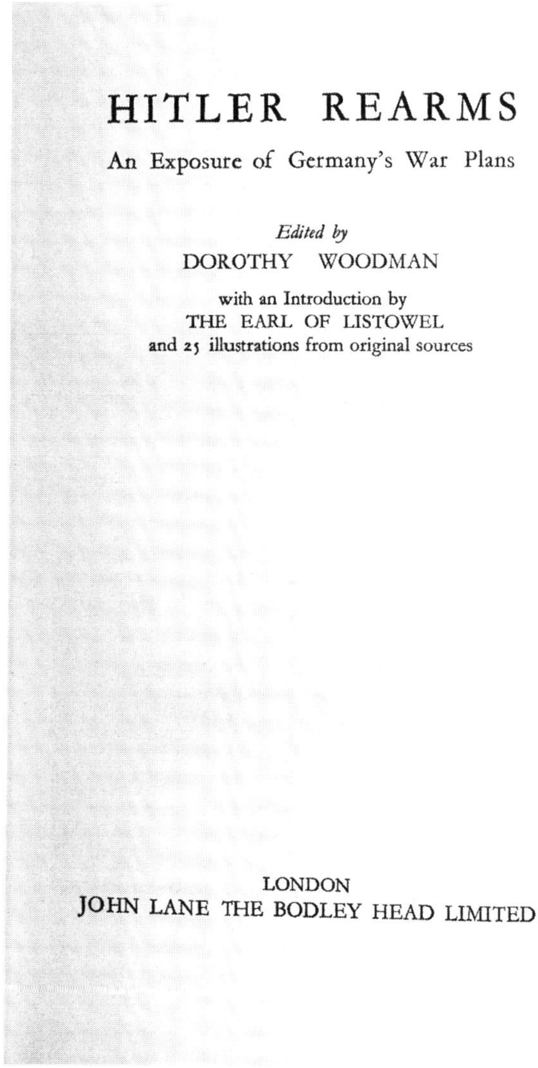

HITLER REARMS

An Exposure of Germany's War Plans

Edited by
DOROTHY WOODMAN

with an Introduction by
THE EARL OF LISTOWEL
and 25 illustrations from original sources

LONDON
JOHN LANE THE BODLEY HEAD LIMITED

The title page of the book.

REICHSWEHR AND S.A. CAVALRY MARCHING TOGETHER

MASSED MARCH OF THE ARMED S.S.

Some photos from the book.

One of the best-informed foreign correspondents officially accredited in Berlin was the American [mistake: *he was British, not American*] journalist [Philip] Pembroke Stevens (1903-1937), who would later meet an early death [in 1937] in the performance of his professional duties during the Japanese bombardment of Shanghai [where he was buried in the Bubbling Well Cemetery].

The English journalist Philip Pembroke Stevens (1903-1937). He was German correspondent for the London *Daily Express*. The author says he was one of the best-informed foreign journalists in Germany. Stevens was expelled from Germany because he refused to reveal his sources. He met an unfortunate death in Shanghai during a Japanese bombardment.

Pembroke Stevens was summoned to the newly established *Propagandaministerium*, where he was interviewed by the head of the department, Councillor Bade, and, laughing and scoffing, refused to disclose any details about the source of his information. After all attempts at surveillance failed, he was finally expelled from the country. The case *"Reports have emerged from within the circle around Hindenburg"* was handed over to the "Special Department Stein", which specialised in exceptional cases of espionage, as none of the police's investigations had borne any fruit. At the time, "Special Department Stein" still operated as a semi-official intelligence unit from its offices in Hotel Steinplatz in Berlin. As a special department for civil espionage and counterintelligence it would later be incorporated into the Security Service of the *Reichsführer SS*, the *SD-RFSS*, and renamed "Security Service for Special Deployment", but it would keep its offices in Berlin's police headquarters, where it had moved to at the end of 1933. The chief of that department was a certain Herr Stein [*the author himself under another pseudonym*], who held the rank of major on the *Reichswehrministeriums's* secret ranking list. As a non-National Socialist and following personal differences with the chief of the *SD* and the Gestapa, Stein was sent to a concentration camp in August 1934. The "Security Service for Special Deployment", the former "Special Department Stein", was dissolved when the mysterious "Chief Stein" – who by then was interned in Berlin's infamous concentration camp Columbiahaus on Heydrich's orders as a "prisoner of honour of the *Reichsführer SS*" – refused to resume his previous official role as a condition of his release. Stein, whose real name was in fact different, then spent nearly a year as a "prisoner of honour", tried in vain to have his case heard at a court of honour, and was eventually quietly and suddenly released.

Columbiahaus, the concentration camp at Berlin in the 1930s, into which the author was temporarily placed as "a prisoner of honour of the Reichsführer SS [Himmler]". He was "eventually and quietly released". There is more to this story than meets the eye, as will become clear in Volume Two. This camp was demolished in 1938 as part of the clearing of the site for the construction of Tempelhof Airport. In addition to being a concentration camp. this large structure also housed the Working Association of Sanitariums and Caretaking Facilities of the Republic, the harmless name of which disguised its true purpose, which was to murder "inferiors", namely disabled and mentally challenged persons by euthanasia. By August of 1941 this organisation had murdered 70,273 such people, all German citizens. It left Columbiahaus and moved to Tiergartenstrasse 4 in April of 1940, where it became known as "T 4".

A short time before its relocation to the police headquarters in Berlin, the "Special Department Stein" was instructed to investigate the "dangerous machinations" of the "circle around Hindenburg". The directive had not come from the Ministry of Propaganda, but had been given by General von Reichenau, the newly appointed chief of the army ordnance office in the *Reichswehrministerium*, which understandably was in a state of agitation following the revelations in the foreign press concerning secret rearmament.

A confidant of the *Reichswehrministerium* at the Siemens works, the former senior boatswain's mate Becker (who operated in the "factory protection service" at the company Siemens & Halske AG), alerted "Special Department Stein" to a certain American lady, "Miss Isabel St". A dilettante "journalist", she was anything but a "spy", but nevertheless turned out to be a conduit to Pembroke Stevens. Miss St., who was in many ways completely harmless, had no inkling of the value of the information that she passed on to her fellow American [*the author did not realize that Stevens was British, not American*]. It also became apparent that Miss St. was a staunch opponent of National Socialism and that she liked to use any opportunity to establish contact with others who shared her dislike of Nazism. Because the "student" Miss St. was a charming companion, had great affection for the fine arts, and even was a dilettante author, poet and composer herself, it came about quite naturally that she should gain access to the "Island of the Respectable". Having been introduced to the club by the head physician of the *Rot-Kreuz* Hospital in Berlin's Landhausstrasse, she soon gained popularity by performing American songs, especially cowboy songs, so competently that even inveterate opponents of American jazz music were quite enchanted; yes, even Wilhelm Furtwängler would applaud enthusiastically.

"Special Department Stein" deployed one of its best female agents against Miss St., namely Jutta [*Jutta Mary*] Baroness von Biel [1909-1965]. Baroness Biel, who came from old Mecklenburg nobility and who had already proved herself during several other espionage investigations, was a money-grabbing, prodigal young woman who craved recognition. She had turned the heads of many men but was never herself in danger of being in thrall to a man through love. She would go on to become one of the *SD-RFSS's* most dangerous senior agents and was used not only for espionage investigations. For a sufficiently large amount of money she would, without batting an eyelid, betray her own father or mother – which in the end she literally did. Baroness Biel was a chilling example of the amorality of certain degenerate circles of nobility, who toadied to the new rulers and sold the honour of their ancient family names for money and official state titles. Their acts were in stark contradistinction to those of many other noble families who, in their loyalty to tradition and according to upbringing and heritage, did continue to serve in the newly established German *Wehrmacht*, but, given their moral convictions, resolutely rejected neo-German Nazism.

Jutta von Biel was able to win the confidence of Miss St. relatively quickly, indeed, to completely put her under her spell and make her entirely compliant: Miss St. fell head over heels in love with the German baroness, for both women had a lesbian disposition. Baroness Biel was introduced to the "Island of the Respectable" by Miss St., where she was received well. Not only did her father bear the name of a venerable family, but he had also been a well-known globetrotter during the time before the World War of 1914–18. Her younger brother had in the past played a role in the various associations set up by Admiral [Adolf Lebrecht von] Trotha (1868-1940; he was Head of the Greater German Youth League, etc.) and had been a successful glider pilot long before the new German *Luftwaffe* had been established. Moreover, Baroness Biel was very well accredited by Dr Edgar Jung, a family friend who was a frequent attendee of the "Island's" soirées, as was already mentioned earlier.

Dr. Edgar Julius Jung (1894-1934, murdered), author and lawyer, vouched for Baroness Jutta von Biel, not knowing that she was a spy. Jung was the speech writer for Franz von Papen. A biography of him has been written: *Edgar Julius Jung, Right-Wing Enemy of the Nazis*, by Roshan Magub (2017), but it mentions nothing about the Jutta von Biel affair.

To come straight to the point: the reports that were compiled by "Special Department Stein" for General [Walter] von Reichenau (who, at that time, in his capacity as chief of the army ordnance office in the *Reichswehrministerium*, still held the rank of major general) demonstrated clearly that no "dangerous machinations" were undertaken by any individuals belonging to the "Island of the Respectable". While agent Baroness Biel did confirm that Miss St. would faithfully report to Pembroke Stevens and other foreign correspondents any scraps of news that she picked up in conversations at the "Island", this clearly had precious little to do with espionage and would have been insufficient for a solid indictment. The "Island of the

Respectable" was certainly not an espionage hub, and none of its members could be accused of espionage. If any important classified *Reichswehr* information concerning armament did actually reach foreign nations from the "circle around Hindenburg", it was certainly not via the "Island of the Respectable". More will be said about Miss St.'s activities later. For now it suffices to say that there were no "dangerous machinations" on part of the "Island of the Respectable", neither in the sense of high treason, nor treason involving foreign nations, which was the sole concern of "Special Department Stein".

The "Special Department Stein"

"Special Department Stein" occupied an ambiguous position, in that its chief was a non-National Socialist who was subordinate to the chief of the army ordnance office in the *Reichswehrministerium* (General von Reichenau). His deputy, a member of the infamous *SD*, naturally kept the chief of the *SD*, Heydrich, informed and made available to him the department's classified reports, despite the fact that at that time Heydrich had not yet been appointed chief of the Gestapa in Berlin, but still held the position of chief of the Bavarian Political Police in Munich. The non-National Socialist Stein had an *SD* member breathing down his neck, who promptly brought about his downfall when it was decided to rid the department of "that inconvenient man". This "Chief Stein" was self-confident in superabundance and seriously thought that he could avoid joining the party while still staying on as chief of "his" special department – even at the point when the "Special Department Stein" had been transformed into the "Security Service for Special Deployment"! And yet this "Major" was only listed on the secret army list (in 1933/34, as part of the small *Reichswehr*); that is to say, he was not even an active officer but was operating only on the basis of a one-year civil employment contract. Nevertheless, until the summer of 1934, his friends celebrated him as "the most influential man in Berlin"; this man who "didn't give a damn about domestic politics" and impertinently reproached the highest Nazi leaders, pointing out their errors and weaknesses, bluntly forcing his own opinion on them and ridiculing the "questionable" ideology of National Socialism. Only his professional competence, which was indeed recognised by the Nazi leaders, saved Stein from being sent to a concentration camp many months earlier. While eventually his friends and benefactors could no longer prevent his imprisonment, they were at least able to ensure that he was not beaten to death during his internment, but instead was held as a "prisoner of honour".

"Special Department Stein" moved from Hotel Steinplatz into its new premises in the Berlin police headquarters. The infamous *SD* man [Staff Master Sergeant, *Stabsfeldwebel*] Josef Pospischil [1902-1948] from the *SD* Senior District East was appointed as Stein's [i.e., the author's] deputy and chief adjutant. Pospischil had until that point been in service with the commander of the *SD* raiding squad, *SS-Standartenführer* [Heinrich Maria "Heinz"] Jost (1904-1964), who was the "liaison officer" between the Munich-based chief of the Bavarian Political Police, *SD*-chief Reinhard Heydrich, and the Berlin-based leader of the Gestapa, Undersecretary Dr Diels. [*Please note that Heinz Jost and Hanns Johst, mentioned later, are different individuals.*] As has been mentioned earlier in these pages, Dr Diels had no idea how irksome liaison officer Jost's presence would turn out to be; and similarly the chief of "Special Department Stein" did not foresee any troubles with his "deputy" [Josef] Pospischil, because he trusted him in the same way that Dr Diels had trusted [Heinz] Jost; indeed, Stein suspected betrayal much less than Dr Diels, who was a much more wary man.

Heinz Jost (1904–1964) at right, and beside him his colleague Otto Ohlendorff (1907-1951, executed). Together they carried our mass murders in Moldova, the south of the Ukraine, and the Crimea, during the War. Jost was, like Pfeifer and Himmler, a Catholic. In the 1930s, as described in the main text, he betrayed his boss Rudolf Diels, while his protégé Josef Pospischil simultaneously betrayed our author.

While Stein was aware of the existence of the *SD-RFSS* and knew of the *SD* Senior District East as well as the other senior districts (indeed, he used them as valuable sources of information for his espionage investigations), he "ignored" the culture of informing and denunciation that was integral to the *SD-RFSS*. Stein did not think there were any timeservers amongst his staff. He would not have dreamt of equating one of his colleagues and "friends" with those questionable and unscrupulous individuals who can be bought, who would do anything for money (or, in misguided ambition, for party or state offices, large or small). In his capacity as chief of an important espionage organisation he did have to deal with such characters, but he had learned to despise them all the more. In his naivety, Stein wanted to be wooed by the party, like a film star whose services a new production company is desperate to attract. He became ever more hubristic in his self-aggrandisement, and ever more exorbitant in the overestimation of his indispensability. But perhaps his professional skills, his intuitive abilities in his field of espionage, were rooted in the fact that, deep down, he was actually a very naïve man, and what is more, an optimist – but not an opportunist. There was no place for men of such naivety in the National Socialist state; sooner or later they would all be brought down or stumble and fall themselves. Their existence was not only a burden on National Socialism, but an utter impossibility.

The planned putsch against the *Reichswehr*

Himmler-Heydrich had just set up their offices at the Gestapa in Berlin, and the "Special Department Stein" had been transformed – in circumstances that will be reported on further in a later chapter – into the "Security Service for Special Deployment", when the surveillance of Miss St. yielded a strange result. Miss St. had reported to a fellow American about an alleged planned putsch by *SA* Chief of Staff Ernst Röhm against —— the *Reichswehr*. The report came into the hands of Heydrich through Pospischil and was passed on to the *Reichswehrministerium* by Stein, where it was asserted that the ministry was already well aware about the rebellious intentions of the *SA* and its chief of staff; indeed, that Röhm's plan was known to the ministry in every detail and that relevant countermeasures were already being prepared.

The facts surrounding the planned putsch by *SA* Chief of Staff Ernst Röhm are these:

The former member of the general staff and retired captain Ernst Röhm – who, apart from the infamous anti-Semite and *Gauleiter* Julius Streicher in Nuremberg was the only man on first-name terms with Adolf Hitler – in his capacity as Chief of Staff of the *SA* had meticulously prepared a precise putsch plan for his *Führer* and friend, *Reich* Chancellor Adolf Hitler. According to the plan, the generals of the *Reichswehr*, bothersome to National Socialism and often appearing restive, were to be forcefully removed; the barracks were to be raided and occupied by armed *SA* troops; and, by incorporating the paramilitary *SA*, the existing *Reichswehr* was to be transformed into a "people's army". In other words: the *Reichswehr*, which was at its core still "apolitical", was to retain its name, but was to be merged with the *SA* and to become a Nazi army, faithfully devoted to the party leader Adolf Hitler; the "people's army", now integrated with the *SA*, was to become a reliable political tool for the use of the Nazi leadership. This plan was to be taken all the more seriously as the organisational talents of its architect Ernst Röhm were undisputed by friend and foe, and the *SA* chief, who was known as a bold and dauntless man, was accustomed to doing outstanding work.

In March 1934 Röhm presented his fully developed putsch plan to the party leader and *Reich* Chancellor Adolf Hitler. Together with Rudolf Hess, he had been brought into government a few months earlier as a minister without portfolio, in an attempt by Hitler to create a counterbalance to the generals of the *Reichswehr* and the "circle around Hindenburg". It had been possible, following the badly orchestrated Reichstag Fire, to sideline the obstructionist Alfred Hugenberg and to curb or even eliminate the conservatives' leverage within the *Reich* government; but, following the first shock, the "circle around Hindenburg" was latterly vigorously opposing the Nazis' terror, which was by now raging "officially" in Prussia and all the other German *Länder*. The Nazi leaders, who were concerned about their positions of power, could not easily attack that circle, as it had the backing of the *Reichswehr*; indeed, the generals of the *Reichswehr* formed the foremost constituents of that circle. Officially, only the *Reichswehrminister*, General von Blomberg, Hitler's "dogsbody", had been a member of the *Reich* government, but he had recently been joined by another general, namely General Baron [*Freiherr*] von Fritsch, in his capacity as Supreme Commander of the army. Nominally, the Supreme Commander of the army did not hold the rank of a *Reich* minister, but *Reichspräsident* von Hindenburg had insisted on Fritsch's presence at all cabinet meetings in which armament was to be discussed. As such matters were almost always on the agenda, the Supreme Commander of the army was, to all intents and purposes, part of the *Reich* government. For this reason, Hitler hastily summoned the chief of his private army, Chief of Staff Röhm, to join the *Reich* government, and promoted him, as well as his deputy Rudolf Hess, the actual leader of the NSDAP, to the position of *Reichsminister*.

The act of elevating Ernst Röhm and Rudolf Hess to the position of *Reichsminister* created a palpable thundery atmosphere. In recognition of the looming storm, which would have the potential to cause much damage to the "National Socialist ideology", Ernst Röhm, together with his cronies, devised a plan for a putsch that would "rescue" National Socialism. The finished plan was presented to Adolf Hitler and the highest party leaders Rudolf Hess, Hermann Göring, Josef Goebbels and Wilhelm Frick. At that time, early in 1934, Heinrich Himmler did not belong to this circle of "highest party leaders"; as *Reichsführer SS* he was not even a *Reichsleiter* of the NSDAP. However, it must be made clear that Himmler not only knew of Röhm's putsch plan from the beginning, but that he even had played a role in the development of that plan; a fact that will be the subject of further investigation later. Once Röhm's putsch plan became known to its opponents, the foreboding thunderous mood turned into a dangerous atmosphere of revolution and civil war. All non-National Socialists, those who had only a hunch and even more so the true insiders, counted on certain victory by the *Reichswehr*. The Nazis in turn were hoping to finally rid themselves of the "reactionary dogs". But while one side, that of the non-National Socialists, was upbeat about its chances of victory and full of a certain satisfaction that "the time of reckoning had come", the other side, that of the Nazis, was full of trepidation and feared an irretrievable loss of power.

The Reichstag Fire had unleashed the "official" Nazi terror. Now, an avenger should arise to ward off that terror and to annihilate Nazism. In the eyes of all politically engaged non-National Socialists, the generals of the *Reichswehr* became the protectors and custodians of the law, who would safeguard against terror and abuse of authority. In the event, of course, the generals of the *Reichswehr* did not become those protectors and custodians of the law.

An atmosphere of civil war, provoked by the Nazis. A feeling of elation among knowing and suspecting non-National Socialists. Amongst the Nazis, fury following the betrayal of Röhm's putsch plan, and hatred against the "reactionary dogs".

In the days between late April and late June 1933, the atmosphere in Berlin was charged; people involved in the various factions were awaiting the "day of reckoning" in nervous, overwrought anticipation.

The German general public, however, was completely unaware. The workers had to endure Nazi terror in a leaderless, torpid and submissive state, and the only way they knew how to avert it was to consign themselves to Nazism, to throw themselves into the arms of the Nazis.

Röhm, the *Reichswehrminister*

In appointing the *SA* Chief of Staff to the position of *Reich* Minister, Hitler hoped to substantially consolidate his own position as *Reich* Chancellor. It was Hitler's intention to skilfully play off the mercenary-like Röhm against the reserved general corps, who were represented by their chief, General Freiherr von Fritsch. According to Hitler's designs, the direct, coarse and ballsy Ernst Röhm would not only be sent in to broach the issue of the NSDAP's various demands on the *Reichswehr*, but he would also act as the *enfant terrible* of the party, enabling Hitler to assume the role of a kind of mediator between the *Reichswehr* and the *SA* (i.e. the party). The more outrageous *Röhm's* demands would become, the more Hitler, in his guise as mediator, expected to be able to extract from the *Reichswehr* for his party. By feigning moderation and seemingly employing delicate negotiating skills, Hitler hoped to shine like a true statesman. In other words: Hitler planned to deploy his tried and tested methods of wirepulling even against the generals of the *Reichswehr*; an approach that would, however, turn out to be a profound miscalculation. The clash of the two opponents Röhm and Fritsch was not a trial of personal strength, but a fight for the party's influence over the *Reichswehr*, or, conversely, the shielding and protection of the *Reichswehr* against the party. Hitler's scheming failed, because – exceptionally – this was not a personal power struggle but a question of matters of true principles.

The new *Reichsminister* Ernst Röhm's first advance against the *Reichswehr* was a spectacular failure: Röhm petitioned for the incorporation of several well-equipped *SA* units into the *Reichswehr*, as part of the – still strictly secret – rearmament. Fritsch's cool and assertive answer came quickly: "No!"

Hitler mediated, telling the *Reichswehr* that "of course" it would have the right to appoint officers as it saw fit, without involvement of the *SA* leadership. Fritsch stuck to his negative response: "No!"

Hitler "humiliated himself" – as Röhm put it – by proposing a compromise, under which the *SA Standarten* would not be incorporated into the *Reichswehr* en bloc, but separated into *Stürme* (an *SA Sturm* is equivalent to a *Reichswehr* company) and distributed amongst several *Reichswehr* regiments, thus merely ramping up the *Reichswehr's* troop numbers through the inclusion of experienced *SA* men. The army command would retain the right to carry out the inclusions on a man-by-man basis. The army chief's answer bordered on impertinence and felt like a slap in the face: he, Fritsch, had really nothing to add to his principled "No!", but he would give the army command's final answer in writing after consulting with the generals! Only several weeks (!) later, the army command issued a solemn declaration "for the attention of the *Reich* government". Over nine typed pages, the general corps laid out its decision: an inclusion – in any form whatsoever – of the *SA* into the *Reichswehr* would never be considered. This statement by the army command was signed on behalf of the general corps and the active German officer corps by General von Fritsch, General Liebmann, and General von Pogrell. It was delivered to *Reich* Chancellor Hitler by – – – *Reichspräsident* Field Marshal General von Hindenburg, who made Hitler renew his promise to respect the integrity of the *Reichswehr*. The competent *Reichsminister*, General von Blomberg, had simply been ignored. General von Fritsch did not even deign to appear at any further meetings of the *Reich* government for the next two months. Eventually the *Reichspräsident* himself (!) called on General von Fritsch to resume his attendance of meetings where questions of rearmament were discussed.

Not only did Hitler renew his promise to the *Reichspräsident* to respect the *Reichswehr's* homogeneity, but he also reassured the chief of army command that he, Hitler, was in fact quite in agreement with the general and that in future he would support a strict separation of the party and the *Reichswehr*. Ernst Röhm, the *enfant terrible*, was incandescent with rage and offered his resignation. Hitler, however, did not accept the resignation, not least because such a step would amount to a public admission of the party's failure. During a private discussion between the two men, who were, after all, on first-name terms, *SA* Chief of Staff Röhm reproached Hitler in a characteristically forceful and coarse manner, and could only be appeased with the insidious suggestion that there were other ways and means to silence the "impertinent, reactionary dogs". But the boisterous Röhm did not want to hear "any more lazy excuses" and went on to develop his detailed putsch plan, according to which the generals of the *Reichswehr* would either be "bumped off", or were made to "keel over"; either way – assuming all went smoothly – the *Reichswehr* would be turned into a Nazi army. And, Röhm continued to argue, decent former members of the general staff could also be found in the *SA*. Many retired generals were only waiting to be reactivated and incorporated into a Nazi army!

As has already been mentioned, Röhm presented his finished plan – which would later be lauded as a military masterpiece even by members of the *Reichswehr* – to his friend and *Reich*

Chancellor in March 1934. The highest Nazi leaders, who in their dual ministerial capacity had witnessed the generals' icy snub and the affront to the party (Göring, Goebbels, Frick, Hess, Darré), were ecstatic about Röhm's plan and launched into veritable tirades of hate against the "reactionary dogs", who, thanks to Röhm's "genius", could now be done away with once and for all. But Hitler, the eternal ditherer in all decision-making matters, fretted about fomenting a civil war and, in contrast to the party zealots, assessed the chances of a successful putsch with much scepticism. He worried that such a putsch attempt might jeopardise the power that had only just been won, and gave his friend Röhm neither a positive nor a negative answer, but instead held out the prospect of a speedy decision. Röhm felt "betrayed by his best friend" and offered his resignation once again, this time in writing and for both his positions, i.e. those of *SA* Chief of Staff and *Reichsminister.* He did not bother to wait for a response, but, in a sulk, went on holiday in Munich. Hitler felt compelled to rehabilitate his friend, and issued a public statement, declaring that Röhm had by no means been relieved of his duties as *SA* Chief of Staff and *Reichsminister*, that he was merely taking a prolonged holiday for purposes of recuperation, and upon his return, would immediately take the reins as a *Reichsminister* once again. Such an explanation on Hitler's part was necessary, as Röhm had vented his anger very noisily and bluntly in *SA* circles, and talked of resigning from his positions. However mendacious Hitler's assurances of friendship may have been, they did have the desired effect: Röhm was calmed down and saw a new glimmer of hope for his planned putsch, for not only had Hitler issued his statement in support of *SA* Chief of Staff and *Reichsminister* Röhm, but at the same time Rudolf Hess and Josef Goebbels arrived in Munich and celebrated veritable "orgies of friendship" with Röhm at his mother's and sister's homes, while Göring and Frick reaffirmed their deep friendship with Röhm in lengthy telephone calls. Röhm's mother received gushing congratulations on her magnificent son, who would now show the generals of the *Reichswehr* the true extent of his genius. The man who felt compelled to indulge in downright nauseating adulation and sycophancy was — Heinrich Himmler, who, as an almost daily guest at Röhm's mother's house, hardly left his boss's side in those days. Showered in premature praise, and puffed up with vain pride in "his" impending great battle, Röhm went back to Berlin, believing with all his heart that nothing now stood in the way of his plan. Back in the capital, Hitler declared himself in agreement with the plan in principle, but still delayed the order for its implementation, as, in his words, the right moment had not yet come. Röhm was appeased and was instructed to do his part to placate all *SA* leaders who were in on the secret plot. The reason given for further delaying the plan's implementation was the recent commencement of the *Reichswehr's* annual spring manoeuvres.

The "betrayal"

By no means all senior *SA* leaders had been let in on the secret of the planned putsch against the *Reichswehr.* As former active army officers, some *SAGruppenführers* were secret admirers of the current *Reichswehr* general corps (or were at least suspected of such quiet veneration). Therefore the *SA* Chief of Staff had only taken his closest friends into his confidence, being satisfied that he would be able to successfully implement his planned putsch with the help of this select group of close associates. Naturally, the Berlin branch of the *SA* was to play a critical role in the implementation of the plan, but, on the day of the putsch, the entire *SA* was to be put on high alert. The various *SA* leaders were to be given their orders – which were expected to be executed with exact precision – only at the last minute. In early 1934, the *SA* Chief of Staff's main offices were still located in Munich, but, in his capacity as *Reichsminister*, Röhm also had a villa available in Berlin's Standartenstrasse, in which some rooms were used as offices for the local *SA* leadership.

SAGruppenführer Count von Helldorff, who as the then leader of the Berlin branch of the *SA* had played a major role in the staging of the Reichstag Fire, had since been appointed as police president for Potsdam.

Count (*Graf*) Wolf-Heinrich Julius Otto Bernhard Fritz Hermann Ferdinand von Helldorf (1896-1944, murdered), who played a major role in starting the Reichstag (German Parliament) Fire on 27 February 1933, blaming it on the communists, and using this false flag incident to help Hitler to absolute power. He then became head of the police for Potsdam, near Berlin. After 1938, he turned against the Nazis and was executed by them in 1944. (Another reason for executing him was that he knew too much.) Otto Strasser says of him that he was "a pervert who was personally short of money". In order to appease his hostility, the clairvoyant Hanussen loaned him large sums of money. Strasser says: "But Helldorff had no intention of repaying this inconvenient creditor. As soon as he became chief of police after Hitler's accession to power, he had him murdered." Strasser points out the irony of the fact that Hanussen was one Jew who was not, as many people thought, murdered by Hitler, but instead by Helldorff to avoid having to repay a debt.

Helldorf was succeeded as the head of the *SA* by a certain Karl Ernst, who had been promoted by the *SAOberführer* directly to the rank of *SAGruppenführer*, thus leapfrogging the rank of *SABrigadeführer*. Ernst was bisexual and lived together with Röhm in the villa in Standartenstrasse. Their quarters were commonly referred to as the "love nest". (In order to avoid a wider scandal, Röhm had recently been engaged and was due to be married.) Along with the infamous *SA* leader [Edmund] Heines, who hailed from Breslau [*now called Wrocław*], and a select group of other choice hooligans, *SAGruppenführer* Ernst was part of

SA Chief of Staff Röhm's most intimate circle of friends. Röhm's entire Berlin *SA* corps had been selected as the command unit for the impending putsch, and the "love nest" in Berlin's Standartenstrasse had been assigned as its headquarters.

Karl Ernst

Karl Ernst, one of the main homosexual lovers of the head of the SA, Ernst Röhm. He lived with Röhm in 'the Love Nest' on Berlin's Standartenstrasse, along with many hooligans and thugs. Röhm's official lover was Count Spreti, but Karl Ernst appears to have been Number Two. He was murdered in the Night of the Long Knives.

Edmund Heines (1897-1934, murdered) of the SA was the Deputy to Ernst Röhm. He was also executed in Stadelheim Prison by the SD as part of the Night of the Long Knives. He was an open homosexual, which many of the Nazis strongly disapproved of. (Bundesarchiv)

It must be mentioned that Röhm and his friends never sought to conceal their homosexual dispositions; the term "love nest" was a common and well-known moniker in all party circles. Between 1931 and 1933, no fewer than 19 separate charges in indictments at the party court for "scandalous homosexual activities" had to be dropped on Hitler's orders. In the days just after Christmas 1933, Hitler had summoned the party's most senior judge, the retired Major and *Reichsleiter* Walter Buch, and angrily ordered him to stop bringing "distracting" charges against *SA* Chief of Staff Röhm. Buch, the highest party judge, was one of the few party officials who had dared, even before 1934, to wage an open war against the homosexual activities of Röhm and his clique; activities that for years had been an open secret both within and outside the NSDAP. In May 1934, at one of his boozy get-togethers at the *Luftwaffe's* headquarters on Berlin's Wannsee, Hermann Göring quipped, to roaring laughter by his audience, that only men who were "at least 50 per cent homosexual" stood any chance of being appointed to the leadership of the Berlin *SA*. And he went on to say about *SAGruppenführer* Ernst: "He is the most enchanting swine I know; I have recommended him to our Doctor (Dr Goebbels), but he says he is only interested in totty." The old "Papa Christiansen", who still liked to be addressed as *"Käpt'n"* by his friends, even though he had long been promoted to the rank of air force general (and would go on to be appointed military governor of Holland), hissed into the ear of a young officer: "Don't listen to him, young man – our dear Herr Minister is getting a bit vulgar! I put it down to bad upbringing..."

Judge Walter Buch (1883-1949), who was a relentless enemy of Ernst Röhm and kept trying to prosecute him. Hitler ordered him to stop it. Buch, who was upright as a prosecutor, had the misfortune to become the father-in-law of the sinister and highly dangerous Martin Bormann. Buch became so terrified of his son-in-law, that Erich Kempka, in speaking of Bormann, says: "His father-in-law Reichsleiter Walter Buch would leave Obsersalzburg in his car in a near panic if he heard that Bormann was coming up."

One of the men in the staff of *SAGruppenführer* Karl Ernst was a former air force officer (during the World War of 1914–18), retired Cavalry Captain [Daniel] Gerth (1891-1934, shot). He had applied to be reactivated in the new *Luftwaffe*, and had been promised later promotion to the rank of major (to be enacted in the autumn of 1934), and the position of *Commodore* of a *Luftwaffe* detachment. For now, the air force man and major-to-be served as an *SA* leader, but Gerth already felt like a reactivated officer. As a member of the "Association of Former Cavalry Men", he asked secretary Herr von Platen to arrange a private interview with the organisation's president. The meeting was arranged and the former cavalry captain Gerth told the president, General Fritsch, about *SA* Chief of Staff Röhm's planned putsch against the *Reichswehr*. Eventually Gerth secretly made copies of the existing putsch plan and passed these on to the chief of the army command. However, the handing over of the documents did not pay off for *SA Führer* Gerth. On June 30, 1934, together with his *SA* chief, Karl Ernst, he was "accidentally" shot in the courtyard of the former cadet school Lichterfelde in the presence of two attending *Reichswehr* generals. When the *Reichswehr* ministry "suddenly" remembered him, and General von Fritsch sent a message to the Generals Witzleben and Rundstedt who were attending in Lichterfelde, it was already too late: Gerth's execution had been carried out; he had been shot without knowing why and on whose orders. The Nazis found out soon enough that the *Reichswehr* ministry knew of the planned putsch, but they only learned the traitor's name after June 30, 1934, when Gerth was already dead. Is it possible that von Fritsch's rescue attempt was *intentionally* tardy, and that the general acted in the spirit of Napoleon's words: "I love treason but hate the traitor"?

Papen sees his chance: the Marburg speech

On June 22, 1934, at the invitation of Dr Goebbels, *Reichsbankpräsident* Schacht gave a lecture on the Haavara Agreement in one of the grand halls (Schinkelsaal) of the Ministry of Propaganda. All foreign correspondents accredited in Berlin had been invited; tea and an abundance of cakes and pastries were served at small round tables, while the Herr *Reichsbankpräsident* addressed the assembled company in arrogant tones from his flower-adorned lectern. But despite the fact that Dr Schacht's exposition was extremely important, not least for all the journalists present, the hall was filled with an almost palpable nervous inattentiveness. There was much secretive whispering between the tables, and now and then someone would point at Vice Chancellor von Papen, who was sitting with *Reich* Labour Minister Seldte at the back of the hall, almost hidden. Two of his stalwarts, the senior councillors Bose and Tschirschky, were sitting with several high officials from the Vice Chancellery at a table in the centre of the hall. With a wry smile on his lips, Bose said to Tschirschky: "If we survive the coming week, we will have won." Senior councillor Bade from the Ministry of Propaganda overheard these words and immediately conveyed them to Dr Goebbels' private offices, where at that time the all-powerful *SS-Oberführer* [Karl August] Hanke (1903-1945) still held office as privy secretary (he would later be appointed as undersecretary and finally *Gauleiter* in Breslau [Wrocław]).

That is SS-Oberführer Karl August Hanke (1903-1945) on the phone behind his boss Goebbels, in the room where Goebbels received his visitors. Hanke went on to become the Head of the occupied Province of Lower Silesia. After the War, he disguised himself as a private and tried to escape, but was caught by Czech partisans. He tried to escape from them by clinging to a passing train, but they shot him and he fell off. They then beat him to death with their rifle butts. (Bundesarchiv)

Senior councillor Bade's news in no way made a sensational impact on the initiates; it was merely one small piece that contributed to the completion of the mosaic. What had happened?

Herr von Papen was informed by his friends in the "circle around Hindenburg" about the existence and nature of Röhm's putsch plan. Von Papen saw this as an opportunity and prepared himself: in his estimation, a clash between the *Reichswehr* and Nazism would doubtlessly lead to the fall of the Hitler cabinet and a crushing defeat for National Socialism; a new *Reich* government would have to be formed with none other than him, Franz von Papen, as *Reich* Chancellor. Von Papen went as far as drawing up a complete cabinet list, after the aged *Reichspräsident* had secured the army command's responsibility for his, Papen's, personal safety, which in the end did save his life.

Herr von Papen wanted to become *Reich* Chancellor once again, after the Nazis had made it abundantly clear that – as *Reichspräsident* Hindenburg's favourite – they did respect him and were willing to grant him the title of vice chancellor. However, they had no plans to concede any real authority or power to him, and did not even take seriously his recently acquired position of *Reich* Commissioner for the Saarland region. Franz von Papen harboured an almost untameable desire to overthrow the government, proved himself as a master of intrigue, resumed old alliances and established new ones, and engaged in an extraordinary level of behind-the-scenes activity.

After the conclusion of Hjalmar Schacht's address, the usual exchange of questions and answers between the foreign correspondents and the speaker ensued, during which Dr Goebbels deftly assisted his colleague Schacht by batting away any difficult questions. Eventually, the American journalist Carl Flick-Steger, who was feared for his sharp tongue and pen, directly addressed Goebbels: "Herr Minister, is it true that because of the Marburg speech your relations with Vice Chancellor von Papen are extremely strained?" Dr Goebbels jumped up from his chair, shouting into the hall: "Herr von Papen! Herr von Paaapen!!" The murmur of chattering and whispering had now ceased, and an appalling silence had enveloped the hall as all present watched the events unfold, fraught with extreme tension. Everyone felt – no, knew – that this would be the major showdown. But Herr von Papen rushed dutifully towards the summoner, who in turn opened his arms, limped two or three steps towards von Papen, embraced him and, almost shouting, exclaimed: "My dear Herr Papen, did you hear that? You and I are supposed to have strained relations! You and I, of all people, when in fact we are the best of friends!" And, turning back to the journalists, Dr Goebbels continued, holding Herr von Papen by the hand: "Gentlemen, I can assure you that no two cabinet ministers have ever had such wonderful relations as do Herr von Papen and I!" The American journalist Flick-Steger, however, was not going to be duped quite so easily and insisted: "My sources tell me that it was precisely you, Herr *Propagandaminister*, who ordered the seizure of the printed version of Herr von Papen's Marburg speech!" Dr Goebbels replied, full of derision: "Lies and deception! You have lousy sources, *mein Herr*! My friend von Papen's Marburg speech was given with the full consent of the *Reich* government! Isn't that so, Herr von Papen?" Vice Chancellor von Papen was visibly so moved that he could hardly speak a word, and, as Dr Goebbels would not release his hand, he simply kept shaking it, approvingly nodding his head.

The background was this: A few days earlier, Franz von Papen had given a speech in Marburg, the stronghold of the staunchly conservative association of former front soldiers, *Stahlhelm*, in which he had rather openly criticised the National Socialist terror regime, especially in the economic sector. The speech had been a clear affront to the NSDAP and its *Gauleiters*. It was given in anticipation of things to come; Herr von Papen wanted to position himself as a future *Reich* Chancellor, in the firm expectation that the downfall of Hitler and his Nazi henchmen, brought about by the *Reichswehr*, was imminent. It was the "circle around Hindenburg" that had encouraged the speech; it was designed to provoke the triggering of Röhm's putsch plan and thereby the initial phase of the *Reichwehr's* counter attack. This is why 500,000 copies had been immediately printed, which were to be distributed by members of the association *Stahlhelm*. But von Papen had barely spoken his last words in Marburg, when Goebbels had the entire print run confiscated. However, the Ministry of Propaganda was unable to retrieve several thousand copies that had begun to circulate in Berlin even before von Papen had travelled back from Marburg to Berlin in his car. Dr Bose, his chief administrative officer in the Vice Chancellery in Berlin's Vossstrasse, had done excellent work, but because of Goebbels' rapid seizure he had only been able to have some 4,000 copies distributed.

The act Dr Goebbels had put on for the foreign journalists was a bluff of the most audacious kind, but one only too typical for National Socialist demagogy. Dr Goebbels, who was the host of the event with the foreign journalists, had arrived late, and *Reichsbankpräsident* Schacht had to delay the start of his lecture on the Haavara Agreement by a good half hour. The fact is that the Herr *Reichspropagandaminister* was still engaged in a hugely important meeting in his private chambers opposite the hall where Schacht and the journalists were waiting. Goebbels kept trying to get Hitler on to the phone in order to — get permission from Hitler for the immediate arrest of Vice Chancellor von Papen! Secret police units had been deployed at all entrances and exits to the Ministry of Propaganda, and had been instructed to arrest – being careful to avoid any sort of scene – Vice Chancellor von Papen, Senior Councillors Bose and Tschirschky and others, as they were leaving the building. Hitler had met Goebbels for lunch that day, and when Goebbels took his leave from his "Führer" immediately afterwards, Hitler had declared that he would give his final orders via a phone call to the Ministry of Propaganda later that day. The secret police units were on standby and Goebbels was waiting impatiently for the call. But after some time, having waited in vain for too long, he walked down a hidden back staircase into the courtyard of the Ministry of Propaganda, had his car take a short detour and then pull up in front of the main entrance. He rushed up the flight of outside stairs, and acted as if he had only just arrived at the ministry, apologising profusely to the assembled press corps for having kept them waiting. Schacht's lecture began, and Goebbels did not show any sign of the inner tension with which he was waiting for Hitler's decision. Waiting on the phone for that message was Goebbels' servile private secretary Hancke. Finally, in the middle of Schacht's speech, Hancke's messenger, the then councillor and later undersecretary Wilfried Bade, appeared, stood discreetly behind Goebbels' seat and whispered into the ear of his minister: "The Vice Chancellor must not be arrested, neither now nor later." The secret police units, which for the action against Papen had been put under Hancke's direct control, were dismissed, and, to conclude his reception, Dr Goebbels would proceed to act out the phoney scenes with his "friend" von Papen. These astonishing acts of fraternisation may seem very theatrical in hindsight, but they appeared very genuine in the moment. The bluff had been pulled off.

Horace Greeley Hjalmar Schacht (1877-1970; in Germany he was only called Hjalmar Schacht). He became a banker in 1903, and after a banking career during the First World War and then under the Weimar Republic, he served under Hitler as President of the Reichsbank (1933-1939) and Minister of Economics (1934-1937); he remained a Minister without Portfolio under Hitler from 1939 until January 1943. It was Schacht who was responsible for the formation of the chemical company I. G. Farben in 1926, by providing its initial funds. Schacht was an intimate friend of the Governor of the Bank of England, Montagu Norman, who was deeply pro-German in his sentiments and became a godfather to one of Schacht's grandchildren. Schacht was credited with the "economic miracle" which made the survival of the Hitler regime possible. By as early as 1924 he had already stabilised the German currency and ended hyperinflation. The early Nazis were furious with him for doing so, because he had destroyed one of their "causes". He was attacked by them and called a Jew, and it was asserted that his real name was Hajim Schachtl. Alfred Rosenberg, the arch anti-Semite made a scurrilous attack upon him. After that, Schacht created a situation where between twenty and thirty billion Deutschmarks flooded into the country, backed by gold, thus bringing some investment into the country. He then suddenly took Germany off the gold standard and forfeited on many debts and international obligations, and seized entire control of Germany's international trade by instituting total currency exchange control. Schacht did not approve of the murder of the Jews and tried to persuade Hitler of a mass emigration plan for Jews instead. He wanted to seize all Jewish private property to raise the funds for their emigration. After the War, during the 1950s, Schacht became a financial consultant to Aristotle Onassis. The author had a very low opinion of Schacht's economic policies, and says of him: "The 'modern art' of spending public funds that do not even exist only became popular under the Hitler regime. The greatest artist in this respect was Herr Hjalmar Schacht, who had already started to perform his monetary acrobatics under the Weimar Republic." Schacht might thus be considered the forerunner of today's "quantitative easing" policies, whereby gigantic sums of fictional currency are "created" out of thin air by central banks and by governments, and everyone then pretends that this non-existent money actually does exist, since it is used to "buy" the bonds of bankrupt governments and keep them on artificial life-suppport. Such policies, now internationally widespread, could justifiably be described as Shachtonomics. Schacht was fiercely pro-Nazi but constantly proclaimed falsely to foreigners his opposition to Hitler, with whom he had closely aligned himself well before Hitler came to power. Schacht joined the Nazi Party early, with Hitler's promise to make him President of the Reichsbank, which Hitler promptly did in March of 1933. Schacht was one of the most devious, brilliant, and unscrupulous schemers of the twentieth century. And his best friend abroad was Montagu Norman, who was the head of the Bank of England throughout the War, and with whom he schemed and conferred often in the safe haven of Basel, at the Bank of International Settlements, which had and still has the independent status of a sovereign state, free from oversight by any laws, and accountable only to itself. (Readers are referred about this to the hair-raising book *The Tower of Basel* by the American journalist Adam LeBor, 2014.)

The company I. G. Farben became famous for its product known as Zyklon B. Hitler found it so useful! It was used to kill the Jews in the gas chambers in the concentration camps. Without the funds raised by Schacht, this essential chemical might never have been made.

Hjalmar Schacht was acquitted at the Nuremberg Trials, along with his two friends Franz von Papen and Hans Fritzsche (at right). Here they are at Nuremberg, looking very happy and relieved. August Franz Anton Hans Fritzsche (1900-1953) was Director of the Nazi Propaganda Ministry under Josef Goebbels. He was in the Berlin bunker with Hitler at the end. He then crossed the Soviet lines in Berlin on May 1, 1945, and offered officially to surrender Berlin to the Soviets. He was taken prisoner and then sent to Nuremberg. He later published an account of his torture by the Russians. He is not mentioned by the author, who probably never met him, as the author had almost no contact with the Ministry of Propaganda, which was run by the bitter rival of his own bosses, Himmler and Heydrich.

The author of the speech is arrested: Dr Edgar Jung

Herr von Papen had narrowly escaped arrest; for reasons of state policy he had been declared "off limits" even before June 30, 1934. But even before that great showdown, before June 30, 1934, another person was targeted and hounded, namely Dr Edgar Jung. He was a well-liked individual in Berlin society, and author of several much-talked-about books that – using a Christian perspective – dealt with questions of the moral and national rebirth of Germany in the years following the war of 1914–18. For some time, Dr Edgar Jung had been associated with the "Young German Order" (usually abbreviated to Jungdo), had good relations with the Young Catholics, and eventually made the acquaintance of Franz von Papen in a Prussian gentlemen's club. Von Papen commissioned him to create a sort of ideological foundation on which he could build his (brief) tenure as *Reich* Chancellor. Whatever this "ideology" might have been, his intentions would have been honest and sincere. For that reason alone it would have stood in stark contrast to the fraudulent and specious ideology of National Socialism; ethical considerations of the kind that were sacred to Dr Jung were completely alien to the Nazis. Before the Nazis' power grab, there existed in Berlin a monthly journal that was little known among the general public, but well respected in intellectual circles, namely *"Die Tat"* (The Deed). Dr Edgar Jung, as a contributor to the magazine, was part of the so-called *"Tat* Circle". After the Nazis' assumption of power and the proclamation of the Third Reich, Dr Edgar Jung began to think of (and frequently refer to) himself as the "spiritual father of the Fourth Reich". In his opinion, National Socialism's power was bound to be of a very limited duration.

After Franz von Papen had installed himself in the Vice Chancellery in Berlin, he repeatedly offered an official position to Dr Edgar Jung, perhaps as a senior councillor, much like his friends Dr Bose and Tschirschky. Dr Edgar Jung rejected the offers with a laugh: "I don't want to be with you when you will all be hanged one day soon!" He did not enter into any sort of direct professional engagement with Franz von Papen, despite the fact that he was not very well off and had to live off his earnings as a writer. Franz von Papen, however, was very keen to secure Dr Jung's valuable, as he saw it, contribution, and as Jung was not in receipt of any fixed salary, he made him his "special" private secretary, who would be remunerated on an ad hoc basis for services rendered to the Vice Chancellor. The sensational speech that was given by Vice Chancellor von Papen in the second half of June 1934 in Marburg had been prepared and printed by Dr Edgar Jung. Yet Franz von Papen decided to withhold an additional fee of fifty *Reichsmark* (50 *Reichsmark*!) from his much-lauded "special" private secretary, which led to a long – and for Franz von Papen downright embarrassing –exchange of letters.

Dr Edgar Jung, the "precious prey", was hounded and cornered by the *SD-RFSS*. The gundog who had retrieved the author of the Marburg speech might have been a pedigree breed, but was one of the most vicious hounds on the *SD-RFSS's* leashes, namely one Jutta Baroness von Biel. Dr Edgar Jung had arranged to meet Baroness Biel, whose father he venerated, in the Hotel Esplanade in Berlin on the day after von Papen's Marburg speech. He confided in her that it was he, Jung, who had written the speech and that now, after the confiscation of all printed copies, he thought it best to get out of the way as quickly as possible and to lie low until the storm had abated. He told von Biel that he had no desire to encounter the wrath of the Secret State Police and – expecting trouble following the speech – that he had already organised travel papers for a trip to Italy in his sports car, where he intended to stay for a few weeks. In the meantime, he added, his all-too-foolhardy friends Dr Bose *et al.* were welcome to put their heads on the chopping block – they that will not be counselled, cannot be helped…

Jutta Baroness von Biel immediately drafted a detailed report and on the same evening took it to *"Sonderbüro Stein"*, where Josef Pospischil [*'Baron Wronski'* in other contexts) was on night duty. Without informing his chief, Stein [*the author himself, under that pseudonym at that time*], the *SD* man Pospischil immediately went to the *SD* Senior District East in Eichenallee, where he found its leader, Dr [Hermann] Behrends, on duty, who in turn immediately contacted the chief of the *SD* and the Gestapa *SS-Gruppenführer* (or, rather, as he was at that time, *SS-Brigadeführer*) Heydrich. Led by Dr Behrends, the men of *SD* Senior District East immediately commenced their hunt for Dr Edgar Jung, who had already set off on his journey. He was located at a friend's apartment and – despite the fact that the *SD* had no official executive authority whatsoever – was arrested and taken to the basement of the Secret State Police Office in Prinz-Albrecht-Strasse in Berlin. The infamous *SD* man *SS-Obersturmbannführer* [Franz Josef] Huber, in his capacity as newly appointed chief of the Gestapa department "Church and Reaction", took on the official handling of the "Case of Dr Edgar Jung". The chief of *"Sonderbüro Stein"* had informed the *Reichswehrministerium* of Dr Jung's arrest, but this came to nothing.

SD Führer Huber was a seasoned criminal investigator. He did not have to wrest a confession from the detained Dr Edgar Jung; the confiscated documents contained everything he needed to know. Quite how unscrupulous, brutal and devious *SS-Obersturmbannführer* Huber could be would be in evidence repeatedly on other occasions, not least when he was deployed as an *SD* special commissioner in occupied territories after the outbreak of war. But the "Case of Dr Edgar Jung" was so straightforward that Huber was able to take on the role of a smooth man of the world – there truly was no role that an *SD* man of Huber's ilk was not ready to slip into. At Heydrich's orders, Huber contacted von Papen and was amused to hear that the Vice Chancellor not only disowned his secretary, but moreover launched into a tirade of abuse directed against Dr Jung.

Despite the fact that the *SD* held copious amounts of evidence against him, Dr Jung unwaveringly refused to make any statements, telling the police to kindly contact his friend Vice Chancellor von Papen for any information they might require. Thereupon Huber had Jung brought before him again and told him about von Papen's denunciation. Dr Jung declared that he did not believe a word of it; rather, it seemed to him to be merely one of those crude Gestapo feints. Huber picked up the telephone, handed Dr Jung a second receiver so he could listen in, and asked him to dial the number of the Vice Chancellery. The connection with Herr von Papen was established. Huber apologised for bothering the Vice Chancellor again, but told him that the detained Dr Jung would not stop referring the investigators to Herr von Papen. The Vice Chancellor's response came: "I have nothing to do with that man! Dr Jung is an impostor, a highly questionable individual, with whom I have never had friendly relations! Kindly spare me the brazen allegations of that notorious liar!" We need not quote von Papen's statement on the phone any further. Dr Jung, who had listened in on the entire exchange, appeared close to a nervous breakdown and was taken away to his cell. Several hours later he drafted and signed an extensive report. That report made by Dr Edgar Jung did not remain in the Secret State Police Office, but was taken to the *SD-RFSS's* secret archive.

Dr Edgar Jung was shot on the morning of June 30, 1934 in the cadet school Lichterfelde. No doubt Dr Behrends' *SD* had smuggled his name onto a list of *SA* leaders who were to be "officially" executed by *Reichswehr* Generals [Gerd von] Rundstedt and [Erwin von] Witzleben, which led to Dr Jung's supposed "accidental" execution. Both the Gestapa department chief Huber and the leader of the *SD* Senior District East, Dr Behrends, subsequently claimed to have had no knowledge of Dr Jung's execution. In truth, both men are likely to have been responsible for the murder. But the man who actually betrayed his friend and associate Dr Edgar Jung was none other than Franz von Papen, at the time Vice Chancellor in Hitler's cabinet.

The role of the *"Stahlhelm"*

Since its founding, the association of former front soldiers from the World War of 1914–18, the so-called *"Stahlhelm"* (steel helmet), had had close ties to the *Reichswehr*, which was, not without good reason, seen as the association's protector. Politically, as a nationalist movement, the *Stahlhelm* was strongly influenced by the German Nationals, but its members came from all parties on the right of the political spectrum, that is to say to a large extent from Hugenberg's German National People's Party and the German People's party, whose most prominent member had been the late German Foreign Minister Gustav Stresemann. Both parties represented the interests of the nobility, the major landowners and heavy industry. (Gustav Stresemann had in the past been the legal adviser to the industrialists' association of Saxony; Alfred Hugenberg had been chairman of the board of the Krupp steel works in Essen from 1909–18, and in the years following the World War of 1914–18 had founded the notorious newspaper group Hugenberg, by expanding the Scherl publishing house and helping the dailies *"Berliner Lokalanzeiger"* and *"Nachtausgabe"* to gain unprecedented popularity and circulation.)

The *Stahlhelm* had been founded by Franz Seldte, the owner of a Magdeburg-based carbonated water factory. It was an association with strict military discipline; Seldte's vision was to provide a sort of first military education for the German youth, but he was only successful to a limited extent, because his regional groups – despite being distributed across the whole nation – only found sufficient numbers of supporters in northern Germany, and even there these were limited to the rural districts that were in the hands of the major land owners, such as in Pomerania, Mecklenburg, East Prussia and the Prussian province of Saxony. (Many of the major landowners, almost all of whom were former military men themselves, would require their subjects to join the *Stahlhelm*.) The *Stahlhelm* was never short of cash – there was a constant stream of funds from the major landowners and heavy industry into its coffers. A large number of war veterans' and reservists' associations that were all affiliated to the umbrella organisation *"Kyffhäuserbund"* (Kyffhäuser League) provided a sort of passive membership for the active *Stahlhelm*. The leader of the *"Kyffhäuserbund"* was retired Infantry General Wilhelm Reinhard. These war veterans' and reservists' associations might have been entirely insignificant politically, but ideologically they would play a sinister role.

Franz Seldte, the leader of the *Stahlhelm*, not only frequented all of the *Reichswehr* officers' messes, but also supplied them with the finest cognacs and spirits. The deputy leader of the *Stahlhelm* was retired Lieutenant Colonel Duesterberg, who, however, was immediately removed from his position following the Nazis' takeover due to the fact that one of his grandmothers was a non-Aryan. Much like the NSDAP with its *SA*, the *Stahlhelm* dreamt of "conquering" Berlin, the *Reich* capital.

The leader of the Berlin branch of the *Stahlhelm* was the aforementioned retired Major Stefanie. Thanks to his excellent connections to the *Reichswehrministerium*, Stefanie had heard about *SA* Chief of Staff Röhm's putsch plan, and, with the *Reichswehr* generals' full knowledge, prepared "his" *Stahlhelm* branch for a joint action with the *Reichswehr* against the *SA*. As a matter of fact, since March 1933 Major Stefanie had been the de-facto leader of the entire *Stahlhelm*, as not only certain factions within the *Reichswehr* but also the leadership of the *Stahlhelm* itself had largely distanced themselves from Seldte, who had been accused of toadying to the Nazis and subsequently was cut out of the preparations for the major action against the *SA*. Duesterberg, too, had resigned from his position in the *Stahlhelm* leadership in March 1933. The only accusation that the *Stahlhelm* elite could level against Duesterberg was that he was "too decent". Major Stefanie, who under Seldte-Duesterberg had already been the actual conduit between the *Stahlhelm* and the *Reichswehrministerium*, was an ardent proponent of the *Reichswehr's* homogeneity, and therefore was strongly opposed to the new Nazi regime, of whose attempts to infiltrate the army with *SA* men he was perfectly aware. Major Stefanie was highly regarded within *Reichswehr* circles for a number of reasons: not only had he been able to arrange a series of valuable arms orders for the *Reichswehr's* secret rearmament and was seen as loyal and discreet, but in 1918/19 he had won special praise by General Seeckt. On the return march from the Western front after a lost war, Major Stefanie marched into Berlin at the head of his battalion at the very moment when rebelling seamen had occupied the Marstall building opposite the Berlin Palace in an attempt to bring down the Social Democratic government of Ebert-Noske-Scheidemann, which they saw as not sufficiently revolutionary. Having just arrived on the scene, Major Stefanie stormed the Marstall building with his troops and achieved a victory over the mutinous seamen.

During the war of 1914–18, in Major Stefanie's battalion there was a certain Fritz Ponath, who at first was an officer cadet, but then rose through the ranks to become leader of a machine-gun platoon and finally a company commander. He retired in 1918 as first lieutenant, joined the Saarland branch of the *Stahlhelm*, and, in autumn 1933 only managed to escape arrest by the Nazis by swiftly being appointed as head clerk in *"Sonderbüro Stein"*. Later he would be sent to a concentration camp as a "prisoner of honour", along with his friend Stein. In the spring of 1937 – at the intervention of the then Major General [Paul] Otto {1991-1061), Chief of the 12th Infantry Group in Magdeburg – Ponath was reactivated and, in his capacity as a machine-gun specialist, later promoted to the rank of major. He is said to have fallen in France in 1940, as a colonel decorated with the Knight's Cross.

Fritz Ponath on many occasions characterised his former battalion commander Major Stefanie as an obnoxious striver and busybody, who, in interactions with officers who outranked him, was overcome with extreme awe and an almost zombie-like obedience. It is this characteristic that was said to be the reason for his popularity in the highest military echelons, the regiment and division staff and later in the *Reichswehr* general corps. According to Ponrath, Stefanie was seen at the head of his battalion only once, namely at the march into Berlin, on the way back from the front; for during the war he was only ever to be found right at the back, in the foxholes of the regiments and battalions. During the storm of the Marstall building, too, he apparently made sure to stay well out of shot at all times. When the chief of *"Sonderbüro Stein"* [*the author*] excitedly let his head clerk [Ponath] in on the secret of Major Stefanie's preparations against Chief of Staff Röhm's *SA* and expressed his profound hope for a victory by the *Reichswehr* and the *Stahlhelm*, Ponath replied resignedly: "Major Stefanie's involvement spells disaster for our cause. He is a busybody, but not a leader. He can't even give clear orders, but is incredibly overbearing in his dealings with his subordinates or others he feels superior to. He and Herr von Papen – what a pair! When Franz von Papen was appointed *Reich* Chancellor in 1932, his aged mother, upon receiving the news, is said to have exclaimed: 'What, our little Franz has become *Reich* Chancellor? Poor old Germany!' But I say: when the generals of the *Reichswehr* rely on people like Major Stefanie, then it is 'Poor old *Reichswehr*'!" Fritz Ponath, this quiet, pensive and always pessimistic man, who in May 1934 grew uncharacteristically excited as he uttered these words, was to be proved right in his pessimism. He hated war and he hated the Nazis, and only agreed to be reactivated in order to get the Nazis off his back.

In 1936, just before his reactivation, he, the eternal pessimist, thought an impending war an utter impossibility, because he could not imagine that any honest soldier who had experienced the horrors of 1914–18 would ever agree to serve again in another war. He loved his country with all his heart and believed that there was justification for the creation of a powerful German *Wehrmacht*, for, in his opinion, this would reinstate the international standing of his fatherland in a peaceful manner by inspiring respect. Ponath believed that respect for a powerful German *Wehrmacht* should be created not only abroad, but also at home; he was of the opinion that the *Wehrmacht* was the only power able to rein in the Nazis, and to curb and eventually break Nazi terror. Fritz Ponath, a decent man and representative of the guild of war craftsmen, but at the same time an upstanding opponent of war, died a hero's death for his beloved fatherland, in devoted performance of his duties – like so many before him and so many after him. He adored Goethe, loved to quote Christian Morgenstern and Eduard Mörike and immersed himself in the verses of Angelus Silesius (aka Johannes Scheffler). Over a good bottle of wine he would ponder developments in military technology, would seek respite and edification with the classical and romantic German composers, and eventually, full of resignation and discord, died a fearless hero's death for a National Socialist regime with which he had nothing in common and for his entire life did not want to have anything in common with. Much like Fritz Ponath, who had been decorated with the Knight's Cross and killed in the Nazis' war, there were millions of decent Germans who, after the war, were held responsible for the Nazis' crimes, despite the fact that Nazism was entirely alien and abhorrent to them. [*Fritz Ponath seems to have served in a Panzer Division in France, where he was killed. He received a medal in 1941, which may have been awarded posthumously.*]

The retired Major Stefanie, leader of the *Stahlhelm*, thought that his apartment was bugged by the Secret Police, and decided to hold all leadership meetings of the Berlin branch of the *Stahlhelm* in the apartment belonging to his girlfriend Brigitte Helm. Brigitte Helm – the celebrated UFA film star!

Her major successes had been during the silent film era, but now her star had noticeably begun to wane; a fact that she did not want to admit. She held Nazism in honest contempt, which intensified into hatred after one day she was stopped and fined for dangerous driving by a Nazi traffic patrol. Following her spell in prison in the winter of 1934/34 Brigitte Helm had become rather unsociable and afraid of people. In July 1934, having carefully prepared her steps, she managed to leave Germany; she simply did not return to Berlin after a trip to the French Riviera.

Major Stefanie had found a companion for his girlfriend Brigitte Helm, namely one Fräulein Jucki de L., a lady of some thirty years of age, who came from old, impoverished Huguenot nobility. Jucki de L. was a deeply damaged and unhappy person who greatly suffered under Brigitte Helm's mood swings, and in early 1934 fell in love with the American Miss Isabel St. In order to ingratiate herself with Miss St., Jucki de L. – who knew of Miss St.'s hobby, namely journalistic dilettantism (it truly never did amount to more than a hobby) – tried to satisfy Miss St.'s curiosity by relating all gossip about the goings-on in the house of Brigitte Helm. Every minor and major episode that took place in that house during the months of April-June 1934 was faithfully reported by Jucki de L. to her adored Miss St. But as Miss St. was in turn completely in thrall to her lady friend Baroness Biel and did whatever she asked of her, Jutta von Biel would hear any news coming from Brigitte Helm's Grunewald villa within hours and would immediately relate any scrap of information to the *SD* Senior District East in Eichenallee.

When the situation became ever more critical, *SD* chief Heydrich needed more than indirect surveillance of the Berlin leadership of *Stahlhelm* by Baroness Biel, and so Dr Behrends' *SD* Senior District East was tasked with its simultaneous and direct surveillance. An *SD* operative disguised as a telecommunications engineer replaced the telephone in Brigitte Helm's villa. Now all conversations held in Major Stefanie's office could be monitored – not only conversations conducted over that telephone line, but any word spoken within the room, for the telephone receiver had been adapted to function as a microphone even when it was not in use. Soon, however, it became clear that many of Major Stefanie's meetings were held in Brigitte Helm's salon. The *SD* Senior District East instructed a part-time agent, an Italian man who spent his time in Berlin as a peddler and film extra, to approach the maidservant with a selection of fine fabrics, and to do this at a time when Brigitte Helm was out of the house, the cook was busy in the kitchen, and Jucki de L. was with Isabel St. The Italian distracted the domestic staff for over half an hour, during which time a group of *SD* men entered Brigitte Helm's villa via the garden, like burglars. They installed a hidden microphone in the salon and ran an electric cable straight through the garden to the nearest connection in the street. (In late May / early June 1934 the "unofficial" *SD-RFSS* still had to employ such burglars' tricks to achieve its goals. Later it would become more audacious but also more crude in the execution of its criminal deeds.)

The film actress Brigitte Helm (1906-1996), star of Fritz Lang's famous film *Metropolis* (1927). The SD had to install microphones to bug her house and record all the "goings-on" there.

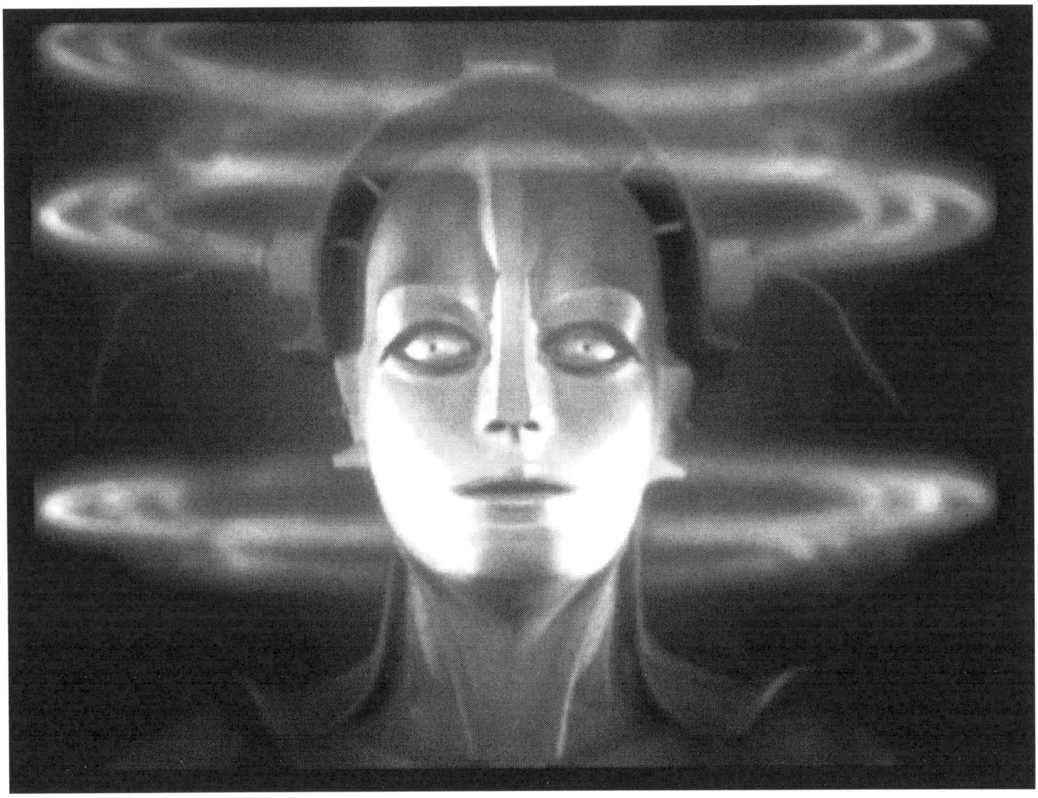

Brigitte Helm in *Metropolis*. Brigitte was not like other girls.

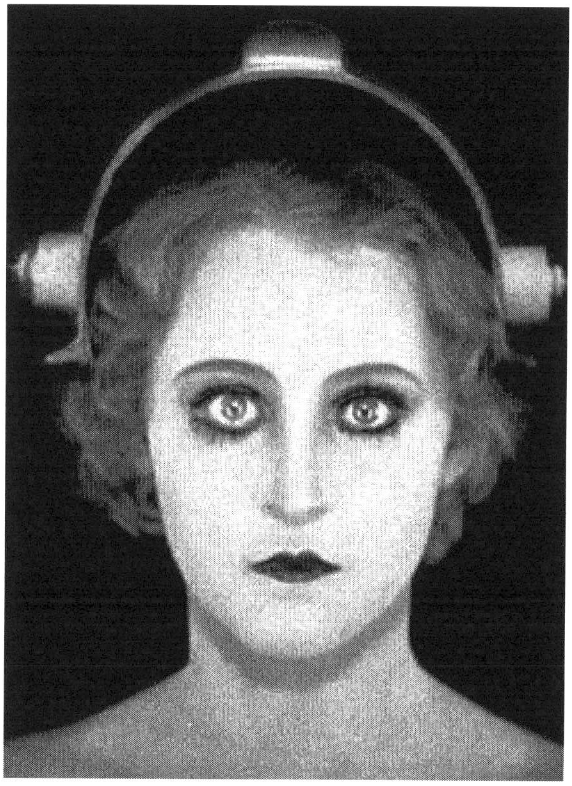

Brigitte Helm in *Metropolis*. She must have been this surprised when she learned the SD were bugging her.

Major Stefanie was a careful man. He never discussed sensitive matters on the telephone, and even used motorcycle or motorcar couriers to announce his visits. His own driver boasted to an *SD* man whom he had befriended about the fact that a state-of-the-art rapid-fire machine gun had been installed in the major's private car. And because the *SD* man revealed himself as a former non-commissioned officer and began to curse the "damned Nazis" in impeccable Berlin slang, the show-off chauffeur could not stop himself from demonstrating the built-in machine gun and explaining its construction to his new friend. The name of the *SD* man was Brunow, an *SS-Obertruppführer* in the staff of the *SD* Senior District East.

All the safety measures put in place by *Stahlhelm* leader Stefanie were in vain. The *SD* (and therefore also *SD*-chief Heydrich, who had recently been appointed chief of the Secret State Police Office) was not only informed about all of Stefanie's personal movements, but knew the precise details of every important discussion and was acquainted with the minutiae of all actions the *Stahlhelm* was preparing against the *SA* and the NSDAP. The sexual aberrations of some harmless and gullible women and other, more licentious characters (such as the denunciator Baroness Biel) had done important service for the spy apparatus of the *SD-RFSS*. Heydrich's motto had proved successful in the most repulsive manner: "If you know it, it is well, but you have to know it!" Spying, denunciation, provocation, exploitation of human weaknesses – these were the preferred means with which National Socialism strengthened its grip on power in the state. This was in addition to propaganda; the nature of which was clearly described in Adolf Hitler's book *"Mein Kampf"* and about which he said: "The bigger the lie, the more easily it will be believed." One needs only to read what the Führer of National Socialism said about the "psychology of propaganda" in his chapter on "war propaganda" (*Mein Kampf*, pp. 193ff):

"The most cruel weapons were humane if they brought about victory more speedily, and only those methods were beautiful that helped the nation to achieve the dignity of its freedom... All propaganda has to be popular in nature, and its intellectual level has to be adjusted to the capacities of the most dull-witted among those it is directed at. However, if the aim – such as in the case of propaganda for the endurance of war – is to draw an entire people into its sphere of influence, then one can not be careful enough in the avoidance of undue intellectual requirements. The more modest its scientific ballast... the more resounding will be its success. It is wrong to imbue propaganda with the intricacies of, say, scientific instruction. The receptivity of the masses is only very limited, comprehension is minimal, but forgetfulness, on the other hand, is considerable. Given these facts, any effective propaganda has to be limited to a few points, and these catchwords have to be hammered home until it is certain that even the last person has buckled or is able to imagine that which is intended. However, the most important prerequisite for any propaganda was the least well understood of all: the need for any propaganda to provide inherently subjective and one-sided commentary on any topic it deals with... The public at large is not made up of diplomats or even teachers of constitutional law, indeed, not even reasonable individuals of sound judgement, but is made up of wavering creatures inclined towards doubt and insecurity. As soon as one's own propaganda admits only the slightest glimmer of virtue for the position of the other side, a seed of doubt in one's own rightfulness will have been planted."

Lies, deception and bluff, combined with denunciation, terror and assumption of power. And yet the Nazis were about to lose their grip on power in June 1934! But if one were to ask, "How could the German people fall for the methods employed by the Nazis?" one could answer: not only the German people, but even such clever statesmen as Neville Chamberlain, the British Prime Minister, and his Foreign Secretary Lord Halifax were tricked by the Nazis' methods – not to mention other major statesmen and diplomats, such as Édouard Daladier, André François-Poncet etc. Treaties were signed, among them the Anglo-German Naval Agreement. The horror stories were not believed, and one hoped for advantages for one's own nation to result from the expansion of that new power; and all around the globe, in members of all nations, Nazism had its admirers.

The *SD-RFSS* spies on Göring

Hitler had made a miscalculation. He had banked on the forgetfulness of his *SA* leaders on the one hand, and that of the generals on the other. When it was no longer possible for him to evade the pressure to make a positive statement on Röhm's putsch plan, he simply made himself scarce and drove off; only very few men were told about the Führer's whereabouts. Among this group of confidants were Dr Goebbels and Rudolf Hess; but not the ministers Hermann Göring and —— Ernst Röhm.

Time and again, Hermann Göring had drawn attention – perhaps too much attention – to his friendship with Ernst Röhm, but at the same time had brought to Hitler's attention all of his reservations about the putsch plan devised by the *SA* Chief of Staff. Göring was – wrongfully – seen as moderate not only by the general public, but also in party circles. He was considered a moderate because he had repeatedly warned the party leadership of the striking power of the small 100,000-strong *Reichswehr* and the stubbornness of the *Reichswehr* generals. He counselled the party to respect the homogeneity of the *Reichswehr* and its officer corps, and was suspected by his own party comrades of being an "avatar of Old Prussian officer virtue". Göring had been awarded the highest Prussian war decoration of the World War of 1914–18, the medal "Pour le mérite", and thus was a member of the noble Prussian Knight's Order by the same name, whose Master General was the aged Field Marshal General August von Mackensen. (In officer circles Mackensen was often referred to as Emperor Wilhelm II's "stirrup holder". The medal "Pour le mérite" was not only awarded for services in war; there was a separate, non-military class that was awarded for services to the arts or sciences. This separate order had 30 life-long members, to be replenished by co-optation in the case of death. Field Marshal General von Mackensen also acted as Master General for this non-military class of the order.)

Hermann Göring had earned his "Pour le mérite" as the commander of the famous fighting squadron "Richthofen" (1914–18). Adolf Hitler skilfully deployed and then sidestepped (1932–33) the highly decorated war hero Hermann Göring in the struggle for power, because naturally an awardee of the "Pour le mérite" was held in the highest regard by *Reichspräsident* Paul von Hindenburg and could not be ignored by the "circle around Hindenburg". It was only thanks to his war decoration from the World War of 1914–18 that in 1933 Hermann Göring was appointed "General of the Infantry", the first and only Nazi leader to receive that honour. However plucky a general Hermann Göring might have been during the years of 1914–18, he turned into an equally brutal and unscrupulous Nazi leader during and after the time of the power grab. The blood sacrifices of this brute speak such a clear language that it remains utterly incomprehensible how such a maniac could time and again have been described as moderate, and remained a "moderate" in the view of the public, even after he had openly demonstrated his brutal Nazism with unparalleled cynicism during the Reichstag Fire trials.

At the end of March 1934, Hermann Göring, the absolute ruler in the state of Prussia, was relieved of his duties in the Secret State Police Office. But as the Minister President of Prussia, an office he had since been appointed to, he still controlled the regular police, as well as a substantial personal police force, the so-called "*Landespolizeitruppe* Hermann Göring", which was in addition to his battalion-sized personal body guard, the so-called *Feldpolizei.* While the "*Landespolizeitruppe* Hermann Göring" was very well equipped and trained, the technical equipment (that is to say, the firepower) of the *Feldpolizei* left much to be desired. After June 30, 1934, the "*Landespolizeitruppe* Hermann Göring" was put under the command of the Ministry of Aviation and remodelled as two air force regiments, the *Flak* Regiment I. in Brandenburg and – in a later separation – the Paratrooper Regiment I., which was housed in newly built barracks in Berlin-Gatow.

In the lead-up to the Röhm putsch, the radical elements within the NSDAP began to ask questions about Hermann Göring, and in *SA* and *SS* circles there was uncertainty about what his actions would be. The *Reichsführer SS*, Heinrich Himmler, and the chief of the *SD-RFSS*, Reinhard Heydrich, both of whom had just been called to service in the Secret State Police Office in Berlin, spent the handsome sum of 80,000 *Reichsmark* in order to determine which side Hermann Göring would take in the eventuality of Röhm's putsch going ahead, that is to say whether he and his police troops would side with the *Reichswehr* generals or the *SA.* Heinrich Himmler, the Inspector of the Gestapa, and Reinhard Heydrich, Chief of the Gestapa, deployed the entire *SD-RFSS* spy apparatus that was at their disposal in Berlin in order to monitor and spy on their eminent chief Hermann Göring, to whom, after all, the entire Gestapa was still subordinate in his capacity as Minister President of Prussia. Of course it was nothing new that the chief of the *SD* had the highest Nazi officials spied upon; but it was characteristic that the surveillance of the Minister President of Prussia was among the first official acts carried out by the *SD* chief Heydrich and the *Reichsführer SS* after being appointed in Berlin, at a time when they were still formally subordinate to the Minister President, and while neither man missed an opportunity to prove his loyalty and devotion! In any case, during the months of May and June 1934 a considerable body of evidence against Göring was assembled, all of which disappeared in the secret archive of the *SD-RFSS* after being carefully examined. These spy reports in their entirety testified against Göring and cast on him the suspicion of conspiracy with the generals of the *Reichswehr*. "If you know it, it is well, but you have to know it!" This motto, which was wheeled out by Heydrich at any given opportunity, was of precious little use to the radical faction within the party, as for the time being Herman Göring was much too powerful a man in the new state, and nothing could be done about him. The inseparable twosome Himmler-Heydrich were so afraid of Göring that all reports that had been compiled against him were not filed in triplicate, as was customary, but only single copies were produced, which were kept in a red-rimmed secret file in a separate secure location within the secret archive. And as no-one trusted anyone, some special agents were visited by officials from the *SD* Senior District East, who would carry out "friendly" but very thorough house searches, in order to eliminate any possibility of any *SD* spy having produced a copy of any of the reports for his own safekeeping, or having kept any other incriminating evidence.

It cannot be stressed enough: during the last days of June 1934, ever more grand declamations were made at the *SD* Senior District East in Berlin's Eichenallee, praising the great *SA* Chief of Staff Ernst Röhm, and lauding the fact that he would finally "deal with" the reactionary dogs (i.e. the generals of the *Reichswehr*). At the Gestapa in Berlin's Prinz-Albrecht-Strasse, the various heads of departments, insofar as they were *SD* members, got together and told stories of the glorious deeds by the strategic genius Ernst Röhm, who was, after all, their highest leader (within the *SS*); a fact, they admitted, that should be acknowledged ungrudgingly. Plenty of premature praise was dished out, perhaps in order to cover up the simmering fear and apprehension of the impending grand reckoning. There was much unease among the officials in the Gestapa premises: diagonally opposite, in the garden of the former regional parliament building, Hermann Göring had deployed a sizeable detachment of his "*Landespolizeitruppe* Hermann Göring"; there was much speculation about the number of machine guns that were in position, and rumours were spread about newly installed rapid-fire guns and so on. There was also a general sense of unease among all other Gestapa officials, despite the fact that the majority had no idea what was going on. Low- and mid-level officials were still trembling with fear following the purge Heydrich had initiated on his first day in office as the chief of the Gestapa; they feared further expulsions of their members. And what happened on June 28, 1934?

The evening of June 28, 1934

Chief of Staff Ernst Röhm had once more secured reassurances by the party leaders Rudolf Hess and Josef Goebbels for their support of his putsch plan against the *Reichswehr*. At the same time, Röhm was being urged more and more strongly by his friends (that is to say, *SA* leaders who were in the know and who could not understand why Adolf Hitler, Röhm's best friend, was delaying an answer and a definitive decision for so long), and so, at Rudolf Hess's advice, Röhm decided to get together with his faithful. He wanted to once again placate the *SA* leaders who were in on the secret of the planned putsch, and to urge them to be patient, because, he would tell them, Hitler, in principle, was all for the plan, but wanted to implement it only later in the summer! Röhm was not making excuses, he simply related to his faithful the assurances Hitler had given him. In order not to draw any undue attention to the gathering, it was made out to be the chief of staff's usual weekend trip away; the group of close-knit friends met at Oberwiessee near Munich. As usual, three units from the *SA's* Munich branch had been mobilised, who were to offer the usual salutes and tributes to the various *SA* leaders arriving at the airport in Dachau near Munich. This had nothing to do with any sort of high alert; it was part of the normal set of duties with which the popular *SA* Chief of Staff Röhm was honoured when he came from Berlin to Munich in order to spend some time there. It was also not unusual, for it happened like this every time, that the *SA* guards would make available their fleet of vehicles for the onward transport of the various *SA* leaders from Munich to Oberwiessee.

The gathering had been planned for June 29/30 and July 1, 1934. Rudolf Hess, in his capacity as Deputy Führer and leader of the NSDAP, had officially been informed of the get-together. On the evening of June 28, 1934, a small farewell dinner was given in the villa in Berlin's Standartenstrasse, the Berlin *SA* staff headquarters. Röhm had organised the farewell dinner in honour of his friend, the Berlin *SA* leader Ernst; for Ernst was not supposed to take part at the meeting in Oberwiessee, but instead, was to go — on his honeymoon! Another man present at the dinner was Röhm's old friend, comrade-in-arms and subordinate, *Reichsführer SS* Heinrich Himmler. Röhm's private chef, whom he had summoned for the occasion from the Carlson Hotel in Hanover, had not only produced wonderful food, but also procured the finest wines. Food and wine were consumed in abundance; Heinrich Himmler presented the newest jokes. When the party was in full swing, *Reichsführer SS* Heinrich Himmler gave a speech, which was laced with solemn affirmation of friendship, eulogising the great leader Ernst Röhm, who would "get rid of and slaughter the reactionary pigs". To much cheering and howling, the celebrated chief of staff promptly replied that he was quite happy to organise the "getting rid of", but that "the "slaughtering should be left to our Heini – he's better at it!" This in turn prompted much noisy protestation by the present *SA* leaders, who also wanted to try their hand at some "slaughtering" and envied their "Heini" his position.

III. Reversal of fortune
The events of June 30, 1934

As has already been reported in a previous chapter, on the morning of June 29, 1934, the chief of army command, General Freiherr von Fritsch, made an historic call to the Minister President of Prussia, Hermann Göring: "Either Röhm and all involved *SA* leaders are immediately sentenced by a special court, or the Berlin garrison will get its marching orders on July 1, 1934!"

Hermann Göring needed to give only a brief explanation to Goebbels for the *Reichspropagandaminster* and *Gauleiter* of Berlin to yield. A heated meeting with Rudolf Hess ensued, who, after only a few brief minutes, accepted that the betrayal of his friend had become a "national policy imperative". Nevertheless, he and Dr Goebbels continued to send pacifying reassurances to Chief of Staff Röhm. *Reichsführer SS* Heinrich Himmler, who had been singing the most heartfelt choruses of praise to his chief Ernst Röhm only half a day ago, was immediately willing to guarantee to Minister President Hermann Göring the upkeep of law and order in Berlin. Major Buch travelled in a special plane from Munich to Berlin and a few hours later boarded another plane with Dr Goebbels, in order to see Adolf Hitler in Godesberg. If truth be told, in his capacity as the NSDAP's highest judge, Major Buch had been the only honest opponent of Chief of Staff Röhm from the beginning. Despite all the trouble it had caused him, he had never made a secret of his dislike of Röhm's character and the man's sexual abnormalities. And so it is no wonder that Röhm's old Berlin buddies, who had just turned against him, straight away sought the assistance of that old enemy of Röhm's, even before approaching Hitler in the matter.

Dr Goebbels was seen as a master propagandist. He not only understood how to influence and mobilise the masses, but he was equally adept, on June 29/30, 1934, at manipulating his Führer Adolf Hitler and instilling the required hatred in him against Ernst Röhm, for which purpose he required Walter Buch, the party judge, to list all of Röhm's misdemeanours and iniquities.

Indeed, Hitler was faced with a most serious political decision, which would have the gravest consequences whichever course of action he was to choose. He could either decide on a coup, by implementing the *SA* Chief of Staff's putsch plan, or he could comply with the wishes of the *Reichswehr* generals, by putting the *SA* Chief of Staff and the highest *SA* leaders on trial for high treason (without, of course, ever allowing legal proceedings to actually take place). The element of surprise that would have been required for a coup was missing; indeed, as General Fritsch's telephone call proved beyond doubt, one would have to expect the *Reichwehr's* intense resistance. A civil war, on the other hand, in which Hermann Göring's Prussian police forces might conceivably fight on the side of the *Reichswehr*, was much too dangerous, given the state of affairs at the time, and would probably lead to an all-out loss of power. Given these circumstances, the party leader Adolf Hitler's political "wisdom" inevitably led him to betray his friend, as well as his own guard, the *SA*. Röhm's erstwhile friends, the party leaders Rudolf Hess, Dr Goebbels, Heinrich Himmler etc. – not to mention Hermann Göring – all advised Hitler to take that course of action.

The generals of the *Reichswehr* awaited, firm and calm, what was to come; they did not see the need to put their troops on alert. In contrast, the *SS* was put on high alert across the entire *Reich* on the evening of June 29; the order had been given by Adolf Hitler on the telephone to Goebbels, who in turn alerted Göring, who passed on the order to Heinrich Himmler. At the same time, all *SD* leaders were required to ready themselves in their quarters for 5am on June 30, 1934. From midnight onwards, Göring alerted all Prussian police troops, via orders given by the head of department in the Prussian Ministry for the Interior, Police General Kurt Daluege, who at that time was also the highest *SS* leader of Greater Berlin. The low- and mid-level *SS* leaders simply thought that now the grand reckoning against the *Reichswehr* had come, and that they would fight side by side with the *SA*. To their great surprise, they were to be disabused of that notion when orders came in the early hours of June 30, 1934.

The *SA* had *not* been put on alert! Furthermore, the Berlin branch of the *SA* was without a leader on June 29 and 30, 1934, as *SAGruppenführer* Karl Ernst was on his way to Hamburg, in order to embark on his honeymoon there. The only *SA* units on standby were three *SA Stürme* at Munich airport, who jubilantly greeted their Führer Adolf Hitler when he unexpectedly arrived there along with Dr Goebbels and party judge Buch. This legitimate "readiness" of three *SA* units in Munich would later serve as a welcome pretext for the assertion that the *SA* had secretly been alerted.

An entire *SS Sturm* detachment from Hitler's personal bodyguard *"Leibstandarte Adolf Hitler"* had been flown from Berlin to Munich using passenger planes. Once there, these troops were put under the direct command of party judge Buch, who held the rank of *SS-Gruppenführer*. Hitler arrived in Oberwiessee some time between 5am and 6am, where he angrily proceeded to wake up all *SA* leaders who were encamped with Röhm, theatrically ripped the epaulettes from the uniforms they had hastily thrown on, and declared the *SA* leaders, who had no clue what was going on, to be under arrest. They were driven to Munich airport and immediately flown to Berlin, where they were taken to the barracks of *"Leibstandarte Adolf Hitler"* in Berlin Lichterfelde. When they were arrested, the *SA* leaders must have thought Hitler had lost his mind; during the first moments of surprise, half asleep, as they were, they had found no words of protest. Adolf Hitler screamed and raged like a madman, but soon his Chief of Staff Röhm would be shouting even louder. He had quickly understood the situation, confronted Hitler and lunged to strike him, but was held back by some burly *SS* men. In his outrage, he spat in Hitler's face, shouting: "You scoundrel, you have just betrayed National Socialism!" Ernst Röhm was led away and taken to a cell in the Munich courthouse. There he was ordered to shoot himself, for which purpose he was handed a gun loaded with a single bullet. Röhm however kept shouting, demanding a proper trial. Eventually, Dr Werner Best appeared. (At the time Best was Heydrich's deputy and thereby chief of the *SD* Senior District South and chief of the Bavarian Political Police.) He had come to talk Röhm out of the nonsensical notion of a trial and to explain to him: either he would shoot himself during the course of the next half hour, or he would be shot. Röhm answered Dr Best, whose demeanour, as ever, was extremely arrogant: "Thank your lucky stars, you rascal, that I'm not putting that bullet into your skull." He took the revolver and threw it through the open cell door. As it turned out, Röhm was not shot that day (June 30), but only the day after: the cell door flew open and several *SD* men, under the command of *SD* chief Dr Werner Best, fired their automatic rapid-fire guns. *SA* Chief of Staff Ernst Röhm collapsed dead, having been killed by more than a dozen bullets. The rough mercenary, who, despite all his questionable characteristics, had been a rather straightforward man, had been betrayed and murdered. The name of this man, who had created a million-strong private army for his friend and party leader, was not to be uttered again; his memory would be publicly sullied by his own party comrades.

In the meantime, in the former cadet school Berlin-Lichterfelde, now the barracks of *"Leibstandarte Adolf Hitler"*, a hastily convened "revolution tribunal" was meeting. General von Witzleben and General von Rundstedt were in attendance as the *Reichswehrministerium's* representatives. They were to satisfy themselves of the fact that the putschist *SA* leaders had actually been shot. *SS-Obergruppenführer* Sepp Dietrich, the commander of the *Leibstandarte,* was in charge of the execution squad.

Josef "Sepp" Dietrich (1892-1966) was in charge of the execution squad which carried out the murders of the Night of the Long Knives. He had previously been Hitler's chauffeur and personal bodyguard. He was buried with honours, attended by over a thousand veterans, in Germany in 1966.

In the general confusion and excitement of the moment, the two generals did not even notice that Dr Edgar Jung was also about to be shot. They probably did not even know who this Dr Jung was. When the *SA* leaders, who had been put against a wall awaiting their execution, caught sight of the generals and their adjutants, many of them erupted in fanatical cries of "Heil Hitler", for they believed that their Führer Adolf Hitler had carried out a failed revolt against the *Reichswehr*, which is why, they thought, they were now being shot as upstanding National Socialists. And so, amongst others, the leader of the Berlin branch of the *SA*, Karl Ernst, died with his arm raised in the Hitler salute; only the men arrested in Oberwiessee had been "informed" by Hitler himself. All in all, 87 executions were carried out in front of the generals. The men who were to be executed had been dressed in grey-blue shirts that had been confiscated during the dissolution of the association *"Das Reichsbanner"* (which had been the Social Democrat equivalent of the Communist *"Roter Frontkämpferbund"* and the radical right-wing *"Stahlhelm"*.)

The situation in Berlin

While Hermann Göring had at various points sent assurances of friendship to *SA* Chief of Staff Ernst Röhm, he had never made a secret of his dislike of *Reichsführer SS* Heinrich Himmler. Nevertheless, Göring had to eventually accept the appointment of Himmler-Heydrich at positions in "his" Gestapa, which led him to veritable temper tantrums. Naturally, the rivalry between Göring and Himmler could not be allowed to be on show openly; when Himmler had moved to Berlin with Heydrich, all required forms of decorum and civility were observed. Incidentally, Dr Goebbels had also never been on especially good terms with the *Reichsführer SS*, and continued to treat him with much condescension even during the years of 1935–38.

As the *SS* was still formally part of the *SA* until June 30, 1934 – which was in evidence not least by the fact that until then the *Reichsführer SS* was a subordinate of the *SA* Chief of Staff – the *SS* leadership feared that on June 30, 1934 the Prussian Minister President might use the purge of the *SA* as an opportunity to also take action against the *SS* and to rid himself of the bothersome police chiefs Himmler and Heydrich. As a matter of fact, until midday of June 30, an occupation of the Gestapa building by the *"Landespolizeitruppe* Hermann Göring" was thought to be imminent. The situation was rather grotesque. The main gate was kept shut all day, all passes were declared invalid, no person was allowed to leave or enter the building. Any senior *SD* or *SS* leaders whose visits had been requested by Himmler or Heydrich, irrespective of their name and rank, had to first report to the *Kommandant* of the house. During that time of high alert, that *Kommandant* was Senior Councillor Patschowsky, *SD* leader and chief of the Main Division III. Patschowsky had installed his command post on the ground floor of the building. Any person arriving whose name was not on a list of individuals who had personally been summoned by Himmler or Heydrich, was, without fail, sent back out by the guard. Individuals whose names could be found on that list, would be guided under guard through a labyrinth of machine guns and command posts, all the way through to Himmler-Heydrich's anteroom. And yet, from a military point of view, all such "war games" were pointless, as Hermann Göring's machine guns could have shot to pieces the entire army camp set up by Himmler in no time.

The *SD-RFSS's* infamous "special actions" were not instigated by the Gestapa in Prinz-Albrecht-Strasse, but instead by the *SD* Senior Division East in Eichenallee, where Heydrich had spent several hours that day. A raiding squad under the command of *SS-Obersturmführer* [Johannes] Schmidt was sent out by the *SD* Senior Division East, which would "accidentally do away with" General Schleicher. The *SD* Senior Division East dispatched a second raiding squad, under the command of *SS-Sturmführer* [Ulrich] Graf (1878-1950), which would track down Undersecretary [Erich] Klausener, the leader of the group *Katholische Aktion*, and shoot him.

Dr. Erich Klausener (1885-1934), the head of the Catholic Action Association. On Heydrich's orders, the SD sent out a raiding party to find and kill him. He was assassinated on June 30, 1934. The raiding party was, as the author says, under the command of Sturmführer Ulrich Graf, who had been Hitler's personal bodyguard from 1920 to 1923 and on one occasion threw himself in front of Hitler to prevent Hitler being shot, and was himself wounded instead. (He became Brigadeführer by 1943.) The official story is that Klausener was killed by another bodyguard of Hitler's, Kurt Gildisch (1904-1956). Perhaps that is true, if Gildisch was under Graf's command and atually fired the shots. We must however accept that Graf was in command, since the author knew these men personally and was deeply involved in the general actions of the Night of the Long Knives, and was an eye witness to the murder of Röhm. (Bundesarchiv)

The man at right in this early photo is Kurt Gildisch (1904–1956), credited with firing the shots which killed Erich Klausener. Seated at left is Ernst "Putzi" Hanfstängel. They must have been discussing Hitler's personal security, as there is an armchair in the background and the setting is a residence.

SS-Sturmführer Ulrich Graf (1878-1950) who led the raiding party that assassinated Dr. Erich Klausener. As Hitler's bodyguard he had previously thrown himself in front of Hitler to take some bullets intended to kill him. (Bundesarchiv)

Another raiding squad was sent out not by the *SD* Senior Division East, but instead by the *SS* barracks in Berlin-Lichterfelde. Under the command of *SS-Hauptsturmführer* [Friedrich Karl, Baron *Freiherr*)] von Eberstein (1894-1979), a Bavarian, the squad went to the Vice Chancellery in Vossstrasse, where Senior Councillor [Herbert von] Bose [he was *Oberregierungsrat*] was murdered in his office. Senior Councillor Tschirschky was able to flee in time, and Vice Chancellor von Papen barricaded himself in the top floor of the chancellery, where he found a telephone, with which he was able to call General Fritsch and thereby alert the *Reichswehr*. When Franz von Papen could hear the *Reichswehr* arrive in the streets below, he left his hiding place, only to run straight into the arms of *SS-Führer* von Eberstein. When the SS-man tried to arrest von Papen and lead him away, von Papen cried: "How dare you? I am Vice Chancellor von Papen!" To which von Eberstein replied: "Ah, you are von Papen, – just the man I'm looking for!" and whacked him in the mouth with his fist, breaking his two front teeth. But before he could strike him again, a *Reichswehr* officer had arrived at the scene, and the *SS* unit had to make a quick get-away.

SS General Baron (*Freiherr*) Friedrich Karl von Eberstein (1894–1979).

According to the author, the violent and arrogant Eberstein (whom he knew personally as a colleague) struck Vice Chancellor von Papen in the face and broke his two front teeth. He wanted to take him away to execution, but von Papen was saved by the arrival of a Reichswehr officer, so that Eberstein had to flee.

Snapshot view of Karl von Eberstein at left, with his friend Ernst Röhm, the head of the SA.

Official American front and side views of von Eberstein after he came into American custody when the War had ended.

Only those who experienced June 30, 1934 from the inside will know to what extent the atmosphere was charged before, during and for a long time after June 30. For example, an

SAStandartenführer by the name of Schmitt – the adjutant of *SAObergruppenführer* [Edmund] Heines, who had since been shot in Berlin-Lichterfelde – was sought by the *SS*. Over the course of three days, no fewer than eight (!) men named Schmitt were shot, and the "right" Schmitt was not even among them. He was only found many months later in Hannover, where he had been in hiding. And what about the "accidental" shooting of General von Schleicher and his wife! *SS-Obersturmführer* Schmidt from *SD* Senior District East (not to be confused with the aforementioned *SAStandartenführer* Schmitt) and his *SD* men had been given the order to arrest General von Schleicher and to take him to the *SD* Senior District. *SS-Obersturmführer* Hans Schmidt was a young man at the time; he had only just gained his doctoral law degree, but had already made a name for himself as the chief of Division I (Information) within the *SD* Senior District East. He and his *SD* men had just been issued with new automatic pistols equipped with 40-shot cylinders. They had not received any active training on these new weapons; they had merely received some verbal instruction explaining the mechanism. And now these guns were virtually burning in the hands of boys who had only just reached adulthood. All they had to do is pull the trigger and forty shots would rattle... The *SD* men surrounded the general's villa, and the *SS-Obersturmführer* asked to be announced; in actual fact, he and three of his men walked directly behind the housemaid into the study. The general was sitting behind his desk and did not consider it necessary to get up and walk towards the intruders. He snapped at them gruffly and asked what the whole scene was about. Hans Schmidt gathered all his courage, which was in danger of faltering, and, in his excitement, exclaimed loudly: "General, you are under arrest! Please follow me and hand over all keys to the house!" As if to underline his words, he pointed his automatic pistol at the general. Kurt von Schleicher was not in the mood for such pranks and jumped up from his chair, at the same time apparently reaching for his right desk drawer. In this moment Hans Schmidt pulled the trigger on his automatic pistol, either unconsciously, in the heat of the moment, or because he perceived a threat. To make things worse, the general's wife burst into the room through a side door and, as if to protect the general, threw herself in front of her collapsing husband. Hans Schmidt's fingers were clenched and in a cramp, much like the entire man himself. The cramp only loosened once the last bullet had been discharged from his pistol. The three *SD* men and their leader Hans Schmidt started to scream as if it were they who were about to be murdered. Eventually Schmidt ran outside to fetch the other men. They took control of the villa, left the dead husband and wife lying in the spot where they had fallen, and *SD-Standartenführer* Hans Schmidt and his driver raced to the *SD* Senior District East in a mad rush. Schmidt was much closer to crying than to laughing; he felt like a murderer and expected to be punished as such, as he had not carried out his orders according to the instructions. The murderer Hans Schmidt was genuinely surprised when at the *SD* Senior District East, against all expectations, he was not given a dressing-down, but instead was greeted and celebrated as a hero. His immediate superior, who instigated the howls of jubilation, was none other than the aforementioned Dr Behrends from Wilhelmshaven, leader of the *SD* Senior District East in Berlin.

The special commission "*in causa* Ernst Röhm"

As already reported in a previous chapter, on June 30, 1934 the chief of the *SD* Senior District East in Berlin was appointed as "Special Commissioner of the Gestapa" and as such tasked with "clean-up operations within the party and state". The chief of the *SD* Senior District East, Dr Behrends, was 27 years of age, neither particularly intelligent nor exceptional in any other positive sense. But he was a submissive tool in the hands of his lord and master Reinhard Heydrich, to whom he was loyally devoted. He did not have any qualms or concerns of his own, but instead carried out all orders given to him with exceptional rigidity and boldness. He was the most eager sniffer dog within the *SD-RFSS*, a skill that qualified him to lead the most important *SD* senior district of all. A fair-skinned northerner, whose face bore a number of duelling scars, with a stout body on bow legs: that was Dr Behrends, the "dachshund", as was his nickname.

During the night from June 30 to July 1, 1934, Dr Behrends moved into the new offices that had been readied for him on the third floor of the Gestapa building, and with his staff installed himself as the "special commissioner". He considered it essential to move from Eichenallee to Prinz-Albert-Strasse, in order to be in constant proximity of the *SD* chief and leader of the Gestapa, Reinhard Heydrich. In actual fact, Behrends' post as "special commissioner" amounted to nothing more than a kind of privy secretary and assistant to Heydrich. The "clean-up operations within the party and state" commenced, all of which, without a single exception, can be personally attributed to Heydrich and his assistant Behrends.

In the cadet school at Berlin-Lichterfelde, the "official" executions had been carried out by the *"SS Leibstandarte Adolf Hitler"* at the indirect order of the *Reichswehrministerium*, and in the presence of General von Rundstedt and General von Witzleben. In the meantime, Himmler-Heydrich – through their "special commissioner" Dr Behrends – were committing well over 200 murders. In the basement of the Gestapa building, Gregor Strasser was shot in his cell by Dr Behrends' *SS* men. The eight wrong Schmitts were murdered at the orders of Dr Behrends. The former leader of the *"Stahlhelm"*, the retired Lieutenant Colonel Duesterberg, was taken to the Gestapa prison and concentration camp "Columbiahaus", but had to be released again after only a short time. Dr Sack, who had acted as the defence lawyer for the Communist Ernst during the Reichstag Fire trials, an old NSDAP member, came across some *SA* leaders in "Columbiahaus" with whom he was acquainted, and who, like him, had been held for weeks, until some good friends within the party obtained their release after petitioning with Hitler and Hess. Special Commissioner Behrends dashed to East Prussia with his boss Heydrich and discharged the well-known *Gauleiter* Erich Koch. He was to be put on trial, but the cunning *Gauleiter* Koch had gathered such a large amount of incriminating material against senior *SS*-leaders that his own misdemeanours paled into insignificance. Instead of him, two *SS-Gruppenführer* as well as two of his close associates were shot; Koch himself was reinstated in his position at Hitler's express orders and thus triumphed over Himmler-Heydrich.

Erich Koch (1896-1986) was a Gauleiter of the Nazis in East Prussia. He was one of the few people to survive Himmler and Heydrich's desire to kill him. He did this through blackmail, because he possessed so much incriminating information about various SS officers. This led to Hitler saving him, so that Himmler and Heydrich never got him. He went on to become Reichskommisar for the Ukraine from September 1941 to August 1944, keeping well out of Himmler's way by staying the the East. He was responsible for the mass murder of 400,000 Polish civiians and countless Ukrainians and Ukrainian Jews. He was thought to know the whereabouts of the Tsar's famous Amber Room, but he never revealed it if he did know it. Despite being a mass murderer, he insisted that he was a Christian, and he claimed that Nazism had correctly evolved from "Luther's unfinished Protestant Reformation". (He may have regarded the Polish Catholics as enemies of Lutheranism? These strange theories of his probably are incapable of rational explanation.)

Eventually the *SD* leaders Heydrich and Dr Behrends made the mistake of laying hands on the brother of *SAObergruppenführer* Wilhelm Brückner, Adolf Hitler's chief adjutant. This brother had only become a National Socialist in March 1933, but enjoyed the close friendship of Hermann Göring, a fact that allowed him to enrich himself in a scandalous manner. He was arrested, but Göring responded to the arrest by promoting Brückner, who had proven himself as an officer in the World War of 1914–18, to the rank of Major General of the *Luftwaffe*, and thus he had to be released from prison.

SAObergruppenführer Wilhelm Brückner (1884-1954), Hitler's Chief Adjutant. Don't mess with his brother! Heydrich and his little "dachshund" Behrends had gone too far.

Hitler in a leather flying cap consulting with his chief adjutant Wilhelm Brückner (at right) about what appear to be some aerial maps or flight charts, prior to taking off.

With the arrest of Brückner's brother in Breslau [*Wrocław*], the two *SD* leaders Heydrich and Behrends had gone too far. They were ordered to immediately return to Berlin, after which Special Commissioner Behrends gradually fell from favour. At the end of 1934, the special commission was dissolved, Dr Behrends was no longer to be seen at the Gestapa, and, as the chief of the *SD* Senior District East, moved back into his old offices in Eichenallee. While still special commissioner, he had also arrested the former deputy leader of the *"Freikorps Oberland"*, Dr Beppo Römer, who subsequently had to wait months for his release, but at least was able to bring to bear enough important connections to avoid being shot.

Dr. Jur. Josef "Beppo" Römer (1892-1944, executed). He was able to avoid being shot in 1934, but he was executed in 1944 at last, having been imprisoned at Dachau. He was always an opponent of Hitler and had plotted for his assassination in 1934. It is interesting that the author does not mention Römer's history as an anti-Hitler plotter, presumably because he was anti-Hitler himself and did not wish to provide any background that could be interpreted as an excuse for Heydrich and Behrends to have arrested him.

As part of a revenge action against the hated reactionary forces and their victory in the cadet school at Berlin-Lichterfelde, two further arrests – which bore some resemblance to that of the retired Lieutenant Colonel Duesterberg – were carried out: Freiherr von Müldner (the former adjutant to the German crown prince) and Freiherr von Medem were detained and sent to the concentration camp "Columbiahaus". However, both had to be released soon after, despite the fact that every single file had been gone through with a fine-tooth comb, in an attempt to find material to support at least some allegations of corruption.

In the course of his purges, Special Commissioner Behrends also arranged the forcible liquidation of all intelligence services operating for the party's ancillary organisations, despite the fact that none of them were in any way connected with the Röhm affair. The way in which these intelligence services were dissolved was characteristic of the cold cynicism of Himmler-Heydrich and the manner in which they sought to gain a certain reputation among their own party comrades. No official resolutions for the liquidation of the intelligence services were obtained from the party leadership, and no official representations at the relevant authorities were ever made in the matter. Instead, when the opportunity seemed right during the general purges carried out after June 30 1934, arbitrary arrests were made of bothersome party comrades.

The special commissioner's actions against one of Alfred Rosenberg's closest aides was typical. The "party philosopher" Alfred Rosenberg regarded himself, alongside Adolf Hitler, as the greatest National Socialist. This manifested itself in the fact that in every room of the "NSDAP Office for Foreign Affairs" (which was led by Alfred Rosenberg), next to the Führer's portrait there had to be displayed a picture of Rosenberg of at least the same size. In some offices an over-sized portrait of the party philosopher was the only decoration on the walls; even the Führer's image was missing. Alfred Rosenberg attempted in all seriousness to create a special "myth" around his own person, which also included the fact that he enjoyed – much like Hitler – the adoption of a peculiar "asceticism", always travelling in a small open-top car, without a driver or any other entourage, from his apartment to the villa that housed his offices in Berlin's Tiergartenstrasse. The cult that Rosenberg created around himself (and that all officials in his department had to play along with) had long incurred Hitler's disapproval. The result was that Rosenberg – despite all his ambition and abilities that distinguished him from other Nazi leaders – was not able to become a minister of the *Reich*, or even some other senior ministerial official, i.e. the sort of position he would have eventually accepted, if only to use it as a springboard. In Prussia, not only Hermann Göring but also Kurt Daluege stood in his way; Himmler-Heydrich had long outranked Rosenberg within the hierarchy of the political police; and in diplomatic circles – which Rosenberg felt especially attracted to – he had to take second place behind Ribbentrop, who was not even a *Reichsleiter* nor an old party fighter, like Rosenberg. He had to stand aside, in a sulk, and was not allowed to participate in the many events that finally led to June 30. And while he was still feeling sorry for himself and kept himself away from the party's affairs like an affronted deity, a group of *SD* men appeared at his offices, arrested [SS Standartenführer] Arthur Schumann (*Born 1899 at Leipzig, became Standartenführer in 1933, degraded in rank to a private in December, 1934, and thrown out of the SS; no further information*], the head of the department and chief of the intelligence service of the "NSDAP Office for Foreign Affairs", took him to the concentration camp "Columbiahaus", and turned his offices upside down and inside out. Alfred Rosenberg was speechless following this impertinence. When he could finally bring himself to remonstrate with his party leader, Adolf Hitler, he found that neither Hitler, nor Göring, nor Himmler were available to talk to him in the days around June 30, 1934. What was more, Alfred Rosenberg discovered – much like other senior party officials – that suddenly the two letters *SD* sufficed to seal lips, to deny access to pending proceedings, and to block the sharing of information. Like others, Alfred Rosenberg had to learn that to maintain one's own spy network, one's own "information service", even if this was done in the context of a party organisation, would be done at the peril of one's life. Only once he had understood these facts was his friend Schumann released from detention; more than three months had passed in the meantime. Forevermore Schumann, but also *Reichsleiter* Alfred Rosenberg, had lost the appetite to get involved in matters that were the sole concern of the *SD-RFSS*.

The leader of the German Labour Front, Dr Ley, had a similar experience to Alfred Rosenberg, with the difference that Dr Ley was a faster learner than Rosenberg. This is why Dr Ley's heads of department, Schäfer and Gruber, who had been involved with intelligence operations for the German Labour Front, were released after only a few weeks. However, independent intelligence services, such as the one maintained by Walter Korodi (a former member of the German National party, who in March 1933 quickly tried to align himself with the new political realities and became a member of the NSDAP), were simply broken up. His "National Defence Centre against Communist Activities" – which was nothing more than a somewhat questionable and intentionally tendentious press agency – disappeared, and Walter Korodi was given the choice to either spend an unspecified amount of time in the concentration camp "Columbiahaus", or to become a paid agent for the *SD-RFSS*. Korodi decided on the latter option, and was subsequently sent on a "special mission" to Romania. [*For an account of this momentous "mission" to Romania see Volume Two. Korodi accompanied the author on this mission as an assistant, since Korodi was a Saxon (German minority) who had been born in Transylvania and had local knowledge and probably knew some Romanian. Korodi was still alive at the time of publication of this book, so the author had to be very careful what he said about him, as Korodi was unscrupulous, dishonest, and volatile. The Swiss Government had officially pronounced Korodi 'a confidence trickster'.*] When he was ordered back to Berlin to give a full statement on some alleged transgressions, out of fear of his superiors he found the courage to become a renegade [by becoming a political refugee in Switzerland]. Despite his markedly nationalistic stance and his reports that were brimming with the "correct" phrases, Walter Korodi was classified by the *SD-RFSS* not as a V-man, but merely as a Z-man (the category for "informers"). In those days, many other intelligence specialists shared Korodi's fate, with the difference that once they had become *SD*-men they were no longer able to bail out.

Ramifications

We have previously ventured to contrast the two dates June 30, 1934 and July 20, 1944. However, the second major turning point in recent German history, in the history of the enslavement of the German people by National Socialism, should be identified with August 8, 1944, the day on which eight German generals were *executed by hanging*, rather than July 20, 1944, the day of the attempted assassination of Adolf Hitler.

June 30, 1934 was a clear victory of the *Reichswehr* generals over Nazism. It was a great tragedy for the German people that the generals were unable to exploit that victory. The generals got "cold feet"; they did not feel equal to the extraordinary unscrupulousness and brutality that National Socialism was ready to use in order to rescue and preserve its position of power in the state. The level of terror Nazism was ready to employ in the course of the events of June 30, 1934; the manner in which it went on the rampage within its own ranks using the tools of the *SS* and *SD-RFSS;* the unscrupulousness with which it not only betrayed and exposed, but single-handedly murdered its own radical elements –such demonstrations of violence not only terrified the opposition within the party, but even more so the external opposition. The Nazis demonstrated a maniacal obsession with power that was unparalleled in modern human history. Power at any cost!

The oldest friends were sacrificed and the most loyal supporters bludgeoned and murdered, all in the name of retention of power. Ideals were betrayed in the grossest form of opportunism, if it meant that the grip on power could be maintained or increased. "If I retain and enlarge my power," so the argument went, "then a time will come when I am so powerful that I can realise my 'ideals', or whatever I imagine my 'ideals' to be; and then I will no longer have to compromise. Promises and treaties are only a means to cement my power; once this has happened, I will be able to break them, as they will no longer be of value to me; they would only impede the expansion of my power. Whatever in the past might have served as a springboard has now become an impediment. Away with it!"

On June 30, 1934, the generals of the *Reichswehr* had won a victory over the party. This fact is best illustrated through the following words by Adolf Hitler, taken from a speech given on July 13, 1934:

"My promise to the *Reichspräsident*, to preserve the army as an apolitical instrument, stands firm —"

And, as if to taunt all those who knew of Hitler's efforts to support Röhm's demands on

General Fritsch as recently as the spring, Hitler added:

"—— out of my innermost conviction and in accordance with the pledge made by me."

And he concluded solemnly:

"As of today there is only one authority in the state that bears arms: the *Wehrmacht*!"

But no sooner had he uttered these words than the *SS* was expanded into a formidable opponent of the *Wehrmacht*, an armed rival of military strength and firepower fit for war.

After the upheaval of June 30, 1934, the generals of the *Reichswehr* committed a catastrophic mistake by surrendering power in the state to the NSDAP. Step by step, the generals had to retreat; they were simply not equal to the non-stop breaches of promises, the level of nonchalant unscrupulousness, and the extent of the ruthless and maniacal obsession with power. They had to relinquish the remaining positions of authority one after the other. Eventually the generals were even forced to abandon the homogeneity of the *Reichswehr* and its officer corps; in return they received the Greek gift of a million-strong army and lavish rearmament. The supreme commander of the army, Colonel-General Freiherr von Fritsch, the victor of June 30, 1934, resigned his leadership position in protest, as did more than a dozen other commanding generals, among them Generals Beck and Liebmann. The hour had come for ambitious careerists. The Nazis showed that unscrupulous fanatics are unable to forget or even forgive: General von Fritsch was forced to die a "hero's death" at Warsaw; venerable generals were wasted in the war that would be started so carelessly.

And at last the Nazis saw the long-awaited opportunity to get even with the reactionaries: the failed officers' assassination attempt on Hitler took place, and with it came the day of the greatest humiliation and ignominy ever inflicted on German generals and the entire German officer corps: the day on which eight generals were executed by hanging. General von Witzleben, the attendee and overseer of the revolution tribunal at the cadet school in Berlin-Lichterfelde, was brought to the gallows. The other overseer, General von Rundstedt, was forced to preside over the military court that expelled his friend and comrade in arms General von Witzleben from the *Wehrmacht* and delivered him into the arms of the Nazi hangmen.

June 30, 1934: a victory by the *Reichswehr* generals over the party!

July 20 and August 8, 1944: a victory by the party over the generals!

Using terror and lies, and a network of spies and denunciators that turned against everyone, the Nazis established their power in the state, and then brutally and violently used it; at first against the German people and then, during the war, against foreign nations. The concentration camps within Germany –which were established long before those in the occupied territories – were the memorials of this maniacal obsession with power. In a truly diabolical manner, the German people were internally "organised" and terrorised before the terror began to rage outwardly.

For the Nazis, power was synonymous with violence, and the expansion of power synonymous with violent means. During the last stage of their intoxication with power, these maniacs were literally running amok; woe betide anyone who got in their way. The first conspicuous victims were the eight generals murdered on August 8, 1944.

June 30, 1934 was a Pyrrhic victory by the generals over the party.

Was August 8, 1944 truly a victory by the party over the generals?

The generals, who at first had resigned their leadership positions, went on to carry the flags of National Socialism from victory to victory and to convey power in the occupied territories to the Nazi cohorts; much like they had left power in the Nazis' hands within Germany, despite the fact that on June 30, 1934 it would have been possible for them to wrest that power from the Nazis. On August 8, 1944, the generals were made to pay for the fact that on June 30, 1934 they had forced the Nazis to carry out a purge within their own ranks; for the victories they had achieved for the Nazis after the outbreak of war counted for nothing after the onset of defeat.

But what of the opposition of that part of society that had gathered together in the "Island of the Respectable"? Without a doubt, they had imagined the *Reichswehr's* victory to play out differently, if indeed they ever did have a clear picture of such a victory or its subsequent exploitation.

Well, there was no need for the Nazis to shatter the "Island of the Respectable", for this cultural association never manifested itself as any sort of actual organisation. The chief of the Secret State Police and the *SD-RFSS* had once put it succinctly: "Even a million or more dissatisfied people do not pose the slightest threat as long as they are unable to organise themselves!" The so-called refined society of Berlin had no intention of organising itself against the Nazis, not before June 30, 1934, and certainly not after that date. Yes, in fact, they were abundantly impressed by the terror the *SS* waged within the party! Among that section of society, the proletarian *SA* had been seen as the *enfant terrible* of the party; *SA* Chief of Staff Röhm had not only incurred their disapproval because of his personal faults and weaknesses but all the more so because he deeply scared them as an "extreme left-wing bandit chief". Now Röhm and the wildest *SA* leaders were dead, and it is no wonder that the achievements of the *SS* impressed the members of the "Island". The *SS* was seen as the right wing of the party, and anything from the right was considered to be conservative and thereby at least preservative. Besides, none of these individuals had had any insight into the way the events had unfolded or knew anything about the true background, such as the last-minute turn by the *SS* and its leader Heinrich Himmler and the betrayal and murder of their erstwhile friends. They had heard something – it was more guessing than knowing – about an impending putsch attempt by the *SA* against the *Reichswehr*, and now the *SS* had intervened and thwarted that SA putsch plan, without the *Reichswehr* having to fire a single shot. And had Adolf Hitler not emphatically pledged allegiance to the *Reichswehr* (on July 13, 1934)? Had he not condemned the despised *SA*leaders beyond their deaths, and solemnly guaranteed the inviolability of the *Reichswehr* and its officer corps? Had Hitler not begun to use all of his power to guarantee the expansion of the *Reichswehr* and the creation of a glorious new *Wehrmacht*? Had he not, in doing so, expressly built on old traditions that were sacred within those circles? And had the *SS* not just proven its willingness to establish peace and order, even putting troublemakers from within its own ranks against the wall, without mercy?

Such considerations might have led to the fact that after June 30, 1934, party officials were suddenly considered to be socially acceptable, especially the National Socialist dignitaries in *SS* uniforms. Soon it became almost *de rigueur* to be made an honourable member of the *SS* and to occupy a senior position within it. The *SS* immediately realised the golden opportunities that would arise from that fact, and so, for instance, the former leader of the German National Party, Alfred Hugenberg, was made an honorary *SS-Standartenführer*. The non-National Socialist ministers of the *Reich* were awarded the Golden Party Badge, and thereby made party members *nolens volens*; among them the former Foreign Minister Freiherr von Neurath, the *Reichsbankpräsident* Hjalmar Schacht, Minister of State Meissner, State Secretary Ernst von Weizsäcker, and many others. To top it all, most of them were promoted to the rank of *SS-Gruppenführer* for outstanding services.

On June 30, 1934, the generals of the *Reichswehr* had won a victory over the party. Using betrayal, murder, terror and masterful dishonesty, the Nazis managed to transform the defeat into a victory. Not only were they able to hold on to power, but over time they expanded their positions of power to such an extent that they turned the erstwhile victors into losers: they became the absolute masters in the state, and their *SS* became a scourge for the German people.

Foreign nations studiously ignored the cries for help of those being abused, and instead preferred to engage in friendly relations with the tormentors of the German people. Germany, the "nation of poets and thinkers" in the heart of Europe, had been turned into an enormous prison where all norms had been reversed – the criminals were the guards, and decent men and women were languishing in cells and basements. Foreign nations praised the spotless walls and the immaculately clean corridors of the prisons and did not care a fig about the inmates; instead they hoped to do good business with the prison guards. And only when those guards set about turning other nations into prisons, did general outrage eventually begin to emerge.

In his book "*The Myth of the Twentieth Century*", Alfred Rosenberg sneered and scoffed at the Christian doctrine of love, and juxtaposed it with a cranky Germanic sense of honour. In his book "*Mein Kampf*" and almost all of his speeches, Adolf Hitler would speak about a relentless hunger for power and a brutal determination to seize it; and even if at times he omitted the adjectives "relentless" and "brutal", the nature of his will and determination was abundantly clear. Let us quote from "*Mein Kampf*", a book that he had already finished by 1925! On page 441, which is entitled "World history is forged by minorities", he writes:

"We are faced with an infinite army ... of individuals who are invested in keeping the status quo. The magnitude of our task ... is illustrated by the seeming futility of our immense struggle. The battle cry, which either frightens away small minds straight away or will soon make them despair, shall be the signal for true fighters. One thing must be clearly understood:

"If a certain amount of ultimate energy and vigour is extracted from a people and directed at one aim, and this energy and vigour is therefore irredeemably stripped away from the indolence of the masses, a few per cent will rise to be the masters of the total number. The history of the world is forged by minorities only when this numerical minority embodies the majority of willpower and initiative."

Well, by continuously talking about relentless willpower and brutal determination, Hitler only painted a portrait of himself. Now that National Socialism has perished, we oppose it with will and determination that are not brutal and relentless like Hitler's, but instead are calm, steadfast and unbreakable. We happily acknowledge the "ecclesial-Christian compassion that has resurfaced in a new form in Masonic humanism" (Alfred Rosenberg). We acknowledge both the "forced doctrine of boundless love and the equality of everything human in front of God", as well as the "doctrine of a 'human right' that is democratic, non-racial, and not sustained by a sense of honour rooted in national thought" (Alfred Rosenberg). We are unburdened by sentimentality and erroneous deference in our desire to stamp out National Socialism and with it German militarism. We agree with the great German thinker and poet Matthias Claudius, who can hardly be suspected of being a Roman hireling:

"Shall love, faith and trust forevermore continue to love, keep faith and trust, so that they shall be betrayed and abused in eternity? —— Shall the many renounce their rights, so that a few can inflict violence and injustice without punishment? —— It shall not be! Betrayed love is like human blood; it screams for revenge. No! Justice has to be justice and remain justice. I do not struggle against, but for the people – and when injustice and violence are inflicted on even a single, small person, I do not wish to be known as the son of Pharaoh's daughter."

PART THREE

A POLITICAL KALEIDOSCOPE

A. ESPIONAGE AND COUNTER-ESPIONAGE

General remarks

It is not the purpose of this chapter to provide a complete mosaic image of the close-meshed, widely ramified and well-nigh boundless net of espionage that was created and expanded during the years of the Nazi regime. Instead, a mere outline of the espionage and counter-espionage activities of National Socialist Germany will be given, in order to demonstrate how these endeavours became an integral part, if not the essence, of Nazi politics.

It is difficult – indeed, at times impossible – to draw a sharp distinction between National Socialist diplomacy in the strict sense, and National Socialist espionage in general. Ultimately, there was virtually no aspect of public life – neither diplomatic-political, nor economic, nor cultural – that was not appropriated by National Socialist espionage for its purposes. Diplomats and journalists, merchants and industrialists, artists and academics were roped into the Nazi espionage apparatus in order to advance the expansion of National Socialist power. Some of these individuals acted consciously and voluntarily; others did so unwittingly or were coerced.

Covert transmission of information – and thus espionage – has existed at all times and in all nations, and is a direct consequence of conflict between peoples. Nations maintain mutual diplomatic missions – the so-called embassies and consulates – according to a strictly defined and internationally accepted set of regulations. These diplomatic missions, too, act as centres for exchange of partly overt, partly covert information. Of course, the ambassadors and diplomats – who, along with their extensive staff of embassy counsellors, envoys and attachés, are generally a rather punctilious bunch – would strenuously object to being characterised as "spies" or suspected of espionage. But there is probably no diplomatic mission that does not secretly – unbeknownst even to the relevant ambassador – harbour an agent from its country's espionage headquarters (who, of course, would be in possession of a regular diplomatic passport). Each of these officially accredited diplomats can claim – with all the appearance of legality – not to have anything to do with "espionage". (This type of espionage, which takes place under the protection of the extraterritorial jurisdiction within embassies or consulates, is often referred to as "the underworld of diplomacy".)

An incident that exemplifies the punctiliousness of, in this instance, the British diplomats took place in the British embassy in Berlin in 1921:

The Russian émigré and "journalist" Harald Siewert, who was mentioned in an earlier chapter in the context of his friendship with Alfred Rosenberg, was well known within the *Reichswehr*, the police and at all party offices in the Weimar Republic as an informer. Harald Siewert was embroiled in the trial of Vladimir Orlov, and was implicated in all manner of shady espionage affairs. There is even suspicion that he was in some way involved in the deception and murder (in Soviet Russia) of the British Captain Sidney Reilly. One day, Harald Siewert walked into the British embassy in Berlin, carrying with him important materials concerning the Russian intelligence service, and offered his services for an espionage operation. As soon as he had finished speaking, the British attaché rose brusquely from his chair and declared curtly and with much indignation: "My dear fellow, the government of His Majesty, the King of England, does not engage in espionage! I must ask you to leave these premises immediately."

Any other informer, however well-connected, would share the fate of that dubious individual Harald Siewert, if he dared to approach a British diplomatic mission, at any time or in any place, regarding some espionage business. (The fact that the same informer would usually be visited by a "private citizen" soon after and possibly would still be engaged in some "business" is of course a different matter altogether.)

Until the "Ribbentrop era", perfect propriety was taken for granted for all German foreign diplomatic missions, even under the Nazi regime. But already the founding of the "Special Bureau Ribbentrop" was an affront to the internationally accepted norms and rules of diplomacy, and the hubris and impertinence with which Joachim von Ribbentrop conducted himself in his capacity as Nazi ambassador in London and later as *Reich* Minister for Foreign Affairs was time and again excused as the "wind of change" that was said to be blowing following the installation of National Socialism in positions of power. The way in which the Nazi regime's foreign policy – in contravention of all conventions and agreements – was pervaded with espionage, disinformation, bribery and defamation, and how the Nazis developed espionage of the worst kind in their dealings with other nations, will be described in detail at a later point.

I. Foreign espionage organisations
The British "Secret Service", also known as "Intelligence Service"

Before embarking on a report on the various espionage agencies of the Nazi regime, we consider it useful to provide a brief overview of the antagonists of National Socialist espionage. In the course of doing so, we will not betray any secrets, for what we have to say about foreign organisations will be well known to any specialist in the field of military intelligence.

For laypeople it might be interesting to gain some insight into the structure of this "profession", which is entirely invisible from the outside and shrouded in an enigmatic mystique, and as such has famously been the subject of much public discussion and curiosity. It is our belief that an exposition of other nations' usual practices of espionage will provide a useful reference point for the assessment of typical Nazi espionage. Let us start with the British "Secret Service".

The American lexicon "Webster's New International Dictionary" contains the following entry on the "Secret Service": "A covert British political institution that is not accountable to parliament for its expenditure."

With its venerable tradition, the British "Secret Service" occupies a special place among all intelligence services in existence today. Its inception dates back to 1329, when Edward III of the House of Anjou-Plantagenet sent his agents to all corners of the known world and, following the example of the Doges of Venice, created a special staff of secret informers. Under Sir William Clifford (during the reign of Henry VII, 1485 – 1509), the network of agents was further expanded, and already during the time of Cromwell it was an invaluable tool for the consolidation of British global power.

Perhaps it is this long tradition that leads to the fact that – quite unlike most other nationals – every Englishman would consider it a special honour to be called upon to do duty with the "Secret Service". Every lord, however noble, and every British financier, however distinguished, would see it as an honour to be a member of the "Secret Service".

Another peculiarity of that intelligence service is the fact that it operates without any government subsidy but instead is financially independent. The "Secret Service" holds a substantial stock portfolio in the shipping and petrochemical industries and other industrial enterprises, and is a major stakeholder at Lloyd's of London, the global insurance corporation, among others.

The "Secret Service" consists of six, or rather, seven, separate bureaux, each of which is an enormous operation in and of itself and operates entirely independently of the others. The agents and employees of each bureau have no idea of the existence of their colleagues in the other bureaux; only the most senior officials are acquainted with one another. Each of the six (or seven) bureaux is headed by a director, and it is these seven directors who elect their highest chief, according to a ceremonial procedure that dates back to the time of Cromwell. Once that highest chief has been elected in a "round table conference", he is presented with the symbol of his supreme power in a solemn ceremony (a ritual that for anyone other than the English would appear quite incongruous for a modern spy apparatus): a golden key giving its holder access – at any time of day or night – to the private chambers of the King of England and the Emperor of India. Upon receipt of the golden key, the highest chief of the "Secret Service" inevitably loses his name and thenceforth – within Whitehall, and for the purposes of contracts, directives or orders – is only known as the "Unknown Quantity"! He even signs documents using that name. (Some readers will be tempted to view all of this as mere hocus-pocus. But anyone who knows the English will be aware of the importance of traditional ceremonies in that country. We can reveal to any doubting readers that in such ceremonies there is also no shortage of powdered perukes and black silk breeches!)

What follows is a short description of the six (or seven) bureaux, which, taken together, form the "Secret Service". It must be made clear, however, that each bureau does not just employ a veritable army of agents and specialists of every kind, but is further subdivided into a myriad of offices and ancillary organisations.

1. WOID, War Office Intelligence Department. Operates on behalf of the British general staff and deals exclusively with military espionage.

2. FOID, Foreign Office Intelligence Department. The most important bureau of the "Secret Service"; it is in constant contact with all British diplomatic missions. The members and employees of this bureau are ministers, diplomats, high-ranking individuals, members of the nobility, parliamentarians and other individuals from the most exclusive circles in society. This bureau deals with political intelligence.

3. BOTID, Board of Trade Intelligence Department. The hub for all commercial espionage. This bureau also concerns itself with technological developments with potential military applications and runs a separate dedicated department for sabotage.

4. NID, Naval Intelligence Service Department. A bureau that deals mainly with counter-espionage. It is responsible for the captains and crew of the military and merchant navy in all ports, and maintains sub-offices with every squadron in the fleet.

5. HI, Home Intelligence Service. This bureau works in conjunction with the immigration authorities and is responsible for all foreign nationals, immigration, emigration and naturalisation.

6. CID, Colonial Intelligence Department. This bureau is responsible for all intelligence operations in the British colonies and dominions. Additionally, it supports insurgents in the overseas territories and controls tribes that are prone to rebellion.

The CID must not be confused with the "Criminal Investigation Department", an organisation that uses the same acronym (however, with the inclusion of three full stops, i.e. C.I.D.) and in times of war often performs important supporting tasks for the HI through the monitoring of foreign nationals.

The IID, the Indian Intelligence Department, is affiliated to the CID, the Colonial Intelligence Department. This bureau has its own director, who, along with the other six directors, is entitled to vote in the round table conferences that elect the highest chief of the "Secret Service".

(It is often alleged that prior to his appointment as First Lord of the Admiralty to Neville Chamberlain's war cabinet in 1939, Winston Churchill was the "Unknown Quantity" for several years, that is to say the highest chief of the "Secret Service" and holder of the golden key. Given the strict secrecy surrounding the identity of the "Unknown Quantity", it will probably be impossible to ever corroborate any such claims.)

In certain films and tales of derring-do, "spies" are often portrayed as men handling guns. Generally, however, possession of a handgun would only be a liability for an espionage specialist operating abroad. Disregarding the fact that without "betrayal" – be it the reckless exposure of a secret, or betrayal for remuneration – successful espionage would be almost impossible, it is clear that the actual espionage specialist, the intelligence officer, has to be imbued with an extraordinary sense of responsibility and naturally has to be equipped with characteristics such as courage, tenacity, stamina and reliability. Master spies are true artists in their field, and, as a matter of fact, unmusical people are rarely cut out for high-level espionage. An espionage specialist must be equipped with a very keen sensory apparatus to detect and scrutinise the most delicate threads that form the opponent's spy web, as well as a highly developed ability to empathise and adapt and an intuitive power of deduction. The most important personal requirement for the espionage specialist, however, is steadfastness. Dirt, filth, hatred, passion and avarice must not touch him, but instead must be deflected by an imperturbable sense of responsibility and duty.

It is no accident that Englishmen were among the most brilliant master spies. Let us at this point remember a man of the highest ethical standards: Colonel Lawrence. Not only did he distinguish himself with invaluable services to his country, but he also fought a tenacious battle against his superiors for decades in order to ensure that promises that had been made to the Arabs during 1914–18 in the name of his government were actually kept; he eventually was able to force the British government to honour the pledges that he had made on behalf of his country. No less a figure than Prime Minister Winston Churchill wrote a revering obituary for Lawrence of Arabia, and to this day Churchill is more than a little proud to have been one of the few personal friends of that great man. Incidentally, Colonel Lawrence was not only a brilliant spy, but also a master of the English language, his book "*Seven Pillars of Wisdom*" being a first-rate literary accomplishment.

And let us briefly commemorate another master spy of the British "Secret Service": Lord Baden Powell, who went on to found the world-famous Scout movement. General Baden-Powell recorded his experiences in his book "*My Adventures as a Spy*" and was also a man of impeccable personal honour.

It would be wrong to simply equate espionage with the activities of informers and denouncers. Despite all the rigour and intractability with which British officers have always done their duty for the "Secret Service", their actions have always been underpinned by a commendable ethos. However dangerous the tasks at hand may sometimes be, Englishmen approach them with sportsmanship, and a sense of fairness and responsibility.

It is only in states that are devoid of protection of the law, and tyrannies ridden with unrestrained police despotism, that espionage is synonymous with the business of spying and denunciation. In nations, on the other hand, where individuals truly enjoy the protection of the law, where the police force is subordinate to the public prosecution department and acts for the protection of citizens, it will never happen that denunciation and informing will be at the heart of espionage. In the great democracies of Britain and America no espionage organisation – however deeply embedded in the apparatus of the state it may be – would dare to encroach on the private lives of its citizens on the basis of unfounded denunciation. Any hubristic assumption of power by an espionage organisation and thereby any police despotism would falter in the face of the law and be dismantled by a judge. There can be no law that "serves the state" but vilifies the individual. If the "Secret Service" were merely an organisation of informers, it would not be held in such high regard by the British people. No decent Englishman would enthusiastically put himself forward to serve as an agent with the "Secret Service" if in doing so he would turn himself into a cheap informer or common denunciator. Only under the National Socialist regime did espionage become synonymous with the methods of informers and denunciators.

The *"Deuxième Bureau"*

The French Deuxième Bureau in the old days. Spies have to have their coffee breaks with their buddies.

The French intelligence service, the *"Deuxième Bureau"*, was founded in 1875. A war had been lost against the German *Reich*, and the French intelligence system had to be overhauled. Division II of the French general staff became the *"Deuxième Bureau"*, which was formally responsible for military espionage.

In close co-operation with the *"Sûreté Générale"* (essentially a political security police force), *"Deuxième Bureau"* eventually dealt with all matters connected to espionage, that is to say, not only military espionage, but also covert political operations, industrial espionage, and, not least, counter-espionage. The *"Deuxième Bureau"* had been at the heart of France's espionage operations long before the World War of 1914–18, and the French Ministry of War and the Foreign Ministry on "Quai d'Orsay" were provided with a continuous stream of information by the *"Deuxième Bureau"*, for which purpose the French foreign diplomatic missions were put at the bureau's disposal. Under the protection of extraterritorial law and at the direct orders of the *"Deuxième Bureau"*, high-ranking French consular officials in Berlin, Hamburg and Nuremberg engaged in such blatant espionage activity in 1910, that the German government felt compelled to lodge vigorous complaints with the authorities in Paris. At the outbreak of war in 1914, the leader of the *"Deuxième Bureau"* was Colonel (later General) Dupont, who was infamous for the unscrupulous deployment of the French espionage apparatus.

General Charles-Joseph Dupont, the head of the Deuxième Bureau, the French spy service. Very few people knew what he looked like, and he wanted to keep it that way. Heads of spy agencies like to be "men of mystery".

The *"Deuxième Bureau"* was famously operating with very large numbers of lowly informers and petty denunciators. Virtually every ballet dancer, no matter if she performed in Paris, the provinces or abroad, was in the service of the *"Deuxième Bureau"*. Nightclub hostesses and gigolos, almost the entire Parisian *demimonde* (which was notorious and popular in equal measure), and all French prostitutes (who were under official government control) were directly or indirectly given the "honour" of performing espionage tasks for the *"Deuxième Bureau"*. There was hardly a French dance troupe on foreign tour that was not roped into some form of espionage activity by the *"Deuxième Bureau"*. For those in the know, the term *"Deuxième Bureau"* immediately conjured up images of cramped and dirty backstreet hotels and night lodgings. The term – in stark contrast to the British "Secret Service" – had something sleazy, sordid and often even suspicious about it. This fact perhaps also derived from the fact that the *"Deuxième Bureau"* was not exactly fussy in the choice of its espionage methods.

Like every other major espionage organisation, the *"Deuxième Bureau"* could not do without some star agents. Monsieur Gérard, who was engaged by the German Empress Augusta as her French reader, was evidently such a star agent. In addition, the *"Deuxième Bureau"* commanded a large number of excellent French intelligence officers, who not only made life difficult for German and (before the World War of 1914–19) Austrian counter-espionage, but also kept the British "Secret Service" in the Mediterranean on its toes. Nonetheless, these French intelligence officers, much like their respective chiefs, had a distinct whiff of unscrupulousness about them. In the main, however, the *"Deuxième Bureau"* relied on strength in numbers. Germany was crawling with hordes of agents, frontier workers and "neutral" informers. In Holland, Belgium, Luxemburg and Switzerland the *"Deuxième Bureau"* maintained well-disguised espionage offices that operated against Germany. In Berlin, there was much disdain for the so-called "rent boys" of the *"Deuxième Bureau"*, despite the fact that it was clear that the *"Deuxième Bureau"* drew considerable strength from the sheer numbers of such petty agents on German soil.

During the construction of the so-called Maginot Line (a vast array of border fortifications), the *"Deuxième Bureau"* was given the special task of organising counter-espionage within the fortified territory in co-operation with the *"Sûreté Générale"*. Along France's eastern border, newly appointed *"commissaires spéciaux"* were appointed in all important border towns and invested with exceptional authority. Such high-ranking officials of the *"Sûreté Générale"*, who also acted as political commissioners for the *"Deuxième Bureau"*, were installed in Thionville [Diedenhofen], the border crossing point to Luxemburg; in Forbach, the border crossing point to the Saarland; in Strasbourg; and in Annemasse (on the Swiss border, just across from Geneva). They were directly subordinate to the two *"directeurs généraux"* of the two (also newly-created) bureaux for counter-espionage within the fortified area (whose headquarters were in Metz and Strasbourg respectively), but were neither answerable to the "Special Bureau for Defence against Nazism" in Nancy, nor to the "Central Military Department East for Espionage and Counter-Espionage" (which was also headquartered in Nancy). Both *"directeurs généraux"* were high-ranking officers from the French general staff; they received their orders directly from the French Ministry of War. Because he hailed from the Alsatian region, Monsieur Becker, the *directeur général* in Strasbourg, had also received thorough training at a German war academy before the World War of 1914–18. The special status afforded to the two general directors and the *"commissaires spéciaux"* is best illustrated by the fact that they were in a position to act on their own authority, without consulting with the relevant prefects (a position equivalent to the Prussian police presidents), and were not in any way accountable to the prefectures.

Despite the uncompromising methods employed by the *"Deuxième Bureau"*, it has to be said that it was at a clear disadvantage compared to the far more rigorous and in every respect more unscrupulous methods brought to bear by the Nazi espionage organisations. What is more, however capable individual officials may have been, French counter-espionage as a whole simply failed to prevent information on the Maginot Line leaking into Germany and its Nazi regime. The idea for the Maginot Line did not originate – as might be assumed, given its name – with the French Member of Parliament, André Maginot (a man straightforward, choleric and reckless in equal measures), but with the former French Minister of War, Paul Painlevé, who, in December 1927, was able to win over the former front soldier and then Member of Parliament, André Maginot, for his plan. The plucky deputy Maginot was able to force the approval for construction through parliament, was appointed under-secretary and later Minister of War himself, and, with his stirring patriotism, was eventually able to push through the plans for the construction.

Paul Painlevé (1863-1933), former Prime Minister of France who in the 1920s was French Minister of War. It was he, not Maginot, who thought of the Maginot Line. He died only one year after Maginot, and seven years before the Nazi invasion, so he did not live to see his pet project fail utterly.

André Maginot (1877-1932). He did not think of the Maginot Line himself, he merely pushed it through Parliament and got it approved. He died of typhoid long before it was completed.

Until 1940, the Maginot Line was seen as impenetrable, but it would eventually not be able to withstand the German onslaught. The manner in which major contracts for the all-important concrete works were awarded was also ill-fated: the good relations that some bosses of private firms enjoyed with members of the Chamber of Deputies would have disastrous consequences. The small building firms that were entrusted with the construction of important fortifications needed to employ – almost overnight – an enormous workforce of engineers, technicians and labourers. Once construction was completed, most of these newly recruited workers found themselves out of work and thus were vulnerable to exploitation by German espionage. When, in August 1935, a monument honouring Maginot was unveiled with much pomp by President Lebrun in Souville, German espionage was already in possession of detailed plans of virtually all fortifications that formed the Maginot Line, despite *"Deuxième Bureau"*, *"Sûreté Générale"*, the two *"directeurs généraux"*, and the *"commissaires spéciaux"*. In addition to the general failure of French counter-espionage, the fact that the *"Deuxième Bureau"* over the years had become increasingly reliant on reports by emigrants had dire consequences in 1940, when the Nazi armies lashed out against France in major assaults. These seemingly reliable reports contained exactly what the French wanted to hear: the Nazi regime was portrayed as facing imminent collapse, the differences between the *Wehrmacht* and the party were exaggerated, distorted or misrepresented, many thousands of misleading calculations demonstrated the Third Reich's utter lack of combat readiness, and its military clout was put in doubt or ridiculed. The *"Deuxième Bureau"* adopted the emigrants' often seemingly coherent reasoning and in so doing made itself complicit in the military defeat.

Soviet Russian espionage

The terms *Cheka* and *GPU* are well-known today, despite the fact that neither is used for the Soviet Russian espionage operations any longer.

Under the Tsarist regime, there existed an infamous secret police force called *Okhrana* ("Protection") or, to give its full name, *Okhrana Otdeleniye* ("Protection Department"). It was founded in 1881 in order to quell revolutionary activities against the Tsarist regime and was especially active between the revolution year of 1905 and the outbreak of war in 1914. After the establishment of the Soviet regime it was replaced by *Cheka* (*"Chrezvycháynaya Komíssiya"* – "Extraordinary Commission") for the fight against counter-revolutionary forces. The first chief and organiser of *Cheka* was the Polish revolutionary Felix Dzerzhinsky, who would later go on to chair the Transport Commissariat. The founding date of *Cheka* was November 2, 1918; on February 6, 1922 it was remodelled as the *GPU* (*"Gosudarstvennoye politicheskoye upravlenie"* – "State Political Administration"), and soon after, in July 1923, it was reorganised as the *OGPU* (*"Obyedinyonnoye GPU"* – "United State Political Administration"). The *OGPU* would provide the blueprint in Nazi Germany for the creation of the Gestapo, the Secret State Police. It became an important espionage tool for Soviet foreign affairs and would cast its web across the entire civilised world. A spy apparatus was created whose only equal was the National Socialist *SD-RFSS*, the Security Service of the *Reichsführer SS*. An *OGPU* commissioner, who was not only tasked with espionage activities but also the monitoring of the activities of the Soviet ambassador and his diplomatic staff, was installed in every Soviet foreign diplomatic mission. A general of the *OGPU* resided in a special office in Amsterdam, where all threads of the Soviet spy web converged, while another *OGPU* general had been installed at the Russian Trade Mission in Berlin, from where all Soviet industrial espionage in the Western hemisphere was orchestrated.

Today, Russian military espionage is the domain of the Revolutionary Military Council of the Soviet Union, with Division I.A. of the general staff of the Red Army forming the central department. All police authority, including the command over the political police, rests with the People's Commissariat for Internal Affairs *(NKVD)*. Much like the *SS*-leadership of the Hitler regime, the *NKVD* maintained a highly-trained and well-equipped police army of some 1,800,000 men throughout the war, who – even during times of dire military pressures – were never drafted into war service and apparently were held in reserve by the Soviet leadership to focus on special tasks after the conclusion of the war. This menacing, almost two-million-strong army of political police officers and fanatics was comprised mainly of Asians.

Without a doubt, the Soviets ran the most effective counter-espionage operation of all countries and nations, though it must be taken into account that the almost hermetic isolation of internal Russia was a clear advantage in this respect. However, the Soviets excelled not only in the field of counter-espionage, but also in active espionage outside of Russia. The Soviet political intelligence service was no less effective than the British "Secret Service", while their capabilities in industrial espionage were unparalleled, which enabled the Soviets to get the better of even the Nazis' operations on many occasions. The successes of their military espionage will probably remain shrouded in secrecy for a long time to come. Organised labour, wherever in the world it may be, will lead to legally or illegally organised Communism. Every political activist or labour organiser of any Communist party is also an agent of the Soviet espionage apparatus, usually without his knowledge or volition but nevertheless with exceptional reliability. Officially appointed Soviet agents carry out their espionage tasks with tireless tenacity and the sort of fanaticism that usually can only be found in the Japanese. Oftentimes a lowly labourer will conduct an entire orchestra of well-paid *bon vivants*, corrupt chief engineers and bejewelled *demimondaines*, without ever being tempted to live beyond his own modest means; and he would not – even for a moment – consider siphoning off even the tiniest fraction of the wealth that is flowing through his fingers to benefit his own wife or child.

Other foreign espionage organisations

Until the outbreak of war in 1939, the USA did not maintain a large espionage apparatus in Europe, but instead made do with the information that flowed – entirely legally – from Europe to Washington via foreign diplomatic missions, embassies, consulates and other delegations. Within the USA, an especially dogged and fierce battle was fought against the substantial Japanese espionage operations, and, insofar as an active American espionage organisation existed at all, it was most probably operating mainly in the vast stretches of the Pacific Ocean, in Japan and in China. Nowadays, the American War Office, the Ministry of War in Washington, is said to be in constant contact with the British "Secret Service". In the same way that the USA draws on the expertise of the "Secret Service" for its espionage operations in Europe, the British Empire avails itself of the assistance of the American War Office and its espionage organisation for British intelligence operations in the Far East.

In the years following the World War of 1914–18, Polish espionage operations were rather bothersome for Germany. Polish espionage – which, much like the Czechoslovakian intelligence service, had been founded and organised by the chief of the French *"Deuxième Bureau"*, General [Charles] Dupont – was modelled closely on the *"Deuxième Bureau"* and was just as unscrupulous in the selection of its methods. For a period of time General [Charles-Joseph] Dupont had acted as the chief of the French military mission in Warsaw, with the sole purpose of establishing a kind of sub-branch of the *"Deuxième Bureau"* in Poland and Czechoslovakia. The Polish central department for espionage and counter-espionage was an important division of the Polish general staff in Warsaw and was headquartered in a villa in Warsaw's Senatorska. That central department was called "Defence", but, despite its perhaps misleading title, was actually rather active. Over the years, the Polish "Defence" had become entirely autonomous and independent of Paris, but, much like the *"Deuxième Bureau"*, it operated with vast numbers of cheap informers and so-called "rent boys". In addition, the Polish espionage organisation – much like the *"Deuxième Bureau"* – shamelessly abused the extraterritorial rights of the diplomatic missions in Germany for espionage purposes to such an extent that the German diplomatic mission in Warsaw was repeatedly forced to demand the immediate recalling of Polish consuls and attachés. During the period when Danzig [Gdansk] was under the protection of the League of Nations, the permanent Polish military mission and the so-called Polish Ministry in the city played a significant role in Polish espionage operations.

Very little is known in Europe about Japan's espionage activities, simply because its principal area of operation was not Europe, but the vast area of the Pacific Ocean and North America, especially the USA. What is known, is that the Japanese authorities equipped an entire fleet of fishing boats for deployment in reconnaissance purposes, and that an elite squad of master spies was trained and maintained. A Japanese citizen would regard it as the highest honour to be sent abroad to do service for his fatherland; much like the British "Secret Service", the Japanese intelligence service was held in very high regard by its citizens.

The espionage organisations of Europe's smaller nations – with the exception of the

Balkan states – did not amount to very much. Small nations almost always made do with the information provided by their foreign diplomatic missions, or were tacit beneficiaries of foreign espionage that invariably took place within their territories. Foreign espionage organisations established more or less well-disguised espionage bureaux on neutral soil, in order to inconspicuously direct their agents. The benefit for the small nations would arise from the secret monitoring and covert consent of such bureaux, or, instead, through unofficial deals regarding overt consent.

The espionage operations of fascist Italy

[Note: the author was fluent in Italian, had done espionage work in Italy, and was particularly well informed about the Italian security services.]

During the months and years leading up to the outbreak of war in 1939, fascist espionage increasingly became subsumed into National Socialist espionage. This is especially true for *OVRA (Organizzazione per la Vigilanza e la Repressione dell'Antifascismo)*, the fascist secret police, which increasingly turned into a sub-branch of the Gestapo. Initially the *OVRA* was tasked merely with the surveillance of antifascists, but soon it would also deal with counter-espionage and active espionage abroad. Military espionage fell under the remit of the *SIM (Servizio Informazioni Militare)*, which co-operated closely with the *OVRA* in all espionage matters. Early in 1945, court proceedings were started in Rome (which had by then been liberated) against General [Mario] Roatta, who had been the chief of *SIM* for several years. The general was able to evade conviction as a war criminal and extradition to Yugoslavia by escaping from the secure hospital where he had been held, but the trial laid bare the machinations of the fascist espionage authorities, and the close co-operation between *SIM* and *OVRA* on the one hand, and *SD-RFSS* and Gestapo on the other, was clearly demonstrated by the court.

General Mario Roatta (1887-1968), Head of the Military Intelligence Service (*Sevizio Informazioni Militare*, or "SIM") of Italy under Mussolini. He was known as the "Black Beast of Yugoslavia" for his repression there. SIM was entirely controlled by the SD and the Gestapo, as the author describes. He informs us that Heinrich Himmler frequently travelled to Rome to reorganise SIM and improve its performance, which involved frequent consultations with Roatta.

Another photo of General Roatta, in his office. He was responsible for the torturing and killing of countless patriotic Serbs in Yugoslavia. In fact, he gave orders for every Serb in uniform who had no identification card on him to be shot. He carried on in the same way in Montenegro and Herzegovina, apparently going so far as to crucify some patriots. And then in September 1943 he was entrusted with the entire reorganisation of the Italian Army in the South. The author points out that he evaded conviction as a war criminal in 1945.

The entire fascist espionage apparatus had been turned into an organisation of informers and denunciators, who did not even shy away from murdering Italian emigrants abroad (such as in the case of Carlo Rosselli).

Carlo Alberto Rosselli (1899-1937). The author says that this Jewish Italian socialist living in exile, a prominent opponent of Mussolini, was assassinated along with his brother by Italian Military Intelligence in France [in June of 1937). A French fascist group was blamed, but it was really an official Italian "hit", as Pfeifer was in a position to know, being fluent in Italian and having spent some time as an Italian specialist within the SD, as well as being a colleague of "Wolffie", who is described below..

The consular and diplomatic service was abused for espionage purposes; often at the personal orders of Foreign Minister Count Ciano, but always with the Duce's, Mussolini's, knowledge and approval. Indeed, the secret police received its orders directly from Mussolini, and the chief of the *SIM* was directly answerable to Mussolini and only formally subordinate to the Italian general staff.

Heinrich Himmler repeatedly travelled from Berlin to Rome in order to "re-organise" the *OVRA* and the *SIM*, and eventually one of Himmler's closest associates, his chief adjutant, *SS-Obergruppenführer* [Karl Friedrich Otto] Wolff [1900-1984], was assigned the role of permanent representative and liaison officer to the fascist espionage operation, in order to safeguard *OVRA's* and *SIM's* full compliance with Berlin's wishes. It is noteworthy that following the expulsion of the fascists from Southern Italy and Rome, *SS-Obergruppenführer* Wolff was appointed as supreme police commander in neo-fascist Northern Italy, where he officially had authority over all fascist police units.

SS-Obergruppenführer (later General) Karl Friedrich Otto Wolff (1900-1964), whom Hitler called "Wolffie". According to the author, he was appointed to exercise full Gestapo and SD control over the ostensibly independent security services of Mussolini's fascist Italy. Later he became the principal liaison between Himmler and Hitler. He was considered "the ideal Aryan". Wolffie was a great favourite at Hitler's private dinner parties. He later became a close friend of Allen Dulles, with whom he negotiated a secret deal on behalf of his boss Himmler as the War was nearing its end, against the specific orders of President Franklin D. Roosevelt. (Bundesarchiv)

Despite some measure of success in the Arab world, in the Near East and North Africa, Italian espionage remained a second-tier affair, never equalling the importance of the espionage operations of the global powers. It was, however, at times quite successful at gaining influence in the Balkans and exploiting the various currents and trends in opinion, by fomenting hatred and fuelling the sort of instability that was seen as advantageous for Italy. Its involvement in the murder of King Alexander I of Yugoslavia in October 1934 in Marseille – during which the French Minister of Foreign Affairs, [Jean] Louis Barthou (1862-1934, shot to death), was also killed – is an open secret.

King Alxander I of Yugloslavia (1888-1934, assassinated). The Italian secret service under General Roatta planned his murder and arranged for Crotian fascists to carry it out.

Jean Louis Barthout (1862-1934, shot to death). In 1913 he was Prime Minister of France for eight months. In 1934 he was French Foreign Minister. In October 1934, King Alexander I of Yugoslavia made a state visit to Marseilles, where he was assassinated. Barthoud was required to be there to receive him. Barthoud also died of a gunshot wound, but it was not until 1974 that the French Government admitted he had been caught in the crossfire and had actually been killed by a French policeman. The account of these events on Wikipedia does not mention the involvement of the Italian secret service, though it is admitted the planning took place in Rome. Our author seems to be the only source giving the true history of the planning of these two assassinations.

Domestically, the *OVRA* embodied the fascist terror regime, much like the Gestapo and *SD-RFSS* did in Germany. The *SIM* and *OVRA* are responsible for a substantial number of murders, but not that of the Italian Socialist leader Giacomo Matteotti in 1924. His assassination was carried out by the so-called *"Arditi"*, former members of the faction around Gabriele d'Annunzio during his seizure of Fiume [Rijeka]. After Mussolini's march on Rome, these *"Arditi"* were first turned into a covert special unit within the fascist militia and, after being officially banned following Matteotti's murder, were fully absorbed into it. Regrettably it is not possible, within the scope of this book, to report more fully on the *"Arditi"* and the significance of Matteotti's assassination to Italian domestic politics – an event that almost cost the dictator Mussolini his position of power.

Major Dordon [*sic: probably should be Dordoni*], who had not only been in charge of Italian espionage operations in the Balkans for many years before the war, but also uncovered the theft of the Italian secret encryption codes at the embassy in Berlin, was one of fascist Italy's most able intelligence officers. The codebook had been stolen by an envoy's secretary, but the envoy, Garbeccio [*the author may have meant Garbaccio, which is a common Italian surname, whereas Garbeccio is apparently unknown*] by name, had been too afraid to report the theft for many months. Finally he was put on trial in Rome, and Ambassador [Luigi] Aldovrandi (Marescotti, Count of Viano; 1876-1945) and three other members of the diplomatic staff were recalled from Berlin. Another notable intelligence officer was the *Carabinieri* Captain Umberto Dermidov (who was Caucasian by birth and not, as the name might suggest, a Bulgarian; his name had temporarily been slavified in 1917). He had repeatedly been put in charge of special personal missions by Mussolini and for a time had been appointed as "assistant of the trade commissioner" (!) at the Italian consulate in Bern. The infamous Georgian Schalwa Karumidze, who will be the subject of further investigation later, was a personal friend of Dermidov's.

Apart from the usual star agents and the activities of fascist intelligence officers disguised as consular staff under the protection of extraterritorial law, the fascist espionage apparatus tended to use Levantines as agents. However, both the *SIM* and *OVRA* repeatedly found that the Greeks, Macedonians, Bulgarians, Yugoslavs, Syrians, etc. in the fascist espionage service could not always be entirely relied upon. In particular, Count Ciano – who often felt compelled to personally oversee espionage matters, which, in his capacity as Minister for Foreign Affairs, were clearly none of his business – committed a whole series of espionage blunders with individuals hailing from those nations.

Count Ciano, at left, enjoying the company of Ribbentop at right.

Incidentally, Police Commander Caruso, who has since been shot in Rome, once made a very disparaging remark about Count Ciano. The then chief of the NSDAP in Italy and legation councillor at the German Embassy in Rome, Erwin Ettel (1895-1971, after 1945 known by the pseudonym of Ernst Krüger), had sought an audience with Caruso in order to reproach him for the fact that – virtually under the eyes of the fascist secret police – important information had leaked from the fascist Ministry for the Exterior. Incensed, Caruso replied: "Well, what do you think? The English or the French have only to put a beautiful and witty woman in our Foreign Minister's bed and the vain and flattered Count Ciano will pompously betray any secret." When Herr Ettel implied that perhaps Countess Ciano might also have committed some indiscretions, the police chief laughed and replied: "Of course, Countess Edda gets through more lovers than handkerchiefs, but you would not be able to elicit any state secrets from that woman – not even during the most ecstatic orgies of love."

SS Brigadeführer Erwin Ettel (1895-1971), known under the pseudonym Ernst Krüger after 1945. He implied that "perhaps Countess Ciano committed some indiscretions". (She was the wife of the Italian Foreign Minister.) She certainly had! But she never gave away state secrets, "even in the most ecstatic orgies of love". (Bundesarchiv)

II German espionage
Military espionage under Emperor Wilhelm II

German espionage was perfected and refined only relatively late. Of course, the German ruling powers never eschewed the opportunity to be informed about secret goings-on in foreign nations, but a scientifically accurate apparatus, able to register, process and evaluate, was only created in 1910, and then brought to exaggerated perfection under National Socialism.

Germany had always had very able spies at her disposal and had been able to produce some veritable "gems" of espionage, but a proven system, tested globally through decades of experience, had not been developed. One reason can perhaps be found in its volatile, undemocratic form of government that always tended to value achievements by individual personalities very highly. Moreover, the tendency to talk of success is deeply rooted in the German character.

Since the time of Emperor Wilhelm II, the military attachés at the German diplomatic missions abroad had occupied a special position. On a formal level, they were indeed subordinate to the relevant ambassadors or consuls, who, as commissioned ministers, were responsible for the representation of His Majesty's government abroad. In reality, however, they were Wilhelm II's special envoys on secret missions, and directly reported to the Emperor, thus bypassing the Foreign Office. It was a state of affairs that even old Bismarck described as untenable, but his opposition to the Emperor's irregular practices was futile. Despite all protests, Wilhelm II required "his" military attachés to send their secret reports directly to the court. The Foreign Office might then get its hands on those reports at a later stage via the Emperor (if His Majesty deigned to permit it), or, as was the case more often, would never see them at all. All of this led to a situation in which the Emperor at times gave direct orders to his military attachés; that is to say, directives of which the Foreign Office and the responsible German diplomats had no knowledge whatsoever.

Espionage was much frowned upon in imperial Germany, and intelligence officers, however capable, were not regarded as "socially acceptable", which is why no self-respecting officer would ever allow himself to be dragged into the intelligence service. In reality, however, the military attachés were nothing but imperial spies, and the impertinence with which they frequently carried out their espionage "for their supreme Lord" repeatedly led to serious diplomatic incidents. In this context we would like to mention the performance of the German military attaché in Washington after the outbreak of the First World War of 1914–18, who ruined all attempts by his ambassador to prevent the USA from entering that war, and whose *"pièce de résistance"* it was to leave behind on a train a folder with secret reports on future and past acts of German sabotage within the USA. This "imperial spy" and military attaché in Washington was none other than Franz von Papen, the later *Reich* Chancellor, Nazi Vice Chancellor, and Nazi ambassador in Vienna and Ankara.

Until May 1913, the chief of German military espionage was not even a regular member of the Grand General Staff! He was not among the 179 members of that body, but instead acted as a mere assistant to the chief of the operations department. When in 1912 General Ludendorff was appointed chief of the operations department at the Grand General Staff, he quickly recognised the importance of military espionage, and in 1913, at Ludendorff's instigation, Major [Walther] Nicolai {later Colonel; 1873-1947) was tasked with the running and reorganisation of German espionage operations. As chief of Department IIIB, Major Nicolai became a regular member of the Grand General Staff.

Major (later Colonel) Walther Nikolai (aka Nicolai, 1873-1947, died in custody in Russia), the Head of Intelligence and Member of the Grand General Staff for Germany during the First World War. He was the "handler' of the notorious female spy Mata Hari. He reorganised German espionage operations. The author praises him highly, saying Nikolai operated on a small budget and hired few agents, concentrating instead of "tehnically versatile star agents", and he admired his other clever techniques, such as hiding his headquarters behind five different import and export companies, which were "fronts", with his secret office being on the third floor of a commercial building and impossible for any outsider to enter. He was in charge of the German secret service from 1913 to 1919. In 1917 he founded the German Fatherland Party, which was a far right political party. In 1926 he helped found the National Security Service of Turkey.

A portrait drawing of Major (later Colonel) Walter Nikolai, which better shows what he looked like than any publicly available photograph. As a true spymaster, he was careful not to have photos of himself in circulation, so that he could go about and not be recognised.

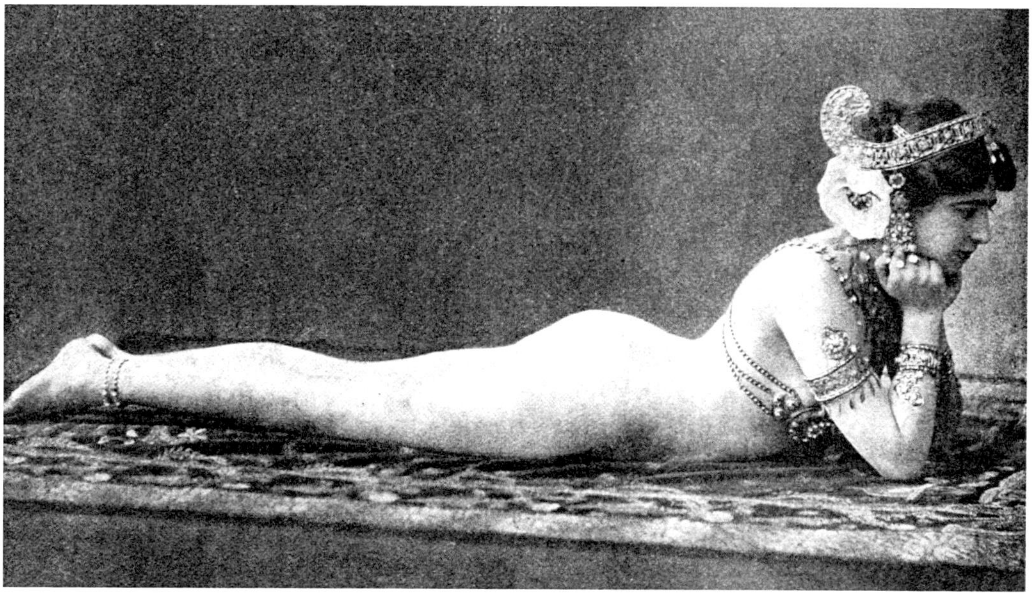

Major Nikolai had been the "handler" of Mata Hari, but as may be seen here, there was rather a lot of her to handle.

Mata Hari, who was not shy in other ways, had a particular obsession: she would never expose her breasts in public, whatever else she showed. Speculations are rife, but it has been suggested that she was worried that her breasts were too small and that people might laugh. It was the French firing squad, however, that had what might be called, if we excuse the pun, the last laugh.

His predecessor in the post of chief of military espionage had been the then Colonel Wilhelm Heye, who later, in post-war Germany (between 1926 and 1930), as Colonel-General, would become Chief of the *Reichswehr* (chief of army command).

Colonel (later Colonel General) August Wilhelm Heye (1869-1947). He was the Head of Military Espionage for Germany prior to Colonel Nicolai. He rose to become Head of the Army Command under the Weimar Republic.

Before Colonel Heye had become chief of German military espionage, there existed a separate Chief of Espionage East (the former German military attaché in St. Petersburg, Colonel [Ernst August Anton Hermann Otto, "Otto"] von Lauenstein (1857-1916), who had fallen out of favour with Wilhelm II and had thus been recalled from St. Petersburg), and a Chief of Espionage West (Colonel [Karl] Brose [later major General, 1855-1930]); both of whom acted as assistants to the chief of the operations department.

When Major Nicolai commenced his service as chief of German espionage, he had a budget of 450,000 *Reichsmark* at his disposal. With this relatively small sum he was supposed to cover all expenses of German military espionage, pay his agents, acquire documents, and pay out funds for special bonuses etc. Therefore, from the very outset, Major Nicolai refrained from engaging large numbers of agents, but instead designed his espionage apparatus around a small group of reliable, technically versatile star agents. By appointing Legation Councillor Muthesius to his office, he created a strong link to the German diplomatic corps, thus securing the co-operation of the Foreign Office, which would prove to be invaluable. At the same time he relocated his central office from Bülowstrasse to Königgrätzerstrasse 58, where he occupied the entire building and thus established himself in the immediate vicinity of the Anhalt and Potsdam railway stations. Well-disguised commercial operations meant that agents were able to frequent the locale without attracting any attention: the premises at Königgrätzerstrasse 58 were home to no fewer than five separate export- and import firms, which in reality were nothing other than subdivisions of the espionage headquarters. The third floor of the building was home to the now infamous secret laboratories of German espionage. For a visitor to gain access to that third floor, where one would be personally received by Major Nicolai or Legation Councillor Muthesius, he (or, indeed, she) had to either be one of the chief agents or an important German intelligence officer.

German pre-war and wartime espionage (during the World War of 1914–18) is inseparably linked with the influence and activities of a particular woman. This woman was much more than a leading star agent; already during the years of 1913–18, as a close associate of Major Nicolai, she truly was the heart and brains of the German espionage apparatus. Her influence is most strikingly epitomised by the fact the she was referred to as Major Nicolai's chief of staff, despite the fact that for a woman no such title had ever officially existed. She was extraordinarily active and the most successful female spy in the history of German espionage, if not espionage anywhere in the world. When she was not "on the move", she occupied an office on the third floor of the building in Königgrätzerstrasse 58, and her extraordinary status is further underlined by the fact that her permanent living quarters were also located in the premises of the German espionage headquarters. This woman did not act for the sake of material gain, but out of true devotion to her fatherland, a thirst for adventure, and death-defying courage, which was instilled in her through an unhappy love affair with a German intelligence officer, who gave his life in 1913 in faithful performance of his duties. The actual name of this woman is Annemarie Lesser, who was born into a good family in the Rhineland. Over the years, there have been multiple reports of her death, but she is probably still alive to this day. As "Mademoiselle Docteur" she became the nemesis of the *"Deuxième Bureau"*; her competence and reliability were unparalleled, and, despite her extreme daredevilry, she was never caught. A veritable web of legends has been spun around her identity, novels and questionable "eye witness reports" have been written, and films have been made depicting her actions as a spy. The most ridiculous allegations have been made; among them some that claim that she spent her last years in a mental institution in Switzerland. We shall meet her again later in this book, in her capacity as advisor and "secretary" in the office of Admiral Canaris, the later chief of German military espionage under the Nazi regime. [*Eglantyne has discovered what is probably the only surviving photo of her, which is reproduced on pagepage 384.*]

Major Nicolai was promoted to the rank of lieutenant colonel, and later, during the World War of 1914–18, the rank of colonel. He knew how to top up his department's meagre funds by making accessible new sources of money, which were uncontrollable and inexhaustible in equal measure: the German counter-espionage apparatus began to receive funds from the German steel and coal industry. This connection is rather unsurprising, given the fact that the German arms industry was directly interested in the existence of an efficient counter-espionage operation. And since counter-espionage and active espionage are closely connected, ever more funds flowed from industry into the coffers of German military espionage.

In the same way that Portugal increasingly became the hotbed of international espionage after the outbreak of war in 1939, Spain had played that role during the World War of 1914–18. San Sebastián was the Spanish base for German agents operating against France, but one particular intelligence officer, who enjoyed a high degree of confidence by the central authorities in Berlin, was stationed in Madrid, namely Lieutenant Canaris. Later, as an admiral, he would succeed his chief, Colonel Nicolai, but at first his official title was "assistant of the military attaché" at the German embassy in Madrid, from where he co-ordinated German espionage in the Atlantic and the Western Mediterranean, making crucial contributions to the success of the German *U-Boot* war against the allies.

By the outbreak of the World War of 1914–18, Colonel Nicolai had become a significant player within German imperial militarism, and after 1916 he was seen as one of the most obstinate among those dogged militarists who quashed any possibility of peace. In every civil or military gubernatorial office in the occupied territories of Belgium, France and Poland, Nicolai had installed compliant intelligence officers, who would make many significant administrative interventions. Similarly, he had reliable espionage officers infiltrate every general corps of the various army groups, who would accomplish some astonishing feats. Despite the fact that at the outbreak of war, in September 1914, his entire cadre of agents in England was exposed, he was able to achieve major successes with his star agents. He was especially in favour with General Ludendorff; and therefore from August 1916, when Ludendorff as First Quartermaster General had effectively become the supreme leader of all military operations, Colonel Nicolai's position was essentially unassailable. Since the outbreak of war in 1914, Nicolai had not in any way been choosy in the application of questionable tricks and methods of espionage. Like many inveterate military men, he had adopted the motto: "Every means is justified, if it contributes to the victory of German militarism!" Personally, he remained convinced of the "victory of German arms" until the autumn of 1918, and to him it was utterly inexplicable why his revered generalissimo Ludendorff sued for an immediate armistice.

Colonel Nicolai was seen as an intuitive go-getter. As chief of Division IIIB of the German general staff, since 1916 he increasingly dealt with censorship of the press and the ideological training for perseverance in war at the German war academies. He did not shy away from quickly arresting Arnold Rechberg (a personal friend of the German Crown Prince) and embassy councillor Freiherr von Eckartstein when he learned about the two men's secret peace negotiations. Due to a vigorous intervention by the Crown Prince he was unable to drag the pair in front of a military court and have them sentenced to death, but the Colonel did not relent and kept them in detention until the end of the war in 1918. When in November of that year the armistice talks commenced, Colonel Nicolai's position became untenable, and army command was forced to forsake one of its most influential officers. The French General Dupont, chief of the *"Deuxième Bureau"* and Colonel Nicolai's direct adversary, entered Germany as the chief of the Allied military mission, and was put in charge of disarmament and dissolution of the German army.

A necessary digression

According to the Treaty of Versailles, Germany was to be completely disarmed. Article 160 set the maximum strength of the German army at 100,000 men, stating explicitly: "The army shall be devoted exclusively to the maintenance of order within the territory and to the control of the frontiers [...] The Great German General Staff and all similar organisations shall be dissolved and may not be reconstituted in any form."

Following military collapse, Germany was proclaimed a republic on November 9, 1918. Only a few hours later, Friedrich Ebert sealed his agreement with General Groener "for the preservation of public order and safety". It soon became apparent that this agreement would demonstrate the majority parties' inability to create a small domestic army – the *Reichswehr* – and to imbue it with a new spirit. Out of fear of Communism and Socialism, the Weimar Republic stooped to "give sanctuary to a Prussian army that had miserably collapsed for the second time in its history" (Karl Thieme).

The German military machine has since then been shattered by the armies of the United Nations, and now there is an urgent need for a comprehensive reckoning with Frederick II of Prussia and Bismarck. It is staggering how many facts are distorted and misrepresented –which in itself would not need to bother us too much if it did not undermine the matter in hand. If, sadly, we are forced to point out the many errors that were made by the Weimar Republic's majority parties, then let us at least endeavour not to repeat them. We therefore consider it appropriate to state emphatically that domestic policies – as pursued by the majority parties – were in many important respects determined by international politics. That is to say: the victorious powers, which had dictated the Treaty of Versailles, decisively influenced German domestic politics. Many of the mistakes made by the German majority parties, in effect, were inevitable because of the influence of the victors of 1918/19. The victorious powers stabbed the government of the Weimar Republic (i.e. the majority parties) in the back and did not support it when it would have been crucial to do so. It will be left to future historiography to objectively determine the exact extent of the influence of the major powers of the Treaty of Versailles on domestic policies of the Weimar Republic; to precisely establish the share of the blame attributable to foreign nations for the domestic policy errors made by the majority parties; and to ascertain to what extent foreign nations were complicit in the emergence of National Socialism and militarism in Germany.

Conversely, it would of course be equally wrong to fully exculpate the Weimar Republic at the expense of foreign nations, but this does not negate the fact that the Weimar Republic was forced onto an inescapably wrong path by other nations. We feel that we are entitled to make such allegations, as we repeatedly pointed out the failures of the men of the Weimar Republic in the past, and, with hindsight, feel compelled to carry on doing so. There is no doubt that the representatives of the Weimar Republic, such as Wirth, Brüning, Braun etc., were driven by honest motives and aspirations. They failed – and to an extent, had to fail – because foreign nations time and again frustrated certain measures that could have saved the Republic. Only two such measures will be mentioned here: a customs union with Austria (as proposed by *Reich* Chancellor Brüning), and the planned enlargement of the *Reichswehr* to 300,000 men. Both measures could have taken the wind out of National Socialism's sails for a long time.

What has to be reaffirmed time and again is the fact that Germany, a republic under the Weimar constitution, had committed herself to full disarmament and had contractually bound herself to an eradication of the former Wilhelmine military machinery, bar a small army of professional soldiers with the explicit remit of "upkeep of law and order". An inter-Allied control commission had been appointed, which was tasked with the monitoring not only of disarmament, but also the intended purpose of the small professional army – the *Reichswehr* – that was about to be formed. At the head of that commission stood a man of impeccable credentials in all matters of espionage and secret intelligence: the French General Dupont. And yet, as already reported earlier in these pages, an utterly paradoxical situation arose, where the Supreme Court of the *Reich* was allowed – completely openly and blatantly – to engage in legal proceedings prosecuting "betrayal of military secrets"! Not a single person – not within Germany nor abroad, and especially not in the victorious nations, whose foremost concern it would have been and who maintained a permanent control commission for that very purpose! – asked the question why such trials were being held in Weimar Germany, when there should not have been any military secrets of any kind. (The Supreme Court of the *Reich* refused to put up with any foreign meddling and instead insisted on the *Reich* government's sovereignty, as granted by the Treaty of Versailles!)

In the spring of 1920, Wolfgang Kapp (1858-1922), the founder of the German Fatherland Party and East-Prussian director of the Agricultural Credit Institute, together with General [Baron, *Freiherr*, Walther Karl Friedrich Ernst Emil] von Lüttwitz (1859-1942) and General [Paul Emil] von Lettow-Vorbeck (1870-1964), carried out a putsch against the Weimar government.

Wolfgang Kapp (1852-1922) led the "Kapp Putsch" of 1920.

Lieutenant General Baron Walther von Lüttwitz (1858-1942), who joined with Wolfgang Kapp for the "Kapp Putsch" of 1920.

General Paul Emil von Lettow-Vorbeck (1870-1964) who joined with Kapp and von Lüttwitz for the "Kapp Putsch" of 1920.
(Bundesarchiv)

The vast majority of the German people responded with a general strike, and swept away the putschists within a few days. At roughly the same time, Dr Otto [Karl] Gessler (1875-1955) was appointed as *Reichswehrminister*, and the creation of the *Reichswehr* commenced, secretly and silently. One year later, General Hans von Seeckt [1866-1936] was appointed as its first "chief of army command", who asserted himself as the guarantor of the *Reichswehr's* homogeneity and who ensured that the responsible *Reichswehrminister* continued to be nothing more and nothing less than the highest military official. Not only did General von Seeckt install himself as the supreme lord and master of the new *Reichswehr*, which he was in the process of creating and organising and which only formally acknowledged the *Reichspräsident* as its supreme commander, but, as the "grand organiser", he also set the tone for neo-German militarism and took on the mantle of avatar and custodian of the Old-Prussian military spirit.

By the time General von Seeckt had to relinquish his command over the *Reichswehr* to the dangerous schemer General Wilhelm Heye in 1926, military intelligence offices had been established very close to the border with the so-called demilitarised zone (among others, in

Darmstadt and Kassel), whose sole remit was espionage and counter-espionage. Within the *Reichswehrministerium* (that is to say, for the chief of the army command), Main Division V (the so-called "Fifth Office") had been created, the central department for all military operations of the *Reichswehr* and later the *Wehrmacht*.

Colonel General August Wilhelm Heye (1869-1947). According to the author, he was "a dangerous schemer". (Photo by Nicola Perscheid, 1864-1930)

German military espionage under the Weimar Republic

Not long after General Hans von Seeckt had been appointed as chief of army command, another officer was installed at the newly created *Reichswehrministerium*, whose name should have been very familiar and highly suspicious to anyone in the inter-Allied control commission, but especially to its chief, the French General [Charles-Joseph] Dupont [1863-1935], former chief of the notorious *"Deuxième Bureau"*: that officer was none other than Vice-Admiral Canaris. As an officially accredited "assistant of the military attaché" in Madrid, with the rank of lieutenant, Canaris had been one of Germany's most important intelligence officers and espionage chiefs during the World War of 1914–18. Now, that cold calculator and – as he was known amongst his friends – "green-table spy" was appointed as chief of Main Division V (a department that was created for and then partly by him) and thereby as chief of the entire military espionage apparatus of the German *Reichswehr*.

Colonel General Johannes "Hans" Friedrich Leopold von Seeckt (1866-1936) It was he who appointed Canaris to the spymaster post in which he was to become so famous.

After the appointment of Vice-Admiral Canaris as chief of Main Division V, mostly officers drawn from the navy were installed in key positions as intelligence officers. Before long, virtually every army officer at the central department of the intelligence service had been replaced by a navy officer, which contributed to the fact that Vice-Admiral Canaris was very unpopular with members of the general staff at the *Reichswehrministerium* from the outset, and, unlike Colonel Nicolai before him, was never given a leading role at the ministry. Quite generally, the differences between Vice-Admiral Canaris and his predecessor and former boss, Colonel Nicolai, could not have been starker. In dealing with his colleagues, Vice-Admiral Canaris had a jovial and relaxed manner, foregoing the forceful and brittle commanding tone that was usually adopted by high-ranking officers, much to the dismay of his comrades. He liked to play the grumbling, grouchy sea dog, despite the fact that he had never been a "sea dog". Neither was he as ballsy and intuitive as Nicolai, but instead much more systematic and perhaps more tenacious; qualities that unjustly earned him a reputation as a bureaucrat. He was also accused of sabotaging the reactivation, that is to say, the re-commissioning, of Colonel Nicolai. The truth is that Vice-Admiral Canaris did not have the slightest influence on a potential reactivation of Colonel Nicolai. In actual fact, after the collapse of Wilhelmine militarism, the "warmonger" and espionage chief Nicolai had become an untenable proposition for the nascent *Reichswehr*, and General von Seeckt, usually a rather rigorous and pompous chief, even denied Colonel Nicolai admission to the so-called border control forces or the unofficial *Schwarze Reichswehr* at the time of the clashes with Polish insurgents in Upper Silesia. A person as tainted as Colonel Nicolai could no longer be supported by the new *Reichswehr*; much like the prominent Generals Ludendorff and Hoffmann, who were at the time sulking in Munich. And when, in 1926, Wilhelm Heye was appointed as supreme commander of the *Reichswehr*, every last chance of reactivation evaporated for Colonel Nicolai, for purely personal reasons. General von Seeckt's successor and new chief of army command was none other than General Heye, previously the chief of espionage operations and, as such, Nicolai's former boss. Heye had never forgotten and still considered a personal affront the fact that Nicolai, as espionage chief, had been able to advance to the position of an independent head of department and had become a recognised member of the Grand General Staff, whereas he, Heye, had merely been considered an "assistant of the chief of the operations departure" during his tenure as espionage chief. The daredevil Nicolai, then a lowly major, had surpassed the schemer Heye, who then held the rank of Colonel; a fact that a man like Heye would not be able to forget for the rest of his days.

Vice-Admiral Canaris' appointment had attracted surprisingly little attention among the members of the inter-Allied control commission. What was noticed even less was the fact that the new espionage chief arranged for Corvette Captain [Richard] Protze to leave his position in Kiel and to join him in Berlin; the same Protze, who, after a stint in *"Sonderbüro Stein"*, would later become the deputy of Vice-Admiral Canaris. [*Traugott Andreas Richard Protze, alias Paarman, formerly a naval captain, was head of Abwehr Counter-Intelligence under Canaris until 1938. After that, he ran an "independent" intelligence bureau in the Netherlands named "Stelle P", on Kalverstraat in Amsterdam, on behalf of Canaris, specifically targeting British intelligence.*]

The members of the general staff at the *Reichswehrministerium* in Berlin perceived Corvette Captain Protze's appointment at the ministry as a disgraceful affront to their Prussian *esprit de corps* – a violation of, or at least disregard for, their "officers' honour" by the "green-table spy". For a time a "palace coup" seemed to be on the cards, which could have cost the Vice-Admiral his position had he not been truly indispensable for the time being.

Why such an uproar, just because of Protze's appointment to the *Reichswehrministerium*? At the beginning of the World War of 1914–18, Protze had been an ordinary deck officer, that is to say, he held the highest rank available to a non-commissioned officer of the navy, while simultaneously holding the lowest officer rank, namely that of a "deck officer". The navy rank of "deck officer" was equivalent to the army rank of *Feldwebelleutnant* (lieutenant sergeant), with the difference that the army rank of *Feldwebelleutnant* could only be achieved by veteran non-commissioned officers during a time of war (i.e. the World War of 1914–18), while the rank of *Deckoffizier* until 1914 was available to navy petty officers also during peacetime. Both ranks, however, represented the highest officer class that a rank-and-file non-commissioned officer could ever achieve. With it, he had achieved officer status, which, for example, allowed him to enter an officers' mess, but nevertheless he would always remain a pariah, who would not be taken seriously by any fully-fledged member of the officer corps. In later years, the rank of *Feldwebelleutnant* and *Deckoffizier* would no longer be available without previous officer training. One can only imagine what it meant for the arch-conservative members of the general staff and army command that they were supposed to welcome, as a social equal, a "common man" into their circle, even if he had in the meantime advanced to the rank of Corvette Captain; a man who had neither attended cadet school or one of the war academies, nor was descended from one of the old officers' families. The venerable *esprit de corps*, which, in the officers' minds, was on the point of being newly cultivated and preserved, was now shamefully being betrayed by the new head of department, who might well have proven himself as capable, but certainly was himself a man without the correct background and thus devoid of "refinement". The old thesis – according to which navy officers lacked tradition and, as lowly merchants' sons, could never be proper officers in the Old Prussian sense – seemed to be reconfirmed.

Corvette Captain Protze had made a name for himself as an intelligence officer at the naval base in Kiel. He truly was an unrefined "common man" with bad manners; and if a surname can ever reveal the character of its bearer, this was true in the case of Protze, who indeed was a braggart [German *protzen* = to show off]. His arrival at the *Reichswehrministerium* in Berlin rather furthered the notion that it was unseemly for an army officer to engage in espionage and to pursue a career as an intelligence officer. All the prejudices that had – thanks to Colonel Nicolai's powerful position during the World War of 1914–18 – almost been overcome, were being newly stoked by the appointment of Corvette Captain Protze in Berlin and by the general demeanour of Vice-Admiral Canaris (restrained though this might have been in comparison to Protze's), who alone was responsible for Protze's appointment. It was therefore inevitable that army command allocated increasingly unqualified, if not to say inadequate, army officers to work on intelligence- and counter-intelligence tasks with that "spying navy chap". As a result, Canaris was forced to run his espionage apparatus with the inclusion of ever fewer army officers, and instead turned to the navy for the training of intelligence officers. It took the tragicomical failure of an intelligence officer of the army, namely one Major [H. K.] Schneider of the intelligence department in Darmstadt, for army command to comprehensively reconsider its negative stance towards Vice-Admiral Canaris' approach to the organisation of espionage operations. More will be said later about the embarrassing "Major Schneider Case".

Corvette Captain Protze proved his considerable abilities through an impressive number of "counter-intelligence successes", and it soon became clear that he would also make for a first-rate espionage specialist. This was especially apparent in such cases where counter-espionage and active espionage overlapped and went hand in hand. One of Protze's major coups was the "Sosnowski Case", which will be discussed later. But he enjoyed his greatest "success" when he was able to track down one of Colonel Nicolai's former associates and to find a new position for her with his boss, Vice-Admiral Canaris. That former associate was none other than Fräulein Annemarie Lesser, formerly also known as "Mademoiselle Docteur". While she would thenceforth act "only as a secretary", with her vast knowledge, her insight into human nature and her powers of deduction she was able to render invaluable services to the central German military operations at the *Reichswehrministerium*. And wherever Corvette Captain Protze, a.k.a. "Uncle Richard", would appear, one could also be sure to find "Auntie Lenchen". No uninitiated person would ever have entertained the idea that this spinsterish lady, who worked as a "secretary" and indeed had something of an ageing aunt about her, had in fact in the past been Germany's greatest female spy, perhaps the greatest of them all during the World War of 1914–18.

The "green-table spy" Vice-Admiral Canaris (or "Papa Sea Dog", as he was called by those close to him) operated behind the scenes, while the inseparable Corvette Captain Protze (the no longer altogether youthful but still quite laid-back "Uncle Richard") and Annemarie Lesser (his "Auntie Lenchen") were active in the foreground. It was they who transformed German military espionage into a perfect espionage apparatus for the *Reichswehr*, and they would remain at the forefront of operations beyond the Nazis' takeover.

The man in the car is Corvette Captain Traugott Andreas Richard Protze (alias also Parman or Paarman), of the Abwehr. Beside him is the notorious female super-spy Annemarie Lesser, who posed as his "secretary", and amongst whose aliases were Helena Skrotzki and Helen Schneider. She also posed as Protze's "Auntie Lenchen" or "Auntie Lene". And he sometime posed as "Uncle Richard". They were two of the most brilliant and dangerous German spies of the War. The woman in front is their colleague Clara Böning, alias Frau Robberts/ Mrs. Roberts. This photo was taken in the Netherlands in 1939 or 1940. It is believed to be the only existing photograph of Annemarie Lesser, whose anonymity was key to her success as one of the most brilliant female spies in history. The author calls her the most successful female spy in the history of German espionage, and possibly of the world. She had a brilliant spy career as Chief of Staff to Major Nicolai in World War One, when she was known as "Madame Docteur" and drove the Deuxième Bureau crazy because they could never find her. It was Protze who tracked her down in retirement and brought her back into active espionage work. The author says of the two of them: 'They transformed German espionage." A false story has been circulated, and may even be found on Wikipedia, that "Mademoiselle Docteur" was a woman named Elspeth Schragmüller (1887-1944). Although Schragmüller may very well have done good intelligence work in Belgium during World War One, where it seems that she became head of a spy ring in Antwerp, an attempt to identify "Madame Docteur" with her is a guess which is no longer convincing, since it is contradicted by Heinrich Pfeifer's clear and detailed testimony, who had close connections with the Abwehr and probably knew Protze personally.

★ *Canaris stuurde "een vos onder de vossen", een specialist van de oude Marine-nachrichtendienst naar Den Haag; kapitein-luitenant ter zee Traugott Andreas Richard Protze. In de herfst van 1937 installeerde deze oude beroeps-spion, die iedereen als schuldig beschouwde tot hij zijn onschuld had bewezen, zich in een villa aan de Bloemcamp-laan 36 in Wassenaar.*

A Dutch newspaper clipping from 1973 showing the modest villa in which Protze and Lesser lived quietly and obscurely to conceal their espionage work. This villa was at 36 Bloemcamp-laan in Wassenaar, a suburb of the Hague by the coast, and they originally moved in in 1937, before the German occupation, to run espionage against the Dutch in preparation for the future invasion.

The newly created *Reichswehr* wanted the espionage department to concern itself mainly with the safeguarding of information around secret rearmament, and therefore was interested in the department's development of sound and well-organised counter-espionage operations. In this, Vice-Admiral Canaris was able to demonstrate his capabilities to the full: he planned, calculated and organised with the utmost care and foresight. This required not so much "intuition" (of the kind possessed by Colonel Nicolai), but hard-nosed calculation. Any amount of recklessness would have been ill advised, for a single misstep could have blown all fuses. The task of developing a reliable counter-espionage apparatus of the highest standards, which would be able to safeguard the secret rearmament in every conceivable regard, did indeed require some of the quiet composure, clear foresight, cool calculation and rigorous precision of a seafarer. A waspish and brash army officer would have been the wrong man for the job.

The Social Democrat *Reichswehrminister* Noske and his successors

So far there has been no mention of the first *Reichswehrminister*, the Social Democrat [Gustav] Noske (1868-1946). As it happens, Noske had nothing to do with the re-establishment of the 100,000-strong professional army. Instead, as the responsible minister, it was his task – in close co-operation with the Wilhelmine Quartermaster General Dr Wilhelm Groener – to implement the disarmament and dissolution of the defeated German army of millions in 1918/19. Once that task had been carried out, under the watchful eye of the inter-Allied control commission, Noske was removed from his post, and from then onwards no other Social Democrat or member of any other majority party would ever become *Reichswehrminister*. The former "revolutionary" Noske had discharged his duties to the full satisfaction of the officers and generals who returned home after the war. During this time of "upheaval", that is to say, just after the collapse of Wilhelmine Germany, it was Noske, of all people, who for those returning officers had become the guarantor against the socialisation ambitions of the parties on the left ("Spartakists", Independents and the left wing of the Social Democrats). However, he was not seen by the officer class as one of their own kind or a sufficiently kindred spirit to be entrusted with the safeguarding of "Old Prussian tradition". And so Noske had to go; he was not ousted by the government of the majority parties, but by the German officer corps.

Reichsminister Gustav Noske (1868-1946). He carried out the disbanding of the German military forces at the end of World War One. He was the last Social democrat to be Reichsminister. He was eventually ousted by the German officer corps, according to the author.

In 1920 no-one would yet have dared to appoint a general as *Reichswehrminister*, and so at first the staid Dr Otto Gessler had to do. However, from the outset it was made certain that the authority of Dr Gessler's position within neo-German militarism, as later devised by General von Seeckt, would be limited.

Dr. Otto Karl Gessler (1875-1955), who succeeded Noske as Reichsminister. The author says he was very staid. By 1928 he too was ousted. (Bundesarchiv)

By 1928, when General [Wilhelm] Groener (a friend and confidant of Field Marshal General von Hindenburg, by then *Reichspräsident*) was appointed as *Reichswehrminister*, the "chief of army command" with his staff had gained such a high level of independence that the *Reichswehrminister* had lost any power to influence the command of the *Reichswehr*.

General Karl Eduard Wilhelm Groener (1867-1939). He succeeded Gessler as Reichsminister, thus re-establishing the official status of the generals. He expanded the Army. But he was later dismissed by Hindenburg because he wanted to disband the SS.

One of his successors, General [Kurt] von Schleicher, made the fatal mistake of presuming powers of command that – in the opinion of the new generals of "army command" – the *Reichswehrminister* was not entitled to. General von Schleicher was betrayed and sacrificed in order to clear the path for Adolf Hitler's assumption of power on January 30, 1933; von Schleicher was forced to resign from the position of *Reichskanzler* not least because he had been disavowed by the entire general corps. But after General von Schleicher's execution at Hitler's order on June 30, 1934, "army command" did muster enough *esprit de corps* to demand the rehabilitation of von Schleicher's reputation by his murderers (von Schleicher had, after all, been a general!), without of course laying a finger on these murderers. Indeed, despite the *Reichswehr's* great victory over the murderous party on June 30, 1934, the generals continued to make pacts with that very same party, in the knowledge that National Socialism alone would be able to guarantee the large-scale construction of a new German *Wehrmacht*. The generals and officers of the general staff seriously thought that by sometimes "turning up their noses" they would be able to sufficiently distance themselves from the "evil Nazis". However, their opposition to the political movement of National Socialism – which was never serious opposition, but rather some vague noises of disapproval – amounted to nothing more than the sometimes downright naïve adherence to prestige, which was happily tolerated by a man like Hitler. And so Adolf Hitler made himself their lord and master and preserved their "prestige" – as long as it seemed opportune to do so – even against National Socialism. In return, they willingly became the most dreadful instrument of National Socialism's foreign policy, and therefore are complicit in all of National Socialism's crimes, and no amount of "opposition with hindsight" will exculpate the general corps. The generals had devoted themselves to National Socialism, which grew into the most dangerous and hopefully last exponent of German militarism, and mercilessly dragged that militarism down into the abyss with itself.

"Only the NSDAP as the party of government and Adolf Hitler as *Reichskanzler* will guarantee general conscription and thereby the creation of a new army of millions!" With these words, the young [Udo von] Woyrsch, the son of the generalissimo Remus von Woyrsch, won over his friend Walter von Reichenau for National Socialism in the summer of 1932(!) in Königsberg [Kaliningrad]. The Chief of Staff, Walter von Reichenau, was in turn able to win over his boss, Division Commander Werner von Blomberg, who would go on to serve as the first *Reichswehrminister* in the Hitler cabinet. He used the same argument to convince the *Reichswehr* and the initially reluctant General Werner Freiherr von Fritsch at army command. Let us not forget that the young Woyrsch at that time was an *SS-Gruppenführer* and a close friend of *Reichsführer SS* Heinrich Himmler, and that the first contact between Blomberg-Reichenau and Adolf Hitler was personally arranged by Himmler. Reichenau received his golden cufflinks engraved with the *SS* runes, was made an honorary member of the *SS* (for which he was *wrongly* decried as a die-hard Nazi general), but eventually had to pay with his life for his later, often very strident, opposition to National Socialism and especially to the misdeeds of the *SS* police during the campaign in Russia. Reichenau supposedly died of a heart attack; but what kind of "attack" he actually suffered will probably never come to light. In any case, his personal opposition was much more forceful than that of any other general, including Fritsch's! Reichenau's critical stance was taken very seriously, especially by Himmler. Walter von Reichenau, probably the most able member of the general staff of the new *Wehrmacht*, was promoted to the rank of Field Marshal General, but out of fear of his opposition – which was never directed against Hitler and National Socialism itself, but always straight at the savage mob controlled by *Reichsführer SS* Heinrich Himmler and his political police – he was never able to become one of the "heroic" leaders of an entire army group during the war. He was only ever given command over certain divisions – important, but subsidiary army units. The life and death of Field Marshal General Walter von Reichenau are but one chapter in the tragedy of the neo-German officer caste, the generals of the *Wehrmacht*. At a crucial moment, Reichenau had become the "stirrup holder" for the advancing power of National Socialism, and was unable to extricate himself for the rest of his life. He fought against certain elements within it and as a result was murdered. Try as he might, as a die-hard militarist he was unable to understand clearly the spirit and purpose of National Socialism and its fatal, systematic and catastrophic policies.

The "factory protection service" in the arms factories

Without the preparatory steps taken by the various governments of the Weimar Republic, it would later have been impossible for the Hitler government to achieve armament on such a massive scale and to assemble a well-equipped army of millions in such a staggeringly short amount of time. With the advent of the Hitler regime, military rearmament was conducted more or less openly; indeed, very soon the Nazis started to publicly brag about it, both at home and abroad. In earlier years it had not always been easy to maintain strict secrecy around the preparatory armament operations. While it was relatively straightforward to conceal these efforts within the purely military sphere, it was more difficult to maintain secrecy in the economic-technical domain, where the contracts given to major industrial enterprises blatantly exceeded the requirements of a 100,000-strong army. A separate chapter, far exceeding the scope of this book, would be needed to describe how, for instance, the Centrist Heinrich Brüning – a highly respectable and honourable man and without a doubt one of the most able *Reich* Chancellors of the Weimar period – could time and again be won over to support the policy of secret armament, sometimes willingly, at other times less so. Chancellor [*from 1930 to 1932*] Heinrich [Aloysius Maria Elisabeth] Brüning (1880-1970), a typical Prussian reserve officer, more than any of his predecessors created the conditions for the subsequent large-scale armament operations under the Hitler regime. Whenever scruples arose within him, they were brushed aside by heavy industry warning of renewed, massive unemployment, even worker redundancies! However, when Brüning – whose actions may have been contentious, but whose personal integrity was beyond reproach – in all sincerity set about exposing the so-called "Eastern Aid scandal", he was insidiously betrayed by the "circle around Hindenburg" and subsequently dismissed. The question remains open as to whether Brüning was aware that he was about to assail one of the three major factions that embodied "Old Prussian tradition" and its arch-conservative spirit: namely the major landowners, who, relative to the officer caste of the new *Reichswehr* and heavy industry, in those days were the weakest and at the same time most corrupt of the three factions. (History repeats itself in men such as Brüning and Reichenau: willingly or unwillingly, they paved the way for neo-German militarism and National Socialism, and their subsequent criticism of any wrongs or excesses was futile, as they were unable to correctly identify the root cause of the evil, l*et al*.ne remedy it.)

After carrying out the dissolution of the defeated Wilhelmine army, Noske was succeeded by Dr Gessler, while General von Seeckt set about organising the new *Reichswehr*. The German arms industry immediately offered its services and soon was awarded the first secret contracts. Vice-Admiral Canaris was appointed as espionage chief at the *Reichswehrministerium*, and was tasked with the concealment of the incipient rearmament effort. And conceal it he did!

Officials at the *Reichswehrministerium* in Berlin soon realised that the inter-Allied control commission was best deceived by passing off the secret arms contracts as orders for the burgeoning German merchant navy. For example, measuring instruments manufactured by Siemens & Halske, radar equipment produced by AEG, and other weapons components manufactured by various precision mechanical engineering companies were diverted via dockyards in Hamburg, Kiel, Wilhelmshaven and, most notably, Elbing: the first orders of cutting-edge weapons for a small, but eventually extremely well-equipped, professional army were all fulfilled via such circuitous routes. In those shipyards, the *Reichswehr's* first armouries were established, and, nestled among the dunes between Stettin [Szczecin] and Zoppot [Sopot], the first small airbases (home to the *Reichswehr's* gliders) were founded, long before there were any public outings of the glider planes in Silesia or on the *Wasserkuppe* mountain. The *Krupp* steel works registered an interest in the *Reichswehr's* secret arms contracts, the *"Stahlverein"* (the steel industry association) and *Thyssen* competed as suppliers of steel, the *"I.G. Farbenindustrie"* (a chemical and pharmaceutical conglomerate) produced the latest explosives (first in Oppau and later in Ludwigshafen), and, in the vicinity of the *Reich's* capital, between Johannisthal and Nieder-Schönweide, *Borsig* established the first small arms factory that produced weapons exclusively for the *Reichswehrministerium.*

Step by step, cutting-edge military hardware was developed, the number and magnitude of contracts handed out to the arms industry multiplied with every passing month and year, and ever more factories were transformed into war plants. At the same time, the task of keeping these operations secret became increasingly difficult for the chief of espionage and counter-espionage, Vice Admiral Canaris.

What had existed only in a rudimentary form before the World War of 1914–18 was expanded and developed into a well-thought-out system by Admiral Canaris: the so-called "factory protection service" was established in all notable arms factories. As a first step, all personnel managers of the major factories that supplied the nascent German *Wehrmacht* were nominated "confidants of the *Reichswehr*", and as such were expected to work hand in glove with Admiral Canaris' central bureau. Of course, the position of personnel manager was not only important to the *Reichswehrministerium*, but also for each firm itself. Usually the personnel manager was a senior director of the company or even a board member, who would have an especially trustworthy authorised clerk at his side acting as a personnel officer. With much skill, Vice-Admiral Canaris was able to fill all relevant posts within private industry with his own confidants. Captain Schumacher was installed in the influential position of chief of the personnel department at Siemens & Halske, despite the fact that no less a figure than Herr von Winterfeldt, the son-in-law of Herr von Siemens himself, was the actual and highest chief of the personnel department. After having been installed at the firm, Captain Schumacher, together with Admiral Canaris, set about establishing an exemplary "factory protection service", whose remit it was to keep a close eye especially on those departments within Siemens & Halske that were almost exclusively concerned with the production of military hardware (such as the *ZL – Zentral-Laboratorium)*, and to closely monitor all information that flowed into and out of the company. Under the auspices of retired Navy Lieutenant Jorger, an entire squad of former members of the imperial navy in Kiel was appointed to form the "factory protection service", which would be responsible for all Siemens plants in Germany, that is to say for Siemens & Halske, Siemens & Schuckert, the cable-manufacturing plants in Nuremberg, etc.

The "factory protection service" at Siemens would serve as a blueprint for similar operations at other notable arms manufacturers – all established at Vice Admiral Canaris' instigation and headed by his cronies. At "I.G. Farbenindustrie", each of the eight giant subsidiaries within the conglomerate initially had its own independent "factory protection service", but these separate operations (which were frequently and unwittingly working against each other, rather than with each other) were soon unified and put under the combined leadership of the aged Counsellor Wagner of the chemical works in Ludwigshafen. Counsellor Wagner (who always seemed rather absent-minded, but in truth was able to act boldly and with extreme rigour) had made a name for himself during the French occupation, when, thanks entirely to his own personal initiative, he was able – in the nick of time and at great peril to his own life – to get patents and classified industrial information to safety across the Rhine and out of reach of the French. He had been a personal friend of Admiral Canaris since 1916.

The Krupp works in Essen, too, redesigned their existing protection service along the lines of the Siemens model. A retired detective superintendent from Cologne was appointed as the chief of the new "factory protection service", but was soon replaced by one Freiherr von Kuenheim, who was allowed to style himself "director of the Krupp works". This Freiherr von Ku-En-Heim (as he liked to pronounce his name when introducing himself) was a somewhat quaint character who was rather ill-disposed toward Wilhelmine Germany. He was of the opinion that he and his noble kin in East Prussia had been deeply humiliated by the fact that Emperor Wilhelm II had conferred a title of nobility onto a Jew who also called himself Kuenheim (but whose name was pronounced with an *Umlaut*!). Eventually, the hoary Freiherr von Kuenheim was able – but only with the greatest difficulty – to force "that low-down bastard of a Jew" to spell his surname with an "h", so that the newly-ennobled Jew thenceforth was not called Kuenheim, but Baron von Kühnheim. Despite all this, it would be wrong to assume that the chief of the "factory protection service" at the Krupp works,

Freiherr von Kuenheim, was a fool. On the contrary, he was a master of his trade.

The chief of the "factory protection service" at *Rheinmetall* in Düsseldorf was a former first lieutenant of the navy by the name of Meinecke, who, incidentally, had been one of Vice-Admiral Canaris' cadets. An aged major general with the not uncommon surname Meier later became the chief of the "factory protection service" at the sprawling *"Stahlverein"* conglomerate. Despite the fact that this major general by no means came from nobility, in order to distinguish himself from other men called Meier, he liked to call himself "Meier zur Kapellen". It was said to have been the bitterest disappointment of his life to be discharged as a major general, before achieving the rank of lieutenant-general, which would have brought with it the coveted title of "Excellency". All the same, Herr "General Meier zur Kapellen" (who, it would seem, did not live to see the outbreak of war in 1939) was a first-rate counter-espionage specialist and an excellent leader of his "factory protection service".

Apart from the chief, the most important person within every "factory protection service" was the man tasked with keeping in constant contact with the authorities; a go-between installed in each arms factory by the espionage service, who would report both to Vice Admiral Canaris' central office and to the local police authorities. All of these "officials", much like their respective bosses in each private arms factory, were personal confidants of the espionage chief, to whom they certainly had greater allegiance than to the factory management on whose payroll they were. In the case of Siemens, this "official" was a former "imperial" petty officer of the *Kriegsmarine* by the name of Becker (also known as Bach), who was mentioned earlier in the context of a report on the *SD-RFSS*. He arrived at Siemens at the same time as the (by then retired) Lieutenant Jorger.

Each of these "men of confidence" had been issued with a special "Open, Sesame!", namely one of the famous identification cards with a red line on a white background, which allowed the holder unimpeded access to the *Reichswehrministerium* (that is to say, to the infamous Division V), as well as to Division IA in Berlin's police headquarters. It was the ultimate aim of every espionage agent to be issued with such an identification card; a dream that would remain unfulfilled in most cases, as only active intelligence officers, or, in other words, the go-betweens in the "factory protection services", were eligible.

Lay people will find it difficult to get a true sense of the enormous importance that was attached to the foundation of each "factory protection service" in the arms factories. These operations were crucial for the functioning of Vice Admiral Canaris' military and industrial counter-espionage apparatus. It was Canaris' strategy to tackle the evil at its root, as it were, by controlling and closely monitoring the production process of each new weapon and each military innovation. In some sense, staff surveillance in arms factories certainly was nothing new, but the "factory protection services", with their strict centralisation and the direct surveillance of each and every arms manufacturer by Canaris' central office at the *Reichswehrministerium*, did represent an innovation. The contact between each "factory protection service" and the central office of military espionage at the *Reichswehrministerium* was so close and organised with such military discipline, that the "officials" in each "factory protection service" were, in effect, well-drilled subordinates of Admiral Canaris.

Apart from the precise collaboration between the "factory protection services" within industry and the counter-espionage apparatus in the *Reichswehrministerium*, which manifested itself as unconditional submission to Vice Admiral Canaris' authority, the creation of the "factory protection services" was an ingenious strategic move by Canaris in a separate regard: private enterprise, that is to say, the arms industry, now had to pay for military espionage out of its own coffers. Of course, the *Reichswehrministerium* did not pay a penny towards Admiral Canaris' "factory protection services", for they were the "private" operations of each individual arms factory. This was a matter of the greatest importance, because any money saved in counter-espionage could be put towards active espionage operations. At first, the nascent *Reichswehr* had access only to very limited funds, and it was not always possible to avoid the irksome expenditure controls imposed by the *Reich* government (that is to say, the *Reichstag*), or the inter-Allied control commission, which was still operational in the early stages of the *Reichswehr's* foundation. However competent the *Reichswehr* might have been at concealment, even the most skilfully disguised funds did have to actually exist before they could be spent. (The "modern art" of spending public funds that do not even exist only became popular under the Hitler regime. The greatest artist in this respect was Herr Hjalmar Schacht, who had already started to perform his monetary acrobatics under the Weimar Republic.)

The arms industry's agencies abroad

Admiral Canaris had established his "factory protection services" in all major industrial companies that received an appreciable volume of orders from the *Reichswehr* – which, in effect, meant almost all large firms. These "private" organisations had become an integral part, if not the core, of all German counter-espionage operations. With the aid of his "men of confidence" who were "officials" within private industry but bound by military obedience to Canaris, the Vice Admiral was able to involve German industry also in *active* espionage.

Over and over, German industrialists denied any involvement of their factories in active German espionage. The directors of the foreign branches of Siemens, AEG, I.G. Farbenindustrie, or the major mining corporations always pointed to the independence of their enterprises in Paris, Brussels, Warsaw, Milan, in South America, Spain, or wherever else they might have been located, and produced legal documents that proved that their businesses were not conventional sub-branches of a German parent company, but instead "associated companies" that were independent and strictly national (i.e. French, Belgian, Polish, Italian etc.). As a matter of fact, the boards of these "associated companies" were filled with honourable local Frenchmen, Belgians, and Poles etc., who knew nothing of "espionage"; indeed, who *could not* know anything of such matters. Even the directors of the parent companies or their delegates at the "associated companies" abroad would have rejected any suspicion of espionage with much indignation. Nevertheless there can be no doubt that all of these so-called "associated companies" of major German industry concerns were systematically abused for espionage purposes and that they formed an integral part of the espionage web created by Vice Admiral Canaris.

What follows is an account of a textbook case of the integration of a German arms manufacturer's foreign agencies into Canaris' espionage organisation. The name of that well-known company is Siemens.

The president of the supervisory board for all of Siemens' foreign "associated companies" was no less a figure than Herr [Ludwig Gustav Moritz] von Winterfeldt (1880-1958), the son-in-law of the venerable Herr [Werner] Siemens (head of the family that was the majority share holder of both Siemens & Halske and Siemens & Schuckert, i.e. the entire Siemens concern). *[Actually, Winterfeld's wife Charlotte was the granddaughter rather than the daughter of Siemens.]* Not only did Herr von Winterfeldt play an important role on the administrative board of the Siemens works in Berlin and Nuremberg, he also held the crucial post of highest chief of the personnel department at Siemens & Halske. The head of the personnel department was the aforementioned friend of Admiral Canaris, the retired Captain Schumacher, who was also in charge of the "factory protection service" at Siemens, including its boss, the retired Captain Jorger. As is by now well known, the man who had been installed as the go-between to the *Reichswehrministerium* was the former petty officer Becker, also known as Bach. On occasion, when especially large foreign contracts were being transacted, the espionage chief Canaris wanted to shield his friends (or rather, subordinates!) Schumacher, Jorger and Becker from the Siemens supervisory board. To achieve this, he would send one of his agents, an active espionage officer or an official from the *Reichswehrministerium*, to call on Herr von Winterfeldt at Siemens. The great industry captain von Winterfeldt time and again would feel honoured to receive such an important visitor from the *Reichswehrministerium* – which is why the sly fox Canaris kept arranging these courtesy visits. Some general talk of "national concerns" and "important missions in the national interest" would ensue, and Herr von Winterfeldt would immediately "make available" his head of department Schumacher, after visibly revelling in the "supreme honour of a visitation from the *Reichswehrministerium*", as he liked to put it himself. In the presence of the official, the head of the personnel department Schumacher then received his instructions from Herr von Winterfeldt:

"The *Reichswehrministerium* requires our assistance. Captain Schumacher, please make available to the gentlemen from the ministry anything they require and make all necessary arrangements according to your own judgement."

This was quickly and inevitably followed up with the routine "exoneration" of the industry captain von Winterfeldt:

"You will understand, gentlemen, that I cannot and do not wish to be involved in the whole affair myself. And so I do not want to learn any details from you, Captain Schumacher, and, in fact, I truly have no idea what this is all about. Other than that, it is your personal responsibility to ensure that this whole affair will not inconvenience the company, so be careful when you choose your people."

The interview was concluded jovially:

"Well, I know that I can rely on you, my dear Captain!" – and, turning to the official:

"Please do convey my best wishes and my deep esteem to the Admiral. I am always at his disposal and am, as ever, pleased to be able to render a small service to him. I only ask – please do understand – that my person must not be connected to the whole affair."

Following such conversations, a Siemens engineer would be sent to Paris, Brussels, Warsaw, Madrid, or wherever else, carrying in his luggage important instructions or well-disguised design plans, along with some ordinary business papers. The engineer had no idea about the nature of the documents; he only knew that some specially designated construction plans or certain "harmless" business letters were to be delivered to a particular person, or a particular office at a Siemens foreign branch, i.e. an "associated company". On the same train as the engineer usually would travel Herr Becker (a.k.a Bach), who naturally was not carrying any potentially incriminating documents. He would keep an eye on the unsuspecting Siemens engineer and would satisfy himself that the disguised secret documents were handed over at their intended destination without a hitch. Only on rare occasions Becker would personally carry out the all-important "correct delivery" of documents at the Siemens branch.

Such were the goings-on at Siemens, at AEG, at I.G. Farben, and any number of other major industrial concerns and their foreign "associated companies".

Herr von Winterfeldt "was not aware of anything", neither were the gentlemen in the general directorate or those on the supervisory boards of Siemens, AEG, I.G. Farben or any other internationally established firm, and all of them would have been "filled with genuine indignation" had they or their firms been suspected of espionage.

The gentlemen in the directorates abroad would have been equally indignant had there been attempts to accuse them or their firms of espionage, and in reality they were entitled to voice rejection of any suspicion of espionage, as in almost all cases they were truly "not aware of anything".

Naturally, the route via the foreign branches was not the only one that the espionage chief Canaris would avail himself of in order to contact his agents and spies abroad; in actual fact this conduit was rarely used for the transmission of documents and information. However, for a substantial number of leading agents of German active espionage, the "foreign branches" of the German arms industry functioned as "finance departments", through which remittances were paid and the well-disguised espionage offices they maintained for the German espionage apparatus were financed. Only a very small number of individuals at every industrial concern would really know, or even have an inkling, of what was actually going on.

Incidentally, one of Admiral Canaris' most important "transhipment points" was Brussels, where the local sub-branch of Bayer-Leverkusen (I.G. Farben) rendered crucial services to the espionage chief. In every instance, Admiral Canaris liaised – either directly or indirectly – with the "official" at each "factory protection service", who at the same time was the go-between to the *Reichswehrministerium* for each factory.

The firm of Bayer-Leverkusen in Belgium, seen in this drone shot, is presumably much larger today than it was when it was acting as a "transhipment point" for the Nazi *Abwehr* under Admiral Canaris, and of course is today devoted solely to commercial business activities.

German espionage after Hitler's takeover

It has to be reiterated at this point that we are not in a position to give a complete account of the entire German espionage apparatus. This applies both to what has already been said, and to what is to follow. We merely aim to provide an outline of the structural design of the espionage machinery, and it is decidedly not the purpose of our report – in contrast to many other publications on alleged espionage cases – to blatantly serve a lust for sensationalism.

Of course, the history of German espionage after Hitler's takeover is closely intertwined with the history of the *Reichswehr* and the German *Wehrmacht*. We must therefore be mindful of the fact that it was only after the dismissal of General Fritsch (which occurred immediately prior to the "invasion" of Austria) that Hitler and National Socialism as a whole were able to gain a decisive and transformative influence over the new German *Wehrmacht* that had been created through the reintroduction of general conscription; for only after the dismissal of Freiherr von Fritsch was it possible for the party to gain a foothold within the *Wehrmacht*.

Until 1938, Admiral Canaris was the undisputed lord and master of the military branch of German espionage, and essentially he remained in control until the fateful day of July 20, 1944; that is to say, for the best part of World War II. He knew very well how to take advantage of the National Socialist's general espionage activities without relinquishing control over the military espionage apparatus.

In an earlier chapter we have already hinted at the attempts of the chief of the *SD-RFSS* and the Gestapo, *SS-Gruppenführer* Heydrich, to sidle up to the chief of espionage in the *Reichswehrministerium*, Admiral Canaris. We described the scenes of fraternisation between Heydrich and Canaris in front of the assembled staff that had been arranged in 1935 by Heydrich's ingenious assistant, deputy chief of the *SD* and the Gestapo, Dr Werner Best (who, after the outbreak of war, was first appointed as Chief of the Gestapo in France and later as *Reich* Commissioner in Denmark).

Heydrich – organiser and chief of the *SD-RFSS* and the Secret State Police, gifted performer of Mozart's piano works, and originator of the idea for the first concentration camp in Dachau and later the office of "Inspector of the Concentration Camps" – had sought to ensure from the outset the best possible relations between the Gestapo and Admiral Canaris' Main Division V. Against all expectations, Heydrich was able to bring about close co-operation between the *Reichswehr* and the Nazi police on matters of espionage, at a time when in other spheres there was still much friction between the party and the *Reichswehr*. While relations temporarily cooled following the transformation of *"Sonderbüro Stein"* into the *SD-RFSS* office "for special deployment" (which, incidentally, also led to the incarceration of Herr Stein in the concentration camp Columbiahaus), the scenes of fraternisation orchestrated by Dr Best in the spring of 1935 seemed to go a long way to clearing the air. Together with the Secret State Police, Heydrich's security service controlled all of the party's activities in matters of civil espionage. Thanks to the work of *"Sonderbüro Stein"* a stop had been put to the brutal attacks by hordes of partisans and *SS*-men in the border regions. The transformed *SD-RFSS* office "for special deployment" was dissolved as it had fulfilled its remit as the umbrella organisation for joint espionage and counter-espionage, and its chief (who had been a thorn in Heydrich's side and thus imprisoned) was eventually released, in order to "smooth ruffled feelings", albeit only several months after the alliance between the two grand chiefs.

Nevertheless, Heydrich, highly intelligent though he was, had miscalculated when he thought that he could impress and manipulate the sly fox Canaris (the "geriatric", as Heydrich liked to refer to him derisively). Police Chief Heydrich thought it best to lay his cards on the table, whereas Canaris decided to keep them close to his chest in order to ensure Heydrich's continued "courtship", which was to last well beyond the outbreak of war.

Heydrich made available to Canaris the entire police apparatus. Canaris had always been on good terms with the police, but, thanks to Heydrich's abilities, the Nazi regime's police apparatus had rapidly grown and now far exceeded its size and importance during the times of the Weimar Republic. Canaris made extensive use of Heydrich's offer, but he had no intention of reciprocating by disclosing to Heydrich all the secrets of Main Division V in the *Reichswehrministerium*; instead, from the outset, he would make information available only on a case-by case basis. Admiral Canaris remained as the undisputed leader of German military espionage, and Heydrich played no significant part in that leadership. Conversely, however, Canaris did secure for himself a significant say in all matters of civil espionage, to the extent that Heydrich could never claim to be the sole leader of that branch. The situation is clearly characterised in the distribution of roles of a later joint creation (which will be reported on in more detail later), namely the Fifth Column. (It is worth noting, by the way, that the designation "Fifth Column" was never in official use.)

Nevertheless, in his capacity as chief of the *SD-RFSS*, Heydrich did hold an important trump card in his hand, which he would frequently use against Admiral Canaris. The Admiral himself was astounded at Heydrich's skill in deploying that trump, and would often compliment his "young colleague" on his ingenuity. At times, Heydrich's trump card was indeed worth more than the entire "deck of cards", i.e. Admiral Canaris' espionage apparatus. Heydrich's unique asset was the so-called "Cross-national Cultural Association", and the way Heydrich's *SD-RFSS* shaped, expanded and corrupted it. The fact that this "Cross-national Cultural Association" would form a significant component of the publicly much-debated "Fifth Column" was sadly completely overlooked abroad.

Before reporting on the "Cross-national Cultural Association", we would like to make the following observation:

In the spring of 1936 – shortly before Himmler's appointment as the "Chief of the German Police" (with Kurt Daluege as deputy and "Chief of the Regular Police Force" and Heydrich as "Chief of the Security Police" and thereby chief of all German criminal police forces) – that notorious "social evening" took place in the "House of the Aviators" in Berlin's Prinz-Albrecht-Strasse. Immediately afterwards, Heydrich issued an order via police radio to all Gestapo department heads, demanding "closest comradely co-operation" in all espionage matters with all *Reichswehr* offices. Heydrich was exactly the sort of man who was able to enforce the strictest compliance with such an order. While it had been commonplace even during the Weimar Republic for an officer from the *Reichswehrministerium* to be present at important interrogations of spies and traitors where there was any suspicion of "betrayal of military secrets", that officer would always play the role of "that taciturn civilian in the background" whose cover was not to be blown under any circumstances by the interrogating officials. (The same script was followed at interrogations carried out by an investigating judge or a public prosecutor!) Now, however, Admiral Canaris' officers, disguised as civilians, would often intervene resolutely in the Gestapo interrogations. Furthermore, every officer had the right to immediately demand a copy of the transcript of the interrogation; previously such documents had only been made available through official channels and after the conclusion of the police investigation. The officers of the Main Division V in the *Reichswehrministerium* not only came and went as they pleased at all provincial offices of the Secret State Police, but they even made themselves rather "at home" in the offices of the Secret Police's Main Division III. On the other hand, if ever a Gestapo officer would attend an office at the *Reichswehrministerium* in official espionage matters, he would be politely received as a "visitor", but there was certainly no notion of the Gestapo man "feeling at home" at the ministry. The Gestapo men, whose demeanour within their own offices was so overbearing and high-handed, would turn into tame and gentle lambs at the *Reichswehrministerium*, the Ministry of War or the provincial *Wehrmacht* offices. This was the reality between 1936 and 1940 and remained the case until Heydrich's death.

The "Cross-National Cultural Association"

Nominally, the Cross-National Cultural Association was an umbrella organisation of all foreign cultural associations within Germany, whose aim it was to promote the "exchange of cultural ideas". Much was made of the "protection of foreign cultural heritage" by the German side, and German scholars and researchers as well as their foreign colleagues living in Germany were called upon to make themselves available for the "lofty ambitions" of the Cross-national Cultural Association. Indeed, many renowned artists and scholars were among the members of the various national branches of the Cross-national Cultural Association, often taking leading roles in the managing committees. The official objective of the project was "a lively cultural exchange for the purpose of the establishment of friendly relations and becoming acquainted with one another".

The individual cultural associations certainly were not the creation of the Nazi regime. Even under the Weimar Republic, they had played an important role in society; for instance, the German-American cultural association "Carl Schurz Club" had done important work fostering German-American cultural relations and was held in high esteem both in Germany and in America. German university professors were invited to give lectures for the "Carl Schurz Club" in the United States, well-known American personalities came to Germany to be introduced by the "Carl Schurz Club" to a select audience, educational trips were organised and scholarships given for mutual exchange of students, and charitable foundations were established. In the same way that the "Carl Schurz Club" aimed to foster honest German-American cultural exchange, all the other cultural associations promoted similar ideals. That was the situation during the Weimar Republic.

The Nazi regime very soon started to take an interest in the existing cultural associations. Not only did it allow the continued existence of the associations that had been established during the Weimar Republic, but it expanded them, made increased amounts of public money available, and finally centralised them in the department entitled Cross-national Cultural Association. As before, lectures and soirées were organised, at which a decidedly "civilised" and genteel atmosphere prevailed. These gatherings continued to be social events of the first order, with elite member from the various state institutions, the *Wehrmacht* and the party attending in the company of their wives.

As has been reported, the new masters of the state, the prominent leaders and senior members of the NSDAP, initially found it very difficult to become socially acceptable and to gain access to the salons of the so-called "refined society". Yet – it has to be said again and again – eventually it became *de rigueur* not just to be an ordinary party member or to hold a position within the plebeian *SA*, but to gain membership of the *SS* or the *NSKK*, the National Socialist Motor Corps. After the Röhm revolt of 1934, formerly decidedly conservative personalities increasingly attended "events of the refined society" dressed in the becoming black uniform of the *SS*, and the *Reichsführer SS* put ever greater store on the practice of bestowing "honourable membership of the *SS*" on distinguished personalities, with the awarded rank reflecting the individual's social standing. Even a man such as Alfred Hugenberg was made "honorary" *SS-Standartenführer*. At the same time, officers of the *Wehrmacht* were awarded the Blood Order of the NSDAP, which actually was supposed to be reserved for participants of the Munich putsch in 1923. Thus the new chief of the *Wehrmacht*, General Keitel, was awarded the party's Blood Order, and he wore it proudly, like a front officer wears a medal earned in combat.

Berlin's cultural associations, which indeed had a decisive influence on social life in the city, had always counted many *Reichswehr* officers (usually well-known representatives from the *Reichswehrministerium* and the *Reichswehr* leadership) amongst their members. From the autumn of 1934 onwards, the new leaders of state and party, clad in the uniforms of the SS, would appear alongside the *Reichswehr* officers at events organised by the cultural associations. And before long, even some retired, venerable military men quite unashamedly put on the uniforms of the *Reichsführer SS*, thus offering their services to the party, purely for personal gain.

Through the creation of the department "Cross-national Cultural Association", the cultural associations were tightly organised and centralised. The men who occupied leadership roles were left in their positions wherever possible; they were simply clothed in dapper, black *SS* uniforms and assigned reliable party members as their deputies.

SS-Gruppenführer Werner Lorenz, a man of suave manners and handsome appearance, who was until that point little known among the general public, was appointed as the president of the Cross-national Cultural Association. He was a close associate of Heinrich Himmler, a member of the staff of the *Reichsführer SS* (as was Ribbentrop), and – more importantly – a close friend of Reinhard Heydrich, the chief of the Gestapo and the *SD-RFSS*. For many years, the close co-operation between the leader of the Cross-national Cultural Association and both the *SD-RFSS* and Gestapo remained a well-guarded secret. Only in August 1939 was the department "Cross-national Cultural Association" officially affiliated with the *SD* Main Office, and even then the general public – especially abroad – took very little notice of that important fact.

SS-Gruppenführer Lorenz made a decisive contribution to the activities of the so-called Fifth Column in all countries, for it was only because of his work, which proved to be so successful for the Nazi regime, that Heydrich, Himmler and Best were able to use the Cross-national Cultural Association for extensive espionage and subversion activities, and to deploy the purported "exchange of cultural ideas" as a means to render a nation "ripe for attack". All such operations took place in downright cordial co-operation between *SD* chief Heydrich and the *Reichswehrministerium's* espionage chief Canaris. It would be entirely wrong to one-sidedly make Heydrich-Himmler-Best and their functionary Werner Lorenz responsible for the abuse of the Cross-national Cultural Association. Admiral Canaris, the entire leadership of the *Wehrmacht* and the German general corps misused the association with equal shamelessness and were deeply complicit in making the Cross-national Cultural Association a primary tool of German espionage. Canaris, the "grumpy old bear", on several occasions lavished rare praise on the "ingenious chess move" thought up by his "young colleague", that is to say, the tactical move of involving Werner Lorenz and the Cross-national Cultural Association. On such occasions Canaris would go as far as calling Heydrich a "hell of a guy".

On August 21, 1939, a reception was given for English archaeologists at the Hotel Esplanade in Berlin by the German-British Society. (Incidentally, on the same night the signing of the German-Russian friendship pact was announced). In one corner of the large ceremonial hall a dignified British scholar was engaged in a conversation with a young man in *SS* uniform, who listened to him politely and modestly. Mr Ross (the Third Secretary of the British Embassy, who had only recently been transferred to Berlin), sipping a glass of Scotch, asked his colleague Mr [Neville Meyrick] Harrison [later Sir; 1882-1942] (the First Embassy Secretary) [subsequently Ambassador]: "Who is that nobody over there, listening so intently to Professor X?" That "nobody" was none other than *SS-Gruppenführer* Werner Lorenz, who at that time had already made all preparations for the deployment of the Cross-national Cultural Association as the "Fifth Column". [*Note: Mr. Ross was probably the subsequently knighted diplomat Sir Archibald David Manisty Ross, 1911-1996, who later became Ambassador to Portugal, 1961-1966, and Ambassador to Sweden, 1966-1971.*]

Apart from Werner Lorenz, the following persons held leadership positions at the Cross-National Cultural Association:

Dr [Axel] Springer (First Vice President), and
Dr Heinevetter (Second Vice President);
both of whom were members of the *SD-RFSS*.
[*Note: Werner Lorenz's daughter Rosemarie married Axel Cäsar Springer, the famous publisher (1912-1985). It may be safely presumed that "Dr. Springer" above can only be Axel Springer, which presumably means that Axel Springer's youthful membership in the SD has never previously been recognised.*]

In addition:

Reich Office Director [Walter] Malletke (1884-1944, or some say, 1970) acted as a permanent liaison officer to Alfred Rosenberg's Foreign Office (and his deputies at the Foreign Office, Herr Stechow and Herr Gottlieb).
Herr Gutjahr (Academic Exchange Service),
Dr Kuhn (University Foreign Department),
Legation Councillor Ripgen (Büro Ribbentrop),
Major [Hans-Jürgen Erdmann] von Cramon [von Cramon-Taubadel, 1901-1985] (General Staff),
SS-Brigadeführer [Rolf Egbert] Humann-Hainhofen,
Herr Örtel (*Reich* Youth Leadership),
Senior Councillor [Franz] von Weyssenhoff (Ministry of Propaganda), and his deputy, the Chief of the Foreign Press Department, Senior Councillor Bade.

All these men were well aware of the fact that the Cross-national Cultural Association was being used for espionage purposes, but it is not clear whether Envoy von Twardowski – who, as the Foreign Office's official representative, was a member of the presidium where he was occasionally deputised by Legation Councillor Busse – was equally cognisant of the circumstances. Envoy von Twardowski was the head of the Cultural Policy Department in the Foreign Office.

SS-Gruppenführer Werner Lorenz had installed a personal confidant in every single cultural association, who, through their activities within the association, would organise and monitor all espionage activities. Ideally, that confidant would hold the post of president or vice president, but in many cases long-standing officials had to be left in their leadership positions, either because they were not willing to engage in active espionage or because they were the sort of person with whom one simply would not discuss any espionage matters. In what follows, several important cultural associations will be listed, but it is not possible to claim that all individuals mentioned had been recruited by German espionage with their full knowledge and volition. What is certain, however, is that every single one of them *was* being used for German espionage in one way or another: some unknowingly, others in full knowledge of the fact that they were carrying out crucial espionage tasks. For all members of the *SD-RFSS* there is no doubt that they were fully aware of their services to German espionage.

German-British Society [*Deutsch-Englische Gesellschaft*] [Dissolved in 1939]
President: Herr [Eugen] Lehnkering (member of the *SD-RFSS*).
[*Note: the other President of this organisation had been Duke Carl Eduard of Saxe-Coburg and Gotha.*]

[*Note: There was also an Anglo-German Fellowship, whose President was Ernest William Dalrymple Tennant OBE, 1887-1962, an English merchant banker and industrialist. He was related to the British Intelligence officer of the SOE Sir Peter Frank Dalrymple Tennant, 1910-1996, who was involved in fantastically complex intrigues in the Stockholm and Paris embassies during the War concerning Himmler's secret peace negotiations with the Allies, which are impossible to summarise here and have frankly never been wholly understood or explained, and which Tennant himself said he never entirely comprehended.*]

German-French Society [*Deutsch-Französische Gesellschaft*]

President: *SA-Brigadeführer* [later *SA-Gruppenführer*] [Professor Dr. rer. pol. Achim] von Arnim [died 1940] [*He was also President of the German-Polish Society, or* Deutsch-Polnische Gesellschaft, *and of the German-Italian Society, or* Deutsch-Italienische Gesellschaft.] [*Note: There was a Major Achim von Arnim (1894-1978) who was a Panzer tank commander, clearly a relation, but the exact relationship between the two men of the same name is unknown.*]

[*His Vice President for the French society was Hanns Oberlindober*] Other members of the presidium included: *SS-Brigadeführer* [Rolf Egbert Wennemar Paul Anton Maria von] Humann-Hainofen (member of the *SD-RFSS*), [Heinrich] Otto Abetz [1903-1958] (later ambassador in Paris), [Roland] Krug von Nidda [1895-1968] (later envoy in Vichy, member of the *SD-RFSS*).

Gilbert Arvengas (the *French* Consul General in Hamburg) was seen as being especially close to Lorenz until his transfer to the French Foreign Ministry in the spring of 1939. [*Note: In 1946 Gilbert Arvengas was appointed to be the French Ambassador to Egypt.*]

FRENCH AMBASSADOR IN CAIRO: M. GILBERT (SECOND FROM LEFT) AFTER BEING RECEIVED BY KING FAROUK.

an Foreign Ministry announced on November 24 that
ın Legation in Paris and the French Legation in Cairo
ised to the status of Embassy. To mark the occasion
appointment in Cairo, the Ambassador, M. Gilbert
visited King Farouk, and presented his Letters of
ce. He is shown leaving after the ceremony.

Gilbert Avengras is second from left in this photo taken after the ceremony of presentation of his credentials to King Farouk in November of 1946 as the new French Ambassador to Egypt. At the same time, the French Legation at Cairo was raised to the status of an Embassy. According to the author, Avengras became close to Werner Lorenz during the time he was the French Consul General in Hamburg in the 1930s, and the implication is that the sympathies of Avengras were pro-German.

Heinrich Otto Abetz carried out espionage for Germany as a member of the praesidium of the German-French Society, coordinating his activities with the author's colleague and friend Werner Lorenz of the SD-RFSS. Abetz was the head of the German espionage network in France, and he later became Germany's Ambassador to France. He died in 1958 in a car crash.

German-American "Carl Schurz" Society

[*Technically, the National Carl Schurz Association, established in 1930 as the Carl Schurz Memorial Foundation and named after a famous German-American politician of the 19th century; commencing in 1934 this society published* The American-German Review. *One of the initial founders of this society was the banker Paul M. Warburg. It was supported by the Oberländer Trust founded by Gustav Oberländer (1867-1936). Its name in German was* Vereinigung Carl Schurz.]

Honorary President: Colonel von Giese [*sic: should be Gise*]

[*Note: This is apparently Group Colonel Baron (Freiherr) Ernst August Maximilian Josef von Gise, 1888-1945; Gise and Giese are pronounced exactly the same. During the War, he commanded a somewhat mysterious Divisonal Group described as a* Sicherungsregiment, *meaning 'safety regiment' or 'security regiment'; it is not at all clear what their purpose was.*] President (?): *Generalarbeitsführer* [Wolf-Dietrich] Freiherr Löffelholz von Colberg [sometimes aka Kolberg] Vice President: Dr. [Hans] Dräger (a confidant of Lorenz).

Dr. Hans Dräger (1896-date of death unknown, probably escaped after the War to a location abroad under an assumed name, possibly Sweden where he knew all the important local Nazi sympathisers). By 1930 he was effectively the real head of the Carl Schurz Association in America. Despite having been active on behalf of Nazism for some time, not least as a major spy for Germany before the Nazis came to power, he officially joined the Nazi Party in 1932. By 1933 he was the Head of the Scandinavian Friendship Association in Berlin, and later became the President of the German-Swedish Association (*Deutsch-Schwedische Vereinigung e. V.*) in Berlin. By 1933 he became Head of the Foreign Division of the Propaganda Ministry. In 1933 he also published the book *The Versailles Treaty, the Basic Cause of the German Calamity* (in German). During the War he ran the office of Reichsminister of the Interior, Dr. Wilhelm Frick. Dräger was thus probably the most important person in the Nazi hierarchy for conceiving and coordinating propaganda and disinformation for foreign consumption. (Bundesarchiv)

German-Belgian Society [*Deutsch-Belgische Gesellschaft*] President: Dr Otto (Mayor of Düsseldorf and member of the *SD-RFSS*]

[*Note: He was Dr. Dr. Gustav Matthieu Helmut Otto, 1892-1974, who was Mayor of Düssseldorf from 1937 to 1939. He was both a Doctor of Law and a Doctor of Medicine. He became Reich Commissioner for Warsaw after the German occupation of Poland, and from mid-June 1940 until 1944 he acted as the Chief Medical Doctor to the Wehrmacht in Brussels, and in early May 1945 to the Hamburg Medical Corps. He was imprisoned until July, 1948.*] Vice President: (retired) General Vogt [possibly Voigt]

[*Note: Identity uncertain, but this may be Major General Hans Voigt, 1896-1969, who reported directly to Heinrich Himmler, and about whom little information survives, even his Knights Cross of the Iron Cross having been bestowed upon him privately at the age of 73 by Himmler on April 28,*

1945 (why?), and never entered into the official records; this was only two days before the death of Hitler and suggests that Voigt's presence in Berlin then and intimacy with Himmler meant that he had a highly important secret status which was kept out of the official records, as was the case also with our author.]

Dr Fonck (a Belgian national, Director General of the Brussels Trade Fair) was seen as a close confidant of Werner Lorenz.

[Presumably André Charles Albert Fonck, born February 15, 1917. His connection with the British SOE commenced in 1939 and in connection with an operation called "the Balaclava Mission" in Belgium in 1942. Perhaps he was a double agent, in which case his primary employer would be the Germans, and he would have been an infiltrator of the SOE. His files should be examined. They were officially closed until 2017, and have not been digitised. The author would probably have known him personally, because of his close connection with Werner Lorenz.]

German-Dutch Society [Deutsch-Niederländische Gesellschaft]

Honorary President: Duke Adolf Friedrich von Mecklenburg (Herzog zu Mecklenburg-Schwerin; 1873-1969) (the brother of the late prince consort of the Queen of the Netherlands)

President: Undersecretary Freiherr von Rheinbaben

[Presumed to be Wilhelm Louis Alfons Victor Freiherr von Rheinhaben, 1884-1957.]

Also in the presidium: Herr Ebert (from Alfred Rosenberg's Foreign Office, Lorenz's confidant).

[Note: The Duke of Mecklenburg-Schwerin above was also Vice President of the German Colonial Society for Southwest Africa.]

German-South African Society [Deutsch-Sudafrikanische Vereinigung

President: Professor [Dr Ing.] Hermann Bohle *[Father of the SS official Ernst Wilhelm Bohle, 1903-1960, who was monitored by the British from 1942, who called him Ernest Bohle. Ernst Bohle was Leader of the Foreign Organisation of the Nazi Party from Fenruary 1934 to 1945, also known as the Organisation of Germans Living Abroad* (Auslands-Organisation); *from late 1935, Ernst Bohle also became a member of the Liaison Staff under Rudolf Hess. In fact, Ernst Bohle, who strangely enough was born in Bradford, England, was one of Hess's few intimate friends. Hermann Bohle was a naturalised British subject who lived in Capetown. He formed the first Nazi spy cell in South Africa in 1932, so that the German-South African Society became the centre of German espionage effort in South Africa. In 1933 he was made Territorial Group Leader. But because Bohle was considered too cautious, his place was taken by Major Heinrich Weigel, who lived in Windhoek and was the Head of the South African Nazi Party, which Weigel had founded as early as 1929]*.

Also in the presidium: Dr [Werner] Schmidt-Prätoria [aka Schmid-Pretoria; 1902-1991; he was born Werner Schmidt, but he adopted the pseudonym Werner Schmidt-Pretoria] (Lorenz's confidant). *[The author would have known him personally, as Lorenz was the author's close colleague. Werner Schmidt-Pretoria, under that spelling, published several books about South Africa.]*

Ibero-American Society:

President: Ambassador General [Wilhelm Freiherr von] Faupel [1873-1945, suicide] (a personal friend of Admiral Canaris). [*Note: Faupel was a military advisor in both Argentina and Peru for seven years after World War One, and his Spanish was later to be useful for his activities in Spain.*]

Berliner Illustrirte Zeitung

FESTTAG in SALAMANCA

Nach der feierlichen Diensteinführung des deutschen Botschafters bei der spanischen Nationalregierung.

Auf dem Balkon des berühmten Rathauses von Salamanca: General Franco und General Faupel danken mit erhobenem Arm für den jubelnden Empfang.

Lieutenant General Baron Wilhelm von Faupel (1873-1945, suicide with wife in Berlin) standing on the balcony beside Franco in Salamanca and giving the fascist salute upon becoming Germany's Ambassador to Spain in 1937. He had become the head of the Ibero-American Institute in Berlin early in 1934, which he transformed from a scholarly institute concerned with Latin American culture into an organisation devoted to penetrating the whole of Latin America in the interest of the Nazi state, and he expanded the Institute to cover also Spain, in order to bring Franco's fascists into it, including Spanish industrialists, bankers, army officers, and prominent personalities who were suporters of Franco. The Institute then became an instrument of the SS and the Gestapo not only for espionage purposes, but also for establishing links and transactions with countries such as Argentina and Uruguay, where Nazi colonies would later be formed. Faupel himself, as a friend of Canaris, worked closely with the Abwehr in his espionage work.

German-Iranian Society

President: Privy Councillor Flach

Also in the presidium:

Herr Schneider (Director of the Mellieh Bank, member of the *SD-RFSS*)

[*Note: Mellieh Bank is now called Bank Melli Iran. It is interesting that this Iranian bank had as a director a member of the German security services. There is still a Schneider working for that bank in Germany today, though that must be a pure coincidence. In Iran today there is a company, Schneider MCB Exporters, also apparently another coincidence. The identity of Herr Schneider is not established.]*

Herr Phillips (President of the Oriental Association, member of the *SD-RFSS*).

German-Bulgarian Society [Deutsch-Bulgarische Gesellschaft]

President: *SS-Gruppenführer* and retired General Freiherr Ewald [Robert Valentin] von Massow (member of the staff of the *Reichsführer SS*, Lorenz's confidant) (1869-1942, heart failure]

Vice President: *SS-Brigadeführer* [Rolf] von Humann-Hainhofen (1885-1961) (also a member of the presidium of the Cross-national Cultural Association and a member of the German-French Society, member of the *SD-RFSS*).

German-Yugoslav Society [Deutsch-Jugoslawische Gesellschaft]

President: Professor [Dr. Dr. Emil Heinrich] Meyer

Vice President: Admiral [Albrecht] Freiherr von Freyberg [Freyberg-Eisenberg-Allmendingen, 1876-1943] (a close friend of the espionage chief Canaris)

Also in the presidium: Ministerial Director [Walter] Gramsch (born 1897). *[He went over to the Communists of East Germany and spied against his former colleagues in the Gehlen Organisation after the War.]*

German-Hungarian Society [Deutsch-Ungarische Gesellschaft]

Director in Vienna: retired Minister [Professor Doctor Edmund] Glaise-Horstenau (1882-1946, suicide)

Edmund Glaise-Horstenau (1882-1946, suicide). The Austrian Nazi who was Director in Vienna of the German-Hungarian Society, through which he supervised espionage in Hungary. Under pressure from Hitler, Chancellor Kurt Schuschnigg of Austria appointed him in 1938 Austria's Vice Chancellor. Shortly afterwards, the Anschluss happened. He then became a General in the Army (Wehrmacht) and was appointed Plenipotentiary General to Croatia. He was horrified however at the terrible atrocities committed by the Croatian Ustaše fascist regime and attempted to overthrow them, but failed. He was removed from his post on September 25, 1944, hated by both the Nazis and the Croatian fascists. Six months later he was captured by American forces but committed suicide rather than be sent back to Croatia where torture and death awaited him.

Director in Berlin: Admiral [Albrecht] Freiherr von Freyberg (1876-1943). (also Vice President of the German-Yugoslav Society).

Vice Admiral Baron (*Freiherr*) Albrecht von Freyberg-Eisenberg-Allmendingen (1876-1943). He was the Berlin Director of the German-Hungarian Society and Vice-President of the German-Yugoslav Society, which infiltrated Gestapo spies into Hungary and Yugoslavia. (Hungary's President Miklós Horthy, who was technically Regent of the Kingdom of Hungary, was an Admiral so perhaps that is why Freyberg was chosen for his role in the German-Hungarian Society, so that he and the Hungarian president could chat about maritime matters and make Horthy feel good.)

This list is not intended to be exhaustive. It corresponds to the actual state of affairs in the summer of 1939; that is to say, just before the outbreak of war.

It is beyond doubt that without the subversive activities of the listed societies, centrally co-ordinated by the Cross-national Cultural Association, the rapid conquests of Holland, Belgium, France, Yugoslavia, Hungary etc. would not have been possible. An entire tome could be written detailing the espionage activities carried out by the Cross-national Cultural Association.

According to remarks made by Werner Lorenz, it was entirely thanks to the espionage and subversive activities carried out by the German-Bulgarian Society that it was possible to annex Bulgaria without active combat, merely by steadily "infiltrating" the country with German troops. Following preparatory work by the German-Iranian Society, it was possible to foment an insurgence in Persia, after the "Oriental Association" and a bank owned by the *SD* member Schneider provided the necessary slush funds.

Through their functionary Werner Lorenz, the trio of Heydrich, Himmler and Best (Dr Werner Best at that time still was Heydrich's deputy) had transformed the Cross-national Cultural Association into an effective tool for civil espionage. Without the Cross-national Cultural Association, the activities of the so-called "Fifth Column" would have been almost impossible to carry out. In actual fact, the fictitious "Fifth Column" in essence was nothing more than the practical exploitation of the espionage activities carried out by the Cross-national Cultural Association. Admiral Canaris, too, had reason to be satisfied with the work of the Cross-national Cultural Association, for his military espionage apparatus also benefited greatly from its operations.

The German-Polish Society, against which the Polish counter-intelligence, the so-called "Defensive", fought a futile battle, is missing from the above list. Despite clearly recognising the toxic nature of the German-Polish Society, the "Defensive" was unable to constrain its activities for a long time due to the existence of the German-Polish friendship pact. When that pact was officially breached, it was too late. In an act of brazen shamelessness – indeed, it was seen as an "honourable" course of action – in late October 1939, after the seizure of Poland, the Nazis awarded the golden NSDAP party badge to the snoopers within that society. *SS-Gruppenführer* Werner Lorenz had his photograph taken with his stalwarts: Herr Weiss from the Jarotschin [Jarocin] office, Herr Ulitz from Katowitz [Katowice], Ludwig Wolff (1908-?) from Lodz [Łódź], Herr [Rudolf Ernst] Wiesner (1890-1973) from Bielitz [Bielsko-Biala], and the two "leaders of ethnic Germans in Poland", Dr [Dr. Jur. Hans Joachim] Kohnert (1905-1972) [*who joined the SS in 1938 and who later became the Landesbauernführer of Poznan under German occupation*] and Dr Hasbach, who were both prominent members of the "German-Polish Society", whose German president for a time had been Herr [Rudolf Christoph Freiherr von] von Gersdorff (1905-1980).

Rudolf-Christoph Freiherr von Gersdorff (1905-1980) was President of the German-Polish Friendship Society. As a junior officer, he subsequently took part in the invasion of Poland in 1939. He was an intelligence operative of the Abwehr (German Military Intelligence). In 1943 he personally supervised the excavation of the graves of the Polish officers who had been massacred at Katyn by the Soviets. Gersdorff was an opponent of Hitler and was one of the few memers of the July plot to kill Hitler who managed to avoid detection and thus survived. After the War, he tried to join the German Army but was refused because they considered him a "traitor" for having plotted to kill Hitler. He co-operated with the Americans on historical work and archives concerning the War. His memoirs were published in 1982, two years after his death. Pfeifer knew all the details of the German espionage against Poland intimately, as he had personally made a fake defection to the Poles prior to the invasion, was hosted by the Polish General Staff and given a Polish passport. It is unknown whether he knew Gersdorff personally, but he certainly knew all about him and every aspect of the functioning of the German-Polish Society, which is why he has given it special attention here. (Bundesarchiv)

Dr. Rudolf Ernst Wiesner (1890-1973), born at Bielitz. One of Werner Lorenz's main German agents in the German-Polish Friendship Society. Under the German occupation of Poland, he was overtly revealed to be an Oberführer in the SS, and he was close to the notorious mass murderer Hans Frank, the German Governor of Poland.

SS Standartenführer and Obersturmführer Ludwig Wolff (1908-?) of Łodz, who prior to the invasion of Poland was a secret agent for the SS holding the concealed position of a national leader of the German minority in Poland. As early as 1934 he became secret leader of the Deutsche Volksverband in Central Poland. He joined the SS officially as an officer in 1940. He served at the front for two years and was awarded medals, but there is no record of his fate after the War or of his death. (Photo from the *Illustrieter Beobachter*, December 30, 1943.)

Until the outbreak of war, Werner Lorenz had played the role of the "unassuming man in the background" for Heydrich-Himmler-Best, and, as president of the Cross-national Cultural Association enjoyed popularity and a good standing in society. Not many would have thought that this "insignificant young man", who was so polite and modest, would be capable of occupying a decisive role within German espionage. When his position became obsolete with the outbreak of war, Werner Lorenz, who had by then been promoted to the rank of *SS-Obergruppenführer*, was appointed as chief of the "Co-ordination Centre of Ethnic Germans", which was responsible for the "resettlement of ethnic Germans". Given the fact that such "resettlement" usually involved the expulsion and forcible deportation of those of "other races", *SS-Obergruppenführer* Werner Lorenz became one of the men with primary responsibility for the deportation and systematic, large-scale murder of Polish Jews.

Werner Lorenz's Cross-national Cultural Association was affiliated to the *SD* Main Office, while the "Co-ordination Centre of Ethnic Germans" was subordinated to the "*SS* Race and Settlement Main Office".

Werner Lorenz, president of the Cross-national Cultural Association, was an old friend of Alfred Rosenberg, the *Reichsleiter* of the NSDAP Office for Foreign Affairs. They were in constant contact through their various liaison officers and, when Rosenberg was appointed as minister for the occupied Russian territories, the two men forged even closer ties in the context of the "resettlement of ethnic Germans". In any case, through his own field of activity, for which he bore sole responsibility, Werner Lorenz was one of the most heinous exponents of the *SS Reichsführung*. He is not only responsible for the actions of the Fifth Column, but also for all "resettlements", forced deportations and murders that were carried out on his orders.

German foreign correspondents

The work of major newspapers' foreign correspondents has traditionally been taken very seriously. Much like diplomats, journalists had to be licenced and officially accredited by the governments of their host countries. Indeed, their remit is not altogether dissimilar to that of the diplomatic missions of their native countries. It is the diplomat's duty to inform his government on events and the state of affairs in the country where he is accredited, while it is the task of the foreign correspondent to inform the public in his home country by filing reports with his newspaper. Naturally the host country is anxious for the tone of such reporting to be as amicable as possible.

The reporting by foreign correspondents can be inconvenient, especially for nations with military dictatorships; all the more so if a journalist feels compelled to report on disagreeable matters that the host country would rather keep under wraps. At times, however, the journalists' activities are precariously close to espionage (be it industrial espionage or "betrayal of military secrets"), which on occasion results in the expulsion of the foreign correspondent in question. No journalist can be compelled to lift the cover of professional secrecy, that is to say, to betray his sources of information, and therefore expulsion is the only option for the host country.

In the same way that a diplomat (say, an envoy of a democratic nation) must not be labelled a "spy", it is also not permissible to tarnish a journalist with that brush. It is a well-known fact that there exists a professional code of conduct for all foreign correspondents that is internationally accepted, respected and strictly adhered to. The Nazi regime, however, did not give a jot about international codes of conduct – neither in the realm of diplomacy nor that of foreign journalism. Instead, with deliberate disregard for all international norms, it sought to integrate its diplomats and representatives abroad into the German espionage apparatus, and, with a staggering lack of conscience and regrettable success, was able to misuse its foreign correspondents for espionage. There can be no doubt that without the actions of German foreign correspondents the elusive "Fifth Column" would have been much less effective, and that German foreign correspondents were amongst its most important exponents.

Under the dictatorship of Hitler's Third Reich, no piece of journalism was published without the Nazi government's knowledge and approval, and so it would have been perfectly possible to keep secret certain reports filed by foreign correspondents and to reserve them for the sole use of the espionage authorities. But German foreign correspondents were much more than "only" unwitting spies who sent important information to their home country. Many of them were actual intelligence officers and agents – or even members! – of the *SD-RFSS*, who, disguised as foreign correspondents, were tasked with spying out the minor and major weaknesses of leading personalities in their host countries, handing out bribes, corrupting politicians, and frequently brokering lucrative deals with local parliamentarians or leading industrialists.

In carrying out their "cultural mission", German foreign correspondents acted as agents or members of the "Cross-national Cultural Association". For every "cultural association" in Nazi Germany there existed a corresponding organisation in the host country. For instance, the "German-French Society" that existed in Germany was mirrored by an analogous "French-German Society" in France, where the local German foreign correspondent would feel very much "at home". (He would, in fact, actually have been "at home", for the offices of the "French-German Society" were located in the "German House" in Paris!)

It has already been mentioned that German military espionage, run by Vice Admiral Canaris, was actively involved and directly interested in any espionage and subversive activities carried out by Nazi agents abroad. If ever there should be further attempts by German militarists to distance or even absolve themselves of any war guilt at the expense of the Nazis, the following facts should be emphatically restated: German militarism not only knowingly and happily profited from all Nazi activities, but was directly and actively involved in its machinations. This is especially true for the entire field of espionage and subversive operations abroad. If the term "Fifth Column" (which, as is well-known, was never used as an official designation) has any validity at all, it must be remembered that one of the foremost representatives of German militarism, namely Vice Admiral Canaris, was one of the most important initiators and leaders of that "Fifth Column" (as well as any other ancillary schemes described as "activities of the Fifth Column"). During a visit to the *Führer's* headquarters in January 1940 (that is to say, after the outbreak of war), an overjoyed Admiral Canaris declared in a conversation with Legation Councillor Hewel (Ribbentrop's deputy): "Truly, these foreign correspondents are our best sniffer dogs!"

In order to clarify matters, it may be useful to list the names of some of these foreign correspondents, who, as agents of the "Cross-national Cultural Association", were travelling in foreign nations immediately prior to and after the outbreak of war. They were, almost without exception, important operatives of German espionage, and carried out "valuable" and questionable work for that "Fifth Column":

In France:

Roland [Hans] Krug von Nidda [1895-1968], a member of the *SD-RFSS*, active as a "harmless" journalist in France and Belgium as late as summer of 1939; later Hitler's special envoy in Vichy.

Hans E. Friedrich, a German intelligence officer who sent seemingly apolitical cultural reports from France to Berlin. Shortly before the outbreak of war he lived in southern France, after British soil had become too dangerous for him.

[*Note: His identity is uncertain but perhaps he was Hans Eberhard Friedrich, 1907-1980, two of whose brothers, a sister-in-law, and a niece were all journalists.*]

Helen Grund [aka Helen Hessel] (1886-1982) who was engaged in German espionage in Paris, where she wrote her dangerous "fashion columns" for a Berlin newspaper.

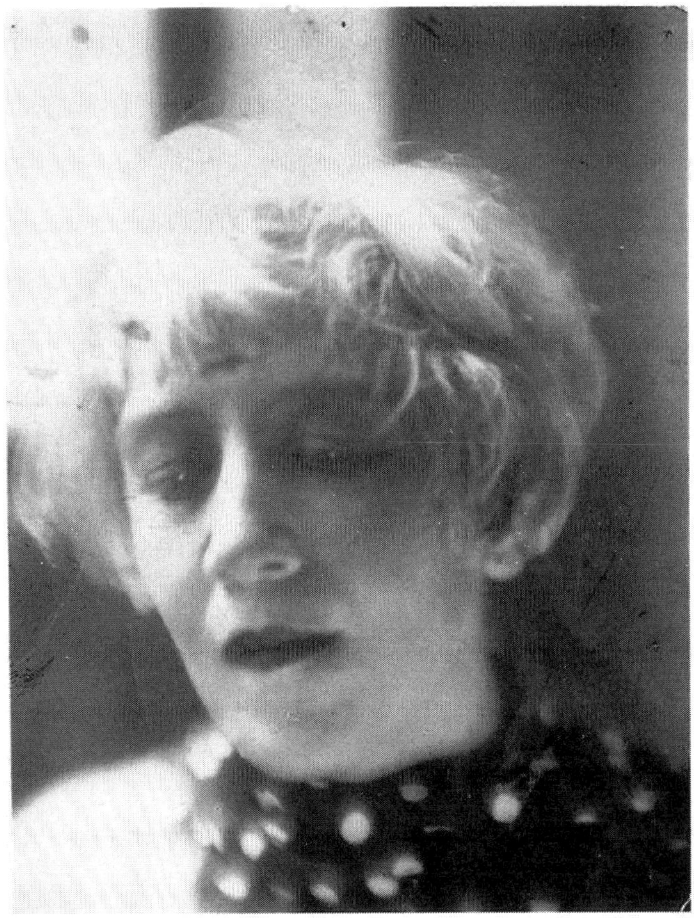

Helen Grund, aka Helen Hessel (1886-1982) was a German spy in Paris disguised as a fashion journalist. From Paris she sent fashion columns to a Berlin newspaper and to the *Frankfurter Zeitung*, and thereby transmitted her information to Germany without any suspicion. She had one real husband and one pretend husband: she married Franz Hessel (born 1880 in Szczecin aka Stettin, Poland) in 1914, and had two children. Hessel translated Marcel Proust into German. Helen "married" secondly (who was in fact merely separated, not divorced, from his first wife in 1933) Henri-Pierre Roché (born 1879 in Paris), died 1959), a poet, playwright, author, translator, early member of the Dada Movement, art collector and friend of Picasso, Duchamp, Picabia, Brancusi, Man Ray, Marie Laurencin, and others. In addition to fashion articles and columns, she also wrote travel articles. Later in life, she translated Nabokov's novel *Lolita* into German. Despite her being secretly a German spy, her son Stéphane Hessel (1917-2013) was arrested in 1944 under the German occupation as an active member of the Resistance and sent to Buchenwald Concentration Camp. She and her two husbands had a long-standing love triangle relationship which was the inspiration for Francois Truffaut's famous film *Jules et Jim*, in which she was played by Jeanne Moreau. (Truffaut took the story from her second husband Roché's autobiographical novel of the same title.) This has been discussed in several books in both French and German. She died at the age of 96 and was buried near her home in the 14th District of Paris, in the Montparnasse Cemetery amongst the many famous literary and artistic figures whom she had known in her long life.

This is probably the most popular photo taken from Francois Truffaut's film *Jules et Jim* (1962). Jeanne Moreau, at left, portrays Helen Hessel, having drawn a false moustache on her face, and she wears a jaunty cap. The three characters are racing across a bridge in one of their many mad antics. The actor in the centre is Henri Serre, who plays "Jim" (Henri-Pierre Roché), and at right is Oskar Werner, who plays "Jules" (Franz Hessel). The film was a huge international success, and the entire world audience was fascinated at this intimate portrayal of a *ménage à trois.*

The cover of a biography of Helen Hessel, the title of which in English is *Helen Hessel, the Woman who Loved Jules and Jim.*

Henri-Pierre Roché, the real "Jim", in a fun-loving mood, similar to some of the carefree scenes in the film.

The real Jules and Jim together. At left is "Jules", Franz Hessel, and at right is "Jim", Henri-Pierre Roché.

Franz Hessel, husband of Helen.

Clemens Heschhaus, who was able to pen exceptionally beautiful feuilletons but in truth was spying for the *SD-RFSS* in France.

In England:

Dr [Baron] Kurt von Stutterheim, who posed as an anti-Nazi activist in London, but actually was one of the most successful informers for the *"Büro Ribbentrop"*. In the summer of 1939 he relocated his activities to Canada, in order to "test the waters" for Herr von Ribbentrop. His last report, before the outbreak of war, was sent from Edmonton in the province of Alberta.

A portrait photo of Kurt von Stutterheim and his wife. According to the author, he was the leading Nazi spy in London until the summer of 1939, at which date he moved to Canada, working as a travelling journalist, and thence onwards to South Africa and Australia. This photo is courtesy of the Australian Government's official portrait archives.

Fritz von Globig [1911-1990], who supplied both Admiral Canaris and the *"Büro Ribbentrop"* with important intelligence.

Hans E. Friedrich, a German intelligence officer who, as mentioned above, had to get out of London, relocating his activities to France in the spring of 1939. [*He was apparently Hans Eberhard Friedrich, 1907-1980, author, journalist and translator.*]

In Ireland:

Carl Heinz [Edwin Ernst] Petersen [*alternatively, Karl-Heinz*] (born 1912 in Hamburg), an important agent of German espionage in Dublin at the outbreak of war, well disguised as a German foreign correspondent.

[*note: Listed as Karl Heinz Petersen, he was posted to Dublin as a journalist in 1939 ostensibly representing the German newspaper the* Deutsche Allgemeine Zeitung. *He later became the Press Attaché at the German Legation in Dublin, was known to be definitely a Nazi and "a notorious propaganda agent" in the bulky 56-page file about him now numbered as KV 2/2094 in the National Archives at Kew. He was under the most intense observation, and the documentation concerning him is very extensive. Including a copy of his passport, letters to his parents in Germany, press cuttings about his marriage to an Irish girl, etc. He remained in Ireland after the War.]*

In Spain:

Heinz [F.] Barth [1910-1974], a member of the *SD-RFSS*, whose provocative actions as a foreign correspondent in Madrid and Burgos were so blatant that the Spanish government soon realised he was an important agent of German espionage.

In Cape Verde:

Dr G. [Georg] Thimm, who, as a well-disguised foreign correspondent, was one of the most able German chief agents for Admiral Canaris. [*Note: During the 1930s he was elected as a member of Parliament for Danzig.*]

In Denmark:

E. Rose and Karla [Alexandra] Hõcker [1901-1992], who posed as feature writers while playing a decisive role in the preparations for the German attack on Denmark.

In Turkey:

Martin Bethke, who, at the direct orders of the *SD-RFSS* in Berlin, and bypassing Ambassador Franz von Papen's espionage department, carried out espionage in Ankara. [*Martin Bethke was apparently born June 5, 1907.*]

In the Middle East:

Count [*Graf*] C. E. [Carl Erdmann] Pückler [1906-1941], a busy foreign correspondent, who variously popped up in Jerusalem, Tehran or Syria, and was seen as a "master spy" by the authorities in Berlin. [*He had also been a London Correspondent.*]

P. [Petra] W. Vermehren [correctly: Wilhelmina Petra Vermehren, though called Petra; 1893-1971, née Schwabroch], who, disguised as a journalist, was a very able purveyor of information. She was active in Iran after the outbreak of war, after performing "valuable tasks" in Greece. She was held in high esteem in Admiral Canaris' office. [She was a foreign correspondent in Athens, in Istanbul, and by 1941 Lisbon. Her activities in Iran seem to be unrecorded elsewhere. She was married to the lawyer Kurt Vermehren, 1885-1962, with whom she had three children.]

Dr Paul Schmitz, a foreign correspondent and one of the most prominent members of the *SD-RFSS*. He carried out several "special missions" in Egypt and Palestine, from where he was expelled twice "under protest".

[*Note: Paul Schmitz was sent to Saudi Arabia by the Gestapo to assist the Grand Mufti of Jerusalem in setting up a shadow Nazi Government which could administer the "German Middle East" on behalf of Nazi Germany. The Muslim Brotherhood, so generously subsidised by the Nazis, was to provide the civil service for this enterprise. Anti-Semitism was to be the criterion for acceptance into that civil service.*]

H. G. [Hans Georg] von Studnitz [1907-1993], who composed "delightful" articles for the *"Berliner Lokalanzeiger"* and travelled the Middle East on Admiral Canaris' orders.

In Bulgaria:

Albert Nachbaur, a member of the *SD-RFSS*, who engaged in "lively" journalistic activities in Bulgaria.

Georg Engelbert Graf [1881-1952], who posed as a harmless journalist but in reality carried out essential preparatory tasks for the "infiltration" of Bulgaria by German troops. [*He posed for most of his life as a Social Democrat but was really a Nazi spy.*]

Georg Engelbert Graf (1881-1952). The Nazi spy who posed all his life as a Social Democrat. While doing journalism as a cover, he helped prepare the way for the German occupation of Bulgaria.

In Poland:

Max [Walter] Clauss [1901-1988], a journalist who had come to Warsaw in 1939 with Ribbentrop, but only showed his true character after the German attack on Poland. [*In 1952, he published the book* The Road to Yalta: Calling President Roosevelt to Account (in German).]

In South America:

[Count/*Graf*] Dieter [Werner Albrecht] von der Schulenburg and Hannes D. Rahs, who both travelled around South America under the guise of journalism and carried out important secret missions for Herr von Ribbentrop. [*Note: He was possibly Johannes Rahs born May 21, 1886, at Remagen, son of Christoph Rahs (born 1860) and Anna Gertrud Haas (1863-1942)*].

These are but a few of the German foreign correspondents who played decisive roles in

German espionage and made important contributions to the preparations for war. They were not always able to act as exponents of the "Fifth Column", as this was not a possibility everywhere, nor always the intention of the central leadership in Berlin. One thing, however, is certain: when using the term "Fifth Column", one must never underestimate the role foreign correspondents played in its activities.

We should point out an important characteristic of these German foreign correspondents: most of them were not longstanding party members of the NSDAP, but instead came from archconservative circles. As their positions and standing became increasingly under threat, they became ever more willing tools of the Nazi regime. As former non-National Socialists, they were all the more useful for well-disguised espionage operations.

Two examples:

A dress rehearsal for the "method of conquest": the Saarland

The "conquest" of the Saarland by National Socialism is a textbook example of Nazi subversion, espionage, incitement and entrapment, and the process of rendering a nation "ripe for attack" employed by the Nazi espionage apparatus. At the same time, it is also a prime example of how the Nazi clique itself was riddled with intrigue and defamation.

At the point of "seizure of power", the Saarland was still under the control of the League of Nations, which had installed an interim government under the leadership of the British diplomat [Sir] Geoffrey [George] Knox (1884–1958), with the Frenchman Heimburger acting as police chief. With the onset of Nazi terror in 1933, many honest Germans fled to the Saarland, where some of them found temporary employment thanks to their good relations with the Social Democratic party of the Saarland. For example, *Reichstag* member [Heinrich] Georg Ritzel [*a Social Democrat*], the former mayor of Michelstadt and later Senior Councillor in Giessen, was appointed as chief of the customs investigation office in Saarland; a Social Democrat police officer from Berlin by the name of Machts [or perhaps Macht] became a police lieutenant in Saarland; and Emil Kirschmann, department head at the Prussian Ministry for Interior and Social Democrat member of the regional assembly, established himself in the offices of the newly launched newspaper *"Die Freiheit"* ("Freedom"), which was the mouthpiece of Max Braun (a.k.a. "Matz"), the leader of the Social Democrats in Saarland. [*Mathias Josef Braun, aka Max Braun and Matz Braun, 1892-1945 in England.*]

Briefly, the situation in Saarland was this:

Until Hitler's assumption of power, the Saarland's Social Democrats and *Zentrum* party (which was very powerful thanks to highly influential local Christian trade unions) *supported* the joining of the Saarland with Germany. However, following Hitler's seizure of power and the ensuing terror in Germany, they had to reverse their position and now argued *against* joining. They hoped to be able to create a "status quo" by seeking the support of the French, and perhaps by keeping in place an Allied governmental commission.

The French had some interests in coal mining in the Saarland (they had established the French mining directorate in the region), but these had been declining for some years. It had become clear that Saarland coal was of inferior quality compared to coal mined in the Ruhr area, and therefore only of limited use for the smelting works in Lorraine. Within the Saarland this fact manifested itself in giant stockpiles of coal for which no buyers could be found.

Even after Hitler's seizure of power, Councillor of Commerce Hermann Röchling, owner of large smelting works in Völklingen and chief of the Röchling Corporation, remained a powerful advocate for the connection of the Saarland to Germany. Much like the French industrialists in Lorraine, he was dependent on coal mined in the Ruhr area, and he was therefore eager for any trade barriers to be removed between himself, that is to say, his smelting works in the Saarland, and the Ruhr area in Germany. Any continued segregation of the Saar area would only be disadvantageous for him. In addition, he was keen to be considered in the awarding of forthcoming large-scale contracts following the re-armament of the German *Wehrmacht*.

The political parties in the Saarland were essentially the same German parties that had existed during the times of the Weimar Republic. As the terms of the League of Nations mandate would not tolerate local parties to exist as mere "sub-branches" of the party headquarters in Berlin, the parties in the Saarland had been forced to become autonomous and to appoint their own leaderships that were independent of Berlin. Of course the NSDAP was among these parties. At first, the NSDAP's responsible *Gauleiter* was the leader of the *Gau* "Saar-Pfalz", Josef Bürckel, who would go on to gain much notoriety. However, he was forced to relinquish control over the Saarland to a separate *Gauleiter* when the youthful hooligan Alois Spaniol, who hailed from Liestal in the Saarland, was appointed as *Gauleiter* of the newly established, separate *Gau* "Saarland". A battle ensued between Göring (Prussia) and Bürckel (Rheinpfalz/ Bavaria), which can best be understood when considering the fact that parts of the Saarland had formerly belonged to Prussia, while other, smaller, regions had been part of the Bavarian Rheinpfalz province.

Prussia's new master, Hermann Göring, appointed the thuggish Spaniol as a Councillor of the State of Prussia and in doing so firmly bound him to his side. Josef Bürckel, the undisputed master of the Palatinate region and at the time known in party circles as "red Bürckel", started his covert battle against Göring-Spaniol. Two things were in his favour:

Firstly, the young *Gauleiter* Spaniol conducted himself in a provocative and offensive manner and thus did not serve the NSDAP well at all, it being in a precarious situation in the Saarland already. Secondly, Bürckel had the considerable advantage of knowing the conditions in the Saarland from his own experience and, as a former leader of the party in the Saarland, had close ties to the region, none of which could be said for Göring. Bürckel received all of his reports at first hand, had messengers and cross-border informants deliver a constant stream of information to him, and counted many leading functionaries of the NSDAP in Saarland among his close friends, who hankered after a return to the Bürckel era, as the stupidity of the new *Gauleiter*, Spaniol, instilled disquiet and alarm in them.

During those times, the Saarland was a hotbed of active espionage both by and against France. In addition to the aforementioned honest Germans who had found refuge and protection in the Saarland, there were large numbers of opportunistic emigrants who not only made themselves available as informers to the French, but were equally happy to be bought by the Nazis for the same purposes. Many became cross-border informants for the German espionage apparatus, making forays into Lorraine and deep into Alsace; that is to say, into the fortified area of the Maginot Line. After a tour of inspection in the Saarland, a then leading espionage functionary paid a visit to *Gauleiter* Bürckel in Neustadt an der Hardt, complaining bitterly about the "pranks" performed by Spaniol and his entourage. He urged Bürckel (and later also the authorities in Berlin) to take decisive steps against the various forms of "espionage at any cost", and against the prevailing culture in which everyone thought they were entitled to engage in their own personal form of espionage, in the process "smashing much valuable porcelain". The complainant was the chief of the aforementioned *"Sonderbüro Stein"*, and his allegations against Spaniol and his henchmen were grist to Josef Bürckel's mill. When Bürckel expressed his powerlessness against Spaniol *et al.* (who enjoyed Göring's support), the chief of *"Sonderbüro Stein"* suggested: "Why don't you simply dissolve the NSDAP and arrange the appointment of a *Reich* Commissioner for German affairs in the Saarland!" As soon as he had heard these words, Bürckel leapt up from his chair and enthusiastically declared his support for the idea. Over the next two days and nights, a meticulous plan was jointly developed, detailing the establishment of a *"Deutsche Front* on the Saar". (That name, incidentally, was not thought of by Bürckel, but instead by Rudolf Hess in Berlin.)

The unlikely pair of Bürckel and the chief of *"Sonderbüro Stein"* [*the author*] travelled to Berlin, and before 24 hours were up the plans were finalised in a luxurious mansion on Berlin's Leipzigerplatz, namely at the offices of Robert Ley, the leader of the German Labour Front and a close friend of Josef Bürckel. Also present were Rudolf Hess and Ley's office manager, Klaus Selzner; and thanks to the initiative of Hess (who was the de facto leader of the NSDAP) the plans were quickly approved by Adolf Hitler. The *"Deutsche Front"* was proclaimed in the Saarland, the NSDAP was dissolved, Spaniol lost both his post and influence, and the *Reich* government installed a *Reich* Commissioner for the Saarland. Against all expectations, however, it was not Josef Bürckel who was appointed as the first *Reich* Commissioner of the Saarland, but the then Vice Chancellor of the *Reich* government, the Catholic Franz von Papen.

Franz von Papen was owner of the firm Villeroy & Boch, which controlled vast quarries in the Saarland. [*This famous company still exists and is thriving, and has an office at Chelsea Harbour in London, and its products for sale at Harrods. It was this company which was Pfeifer's original employer, and which sent him to work in its offices in Madrid and Milan.*] Furthermore, Franz von Papen's family residence was also located in the Saarland, namely in Wallerfangen near Saarlouis.

Front of a postcard sent by Franz von Papen to a friend in America in 1957, with a photo of his house at Wallerfangen. *(Collection of Eglantyne.)*

Back of the postcard.

In his capacity as *Reich* Commissioner, Herr von Papen quickly embarked on a wide variety of activities. He behaved in an exaggerated "Catholic" manner – which, once again, was very damaging for Catholicism itself and only served the interests of National Socialism. He persuaded the *Zentrum* Party to disband and instead to join the *"Deutsche Front"* proclaimed by Berlin and the Nazis. He also won over Labour Secretary Kiefer, an upright Catholic, for the Nazi project *"Deutsche Front"*, and dished out promises to clerics and Catholic Labour functionaries, but equally to representatives of the *Deutsche Volkspartei* and the *"Stahlhelm"* – promises that, one and all, he would not be able to keep. After Herr von Papen had done such "excellent work" for the Nazis in the Saarland, he was recalled as *Reich* Commissioner for the Saarland and in his place *Gauleiter* Josef Bürckel of Neustadt an der Hardt was "finally" appointed as *Reich* Commissioner. It is worth noting that it was neither Spaniol nor Bürckel, but Franz von Papen, who prepared the Saarland for the assault by National Socialism. The Nazi regime consolidated its grip on power in Germany using lies, deception, promises, terrible threats, bluffs and a hitherto unknown level of police terror. The same tools were deployed in the foreign territories the Nazis intended to occupy, and Josef Bürckel was the master craftsman. The system was first applied in the Saarland, and later the process was repeated with great success in Austria. The procedure was the same every time: once the first milestone had been passed and power had fraudulently been seized, terror tactics were deployed in order to consolidate the grip on power. The "official" espionage apparatus, in concert with common informers and denouncers, played a decisive role in the assumption of power in every instance.

Regrettably it would exceed the scope of this book to describe in detail the appalling methods of espionage deployed in the Saarland prior to the referendum on the region's territorial status. A separate book comprising many chapters could be written on the topic. With the help of corrupt police officials, documents were stolen from the secret archives of High Commissioner Geoffrey Knox, copied, and carefully replaced in their original position. It is likely that Mr Knox only became aware of the intrusion by the German espionage apparatus into his offices during the referendum period, when copies of his documents began to be widely circulated. The entire Maginot Line was spied upon from the Saarland, and photocopies of the design plans of all fortifications were sent to Berlin. All French diplomats and all German party members who had not joined the *"Deutsche Front"* were kept under surveillance. Antifascist delegations from the Saarland travelled to League of Nations meetings in Geneva and Paris, and among them sat Nazi agents and German spies who would report on every word spoken amongst the members of the delegations. Every evening, instead of being incinerated, the contents of the waste bin of every provisional member of government were transported across the Saarland's border, and by the next morning would form a neat pile on the desk of the jubilant espionage chief in Berlin.

The Röchling Bank put an authorised signatory at the disposal of the German espionage apparatus for the sole purpose of payment of spies' salaries and bribes. This accredited clerk, a man by the name of Narzissus Quindt, but known to all simply as "Hansi", first became a "V-man" and later a tried-and-tested full member of the *SD-RFSS*, despite the fact that as late as 1933 he had held a leadership position in *"Stahlhelm"*, an organisation with a rather anti-National-Socialist stance.

One incident exemplifying the aforementioned conditions in the Saarland shall be singled out for a more detailed account. The newly appointed chief of the customs investigation office, retired Senior Councillor H. G. [Heinrich Georg] Ritzel, had managed to arrest a *Reichswehr* counter-intelligence officer from Darmstadt, one Major Schneider, in the border town of Homburg.

Major Schneider was more than a little surprised that a German officer could be arrested in the Saarland and that he should suffer this ignominy on "German soil". For months and years he had become accustomed to being able to travel to the Saarland from any other territory of the *Reich* without impediment. Therefore, as a "well-known intelligence officer", he began to disregard the most basic precautionary measures. The chief of the customs investigation office must have been astonished to find a list of 32 (!) names of German spies and Nazi agents in the Major's notebook, complete with their exact addresses in the Saarland. Three of them were prominent spies in the service of Admiral Canaris, the chief of German military espionage, who were based and active in Alsace-Lorraine. Following their exposure, two of them were arrested in Alsace and later shot; only one managed to flee and thus evade arrest.

The Saarland's highest court was the Higher Regional Court in Saarlouis. It was to this court that 29 German intelligence officers and Nazi agents were summoned in the wake of Major Schneider's downright incredible acts of negligence. It was reasonable to assume that all defendants would receive long custodial sentences and that some would be handed over to the French authorities, in order to stand trial at a French military court for military espionage at the Maginot Line. However, the German counter-intelligence authorities and the entire network of Nazi informers in the Saarland were mobilised in order to put pressure not only on all potential judges for the trial, but also the relevant representatives of the prosecuting and investigating authorities for the "Schneider Case" at the Higher Regional Court in Saarlouis. The Röchling Bank made available as slush funds the preliminary sum of one million Francs (then the official currency in the Saarland) to their authorised officer Narzissus Quindt, the man of confidence of German espionage. By the start of the trial, a total of 2.3m Francs had been paid in bribes, which at the time was equivalent to no less than 250,000 *Reichsmark*. Significant promises were made to many individuals; some of which were even kept after the completion of the referendum. After the incorporation of the Saarland, some of the judges involved in the "Schneider case" were rewarded with very senior positions within the *Reich*. Threats were made and several family members of two leading personalities of the Old *Reich* were intimidated. Theses tactics led to the desired result: what was intended to be a sensational trial descended into a ridiculous farce. Using bribed witnesses, a more than questionable proof of innocence was fabricated, and some nominal penalties were imposed. In addition, most of the defendants were given bail and had left detention long before the trial even started.

The entire case, so carefully prepared by H. G. Ritzel, had come to nothing. Corruption had triumphed, and the Nazi spy machine was able to celebrate a victory over the League of Nations and to deride the reliability of the interim administration's civil service.

EUROPA NACH DEM KRIEG

HANS BAUER / H.G.RITZEL

Von der eidgenössischen zur europäischen Föderation

Europa Verlag Zürich/New York

After he defected and fled to Switzerland, H. G. (Heinrich Georg Johannes) Ritzel (1893-1971) published this book with his friend Hans Bauer: *Europe after the War: from a Confederation to a European Union.* His admiration for the League of Nations had been insulted by the bribery and corruption of the Nazis, so he envisaged this possible ideal solution for Europe.

Ritzel and Bauer published this other book in Zurich, the title translated being *Struggle over Europe, as Seen from Switzerland*, in 1945.

The first major instance of "disinformation"
Intelligence officer Major Jerzy Sosnowski steals the "German plans for the invasion of Poland"

Major Jerzy ("Jurek" Ksawery Franciszek) Sosnowski (1896-1944), the Polish master spy. His nickname was "the Black Angel". He carried out one of the greatest possible acts of espionage on behalf of his native Poland, only to have it backfire because he was outwitted, as the author describes in detail. It was the author himself who "cracked the Sosnowski Case", one of the most bizarre of his entire career. Sosnowski was a super-spy who had exposed 54 Nazi agents. After the German occupation of Poland, Sosnowski went to Russia and became an agent of the NKVD spy service to work against the Germans, and was promoted to Colonel. In 1944 he found himself in Warsaw at the time of the Rising, and is believed to have died then, although he may have been executed by the Soviets, and one story says that Nikita Krushchev gave the order for his execution. Like most important spies, Sosnowski had a variety of aliases and pseudonyms and was always wreathed in mystery.

It would be worth describing the "Sosnowski case" in minute detail, but unfortunately we will have to limit ourselves to an outline of its most important aspects. In the summer of 1934, sensational reports were printed in the German-language émigré press in Paris, the Saarland and in Prague, which were soon followed by countless others elsewhere. According to these reports, a Polish spy by the name of Sosnowski had been arrested in Berlin, along with dozens of implicated leading personalities from the capital's "refined society". Film stars, ladies associated with the general corps and even princes of the Hohenzollern dynasty were named, and shocking tales were told about a supposed Persian princess. The Polish spy Sosnowski was celebrated both as a master spy and a womaniser, and the Secret Police was partly ridiculed, partly praised for its "rigorous clampdown" that apparently did not even spare the highest dignitaries.

In the spring of 1935, the first judgment by the People's Court in relation to an espionage case was announced: two of Baron Sosnowski's lovers, Frau [Baroness Benita 'Kitty'] von Berg-Falkenhayn and Fräulein [Renate "Gerda"] von Natzmer (1898-1935, executed by axe), were sentenced to execution by decapitation by axe for high treason and betrayal of military secrets.

Baroness Benita ('Kitty') von Berg-Falkenhayn (née Zollkofer-Altenklingen) (1900-1935, executed), who was executed with an axe for espionage against Germany on behalf of Polish Intelligence. The author was personally involved in investigating this case under his then pseudonym of Heinz Stein, head of the 'Special Stein Office' of the SD, on the personal orders of Heydrich. (Only Himmler, Heydrich, and Werner Best knew the true identity of 'Heinz Stein'. Such extreme precautions of secrecy as disguising the name even of an important official from his own working colleagues and subordinates was very rare in the SD, and shows how confidential and secret many of his activities were. Also, the SD did not want Admiral Canaris to know who 'Heinz Stein' really was, because of the rivalry with his organisation.) It was the author who proved the guilt of Renate "Gerda" von Natzmer, who was also executed.

The Polish intelligence officer Jerzy Sosnowski received only a life sentence, as, according to international conventions, "officers of friendly nations" could not be sentenced to death in espionage cases. The death sentences on the two women were carried out in the courtyard of the detention centre in Berlin Tegel, while – after the necessary paperwork had been completed – the Polish officer Sosnowski was exchanged for three German intelligence officers who had been convicted of espionage in Poland. He went back to Warsaw and one could be sure – as is the norm in such cases – that he would never set foot on German soil again. What had happened?

In February 1934 a performance had been given at the Bachsaal in Berlin by the hitherto fairly obscure dancer Lea Niako.

Lea Niako may have been obscure then, but she became notorious later. The author discovered that she was really a German girl whose name was Frieda Kruse. (Wikipedia mistakenly calls her Maria Kruse. IMDb does not mention her real name at all.) She was born at Hamburg in 1908 and murdered in Berlin in 1945. She appeared in five films, the last released in 1941. One of her films was based on a play by Somerset Maugham called *The Letter.* She was a girlfriend of the Polish agent Jerzy Sosnowski, and was the guest of honour at his party which was raided by the Secret Criminal Police when they were all arrested in their evening gowns and dinner jackets. After the failure of the Berlin Police to get anywhere with the case after many days, the author was in charge of the further interrogations of the huge crowd of over one hundred guests, Sosnowski, and 'Lea Niako' herself, and he managed to get to the bottom of everything.

Despite her Mediterranean temperament and looks, by birth she ('Lea Niako') was actually a very German Frieda Kruse. Jerzy Sosnowski had bought 100 tickets to the event and shared them out amongst his friends in order to ensure that the performance by the questionable Lea Niako would be well attended and successful. The young and gallant Sosnowski, generally known and admired as "Herr Baron", had organised a soirée in honour of his dancer friend, which was held in his elegant apartment in Berlin's Budapester Strasse straight after the dance performance. Some 100 guests were enjoying a nocturnal meal in the company of their host, when suddenly a dozen officers from the Secret Criminal Police Office, led by none other than *SS-Standartenführer* Senior Councillor Dr Patschowsky (the chief of Main Division III and member of the *SD-RFSS*) entered the apartment. In a less than polite tone he declared every single guest to be under arrest. The host, who remained very calm, asked the police chief for a private interview in his study, where the two men were joined by the also present Polish trade commissioner in Berlin. Jerzy Sosnowski demanded that his guests should not be inconvenienced, especially not the ladies in their elaborate evening gowns, for whose reputations Sosnowski said he felt personal responsibility. Might it not be possible to leave them to enjoy the rest of their evening meal in peace? He, on the other hand, was ready to go with the officers there and then. Sosnowski's request was dismissed by Senior Councillor [Günther] Patschowsky with a derisive laugh. Everyone present was crammed into the waiting police cars and taken, in the middle of the night and along with their host Sosnowski, to the police prison in Berlin's police headquarters on Alexanderplatz. Even "Baron" Sosnowski's servant did not evade arrest. Only the Polish trade commissioner could not be arrested as he was in possession of a diplomatic passport. He also firmly refused to allow any examination of the documents that were on his person.

At around one o'clock in the morning, when the ladies in their evening gowns and gentlemen in their tail coats and dinner jackets began to be led to solitary cells by the officers in the police prison, there was much hysterical screaming, raging and crying. The names and appearance of the detainees, especially of the ladies, truly made for an exquisite gathering. Among them were Anita von Berg, the divorced Baroness von Falkenhayn; Frau von Thielemann, the assistant head of a government department; Baroness von Engelhardt; Frau Heuser, née von Engelhardt; Frau Katja Berberian, a Persian "Princess of the Rising Sun"; the film star Maria Paudler (1903-1990); and, not least, the dancer Lea Niako, who was detained under her common name Fräulein Frieda Kruse. The most dramatic scenes were caused by Frau Maria Paudler, who, kicking and screaming, kept insisting that she was a personal friend of *Reichspropagandaminister* Dr Goebbels. And indeed, as a result, she was released the very next morning.

The film star Maria Paulder (1903-1990) was arrested in her evening gown, but she kicked and screamed and claimed that she was a friend (doubtless a mistress) of Josef Goebbels, and she was released as a result.

At Main Division III of the Secret State Police Office, a great multitude of interrogations were held, all of which were concluded without any real results. A few weeks later *SD* Chief Reinhard Heydrich was appointed as leader of the Secret State Police Office instead of Dr Diels, and he succeeded in persuading the *Reichswehrministerium* to commission *"Büro Stein"* to carry out a special investigation into the "Sosnowski case". Thus far, the Gestapa officials tasked with the official police investigation of the case – namely Detective Superintendent [Dr. Walter] Kubitzky 1891-1945, suicide), chief of Division East in the Main Division III, and Detective Superintendent Dr [Kurt Arthur Franz Josef Friderik] Riedel (1903-1945), the case officer for Poland, Czechoslovakia etc. – had achieved very little success, and as a result more and more of the detainees had to be released from investigative custody for lack of evidence. The fact that the *Reichswehrministerium* seemed utterly incapable of assisting in the solving of the case led to many angry complaints by Gestapa officials. The head of Main Division V in the *Reichswehrministerium* and chief of military espionage, Admiral Canaris, maintained a stubborn silence around the whole issue, as did his assistant, Corvette Captain Protze. It was hoped that a solution would be found by *"Büro Stein"*, not least because of that bureau's close ties to the *Reichswehrministerium*.

A photo of Dr. Kurt Riedel as a student in the mid 1920s. He was SS Sturmbannführer (Major) Dr. Kurt Arthur Franz Josef Friderik Riedel (1903-1945, suicide). He became not only a police investigator, but a Gestapo spy. He joined the Gestapa (later called the Gestapo) in 1933. He had achieved little in solving the Sosnowski Case until the author and his colleague Günther Patschowsky stepped in. The author came to know Riedel very well. In November and December 1944 Riedel became a leading member of the Gestapo staff in Warsaw.

The ensuing investigations revealed that *SS-Standartenführer* Senior Councillor Patschowsky had personally rented the apartment directly above that of Jerzy Sosnowski, where he had been lying in ambush like a sleuth dog for days on end. It also came to light that a certain Countess Buchholz had suspected Jerzy Sosnowski of large-scale espionage for Poland as early as the autumn of 1932 and that she had reported her suspicions at Division IA of the Berlin police headquarters. However, that report had been dismissed by Admiral Canaris as an act of revenge by the disgruntled Countess Buchholz. It was shelved, and orders were given by the *Reichswehrministerium* prohibiting its onward transfer to the public prosecution department or any other further investigation by the police. What caused the biggest stir, however, were findings by *"Büro Stein"* that proved beyond doubt that Fräulein von Natzmer, an employee and secretary of the chief of the operations department in the *Reichswehrministerium*, had stolen important documents for Jerzy Sosnowski, which were then smuggled out of the premises of the *Reichswehrministerium* by Anita [*sic*, he means Benita] von Berg-Falkenhayn. A brief outline of the facts: Fräulein von Natzmer was the daughter of a retired general from Silesia, for whom she cared with much loving kindness. Somehow she had come under Sosnowski's spell, despite the fact that she was not exactly a beauty. It must be assumed that she rendered her important services to Sosnowski because she was in some way devoted to him, rather than for money – despite the fact that she was the exemplification of impoverished Prussian officer nobility. The beautiful and adventurous Anita von Berg was the exact antithesis to Fräulein von Natzmer. She was the wife of one of the most ingenious engineers at Siemens-Stern, the aircraft engine manufacturers. Her liaison with Sosnowksi did not hinder her from living in good relations with chief engineer Dr Berg, who was utterly consumed by aviation technology and quite divorced from the real world. She also maintained very good relations with her former husband, Freiherr von Falkenhayn, a man from venerable military stock. It must be said in Jerzy Sosnowski's defence that he would always seek to exonerate the women who were so utterly devoted to him. He even went as far as offering himself in marriage to the incarcerated Anita von Berg, in an attempt to save her – as a married Polish woman – from the guillotine. Her husband, the engineer Dr Berg had committed suicide out of sorrow, following his wife's arrest. It was absolutely certain that he was in no way involved in the Sosnowksi espionage affair.

Another of Major Sosnowski's girlfriends was the Circassian Katja Berberian, née Unanov. Her divorced husband lived in Paris, and a Persian prince who had fallen head over heels in love with her had bestowed on her the title of a Persian "Princess of the Rising Sun". The investigations revealed that, while she was aware of some espionage activities, she had no personal involvement in any of the machinations of her adored Major Sosnowski. At the request of the chief of *"Büro Stein"* she was temporarily released from detention to be closely monitored. She was able to evade re-arrest by joining *"Büro Stein"*, however not in relation to the "Sosnowski case". Later she was taken on by the *SD-RFSS*, and at the outbreak of war proved herself as one of the most dangerous star agents of the *SD*.

The "Sosnowski case" later gave rise to close co-operation between the Gestapa's Main Division III and the *SD-RFSS* on the one hand, and the military espionage of Admiral Canaris in Main Division V at the *Reichswehrministerium* on the other. One of the most important findings by *"Büro Stein"* (which had by now been remodelled as the "Security Service for Special Deployment") suggested that the Polish intelligence officer Sosnowski had stolen the invasion plans for Poland from the operations department at the *Reichswehrministerium*, and smuggled them across the border to Warsaw. What was peculiar, however, was the fact that none of these findings were to be included in the written interrogation records.

The "Sosnowski case" was the first major espionage trial of the Nazi regime. As such it was heard at the newly established People's Court, and not, as would previously have been the case, at the *Reich* Court in Leipzig. Chief Prosecutor Dr Parisius – who at that time was not yet a prosecutor of the *Reich*, but, as is generally known, was appointed as president of the People's Court just before his death – led the proceedings for the prosecution. His deputy at the time was the ambitious young public prosecutor Dr Rudi Kempter, who, without the knowledge of his superiors, was an eager member of the *SD-RFSS*. Since his appointment at the *Reich* Court in Leipzig he had rendered valuable informer services to *SD* chief Heydrich from within the highest German legal agency, and, thanks to Heydrich's connections, had then been called to the People's Court in Berlin. The scheming of that "worthy" member of the *SD-RFSS* alone could fill an entire volume.

As has already been mentioned, the "Sosnowski case" gave rise to an elaborate staging of scenes of fraternisation between Admiral Canaris and *SD* chief Heydrich. But it also represented a trial of strength between the *Reichswehr's* espionage and counter-espionage apparatus on the one hand, and that of the *SD-RFSS* and Secret State Police on the other. The chief of military espionage, Admiral Canaris, had no intention whatsoever to reveal his secrets to the "upstart" Reinhard Heydrich; and all spying attempts by the lowly prosecutor Dr Rudi Kempter proved unsuccessful. Admiral Canaris was able to maintain strict secrecy even vis-à-vis the newly established People's Court, which he – rightly – viewed as a Nazi agency. When the "Sosnowski case" came to court, the *Reichswehr* demanded that the issue of the theft of the German plans for an invasion of Poland would be brought up neither during the court hearings, nor at any other point during the police investigations or preliminary juridical inquests. The facts were these:

The Polish intelligence officer Jerzy von Sosnowski had been able to accomplish – seemingly against all expectations – the most ingenious coup of military espionage. He was able to steal a supremely important secret document from the German *Wehrmacht's* operations department; the type of document that around the world is most closely guarded by the military, namely an invasion plan, a so-called "A-plan"; that is to say the sort of document that would reveal to the opposing side all aspects of the eventual mobilisation and attack in the most minute detail.

When Sosnowski presented his "A-plan" in Warsaw, the Polish generals were divided in their opinions about the value of the document. Some believed in its authenticity, while others doubted it. The chief of the Polish espionage and counter-espionage operations ("Defence"), Colonel Lipinski, resigned, as he was unable to assert his views about the document's inauthenticity. The remaining generals arranged Poland's defence strategy according to the "A-plan" stolen in Berlin and – – – lost the war in the shortest possible time.

In actual fact, it had all been an ingenious feint: German espionage had intentionally allowed the Polish agent to steal a specially prepared document that contained a misleading invasion plan – and the enemy promptly fell for it. (Another authoritarian state would use the method of "disinformation" in an even more unscrupulous manner. The Soviet dictator staged a "paltry", yet extremely bloody, invasion of Finland, sacrificing countless lives, in order to mislead the world about the real strength and condition of the Soviet armies.)

There can be no doubt that Jerzy Sosnowski had acted in good faith, and that he believed in the document's veracity when he brought it to Warsaw. Following his return from Germany, he was detained – albeit in "honourable captivity" – for almost a year by the Polish espionage chief. Eventually, after a positive opinion of the document had prevailed amongst the generals despite all misgivings, he had to be eventually released and rehabilitated; not least in light of the fact that he had kept silent about his grandiose coup during the trial in Berlin. The German chief of espionage, Admiral Canaris, had pulled off the most significant case of "disinformation" in the most recent history of espionage. The successful campaign and attack on Poland proved this fact beyond doubt.

The "Sosnowski case" demonstrated the uniquely unscrupulous methods the German espionage authorities were willing to employ; not only the Nazi authorities, but to an even greater degree the military authorities. Two women from honourable families were inveigled by Admiral Canaris' henchmen into participating in high treason and the betrayal of military secrets, and subsequently sent to the guillotine without qualms. In a state of extreme agitation, a clueless member of the general staff, the young Lieutenant Colonel R., put a bullet through his head. The engineer Dr Berg, who was widely held in high esteem and highly qualified both personally and professionally, committed suicide. All this, only in order not to derail Admiral Canaris' grand coup of "disinformation". The scheme, which in itself was ingenious, had been developed over months of painstaking work by two model students who had been put to work day and night at the war academy in Dresden. Some less well-informed people claim to know that the idea of deploying "disinformation" originated with Annemarie Lesser, the formidable First World War agent "Mademoiselle Docteur".

PART THREE

A POLITICAL KALEIDOSCOPE

B. TOWARDS WAR

The *"Büro Ribbentrop"*

Much has been written about Joachim von Ribbentrop, the Nazi Foreign Minister. Most opinions are disparaging in nature, but there was also much glorification of the man at the time of his so-called successes. He had travelled the world as the son-in-law of the proprietor of Henkel & Co., the sparkling wine producers, and in the years before Hitler's takeover had been a welcome guest at many an English country house, supplying the lord of the manor with fine wines and liqueurs. His business connections in England instilled in him the erroneous belief that he was an expert on the British mentality, which in turn led him to pass on an entirely false understanding of Britain's political position to his *Führer* and *Reich* Chancellor. The character of this slippery Rhinelander, Joachim von Rippentrop, was a curious amalgamation of questionable cosmopolitanism, occasional displays of diffidence, and sudden eruptions of brazen insolence. Long before he was appointed as Minister for the Exterior, he was seen as "that modest young man", who would only be invited to a dinner party if the host needed to fill the last seat. Later he would compensate his purported modesty with a downright provocative arrogance.

From the earliest stages of his political career, much too little attention was given to the fact that Ribbentrop occupied a very senior leadership position within the *SS*. As a mere functionary of the NSDAP he would never have been able to play as decisive a role in German foreign policy as he was able to as a leading exponent of the *SS*.

Ribbentrop was not a long-standing member of the NSDAP. He only joined the party in the summer of 1930, and won his first accolades when, in the election year of 1932, he was able to draw Rhenish-Westphalian heavy industry towards National Socialism. It is likely that it was Ribbentrop's recommendation that led the banking house Schröder to make available to the NSDAP large sums of money, without which the party would never have been able to spread its propaganda on such a massive scale. Moreover, the influence of the *"Pour le mérite"* awardee Hermann Göring alone would not have sufficed to sway *Reichspräsident* Hindenburg to eventually entrust Hitler with the office of *Reich* Chancellor. It should not be forgotten that Joachim von Ribbentrop was a keen member of the *"Kavallerie Verein"* (an association of cavalry officers), whose then president was General Werner von Fritsch and on whose board were many prominent personalities, among them Cavalry General Günther Freiherr von Pogrell [1879-1944].

The *"Kavallerie Verein"*, which was based in Berlin, played a fateful behind-the-scenes role in the Weimar Republic. To support its rearmament ambitions, the *Reichswehr* had installed one of its representatives in the association, namely the retired Major [General] von Platen, who was on excellent terms with many in the general corps. He also held a position as a secretary at the so-called *Mühle Konzern* (a milling company), as part of which he ostensibly dealt with the grain supply for the *Reichswehr*. In truth, however, he shuttled back and forth between East Prussia, Pomerania and Brandenburg on secret missions for the *Reichswehr*. He deserves a mention not least because of the fact that, as a "gentleman rider", he acted as the association's secretary. One of his closest friends was the infamous *SA* leader Count Wolf-Heinrich Julius von Helldorff, whose friendship Joachim von Ribbentrop had been seeking for some time. It will clarify matters further to mention the fact that Ribbentrop, too, had been a cavalry officer during the World War of 1914–18, and for some time had acted as a liaison officer in the staff of Field Marshal [Anton Ludwig Friedrich August] von Mackensen (1849-1945) in Constantinople. Much like General von Reichenau, Ribbentrop was introduced to Himmler by von Woyrsch, then a young and active member of the *"Kavallerie Verein"*. (As mentioned previously, *SS-Truppenführer* von Woyrsch was the son of the late generalissimo Remus von Woyrsch.) In any case, during those days before the "assumption of power", in the election year of 1932, anybody who was anybody came together in Berlin's *"Kavallerie Verein"*, and before long the entire membership enthusiastically sided with National Socialism. Prominent members included Joachim von Ribbentrop, von Woyrsch, Count Welldorf, [Hartwig] von Platen, [Major General Hans] von Hanstein (1883-1975) and – last, but not least – the former *Reich* Chancellor Franz von Papen.

It cannot have been a pleasant spectacle for the archconservative generals to witness many close friends suddenly changing sides and joining the hitherto frowned-upon movement of National Socialism, but perhaps these "conversions" made it easier for people like Fritsch and Pogrell to eventually also make themselves available to the Nazi Chancellor Hitler, albeit at first somewhat sulkily and with a certain reluctance. (Incidentally, the Hohenzollern Prince August Wilhelm, the well-known *SA* leader "Auwi", was also a keen member of the *"Kavallerie Verein"*.) [*Note*: Field Marshal von Mackensen's son Hans Georg von Mackensen (1883-1947) had been Auwi's Adjutant as well as boyhood friend.]

The support of the *SS*-leadership enabled Joachim von Ribbentrop to become Nazi Foreign Minister, despite the fact that he had only relatively recently joined the NSDAP, and the fact that there were other, more prominent representatives of National Socialism, such as Alfred Rosenberg, who thought they were a shoo-in for that office. Perhaps Ribbentrop initially only joined the *SS* because in those days it was seen as the most genteel, not to say "aristocratic", party structure. It soon became clear that Ribbentrop knew very well how to represent the concerns of the *SS* in foreign policy, and that, as a foreign-policy tool for the *SS* leadership, he indeed was compliant and "worthy" in equal measure. For example, its ideas on race led the *SS* to seek some sort of understanding with "Germanic" Englishmen on the matter of a war against the "non-congeners" in the East. Nothing is more typical of the peculiar and cranky "idealism" within the *SS*-leadership than the fact that these people seriously believed there might be some sort of rapprochement with Britain, and that it was thought that they would be able to achieve their ideals of a master race with the tacit consent of the British, if not their full-blown co-operation.

When Hitler became *Reich* Chancellor in 1933 and formed his first cabinet, he kept Konstantin Freiherr von Neurath in office as Foreign Minister, who would go on to lead German foreign policy under the Nazi regime until 1938. It was part of Hitler's overall foreign-policy plan to establish friendly relations with Britain, and the *SS*-leadership presented him with the man perfectly suited for the job: Joachim von Ribbentrop. Thanks to Ribbentrop's supposed excellent personal relationship to the British, the *SS*-leadership established a special office, namely the *"Sonderbüro Ribbentrop"*, as early as 1933. The establishment of this office alone represented a blatant break by the Nazi regime with the time-honoured traditions of the Foreign Office in Berlin's Wilhelmstrasse, for the *"Sonderbüro Ribbentrop"* was neither affiliated to the Foreign Office nor subordinate or even answerable to the Foreign Minister. At the same time, the establishment of the *"Sonderbüro Ribbentrop"* was a clear affront to Alfred Rosenberg's "Foreign Office of the NSDAP". Rosenberg thought that he would be able to cut his own path, independent of the *SA* and the *SS*. He had a reputation as a stubborn loner, and arrogated the right to ignore the "*SS* Race and Settlement Office". Even before Hitler's takeover, he had repeatedly fallen out with the highest leadership of the *SA* – and therefore also that of the *SS* – and put himself in direct opposition to the party and its then leader, Rudolf Hess. His self-aggrandisement, with which he frequently put himself on the same level as Hitler, was met with much disapproval. Therefore the establishment of *"Büro*

Ribbentrop" was a dual strike by the *SS*-leadership: on the one hand, against the Foreign Office, and, on the other, against Alfred Rosenberg and the "Foreign Office of the NSDAP", which entirely revolved around him. Joachim von Ribbentrop was given the rank of *SS-Gruppenführer*, the first title bestowed on him by the party.

During the years of 1934/35, anyone who approached the "special representative" Joachim von Ribbentrop for any kind of information would be turned away by the "modest man with the winsome smile" and the words: "You do know that I am a mere figurehead, a simple representative of my office? If you require specific information, kindly contact Herr von Raumer; he alone is authorised!" And indeed, the goateed Herr von Raumer was the "brains" of *"Büro Ribbentrop"*. A former German envoy in Warsaw, he had initially been seen as conservative and, before the takeover, had been an official member of Alfred Hugenberg's German-National People's Party. This, however, did not stop him from becoming a secret member of the NSDAP as early as 1931, from performing valuable informer services for Himmler-Heydrich, or from being a well-respected agent of the *SD-RFSS* in the Foreign Office. Joachim von Ribbentrop had been made an "honourable" member of the *SS* and appointed directly as *SS-Gruppenführer*, whereas the envoy Raumer had climbed every rung of the *SS* hierarchy to reach the rank of *SS-Standartenführer* and was now suddenly appointed as head clerk of *"Büro Ribbentrop"*. In the early stages of Ribbentrop's career he had even been his chaperone, or, as Ribbentrop liked to say within his family circle, his "watchdog". Later, when Ribbentrop had proven his loyalty and devotion to the *SS*-leadership to a sufficient degree and had become Hitler's confidant, it was only natural that he rid himself of his "chaperone" and that Herr Raumer faded into obscurity.

In blatantly sidestepping the Foreign Office, Ribbentrop was appointed as Hitler's special envoy and, as such, was responsible solely to the *"Führer and Reichskanzler"*. (Ribbentrop was clever enough – until the inglorious end of his career – to pointedly and unmistakeably remain a representative of the *SS* leadership and to act as such; in other words, he never failed to secure the *SS* leadership's backing for all his foreign policy schemes. This can be the only explanation for why he could never be deposed, even after the many later failures of his foreign policy decisions.)

Ribbentrop had two secretaries, both of whom were integral to the workings of *"Büro Ribbentrop"*. Both men were Ribbentrop's confidants and closest associates, whom he could trust implicitly: Legation Councillor [Walther] Hewel [1904-1945, suicide] and Embassy Councillor [Heinrich Georg] Stahmer (1892-1978).

Walther Hewel (1904–1945) and his wife Elizabeth 'Blondie' Blanda, a Red Cross nurse who had nursed him when wounded. Hewel was one of Hitler's oldest and closest friends and has generally thought to have been with him in the bunker at the end. However, Erich Kempka, who carried Eva Braun's body from the bunker to be cremated, recorded in his memoirs: "After the war I discovered that Hewel shot himself in the cellar of the Schultheiss Brewery on Berlin's Schönhauser-Allee after the break-out from the Reich Chancellery. ... Hewel had previously promised to take his own life to avoid capture."

Heinrich Georg Stahmer (1892-1978) standing beside Josef Stalin and smiling while Molotov signs a treaty.

Heinrich Georg Stahmer (1892-1978), Nazi Ambassador to Japan and effectively Ribbentrop's "number two".

After the outbreak of war, Legation Councillor [Walther] Hewel (1904-1945, suicide] originally Ribbentrop's private secretary, became his master's permanent representative at the Führer's headquarters. His young wife [Elizabeth "Blondie", née Blanda, a former Red Cross nurse] was for some time one of the few women who had a great influence on Hitler and enjoyed the Führer's special favour. According to credible reports, Frau Hewel was the only person, other than Eva Braun, who was allowed into the hospital room where the injured Adolf Hitler was cared for following the officer assassination attempt of July 20, 1944.

During the war, Embassy Councillor Stahmer was appointed to the crucial post of German ambassador in Tokyo, replacing General [Eugen] von Ott, who, following the interim recalling of the Japanese ambassador in Berlin, General Oshima, had fallen out of favour with Hitler and Ribbentrop. However, Stahmer was also not able to perform the miracle that was expected of him, namely to induce the government in Tokyo to declare war on the Soviet Union.

In all matters of Ribbentrop's foreign policy planning, Hewel and Stahmer were probably his closest associates, but the activities of another man, *SS-Hauptsturmführer* May [*note: This man may have been Erich May, who was promoted to this rank in 1935; his brother Fritz May was younger and promoted later; recorded facts about May are however very few and this identity is not at all certain.*], were at least of equal importance. May was a full member of the *SD-RFSS*, whereas von Raumer was only an agent and "V-man" for that organisation. When May joined *"Büro Ribbentrop"*, von Raumer's influence was already waning, whereas May would stay at Ribbentrop's side as his permanent deputy and liaison officer to the *SD-RFSS* until the end. It was his task to evaluate all incoming secret reports and make these available to the *SD-RFSS*, as well as to ensure perfect co-ordination and smooth planning of all aspects of civil espionage abroad. Further, it was not the envoy von Raumer, but May, who was quickly promoted to the rank of *SS-Standartenführer*, and, in his capacity as liaison officer to the *SD* Main Office, acted as Ribbentrop's espionage chief.

As is well known, a certain Dr Heinevetter was not only a full member of the *SD*-RFSS, but also a member of the presidium and Second Vice President of the "Cross-national Cultural Association" (with *SS-Obergruppenführer* Lorenz as president). This Dr Heinevetter was subordinate to *SS-Hauptsturmführer* May in *"Büro Ribbentrop"*. The official representative of *"Büro Ribbentrop"* was Legation Councillor Ripgen, while the Foreign Office was officially represented by Legation Councillor Busse.

All of these cross-connections are important, as they increasingly helped to consolidate Ribbentrop's well-nigh limitless power and influence on German foreign policy under the Nazi regime. When Ribbentrop was appointed as Foreign Minister, *"Büro Ribbentrop"* continued to operate alongside the Foreign Office rather than being dissolved – a fact that regrettably is all too often forgotten. This can only be understood in light of the fact that *"Büro Ribbentrop"* was in reality an instrument of the *SS* leadership and that Ribbentrop remained an exponent of that *SS* leadership when he was already Nazi Foreign Minister and the confidant of and advisor to Adolf Hitler. Especially in his new role as Foreign Minister, Ribbentrop did not want to do without the vast *SS* spy machinery, and the continued operation of *"Büro Ribbentrop"* ensured access to that apparatus.

It is not our intention to plot all stages of National Socialist foreign policy under Ribbentrop's leadership; instead, only one event will be singled out. In 1935, Ribbentrop, in his capacity as Hitler's special envoy, negotiated the signing of the Anglo-German Naval Agreement, which would later gain much notoriety. A feat that had been beyond the wildest dreams of the Foreign Office in Berlin's Wilhelmstrasse had single-handedly been achieved by the "outsider" Ribbentrop, without any assistance from the competent Foreign Minister, Baron von Neurath. There was much jubilation and rejoicing in senior Nazi circles in Berlin, especially among the *SS* leadership. It was honestly and firmly believed that a major step had been taken and that now nothing stood in the way of a close friendship between Nazi Germany and Great Britain. Ribbentrop had delivered his masterpiece and subsequently, in 1936, was appointed Nazi ambassador in London. On the occasion of presenting his letter of accreditation as German ambassador of the *Reich* government and special envoy of Adolf Hitler, he greeted the King of England with the Nazi salute and a spirited "Heil Hitler!" In doing so, he offended the British and provoked consternation and laughter in London, but at the same time he ensured his Führer's and *Reich* Chancellor's complete trust and special favour as well as the deep respect of the *SS* leadership in Berlin. In order to impress his British acquaintances and benefactors, Ribbentrop had an old friend from the *"Kavallerie Verein"*, namely General Walter von Reichenau, appointed as president of the Olympic committee. He introduced the general to London's "high society", before sending him off on special missions for his

"Büro Ribbentrop" to the Mediterranean and the Arab world. General Reichenau, usually an intelligent man, in London conducted himself in such a markedly "Teutonic" manner that he alienated even those who had shown a semblance of affinity toward the German cause. The more provocatively and offensively Ribbentrop behaved in London, the more his reputation grew in Berlin. Eventually he was seen by Hitler and the *SS* leadership as "unconditionally reliable", and in 1938 was appointed as German Foreign Minister, replacing Freiherr von Neurath. Thanks to the connections he had established through his *"Büro Ribbentrop"* and Hitler's personal confidence, Ribbentrop became the undisputed and imperious leader of German foreign policy, far exceeding any level of authority Baron von Neurath had ever managed to establish.

Following Ribbentrop's appointment as Foreign Minister, *"Büro Ribbentrop"* was not incorporated, integrated or subordinated to the Foreign Office, or perhaps preserved only notionally. Far from it, it not only became the guarantor for further, especially close co-operation with the *SD-RFSS* and the *SS* leadership, but its continued existence also ensured that the new Nazi Foreign Minister would by and large stay connected to the entire spy and informer apparatus of the Nazi regime. Indeed, Joachim von Ribbentrop's very existence was deeply rooted in the Nazi system of espionage and informing.

The intrinsic logic of history dictates that evil forces will always wipe out last that which united them in the first place. It is possible to impress one's unsuspecting environment with lies, deception, bluffs and threats for a certain while, but there comes a time when the vessel of deceit can hold no more, at which point only terror can ensure continued outward success, which will continue until he who inflicts the terror is shattered by his own lies. For in the end, that which is right and that which rests within God Himself will always succeed.

The methods of National Socialist foreign policy, which under compulsion had turned itself into an exponent of German militarism, inevitably had to lead to a World War. Each lie was followed in its wake by an even bigger lie. Eventually there must come a point when the rest of the world has to take a stand against these lies, even if the world has kept its eyes shut in primitive complacency forever and a day. When lies and deception are systematically deployed as "politics", war must inevitably follow. The perturbation of the spirit caused by these lies often continues long beyond the end of war, and acts like a disease that can only be curbed and eventually cured by the most skilful doctors.

The foreign policy of Hitler and Ribbentrop was nothing but a lie. By its very nature, it inevitably had to lead to violence, brutality and war. It sowed hatred and brought forth a boundless bewilderment of the spirit, which ultimately and necessarily also affected the powers that were victorious in the war.

Schalwa Karumidze and the Anti-Comintern Pact

During the World War of 1914–18, a Georgian by the name of Schalwa Karumidze performed valuable services for Germany in the Black Sea / Caucasus region. He secretly supplied German submarines that had advanced into the Black Sea with fuel, smuggled arms for Germany, and later induced the *Reich* government to grant *de facto* recognition of sovereignty to his beloved Georgia. Unfortunately the joy derived from the recognition of the state of Georgia by Germany did not last very long, and Karumidze had to flee the country when the Soviet armies approached.

Karumidze was a true adventurer. He gathered a throng of displaced Georgians around him who bestowed on him the honorary title "Schalwa", which can be translated as "master" or "sage". He had made Stalin's acquaintance, and later there would be a certain marshal in the Red Army, with whom Karumidze would remain in constant covert contact. In Geneva, Karumidze sought the favour of the then Swiss Foreign Minister, Federal Councillor Motta, and, due to Motta's subsequent tacit consent, Karumidze was able to establish a "committee for the liberation of the Caucasian peoples" in Geneva. Soon Karumidze and his associates in the committee had large sums of cash at their disposal, which had been made available by Henri [Wilhelm August] Deterding [1866-1939], the chief executive of the British oil trust Shell [*the Royal Dutch/Shell Corporation, of which Deterding was the majority shareholder*].

Henri Wilhelm August Deterding (1866-1939) the "oil king" who funded a movement to free the Caucasian peoples. He hated the communists and had financially assisted many White Russian emigrés. He had close connections also with the British Intelligence Service and Lord Killearn, then Colonel Miles Lampson.

Many sensational reports and countless books have been written about the history of oil and the major oil tycoons. Strangely, the role played by the three Nobel brothers in the story of oil has rarely even been given a mention. While one of the three brothers has entered the history books as the inventor of dynamite and the founder of the international Nobel Price for Peace, the other two brothers were the architects of the Caucasian-Russian oil trust under the Tsarist regime. Many minor and major Caucasian princes were interested in the Nobel brothers' oil trust. It is worth noting that in the Caucasus anyone who owned a larger flock of sheep and the required pasturage (i.e. land) would call himself a "prince". Karumidze, however, had not been a "prince" prior to the World War of 1914–18, but a wealthy wool merchant, sometime arms dealer, and keen speculator with oil shares on the stock exchange, and as such connected to the Nobel brothers. When war broke out in 1914, he became a well-paid agent in Mackensen's army group, and when the German army finally collapsed and the Soviet Union seized the Caucasus, Karumidze, who was politically heavily tainted and decried in his country as a rich "bourgeois", had to flee. He escaped with little more than the clothes on his back, and finally threw in his lot with the oil tycoon Deterding of the Shell trust. On Deterding's behalf, Karumidze bought large amounts of shares in Caucasian Nobel oil from Russian émigrés. In the process, he was able to divert a handsome sum of money into his own pockets, but the lion's share of the proceeds had to be handed over to the aforementioned "committee for the liberation of the Caucasian peoples", as whose secretary Karumidze had been appointed. Deterding was smart enough to only pay a fraction of the nominal value of the acquired Nobel shares, and to divert a portion from that fractional part for the purpose of funding an anti-Soviet revolutionary movement. No one knew better than Henri Deterding that those shares would remain worthless while the Caucasus was under Soviet rule.

The committee established by Deterding in Geneva had several million Swiss francs at its disposal. While Karumidze had been able to have himself appointed as its secretary, he by no means had the exclusive right of disposal of the funds. A personal friend of Deterding's, the industry magnate Hirth – a very reserved elderly gentleman with excellent connections to England, who was held in equally high esteem at the Foreign Office in Berlin as he was in the City of London and at the stock exchange in Amsterdam – also had a right of co-determination. Hirth had major business interests in Focke-Wulf, the aircraft manufacturer, and owned a handsome wad of Shell shares, which he had been able to hold on to, despite Germany's defeat in the war.

By founding the "committee for the liberation of the Caucasian peoples", Karumidze turned himself into a high-profile intelligence agent acting on the world stage. Through his affiliation with Deterding he had made connections to the British "Intelligence Service", where occasionally he would liaise with Colonel Lampson [*note: It seems impossible that this could be Miles Lampson, later Lord Killearn, or his cousin Oliver Locket-Lampson, and it presumably refers therefore to the brother of the latter, Godfrey Locker-Lampson, 1875-1946, whose career at this time is suspiciously opaque, suggesting an intelligence role.*]; while for Germany he repeatedly carried out espionage missions in France. From early on, Karumidze had maintained close relations to prominent personalities in the Arab and Muslim world, and therefore – given France's strong regional interests in Syria – Karumidze was also able to curry favour with the French. Among Karumidze's friends was Tabatabei [Tabata Bey?, Tabatabai?], the former Iraqi Minister and advisor to Ibn Saud of Arabia.

By his countrymen, Schalwa Karumidze was shown ill will and veneration in equal measure. One individual who would almost explode with rage at the mere mention of the name Karumidze was "Prince" Paul Awaloff-Belmont, who was also a native of the Caucasus region. Karumidze simply laughed off the prince's hostility, putting it down to the fact that he had once been forced to refuse credit to the "profligate little Paul", lest the prince ruin him financially.

Karumidze was accused of offering his services as an agent one moment to one nation, and the next moment to another nation, of always "carrying water on both shoulders". Karumidze was able to counter such claims with the argument that, as a Georgian, he was ready to associate with anyone who would potentially be able to contribute to the liberation of his homeland. One fact was beyond doubt: during the World War of 1914–18, Karumidze had developed boundless respect for German soldiers and German militarism, which is the only possible explanation for his almost naïve veneration of the Generals Ludendorff and Hoffmann.

During the Weimar period, Karumidze's permanent representative among the Munich coterie of out-of-work militarists, minor-league former members of the general staff and adventuresome mercenaries was his secretary Basilius Sadathieraschwili. This man, also a native Georgian, acted as a sort of go-between for Karumidze to his friend and benefactor, General Hoffmann. And it was General Hoffmann who beguiled the otherwise rather level-headed Karumidze into getting involved with the risky business of the *chervonets* forgery. When that downright ridiculous adventure tale was prematurely exposed and went to trial, Karumidze did not even hint at General Hoffmann's involvement, and his power over his accomplices was so great that none of those who sat next to him in the dock dared utter the general's name either. (Incidentally, the *chervonets* forgery affair in Munich was a sham, especially from the Soviet Union's perspective. While Karumidze was given an eight-month prison sentence for forgery of banknotes, neither he nor any of his accomplices ever served a single day of their sentences.)

Karumidze's feet were too firmly on the ground for him to be ignorant of the fact that his friendships in Munich were only of limited value. Consequently he assured himself of the allegiance of the chief of German military espionage in the *Reichswehrministerium*, Admiral Canaris, for whom he performed valuable services on occasion. He installed the Georgian Kornali, a former Tsarist police colonel in Warsaw, as a permanent conduit to the *Reichswehrministerium*, who, funded by Karumidze, established a small taxi firm in Berlin-Charlottenburg.

When a militarily reinvigorated Nazi Germany, in concert with Fascist Italy, began to develop an interest in the Middle East, the Arab World and the Islamist movements, it seemed that Karumidze might be on the threshold of achieving great importance. As a matter of fact, to begin with, he and his secretary Sadathieraschwili were detained by the suspicious Gestapa chief Dr Diels, who wanted to satisfy himself that Karumidze's association with the British Colonel Lampson at the "Secret Service" had not, in fact, been detrimental to Germany. However, soon after Himmler-Heydrich had taken over the leadership of the Secret State Police, Karumidze had to be released at the request of the *Reichswehr's* espionage chief, Admiral Canaris. Karumidze's rehabilitation by Canaris himself was the prelude to the Georgian's major espionage activities for the "axis" Berlin-Rome-Tokyo. Sadathieraschwili, who had previously relocated his place of residence from Munich to Berlin following Hitler's takeover, moved to Rome, while Kornali remained in Berlin. The connections to the *Reichswehr* were becoming ever closer, and, in a new development, Karumidze and his people established friendly relations to *"Büro Ribbentrop"* and therefore also the *SD-RFSS*.

One evening after the Italian invasion of Ethiopia (the "Second Italo-Abyssinian War"), Karumidze dined with Mussolini at the Palazzo Chigi in Rome. As early as 1933, while he was in Geneva, Karumidze had ingratiated himself with the Italian delegate to the League of Nations, Baron Aloisi, and now Karumidze became Italy's intermediary to the Arab world. When Nazi Germany, too, sought to gain direct influence over the various Arab movements via its *"Büro Ribbentrop"*, Karumidze deployed his duplicitous manipulations as skilfully for the Nazis as he had done for the Fascists. But much like the Gestapa chief Dr Diels (who had by this point been replaced), the *SD-RFSS* never fully trusted Karumidze and his people, as Karumidze did not seem willing to give up his connections in England once and for all. Only when a third major power registered an interest in the Arab world did Karumidze finally fully side with the axis Berlin-Rome-Tokyo. That third major power that wanted to gain a foothold in the Middle East and for that purpose sought to enlist the help of Karumidze was none other than – – – Japan!

At the League of Nations in Geneva, a diminutive man of slight build could often be seen; he talked very little, always had an obliging smile on his lips and modestly kept himself in the background. This man was the Japanese Major [Masanobu] Tsuji [*the author mistakenly, evidently from faulty memory of a Japnese name, calls him* "Usuj"), to whom no-one at the League of Nations paid much attention, for he did not seem to play an especially important role even within the Japanese delegation. The inconspicuous major would often, as if coincidentally, meet with Schalwa Karumidze, who was also present in Geneva during those days, and was all ears when the vivacious, heavily-set Georgian would eloquently hold forth about his cunning plans concerning an encirclement of the Soviets. And one fine day, the otherwise so taciturn Japanese officer revealed himself as the adjutant of the Supreme Imperial War Council of Japan, on whose orders he was travelling the European states while establishing connections to the Middle East and other Asian states.

Major (later Colonel) Masanobu Tsuji (1901-1961, missing, declared officially dead in 1968). The author describes him as "a diminutive man of slight build ... modestly kept himself in the background" to whom no one paid any attention in Geneva. But then he was revealed as a special emissary of the Supreme Imperial War Council of Japan, and he schemed with the Georgian Schalwa Karumidze about a plan for the encirclement of Russia. He then came to Berlin in the winter of 1935-6 and continued negotiations with the Germans. As the author describes, he was eventually able to negotiate arrangements directly with Admiral Canaris and Ribbentrop, overcoming initial hesitancy by the German Army generals. Later, it was Tsuji who planned the Japanese invasion of Malaya, and he was deeply implicated in the most atrocious Japanese war crimes. He was one of the most extreme of all the Japanese militarists.

When Major Tsuji arrived in Berlin – that is to say, in the winter of 1935/36 –Baron [Konstantin] von Neurath was still at the Foreign Office. The imperial adjutant from the "Land of the Rising Sun" took up quarters with the then military attaché of Japan, Major General [Baron Hiroshi] Oshima (1886-1975), and made his initial contacts with the *Reichswehrministerium.* [*Oshima had been a member of the extremist young officers in the early 1930s who wanted to overthrow or murder the members of their Government because they were not sufficiently extreme, chauvinist, and imperialistic. Some Government ministers were actually murdered by these fanatics. In 1933, Oshima became very friendly with Colonel Eugen Ott, who had been sent to Japan for espionage purposes by Colonel Nikolai. By 1934 Ott became military attaché in Japan and Oshima became military attaché in Berlin, thus facilitating their mutual plotting.*]

Lieutenant General Hiroshi Oshima (1886-1975). He was the Japanese military attaché in Berlin from 1934, while still a Colonel (promoted to Major General in March, 1935). The Japanese Ambassador then was Admiral Shigenori Togo. Oshima spoke almost perfect German. He was befriended by Ribbentrop, who introduced him to Hitler. In October 1938 he was promoted to Lieutenant General and became the Japanese Ambassador in Berlin. He wished to assassinate Stalin and bring about the disintegration of the Soviet Union, which he plotted with Himmler. During the period discussed by the author, Major Tsuji (called by the author, from defective memory, "Usuj", unless that error was typographical), emissary of the Supreme Imperial War Council of Japan, stayed with Oshima, and jointly they pressed forward the Japanese alliance with Germany. It was Oshima who was the Japanese who, with the German Eugen Ott (1889-1977), co-drafted the November 1936 Anti-Comintern Pact between Japan and Germany.

Ribbentrop, at left, chatting with General Oshima, at an official reception.

[The overall head of the Japanese espionage operations was Major General Kenji Doihara, operating under the harmless-looking name of the Continental Service. Doihara, like Oshima, spoke fluent German. But he also spoke seven other European languages and various Asian ones. He was a bit of a genius, certainly where languages were concerned. The author's account of the Japanese intelligence services was omitted from his volume, probably because, although the War in Europe was over by the time of publication of his book, the War in the Pacific was still continuing, so that it was important to withhold that information.]

Major General Kenji Doihara (1883-1948, hanged), the head of the Japanese espionage services. He was deeply involved in the invasion of Manchuria. In 1948 he was executed as a war criminal.

Despite treating the imperial envoy with impeccable courtesy, neither the chief of the general staff, General Beck, nor the chief of army command, General Fritsch, seemed particularly sympathetic to his proposals. Someone else, however, did perceive an opportunity both for himself and his specialised field in the Japanese proposals: the chief of military espionage, Vice Admiral Canaris. He was not able to engage in direct contact with the Japanese Major, as he could not be seen to blatantly take a stance in opposition to that of the chiefs of the general staff and army command, but an opportunity presented itself to go through the versatile and tested Schalwa Karumidze. The Georgian made the Japanese sit up and take notice by immediately proposing direct contact to the office of Adolf Hitler's special envoy, thus sidestepping the Foreign Office. Karumidze set up the connection to *"Büro Ribbentrop"*, and, in a traditional wine bar in Potsdam, a first exploratory meeting took place between the "private" Herr von Platen and Major Tsuji, in the presence of Schalwa Karumidze. The shrewd Herr von Platen quickly smoothed all paths of communication, so that soon secret talks could take place not only between Ribbentrop and Major Tsuji, but also between Admiral Canaris and the Japanese officer.

Nazi Foreign politics availed itself of the same means over and over: lies, deception, bluff and grand promises, interspersed with threats. However, during those days Herr von Ribbentrop believed that he required additional leverage in order to lend sufficient weight to his political overtures in London. This is how the Anti-Comintern Pact came into existence. While it is true that the pact with Japan was officially directed against Soviet Russia, in actual fact it was as much of an affront to the British Empire. The lines of thought that the architects of the pact followed in their secret negotiations at the Berlin villa of the Japanese military attaché Oshima were these: the Japanese fleet, as an ally of a militarily reinvigorated Germany, had to become a dangerous adversary of the British Empire in the Pacific Ocean, and Japan was to assert a claim against British possessions in the Pacific. It was assumed with all certainty that the USA would remain neutral if war was to break out, because according to the opinion of the espionage chiefs, who were bound to be in the know, the USA would be unable to afford a war due to its isolationist stance.

Naturally the original idea behind the Anti-Comintern Pact had been the complete encirclement of the Soviet Union. But when Major Usuj travelled to Poland and Romania for negotiations in the matter, he was surprised that his requests were met with blunt refusal by the two nations, despite all the support given by National Socialist Germany. Even the Polish Foreign Minister, Colonel Beck, usually a rather pliable character who generally was submissive to Berlin, thought it best to advise against Poland's signing of the pact; not so much out of fear of Moscow, but out of regard for London.

The Anti-Comintern Pact brought with it a very important development: the co-ordination of the signatories' espionage operations. Before long, Fascist Italy joined the pact that had been signed in Berlin, and the ensuing co-ordination of espionage efforts had an immediate advantageous effect for all participating nations, especially in the Eastern Mediterranean. The British not only keenly felt the impact of Japanese dumping in the Middle East and Far East, but they also soon registered an increasing influence of the allied nations of Italy, Japan and Germany over the entire Arab world. Very alarming difficulties arose for Britain not only in Iran and Iraq, but even in Egypt.

In order to affirm the newly entered pact, and in contravention of all conventions, the Japanese military attaché in Berlin, General Oshima, was appointed as ambassador, while General [Eugen] von Ott, a member of the general staff, was appointed as German ambassador in Tokyo. By elevating military men to the rank of ambassador, the significance of the military pact was to be underlined; but in truth, no actual military alliance had come into existence. Yes, *"Büro Ribbentrop"* had developed a political plan of action, but the alliance that had been forged was in the main an espionage agreement, because its main purpose was to agitate and to disturb the peace in the region to the south-east of the Soviet Union, that is to say, in Iran, Iraq and elsewhere in the Orient, as far as the Islamic regions of India. In actual fact, therefore, British interests were undermined to a much greater degree than those of Russia. Naturally, agitation in the Caucasus region also formed part of Ribbentrop's plan of action; Schalwa Karumidze, who had played a role in the development of the plan, had made sure of that. A full military alliance with Japan had been opposed by Generals Fritsch, Beck and Liebmann, and even the fact that Admiral Canaris, head of military espionage, would go on to play a very active role in the preparation of the plan did little to change the generals' stance. The action plan, as devised by *"Büro Ribbentrop"*, was merely supplemented with a military "action treaty", which would be triggered in case of a Soviet attack on Germany or Japan.

"Büro Ribbentrop" regarded the Anti-Comintern Pact as much as a stick as a carrot for Great

Britain. The pact was signed by Germany and Japan in 1936, with Fascist Italy joining in 1937. Japan's assault on Shanghai and the advance along the coast, which brought Japanese forces into the immediate vicinity of the British crown colony of Hong Kong, also took place in 1937. It is staggering that in 1935 Ribbentrop had been able to enter into a naval treaty with the British, and that, after he had been appointed as ambassador in London, his *"Büro Ribbentrop"* signed a pact with Japan that was an unambiguous threat to British interests.

The obstinacy of high Nazi officials, among them Ribbentrop, is breathtaking. They seriously believed that their crude tricks and threats – such as the Anti-Comintern Pact directed against Britain – would have the desired effect. Nazi foreign politics truly knew no form of proposal of friendship other than *"if you refuse to be our brothers, we shall break your skull"*.

Another word about Schalwa Karumidze: when he travelled abroad, he usually used a Bulgarian passport in the name of "Karumidiev". He was briefly interned in Switzerland, where he fiercely demanded an interview with the German envoy in Bern, and was subsequently released to Germany. As long as the Nazi regime achieved success upon success, he was "loyally devoted" to the Nazis; he was "their man". After his return to Germany from Switzerland, for a time he was an agent of the *SD-RFSS*, after which there is no further trace of him. It is said that he met an inglorious end.

The war in Spain and the "Condor Legion"

The start of the Spanish Civil War was marked by an act carried out by "volunteers" of the new German *Luftwaffe*, which would have a profound effect on the further course of the conflict. These supposed "volunteers" were pilots, engineers, designers, anti-aircraft specialists and ground personnel who had been painstakingly selected by the Ministry for Aviation in Berlin. They arrived in Morocco with twenty aircraft manufactured by "Junkers", and established the transport company *"Hisma" ("Hispano-Moroccan Transport Inc. Tetuan-Sevilla")*. This supposed "haulage firm" was of crucial importance to General Franco, as it was able to transport, within a few days, 15,000 Moroccan troops that were devoted to Franco (legionaries, *Regulares*, and Moroccan police units) from Morocco to southern Spain. In November 1936, *Hisma* was remodelled as the "Condor Legion".

The chief of the transport company *"Hisma"* was Colonel [Walter] Warlimont [1894–1976], a member of the general staff of the German *Luftwaffe*, who was also the German *Wehrmacht's* authorised representative with General Franco in Morocco at the outset of his rebellion.

Colonel Walter Warlimont (1894-1976), later to become Deputy Chief of Operations for the Oberkommando, helped Franco secure control of Morocco. In 1939 he helped plan the invasion of Poland, plans which were intentionally contradicted by information fed to the Polish High Command by the author on his secret double-agent spy mission canoulflaged by a simulated quarrel with Reinhard Heydrich and a phoney "SD arrest warrant". After the War, Warlimont was imprisoned until 1954. In 1962 he published the book *Inside Hitler's Headquarters, 1939-1945*. (*Bundesarchiv*)

When the German *Wehrmacht* officially intervened in the Spanish Civil War and ever more "volunteers" arrived from Germany, the later Field Marshal General of the *Luftwaffe* and then Major General [Hugo] Sperrle [1885-1953] was appointed as the first commander of the "Condor Legion". With his "Condor Legion", General Sperrle not only ensured air superiority in the Burgos-Seville-Madrid area and established a first-rate transport fleet, but in Spain he also created those fighter squadrons that, under the name *"Stuka"*, would have such a terrible impact on the World War that was to follow.

General Hugo Sperrle (1885-1953) of the Luftwaffe secured control of the air for Franco in Spain. While in Spain, he created the fighter plane squadrons known as *Stuka*, which were to be so important in the world war to come.

The "Condor Legion" was much more than just an excellent air force formation. Its anti-aircraft guns were not only used against airborne enemies, but also increasingly deployed as weapons of artillery in ground attacks. A special section of the legion were the so-called *"Imker"* ("bee keeper") units, who, as early as 1936, had started to rigorously train the rebelling Spaniards in the use of modern weaponry. It would fall to the German General Sperrle and his staff to present to General Franco the operational plan for the flanking manoeuvre along the 600-kilometre-long northern front, which on March 31, 1936 led to the major offensive along the entire front between Bilbao and Santander. The Italian "Novarra Corps" also made three of its brigades available for that venture. (Field Marshal General Stukke would fly into the most extreme fits of anger when he raged against the "wimpish conduct" of his Italian allies. He blamed the Italians for the fact that the "iron belt" around Bilbao could only be breached in June and the town taken much later than anticipated.)

During the course of the Spanish Civil War, the "Condor Legion", which initially had operated almost exclusively with planes manufactured by Junkers, began to experiment with many other types of German aircraft. With supercilious smiles on their faces, former members of the legion nowadays boast about how Junkers planes flying in close formation had dropped the first 250kg bombs, how several squadrons of Heinkel planes had carried out the first low-altitude machine-gun attacks, and how Messerschmidt planes had experimented with dive bombing for the first time.

Alongside the Luftwaffe, the army and navy, too, deployed new weaponry in the Spanish Civil War, testing its "war readiness" for German High Command. The training unit *"Imker"* was supported by the *Panzer* unit *"Drohne"* ("drone") and a marine training unit by the name of *"Anker"* ("anchor"). All of these units formed part of the "Condor Legion". The German torpedo boats *"Leopard"*, *"Albatros"*, *"Lux" and "Seeadler"*, the two submarines *"U 33"* and *"U 34"*, and the two armoured vessels *"Admiral Scheer"* and *"Deutschland"* were also deployed in the Spanish Civil War, tasked with the "dangerous defence of German interests" in Spanish waters. Among other actions, they carried out the "retaliatory bombardment" of the harbour of Almeira, which at that time was in the hands of the Spanish Republicans.

A photo of the submarine U 33 leaving its German harbour and sailing to Spain to assist Franco, as mentioned by the author.

Tanks of the Panzer Unit "Drohne", of the Drohne-Imker Group, in Spain during the Spanish Civil War. "Lonja del Pescado" just means a place where the fishermen sell their catch. The actual location of the coastal village where this photo was taken is unknown. It is likely that it was in the north of Spain.

The first commander of the "Condor Legion", *Luftwaffe* General Sperrle, had been succeeded by *Luftwaffe* General Volkmann, the later commander of the *Luftwaffe* academy. Its last commander was *Luftwaffe* General Dr Freiherr von Richthofen. The units of the German *Kriegsmarine* had been under the command of Vice Admiral von Fischel. The chief of the army units *"Imker"* and *"Drohne"* – both subdivisions of the "Condor Legion" – was Colonel Freiherr von Funck. According to the official version, apart from the two listed army units, the "Condor Legion" consisted of the 53rd Fighter Squadron, the 9th Anti Aircraft Regiment, and the 3rd Air Intelligence Regiment.

On June 6, 1939, in Berlin's Lustgarten, a victory parade was staged in honour of the "Condor Legion", which had just returned from Spain. Hitler himself spoke at that grand state ceremony, boasting about the "victories" that had been achieved by the new German *Wehrmacht* in the Spanish Civil War. Many Berlin residents had been obliged to attend the "jubilant reception" on the Unter den Linden boulevard. From their seats on the VIP stand, foreign dignitaries viewed in astonishment the German troops filing past in a victory parade. A foreign land, ravaged by civil war, General Franco's Spain, had been turned into a veritable military manoeuvre area for German special units. Without any scruples, the German Generals – those of the *Luftwaffe* and army alike – were experimenting in Spain. By any measure, the Spanish Civil War had been turned into an "excellent opportunity" for German militarism.

Not only had the German craftsmen of war unscrupulously put their skills to the test in a foreign land and, with the entire civilised world's acquiescence, turned into the murderers of Spanish Republicans, they also used the opportunity during this "dress rehearsal" to perfect the tools of their trade. On top of it all, they were able to rid themselves of other, outdated tools for a good price. German militarists had always been shrewd businessmen also. The general public was not to learn about the dirty business they conducted in Spain. The situation was this: at the time of Hitler's takeover, General Lutz was the commander of the German *Panzer* units. He had consolidated the first motorised units in large formations and created the first *Panzer* brigade for the *Reichswehr*. After the appointment of General Blomberg as *Reichswehrminister*, these tanks were contemptuously described as "tin cans" by Blomberg's chief of staff, Walter von Reichenau. For a short period of time, General von Reichenau acted as chief of the Army Ordnance Department in the *Reichswehrministerium*. After being promoted to the rank of lieutenant general, he was initially appointed as commander of the 7th Army Corps in Munich and eventually as commander of the 4th Army Group in Leipzig, where he became the grand organiser of all German motorised forces. At von Reichenau's behest (while he was still in Berlin), General Lutz was forced to resign and was replaced by General Guderian, the new commander of the *Panzer* forces. (General Lutz would later be appointed as "general for special deployment" and as president of an association of motorised vehicles operations.) Guderian was on friendly terms with Reichenau, and, despite the fact that as a *Panzer* general he was part of the army's supreme command, he was not much more than Reichenau's stooge in Leipzig. Be that as it may, Reichenau and Guderian tried their best to dump as many of their predecessor Lutz's "tin cans" in Spain as possible. While the *Panzer* unit *"Drohne"* of the "Condor Legion" was equipped with the newest models of German *Panzer* technology in order to test them on the battlefield, General Franco and his motorised units were sent the old "tin cans", which were usually quickly shot to pieces and in which many a Spanish tank operator was left to die a "hero's death" for the "honour of German business". The first commander of the "Condor Legion" talked angrily to his officers, blaming the "tin cans" that had been sent to General Franco for the poor progress of the war in Spain and the needless delay to its conclusion.

General Heinz Wilhelm Guderian (1888-1954). He sent "tin cans" to Spain in which many a Spanish tank driver died.

Much later, General Guderian had the unpleasant duty of going to the Eastern Front during the War. Here we see him on his way there.

PART THREE

A POLITICAL KALEIDOSCOPE

C. WAR

Prelude

This book is not a historical work on war; neither is it an exhaustive treatise on National Socialism. It merely seeks to present facts for whose veracity the author can avouch. In the following, a range of facts that necessarily had to lead to war are to be recorded.

On June 30, 1934, at the behest of the *Reichswehr*, the supposed "Röhm revolt" was brutally quelled by Adolf Hitler. The *Reichswehr*, under the leadership of its supreme commander, General Freiherr von Fritsch, had won a victory over the NSDAP, but it simply did not understand how to take advantage of that victory.

On July 25, 1934, the Austrian Chancellor Engelbert Dollfuss was murdered by Nazis in Vienna.

His [Dolfuss's] successor, Kurt Schuschnigg, was given assurances by Mussolini, which the *"Duce"* was later unable to honour. After Dollfuss's assassination, the "NSDAP *Landesinspekteur* for Austria", Theodor Habicht, was appointed as mayor of Wittenberg. Later he advanced to the position of department head in the Foreign Office, with the official title of "undersecretary of state". Put simply, the person who – from his offices in Munich and at the Party's behest – had orchestrated Dollfuss's murder was now "honourably" elevated to one of the highest offices in the Nazi state.

Theodor Habicht (1898-1944, killed in action on the Eastern Front), the Nazi functionary who according to the author organised and planned the assassination of Chancellor Dolfuss of Austria. He had originally been sent to Austria by Hitler in 1931 to oversee the reorganisation of the Austrian Nazi Party, which he then ran jointly with Alfred Proksch (1891-1981). Habicht was very proud of killing Dolfuss, and boasted to Putzi Hanfstängl: "That *schwein* Dolfuss is dead!"

Austrian Chancellor Engelbert Dolfuss of Austria (1892-1934), who was murdered by Theodor Habicht., as a prelude to the Nazis later taking over Austria. (The author's detailed account of this and subsequent events is to be found in Volume Two. He was both an eyewitness of and an active agent in preparing for the *Anschluss.*)

After the death of *Reichspräsident* Paul von Hindenburg, Hitler appointed himself as "Führer and *Reich* Chancellor" and the *Reichswehr* was sworn to his name. It was not only the *Reichswehrminister*, Werner von Blomberg, who swore an oath of allegiance to Hitler, but also – without any protest – the entire general corps, headed by the supreme commander General von Fritsch. (Hindenburg died on August 2, 1934.)

On January 13, 1935, the Nazi regime won a great foreign policy victory in the referendum in the Saarland, and, thus encouraged, reintroduced general conscription on March 16, 1935. At the request of the general corps, the conscription period was doubled from one to two years on August 24, 1936. To much acclaim from his generals, Hitler resolved to "recapture" the Rhineland, and, in direct contravention of the terms of the Treaty of Versailles, German troops marched into the Rhineland on March 7, 1936.

The first days of February 1938 saw the resignations of the "chief of army command",

General Freiherr von Fritsch, and 18 of his staff. These resignations were wrongly interpreted as a protest against the annexation of Austria that took place immediately afterwards, but, in truth, they were nothing more than sulking withdrawals in the face of Hitler's breaches of promises regarding the *Reichswehr's* homogeneity. Around the same time – but independently – *Reichswehrminister* von Blomberg was also forced to resign, as he had lost the trust of the general corps following his marriage to an "unworthy" woman. Thereupon Hitler assumed supreme command of the entire *Wehrmacht* and dissolved the Ministry of War on February 4, 1938. That is to say, he no longer appointed ministers for the three constituent parts of the *Wehrmacht*. Instead, General Wilhelm Keitel, forever a servile character, became "supreme commander of the three parts of the *Wehrmacht*" and "chief of the high command of the *Wehrmacht*". As such, he was tasked with the affairs of a minister of war.

General Wilhelm Bodewin Johann Gustav Keitel (1882-1946; executed by hanging) was the Chief of the High Command of the Army from 1938. According to the author, he was 'forever a servile character'.

One of the few generals for whom Hitler had an inflated level of respect was the ostensibly Nazi-friendly General von Reichenau, who at that time was under suspicion of scheming against the NSDAP's power in the state. Von Reichenau, one of the most intelligent members of the German general corps, was ushered out of the *Reichswehrministerium* with much praise and instead appointed as commander of the 7th Army Corps in Munich, where, together with his staff, he developed plans for the "annexation of Austria". However, he was not allowed to personally lead the annexation, as those around him were wary of him. The "march" of the German *Wehrmacht* into Austria began on the morning of March 12, 1938. Despite the fact that there was virtually no resistance, a startling number of armoured vehicles floundered and broke down during the invasion of Austria, thus proving General Reichenau's assertion that General Lutz's "tin cans" were not fit for purpose. They broke down not due to engine failure but because of malfunctioning tracks that could not cope with the mountainous terrain. Their greatest enemies were --- scree and sharp stones! Reichenau was tasked with the urgent reorganisation of the German *Panzer* units, for which purpose he was transferred to Leipzig, where, as chief of the newly created Army Group 4, he founded the Heavy *Panzer* Force, and, together with his staff, developed plans for the "march on Czechoslovakia" and the "assault on Poland". All these plans were developed in close co-operation with the chief of the general staff, General Beck.

The all-too-peaceable British Prime Minister, Neville Chamberlain, met in Munich with his French counterpart, Édouard Daladier, and in Godesberg with Adolf Hitler. He believed that through amicable negotiations and the abandonment of Austria and later Czechoslovakia he would be able to rescue peace. On October 1, 1938, the "occupation of the Sudeten German territories" commenced, and on March 15, 1939, the German *Wehrmacht* invaded Czechoslovakia and held its "victory march" in Prague. By March 16, 1939, the formal establishment of the "Protectorate of Bohemia and Moravia" and Slovakia's sovereignty, "by the grace of Hitler", were already resolved upon. Colonel General Otto was appointed as the "*Inspekteur* of the German troops" in Slovakia, after a so-called "treaty of protection" was signed with the newly formed government of Slovakia on March 23, 1939. On the previous day, March 22, 1939, the Memel Territory had "returned to the German *Reich*".

Neville Chamberlain arrives in Germany to give a smiling and enthusiastic greeting to Adolf Hitler. Notice how Hitler has positioned himself two steps higher than his lowly British supplicant. (From an original photograph by an unknown official German photographer, Eglantyne Collection. This same image was however also circulated at the time in a larger print by the German Government and reproduced in the press.)

On April 20, 1939, Berlin celebrated Adolf Hitler's 50th birthday with much pomp and ceremony and a parade of the German *Wehrmacht*, the likes of which the world had never seen before.

On the VIP stands, the representatives of the entire civilised world were sitting shoulder to shoulder and, through their presence, paid homage to the "victorious German Führer and *Reich* Chancellor". Proudly, the official German celebratory communiqué announced:

"On Wednesday afternoon, wreaths were laid at the cenotaph "Unter den Linden" by the Führer's foreign guests. Upon arriving at the marble memorial, they were greeted by the commander of Berlin, Lieutenant General Seifert. After a parade by the guard of honour of the Berlin guards regiment, the solemn laying of wreaths commenced at the cenotaph.

Among the honorary guests at the ceremony (apart from all the ambassadors, envoys and military attachés! – author's note) were:

Lord Brocket and retired Major General [John Frederick Charles 'Boney'] Fuller [1878-1966] (Great Britain);

Lieutenant General Deffontaine, army corps commander (Belgium);

The Belgian Lieutenant General Georges François Auguste Deffontaine (1882-1940, died in a German POW camp) is at right in the foreground of this photo taken in mid-April, 1936, in London. Standing beside him is the French Major General Henri Schweissgut, Deputy Chief of the French Army General Staff. They are leaving the War Office after the first round of the British-French-Belgian talks about what to do about Hitler's reoccupation of the Rhineland. Three years later, Deffontaine flew to Berlin to take part in Hitler's 50th Birthday celebrations.

Dr. [Frans Herman] Visman (1888-1972), member of the administration of the Dutch East Indies (Netherlands);

Lieutenant General With, commander of the army and air force, and Vice Admiral [Hjalmar] Rechnitzer [1872-1953], chief of the navy (Denmark);

General [Kristian] Laake (Norway);

The Norwegian General Kristian Kristiansen Laake (1875-1950).

He came from Norway to Berlin specially to attend Hitler's 50th birthday celebration on April 20, 1939. At the time, he was Commanding General of Norway, and he was involved in shrinking the Norwegian Army, which was to have the effect of weakening Norway's defences against Hitler's coming invasion. He was replaced after the Germans launched their attack, but it was too late to counteract Laake's bad decisions and passivity.

Agis Tambakopoulos, Minister of Justice (Greece);

General Ali Fuat Cebesoy (1882-1968), Minister of Public Works, and Colonel General Asim Gündüz (1880-1970), Deputy Chief of the General Staff (Turkey);

Turkish General Alia Fuat Cebesoy (1882-1968) travelled to Berlin to celebrate Hitler's 50th birthday in 1939. He was a member of the Turkish parliament and in 1939 became Minister of Public Works until 1943.

and many others."

All listed personalities had travelled to Berlin as their governments' envoys! It was their mission to support their nations' official diplomatic representatives in their congratulations to Adolf Hitler, and, through their presence, to lend additional weight – and more cordiality? – to those congratulations. Immediately after the attacks on Austria and Czechoslovakia they had made their pilgrimages to the cenotaph "Unter den Linden", in order to demonstrate their countries' special respect for the new German *Wehrmacht.*

Certainly the adulations bestowed on Adolf Hitler on the occasion of his 50th birthday by the representatives of all major nations present in Berlin were seen by the Nazis not as mockery, but as approval, and would have decisively strengthened the entire predatory politics of the Nazi regime. It must be noted that the United States was the only major power – apart from Russia – who refrained from any expression of felicitation and that, in the manner of his participation at the laudatory parade, President Roosevelt's ambassador only upheld the most necessary forms of politeness.

In an act of scornful mockery, Rudolf Hess, the actual leader of the NSDAP, presented his "Führer" with 50 letters written by Frederick II, which had just been confiscated from the Free Masons by the secret state police. The documents were hand-written by the famous King of the Prussians, which he had composed in his capacity as founder and first Grand Master of the Old Prussian lodge *"Zu den drei Weltkugeln"*. The letters had been guarded by the Free Masons like the most precious jewels, and had never been made available for inspection, scholarly study or publication even to the Prussian National Library. As was mentioned earlier, Adolf Hitler had promised to *Reichspräsident* Hindenburg never to dissolve those Masonic lodges that had a special nationalistic and Prussian inclination. Hitler broke his word, the secret state police forced the lodges' "dissolution", confiscated all possessions, and the "Führer and *Reich* Chancellor" was presented with the stolen letters by his trusted deputy with the words:

"You have reconnected the current course of German history with the spirit and purpose of the great Germans of a bygone era – and the spirit of these great men is within you. With this in mind, I am honoured, on behalf of our movement, to present you with these yellowed sheets, which have once been touched by the hand of one of the greatest architects of German destiny, which are written in his hand, and which communicate his spirit to us through the ages. Our movement presents to you – and through you to the entire German nation – 50 letters written by Frederick the Great!"

Futile warnings

In March 1939, a young British intelligence officer received the first reports of an impending arrangement between National Socialist Germany and Bolshevik Russia. As the details concerning negotiations about a German-Russian friendship pact became ever more concrete, they were dismissed with the words: "That's idiocy!" A commission of members of the French and British general staffs travelled to Russia and, on August 23, 1939, were informed in Moscow that a German-Russian friendship pact had indeed been entered into. Upon hearing this, the generals had to immediately travel back to France and England, without having accomplished anything. The German military attaché in Moscow, General [Ernst August] Köstring [1876-1953], received a high-ranking visitor from the *Wehrmacht's* supreme command in Berlin. After his return from Russia, Ribbentrop triumphantly revelled in his success. Always displaying his tried and tested diplomat's smile, the German ambassador in Moscow, Friedrich Werner Graf von der Schulenburg, attempted to negotiate all troubles and obstacles that were soon standing in the way of the new "friendship". In these efforts he was assisted by the German embassy councillor [Kurt] von Tippelskirch [1880-1946], a far less "diplomatic" man. *[He was not the same person as General Kurt von Tippelskirch of the Wehrmacht, 1891-1957.]*

Alexis [Saint-Léger] Léger [*the poet whose pen name was Saint-John Perse, who later won the Nobel Prize for Literature in 1960*], the general secretary at the "Quai d'Orsay" in Paris (a man who played a key role in French foreign policy), and Prime Minister Daladier received warning upon warning, but disregarded them one and all. Despite all concrete details, the veracity of the ominous information was questioned again and again. Across the border, in the small country of Switzerland, general mobilisation was initiated based on the same warnings. War broke out. In his first public speech, Corps Commander Henri Guisan [1874-1960], having been promoted to the rank of general and supreme commander of the Swiss army, made it clear that it had been possible to order general mobilisation of the Swiss army – on precisely the correct day – only thanks to special information received by the well-functioning intelligence service, for which the general showed himself very grateful. [*It is probable that the author knew Guisan personally in Switzerland after his defection and discussed this in person with him. The author worked for the Intelligence Department of the General Staff of the Swiss Army from the autumn of 1938 until September 1, 1941.*]

The Swiss General Henri Guisan who "got it right" when the French "got it wrong".

As was reported in a previous chapter, the deputy chief of the Polish "Defence", Colonel Lipinski, fought unsuccessfully against the supposed genuine invasion plan that had been "stolen" from the *Reichswehrministerium* by the Polish intelligence officer Sosnowski in good faith. The cunning plan spread disinformation and would have disastrous consequences for the Polish general staff. Colonel Lipinski later would heroically defend Warsaw, while his friend, Admiral von Walden, former chief of the Polish military mission in Danzig [Gdansk], became the valiant defender of the Westerplatte near Gdingen [Gdynia].

As early as during the winter of 1936/37, the Polish general staff had at their disposal a 300-page-strong memorandum detailing all weaknesses and deficiencies of the Polish army, but all warnings were eventually swept aside as exaggerations by the Polish generalissimo Edward Rydz-Śmigły [aka Śmigły-Rydz, 1886-1941] who was the successor of Józef [Klemens] Piłsudski 1867-1935].

General Edward Rydz-Śmigły, Commanding General of the Polish Army, 'got it *very* wrong'. He dismissed a 300-page report outlining the deficiencies and inadequacies of the Polish Army, as Hitler's invasion of Poland loomed.

The Foreign Minister, Colonel Beck, flew into a rage, as the memorandum criticised his foreign policy. The political bias of the document culminated in these words:

"If Poland wants to avoid being crushed between two steam rollers, it must seek conciliation with Czechoslovakia and try to forge an eleventh-hour military pact. For unlike Poland, Czechoslovakia has first-rate artillery units at her disposal. The Polish army, on the other hand, commands not only an excellent cavalry but also a well-drilled infantry, which only needs to be better motorised, in line with latest technology. However, both nations lack a combat-effective air force or – equally important – an adequate armoured tank force. Even so, in concert with the Czech artillery, the Polish infantry and cavalry could put up effective resistance, even in a war on two fronts, for an appreciable amount of time. All depends on adequate co-ordination and timely military relief by France and England."

On the basis of this memorandum, the Polish Foreign Minister, Colonel [Jósef] Beck [1894-

1944], speedily arranged for – – – defamation of the irksome admonisher. During the winter of 1936/37, Polish-German relations were still excellent.

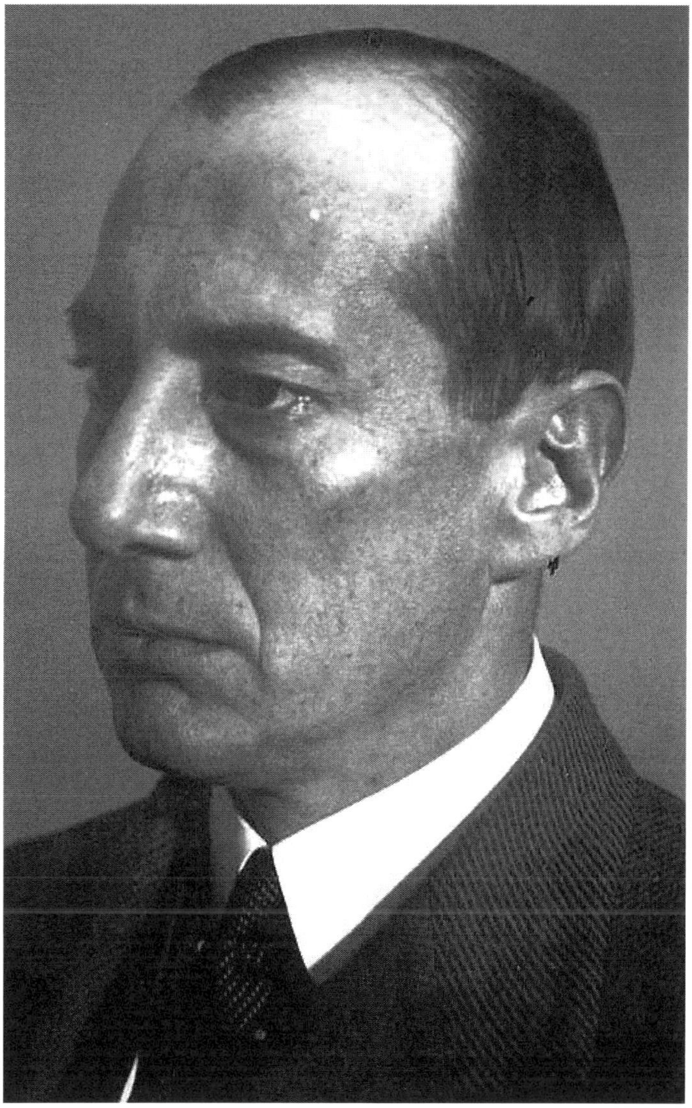

Polish Foreign Minister Józef Beck (1894–1944, died of TB) also disregarded the warnings and continued 'friendly relations' with Germany.

In defence of the Polish generals it must be noted that they were quite open to any kind of critical advice. They were under no illusions as to the present state of affairs, but had to disregard the warnings contained in the memorandum "on higher orders". Unfortunately the course of the German *Blitzkrieg* later created the impression that Polish soldiers were inadequate defenders of their homeland. In actual fact, wherever the Poles were led well, they put up an excellent fight and truly heroic resistance. The Polish officers, too, were by no means inexperienced, but by and large hard-nosed and seasoned commanders of military units. The members of the general staff had all enjoyed excellent training, but their intended defensive strategy was rendered meaningless from the word go by the enemy's cunning deployment of "disinformation", i.e. the "stolen" plan of attack. The German *Blitzkrieg* against Poland meant the country was simply overrun, made possible by inadequate allocation and deployment of troops by the Polish side. Despite the most skilful last-minute improvisation, such comprehensive misdirection of the entire Polish army could not be redeemed.

The *Blitzkrieg* against Poland had been completed; Warsaw had put up a desperate fight. France entered the period of *"drôle de guerre"* ("phoney war"). Alexis Léger, the general secretary at the French Foreign Office, as well as Daladier himself, were told the precise date of the planned assault on Belgium and the Netherlands. Having given them little consideration, both Daladier and Lèger simply shelved the intelligence reports they had received. Later, in an attempt to exculpate themselves, they would deny ever having taken possession of the reports, feigning innocence and surprise. The answer to all warnings and admonitions, however concrete, was a telegram from Paris: "Why are you so pessimistic?" At the end of April 1940 – when within three days of receipt of intelligence regarding an impending assault on Norway the actual deed followed with regrettable precision – one of Monsieur Léger's confidants saw fit to opine: "Your intelligence regarding a German attack on the Netherlands and Belgium is incorrect! I have just heard that the German envoy in Brussels has given credible assurances on behalf of the *Reich* government that Germany will definitely honour Belgium's neutrality. Even if your predictions concerning Norway may in part have turned out to be correct, on this occasion, regarding Belgium and the Netherlands, you are in the wrong. Our intelligence in the matter simply is better than yours. Remember: all of our various intelligence reports independently conform with each other, while they are diametrically opposed to the one single piece of information that you have received."

Alexis Saint-Léger Léger (1887-1975), the General Secretary at the French Foreign Office who disregarded the warnings of the German invasion of Belgium. Under the pen name Saint-John Perse, he was one of the 20th century's greatest poets, and he won the Nobel Prize for Literature in 1960. When the Nazis came to Paris in 1940, they destroyed many of his unpublished manuscripts, and the Vichy regime stripped him of his French nationality. He fled to America, where the Chanler family provided him a place to live and write on the coast of Maine. It was there that he wrote one of his finest and most inspiring long poems: *Chronique*. (He adopted the name of Perse as his pen name because he was descended from the Perse family of Cornwall.) It must be said in Léger's defence, considering his and Daladier's inaction regarding German threats, that the French Foreign Minister, Georges Bonnet, as well as his wife, had been blackmailed by agents of the German Abwehr and were concealing and destroying the intelligence warnings and not passing them on, and were actively aiding Abwehr spies and helping to prepare the way for a German occupation. To have such treason and betrayal at the highest level of the French Government is not surprising, considering the Vichy regime which was soon to follow. Since the Abwehr spies were rivals to our author's organisation, he may not have known at the time that Bonnet had become a German agent for them, and he attributed the otherwise astounding lapses in judgement to Daladier and Léger being idiots, not realizing they had not been shown the information concealed by Bonnet. Of all the people in France from whom Bonnet would most wish to conceal his treachery, it would have been Léger, who was his Ministry's very own General Secretary. In order to protect himself from exposure, Bonnet fired his Ministry's Political Director René Massigli and sent him off to Turkey to get him out of the way because Massigli was questioning his actions and decisions too closely.

The assault on the Netherlands and Belgium came to pass. German tanks advanced into France. The neglected French military aviation apparatus was easy prey for the German *Luftwaffe*. The battle-hardened General Weygand was only called upon when it was already too late.

The Maginot Line was bypassed. Paul Reynaud, who was unflinching in his commitment to absolute resistance, had to resign. The aged Marshal Philippe Pétain was appointed as Prime Minister and capitulated. At the French embassy in Bern extremely turbulent scenes unfolded. The embassy staff were panicking, but the former admonisher and naysayer had suddenly turned into an optimist:

"Allow me to join Weygand! The Nazis have only seven tank divisions left. Resistance in the south *must* lead to success! Let me join Weygand! I stake my life on the fact that my information is correct and with my presence vouch for the possible defensive measures."

The French embassy councillor Saint-Hardouin replied scornfully:

"You, of all people, you, the eternal merchant of doom, now play the optimist! And now, when it is totally misguided!"

And he continued angrily:

"It's all lies! Nothing but lies! Ignorance and stupidity! You talk of seven tank divisions; but only this morning I received reports about a 123rd German tank division! Hahaha!"

No amount of explanation made any difference. Eventually – at midnight – the French ambassador Coulondre decided that a departure for the headquarters of General Weygand was out of the question, especially since any further resistance was now futile. The former pessimist who had turned into a bothersome optimist was seen off with a piece of well-intended advice:

"Get yourself to safety as quickly as possible. We have precise intelligence about an attack on Switzerland within the next few hours. By dawn the Nazis will be outside Bern. Believe us! This time, we are better informed, and your incredulity will cost you your life!"

The French diplomats in Bern truly had lost their heads, and no argument – however conclusive – would thenceforth be effective. It was a time of virulent rumour-mongering.

Prior to the outbreak of war, German émigrés had found a myriad ways of praising the "invincible" *"Grande Nation"*; they labelled the French army the "world's best army". For a credulous global audience they calculated the fact that Nazi Germany was in no position to start a war and presented precise mathematical "proof" to back up their claims. They reported on the impending collapse of the Nazi regime, and wrote entire books about the tensions between the *Wehrmacht* and the party, which, they alleged, would come to a head as soon as war broke out. In the brief interval following the assault on Poland, they seriously asserted that German militarism could not possibly be contemplating an attack on France. They adduced "evidence" they believed proved that Belgium and the Netherlands would not be attacked. They did not even shy away from vilifying the brave Poles with such sentiments as: "That would never happen to the French!"

Anyone who did, with honest unease, warn of the strength of German militarism was suspected of being a Nazi agent, and all who dared to report on a seeming consolidation of the Nazi regime were, without fail, written off as outright Nazis.

Nowhere in the world were the writings of General de Gaulle studied with as much fervour as at the German war academies, along with an excellent book written by General Weygand on the Viscount of Turenne. Paul Reynaud, who himself had been forced to stand on the sidelines for too long, brought de Gaulle into the French Ministry of War only in April 1940, and the great French General Weygand was not appointed as supreme commander (to replace Gamelin) until it was too late. There was no time and opportunity left for him to completely reorganise the French resistance, in order to check Germany's advance, to save Paris and to avoid the Maginot Line being bypassed. Out of a fear of utter chaos he then counselled Pétain to capitulate. On July 24, 1940 [should be June?], the clear-thinking Georges Mandel tried to form a government of resistance in Rabat, Morocco, but he was betrayed, arrested and, together with Daladier and Campinchi, was forced to sail back to his homeland on board the "Massilia". When General Viscount Gort and Duff Cooper landed in Rabat in a hydroplane on June 25, Mandel was already in captivity. The two British emissaries sent by Churchill only found Lord Dillon, who had also travelled to Rabat on a secret mission. France seemed to be irredeemably lost, but her saviour had already arisen in London. General Charles de Gaulle, who had been able to flee France in time, declared his unwavering belief in God and justice, even in the face of all military defeats, in two radio broadcast from London.

The war against Russia

One of the few statesmen who in Berlin had not come under Hitler's spell was the Romanian Foreign Minister Grigore Gafencu. Immediately after Hitler's 50th birthday, as a guest of the *Reich* government, and as a consequence of the lack of action by France and Britain following Germany's annexations of Austria and Czechoslovakia, he had been forced to enter into a friendship pact with Hitler's Germany. However, it is very instructive to review his speeches and toasts given in Berlin, and to notice their distinct lack of gushing praise for Hitler (which was the daily fare of most other statesmen on such occasions). Later Gafencu was appointed as the Romanian envoy in Moscow. However, in Russia he was not exactly a *"persona grata"*, and thus had to be content with quiet observation instead of an active and busy diplomatic schedule. [*The author had a special knowledge of Romanian political personalities: see Volume Two.*]

The Romanian Foreign Minister Grigore Gafencu (left; 1892-1957) was reluctantly forced to deal with Hitler. The author praises his book explaining in great detail the real reasons for Germany going to war with Russia, and regrets that few people read it.

Gafencu wrote a book entitled "Prelude to the Russian Campaign". Sadly, despite its sound basic attitude and the excellent body of facts it contains, it never achieved the circulation it would have deserved. In his book, Gafencu shows how opposite interests collided on the issues of the Balkans, the Dardanelles, and the domination of the Danube, and how these conflicts of interest necessarily had to lead to a war that had neither been desired nor provoked by Russia. What is more, on the German side there were many other factors that all led towards a war with Russia.

According to an agreement between the German and Russian generals, a demarcation line was drawn straight through Poland, and the Baltic states were "shared out" by mutual accord. Latvia and Estonia were declared to be part of the "Russian zone of influence" and thus relinquished to the Red Army, while Lithuania was to be part of the "German zone of influence" according to explicit arrangements. However, the "Soviet-Lithuanian Mutual Assistance Treaty", which, following an increase in tensions, came about on October 10, 1939, suddenly entitled the Soviets to establish Red Army garrisons also in Lithuania. The German general staff only reluctantly agreed; a fierce altercation took place in the Führer's headquarters between Ribbentrop and Chief of General Staff Halder.

On November 29, 1939, the Soviet Union started its first campaign against Finland. After putting up heroic resistance, on March 13, 1940 the Finns had to sign a peace treaty that forced Finland to surrender important stretches of territory. The Germans had to stand back and watch as "their Finns" were ultimately crushed by the superior force of the Red Army. Even so, the Red Army – whether intentionally or unintentionally – demonstrated a military weakness that must have been extraordinary to behold for the German generals. (Encouraged by the German General Hoffmann, the Finns had declared their independence from Russia in 1917. Two years later, in 1919, a German auxiliary corps led by General von der Goltz fought against the Bolsheviks for Finland's liberation, and German troops in co-operation with General [later Field Marshal, Baron Carl Gustaf Emil *Freiherr*] Mannerheim (1867-1951) liberated Helsinki and were the first to march into the Finnish capital. Consequently, the German militarists thought of the Finns as "their Finns", and, following the defeat of the Soviet army in the spring of 1940, that was the case more than ever.)

A 1940 photo of General (later Field Marshal) Baron Carl Gustav Emil Mannerheim (1967-1951). Many Finns consider him "the greatest Finn of all time" because he successfully saved Finland from being absorbed into the Soviet Union. In 1944 he became President of Finland., resigning in 1946 after conluding a peace with the Soviets. Earlier, Mannerheim maintained a very friendly liaison with the German Nazis. He had coordinated closely with the Germans between 1919 and 1920 in fighting the Bolsheviks, and kept close to the Germans thereafter. And as our author reveals, Mannerheim held secret negotiations with the Chief of Staff of the Wehrmacht, Field Marshal Halder, in 1940, which so alarmed the Soviets that the Soviet Foreign Minister Molotov issued a public demand that the Germans stop interfering in Finnish-Russian relations.

As soon as France had been overpowered, during the first days of September 1940 no less a figure than the German chief of general staff, Field Marshal General Franz Halder, personally travelled to Finland and held secret negotiations with Mannerheim and his entourage. But perhaps Halder's trip to Finland was not kept quite as secret as it seemed. On November 12, 1940, Molotov demanded in Berlin that Germany should keep its nose out of the relationship between Finland and Russia. Moreover, Moscow was alarmed by the friendship pact the Axis powers had entered into with Japan (September 23, 1940). Despite all reassurances given to Molotov, especially following the crisis in the Balkans that was spiralling out of control,

Bulgaria was occupied on March 2, 1941, in the wake of which a change of regime took place in Yugoslavia and war broke out in the Balkans. Expecting an attack by Germany, the Kremlin sought assurances of neutrality from Japan. The exact details can be found in any chronicle of the war.

Göring, in his capacity as chief of the German *Luftwaffe*, had pushed for an immediate invasion of the British Isles. In this he was supported by von Ribbentrop and virtually the entire leadership of the NSDAP, as well as the supreme commander of the navy, Fleet Admiral Dr Räder. However, during those days Adolf Hitler was entirely under the influence of his victorious army generals, who were determined to first fight a war against Russia. The facts, which are all too little known, are the following: the Nazis (sic!), with Göring leading the way, wanted an immediate invasion of the British Isles, but the generals demanded a war against Russia! – – – Unusually, Hitler did not listen to his Foreign Minister, but, at the last minute, opted for the generals' plan. The successful campaign in the Balkans and the weakness of the Red Army that had become apparent during the first war between Finland and Russia seemed to justify the generals' desire. Behind the scenes, repulsive intrigues and wild struggles ensued over who would have the decisive influence over the *Führer* and *Reich* Chancellor.

The German Chief of General Staff, General [Franz] Halder, repeatedly demanded a campaign against Russia in the most insolent and unrelenting manner; he was supported by the arch-conservative Generals Fedor von Bock, Gerd von Rundstedt with his chief of staff [Erich] von Manstein, Walter von Reichenau, Wilhelm List, and a good dozen other prominent exponents of the German *Wehrmacht*, led by Field Marshal General von Brauchitsch.

General Franz Halder (1884–1972), Chief of Staff, "repeatedly demanded a campaign against Russia in the most insolent and unrelenting manner", according to the author.

This coterie of generals had influential allies within Hitler's inner circle in General Jodl, the commander of the *Führer's* headquarters; his predecessor, General Rommel, who at that time was still commonly referred to as "the *Führer's* Benjamin"; and – last, but not least – in General Keitel, the "supreme commander of the three elements of the *Wehrmacht*", who many disrespectfully called "Hitler's dogsbody".

General Alfred Josef Ferdinand Jodl, Commander of Hitler's Headquarters, who later became Chief of the Operations Staff of the Army High Command. He was a central member of Hitler's inner circle. He signed the surrender to the Allies. He was hanged at the end of the War.

Against this trio, a man such as *Luftwaffe* Major General [Karl-Heinrich] Bodenschatz (Göring's deputy in the *Führer's* headquarters) had no chance.

Luftwaffe General Karl-Heinrich Bodenschatz (1890-1979), at right, Deputy to Hermann Göring and his personal liaison with Hitler, who according to the author, "had no chance". Here we see him leaving the German Embassy in Carlton House Terrace, London, accompanied by Major General Rudolf Wenninger (1890-1945), at left, the German air attaché, on a secret visit to London of January 1, 1938. The third man at rear is unidentified, but presumably is an assistant military attaché. The real reason for this secret visit to London was revealed long after the War by Putzi Hanfstängl, in his memoirs. Putzi had fled Germany in 1937, and spent some months hiding in Switzerland. From there he went to London where his presence was publicly known. Bodenschatz was sent to meet with him and persuade him to return to Germany. The Nazis were worried that Putzi knew too much, and they must get him back at all costs. Bodenschatz had been told to offer him Göring's personal guarantee of safety, and handed him a letter to this effect signed by Göring. After all, Hanfstängl and Göring had been close friends earlier on, and this was supposed to be an offer which would seem convincing. But Hanfstängl did not fall for this, and when he refused to return, Bodenschatz made these remarks to him: "We can't keep this kind of thing quiet forever. The foreign press people in Berlin are already starting to ask all sorts of awkward questions. If you won't see reason things might become very unpleasant for your family." Hanfstängl replied: "Tell your boss to get any hostages out of his mind. If I hear that one of them has been as much as threatened I shall publish everything I know about the whole Nazi regime. All my records have been in places of safety for some time and I can tell you even Goebbels wouldn't get his trousers on again for a fortnight." Bodenshatz replied: "Very well, I will report back to Göring and ring you from Berlin. There must be some way of settling this." Our author knew nothing of this, as all of these events took place outside the scope or knowledge of the SD, SS, or Gestapo, but were instead coordinated by Göring and Goebbels, the great enemies of Himmler and Heydrich.

Adolf Hitler, who during those days spent most of his time with the general staff, did not pay much attention to the NSDAP party leaders. Hess vented his anger in a conversation with Göring: "The Führer only has eyes and ears for these reactionary generals!" In public, Hitler also underlined his close connection to the German generals, which was neither pomposity nor bluff on Hitler's part, but a true reflection of the reality at that time.

The ambition of the generals of German militarism and their addiction to belligerent activity and "glorious victories on the fields of honour" have – from time immemorial – decisively influenced the German thirst for power and consistently and profoundly affected German foreign policy. Both *"Büro Ribbentrop"* and the members of the personal staff of *Reichsmarschall* Göring thirsted for an invasion of the British Isles until the very end. Not that they sought to avert a war against Russia on moral grounds. Certainly not. All they wanted was the invasion first and then the war against Russia. Why?

Much like most events that occurred under the Nazi regime in Germany, this struggle for power, which took place behind the scenes of the Third Reich, was also not about principles. All the intrigues were designed purely to expand personal power, to gain new medals and decorations, and to satisfy personal ambition. The generals who sat in Army High Command saw no opportunities for themselves in an invasion, for they knew full well that during the all-important initial stages of such an operation the generals of the *Luftwaffe* and the admirals of the navy would be given supreme command. In such a scenario they would have had to unconditionally subordinate themselves to Göring, who, backed by the generals of the *Luftwaffe*, would have presented himself as the ultimate heroic figure after a victorious conclusion of the campaign. Instead they were eager to earn as much acclaim as possible in a ground campaign against Russia, so that the generals of the *Luftwaffe* would not be able to compete with them, however significant their later successes might be. As they saw it, Göring, despite his grand title of *Reichsmarschall*, should remain a deferential rival, who would be "taken in tow" by the army generals following a successful campaign against Russia.

Conversely, Göring calculated that at the commencement of a successful invasion he would automatically be appointed as supreme commander also of the "army lowlifes", which would mean that he would not only be the "most senior", i.e. highest-ranking, officer of the *Wehrmacht*, but effectively also the superior of the entire general corps of Army Supreme Command. For he, Göring, would have the initiative in case of an invasion, and, with it, supreme command.

However banal such considerations may seem, and however primitive such intrigues and wrangling may appear, sadly they are true and irrefutable facts. They are the pivotal trains of thought that eventually led to the war against Russia! In their boundless ambition, the German generals all competed for Hitler's approval. It fell to a former private of the World War of 1914–18 to decide whose ambition would be satisfied first: that of the generals of the *Luftwaffe*, or that of the generals of the Army. Hermann Göring lost his fight for air supremacy high above the British capital, while his fight for Hitler's approval for an invasion was lost in the *Führer's* headquarters. Giant landing equipment had been readied on the shores of Holland, small and medium-sized tanks were to be transported through the air and set down in England by specially constructed "gripper planes", and at the military training area Münster, situated between Celle and Lüneburg, the generals "played invasion" in endless military exercises. Virtually the entire Lüneburg Heath seemed to have been transformed into a gigantic base camp for the impending invasion. But Hitler opted for the plans of "his" chief of general staff, General Franz Halder, and Keitel, Brauchitsch, Bock, Rundstedt *et al.*were "finally" given the go-ahead for the attack on the Soviet Union.

The German generals had demanded from Hitler an immediate war against Russia, against the will of Göring, Ribbentrop and the Nazi party leaders! According to all indications, the generals' plan was correct while Göring's scheme appeared untenable. But when the seemingly unstoppable advances reversed into increasingly rapid retreats, when the fortunes of war finally turned and all the German generals' plans were thrown into disarray, in the end it was the prominent *Luftwaffe* generals who were given supreme command over the army. Field Marshal General Albert Kesselring replaced General von Rundstedt as the supreme commander over the entire Western Front.

The birth of a new *Dolchstoss* Legend

On a warm spring evening, a group of officers from all three branches of the armed services were merrily carousing in the *Luftwaffe's* House of the Aviators on Berlin's Wannsee. Heads of department from the *Reichswehrministerium* and from Army Supreme Command and their navy comrades were hosted by the airmen. *Luftwaffe* General [Ernst] Udet, a man who always enjoyed a bit of banter, was holding court and telling disrespectful jokes about his friend "Hermann", i.e. Göring. Suddenly someone asked: "Why is the lion not here yet?" A newcomer to the group asked: "Who is that, the lion?" And to much laughter from his drinking companions, *Luftwaffe* General Christiansen, "the old *Käpt'n"* who had transferred from the Navy to the *Luftwaffe* during the World War of 1914–18, gave this explanation: "My dear young fellow, who or what is a lion? It is an animal that roars in the desert and defends its young with unequalled devotion!" And even while the "old *Käpt'n*" was still talking, the assembled officers broke into a thunderous song: "Look who's here, in he walks, with giant steps he stalks!" – and Navy Captain Karl Dönitz joined the officers' gathering.

Even at that time, Dönitz was seen as one of the most able officers in Navy High Command. He had been assigned to the staff of Dr Raeder as a *U-Boot* expert, advanced relatively quickly from the ranks of captain and colonel to the ranks of rear admiral and then vice admiral, and, at the outbreak of war, was appointed commander of the submarine force. Hitler promoted him to the rank of admiral and soon after to admiral general, and as fleet admiral he replaced Raeder in his post as supreme commander of the entire *Reichsmarine.* It is said that Hitler personally appointed him as his successor, and as such he would later be involved in the early stages of the surrender negotiations with the United Nations.

Without a doubt, Karl Dönitz was one of the most well-liked officers in the navy. He looked after his men in an exemplary fashion and even among the rank-and-file sailors he was only ever referred to as "*Onkel* Karl". As much as the men feared his proverbial roaring (hence the nickname "The Lion"), even the lowest-ranked among them knew that in any honest dispute they would be able to turn directly to the supreme commander, Karl Dönitz. He loved surprise inspections, and his officers knew that "The Lion" was able to figure out any murky business and that he would go the extra mile to look after each and every one of his common sailors.

Karl Dönitz was never a National Socialist. But he was always ambitious and obsessed with his career and he very well knew that only Adolf Hitler and his National Socialism would be able to present him with opportunities for advancement, and that his career would come to nothing without Hitler and the Nazi regime. And so, Karl Dönitz, this exemplary navy officer, was faithfully devoted to "his" *Führer* and remained so beyond Hitler's death. Until the very end, he saw Hitler as the man who could fight Bolshevism, which he despised, and regarded National Socialism as the guardian against the "global threat of Communism". That said, since his internment in England (1917/18), Dönitz was also well known for his hatred of the British, whose excellent navy he was envious of.

Karl Dönitz was one of the navy's typical "avatars of Old Prussian officer virtue", and he would apply all these "splendid" characteristics and traits to turn himself into a master craftsman of war. National Socialism had positioned itself as the guarantor of a grandiose supply of state-of-the-art tools for the craftsmen of war, and Hitler had managed to elevate himself to the position of "*Führer* of the German People in accordance with divine providence", and so Karl Dönitz consigned himself body and soul to the *Führer* and his Nazi regime. It is indicative of the man's sense of honour that after the defeat he did not try – at least not in public – to distance himself from the Nazi regime and Adolf Hitler and to blame Hitler and the regime for the collapse of German militarism.

Grand Admiral Karl Dönitz (1891-1980), Supreme Commander of the German Navy 1943-1945. He succeeded Hitler as head of state with the title of President of Germany after Hitler's death, and ordered General Jodl to sign the surrender of the German Armed Forces to the Allies. According to the author, he was always referred to by his sailors as either "Uncle Karl" or "the Lion", and was immensely popular with them. The author says he was "well known for his hatred of the British", and had a violent hatred of communism. He was a passionately devoted follower of Hitler, and the author says he "consigned himself body and soul to the *Führer* and the Nazi regime".

The capitulation of German militarism has only just taken place, and already a new *Dolchstoss* ["Stab in the Back"] legend is emerging. For now, this re-emergence is almost imperceptible, but perhaps the extreme danger of the current situation resides in that very fact. Without Grand Admiral Karl Dönitz having any hand in the matter, this new *Dolchstoss* legend originated with him. At first it was said: "Yes, these officers à la Dönitz eventually achieved what they wanted. They allowed the Bolsheviks to penetrate into German territory as little as possible and eventually capitulated to the Anglo-Americans *de facto*, whereas the capitulation to the Russians was only *de jure*!" And straight away wild speculations ensued about a possible war between the Anglo-Saxons and the Russians – either immediately, or "only" in three, five or seven years, when the German militarists could come in very useful. And when such speculations became untenable, the new *Dolchstoss* legend pounced on the generals' "honourableness", and suddenly the individual generals – prominent members of German militarism one and all! – were cleansed of sin, at the expense of the "evil Nazis". The *Wehrmacht* generals' complicity was rejected or at least minimised, and any involvement, either direct or indirect, in the crimes and atrocities committed by the Nazis was denied. Nazi leaders were branded war criminals, but German militarism was more or less exculpated at the expense of the Nazis. Indeed, as a result of the many mistakes, both large and small, made by the occupying authorities, there are already some voices that express the dangerous sentiment: "They are no better than the Nazis!"

An authoritarian state will always be an authoritarian state. At its very essence, National Socialism was nothing other than the incarnation of an intoxication with political power, both in terms of its domestic and foreign policies. What is certain is the fact that wherever victorious militarists were allowed to indulge their intoxication with power, all their actions were infused with the Nazi spirit, which became a disease that by no means always stopped at Germany's geographical borders. All the same: we are convinced that, in principle, the Anglo-Americans have good intentions, as much as we are convinced that National Socialism was intentionally evil. But we would not be able to muster a shred of understanding if the local occupying authorities were to operate in a spirit of revenge and retribution, which would spurn all notions of Christian morality, humanity and honest democracy. It is certain that it will not be possible to inoculate the German people with a spirit of divine love and Christian benevolence through orders given by the occupying authorities. Sadly it is equally certain that some of the calamitous mistakes made by the occupying authorities will serve to stifle such a spirit and make impossible its propagation. And then, despite all energetic attempts to monitor the situation, outrageous claims will spread like wildfire and notions of revenge will reignite: "They are no better than the Nazis!"

We would also regard it as a serious mistake to declare, without exceptions, all members of *SS* units as war criminals. It is a simple and undeniable truth that during the last years of the war more and more young men were forcefully recruited for the *SS* by their local military districts, without their parents' consent or the will of the young men concerned. Without a doubt, such a "watering down" of the *SS* was not done by design on the part of the *SS* leadership, but rather happened as a result of the fact that there was an increasing lack of volunteers. In stating such a "watering down", it is most certainly not our intention to excuse even a single atrocity that was ever committed by an *SS* man.

It would be equally erroneous to regard every boy in the Hitler Youth as a future "werewolf". As is well known, according to the law of the *Reich* every German boy over a certain age had to join the Hitler Youth. It is certainly true that many boys in the Hitler Youth turned into fanatical Nazi supporters. But it is equally true that many of the boys that had been forced into membership of the Hitler Youth turned into vocal critics of the Hitler regime, often at grave danger to their own lives. An increasing number of the boys who were enrolled at universities were amongst the most eager churchgoers and openly acknowledged their allegiance to professors, priests and educators that were suspicious of the Nazi regime. In the end, it was at the University of Munich, of all places, where members of the Hitler Youth revolted against the Nazi regime and paid for their open challenge to National Socialism with their lives.

In talking of a *Dolchstoss* legend, we are mindful of the fact that this term is not always fully applicable. However, over the course of time it has turned into a concept in and of itself, which is why we have applied it to matters that are of a similar nature.

What are the characteristics of this new *Dolchstoss* legend? We feel compelled to reiterate clearly and explicitly what was said at the beginning of the book: "The root cause of the evil is German militarism, and National Socialism is its most dangerous, and hopefully last, exponent!"

We have already spelled it out: the new *Dolchstoss* legend began with the retrieval of the generals' honour and that of German militarism. The "avatars of Old Prussian officer virtue" celebrated their resurrection because – – – in their heart of hearts, they had "never actually been Nazis".

A man who had to fight many a difficult struggle for his own personal conviction once described *subalternity* as the erroneous fundamental attitude that forces individuals onto the wrong track. The focal point of a "subaltern" human does not reside within him, within his own self-worth and conscience. Security and (an often exaggerated) sense of recognition can only be provided to him by external authorisation. In turn, such authorisation can destroy his conscience, as it subordinates independent choice to "orders from above". Do we really have to reiterate the fact that it was the German generals, those peculiar "virtuous heroes" of German militarism, who willingly gave allegiance to a man like Adolf Hitler, as long as he led them "from victory to victory"? That it was the non-National-Socialist generals who carried the Nazi insignia into foreign lands, who found no words of protest within themselves, and, as long as the Nazi regime seemed to guarantee the "victory of German arms", in no way distanced themselves publically from that regime?

During the time of the Weimar Republic, the German generals in some sense had their own political party: the German-National People's Party that had gathered around Hugenberg, and, willingly or unwillingly, had become the stirrup holder for Adolf Hitler and his National Socialism. It was that very German-National People's Party that disseminated the dangerous lie of the *"Dolchstoss von hinten"* (the stab in the back) after the World War of 1914–18, and made sure that among the German people a view gained much currency according to which German militarism had not been vanquished, and that it had therefore returned home undefeated from the First World War. (According to the *"Dolchstoss"* legend, the homeland had betrayed the unbeaten front, thus "stabbing it in the back".) Adolf Hitler took up this lie and inoculated the German youth with it.

Nowadays the new legend is disseminated by the same clique. While they can no longer claim the invincibility of German militarism, they are now cleverly beginning to manipulate the notion of the generals' "honourableness". In so doing, they make National Socialism solely responsible not only for the military collapse, but also for the war itself and all crimes and atrocities committed during it.

The new legend exploits the officers' revolt of July 20, 1944 in a vicious and dangerous manner for the purposes of its propaganda. Not only men like General von Witzleben or General [Erich] Hoepner are being elevated to downright heroic status within the new legend, but also General Halder (who was Adolf Hitler's chief of general staff from 1938 and eagerly carried out all preparations for the coming war on behalf of the Nazi regime) and even General von Brauchitsch (who at the time of the German victories was Hitler's "supreme commander of the army") are now retrospectively portrayed, together with all other conservative generals, as having been fierce opponents of the Nazis "from the earliest days". It is asserted that they were unable to translate their opposition into actions as – oddly enough! – "fate had not allowed it"!

The men of July 20, 1944, who were hanged like common criminals on August 8, 1944, deserve deep respect. A close friend of the author of these pages was among them. When they realised where their assiduity and deference – with which, in their bred-in-the-bone spirit of subordination, they had served the Nazi regime – would lead the German people and their fatherland, a sense of guilt began to weigh too heavily on their consciences and they found within themselves the courage for action; an action that was meant to avert a catastrophe for their people and fatherland at the eleventh hour. The courage of these truly principled and honest men deserves the highest praise, and their good intentions are beyond reproach. Others, however, who were involved to the same extent and who are now to be exonerated through the narrative of the new *Dolchstoss* legend, did not find the same courage within themselves, and, precisely through their tacit acquiescence of the murders of the men of July 20, 1944, again made themselves complicit in the crimes committed by the Nazis.

Adolf Hitler operated according to a principle that, in retrospect, could play a crucial role in the refutation of a new *Dolchstoss* legend: all commanding generals were required to produce "orders of the day" on a regular basis, in which they would confirm their inviolable loyalty to the Führer. These "orders of the day", designed by Hitler to firmly bind the generals to the Nazi regime, had to be signed in the hand of the respective generals. Anyone who reads the "orders of the day" issued by General von Brauchitsch, the "supreme commander of the army", will be astounded by the sheer amount of gushing praise for Adolf Hitler and the explicit recognition of National Socialism, while careful study of the decrees and official reports written by General Franz Halder, the chief of general staff, will render the reader utterly speechless. And what goes for Brauchitsch or Halder applies to each and every one of these ostensibly "fierce" opponents of National Socialism, these commanding German generals of the Nazi regime. It applies to no less a degree to Fritsch, Pogrell, Lutz *et al.*, who all kowtowed to Hitler before resigning sulkily in February / March 1938.

Let us also not forget the speeches given by prominent generals of the German *Wehrmacht* in front of the assembled troops or the "victorious German Führer". Indeed, let us also not forget the speeches made by alleged non-National Socialists, such as those by Freiherr von Neurath. Through years of assiduous allegiance, this conservative and at times decidedly reactionary and anti-working-class clique had made itself complicit in the war and the crimes committed by the Nazis. It was precisely they who carried the banners of National Socialism when foreign nations were conquered and peace-loving neighbours were attacked. Suddenly, however – after the collapse – they wish to be portrayed as non-National Socialists while propagating an insidious new *Dolchstoss* legend. This legend begins with the compurgation of German militarism. This, however, is but the first step towards the birth of a new German militarism of the future; even "newer" than the very recent and ostensibly vernacular "new German militarism" that was National Socialism.

From the New York Times of 1939

Two further observations:

On the one hand, the propagators of the new *Dolchstoss* legend tout themselves as the future warriors against Communism.

On the other hand, in their broadcasts on Moscow Radio, General Seydlitz, General Paulus *et al.* use language that is riddled with tirades against the Nazi regime, but does not castigate German militarism and war itself with a single word. The events of war, and with it, the spirit of German militarism, are not condemned, while Adolf Hitler alone, with his strategies of a "mere private", is given the full blame for the catastrophic collapse of the German military.

General Walther Kurt von Seydlitz-Kurzbach (1888-1976) defected from the German army to Russia after the Battle of Stalingrad, where he had commanded the German troops. In Russia he gave radio broadcasts attacking Hitler and the Nazi regime. But the author complains that he "does not castigate German militarism and war itself with a single word".

How do we recognise the propagators of the new *Dolchstoss* legend? For them, Christian benevolence is synonymous with maudlin sentimentalism and folly, while Christianity itself is, at best, a formality. They use certain phrases regarding democracy to camouflage their true intentions. They are dangerous adversaries, for many of their followers hold the honest belief that they are serving a new form of "Germanity". They have a special trait: whenever German militarism is attacked and the deep complicity of the German generals is demonstrated, they shout indignantly: "A closet Nazi!" And as part of their defence they employ a useful weapon by arguing thus against the attacker: "He assaults German militarism and disparages the German generals, just like the Nazis did on July 20, 1944!"

Among the former adherents of the German-National People's Party, the new *Dolchstoss* legend is proving very popular. If it were to remain confined to that circle, it would never pose a threat. But let us not forget: the spirit of German militarism with its subordination is deeply ingrained in the German soul. Germans are all too ready to stand to attention in front of a venerable general, full of respect and deference, and they are all too easily blinded by the splendid "virtues" of military men. In this context, let us remember many a debate in the *Reichstag* during the Weimar Republic, where members of the parties of the left noisily bragged about their war decorations. There was no greater insult to many parliamentarians on the left than to question their "heroic" war service against Wilhelmine militarism. Social Democrats and members of the *Zentrum* party, senior councillors, mayors and district administrators who were members of any of the parties on the left felt a deep sense of honour when a German general called at their offices to appoint them as "men of confidence of the *Reichswehr*". Despite all experiences of war, their sense of subordination made it impossible for them to expunge their feelings of respect and veneration for a German general.

A certain man, who nowadays purports to represent the new Germany in Switzerland, in a sentimental impulse – after the outbreak of war! – referred to the moment when he was chosen as the *Reichswehr's* man of confidence as the highlight of his life. Once upon a time, during the days of the Weimar Republic, this man was an ordinary parliamentarian of a left-of-centre party. We have chosen this example to illustrate how the new *Dolchstoss* legend may lead to a fresh aberration of the spirit, which might even affect those who are honestly working on the reconstruction of their ravaged homeland.

The Nazi spirit has infected us all in some way, and it most certainly did not stop at Germany's geographical borders. That is why we have been calling, time and again, for a sincere and Christian *"mea culpa, mea culpa, mea maxima culpa"*. We have rejected the notion of the collective and exclusive guilt of the entire German people, as assigned by the Russians, the Anglo-Americans and the French, but at the same time are fully conscious of the fact that the German people will have to atone for the atrocities carried out by the Nazis and the crimes committed by German militarism. However, the elimination of the Nazi spirit requires a simultaneous eradication of German militarism, of the military spirit within the German people; that is to say, the root cause of the evil must be addressed.

As far as the question of individual guilt is concerned, to bring things to a close, we would like to refer to some deliberations included by the National Socialist Hermann Göring in his book *"Aufbau einer Nation"* ("The composition / creation / formation of a nation"), written in 1938:

"Hitler does not seek a personal dictatorship... In the execution of their tasks and duties, he affords his collaborators the greatest degree of freedom. They can operate entirely independently!"

Such words require no further comment. Those who are guilty must be identified and brought to justice. Culpability requires punishment. Even in virtuous Christian nations, the penalty for murder is death. As judges, let us be strict but just. Brutality and violence have never led to justice, and only an absence of retaliatory and vengeful motives can lead to legal certitude. It would be utterly disastrous for the German people if a spirit of revenge and retaliation, aided by a new *Dolchstoss* legend, were to take hold of the German soul again, provoked, say, by the selfsame retaliatory and vengeful spirit on the part of the victors, now in turn intoxicated with power.

On the other hand, it might be fear of clandestine resistance and the still-not-dead Nazi spirit that inveigles the victors to employ methods of terror. Fear and suspicion are eternally the most excellent tools of evil. Out of fear, prudent insights and sensible plans are sacrificed on the altar of violence. This is a clear sign of inner weakness. He who is truly superior will not seek to wrest everlasting self-recrimination from the vanquished. Who could command conscience itself? Rather than eradicating the spirit of servility (the root cause of the problem), such methods would only foment a new spirit of servility within the German people, and the feelings of inferiority that would result from such a development could easily lead to a renewed pathological ambition for power.

After the collapse of National Socialism and German militarism, the German people experienced the power of the victorious nations. But a new spirit is not conceived by power, however abundant that power may be. Force alone will not annihilate the Nazi spirit; if anything, it might lead to the provocation and cultivation of a new version thereof. All depends on the victors' attitude towards the defeated! The fate of future generations depends on this attitude, not just in Germany, but all across the civilised world. If Europe is to heal, if the world is to heal, if the peoples on Earth are to live in peace, this attitude *must* be a Christian one. There is no true democracy and no honest humanity that can do without such a Christian attitude of mind. And how could this Christian attitude be epitomised more profoundly than in the "Song of Praise" sung by the Great Apostle of the People, St. Paul, in the Epistle to the Corinthians:

"Though I speak with the tongues of men and of angels,
and have not charity,
I am become as sounding brass,
or a tinkling cymbal.
And though I have the gift of prophecy,
and understand all mysteries, and all knowledge;
and though I have all faith,
so that I could remove mountains,
and have not charity, I am *nothing*."

For all his rages and threats and affirmations of certainty, underneath it all, such a hysterical man was always full of fear and apprehensions. Hitler was continually afraid of what might come next, watching anxiously to espy his doom.

THE AUTHOR'S CONCLUDING REMARKS

I embarked on the writing of this book in the summer of 1944, after having fought relentlessly against National Socialism and German militarism for almost a decade. One year in a concentration camp in Nazi Germany, fleeing abroad, prison and yet more prison *after* my escape, contempt, ridicule and derision, disparagement of myself as a "vexatious foreigner", eventual internment in Switzerland for one-and-a-half years: these seemed to be the rewards I was allowed to reap. After I was released from internment on the explicit condition that I should refrain from any practical activities directed against Nazism and German militarism, I used the period of a further compulsory stay that had been imposed on me for the composition of this book. Following the advice of my revered mentor and experienced, fatherly friend, and thanks to the initiative of the young and energetic director of the Otto Walter publishing house, I was able to resolve upon writing this book and seeing through the project. It is these two men to whom I am most profoundly indebted. I am also deeply thankful to all those who steadfastly kept faith with me, in the face of defamation and the concomitant danger of malicious gossip, while special gratitude is due to J. Werner Meyer for his corrections of the text.

With each passing page, the task upon which I had embarked increasingly turned into an obligation towards my friends who had remained in Germany and who continued their stoical fight against the Nazi regime despite all the terror, and to my comrades and all like-minded individuals who were being tortured to death in the concentration camps. All of them were good Germans, as I believes myself to be. Living to see that hour – the hour of the death of National Socialism and German militarism! – was not granted to them. They had already passed into eternity through the gates of death; many of them long before their tormentors were or will be summoned before an earthly judge or the judgement seat of the Almighty.

These closing remarks are written on this night, the night from May 7 to May 8, 1945. This "present moment" means: the day of the unconditional surrender of the German *Wehrmacht*! The day of armistice and thereby the end of the most murderous war in the history of the world! The end of the Nazi regime! The end of German militarism! I conclude my work and am holding a silent celebration. Once more I speak to my readers, one last time. At the end of my factual report I address my readers in a very personal manner:

"For me, this 'present moment' – the unconditional capitulation of National Socialist Germany – is a Holy Night, a night of reflection, of communion with myself and of anticipation. A night of the most profound obligation!

I commemorate the dead on the battlefields: my son is among them. He had to die a 'hero's death' for the Nazi regime on the eastern front, while his father was fighting a seemingly hopeless fight against that regime.

I commemorate the millions that were murdered with unthinkable brutality in the concentration camps. Many friends are among them; one of the dearest ones was hanged like a common criminal on August 8, 1944.

I commemorate the millions of Germans, who, as frightened civilians, were scourged through the horrors of war by the furies of National Socialist terror. My wife is among them. She lived through the hell that was occupied Berlin, after having passed through all purgatories of war; and before the outbreak of war, time and again she was fetched for interrogation by the henchmen of the Secret State Police. Is she alive today?

I commemorate the destroyed towns and villages and all the cultural artefacts that have been irretrievably lost. My own property, which I hoped to regain after the end of the war, went up in flames and has been reduced to ash and rubble.

I commemorate a contaminated generation of young people who were torn from their parents by the Nazis, and who – far from their relatives and friends – roam in the mountains of Austria or Southern Germany. My 14-year-old son – who hardly knows his father by name and whom I have not seen for almost a decade – was taken from his mother in a mandatory evacuation three years ago. Is he still alive?

Closing remarks – armistice – silent celebration:

Reflection – communion – obligation!

I found myself in the clutches of a concentration camp as early as 1934; the torture experienced there has made me into a tough fighter. I have survived a hard battle against National Socialism and German militarism; a battle that I fought to the last, with every fibre of my body. (I request that all of my reports, including those that date from the time after my escape, are treated as authentic factual reports!)

The battle is over: National Socialism and German militarism have surrendered unconditionally and lie shattered on the ground. I, too, have made a modest contribution. It is up to us to ensure that they will never rise up again, that their unconditional surrender equates to the death of National Socialism and German militarism. It is up to us Germans, not to the victorious powers!

What is the tangible result at the end of the fighting?
Germany is destroyed and devastated.
Germany is impoverished, starved and ravaged.
Germany, this once beautiful, civilised and cultured nation, is bleeding from thousands upon thousands of wounds!
But do not only blame the victorious powers! Germans, let us all – and the whole world with us – beat our chests and pronounce, out of an honest Christian impulse and truthful aspiration: *mea culpa – mea culpa – mea maxima culpa!* And let us seek and apportion blame where it is due: in National Socialism and German militarism, which was cultivated with much zeal and cheered on by a majority of the population, as long as it led from victory to victory under the Nazi banner, against God and Christianity!

Closing remarks – armistice – silent celebration:

Reflection – communion – obligation!

Our concerns, fears and hopes are reserved predominantly for the youth of Germany, who face such a bleak future and on whom National Socialism has imposed such a heavy legacy. All my struggles, aspirations and wishes have always been for that youth, and not least my own son, the only one who was or is left to me.

As I sit here, I am leafing through the diary that I wrote for my son; the last entry dates from

September 6, 1943 (!). I include this final diary note here, in the final chapter of this book; and, in doing so, I am not only speaking to my son, but to the entire German youth:

My son!

Some months have passed since I last wrote in this diary. (I was released from the internment camp in Switzerland in the spring of 1943, after which I did not keep up the diary. Author's note.) It was not storms and stresses, not titanic volition and not restless powers that have kept your father from writing. No, I was exhausted, injured and wounded, and dangerously close to abject misery and total surrender.

What is it, then, that compels me to take up the pen once again? It is Beethoven's "Missa Solemnis"! Amidst the most hideous murdering and annihilation, amidst the destruction of irretrievable cultural treasures, in a world of hatred and fanatical and rampant thirst for extermination, a small cultured nation in the heart of Europe is staging a music festival of world-class standards. In the Jesuit church in Lucerne, the "Missa Solemnis" is performed, and its harrowing plea, its supplication to God, rings out: "Dona nobis pacem" – grant us peace! You see, my son, this "Missa Solemnis" has reinstated in me the belief in the land of culture that is Europe.

Let me start by saying the following, unequivocally and clearly: the Nazis – degenerate Germans, my son! – unleashed this war!

The Nazis – megalomaniac Germans, my son! – are the creators of this immeasurable anguish, which now, during the final stages of this war, is descending on our own country and people!

We Germans will have much to atone for; the entirety of the crimes committed systematically and with preconceived intent by the scum of this country. Atonement in spirit and atonement through deeds!

And yet:

The "Missa Solemnis" has reawakened in me the belief in humanity and the belief in the land of culture that is Europe. The victors will dictate their terms to the vanquished and will hunt down war criminals, after themselves inflicting death and destruction on innocent civilians, women and children and driving them into the same hell that their enemy – the Nazis! – had cheeringly shown them, threatened them with, and subjected them to in the first place! An inhumane criminal, a semi-educated German with pathological tendencies, in his loathing of himself and all those around him, fanned hostility across the globe, until the hatred turned into a vast sea of flames that finally engulfed also his own country, laying Germany to waste. The rest of humanity – which by no means is entirely innocent – will not forgive us Germans for allowing this maniac to force his satanic will on us and for continuing to follow this diabolical spirit until all of Germany, our youth and our men of military age became fully entangled in it, as if in a deadly spider's web.

In allowing this to happen, do we Germans and all of Germany not deserve to be cast into eternal damnation and perdition? As absurd as it may sound today, your father still dares to assert the following: we Germans, in our heart of hearts, are a people with religious sensibilities, a people on an eternal quest for truth, light and stability – for God! And as outrageous as it may sound today: this is precisely why the Germans, in their faithfulness, time and again succumb to false prophets!

In times of crisis – and by no means only that of the material kind, but all the more so that of the spiritual kind – Germans positively need a prophet, someone who promises a way out of discord and grief. The better this prophet knows how to style himself as a leader sent by God, the more he pretends to serve the truth (by decrying true iniquities!) and to lead towards "light" (by uncovering so-called "shady characters"), the more outward success he can demonstrate and the more splendour he can display – the greater will be the danger that the Germans will follow him blindly, willingly and enthusiastically.

This is the only way to explain the veneration of the "figures of light" of German militarism and the Nazi insanity as part of which a semi-educated dunce was deified by the "people of poets and thinkers"! If ever there was a reason to talk of the tragedy of the "Faustian Germans", this must be it!

The Germans' disgraceful and depraved concept of a master race, their racial delusions, their imperiousness, and their compulsive thirst for domination at any cost cannot be excused in any way. But no matter how many times – over the course of centuries – false prophets and power-hungry demagogues have tried to instil untruths into the Germans: a deeply-instilled desire for the search for truth, for light, for God has empowered Germans to achieve far greater things than those crimes of imperiousness! The Germans did not "only" have false prophets, as a cursory browse through a history book might suggest. The German nation has gifted humanity with a whole host of true, eternally valuable prophets; especially in the most recent period of human history!

And in the same way that some of the temporary successes of false prophets must be explained through the "Faustian" struggle and the religious disposition of the Germans, the awakening and lasting impact of true prophets – despite all egregious and inexcusable aberrations – must also be explained through that deep religious disposition and its striving for (or obsession with) truth, light and God!

Music is said to be the highest of all arts, and at the same time the art form that draws most directly from the soul and connects most immediately to the deepest essence of humanity. And yet, in the essence of their being and disposition, the greatest and most brilliant music creators of all time were archetypal German men:

Bach! – Haydn! – Händel! – Mozart!

and, the most "Faustian" and perhaps greatest of them all:

BEETHOVEN!

Ludwig van Beethoven (1770-1827). The author wishes his countrymen to turn their attention back to the great German composers, Bach, Hadyn, Händel, Mozart, and "perhaps the greatest of them all: BEETHOVEN!"

I do not wish to talk at this point of the "poets and thinkers", who, as good Germans, have enriched the body of thought of humanity in such profound ways. If you were to compile a list of their names – beginning with Goethe – please do not forget the great Cusanus, the towering reformer and prince of his church, Cardinal "Petrus in vinculis", who, in a visionary manner, anticipated the achievements of Copernicus, Galileo, Kepler and Giordano Bruno: namely Nicholas of Cusa.

Nicholas of Cusa (1401-1464). (aka Nicolaus Cusanus, Nikolaus Cryfftz or Krebs, and Nicholas of Kues.) He was born in Kues (now Bernkastel-Kues) on the Moselle River between Trier and Koblenz in Germany. The family surname was Cryfftz (pronounced "crifts"). He was a famous philosopher who acted as an intellectual bridge between the Middle Ages and the Renaissance. He was influenced by Neoplatonism and was a profound mystic, who became a Roman Catholic Cardinal. He was also a mathematician and held advanced astronomical theories as a forerunner of Kepler. He wrote many books, the best known of which is probably *Of Learned Ignorance* (1440). The author says of him: "Please do not forget the great Cusanus, the towering reformer and prince of his Church."

And yet: will we Germans ever be able to erase the burden of guilt that the Nazis heaped upon us through committing their crimes during this last war?

Will we Germans ever be able to remove the stain with which they have besmirched us in front of the whole world?

We Germans not only *have to* atone, but we *will* atone. Atone willingly in the spirit of our true prophets, the antipodes of all false prophets of German politics and the history of the world.

We will reflect on the heritage left to us by our true prophets; a heritage that those who seek to corrupt us can no longer violate. For power (!) was their only response; but power they have no longer. We wish to finally accept the inheritance that our ingenious cultural creators have bequeathed to us; an inheritance that will never be destroyed by war or any amount of bloodshed and destruction.

Let us finally turn towards our true paragons, the actual heroes, whose words and examples will not fade with temporary power. They shall and will help us to conquer and eradicate the spirit of the false prophets within us: the Nazi spirit, the Prussian spirit of German militarism in us and around us! They will help us to recognise truth in its purest form and stand by us as we strive towards the light of divine love.

With such honest aspirations and in the spirit of the "Missa Solemnis", we Germans wish to beseech our true God, who is love itself, to grant us peace; to earn and receive, for ourselves and our children's children, a just peace.

May a new light shine on the smoke-blackened ruins of Germany; may truth, benevolence and the love for God quietly appear in the grief-stricken soul of each and every German: "Dona nobis pacem, oh Lord!"

As mentioned above, these words to my son are dated September 6, 1943. I do not know if my son will still be able to hear them. In addressing my son – who perhaps is no longer among the living on the day when all guns have finally fallen silent – I wish to speak to the entire German youth, with whom I feel an especially close connection on this day; I wish to speak to all Germans; and, in particular, I wish to speak to all of my readers:

The day of armistice.

The day of the end of war.

The day of the unconditional surrender of National Socialist Germany and German militarism.

My son!

This day brings with it an enormous responsibility – for you, for me, and every sincere and honest German.

Today, the poor, suffering German people are setting out on a difficult and dangerous path full of ordeals. We must engage in honest expiation; we must rebuild our ruined homeland and we must overcome the perturbation of the spirit. We must find a new legal system, which can only be built upon the foundations of the ancient, eternal order of natural and divine law, God's moral code and age-old Christian guidelines. We must re-introduce the protection of the law to a Germany that for years has been lawless, and build benevolence upon it.

Whenever you will encounter hardship and inevitable obstacles, remember this, my son: only through love, only through that vast, unspeakable love that is God Himself, can hatred be overcome!

Your father was in a concentration camp when he encountered this love, which is God Himself, when he found the wonderful joy of nearness to God, and when he first felt the exhilaration of God's wonder. And believe me, my son: the hell that is a concentration camp knows no false and maudlin sentimentality! But the love that is God Himself encompasses all justice and embraces all law.

Today, on the day the war has ended and National Socialist Germany has capitulated, I urge you, my son, to make a commitment to love. The divine duty of love! My son, do not let yourself be beguiled by hatred in any of its devious manifestations. Never let faintheartedness, defeatism, captiousness, envy or resentment discourage you from your commitment to love. Once this holy commitment to love has taken root within you, you will learn that even the most difficult penance will lead to cheerful and edifying work, in the spirit of the all-powerful and almighty creator of Heaven and Earth, in the spirit of God, who is love itself!

Set to work, my son!

The work of rebuilding our destroyed homeland!

The work of redemption of the damage inflicted!

The work of overcoming hatred through active love in the spirit of the Lord!

I conclude my appeal to you, written on the day of the collapse of National Socialism and German militarism, with the words of the *Introitus* for Christmastide, from the Second Mass at Dawn:

"Today a light will shine upon us, for the Lord is born to us. And He shall be called Wonderful God, Prince of Peace, Father of future generations."
Gloria in altissimis Deo, et in terra pax hominibus bonae voluntatis!

A

B

C

D

E

F

G

H

I

J

K

L

M

N

O

P

Q

R

S

T

U

V

W

Y

Z